STRUCTURES OF THE
EDUCATION AND INITIAL TRAINING SYSTEMS
IN THE EUROPEAN UNION

EURYDICE
The European Education
Information Network

CEDEFOP
European Centre for the Development
of Vocational Training

European Commission

This document does not necessarily represent the Commission's official position.

Cataloguing data can be found at the end of this publication.

Luxembourg: Office for Official Publications of the European Communities, 1995

ISBN 92-826-9319-8

Printed in Belgium

Preface

At a time when the importance of education and training to the future success of the European Union is becoming more and more apparent, the Commission is very pleased to present this updated and extended document describing the education and initial vocational training systems for young people in the 15 Member States of the European Union and in the two EFTA countries which have signed the EEA Agreement.

Like the previous edition, this document is a joint product resulting from the long-standing cooperation between EURYDICE, the European education information network, and CEDEFOP, the European Centre for the Development of Vocational Training. The increased mobility within the education and training systems which has led to, and been a result of, the European programmes in these fields makes reliable, accessible and readable information concerning these systems an even greater necessity than before.

The increasing obsolescence of the traditional dividing lines between education and training makes a joint publication such as this one of particular relevance and importance.

It has been prepared on the basis of information contributed by the National Units of EURYDICE and the members of CEDEFOP's documentary information network. It has been validated by the competent national authorities. Final editorial responsibility lies with the European Unit of EURYDICE.

We hope that this publication, presenting the richness and diversity of the education systems in the European Union, will be of interest to policy-makers and to education and training practitioners in general.

Dr. T. O'Dwyer
Director General
European Commission
DG XXII 'Education, Training and Youth'
February 1995

Introduction

In general, the present report follows the approach used for the 1991 version of the publication but is more extensive, firstly with regard to the countries it covers and secondly with regard to the content for each country. It now includes 17 countries – the 15 Member States of the European Union (including Austria, Finland and Sweden as of 1 January 1995) plus the EFTA/EEA countries, Iceland and Norway. It provides information on the administration and structure of all levels of education and initial vocational training. Brief information has been added on higher education and on the initial and in-service training of teachers and their status.

As in the previous edition of the document, all countries have been dealt with in a broadly similar way, in order to facilitate comparison between them. Nevertheless, care has been taken to represent the particularities of the different systems.

In almost all cases, the first chapter comprises brief information on the country concerned, the basic principles affecting the education and training systems, the distribution of responsibilities and more detailed information under the headings: administration, inspection, financing, private education and advisory bodies. In some countries, information pertaining to initial vocational training has been integrated under these headings and in others it appears as a separate heading at the end of the first chapter. In exceptional cases, it has not been possible to adhere to this pattern, but the information provided is comparable. Some information on major reforms is also included.

The following chapters cover successively pre-school, primary, secondary (general, technical and vocational) education and initial vocational training for young people and higher education. However, the organization of chapters again takes account of the national situation. For instance, no artificial division has been made between pre-school and primary education, primary and lower secondary education or the different types of secondary education when there is no division in national terms. Sections dealing with curriculum, assessment, teachers and statistics follow a general description of the objectives and organization of each level. In some instances, information on teachers is provided for several levels together, sometimes it is in a separate chapter. Statistical data cover the number of pupils/students, teachers and institutions and, where available, pupil-teacher ratios, attendance or completion rates and the options taken up at different stages. Initial vocational training covers provision which is usually outside the formal education system, such as apprenticeship, youth training and vocational integration programmes and other specific courses. After a general outline, the higher education section includes the following: admission, fees/student finance, academic year, courses, qualifications and assessment.

Diagrams of the systems, with brief explanatory notes, can be found at the beginning of each chapter.

Whilst no direct comparison or evaluation of the systems has been made, certain patterns or trends common to several countries do emerge – the decentralization of administrative and financial arrangements with more responsibility for management at institutional level; regional or local responsibility for training linked to economic and social development; efforts to extend the period of schooling, by lowering the compulsory school entry age, raising the leaving age or by providing incentives for young people to stay on beyond compulsory schooling; efforts to expand or extend pre-school provision; common general education, normally coinciding with the period of compulsory schooling, which usually ends after the lower stage of secondary education; the introduction or reintroduction of more formal assessment procedures during schooling; a diversity of options and routes in (post-compulsory) secondary education and in vocational training; attempts to improve the status of vocational qualifications as compared with academic qualifications; the development of post-secondary and advanced vocational education and training; the introduction of modular courses in secondary education, training and higher education; efforts to improve the diverse forms of initial teacher training.

Contents

Contents

Belgium

French Community

German-speaking Community

Flemish Community

BELGIUM

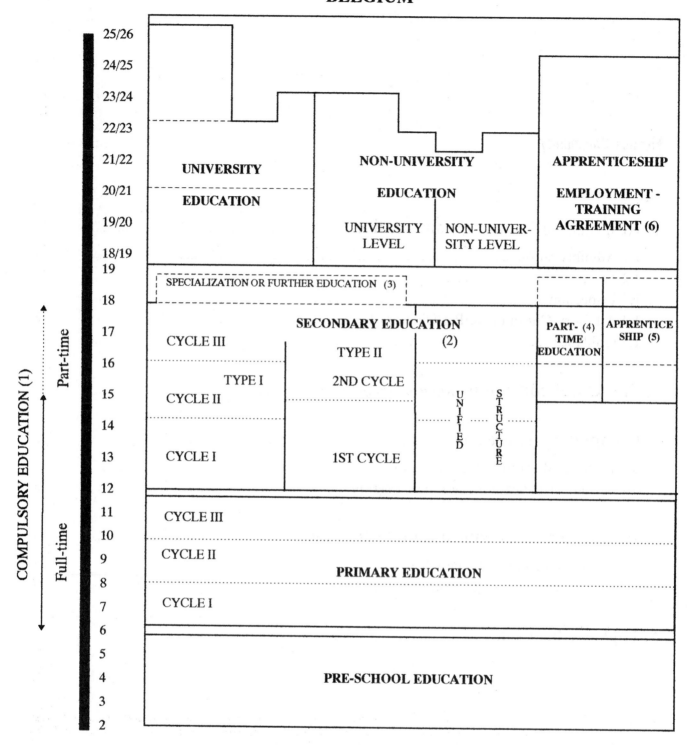

.... = division in the level / type of education.

------ = alternative beginning or end of level / type of education.

1. Compulsory education covers twelve years, from 6 to 18 years of age. It is full-time up to 15 years of age; those who have completed at least the first two years of secondary education and do not wish to continue full-time until 18 may then follow part-time compulsory education. Pupils who have not completed 3 years of secondary education must attend full-time compulsory education until 16 years of age.

2. TYPE I or 'renovated' education comprises secondary education at lower and upper secondary levels, organized in four forms – general, technical, vocational and artistic education – and two main streams, one leading primarily to higher education, the other primarily to employment.

   TYPE II or 'traditional' education comprises secondary education at lower and upper secondary levels comprising general, technical or vocational sections. Type I education is being extended to nearly all schools in the French and German-speaking Communities.

   Type I and II are being replaced by a unified structure in the Flemish Community.

3. A preparatory year for higher education or a year of specialization or further education for employment after 6 years of secondary education.

4. Part-time education is available to 15- or 16-year-olds, and covers the last years of compulsory schooling. It lasts 360 hours in the first year (for 15/16-year-olds) and 240 hours in the following years.

5. The theoretical training of apprenticeship lasts the same time (360 hours in the 1st year and 240 hours in the following two years) as part-time education.

6. The Employment-Training Agreement is available to 18- to 25-year-olds, and lasts 256 hours when provided by an employer and 500 hours when followed in a training establishment.

Belgium

1.1 Background

The State of Belgium was founded in 1830. The Constitution provided the structures of a unitary centralized State, with a constitutional monarch at its head.

Since 1970, after four consecutive phases of reform of the Constitution, Belgium has evolved to a federal State, composed of three Communities (Flemish, French and German-speaking) and three Regions (Flemish, Walloon and Brussels). There are four linguistic areas: Dutch-language, French-language, bilingual (Brussels) and German-language. Each of the Communities and regions has legislative and executive autonomy with respect to its own attributions. The Councils of the Communities and regions, as legislative authorities, pass regulations in the form of 'decrees', which have force of law within their territory.

The Communities are responsible for cultural matters, education, person-related matters (welfare, health care) and language. The regions are responsible for economy, energy, public works and transport, town and country planning and the environment. The federal State retains the main responsibility for foreign affairs, defence, justice, finance and social legislation.

Below the regions there are 10 provinces and 589 communes responsible for provincial and local matters.

Belgium has a population of around 10 million in an area of just over 30,000 square kilometres.

The main areas of employment are industry (27.5%) and the services (7%), with only 2.5% now employed in agriculture. There is a 13.5% unemployment rate.

The Belgian Constitution guarantees the separation of Church and State. There is therefore no official religion. The Catholic Church is the most widespread.

1.2 Basic principles: education

Article 17 of the Belgian Constitution, established in 1831, guarantees **freedom** of education. This principle was meant to eliminate any monopoly on education. It also implies **freedom of choice** for parents, who may enrol their children in any school which subscribes to their philosophical or religious convictions. Only education administered by the Communities is neutral, respecting all philosophical and religious beliefs. All schools organized by public authorities must offer a choice between instruction in a recognized religion or secular moral instruction.

The Constitution also establishes the **right** to education. The corollary of this principle is that access to education is **free of charge** throughout the period of compulsory education.

1.3 Distribution of responsibilities

The constitutional reforms of 1980 and 1989 transferred responsibility for education from the State to the Communities.

Since 1 January 1989, and as stipulated in Article 59bis of the Constitution, only three very specific areas have remained under the control of the federal State:

- fixing the start and finish of compulsory schooling;

- minimum conditions for the award of diplomas;

- the pensions scheme for teachers.

All other educational matters have been transferred to the three Communities. They are responsible for education within their linguistic area and, as concerns the French and Flemish Communities, with regard to French or Dutch-speaking establishments in bilingual areas (Brussels). The educational responsibilities of each Community are vested in the Community Council (legislative power) and the Community Government and Education Minister (executive power).

The federal State continues to administer the tax system for the whole of Belgium and allocates funds to the Communities in accordance with detailed criteria set out in an Act of 16 January 1989. In education, the annual amount is calculated on the basis of the reference year 1987 and adjusted partially each year in relation to population trends. In 1989, the Flemish Community received 56.2% of the funds, the French and German-speaking

Communities 43.8%. A special Act sets the amount of funding the German-speaking Community receives.

The Communities are also responsible for apprenticeships and initial training for the independent professions and for the managers of SMEs, through specialized bodies.

1.4 Compulsory education

According to the Act of 29 June 1983, compulsory education lasts for 12 years, from 6 to 18 years of age.

Children are required to attend school full-time up to the age of 15, completing primary education and at least the first two years of secondary education. Pupils who have not completed the first two years of secondary education are required to attend full-time education until the age of 16. Those who do not wish to continue full-time until 18 may then follow compulsory part-time education up to the age of 18.

Part-time compulsory education is defined as studies in a recognized establishment, in the form of either part-time study or a recognized training course.

1. Responsibilities and administration

1.1 Administration

As a consequence of the recent reforms of the State, policy for education and higher education is the responsibility of the Council of the French Community and its Government, in which there is one Minister in charge of higher education and academic research, and another for education (pre-school, primary, secondary and special education).

In the French Community, except for private schools, there are three main types of education institutions:

– public education institutions organized and managed by the French Community and financed in total from its budget;

– public education institutions subsidized by the French Community, but managed by provincial or communal authorities;

– 'free' education institutions, denominational or non-denominational, subsidized by the French Community.

Each category comprises an 'educational network' composed of one or more 'organizing bodies', each directing one or more schools.

The organizing body of Community education is the Government of the French Community. It administers and manages establishments (at all levels) and the careers of administrators of its own educational network. The organizing bodies of subsidized public education, however, are the provinces or communes, and of 'free' subsidized education, the natural or legal persons responsible.

The network of subsidized public education establishments has developed two structures for coordinating education: the *Conseil de l'enseignement des communes et les provinces (CECP)* and the *Conseil des pouvoirs organisateurs de l'enseignement officiel neutre subventionné (CPEONS)*. The establishments of 'free' education are grouped under the *Secrétariat national de l'Enseignement catholique (SNEC)* and the *Fédération des écoles libres subventionnées indépendantes (FELSI)*.

The Minister grants subsidies to educational establishments under certain conditions.

Establishments must:

– comply with legislation on language;

– adopt a structure approved by the Minister;

– follow a curriculum which meets legal requirements;

– submit to supervision and inspection as organized by the Government of the Community, which is responsible for determining that the level of instruction is satisfactory;

– have a minimum number of pupils per class, section or level;

– be composed of educational facilities which are located in the same complex of buildings and form a whole, and which meet standards for hygiene and cleanliness;

– follow the general scheme for leave and holidays;

– employ staff who are not likely to endanger pupils' health;

– possess the teaching materials and school facilities required to meet educational needs.

If the establishment meets these conditions, the organizing body is free to choose staff, as long as they also meet certain standards. It is also free to choose teaching methods and define the content of curricula, on the prior approval of the Minister.

Assessment is another area where the academic freedom of each organizing body is guaranteed. Within the limits of laws and decrees, each organizing body may define the type of assessment it wishes to use and the means of monitoring and communicating the results of the assessment.

In order to improve cooperation between full-time secondary education establishments, ten geographical zones have been established, each with two Councils, one for non-denominational education and the other for denominational education. The Councils ensure that common teacher periods (*périodes – professeurs*) are used in establishments in the same zone and that the provision of education is harmonized. Their proposals are sent to a cooperation committee (*Comité de concertation*) to be approved and made final. Educational options which have not been approved by the committee cannot be offered.

The cooperation committees and the zonal Councils comprise representatives of the organizing bodies concerned, including the Minister as the organizing body of Community education.

At the level of the school itself, the organizing body is free to choose the organization of cooperation. As regards Community education, since 1990 Participation Councils (*Conseils de participation*) have been set up to make proposals and give opinions on matters such as the pedagogical (e.g. implementation of the school education plan), the material and the administrative organization of the establishment. This Council comprises, *inter alia*, the head teacher, representatives of teaching and administrative staff, parents, unions, pupils and local policy makers.

1.2 Financing

The French Community covers all the costs of Community education and subsidizes public and 'free' education as far as permitted by laws and decrees, according to the level of education, number of pupils, etc. Subsidies cover, for the whole school system including short higher education courses, completely or partially:

– staff remuneration, under the same conditions (qualifications and duties) as those granted to Community education staff;

– operating expenses, on a lump-sum basis, according to regulatory criteria;

– expenses related to construction and development, within the limits of credits provided for in the budgetary decree.

However, certain expenses, such as the purchase of material (school textbooks, exercise books, etc.) and participation in extra-curricular activities, may be covered by parents, associations, etc.

As regards university education, an operating grant is allocated to each institution in accordance with the number of students. This covers the purchase of material, salaries of teaching and administrative staff, etc.

1.3 Inspection

There is a triple system of inspection, consisting of:

– A monitoring service, which ensures that Community subsidies are being used correctly and inspects accounting procedures.

– A dual inspection service:

The service of the French Community, which verifies the level of instruction in Community education establishments and gives its opinion on the qualifications of staff. This service also provides educational support by advising teachers, and contributes to the preparation of curricula and the development of teaching methods. In addition, it verifies the level of instruction in education subsidized by the Community.

The service of subsidized pre-school and primary education, which has a supervisory function (with regard to the fulfilment of compulsory school obligations, material organization, etc.) and an educational one with regard to the value of education provided. Organizing bodies may also have educational advisers for their network.

– A 'homologation committee' (*Commission d'homologation*), whose task is to verify whether secondary-level studies have been completed in keeping with the provisions of legislation and regulations. The committee is also responsible for approving upper secondary school certificates (*certificats d'enseignement secondaire supérieur – CESS*).

The education authorities enforce procedures for the award of other qualifications, such as certificates of vocational qualification, and also validate diplomas awarded in higher education. At university level, there is a ratification committee (*Commission d'entérinement*).

1.4 Consultative bodies

Community Ministers receive the opinions of a large number of councils and committees, of which the most significant have been established by the provisions of laws, decrees or regulations. These include, for example, the Education and Training Council, which has the task, *inter alia*, of determining the basic direction of education and training in the next ten years, and the French Community Parents' Council. In addition, each level of education has bodies for consultation and cooperation (e.g. Commission for cooperation and improvement in secondary education, Council for technical and vocational education, French Community Inter-University Council, Commission for the modernization of pre-school and primary education).

1.5 Guidance

The tasks of guidance and orientation of pupils in pre-school, primary, secondary and special education are the responsibility of the psycho-medico-social centres (*Centres Psycho-Médico-Sociaux – PMS*). These centres are also responsible for school medical inspections. The centres are independent of the schools, but work closely with them and with families. Each centre is composed of an interdisciplinary team made up of educational psychologists/counsellors, social workers, nurses and independent doctors.

Several types of educational activities help young people plan their lives and careers. The methods used combine group activities and individual analyses. In the French Community, the Community and 'free' education networks use computer software to help pupils choose studies and occupations (e.g. *CHOIX*). A software on options in higher education has also been developed (*SOCRATE*).

2. Pre-school education (*Education préscolaire*)

Pre-school education is an integral part of the education system. Pre-school education is optional, free and coeducational, and is provided for children aged from two-and-a-half to six years, and up to seven years in exceptional cases. The pre-school education attendance rate is 95% among three-year-olds, 97% among four-year-olds and 100% among five-year-olds (and above).

Pre-school education has a social function and is a preparation for primary education. The general aim of pre-school education is to develop the child's:

– mental, physical and psychomotor balance;

– intellectual skills;

– capacity for expression and communication;

– independence;

– creativity.

Pre-school education is provided in nursery schools (*écoles maternelles*) which are attached to primary schools. There are nursery schools in the three educational networks. In most cases, depending on their size, nursery schools are organized in groups or 'classes' according to age, but in some rural areas where small schools do not have enough children to set up three age groups, the 'family model', bringing together children of different ages in one class, is often used.

The children are supervised mainly by nursery teachers. Since 1989, each pre-school teacher is responsible for one class, but specific provisions, as well as the internal rules of each establishment, encourage collaboration between teachers.

The organization of classes is very flexible, in order to adapt teaching to children's needs. There are various activities to encourage the child's development – psychomotor, artistic, linguistic, logical and social – but no lessons as such.

There is no formal assessment at this level and pupils automatically progress to the next class.

The school week is structured around five mornings and four afternoons; Wednesday afternoon is free. The school year is from 1 September to 30 June. In addition to traditional public holidays, there is one week's holiday in February (*Carnaval*) and November (*Toussaint*) and two weeks' at Christmas and at Easter.

There are special nursery schools for mentally or physically handicapped children.

Teachers

Nursery teachers have followed three-year concurrent courses (of academic and theoretical and practical teacher training) at a teacher training institution (*Institut d'Enseignement Supérieur Pédagogique*) leading to a teaching diploma (*Instituteur/trice préscolaire*).

Teachers are employed by the organizing body. They may work part-time or full-time.

Participation in in-service training is voluntary and arranged under the responsibility of the different organizing bodies.

Statistics 1991/92

	Pupils	Teachers*	Schools
Community Schools	14,576	894	194
Provincial Schools	314	18	3
Communal Schools	81,301	5,327	1,001
'Free' Schools	65,629	4,038	719

* Number of full-time and part-time teachers.

3. Compulsory education

According to the Act of 29 June 1983, compulsory education lasts for 12 years, from 6 to 18 years of age.

Children are required to attend school full-time up to the age of 15, completing primary education and at least the first two years of secondary education. Pupils who have not completed the first two years of secondary education are required to attend full-time education until the age of 16. Those who do not wish to continue full-time until 18 may then follow compulsory part-time education up to the age of 18.

Part-time compulsory education is defined as studies in a recognized establishment, in the form of

either part-time study or a recognized training course.

3.1 Primary education (Enseignement primaire)

Primary education caters for children aged six to 12. It lasts six years and is divided into three cycles of two years each.

Primary education is provided in primary schools. In organizational terms, these may be:

– independent primary schools;

– primary schools attached to a secondary establishment;

– primary schools attached to a teacher training institution.

In accordance with official measures to promote equal opportunities for boys and girls, primary schools are now usually coeducational. However, there are still a few single-sex schools, mostly in the subsidized 'free' denominational sector. Classes are usually organized by age.

Instruction is provided five days per week, morning and afternoon, with the exception of Wednesday afternoon, for a total of 182 days per year. There are 28 weekly lessons of 50 minutes each. The school year, as at pre-school level, starts on 1 September and ends on 30 June. Holidays are identical to those at pre-school level.

The general aims of primary education may be summarized as follows:

– to encourage the personal development of each child whilst respecting its identity;

– to encourage the child's initiation into society;

– to help the child acquire basic knowledge and skills;

– to overcome the child's inequalities with regard to the school and education.

In 1993, these general aims were made more precise in an action plan intended to promote school success, which, at the initiative of the Minister of Education, brings together all organizations representing organizing bodies.

This action plan provides, *inter alia*, that by the year 2005 all schools of basic education (nursery and primary schools) should be organized in cycles which allow each child:

– to progress in school in a continuous manner at his/her own rhythm from nursery school entry to the end of the sixth year of primary;

– to complete certain essential courses with reference to standards of knowledge and the level of studies.

To this end, all organizing bodies will implement strategies to:

– harmonize the transition from nursery to primary school;

– give meaning to learning;

– assure continuity;

– take individual rhythms into account through differentiated learning;

– avoid making pupils repeat, through the use of formative assessment within the same cycle and summative assessment at its end;

– support schools and teachers in their efforts to succeed;

– associate parents of all backgrounds with school life and ensure real collaboration with them;

– encourage the school to be open to its environment.

Since September 1984, standards for the staff-pupil ratio in primary schools have, as in nursery schools, been based on the system of *capital-périodes*. This fixes a certain number of periods at the disposal of the school in accordance with its total number of pupils. Each unit of 24 periods entitles the school to a full-time teacher. The system enables the school to adapt its structure partially to its pupils' needs.

Curriculum

Since 1971, primary schools have been going through a process of fundamental reform in terms of both educational objectives and methods and teaching content. However, this reform has not extended to all primary schools, a large proportion of which continue to use traditional methods.

As a general rule, the reforms aimed to introduce a greater degree of flexibility into education, to take into consideration the particular ways of learning of young children, to adapt education to the changing needs of the surrounding world and to respect the learning speed and rhythm of the individual child as far as possible.

Curricula are designed to promote the acquisition of 'instrumental knowledge' (such as the general mastery of language and mathematics) rather than 'factual knowledge'.

The timetable includes: French, writing (cycle I), mathematics, history, geography, natural sciences, religion or ethics, physical education, musical education, manual education, civics and road safety.

In some towns and communes (the Brussels region and some localities designated by law), the study of Dutch is compulsory from cycle II. In the rest of the French Community, a second national language (Dutch or German) or English may be taught in cycle III.

Assessment and qualifications

As mentioned above, assessment is an area in which the principle of freedom is guaranteed.

Throughout the year, teachers use a continuous formative assessment to monitor the progress of their pupils. At the end of the school year, the teacher makes a summative assessment, and can use tests to assess pupils. The teacher or team of teachers/Class Council assesses the year's work and the results of the tests (if any) at the end of the year to decide whether or not to allow a pupil to move on to the next class. In this, the pupil's analytical skills, ability to think independently, cooperative spirit and taste for work and for working well must all be taken into account. Report cards regularly keep the child and his or her parents informed of test results, academic progress, behaviour in class and personal development.

It is possible for a child to repeat classes each year and thus within a cycle but it is rare to repeat more than one year at primary level. Pupils who experience learning difficulties can receive special and individualized assistance from a remedial teacher.

However, the progressive implementation of the action plan will generalize the use of formative assessment, with summative assessment only at the end of a two-year cycle.

When they have successfully completed six years of primary education, pupils receive a certificate of primary education (certificat d'études de base – CEB) in accordance with the Law of 29 June 1983. Pupils may also obtain this certificate by passing the cantonal examination.

For pupils having difficulties, the period of compulsory schooling may include seven years of primary education, or even eight in exceptional cases.

Teachers

In most cases, primary school teachers (instituteurs/ trices primaires) are allocated by class and provide all instruction, but, especially in cycle III, instruction may be broken down by subject area. Some courses may be given by specialized teachers (language, physical education or artistic or manual activities), who are employed on the basis of their teaching qualification.

Teachers have received three years of initial training at a teacher training institution (Institut d'Enseignement Supérieur Pédagogique).

Each year the ideal number of days of in-service training is fixed in regulations. The implementation of the action plan has led to an increase in in-service training activities which have also been allocated a specific budget.

Statistics 1991/92

	Pupils	Teachers*	Schools
Community Schools	34,190	2,585	207
Provincial Schools	921	73	3
Communal Schools	130,757	10,327	1,004
'Free' Schools	135,929	9,437	706

* Number of full-time and part-time teachers.

3.2 Secondary education (Enseignement secondaire)

Secondary education, like primary education, is included in the period of compulsory schooling. Full-time schooling may last until age 18, or up to the age of 15 or 16, when part-time schooling may be followed up to age 18.

There are two procedures for entering secondary education:

– the first (which applies to 82% of pupils) allows pupils with a certificate of primary education (CEB) to be admitted automatically into secondary education. Pupils who have completed the sixth year of primary education but have not obtained the certificate may also be admitted under certain conditions;

- the second (applying to 18% of pupils) provides for admission for 12-year-olds who do not have the certificate.

The *CEB* may also be awarded to pupils who did not complete primary education successfully, but have successfully completed the first year of secondary education or the second year of vocational education.

In the French Community, secondary education is divided into two main categories:

Type I: three cycles of two years (known as 'reformed' (*rénové*) education);

Type II: two cycles of three years (known as 'traditional' education); this system now exists in only a few subsidized public establishments.

The introduction of Type I secondary education began in 1969 in the public sector, and has now been extended to all schools organized by the French Community and to nearly all subsidized denominational and non-denominational establishments, and to provincial and communal schools.

The French Community provides secondary education in three types of establishments:

- the Royal *Atheneum* (*Athénée Royal*), organizing the three cycles, or the second and third cycles;

- the Community *Lyceum* (*Lycée de la Communauté Francaise*), organizing the first cycle, or the first and second cycle;

- the Community Technical Institute (*Institut technique de la Communauté Francaise*), organizing the three cycles or the second and third cycles.

Schools are usually coeducational. Secondary schools do not charge fees. They may be attached to primary schools. Classes are generally organized by age and sometimes by subject. In some schools, classes can be organized by level of ability. However, because of repeating, classes sometimes include pupils of various age-groups.

Secondary schools provide 32 lessons of 50 minutes each per week. In sections including practical classes as part of vocational education there may be 34 or even 36 lessons. The school year is organized as at primary level.

Curriculum

Type I

Type I secondary education, under the Law of 19 July 1971, is organized in the following four forms:

- general education;

- technical education;

- vocational education;

- artistic education;

and in two main streams:

- the transition stream (general, technical and artistic education), the objective of which is to prepare pupils for higher education while leaving them the option of entering employment;

- the qualification stream (technical, vocational and artistic education), the objective of which is to prepare pupils for employment, while allowing them the option of entering higher education.

As mentioned above, Type I secondary education comprises three cycles of two years:

- 1st cycle – an observation cycle (usually for pupils aged 12 to 14);

- 2nd cycle – an orientation cycle (usually for pupils aged 14 to 16);

- 3rd cycle – a determination cycle (usually for pupils aged 16 to 18).

In the first year of the **observation cycle**, nearly all pupils follow a common curriculum – religion or ethics, French, a second language, mathematics, history, geography, sciences, physical education and artistic education. In the common second year, the common curriculum is the same, with various basic options: Latin, economics and scientific, artistic or technical education. In the vocational second year, common courses do not include a second language or artistic education. Each grouped option of 12 weekly lessons covers at least two areas of technical activity.

From the beginning of the **orientation cycle**, the four forms of education are distinct, although within each form of education, in addition to the various options, there is a common core which is reduced in volume during the **determination cycle**.

In **the second cycle of the transition stream**, in addition to common instruction, it is compulsory to choose from among the following options: a second modern language, mathematics and sciences (biology, chemistry and physics), Latin, Greek, economics, social sciences, technical and technological education, and physical or artistic education.

In **the third cycle of the transition stream**, a training system incorporating integrated themes (scientific, classical, economic, social science and artistic), or training which combines options, has been introduced from the 1993/94 school year.

In **the second and third cycles of the qualification stream**, in addition to general education, grouped options representing an average of 21 weekly lessons are organized. These cover the following nine areas: agronomy, industry, construction, hotel work, clothing, arts, economics, social service, and sciences.

In **vocational education**, options are also grouped into nine areas. One grouped option represents 25 weekly lessons. At the end of the second cycle of vocational education there may be a year of further education or specialization.

At the end of the 3rd cycle, the following may be organized:

- a preparatory year for higher education (university);

- a year of further education, or specialization in a qualification stream leading to a qualification certificate;

- a seventh year of vocational education leading to an upper secondary school certificate.

Type II

Type II secondary education is organized according to the basic laws on general and technical secondary education of April and July 1957. It comprises two cycles of three years each.

General Type II secondary education is composed of the following sections: Latin-Greek, Latin-

mathematics, Latin-sciences, modern humanities (scientific, economic and human science options).

Two-thirds of technical education courses are theoretical; in vocational education, two-thirds are practical. However, since there are few remaining technical and vocational sections, there are no longer separate schools of technical Type II education.

Assessment and qualifications

Teachers use formative assessment methods on a regular basis. The results of this continuous (periodical) assessment, together with the results of the one or two examination sessions which may be organized, are all taken into account in the decision of the Class Council (Type I) or the teaching staff (Type II), at the end of each school year, as to whether or not a pupil will move up to the next year, with or without restriction or repeat the current year. When they are organized, the examinations are written, oral or practical, depending on the subject.

In both Type I and Type II education, certificates are awarded by the schools concerned. The upper secondary education certificate (*certificat d'enseignement secondaire supérieur – CESS*) is ratified by the 'homologation committee', which ensures that the schools comply with regulations on the organization of studies.

At the end of the third year of general or technical studies, or of the fourth year of vocational education, the pupil receives a lower secondary education certificate (*certificat d'enseignement secondaire inférieur – CESI*).

In Type I education, in the technical or vocational forms, a qualification certificate (*certificat de qualification – CQ*) is awarded at the end of the 4th year, and a pupil may obtain a lower secondary education certificate at the end of the first cycle of Type II secondary technical education.

An upper secondary education certificate is awarded to each pupil who has successfully completed the sixth year of Type I or Type II education in the general or technical sections.

In the vocational sections, a study certificate (*certificat d'études)* and a qualification certificate are awarded at the end of the sixth year of studies. Pupils who go on to a seventh year of vocational studies may obtain an upper secondary education certificate if they already have a lower secondary education certificate, which in vocational education may be obtained at the end of the fourth year.

These certificates are not obtained on the basis of examinations separate from the overall assessment procedures described above and defined by the school itself. They are awarded to pupils who have regularly followed and successfully completed the course concerned.

Teachers

Teachers are subject specialists and are appointed to teach these subjects.

To be appointed to a permanent position in secondary education, a candidate must have one of the following:

- The qualification for lower secondary school teachers (*diplôme d'agrégé de l'enseignement secondaire inférieur – AESI*). This diploma is awarded to students who have successfully completed the three-year teacher training course at a teacher training institution and qualifies the holder to teach in the lower cycle (the first three years). The course comprises general and pedagogical training, including the study of one or two specific subjects. In the third year, about 50% of the time is spent on teaching practice.

- The qualification for upper secondary school teachers (*diplôme d'agrégé de l'enseignement secondaire supérieur – AESS*). This diploma is awarded after at least four years of study (at *candidature* and *licence* levels) at a university and qualifies the holder to teach in the upper three years of secondary education and in short higher education.

The four or five years of academic training is completed by pedagogical training and teaching practice. Pedagogical training is not full-time and may be carried out either in parallel to the degree course from the third year or after its completion as a two-year part-time course.

To be appointed to a permanent position, teachers of technical and practical vocational education must have a qualification for lower secondary technical education (*diplôme d'agrégé(e) de l'enseignement technique moyen inférieur or regent(e) technique*) obtained on completion of three years of study at a technical teacher training college. There are also technical teacher training courses offered by social advancement education which lead to a teaching qualification; these last one, two or three years depending on what level of education the entrant already has.

In-service teacher training is organized by each education network within the legal framework regarding the aims, methods and administration of such training. Participation by teachers is voluntary.

Statistics 1991/92

	Pupils	Teachers*	Schools
Community Schools	89,773	13,643	204
Provincial Schools	29,887	5,079	62
Communal Schools	32,479	4,722	64
'Free' Schools	183,039	24,695	409

* Number of full-time and part-time teachers.

4. Initial vocational education and training

4.1 Part-time compulsory schooling

Beyond full-time compulsory schooling, the training of young people below 18 years of age comes under three types of measures conforming to requirements for part-time compulsory schooling up to age 18:

- part-time education;
- apprenticeship (including industrial apprenticeship);
- recognized training courses.

Part-time education

Under the Law of 29 June 1983 on compulsory education, part-time compulsory education was introduced in 1984 for young people who have either reached the age of 15 and have already had two years of secondary education or who have already reached the age of 16. Pupils who no longer wish to follow full-time education can study on a part-time basis in a centre for part-time education (*Centre d'éducation et de formation en alternance – CEFA*) or in a recognized training centre, such as a centre for training in independent professions (*Centre de formation des classes moyennes*).

The centres for part-time education provide courses combining general education (including social and personal training) with preparation for an occupation. The content of courses is limited, and designed to be a continuation of the full-time education system. The centres are linked to a school providing full-time technical and/or secondary vocational education.

Training lasts for 600 periods of 50 minutes per year, spread over at least 20 weeks. The number of periods devoted to general training in proportion to the number of periods spent on vocational training is partly left to the discretion of the management of the centre, which takes into account the characteristics of the group of pupils concerned. Part-time secondary education may be provided outside the opening hours of full-time education establishments. Evening or weekend courses are allowed. This type of education may also be organized in modules to be determined by the Executive of the French Community.

Part-time education leads to an annual certificate indicating the skills acquired by the pupil, and may also lead to a qualification certificate (*certificat de qualification*), equivalent to the certificate awarded for full-time study.

Apprenticeship

Apprenticeship is a recognized form of part-time compulsory schooling. It is available to 15-year-olds who have successfully completed two years of general secondary education or vocational secondary education, or have passed an entrance examination, or to 16-year-olds.

Apprenticeship lasts for one to three years. Theoretical vocational/technical training lasts for 360 hours during the first year and 240 hours during the following two years. It is provided in a *Centre de formation des classes moyennes* for one to one-and-a-half days per week. Practical training is provided by a craftsman; the apprentice spends three-and-a-half to four days a week in a firm with which he/she has an apprenticeship contract.

Apprenticeship contracts may be concluded for all groups recognized by the *Conseil supérieur des classes moyennes*, that is, commerce, trade, smaller industries and occupations in the services sector.

According to the apprenticeship contract, a monthly minimum salary is paid to the apprentice by the head of the firm on a progressive basis. The training period is subject to continuous assessment and ends in an examination.

The *Institut de Formation Permanente Pour les Classes Moyennes et les Petites et Moyennes Enterprises* (Institute of Continuing Training for Independent Professions and Small and Medium-sized Enterprises) at present provides training to 8,000 apprentices in the French Community.

In 1983, apprenticeships in occupations exercised by salaried workers were recognized under the name 'industrial apprenticeship'. This type of apprenticeship is intended for young people, aged between 16 and 21, with a poor school record, who have lost interest in attending school. It lasts for six months to two years and may take place in several firms successively.

Training in a firm lasts an average of 21 hours per week. The content is established by the representative committee of the sector concerned. Theoretical training is provided in school for 15 hours over two days per week. The apprentice receives an allowance, a percentage of the minimum wage in the chosen sector, from the head of the firm.

The apprenticeship leads to a vocational aptitude certificate (*brevet d'aptitude professionnelle*) and a certificate of apprenticeship (*attestation d'apprentissage*).

Recognized training courses

These courses are given by bodies, usually non-profit-making associations, which are recognized and subsidized by the authorities of the Community.

After the age of 18, the vocational training of young people may be covered either by continuing training intended for adults, or by provisions specifically aimed at 18- to 25-year-olds, that is, the industrial apprenticeship described above and the employment-training agreement described below.

4.2 Employment-training agreement

Set up in 1986, this type of training is available to all young people between the ages of 18 and 25 who are seeking employment, and do not already possess a diploma of long or short higher education or university education, or of technical upper secondary education.

The employment-training agreement involves industrial and commercial firms, non-profit-making associations and the liberal professions. The agreement is signed by the young person and the employer and lasts for a minimum of one year or a maximum of three years. It has two parts: a contract for part-time work of indeterminate duration (at least half-time) and training.

Theoretical training lasts for 256 hours per year when it is provided by an employer in the context of training for independent professions (*classes moyennes*) and 500 hours when it takes place in an education establishment or training centre, in particular in a centre organized by a Community/regional training office such as *FOREM* (Community and regional office of vocational training and employment).

Since 1987, nearly 600 young people have taken part in employment-training agreements in Wallonia and the Brussels region.

*
* *

In the French Community, three other forms of training are specifically aimed at young people over 18 who are from disadvantaged backgrounds and are considered to be at risk:

– apprenticeship training enterprises (*Entreprises d'apprentissage professionnel - EAP*), which offer 18 months of training and professional activity in an enterprise created for this purpose;

– centres for employment promotion (*Centres de promotion de l'emploi – CPE*) offering sandwich courses combining work and training;

– integrated development actions (*Actions intégrées de développement – AID*) based on partnerships between different associations, employers, unions and public services with the aim of reintegrating young people between 18 and 25 years old who are not entitled to unemployment benefit.

5. Higher education

There are three types of higher education: short higher education, long higher education and university education.

Admission

All those who hold an upper secondary education certificate (*Certificat d'enseignement secondaire supérieur – CESS*) have access to all three types of higher education. For some courses (for example, in the engineering sections) an entrance examination is organized.

Fees/Student finance

Registration fees *(minerval)* are paid in all types of higher education. The minimum amount in short and long higher education is fixed by regulations. Universities fix the amount themselves.

Academic year

The academic year comprises 30 weeks of classes and begins between 15 September and the first Monday of October.

Courses/Qualifications

Short and long higher education

Short and long higher education covers an extremely wide range of courses. It prepares students for a variety of activities, providing access to occupations mainly in the following sections: industry, trade, transport, agriculture, paramedical and social, education, translation and interpretation, applied arts and distributive arts.

Courses are given in institutions, bearing a variety of names depending on the specializations taught (e.g. *Institut d'enseignement supérieur pédagogique – IESP*, or higher teacher training institution).

Education comprises two forms:

– short higher education, which is organized in a single cycle of study lasting 3 or 4 years and leads to the diplomas of *gradué* (in various disciplines), nurse, social worker or auxiliary, librarian-documentalist, pre-school teacher, primary teacher, educator, lower secondary teacher (*agrégé*);

– long higher education, which is of the same nature and level as university education. It is organized in two cycles of study, lasts at least 4 years and leads to the following diplomas and degrees: industrial engineer, commercial engineer, upper secondary teacher *(agrégé)*, architect, *licencié* in commercial, administrative or consular sciences, *licencié* in translation, *licencié* in applied communications.

University education

University education is organized in institutions with university or equivalent status. Three universities in the French Community consist of the five traditional faculties (philosophy and arts, law, sciences, medicine, applied sciences) and a variable number of departments, schools and institutes which organize courses in other disciplines (agricultural sciences, oriental studies, business and economics, education, science, etc.).

The aim of university education is to provide theoretical training for managerial staff responsible for research, conception and application of knowledge.

University education is subdivided into distinct levels of study. Each period or cycle of study leads to the award of a degree which is required to be admitted to the next study cycle. As a general rule, the first university degree is the *candidat* obtained after two or sometimes three years of study. It indicates that the student has completed the basic training essential to commence the second cycle. The second cycle leads to a second degree, the *licence*, obtained after two or three years of study. It includes specialized education and the presentation of a thesis. In some disciplines, the second cycle leads directly to the qualifications of doctor, pharmacist, engineer or teacher (*maître*) and thus lasts longer. Some *licences* may be supplemented by the diploma of *agrégé de l'enseignement supérieur (AESS)*, a diploma in upper secondary education, necessary to become a teacher at this level.

University education may also include a third cycle in some specializations. This leads to the award of the title of doctor to students who have successfully defended a thesis at least one or two years after completing the second cycle.

Assessment

Each year of study leads to examinations which determine whether a student may continue to the next year. Examinations are carried out in line with a number of administrative and organizational arrangements. Two examination sessions are held each academic year (the first between 15 June and 15 July, the second after 15 August of the current academic year). Students are prohibited from sitting the same examination more than four times in two academic years and must sit examinations during the first session. Students are, at the end of the academic year, either:

– admitted to the next year of study if they have obtained a score of at least 50% in each test and 60% of the points awarded for the entire examination;

– deferred and required to resit, at the second session, the examinations in which they did not meet the examining board's standards;

– rejected, and must repeat the year.

1. Responsibilities and administration

1.1 Administration

As a consequence of the recent reforms of the State, education policy is the responsibility of the Council of the German-Speaking Community and its Government and Minister of Education.

In the German-speaking Community, except for private schools, there are three main types of education institutions:

- public education institutions organized and managed by the German-speaking Community and financed in total from its budget;

- public education institutions subsidized by the German-speaking Community but managed by communal authorities;

- 'free' education institutions, denominational or non-denominational, subsidized by the German-speaking Community.

Each category comprises an 'educational network' composed of one or more 'organizing bodies', each directing one or more schools.

The organizing body of Community education is the Minister of Education. The Minister directly administers and manages establishments at all levels, and the careers of administrators of the Minister's own educational network. The organizing bodies of subsidized public education however, are the communes, and of 'free' subsidized education, the natural or legal persons responsible.

The Minister grants subsidies to educational establishments under certain conditions.

Establishments must:

- comply with legislation on language;

- adopt a structure approved by the Minister;

- follow a curriculum which meets legal requirements;

- submit to supervision and inspection as organized by the Government of the Community, which is responsible for determining that the level of instruction is satisfactory;

- have a minimum number of pupils per class, section or level;

- be composed of educational facilities which are located in the same complex of buildings and form a whole, and which meet standards for hygiene and cleanliness;

- follow the general scheme for leave and holidays;

- employ staff who are not likely to endanger pupils' health;

- possess the teaching materials and school facilities required to meet educational needs.

If the establishment meets these conditions, the organizing body is free to choose staff, as long as they also meet certain standards, and to choose teaching methods.

With respect to the freedom of subsidized education, the Minister decides on the rational organization of school transport and on the organization of centralized and decentralized in-service training activities.

At the level of each educational establishment, daily management is generally the responsibility of the organizing body or of the head teacher to whom it delegates its responsibilities.

Each educational establishment has total responsibility for the assessment of its pupils.

Within the limits of laws and decrees, each organizing body may define the type of assessment it wishes to use and the means of monitoring and communicating the results of the assessment.

1.2 Financing

The Community covers all the costs of Community education and subsidizes public and 'free' education as far as permitted by laws and decrees.

These subsidies cover, completely or partially:

- staff remuneration, under the same conditions (qualifications and duties) as those granted to Community education staff;

- operating expenses according to regulatory criteria;

- expenses related to facilities, construction and development, within the limits of credits provided for in the budgetary decree.

Financing is partially based on a pupil/teacher ratio. Since September 1984, the rules which govern the pupil/teacher ratio have been based on a subsidizable set of units known as the system of 'capital periods'. This places a certain number of periods at the disposal of the school in accordance with its total number of pupils. Each unit of 20 (secondary) or 28 (primary) periods entitles the school to a full-time teacher. The system enables the school to adapt its structure partially to its pupils' needs.

1.3 Inspection

There is a triple system of inspection, consisting of:

- A monitoring service which ensures that Community subsidies are being used correctly. This service mainly controls the number of regular pupils and students.

- An inspection service which verifies the level of instruction in Community educational establishments and gives its opinion on the qualifications of staff. This service also provides educational support by advising teachers, and contributes to the preparation of curricula and the development of teaching methods. In addition, it verifies the level of instruction in

education subsidized by the Community. Organizing bodies also have a teaching inspection service for their network. Every six months inspectors establish a plan for in-service teacher training activities.

This inspection service is still provided by the French Community, but in the near future, the Minister of the German-speaking Community will have his own inspection service that will cooperate with the inspection services of the two other Communities and of the neighbouring countries.

- A 'homologation committee' whose task is to verify whether secondary-level studies have been completed in keeping with the provisions of legislation and regulations. The committee is also responsible for approving lower secondary school certificates and upper secondary school certificates (*Abschlußzeugnis der Unterstufe des Sekundarunterrichts, Abschlußzeugnis der Oberstufe des Sekundarunterrichts*).

This 'homologation committee' is an inspection service of the French Community, but the German-speaking Community is represented in every section.

1.4 Advisory bodies

The Minister's advisory body is the *Pädagogische Kommission*. This comprises representatives of the different organizing bodies, the *Pädagogische Arbeitsgruppe* (service of the Department of Education responsible for the in-service training organized by the Ministry), the inspection service, the administration, the institutions of higher education and the unions. It advises the Minister mainly on matters of in-service training and educational projects.

1.5 Guidance

The tasks of guidance and orientation of pupils in pre-school, primary, secondary and special education are the responsibility of the psycho-medico-social centres (*Psycho-Medico-Sozial-Zentren – PMS*). These centres are also responsible for school medical inspections. The centres are independent of the schools, but work closely with them and with families. Each centre is composed of an interdisciplinary team made up of educational psychologists/counsellors, social workers, nurses and independent doctors.

The teams deal with assistance and advice to pupils, parents and schools. The main task of these centres consists in helping schools to offer their pupils the best possible chance of developing a balanced personality. That is why *PMS* counselling is of a multidisciplinary nature. In order to fulfil their task properly the centres follow pupils from nursery school up to the end of their secondary education.

Several types of educational activities help young people plan their lives and careers. The methods used combine group activities and individual analyses. The *PMS* centres use computer software (e.g. *CHOIX*) and other interesting means (e.g. *BIZ*-Mobil, a kind of mobile exhibition of information on occupations mainly in Germany and Belgium) to help students choose their studies and occupations.

2. Pre-school education (*Kindergarten*)

Pre-school education is an integral part of the education system. Pre-school education is optional, free and coeducational, and is provided for children aged from two-and-a-half to six years, and up to seven years in exceptional cases. For children aged three and above the attendance rate is higher than 95%.

Pre-school education has a social function and is a preparation for primary education. The general aim of pre-school education is to develop the child's:

– mental, physical and psychomotor balance;

– intellectual skills;

– capacity for expression and communication;

– independence;

– creativity.

Pre-school education is provided in nursery schools (*Kindergarten*) which are usually attached to primary schools. There are nursery schools in the three educational networks.

In most cases, depending on their size, nursery schools are organized in groups or classes based on age, but in some rural areas where small schools do not have enough children to set up three age groups, the 'family model', bringing together children of different ages into one class, is often used. There are 20 pupils per class.

The children are supervised mainly by nursery teachers. Each pre-school teacher is responsible for one class, but specific provisions, as well as the internal rules of each establishment, encourage cooperation between teachers.

The timetable is flexible as there is no academic teaching. There are various activities to encourage the child's development – psychomotor, artistic, linguistic, mathematical, musical, scientific – but no lessons as such. There is no formal assessment and no written reports at this level.

Assessment is mainly based on the teacher's observation of pupils' attitudes and behaviour. Pupils automatically progress to the next class. The *PMS* centres, together with the educational team, measure the degree of maturity and development reached by the child.

The school week consists of four-and-a-half days; Wednesday afternoon is free. In the first year, pupils may attend only in the mornings if their parents choose. The length of the school year is the same as in compulsory education, with two months' holiday in the summer, and two weeks' at Christmas and at Easter.

Teachers

Pre-school teachers have followed three-year concurrent courses of theoretical and practical teacher training at an institution of higher education (*Pädagogische Hochschule*) leading to a teaching diploma [*Vorschullehrer(in)*, *Kindergärtner(in)*]. Teachers are employed by the organizing body. They may work part-time or full-time. In-service training is not compulsory, but

there are normally three in-service days (*Konferenztage*) per year.

Statistics 1991/92

	Pupils	Teachers*	Schools
Community Schools	696	42	10
Provincial Schools	–	–	–
Communal Schools	2,011	149	51
'Free' Schools	217	19	4

* Number of full-time and part-time teachers.

3. Compulsory education

According to the Act of 29 June 1983, compulsory education lasts for 12 years, from 6 to 18 years of age.

Children are required to attend school full-time up to the age of 15, completing primary education and at least the first two years of secondary education. Pupils who have not completed the first two years of secondary education are required to attend full-time education until the age of 16. Those who do not wish to continue full-time until 18 may then follow compulsory part-time education up to the age of 18.

Part-time compulsory education is defined as studies in a recognized establishment, in the form of either part-time study or a recognized training course.

3.1 Primary education (*Primarschulwesen*)

Primary education caters for children aged six to 12. It lasts six years and is divided into three cycles of two years each.

The general aims of primary education may be summarized as follows:

– to encourage the personal development of each child whilst respecting its identity, to stimulate its initiation into society and to participate actively in its education;

– to help the child acquire basic knowledge and skills;

– to overcome the child's inequalities with regard to the school and education.

In the German-speaking Community, there is a special solution for the French-speaking minority according to the Laws on languages (1963): there are French primary schools where the language of instruction is French and the second language is German.

Primary education is provided in primary schools. In organizational terms, these may be:

– independent primary schools;

- primary schools attached to a secondary establishment;

- primary schools attached to a teacher training institution.

There are primary schools in every educational network.

Each school is placed under the responsibility of the organizing body (Community, free bodies and institutions, or other public institutions) on which it depends. There are no entrance requirements. Education is free of charge.

In accordance with official measures to promote equal opportunities for boys and girls, primary schools are now usually coeducational.

Classes are usually organized by age. In low population areas classes may cover two years (one cycle) or more.

Instruction is provided five days per week, morning and afternoon, with the exception of Wednesday afternoon, for a total of 182 days per year. There are 28 weekly lessons of 50 minutes each. The school year starts on 1 September and ends on 30 June. There are three main holidays: two weeks at Christmas, two weeks at Easter and eight weeks in the summer, and one shorter mid-term holiday each term.

Curriculum

Since 1971, primary schools have been going through a process of fundamental reform in terms of both educational objectives and methods and teaching content. However, this reform has not extended to all primary schools, a large proportion of which continue to use traditional methods.

As a general rule, the reforms aimed to introduce a greater degree of flexibility into education, to take into consideration the particular ways of learning of young children, to adapt education to the changing needs of the surrounding world and to respect the learning speed and rhythm of the individual child as far as possible.

Curricula are designed to promote the acquisition of instrumental skills (such as the general mastery of language and mathematics) rather than factual knowledge.

The timetable includes: German, French, observation of the environment (history, geography and science education), mathematics, religion or ethics, physical education, musical education, manual and artistic education, road safety and health education.

The teaching of French is possible from the first year on and compulsory from the third year on. (The Minister has made a lot of efforts to improve the teaching of French and the in-service-training of primary teachers, expecially in French.)

The same subjects are taught to all pupils, and there is little differentiation.

Assessment and qualifications

Each teacher and school have complete responsibility for the process of pupil assessment. As assessment is an area in which the pedagogical freedom of each network is guaranteed, each organizing body can define the type and method of assessment it wishes to use as well as the way it communicates the results, insofar as the relevant laws and regulations are respected.

Throughout the year, teachers use a continuous formative assessment to monitor the progress of their pupils on the basis of all written and oral work and homework. At the end of the school year, the teacher makes a summative assessment, and can use tests to assess pupils. The teacher or team of teachers/Class Council assesses the year's work and the results of the tests (if any) at the end of the year to decide whether or not to allow a pupil to move on to the next class. In this, the pupil's analytical skills, ability to think independently, cooperative spirit and taste for work and for working well must all be taken into account. Report cards regularly keep the child and his or her parents informed of test results, academic progress, behaviour in class and personal development.

It is possible for a child to repeat classes each year but it is rare to repeat more than one year at primary level. Pupils who experience learning difficulties can receive special and individualized assistance from a remedial teacher.

When they have successfully completed their primary education, pupils receive a certificate of primary education (*Abschlußzeugnis der Grundschule*). Schools may award the certificate themselves as long as they respect the terms of the law, or they may register pupils for a cantonal examination (minimum age: 11 years by 31 December of that year). This certificate can also be awarded to anyone who successfully completes either the first year of secondary school (class B) or a second year of vocational education, even though he or she did not obtain it in primary school.

For pupils having difficulties, the period of compulsory schooling may include seven years of primary education, or even eight in exceptional cases.

Teachers

In most cases, primary school teachers are allocated by class and provide all instruction, but, especially in cycle III, instruction may be broken down by subject area. Some courses may be given by specialized teachers (language, physical education or artistic or manual activities) or remedial teachers.

Teachers have received three years of initial training at a teacher training institution. The course comprises academic and theoretical and practical teacher training and leads to diploma for primary school teachers [*Primarschullehrer(in)*].

In-service training is not compulsory, but there are normally three in-service days (*Konferenztage*) per year, and 10 days of training per year are available in special centres. Teachers may work full-time or part-time and are appointed by the organizing body of the school.

Statistics 1991/92

	Pupils	Teachers*	Schools
Community Schools	1,300	101	10
Provincial Schools	–	–	–
Communal Schools	2,990	294	51
'Free' Schools	661	64	5

* Number of full-time and part-time teachers.

3.2 Secondary education (*Sekundarschulwesen*)

Secondary education, like primary education, is included in the period of compulsory schooling. Full-time schooling may last until age 18, or up to the age of 15 or 16, when part-time schooling may be followed up to age 18, combined with vocational training.

There are two procedures for entering secondary education:

– the first allows pupils with a certificate of primary education (*Abschlußzeugnis der Grundschule*) to be admitted automatically into the first year A (general education) of secondary education. Pupils who have completed the sixth year of primary education but have not obtained the certificate may also be admitted under certain conditions (on the agreement of parents, the recommendation of the *PMS* centre and the first year A admission council);

– the second provides for admission for 12-year-olds who do not have the certificate to the first year B (reception or transition class).

Transfer from the first year B to the first year A is possible up to 15 November and from first year A to first year B up to 15 January if the pupil's parents agree and the Class Council so advises.

Schools are usually coeducational. Secondary schools do not charge fees. Schools have an average of 200 – 400 pupils. They may be attached to primary schools. Classes are generally organized by age and sometimes by subject. However, because of repeating, classes sometimes include pupils of various age-groups.

Secondary schools provide 32 lessons of 50 minutes each per week. In sections including practical classes as part of vocational education there may be 34 or even 36 lessons. There are 182 school days per year and there are three main holidays: eight weeks in the summer, two weeks at Christmas and at Easter, and three shorter mid-term breaks each term.

In the German-speaking Community, secondary education now comprises Type I education only, which is divided into three cycles of two years and is known as reformed education.

Type I secondary education, under the Law of 19 July 1971, is organized in the following four forms:

- general education;

- technical education;

- vocational education;

- artistic education;

and in two main streams:

- the transition stream (general, technical and artistic education), the objective of which is to prepare pupils for higher education while leaving them the option of entering employment;

- the qualification stream (technical, vocational and artistic education), the objective of which is to prepare pupils for employment, while allowing them the option of entering higher education.

As mentioned above, Type I secondary education comprises three cycles of two years:

- 1st cycle – an observation cycle (usually for pupils aged 12 to 14);

- 2nd cycle – an orientation cycle (usually for pupils aged 14 to 16);

- 3rd cycle – a determination cycle (usually for pupils aged 16 to 18).

Throughout the first two cycles and to a lesser extent in the third cycle, there is the possibility of transferring from one form of education to another, as well as bridges from vocational education to other types of education.

Curriculum

In the first year of the **observation cycle**, nearly all pupils follow a common curriculum – German, French, religion or ethics, mathematics, history, geography, sciences, physical education and artistic education. In addition, five periods a week are left available to each school to allocate as they wish within a defined and legally fixed framework.

In the common second year, the common curriculum is the same, with various basic options: Latin, economics and scientific, artistic or technical education. Each option of 12 weekly lessons covers at least two areas of technical activity.

Special arrangements exist for pupils who follow vocational education from the second year. They study the same subjects provided in the basic course, but 8 to 10 lessons are available for each school to develop individually as regards, for example, the tradition of the school or the socio-economic environment in which it is situated. In the second year of vocational education the basic course is limited to 16 lessons. Two groups of subjects, a total of 16 lessons, are added to this package. Each of these groups provides an introduction to the theory and practice of the main vocational sectors.

From the beginning of the **orientation cycle**, the four forms of education are organized separately, although within each form of education, in addition to the various options, there is a common core which is reduced in volume during the **determination cycle**.

The common part consists of the basic course.

Basic education from the third to the sixth year consists of the following subjects: religion or non-denominational ethics, French, German, mathematics, history, geography, science and physical education in the transition stream. General academic education also includes a third modern language. In some schools, different subjects are gradually taught in the second language, French.

In addition to the common part, it is compulsory to choose from among the following options:

- in the transition stream: Latin, modern languages, mathematics, sciences, economics, social sciences, technological education, physical education;

- in the qualification stream: agronomy, industry, construction, hotel work, clothing, arts, economics, social services, sciences.

The educational networks enjoy total freedom as regards **teaching methods**. Curricula can contain a list of recommended textbooks, but there is no obligation whatsoever to use a textbook from these lists. The same applies to **teaching materials**.

Assessment and qualifications

The essential instrument in assessment is the Class Council (*Klassenrat*), which is the committee consisting of the entire teaching staff responsible for the education of a specific group of pupils. It assesses their school progress and makes the decision regarding each pupils' promotion to a higher class. It issues certificates as appropriate. The Class Council bases its decisions on various factors, such as:

– the past school career of each pupil;

– the intermediate results from class work, assessments and oral and/or written examinations;

– information from the psycho-medico-social centre (*PMS*);

– interviews with the pupil and parents, as necessary.

Each Class Council has to establish, at regular intervals, an intellectual, social and moral assessment of each pupil. The results of assessments carried out during the year are taken into account in the end-of-year assessments. Tests are compulsory for all pupils.

At the end of the year, the Class Council decides, for each pupil, whether they should be promoted to a higher class – with or without restriction – or whether the promotion should be delayed or refused. Unsuccessful pupils repeat a year, but pupils with learning difficulties may obtain help from remedial teachers.

Certificates are awarded by the schools concerned, and then ratified by the 'homologation committee', which ensures that the schools comply with regulations on the organization of studies.

At the end of the third year of general or technical studies, or of the fourth year of vocational education, successful pupils receive a lower secondary school certificate (*Abschlußzeugnis der Unterstufe des Sekundarunterrichts*).

In the technical section, a qualification certificate (*Befähigungsnachweis*) is awarded at the end of the 6th year.

An upper secondary school certificate (*Abschlußzeugnis der Oberstufe des Sekundarunterrichts*) is awarded to each pupil who has successfully completed the sixth year in the general or technical sections.

In the vocational section, a study certificate (*Studienzeugnis*) and a qualification certificate (*Befähigungsnachweis*) are awarded at the end of the sixth year of studies. Pupils who go on to a seventh year of vocational studies may obtain an upper secondary certificate

Teachers

Teachers in secondary schools in the German-speaking Community are trained in the French Community as there is neither a teacher training institution for that level nor a university in the German-speaking Community itself.

Teachers are subject specialists and are appointed to teach these subjects.

To be appointed to a permanent position in secondary education, a candidate must have one of the following:

– The qualification for lower secondary school teachers (*diplôme d'agrégé de l'enseignement secondaire inférieur – AESI*). This diploma is awarded to students who have successfully completed the three-year teacher training course at a teacher training institution and qualifies the holder to teach in the lower cycle (the first three years). The course comprises general and pedagogical training, including the study of one or two specific subjects. In the third year, about 50% of the time is spent on teaching practice.

– The qualification for upper secondary school teachers (*diplôme d'agrégé de l'enseignement secondaire supérieur – AESS*). This diploma is awarded after at least four years of study (at *candidature* and *licence* levels) at a university and qualifies the holder to teach in the upper three years of secondary education.

The four or five years of academic training is completed by pedagogical training and teaching practice. Pedagogical training is not full-time and may either be carried out in parallel to the degree course from the third year or after its completion as a two-year part-time course.

Teachers of vocational education courses and certain technical courses at secondary level, for which no full-time training is available, may follow part-time teacher training through social advancement courses. Courses include theoretical and practical teacher training and teaching practice and lead to the certificate of pedagogical aptitude (*Fachkundelehrer(in) und Pädagogischer Befähigungsnachweis*).

Teachers may work full-time or part-time. They are appointed by the organizing body. In-service training is organized by the organizing body or the centralized structure and is available for all teachers.

	Pupils	Teachers*	Schools
Community Schools	1,507	306	5
Provincial Schools	–	–	–
Communal Schools	227	50	1
'Free' Schools	2,007	329	8

* Number of full-time and part-time teachers.

4. Initial vocational education and training

4.1 Part-time compulsory schooling

In the framework of compulsory schooling, the training of young people under 18 years of age comes under two types of measures conforming to requirements for part-time compulsory schooling up to age 18:

– part-time education;

– apprenticeship (apprenticeship in the SME sector and industrial apprenticeship).

Part-time education

Under the Law of 29 June 1983 on compulsory education, part-time compulsory education was introduced in 1984 for young people who have either reached the age of 15 and have already had two years of secondary education or who have already reached the age of 16. Pupils who no longer wish to follow full-time education can study on a part-time basis in one of the two centres for part-time education.

The centres for part-time education provide courses combining general education (including social and personal training) with preparation for an occupation. The content of courses is limited, and designed to be a continuation of the full-time education system. The centres are linked to a school providing full-time technical and/or secondary vocational education.

Training lasts for 600 periods of 50 minutes per year, spread over at least 20 weeks. (Part-time education lasts 360 hours in the first year – 15- to 16-year-olds, and 240 hours in the following two years.) Part-time education is provided for 40 weeks a year with an average of 15 hours per week covering, according to need, 8 hours of general (French/Dutch, mathematics), personal and social training and 7 hours of vocational training (technology). The remaining time may be spent on a training placement in a firm. The number of periods devoted to general training in proportion to the number of periods spent on vocational training is partly left to the discretion of the management of the centre, which takes into account the characteristics of the group of pupils concerned. Part-time secondary education may be provided outside the opening hours of full-time educational establishments. Evening or weekend courses are allowed. This type of education may also be organized in modules to be determined by the Government.

Part-time education leads to an attendance certificate (*Bescheinigung über den regelmäßigen Schulbesuch*), and may also lead to a qualification certificate (*Bescheinigung über die erworbenen Kenntnisse*).

Apprenticeship in the SME sector

Apprenticeship is a recognized form of part-time compulsory schooling. It is available to 15-year-olds who have successfully completed two years of general secondary education or vocational secondary education, or have passed an entrance examination, or to 16-year-olds. It aims to train young people to run a business.

Apprenticeship lasts three years. Theoretical vocational/technical training lasts for 360 hours during the first year and 240 hours during the following two years, and is provided in a SME training centre for one to one-and-a-half days per week. The apprentice then spends three-and-a-half to four days a week gaining practical experience in a firm with which he/she has an apprenticeship contract.

Apprenticeship contracts may be concluded for occupations related to commerce, trade, smaller industries, craftmanship and non-manual occupations in the services sector.

The training period is subject to continuous assessment and ends in an examination.

The Community Minister responsible for the SME sector is required to determine the length of training for each occupation or group of occupations within a range of one to three years. They also use the preliminary training during the period of apprenticeship as a basis for deciding whether the duration should be extended or shortened. A monthly minimum allowance, adjusted each year to the consumer price index, is paid each school year to the apprentice by the head of the firm on a progressive basis.

5. Higher education

In the German-speaking Community there is only one type of higher education (short higher education; short non-university level).

For long higher education or university education, students have to study in the French Community, the Flemish Community or Germany. Most choose the French Community, and this is one of the reasons why French is taught from early on in the education system of the German-speaking Community.

Admission

Students must have an upper secondary school certificate (*Abschlußzeugnis der Oberstufe des Sekundarbereichs = Abitur*).

Fees/Student finance

Students pay tuition fees each year, but grants are available from the Community budget and may be awarded on the basis of a means test.

Academic year

The academic year starts between 15 September and the first Monday of October, with a total of 30 weeks of classes.

Courses/Qualifications

Short higher education is organized in a single cycle of studies lasting three or four years, leading to a final diploma and providing direct access to a profession in the German-speaking Community.

This type of education covers two types of studies: paramedical (medical auxiliary education) [*Graduierte(r) Krankenpfleger(in)*] and educational (pedagogical education). It leads to diplomas in various professions: nurse, nursery teacher [*Kindergärtner(in)*], primary teacher [*Primarschullehrer(in)*].

Assessment

Each year of study is sanctioned by examinations which determine whether a student may continue to the next year. Examinations are regulated by a number of administrative and organizational rules. Two examination sessions are held each academic year. Students are prohibited from sitting the same examination more than four times in two academic years and must sit examinations during the first session. Students are, at the end of the academic year, either:

- admitted to the next year of study if they have obtained a score of at least 50% in each test and 60% of the points awarded for the entire examination;

- deferred and required to resit, at the second session, the examinations in which they did not meet the examining board's standards;

- rejected, and must repeat the year.

Assessment comprises the accumulation of results and the award of a certificate. It is based on end-of-year examinations and the submission of a final project or thesis. However, a dossier containing an evaluation of the performance of the students during the academic year, and in particular of their practical work and courses, is studied prior to assessment. Recently, initiatives have also been taken to introduce formative assessment aimed at providing teachers and students with more frequent assessment opportunities.

1. Responsibilities and administration

1.1 Administration

As a consequence of the recent reforms of the State, education policy is the responsibility of the *Vlaamse Raad* (Flemish Council, legislative power by means of *decreet*) and the Flemish Government and the Flemish Minister of Education (executive power by means of *besluit*). The Minister heads the Education Department, which is part of the Ministry of the Flemish Community.

The concept of organizing body (*inrichtende macht*) is central to the organization of Flemish education. The organizing body is the natural or legal person taking the initiative to provide education and being responsible for it. It defines the 'character' of the education provided (except for Community education), and develops the school educational plan.

According to the type of organizing body, there are three educational networks:

– Community education: education set up by the Autonomous Council for Community Education (*Autonome Raad van het Gemeenschapsonderwijs – ARGO*) on behalf of the Flemish Community. The Constitution stipulates that Community education must be neutral.

– Subsidized 'public' education: provincial education, organized by the provincial authorities, and municipal education, set up by the municipal authorities. Schools in this network can be denominational or neutral.

– Subsidized 'free' (private) education: education set up at private initiative by a private person or organization. It consists of denominational (mainly Catholic) and non-denominational private education.

Education organized by the first two networks (the authorities) is called public education. Education provided by the third network is called 'free' education.

A school is subsidized by the Community when it complies with legislation and regulations concerning the organization of studies and with legislation on language.

The organizing body receives the financial resources required to provide education. It is responsible for the correct management of these resources. The organizing body owns or rents the school buildings. The organizing bodies of subsidized education can apply for building grants for school construction.

The organizing body is free to appoint school staff within the limits of the personnel statute and the regulations concerning financing and subsidy.

It is also free to determine its teaching methods, and draws up curricula on the basis of centrally defined minimum goals (*eindtermen*). The curricula are not developed centrally. The minimum goals are the final aims to be achieved at each level of education and are determined by the Flemish Government. They are prepared by the education development service (*Dienst voor Onderwijsontwikkeling – DVO*) and, upon the unanimous recommendation of the Flemish Education Council (*Vlaamse Onderwijsraad – VLOR*), the Flemish Council ratifies them.

The school is responsible for assessment and can award certificates and diplomas on condition that the minimum goals, as ascertained by the inspectorate, are achieved.

In **Community education** the Central Council (*Centrale Raad*) of the *ARGO* receives and manages the financial resources required to provide education. It determines the school educational plan and school curricula, and deals with the recruitment of school staff, the management of the school construction fund and overall educational planning. The local School Council (*lokale schoolraden*) can take decisions on all matters which can be settled at local level. This applies to the provision of materials and financial management, and to teaching and staff policy. It is composed of representatives of parents, local social, economic and cultural circles and teachers. This council ensures genuine co-management. There is also a pedagogical board (*pedagogisch college*), composed of members of the teaching staff of the school. In higher non-university education, the local school council is called *raad van bestuur* (administration council).

In **subsidized public education** each organizing body enjoys full autonomy in conducting its local policy for the school or schools that come within its responsibility. There are two bodies coordinating the different organizing bodies of this network: *Cel voor het Vlaams Provinciaal Onderwijs (CVPO)* for the provinces; *Onderwijssecretariaat van de Steden en Gemeenten van de Vlaamse Gemeenschap (OVSG)* for the municipalities.

In **subsidized free education** the autonomy of the organizing bodies is the same. There are also bodies uniting the organizing bodies. As regards Catholic education, there is the *Vlaams Secretariaat van het Katholiek Onderwijs (VSKO)* at Community level, the *Diocesane Planificatie- en Coördinatiecommissie (DPCC)* at diocesan level and the *Regionale Coördinatiecommissie (RCC)* at regional level.

In subsidized public and free education, there is a Participation Council (*participatieraad*), composed of representatives of the organizing body, parents, staff members and the local community. The Council has the right to information about all matters involving school life. It provides advice with regard to the general organization and operation of the school, planning at school level and general criteria for the counselling and assessment of pupils, and is consulted about the criteria for applying the capital-periods system (number of periods per teacher), the determination and modification of school rules, school transport, and the safety and health of pupils. In subsidized free education, in a limited number of matters, the organizing body cannot make decisions without the consent of the Participation Council.

1.2 Financing

As far as public spending is concerned, it should be repeated that education is a Community matter. In Flanders, the Community and the region coincide politically and therefore all Community and regional matters are financed in total by the Community and the region. In addition to Community spending, contributions are made by the provinces and the municipalities (in subsidized public education), and by private persons and organizations (in subsidized free education).

The basic principle is that the Community covers all the costs of Community schools, and awards the subsidized schools grants to cover the running, maintenance and replacement costs of equipment and buildings. The salaries of all school staff are paid directly by the Education Department.

Access to education is free of charge until the end of compulsory schooling. However, in practice many schools have to cater for additional expenses, to which parents do make some financial contribution.

1.3 Inspection

The inspectorate (*Inspectie*) supervises the quality of all levels of education up to short higher education. To that end, it has to examine whether the minimum goals are properly achieved and whether the other organizational obligations are correctly observed. The inspectorate is not subject-related or meant to check out individual teachers. It operates through team visits aimed at the examination of the whole school.

Quality control in long higher education and at universities is essentially based on self-evaluation and 'visitation committees' (peer review).

The education development service (*Dienst voor Onderwijsontwikkeling – DVO*) can be considered as a scientific staff service belonging to the inspectorate. It defines the minimum goals, and develops the instruments required to measure the functioning of these.

1.4 Advisory/Consultative/ Participatory bodies

The Flemish Education Council (*Vlaamse Onderwijsraad – VLOR*) is the advisory and consultative body for all educational matters. All draft decrees in the field of education must be submitted to the *VLOR*. Furthermore, the *VLOR* can give advice to the Flemish Government at its own initiative. The *VLOR* consists of a general council and separate councils for primary, secondary, higher and adult education. The general council is composed of representatives of the organizing bodies, school staff, parents and socio-economic organizations, university experts and Education Department representatives.

Within the *VLOR* there are two so-called 'participation boards': one for subsidized public education and the other for subsidized free education. Their composition is analogous to that of participation councils in schools. The boards have a mediating role when conflicts arise and they have to establish violations of the participation rules.

The Flemish Socio-Economic Council (*Sociaal-Economische Raad van Vlaanderen – SERV*), composed of representatives of employers and employees, must give advice on all draft decrees, including those in the field of education.

The Flemish Interuniversity Council (*Vlaamse Interuniversitaire Raad – VLIR*) gives advice and makes proposals to the Minister of Education in the field of university education.

1.5 Guidance

Each educational network also has pedagogical counselling services (*pedagogische begeleidingsdiensten*) to assist teachers and schools in the general pedagogical and methodological fields.

Psycho-medico-social guidance centres (*Psycho-medisch-sociale centra – PMS*) deal with assistance and (non-binding) advice to pupils, parents and schools. The task of these centres consists in helping schools to offer their pupils the best possible chances of developing a balanced personality. *PMS* guidance is therefore multidisciplinary, with the team at a centre including doctors, paramedics, psychologists, educationalists and social workers. The centres follow pupils from nursery school up to the end of secondary education. *PMS* centres belong to one of the three educational networks.

2. Pre-school education (*Kleuteronderwijs*)

Pre-school education is optional and is provided for children aged between two-and-a-half and six years, exceptionally seven years, in nursery schools free of charge. The attendance rate is 92% among three-year-olds, 97% among four-year-olds and 100% among five-year-olds (and above).

Pre-school education has a social function and is a preparation for primary education. The general aim of pre-school education is to develop the child's:

– mental and physical equilibrium;

– intellectual skills;

– expression and communication skills;

– creativity and independence.

There are special nursery schools for children with serious mental or physical handicaps

Nursery schools are coeducational and can be attached to a primary school. In most cases, classes are organized into three groups of children by age, according to the size of the school. Teachers are allocated to a different group of children each year.

The school year is organized as at primary level.

Assessment in nursery schools is mainly based on observation. Pupils progress automatically up to the next class. The guidance centres, together with an educational team, measure the degree of maturity and development reached by the child.

Teachers

Intending pre-school teachers are trained in the same way as primary teachers (see 3) but are specialized in pre-school education. Successful students are awarded a teaching diploma (*kleuteronderwijzer*).

Teachers may work full-time or part-time. In-service training is not compulsory.

Statistics 1991/92

	Pupils	Teachers*	Schools
Community Schools	30,278	1,662	327
Provincial Schools	300	15	4
Communal Schools	41,417	2,200	405
'Free' Schools	161,266	8,328	1,336

* Number of full-time and part-time teachers.

There is no pupil/teacher ratio in the proper sense in pre-school education. Since September 1984, the rules which govern the pupil/teacher ratio have been based on a subsidizable set of units known as the system of *lestijden* (capital periods). It puts a certain number of periods at the disposal of the school in accordance with its total number of pupils. Each unit of 24 periods entitles the school to a full-time teacher. The system enables the school to adapt its structure partially to its pupils' needs.

3. Compulsory education

According to the Act of 29 June 1983, compulsory education lasts for 12 years, from 6 to 18 years of age.

Children are required to attend school full-time up to the age of 15, completing primary education and at least the first two years of secondary education. Pupils who have not completed the first two years of secondary education are required to attend full-time education until the age of 16. Those who do not wish to continue full-time until 18 may then follow compulsory part-time education up to the age of 18.

Part-time compulsory education is defined as studies in a recognized establishment, in the form of either part-time study or a recognized training course.

3.1 Primary education (*Lager onderwijs*)

Primary education is for children aged six to 12 years and is divided into three stages of two years each. It is provided free of charge in primary schools. These are usually coeducational; however, a rather limited number of schools are still single-sex.

Classes are usually organized by age. As in nursery schools, there is no pupil/teacher ratio in the proper sense, since standards are based on the system of *lestijden* (capital periods).

Instruction is provided five days per week, morning and afternoon, with the exception of Wednesday afternoon, for a total of 182 days per year. There are

28 weekly lessons of 50 minutes each. The school year starts on 1 September and ends on 30 June. There are three main holidays (two weeks at Christmas, two weeks at Easter and two months in the summer) and one shorter mid-term holiday each term.

The general aims of primary education may be summarized as follows:

- to encourage the personal development of each child whilst respecting its identity, to stimulate its initiation into society and to participate actively in its education;

- to help the child acquire basic knowledge and skills;

- to overcome the child's inequalities with regard to the school and education.

Curriculum

The timetable applied in primary education comprises: religion or ethics, observation of the environment, Dutch, mathematics, drawing, manual activities, physical education, music and writing. In Brussels, the teaching of French is possible from the first year on and compulsory from the third year on. In all other Flemish schools, French may be taught in the third stage (5th and 6th years). In linguistic border municipalities, the teaching of French is compulsory in the second stage (3rd and 4th years). It is also possible to teach consumer education. The same subjects are taught to all pupils, with little differentiation.

Assessment and qualifications

As mentioned above, assessment is an area in which the pedagogical freedom of the organizing body is guaranteed; each organizing body can define the type and method of assessment it wishes to use and the way it communicates the results, as long as the relevant laws and regulations are respected.

Throughout the year, teachers use a continuous formative assessment to monitor the progress of their pupils on the basis of all written and oral work

and homework. At the end of the school year, the teacher makes a summative assessment, and can use tests to assess pupils. The teacher or team of teachers assesses the year's work and the results of the tests at the end of the year to decide whether or not to allow a pupil to move on to the next class. In this, the pupil's analytical skills, ability to think independently, cooperative spirit and taste for work and for working well must all be taken into account. Report cards regulary keep the child and his or her parents informed of test results, academic progress, behaviour in class and personal development.

It is possible for a child to repeat classes each year and thus within a stage. Pupils who experience learning difficulties can receive special and individualized assistance from a remedial teacher.

When they have successfully completed their primary education, pupils receive a certificate of primary education (*Getuigschrift van het Basisonderwijs*). Schools may award this certificate themselves as long as they respect the terms of the law, or they may register pupils for a cantonal examination. However, the latter possibility will disappear in the near future. This certificate (or an equivalent) may also be awarded to pupils who successfully complete either the first year of secondary education or a second year of vocational education, if they did not complete primary education successfully.

Teachers

In most cases, primary teachers are not subject specialists and are allocated by class, but, especially in the third stage, instruction may be broken down by subject area. Some courses may be given by specialized teachers (language, physical education or artistic or manual activities) or remedial teachers.

The initial training of primary school teachers is organized in *Pedagogische Hogescholen*, higher teacher training institutions. It entails three years of study comprising academic and theoretical and practical teacher training. Successful students are awarded a diploma of qualified teacher for primary education (*Onderwijzer*). Teachers may work full-time or part-time. In-service training is not compulsory.

Statistics 1991/92

	Pupils	Teachers*	Schools
Community Schools	54,457	3,883	329
Provincial Schools	702	55	3
Communal Schools	88,178	5,825	508
'Free' Schools	261,436	16,434	1,387

* Number of full-time and part-time teachers.

3.2 Secondary education (Secundair onderwijs)

Secondary education, like primary education, is included in the period of compulsory schooling. Full-time schooling may last until age 18, or up to the age of 15 or 16, when part-time schooling may be followed up to age 18.

Pupils must have reached the age of 12 before they are admitted to secondary education. They may enter the first year A on obtaining the certificate of primary education. After spending a year in the sixth year of primary education without obtaining the certificate, pupils may be admitted to the first year A with their parents' consent and on the advice of the *PMS* centre, on condition that the first year A admission Class Council (*Toelatingsraad*) gives a favourable opinion. Without the certificate of primary education, pupils may be admitted to the first year B from the age of 12. The same holds true – with parental consent and on the advice of the *PMS* centre – for pupils who do not seem to be suitable for the first year A, even though they have the certificate. Transfer from the first year B to the first year A is possible until 15 November and from the first year A to the first year B until 15 January, if the child's parents agree and the Class Council so advises.

As the coexistence of two different structures in secondary education caused quite a number of complicated organizational, budgetary and psychological problems, it was decided to replace the two types – Type I and Type II – with a new general structure for secondary education. As a result of this decision all Flemish secondary schools adopted the new organizational type – progressively from the first year of secondary education from 1 September 1989.

In accordance with the Act of 31 July 1990, the new structure is composed of three stages of two years, the second and third stage comprising four different forms:

- General secondary education (*Algemeen secundair onderwijs – ASO*), which emphasizes broad theoretical training and provides a strong basis for attending higher education.

- Technical secondary education (*Technisch secundair onderwijs – TSO*), which focuses mainly on general and technical-theoretical subjects, and leads to employment or higher education. Practical courses are also included.

- Artistic secondary education (*Kunstsecundair onderwijs – KSO*), which links general and broad development with active art practice, and leads to employment or higher education.

- Vocational secondary education (*Beroeps-secundair onderwijs – BSO*), which is practical education combining the acquisition of specific skills with general education. It may provide access to higher education.

Throughout the first two stages and to a lesser extent in the third stage, it is possible to transfer from one form of education to another, and there are 'bridges' from vocational education to other types of education.

There are three types of secondary schools organized by the *ARGO*:

- Middle Schools (*Middenscholen*) which organize general secondary education in the 2nd and 3rd stages, or the three stages;

- Royal *Atheneum* (*Koninklijk Atheneum*) which organizes general secondary education in the 2nd and 3rd stages, or the three stages;

- Royal Technical *Atheneum* (*Koninklijk Technisch Atheneum*) which organizes technical and vocational secondary education in the three stages.

All Community schools are coeducational. The vast majority of subsidized schools are also coeducational, and it is expected that the remaining single-sex schools will become coeducational in the years to come. Secondary schools do not charge fees.

The smallest schools have some 200 pupils. They can be attached to primary schools or to teacher training institutions. Classes are generally organized by age and sometimes by subject. In some schools classes can be organized by level of ability.

The timetable in secondary schools may vary between 32 and 36 periods of 50 minutes. There is a short break of 10-15 minutes in the morning and in the afternoon. The break at noon must last at least an hour and a half. The school week consists of 5 days, except Wednesday afternoon. The school itself can determine the start and the end of the school day (usually from 8.30 a.m. to 12.00 noon and from 1.30 p.m. to 4.00 p.m.).

The school year is organized as at primary level.

Curriculum

The purpose of the first stage is to provide a broad general basis. This stage should enable pupils to be oriented in the most suitable way towards the different courses available in the second stage.

In the first year, all pupils follow a common curriculum of at least 27 lessons per week consisting of the following subjects: Dutch, French, (English may also be included), mathematics, history, geography, art education, science, technical education, physical education and religion or ethics. In addition, five periods a week are left available to each school to allocate as they wish within a defined and legally fixed framework.

In the second year, almost all pupils follow a basic course of at least 24 lessons per week, consisting of the following subjects: religion or ethics, Dutch, French, English, mathematics, history, geography, art education, science, technological education and physical education. At least 14 of the 24 lessons are followed by all pupils.

Special arrangements exist for pupils who follow vocational education from the second year. They study the same subjects provided in the basic course, except for French and English. Apart from the basic course, 8 to 10 lessons are available for each school to develop its individual character. In the second year of vocational education, the basic course is limited to 16 lessons. Two groups of subjects (a total of 16 lessons) are added to this package. Each of

these groups provides an introduction to the theory and practice of the main vocational sectors.

The remaining periods are free for optional courses (e.g. Latin, Greek, modern languages, additional mathematics, technology).

From the third year up to and including the sixth year, the four forms of education (listed at the beginning of this section) are organized separately, with a common and an optional package. The common part consists of the basic course. Optional subjects are either fundamental (depending on further choices) or complementary.

Basic education from the third to the sixth year consists of the following subjects: religion or non-denominational ethics, Dutch, a second modern language, mathematics, history, geography, science and physical education. General secondary education also includes a third modern language. In vocational education the basic training from the third up to and including the sixth year consists of the following subjects: religion or non-denominational ethics, Dutch, history and geography (the last two subjects may be replaced by an integrated social education course) and physical education.

A wide range of subjects are offered in the optional section to supplement the basic course.

Curricula can contain a list of recommended **textbooks**, but there is no obligation to use a textbook from these lists. The same applies to **teaching materials.**

Assessment and qualifications

The essential instrument in assessment is the Class Council (*Klasseraad*), which is the committee consisting of the entire managerial and teaching staff responsible for the education of a specific group of pupils. It assesses pupils' school progress and makes the decision regarding their promotion to a higher class, and issues certificates where appropriate. The Class Council bases its decisions on various factors, such as:

– the past school career of each pupil;

- the intermediate results from lessons, assessments and oral and/or written examinations;

- information from the guidance centre;

- interviews with the pupil and parents, as necessary.

Each Class Council has to establish, at regular intervals, an intellectual, social and moral assessment of each pupil. The results of assessments carried out during the year are taken into account in the end-of-year assessment. Tests are compulsory or all pupils.

At the end of the year, the Class Council decides whether pupils should be promoted to a higher class, with or without restriction, or whether promotion should be delayed or refused. Unsuccessful pupils repeat a year, but pupils with learning difficulties may get some help from remedial teachers.

At the end of the 6th year of secondary education or at the end of the 7th year of vocational education, pupils receive a secondary education certificate (*Diploma van secundair onderwijs*), which provides access to higher education.

Teachers

Teachers are subject specialists and are allocated to teach one subject. They can be full-time, part-time, permanent or temporary. There is no obligation to follow in-service training.

There are different forms of teacher training.

Teacher training in full-time higher teacher training institutions

This course lasts 3 years, and comprises concurrent general and pedagogical training, together with the study of one or two specific disciplines in the case of future lower secondary teachers. In the third year of studies, half the time is spent on teaching practice. Students completing the course are awarded a diploma qualifying them to teach in lower

secondary education (*Diploma van geaggregeerde voor het lager secundair onderwijs*). They may teach in the 1st stage (1st and 2nd years) and in vocational secondary education.

Teacher training at universities

Students enrolled in university education in certain specialized subjects may obtain a supplementary certificate entitling them to teach. Training comprises an introduction to some of the theoretical aspects of pedagogy, and teaching practice. Students who successfully complete this course are awarded a diploma qualifying them to teach in upper secondary education (*Diploma van geaggregeerde voor het hoger secundair onderwijs*). This diploma also entitles them to teach in short higher education.

Teacher training through social advancement courses (part-time education in the form of evening or weekend classes based on a credit system)

This type of teacher training is meant for teachers giving vocational training courses and certain technical courses, for which no full-time training is available. Courses focus on both the theory and practice of teaching, and students give lessons under the supervision of an instructor. Training leads to a certificate of pedagogical aptitude (*Getuigschrift Pedagogische Bekwaamheid*), which entitles the holder to teach technical subjects at lower or upper secondary level.

Statistics 1991/92

	Pupils	Teachers*	Schools
Community Schools	70,694	10,989	289
Provincial Schools	13,969	1,971	33
Communal Schools	22,775	3,553	80
'Free' Schools	319,877	37,799	657

* Number of full-time and part-time teachers.

4. Initial vocational education and training

4.1 Part-time compulsory schooling

In the framework of compulsory education, the training of young people under 18 years of age comes under three types of measures conforming to requirements for part-time compulsory schooling up to age 18:

- part-time education;

- apprenticeship in the *SME* sector;

- industrial apprenticeship.

Part-time education

Pupils who are no longer required to follow full-time education can study on a part-time basis in a centre for part-time education (*Centrum voor deeltijds onderwijs – CDO*) or in a recognized training centre.

The centres for part-time education provide courses combining general education (including social and personal training) with preparation for an occupation. The content of courses is limited and designed to be a continuation of the full-time education system. The centres are linked to a school providing full-time technical and/or vocational secondary education.

Part-time education lasts 360 hours in the first year (15- to 16-year-olds), and 240 hours in the following two years. Part-time education is provided for 40 weeks a year with an average of 15 weekly periods of 50 minutes (8 periods of vocational training and 7 periods of general education).

Part-time education leads to an attendance certificate (*Attest van regelmatige lesbijwoning*), and may also lead to a qualification certificate (*Kwalificatiegetuigschrift*) equivalent to the certificate awarded for full-time study.

Industrial apprenticeship

This concerns apprenticeships in occupations exercised by salaried workers. It was initially intended for young people aged between 15 and 18, with a poor school record, who had lost interest in attending school. Young people aged 16 who had already completed two years of general secondary education or vocational secondary education, or had passed an entrance examination were also eligible. Since 1987, young people between 18 and 21 have also been able to participate.

The length and content of the apprenticeship is established on the basis of a proposal put forward by the representative committee of the sector concerned. Successive apprenticeship contracts may be concluded with several different firms if required for training in a given occupation. Since 1992, firms with under 50 employees have been entitled to train young people by means of an industrial apprenticeship.

Pupils spend two days in a recognized part-time training centre where they acquire the necessary theoretical and general knowledge, and spend the other three days of the week working in a firm under the guidance of an experienced employee.

Training in a firm lasts an average of 21 hours per week. Training in a centre for part-time education lasts 15 hours per week: 7 hours of general, personal and social training and 8 hours of vocational training (theoretical knowledge, practical skills).

In the case of the unskilled occupations, training must last no less than six months and no more than two years. The representative committee has established a longer period of training for the skilled occupations. The trainee is deemed to be an employee and receives a percentage of the minimum wage in the business sector concerned.

When training has been completed, the employer provides the apprentice with a certificate indicating the period covered by the training and its content.

Apprenticeship in the SME sector

Young people can conclude an apprenticeship contract with an employer-instructor from the age of 15 or 16. They then spend 4 days a week gaining practical experience in the firm with which they have the apprenticeship contract and one day in a training centre supervised by the Flemish Institute for Independent Entrepreneurship *(Vlaams Instituut voor het Zelfstandig Ondernemen – VIZO)*. In the training centre, the apprentices follow a technical/vocational training course and a general social education course. These courses are strongly oriented towards practice.

Apprenticeship in the SME sector is thus a form of alternating training and practical training is an essential part. The head of the enterprise-instructor is responsible for ensuring that the apprentices get a general and technical basic training in the practice of the occupation concerned. The pupils are bound to take the additional courses in the training centre.

Apprentices have the status of pupils since they are still fulfilling their compulsory education obligations. However, apprentices are entitled to a fixed apprenticeship fee from their employer.

The number of occupations covered by apprenticeship is virtually unlimited and includes all occupations that can be practised as a self-employed person. The education service of *VIZO* and the *VIZO* centres continually adjust the apprenticeships available to take into account new developments in SMEs or in educational techniques.

The apprenticeship lasts three years (or less if apprentices have followed preliminary training). At the end, apprentices obtain an official certificate *(Getuigschrift van Leertijd)*.

They can then opt to find a job as an employee or go on to entrepreneur training. A lot of young people who do not intend to become self-employed prefer to follow vocational training within the training programme for the self-employed.

There are 120 hours each of general social education and technical/vocational training in all three years. General social education comprises thematic project work and separate language and mathematics periods. It aims to develop the apprentice's personality. Technical/vocational training is aimed at the acquisition of the basic knowledge needed to practise an occupation. The course is supplementary to the practical training in the enterprise.

In accordance with the legislation regarding compulsory education, 15-year-olds must take an additional course in general social education of 120 hours in the first year. This means that they attend the training centre an extra half-day a week.

Apprentices are subject to continuous assessment throughout the course year. At the end of the first and second years, they have to take a transitional examination, which consists of A and B tests. This examination is intended to assess their progress and determine whether they can continue the apprenticeship.

At the end of the third year, there is a final examination, which consists of A,B and C tests. The A test concerns general social education (Dutch, mathematics, social legislation, civics, history, geography and hygiene), and the B test assesses theoretical technical/vocational knowledge of the occupation concerned. The C test is the practical part of the examination; the apprentices have to carry out a piece of work or an assignment. In both the transitional and final examinations apprentices must obtain 50% in each part of the examination in order to pass. They are informed of the results of the transitional examination by a certificate. At the end of the course, the apprentices who pass the final examination obtain an apprenticeship certificate, signed by the *VIZO*. This certificate provides access to the entrepreneur training and also complies with the legal requirements for most regulated occupations.

Each year, the *VIZO* provides education and training to more than 10,000 young people.

4.2 Employment-training agreement (+ 18 years)

In addition to education and training organized as part of compulsory part-time education, there is also what is known as the employment-training agreement.

Set up in 1986, this type of training is available to all young people between the ages of 18 and 25 who are seeking employment, and do not already possess a certificate of long or short higher education or university education, or of technical upper secondary education.

This initiative is based on granting a temporary reduction in the employer's contribution to the State Social Security system when they hire young job-seekers involved in an employment-training scheme.

The employment-training agreement involves industrial and commercial firms, non-profit-making associations and the liberal professions. The agreement is signed by the young person and the employer and lasts for a minimum of one year or a maximum of three years. It has two parts: a contract for part-time work of indeterminate duration (at least half-time) and training. The training provided under the employment-training agreement must involve courses and establishments which are recognized or subsidized.

Training lasts for a total of 500 hours, except for management training in the context of training for independent professions, where the minimum period is 256 hours.

From 1987, the year in which the scheme was launched, up to 30 June 1990, 842 employment-training agreements were concluded in Flanders.

Legislation on the employment-training agreement falls within the competence of the Employment Minister.

5. Higher education

Higher education can be divided into 3 types:

– short higher education;

– long higher education;

– university education.

Admission

All those who hold a certificate of secondary education are in principle entitled to follow any type of higher education. Access to university education in applied sciences (including architecture) is subject to an entrance examination organized by the universities concerned. Special or additional conditions may be specified to candidates by educational institutions.

Fees/Student finance

Students pay tuition fees for each academic year, but grants are available from the Community budget and may be awarded on the basis of a means test.

Short and long higher education

Higher education establishments providing short and long higher education courses have various designations: Higher Institute, School, Centre for Higher Education, Teacher Training College/ Institute, Conservatory, Academy, etc.

Both short and long higher education cover eight main disciplines: technical, economic, agricultural, paramedical, social, artistic, pedagogical and maritime.

Academic year

The academic year starts between 15 September and the first Monday of October and ends in June.

Courses/Qualifications

Short higher education courses are organized in a single cycle of 3 to 4 years. Study focuses on practical aspects and provides direct access to employment. It is not university level. Courses lead to diplomas in various professions: nurse, social worker, librarian/documentalist, etc.

Long higher education courses are divided into 2 cycles: the first cycle takes 2 years, the second cycle takes 2 or 3 years. The first cycle of general theoretical and academic education is a preparation for a second specialized cycle. At the end of this, the student has to present and defend a thesis. Courses are university level, and diplomas are of equal value to those of universities and confer titles such as industrial engineer, licentiate, commercial engineer or architect. Long higher education trains highly technical staff for executive tasks and applied research.

Assessment

Every academic year is completed by examinations. Students must pass these examinations to be admitted to the next year.

The examinations are regulated by a number of administrative and organizational rules. Two examination sessions are held each academic year (the first between 15 June and 15 July, the second after 15 August of the current academic year). Students are prohibited from sitting the same examination more than four times in two academic years and must sit examinations during the first session. Students are, at the end of the academic year, either:

- admitted to the next year of study if they have obtained a score of at least 50% in each test and 60% of the points awarded for the entire examination;

- deferred and required to resit, at the second session, the examinations in which they did not meet the examining board's standards;

- rejected, and must repeat the year.

Assessment comprises on the accumulation of results and the award of a certificate. It is based on end-of-year examinations and the submission of a final project or thesis. In some sections, however, a dossier containing an evaluation of the performance of the students during the academic year, and in particular of their practical work and courses, is studied prior to assessment. Recently, initiatives have also been taken to introduce formative assessment aimed at providing teachers and students with more frequent assessment opportunities.

University education

(academic education at universities)

Academic year

The academic year runs from early October to the end of September. The courses begin in early October and end in May or June, depending on the university.

Courses/Qualifications

University education provides theoretical training for managerial staff responsible for research, conception and application of knowledge. It is offered at different levels: basic academic courses; and advanced academic courses following the basic academic courses (e.g. teacher training, doctoral programmes and post-academic programmes). The basic academic courses are divided into two cycles: a first cycle of 2 or 3 years and a second cycle of 2, 3 or 4 years.

The first cycle of basic academic education leads to the intermediate academic degree of candidate (*kandidaat*).

The second cycle is concluded by the following academic degrees (equivalent to a Master's):

- licentiate (*licentiaat*);
- dentist;
- physician-medical practitioner;
- veterinary surgeon;
- pharmacist;
- civil engineer-architect;
- civil engineer with further qualification;
- bio-engineer with further qualification;
- commercial engineer.

University education is divided into study years of at least 1,500 and at most 1,800 hours of tuition or other study activities. The volume of study for each year is expressed in terms of study-points and corresponds to 60 study-points per year. One study-point corresponds to 25 to 30 hours of study.

Most courses are compulsory. There are few electives in the first cycle, but there are many in the study programmes of the second and third cycle.

Assessment

Students are assessed in all of the courses of a specific year of study.

The examinations are subject to a number of administrative and organizational requirements, similar to those described under short and long higher education.

Students are awarded a maximum mark of 20 for each subject in which they take an examination. The pass mark for any subject is 10 out of 20. To complete a given study year, students must take all the examinations that are included as part of that particular year of study.

Denmark

DENMARK

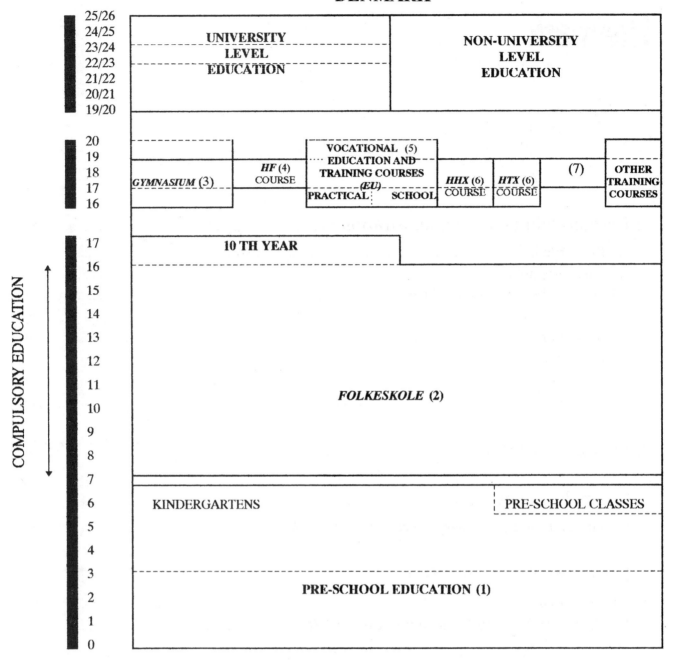

1. In pre-school education there are several institutions catering consecutively or alternatively for the 0 to 6/7 year age range.

2. The *Folkeskole* comprises an optional pre-school class, nine years of full-time compulsory education and a supplementary optional tenth year. It provides general education at primary and lower secondary levels; the Danish education system does not differentiate between primary and lower secondary education.

3. The *Gymnasium* provides a 3-year course of general education at upper secondary level, after the 9th or 10th year of the *Folkeskole*, with the final examination qualifying for university entrance.

4. The course for the *HF* (higher preparatory examination) is a 2-year general course, after the 10th year of the *Folkeskole*, with the final examination qualifying for further and higher education.

5. The basic vocational education and training courses *(EU)* last between 3 and 4 years with approximately two-thirds of the time spent in a company. A typical course consists of a first 20-week school course or practical training in a company of similar length, followed by a second 20-week school course. After that, the course alternates between practical training and school.

6. The courses for the *HHX* (higher commercial examination) and the *HTX* (higher technical examination) are 3-year school-based courses within the commercial and the technical area respectively, leading to a final examination which qualifies for admission to higher education and for direct employment in trade and industry.

7. Social and health education programmes.

- - - - - - - - =alternative beginning or end of level/type of education

1. Responsibilities and administration

1.1 Background

Denmark covers a total area of 43,000 square kilometres, and has a population of around five million. The national language is Danish. Denmark is a country with a very homogeneous population – apart from a small German minority and relatively few immigrants compared with other Western-European countries.

Denmark is a constitutional monarchy. Legislative power lies with the Queen and Parliament; executive power lies with the Queen through the ministries (central administration). The electoral system is based on proportional representation, which has normally resulted in coalition or minority Governments. After the last General Election in 1990, eight political parties were represented in Parliament. The present Government, which came into place in January 1993, is based on the Social Democratic Party, the Social Liberal Party, the Centre Democrats and the Christian People's Party.

Local government is exercised through the 14 counties and 277 municipalities.

The Evangelical Lutheran Church (*Folkekirke*) is the official church.

The main employment sectors are the industrial sector (including energy and water (0.9%), extraction of minerals and chemical industries (1.9%), metal manufacture and machine technology (7.7%), other manufacturing activities (10.4%), building and construction (6.5%)) and the services sector (including distribution (15.9%), hotel, transport and communication (7.1%), banking, finance and insurance (9.3%), public administration (6.7%) and other services (28%)).

In 1992, the unemployment rate was 11.4%.

1.2 Basic principles: education

A leading principle of the Danish education system has always been freedom of choice of education. Whilst the State provides educational opportunities for all, people are free to choose alternative kinds of education, whether it be for ideological, political, educational or religious reasons.

1.3 Distribution of responsibilities

Responsibility for education and training in Denmark is shared between central state authorities, the counties, the municipalities, private bodies and individuals, and the boards and heads of individual education or training institutions. The division of responsibility differs according to the type of education or training institution and the level of education or training.

Pre-school institutions are under the responsibility of the Ministry of Social Affairs and are run by the municipalities or independent or private bodies. Most other types and levels of institutions are under the responsibility of the Ministry of Education. Municipalities are responsible for schools providing primary and lower secondary education (*Folkeskole*); 10% are private schools which are run by their own respective boards of governors. Counties are generally responsible for the majority of upper secondary schools (*Gymnasia*) and institutions offering courses leading to the Higher Preparatory Examination (*Højere Forberedelseseksamen – HF*); one is run by central state authorities, two by municipalities, and some by private bodies. County and Municipal Councils run the schools in conjunction with the individual School Boards.

Private responsibility dominates for a variety of non-university-level higher education institutions, including teacher training colleges and engineering colleges, folk high schools (*Folkeshøjskoler*), agricultural schools, continuation schools (*efterskoler*) and some home economics schools. Universities and other institutions of further and higher education are in the vast majority run by the State.

The Ministry of Education cooperates with the social partners with regard to vocational education and training. Schools within the area of vocational education and training are organized as independent, self-governing institutions (technical schools, commercial schools and agricultural schools).

The Ministry of Cultural Affairs is responsible for higher education offered by the Royal School of Fine Art, the schools of architecture, the academies of music and the schools of librarianship. The Ministry of Labour is responsible for short labour-market courses (*AMU*-centres).

1.4 Administration

Central level

The main responsibility for education lies with the Ministry of Education but, as mentioned above, the Ministry of Cultural Affairs and the Ministry of Labour also have responsibility for education within certain delimited areas. Each Ministry consists of a number of Departments and Directorates.

The Ministries are headed by a Minister, a Permanent Secretary and a number of deputy permanent secretaries.

In legislative and administrative terms, the central bodies and institutions play a very significant role. Most of the important fields of Danish education and training and related issues are regulated by laws adopted by the *Folketing*, the Danish Parliament. These laws set the overall aims and define a general framework for the different types and levels of education and training. This applies with special force to the Act on the *Folkeskole*, which is largely a target and framework Act. The Act has just been

amended with effect from 1994; this means that the legislation pertaining to the *Folkeskole* has on average been revised every 20th year throughout the twentieth century.

The Ministry of Education controls and directs the education and training system through a variety of instruments and measures:

- by issuing decrees, orders and circulars, which lay down the aims and framework for the education and training system and are binding on the education/training institutions;

- by issuing guidelines, directives and recommendations, which have to be considered without being binding;

- by settling certain educational disputes;

- by general supervision and other means, such as the approval of curricula in certain sectors of the system, the general control of final examinations and the appointment of external examiners, and the appointment, or approval of the appointment, of permanent staff at educational institutions in certain sectors of the system;

- by allocating public funds on an annual basis to the various types of education and training institutions (within the framework fixed by legislation).

At *Folkeskole* level, the Ministry of Education lays down regulations pertaining to the aims of teaching in each subject or subject combinations, issues curriculum guidelines and guidelines for the distribution of lessons and establishes rules for the examinations, which are binding for all schools. The written examination papers are also issued from central level.

The central administration of the *Gymnasium and HF courses* is more extensive and detailed than that of the *Folkeskole* education. The Ministry of Education is responsible for the supervision of teaching and examinations. It issues regulations on the aims and content of the curriculum and examinations, sets the written examination papers, and approves new subjects.

Vocational education and training courses (technical and commercial schools) are administered in close cooperation between the Ministry of Education and the social partners. With the reform that came into effect on 1 January 1991, the detailed regulatory management that had been exercised by the

Ministry of Education was replaced by target and general framework management by the Ministry of Education and the social partners, with greater influence being given to advisory bodies and detailed decisions decentralized to school level. The Ministry approves new types of training and prepares regulations concerning training already offered at the recommendation of the Council for Vocational Education, an advisory body. The Minister has competence to make binding rulings, but is required to consider the Council's recommendations. The Ministry is responsible for ensuring that vocational education and training courses are also of the nature of broad youth education.

The **social partners** play an important role within the area of vocational education and training. New legislation and changes or innovations within the area are made in close cooperation with the social partners.

They are responsible for modernizing training schemes and for the practical work experience part of courses, and exert considerable influence on the school parts of the courses. The structure and content of courses, the allocation of time between school instruction and practical training, and assessment are decided by the Ministry of Education and the social partners within 85 sectorial trade committees. The important role of the social partners ensures that labour-market approval of the education and training courses is guaranteed all over the country by both sides of industry.

Higher education is also administered centrally by the Ministry of Education. Universities, university centres and other research-based higher education institutions are subject to the same Parliamentary Act, which empowers the Minister to lay down regulations on admission, the content of courses, the awarding of degrees and the appointment of academic staff. Corresponding framework regulations are found in the Acts pertaining to the engineering colleges, colleges of education and other non-university-level higher education.

The university sector institutions have a high degree of autonomy with regard to the content and organization of courses; other institutions of higher education have less.

County and municipal level

The counties and the municipalities have publicly elected councils.

The Municipal Council has overall responsibility for the supervision and administration of municipal schools (pre-school institutions and the *Folkeskole*). The Municipal Council decides on the aims and the framework of the activities of the schools, and is responsible for the setting up, operation and closing down of schools, the number of schools and their size, the appointment, promotion and dismissal of examiners, head teachers and teaching staff in schools, and the approval of the curricula (including the number of lessons) as proposed by the School Boards. The municipalities (or the individual schools) decide themselves whether they want to follow the centrally drawn up curriculum guidelines for individual subjects. The curriculum is binding on teachers.

Counties are generally responsible for upper secondary schools (*Gymnasia* and other institutions leading to the Higher Preparatory Examination – *Hojere Forberedelseseksamen* – *HF*). The County Council is responsible for the setting up, operation and closing down of such institutions and decides on the appointment of head teachers, the appointment and dismissal of teachers and other staff, and student and class numbers. It may delegate its powers regarding, for example, the number of lessons, classes and pupils and the optional subjects to be offered to the School or Course Board.

Institutional level

The day-to-day management of all public and private education and training institutions is in the hands of one person, usually a public servant, in cooperation with a governing body or board. A number of collegiate bodies are established at most institutions, and these take part in their management to a varying degree.

Since 1 January 1993, a Parents' Committee must be set up in **pre-school institutions**, which influences the running of the institution and the use of its budget. The head teacher has administrative and educational responsiblity and takes account of the decisions of the Parents' Committee.

As from the 1991/92 school year, at each individual *Folkeskole*, a School Board (*Skolebestyrelse*) must be set up consisting of five or seven parents' representatives, two staff representatives and two pupils' representatives. The School Board carries out its activities within the aims and framework set down by the Municipal Council and furthermore supervises the activities of the school. It lays down the principles for the activities of the school, including: the organization of teaching, the number of lessons, the optional subjects to be offered, the allocation of pupils to classes, the distribution of the workload of teachers, and cooperation between schools and parents. As mentioned above, it draws up draft proposals for the curricula to be submitted to the Municipal Council. The School Board also approves the school's budget and teaching materials. The head teacher of the school has administrative and educational responsibility vis-à-vis the School Board and the Municipal Council. In addition, a Pedagogical Council composed of all the teaching staff must be set up at each school to advise the head teacher. At schools with five or more form levels, the pupils set up a Pupils' Council.

The 1994 Act on the *Folkeskole* implies that more responsibility and influence will be placed in the hands of the school and parents. The Minister of Education will continue to lay down the aims of teaching in the individual subjects and draw up guidelines for project assignments, the curriculum etc., but teachers and pupils will fix together the aims which individual pupils will try to achieve.

As from the 1991/92 school year, each *Gymnasium* or *HF* course must also set up a Board, comprising representatives of the County Council, the Municipal Councils of the local area of the school/course, parents, and the pupils and staff of the school/course (the latter must not form the majority). On the recommendation of the head teacher, the Board fixes the capacity of the school (maximum number of pupils in each class), the subjects offered and the holiday plan. It also fixes the budget of the school/course. The head teacher of the school/course is in charge of day-to-day management and is responsible for the activities of the school/course vis-à-vis the County Council, and teaching and examinations vis-à-vis the Minister of Education. Each *Gymnasium* or *HF* course must also set up a Pedagogical Council to advise the head teacher. This consists of the head teacher and all the teachers of the school/course. In addition, a Pupils'

Council must be set up, whose members are elected by and among the pupils of the school/course.

There are no state-authorized **textbooks** or **teaching materials.** The overall responsibility for which books and materials a school uses lies with the School Board of the individual school; the individual teacher chooses what he/she wants to use. All teachers are free to use the **teaching methods** of their own choice.

The **vocational schools** (technical and commercial schools) are self-governing and administered by a Board. Under the reform of school management, detailed planning and execution have been decentralized to the school level. Head teachers and School Boards now have decision-making powers, and the new local Education and Training Committees play a role in the development of the interplay between school and on-the-job training in the alternance-based vocational courses. The head teacher and the Board decide which courses to offer, administer government grants and are responsible for examinations, teachers, school buildings and organization.

Colleges offering **medium-cycle higher education** may be state-run, self-governing or chartered institutions but are all run by a Board and a Rector. Engineering colleges also have various governing bodies (institution council, administration council, subject council and staff-student study committees) which make recommendations and take decisions relating to the appointment and dismissal of staff, the organization of teaching, the curricula and examinations and the distribution of funding.

The Rector has formal responsibility for a **university-level higher education** institution and is responsible for its day-to-day running. The institutions are divided into faculties, departments, etc., and certain collegiate bodies take part in their administration. The Senate, which is the highest collegiate body of the institution, safeguards the interests of the institution in matters relating to education and research. It establishes guidelines for long-term planning and development and approves the budget. The Faculty Council establishes guidelines for long-term planning and approves the budget of the faculty. The department Executive Committee establishes general guidelines for the activities and development of the department and approves its budget. The Study Committee, which represents a specific study programme or cluster of programmes, approves teaching plans, including the assignment of teaching resources, and draws up proposals for curricula.

1.5 Inspection

There is no inspectorate as such in Denmark. Municipal and county authorities are responsible for supervising their schools. Each private school has attached to it an inspector chosen by the parents or appointed by the municipality.

Some municipalities have pedagogical support centres with local advisers, book collections and course activities. A similar system exists in all counties. In addition, the State has a corps of subject advisers. There is one state adviser for each subject of the *Folkeskole* and the upper secondary schools, and the adviser in question covers the whole country.

Within the field of vocational education and training, there are state advisers for the different vocational subject areas. There is no such system for the universities.

1.6 Financing

The State subsidizes all county, municipal and private education and training institutions. The *Folketing* decides how public funds are to be distributed between the various types of education through the Appropriations Act.

Educational institutions run by the counties or by private bodies receive considerable direct state funding, up to 100% of the individual institution's budget in the former and 85% in the latter. The municipal schools are 100% state-funded but do not receive state funding directly. The municipalities receive block grants and distribute funds to the schools. The money is not earmarked by the State. The Municipal Councils are financially responsible for municipal schools, including the budgetary scope of each school. The School Board approves the budget as proposed by the head teacher.

The County Councils are financially responsible for all educational activities in county institutions (*Gymnasia* and *HF* courses), including the allocation of grants and the financial framework of each school. It is the County Council which fixes the appropriations to be granted for the operation and construction of schools/course establishments and which decides whether pupils should pay for certain teaching materials themselves (most are free of charge). The school/course Board decides on the distribution of the budget of the school/course.

Engineering colleges and colleges of education are private but 100% subsidized by the State. Folk high schools (*Folkehøjskoler*), agricultural schools, continuation schools (*efterskoler*) and some home economics schools are also private and receive state subsidies.

Higher education is financed directly by the State. The institutions are, however, able to secure extra income through offering special courses and selling know-how. Teaching expenditure is covered by a fixed amount per active student, whereas the budgets for buildings, administration and research are fixed on the basis of a specific assessment.

From the fiscal year 1994, all levels of the Danish education and training system financed by Central Government are to be funded according to the 'taximeter system'. The Act on Vocational Schools, which came into force in 1990, has already introduced the taximeter system in vocational schools.

The total annual grant consists of teaching grants based on the number of active pupils/students and fixed grants for joint expenditure, which are allocated in the form of one block grant; institutions are free to re-allocate the two grants. They cover the salaries of teachers and other staff, the cost of teaching material and equipment, general management and administration, the maintenance and operation of buildings, mortgage interest and the rent of buildings.

1.7 Private schools

Private primary and secondary schools can be set up by any private organization or group, denominational or non-denominational, as long as they meet certain official criteria. Education must be of a standard comparable to that in public schools and there must be a certain minimum number of pupils.

The 1991 Act on Private Schools introduced a new public grant system for private primary and secondary schools, by which they are allocated a grant for operational expenditure per pupil; in principle, this matches the public expenditure per pupil in municipal schools minus school fees paid by parents.

1.8 Advisory bodies

After the adoption of the new Act on the *Folkeskole*, a new *Folkeskole* Council was set up. It is to act as an adviser to the Minister in all questions relating to the *Folkeskole* and may in this context recommend the initiation of development work and research projects in relation to the *Folkeskole*.

The Council for Vocational Education (*EUR*) is the Ministry's advisory body for questions concerning training policy and the overall objectives and structure of the vocational training schemes.

In order to ensure coherence of policy across the broad range of higher education, five consultative bodies have been established to advise the Minister: the National Advisory Board for the Humanities, the National Advisory Board for Health Education, the National Advisory Board for Natural Sciences, the National Advisory Board for Technology and the National Advisory Board for Social Sciences. Each board consists of ten members appointed by the Minister.

2. Pre-school education

In the Danish pre-school sector there are several institutions catering consecutively or alternatively for the 0 to 6/7 year age range:

— **day nurseries** (*vuggestuer*) for children from birth to 3 years of age;

— **kindergartens** (*børnehaver*) for children from 3 to 7 years of age;

— **integrated institutions** (*integrerede institutioner*) for children up to the age of 14, including pre-school children;

— **pre-school classes** (*børnehaveklasser*) for children from 5 to 7 years of age.

The administration of the first three types of institution comes under the Ministry of Social Affairs. Some are established and run by the municipalities, others are independent or private institutions. Privately managed institutions can be put at the disposal of the municipal authorities which then pay their operating costs. Around two-thirds of institutions are municipal and one-third are private or independent. They are state-subsidized but parents pay part of the costs (up to 35% according to their income).

The administration of pre-school classes comes under the Ministry of Education. Premises for these classes are made available in municipal and private schools. Since the beginning of the 1980/81 school year, all municipalities are required to establish such classes. Parents do not pay fees in municipal pre-school classes. They pay a small fee in private pre-school classes.

Attendance at pre-school institutions is optional. In the first three types, certain categories of children, such as those from socially disadvantaged families or families where both parents work, are given priority. The attendance rate varies between 35% for the younger children in nurseries and kindergartens and 90% for the 5- to 6-year-olds attending pre-school classes.

Most institutions managed by the municipality are open from 6.00 or 7.00 a.m. to around 5.00 p.m. for 200 days per year. The school year begins around 15 August and ends around 20 June. Children may attend full-time or part-time.

A pre-school class must not exceed 22 pupils without being divided or provided with extra assistance. The average size of a child care institution is 40-60 children. There are generally two adult staff members for 10-12 children (between the ages of 6 months and 2 years) or for 20 children (between the ages of 3 and 6 years).

Neither kindergartens nor integrated institutions offer proper 'teaching'. Their aim is to supplement and support the children's home life by offering care and participation in educational activities in order to contribute to the development of the child's personality and creativity. This was also the case for pre-school classes until Act 270 of 1985. Now, however, there is 'teaching' in pre-school classes, and this is defined as 'playing and other activities promoting the child's development'. It is also possible to devote some time to teaching subjects such as Danish and mathematics.

Pre-school classes aim more specifically at preparing children for normal school routine, encouraging them to play and cooperate with other children and thus become more acclimatized to school. Pre-school classes have three to four 'lessons' a day, five days a week.

A change in the law on pre-school education came into force on 1 August 1986. According to the change, pre-school children may be taught together with children in the first two classes of the comprehensive *Folkeskole* for a certain number of lessons per week. Pre-school classes physically belong to the individual *Folkeskole* but have their own premises.

No curriculum guidelines are drawn up for the activities of the pre-school classes. In principle, the staff of kindergartens are free to choose the programme, methods and materials; however, the municipalities can draw up programmes and the Parents' Committee defines the principles of activities.

The teachers at all three types of 'schooling' are qualified educators. As regards the integrated activities of the pre-school class and the first two years of the *Folkeskole*, teachers with a *Folkeskole* teaching qualification take a certain number of lessons.

Teachers

The staff of all pre-school institutions and pre-school classes include qualified teachers and assistants. The latter may have followed short teacher training courses.

As of 1 January 1992, all pre-school teachers follow the same educator training course (*pedagoguddannelsen*). It is provided in non-university educator training colleges (*seminarier*) and lasts for three-and-a-half years, 15 months of which is practical. Prior to 1992, there was a special 3-year programme for kindergarten teachers.

In principle, teachers are employed on a full-time basis. As from 1993, all new teachers in the *Folkeskole* are employed on a group contract basis (i.e. they are no longer civil servants).

3. Compulsory education

In Denmark there are 9 years of full-time compulsory education – for children between the ages of 7 and 16 years. This education mainly takes place in municipal schools (*Folkeskole*, 90%); it is also provided in private schools (10%). Following the 9th year of the *Folkeskole*, pupils can opt to stay on in the 10th year. The Danish education system does not differentiate between primary and lower secondary education.

Primary and lower secondary education (*Folkeskole*)

As mentioned above, the **Folkeskole** are maintained and supervised by the individual municipality and run by the municipality in conjunction with the individual School Boards. Education is compulsory, but not schooling. Parents have a choice between the municipal school and a private elementary school and, in principle, educating the children at home.

Education in the *Folkeskole* is available to all children, is coeducational and is provided free of charge (this also applies to books and other teaching materials). 90% of all Danish children attend the *Folkeskole*. Fees, usually a relatively modest amount, are charged at private schools.

Folkeskole comprise either a pre-school class and the 1st to 7th years or a pre-school class and the 1st to 10th years. The 9th year completes compulsory education; the 10th year is optional. Compulsory education cannot be met fully in the first and pupils have to move school after the 7th year. However, both are organized in the same way. Private schools must comprise at least the 1st to 7th years.

Two other types of schools cater for 14- to 18-year-olds after completion of seven years in the *Folkeskole*: public or private youth schools under the responsibility of the municipal authority; and private boarding schools (*efterskoler*), approved and supervised by the Ministry of Education.

The latest comprehensive reform of the *Folkeskole* was carried out in 1975 (since then, legislation effecting minor changes has been adopted). A new Act on the *Folkeskole*, adopted in June 1993, will come into force in 1994. The Act in force states that the aim of the *Folkeskole* is 'to give pupils the possibility of acquiring knowledge, skills, working methods and ways of expressing themselves which will contribute to the all-round development of the individual pupil'.

The school year begins around 15 August and ends around 20 June, and there are 200 school days per year. Teaching takes place five days a week, Monday to Friday, usually from 8.00 a.m. until 2.00 or 3.00 p.m., with only a short lunchbreak (around half-an-hour).

The number of weekly lessons is fixed according to the age of the children and may vary between 15 and 22 weekly lessons for the youngest children and 24 and 34 for the final class of the *Folkeskole*. One lesson lasts 45 minutes. In the future, the number of lessons will be changed so that the youngest pupils (first and second classes) will have a minimum of 20 lessons a week, and the oldest pupils will have a minimum of 28 lessons a week. Class time varies from four to seven hours per day, depending on the age of the child.

Pupils are grouped by age. In principle, *Folkeskole* education is comprehensive, and pupils remain together as a class throughout their entire school career. They may, however, in the 8th to 10th years, choose an extended syllabus in a number of subjects.

A different teacher teaches each subject. The team of teachers may change each year, but generally follows the same class for several years. As far as organization allows, at least one main teacher remains with the same group of pupils for their entire school career.

Curriculum

According to the Act in force, the curriculum includes:

- **compulsory subjects** which the individual school **must** offer;

- **compulsory subjects** which the individual school **may** offer;

- **non-compulsory subjects** which the individual school **must** offer;

- **non-compulsory subjects** which the individual school **may** offer.

None of this will be changed by the new Act.

During the first two years, Danish, arithmetic/mathematics, physical education and sport, Christian studies, creative art, music and free class discussion constitute a common compulsory curriculum.

In addition, history is compulsory from the 3rd to 9th years, geography and biology are compulsory from the 3rd to 7th years, English is compulsory from the 5th year onwards and physics/chemistry are compulsory from the 7th to 9th years. Needlework, woodwork and domestic science are compulsory for one year or more according to local decisions.

There will be certain changes in the subject range with the new Act. History will continue to be compulsory in the 3rd to 8th years. English will begin in the 4th year, and a new subject area – nature and technology – will be compulsory in the 1st to 6th years. German or French must be offered as a non-compulsory subject from the 7th year onwards (French and Latin may be taken in the 10th year). Vocational studies may be offered from the 8th year onwards; this is defined as 'the knowledge of the range of educational and employment opportunities available and of the conditions prevailing in working life' and includes visits to, and periods of work experience in, firms and institutions.

Educational and vocational **guidance** and work experience are compulsory subjects in the 7th, 8th and 9th years. They include such activities as information and discussions on career options, study visits and short work placements in firms, presentations by representatives of the world of work, visits to training centres and other types of schools, etc. These activities are carried out in close cooperation with the local community. The class/main teacher is responsible for vocational and educational guidance. The individual school has an educational counsellor who acts as a counsellor to the teachers, advises pupils and parents and takes up contacts with business and educational institutions.

From the 8th year onwards, there are also a number of practical subjects (typing, photography, drama, film, electronics and informatics), which schools may offer as non-compulsory subjects to enable more practically-minded pupils to develop their interests and abilities. There will also be minor changes in this area in the future.

Some degree of differentiation has been introduced in the 8th, 9th and 10th years for arithmetic/mathematics and English and German, and in the 9th and 10th years for physics/chemistry, in that basic and advanced courses (leading to the Leaving Examination and the Advanced Leaving Examination respectively) are offered. The final decision as to which course a pupil is to follow is made by the parents, after consultation with the pupil and the school.

In the future (in accordance with the new Act), the *Folkeskole* will be carried through integrally, as the existing distinction between basic course and advanced course will only appear when pupils choose what level to take at the leaving examinations. Classes will not be divided into levels, but kept together. At the same time, teaching differentiation will be a central concept, that is, teaching will be adapted to individual pupils to a greater extent (for example, through the formation of groups within a class).

In addition, instruction must be given in road safety, sex education, Norwegian and Swedish, religious education and health education. Minor changes are on their way in this context.

With regard to the planning of curricula and teaching methods, the individual school and local authorities have a high degree of autonomy. Although Parliament (*Folketing*) sets down the general aims of the *Folkeskole* and the Minister of Education sets down the objectives for individual subjects, it is up to the local education authorities and the individual schools to decide how these aims and objectives are to be achieved.

Assessment and qualifications

The assessment system also reflects the liberal philosophy of the *Folkeskole*. No marks are given in the 1st to 7th years, but schools are required to inform pupils and parents regularly (at least twice a year) of the pupils' progress on the basis of all oral and written work during the year. In the 8th, 9th and 10th years, marks from 0 to 13 are given for the year's work in those subjects in which a leaving examination may be taken. Pupils move up from one class to the next automatically. When they leave school, all pupils receive a leaving certificate indicating the subjects taken, the latest marks for the year's work and the examination results.

There is no overall leaving examination; examinations may be taken on a single-subject basis, and it is the pupils themselves who decide whether they want to sit an examination and in which subjects. Marks are again given from 0 to 13, but there is no minimum pass mark.

The Leaving Examination of the *Folkeskole* (*Folkeskolens afgangsprove*) may be taken in 11 subjects; the Advanced Leaving Examination (*Folkeskolens udvidede afgangsprove*) may be taken in 5 subjects, and only at the end of the 10th year. Only those pupils who have followed the advanced course in the 10th year may sit the latter examination.

Written examinations are standardized; they are drawn up and marked by the Ministry of Education. Oral examinations are administered by the subject teacher in the presence of a teacher from another school.

The Leaving Certificate is obtained by 95% of 16-year-olds.

Teachers

Folkeskole teachers are trained in specialized university-level colleges of education (*seminarier*) for four years. They are trained to teach all forms, and receive training in all subjects, but specialize in two. Training includes a total of 16 weeks' teaching practice.

In principle, teachers are employed on a full-time basis. As from 1993, all new teachers in the *Folkeskole* are employed on a group contract basis (i.e. they are no longer civil servants).

In principle, teachers are not obliged to follow in-service training; it is a local decision. In connection with the new Act on the *Folkeskole*, teachers will be obliged to follow in-service training in certain topics.

Statistics 1992/93

Folkeskole (including pre-school classes)	
Pupils	*525,720
Teachers (full-time equivalents)	50,462
Schools	1,688

* approximately 50,000 in pre-school classes + approximately 5,000 in private schools.

The maximum teacher/pupil ratio is 1: 28, the average ratio is 1: 19.

Private schools	
Pupils	67,302
Teachers	5,817
Schools	403
Efterskoler	
Pupils	16,113
Teachers	1,700 (estimate)
Schools	215

*

* *

Following the 9th year of the *Folkeskole*, those pupils who do not opt to stay on in the 10th year can either go on to the *Gymnasium* or to initial vocational training (see below). Pupils who stay on in the 10th year can go on to the *Gymnasium* or initial vocational training after that year or they can go on to the Higher Preparatory Course (*HF*). About 8% leave the education system altogether after the 9th or 10th year.

Around 50% of children continue with the non-compulsory 10th year. Of those who leave the basic school after the 9th year, the vast majority move on to the *Gymnasium* or to vocational education and training.

Close to one-third of young people opt for the *Gymnasium* or *HF* course.

4. Post-compulsory education

Upper secondary education

Upper secondary education can be divided into:

- General upper secondary education – *Gymnasium* and Higher Preparatory Examination (*Højere Forberedelseseksamen – HF*) courses;

- Vocational upper secondary education (see Initial Vocational Training – higher commercial courses – *HHX* and higher technical courses – *HTX*).

4.1 *Gymnasium*

Gymnasia are separate institutions which (with a few exceptions) offer education at post-compulsory level only. The schools provide a 3-year course, normally for pupils between 16 and 19 years of age, leading to the *Studentereksamen* (upper secondary school leaving examination) which qualifies pupils for university entrance. They are intended for academically able pupils aiming to enter higher education.

The majority of *Gymnasia* are run and funded by the counties. There are also a number of private *Gymnasia*; these are attended by approximately 6% of pupils. Education at the public schools is free of charge; a small fee is paid at the private schools. The Act on Upper Secondary Schools lays down that the County Council shall allocate grants for the transport between home and school of pupils enrolled in youth education. The *Gymnasium/*course lends textbooks to pupils. Other teaching materials may be purchased.

An alternative to the *Gymnasium* is the *Studenterkurser* which offers a 2-year course to pupils who have completed the 10th year, in day and evening classes. There are the same lines, levels and subjects as in the *Gymnasium*.

Pupils are admitted to a *Gymnasium* of their own choice (usually the one closest to their home), provided they have completed the 9th year, on the basis of a statement issued by their *Folkeskole* on whether they are 'qualified' or 'perhaps qualified' for academic studies at this level. Provided the school has enough capacity, 'qualified' applicants must be admitted to the (public) school of their first choice. If the school does not have the capacity, some applicants will be transferred to the school of their second choice. 'Perhaps qualified' candidates are tested at the school they apply to, and if the *Gymnasium* decides that the test results are satisfactory, they are admitted. *Gymnasia* are coeducational.

The school year covers 199 days, extending from around 15 August to that time in May when examinations start. It is not divided into terms, but there are holidays in October, at Christmas and at Easter, and from mid-June to mid-August. Schools are open 5 days per week from 8.00 a.m. to 2.00 p.m., with a short lunchbreak.

Pupils are grouped according to age and their chosen line and subjects. A different teacher teaches each subject. The team of teachers may change each year, but generally follows the same class for several years.

Curriculum

The structure of the (national) curriculum of the *Gymnasium* was changed by the Reform Act which came into effect for pupils starting in August 1988. However, teaching is still provided on two lines – the language line and the science line – as it has been since the 1903 Education Act. 50% of girls and 16% of boys (totalling 35%) choose the language line.

A core curriculum is common to both lines. In addition, there are a number of compulsory subjects in years 1 and 2, and 4 'blocks' for option choices at higher or intermediate level (3 in year 3 and 1 in year 2).

The core curriculum includes Danish, history, biology (1st year), music (1st year), geography (2nd year), art (3rd year), religious studies (3rd year) and classical studies (3rd year) and physical education.

Compulsory subjects in the language line are: English, German or French, a third foreign language (French, German, Italian, Japanese, Spanish or Russian), science and Latin (1st year only).

Compulsory subjects in the science line are: mathematics, physics, English, a second foreign language (German, French, Spanish, Italian, Japanese, or Russian) and chemistry (1st year only).

The options at higher level include music and social studies in both lines and, additionally, English, German and a third foreign language in the 3rd year. In the language line Greek and Latin are also options. In the science line biology and chemistry are options in the 2nd year and, additionally, mathematics and physics in the 3rd year.

The options at intermediate level include art, biology, computer studies, drama, economics, film, music, philosophy, physical education, social studies, technology and geography (3rd year only) in both lines. In the language line Latin is also an option and, additionally chemistry, mathematics and physics in the 3rd year. In the science line chemistry and Latin are also options.

Certain criteria for option choices must be met by all pupils:

– all 4 'blocks' must be occupied, and a subject can only be chosen at one of the levels;

– at least 2 of the subjects must be chosen at higher level;

– language line pupils must choose at least one foreign language at higher level;

– science line pupils must choose higher level in one of the following subjects: biology, chemistry, mathematics, music, physics or social studies;

– higher level in social studies or music must be combined with intermediate level in either biology, chemistry or geography or higher level in mathematics or physics.

The weekly number of lessons (45 minutes) which every school must teach is 32 in the 1st year and 31 to 32 in the 2nd and 3rd years. In the 1st year all 32 are devoted to compulsory subjects; in the 2nd year there are 27 lessons for compulsory subjects and in the 3rd year there are 17.

The Department for Upper Secondary Education issues framework curricula for all subjects/levels which must be taught, but individual teachers and classes jointly decide on the details (e.g. texts, special studies).

Assessment and qualifications

To successfully complete a course of study at the *Gymnasium* pupils must sit the 10 end-of-year external examinations leading to the *Studentereksamen*. Each pupil must sit written examinations in Danish and all higher level subjects at the end of the 3rd year and compulsory English (language line) or compulsory mathematics (science line) at the end of the 2nd year. In addition to these, there are 5 or 6 oral examinations to make up the total of 10 examinations during the three years of study.

During one week in the 3rd year, each pupil is exempt from lessons to write a major assignment in Danish, history or one of the subjects chosen at higher level. The assignment is assessed by the subject teacher and an external examiner appointed by the Ministry. The mark for the major written assignment in the third year counts towards the overall examination result.

Written papers are drawn up by the Department of Upper Secondary Education and are marked by two external examiners appointed by the Ministry. The Department of Upper Secondary Education decides in which subjects pupils in individual classes must sit oral examinations. The Department makes a complete timetable for each school and allocates an external examiner for each subject/class. The mark is decided by the subject teacher and the external examiner.

Pupils' performance is graded on a 13-point marking scale. Pupils who pass the *Studentereksamen* receive a certificate (*Bevis for Studentereksamen*) stating the examination marks, the marks for the year's work and the examination average.

In addition to the examinations for the *Studentereksamen*, pupils' work is assessed by the teachers twice during the school year and at the end of the year. Written examinations are held at the end of each year (May/June), in Danish for all pupils, in English for pupils in the languages line and in mathematics for pupils in the science line. At the end of the second and third years there are also examinations in the optional subjects that pupils have chosen at higher level. 'Term' examinations are held in the period February-April: in English for pupils in the languages line and in mathematics for pupils in the science line in the second year, and in Danish and the optional subjects chosen in the third year. The mark given for each term examination counts towards the general proficiency mark. At the end of the first and second years, three oral examinations are also normally held, including the final examination for the *Studentereksamen*.

Assignments for the end-of-year and term examinations are selected by the subject teacher. Marks for the end-of-term examinations are taken into account when determining the term marks and the marks for the year's work.

Marks are given in all subjects except physical education and sport at the end of all three years. In subjects in which there are written external examinations, two marks are given for the year's work: one for written work and the other for oral work. In other subjects, only one mark is given for the year's work. The mark for the year's work is given by the subject teacher and is an expression of the pupil's proficiency at the end of the school year.

On the basis of the assessment at the end of the 1st and 2nd years, the Teachers' Assembly advises pupils and their parents about advancement to the next class. If the pupil has attended courses regularly, he/she can insist on continuing or, in the case of failure, choose to resit examinations. The pupil and/or his/her parents make the final decision. During the 3rd year, written mock examinations are held locally; the results of these are taken into account when teachers determine the final assessment.

Several of the teachers of the *Gymnasium* are in charge of giving pupils individual **guidance** concerning educational, financial, social and personal matters. Around 20 hours of guidance are given to each group over the 3-year period.

Teachers

Teachers are all subject specialists with a university degree, normally in two subjects at Master's level. In order to follow teacher training, they must be employed or employed on probation at a school. They then follow theoretical and practical teacher training (*pedagogikum*) over six months. The theoretical part consists of a subject-related 2 to 4-day residential course and a 4 to 8-day course in educational theory in regionally established classes. The latter leads to a written examination. Practical training covers a minimum of 120 teaching and observation lessons in the first year of employment, supported by a tutor.

Teachers are employed on a group contract basis in accordance with an agreement between the Association of County Councils and the National Union of Upper Secondary School Teachers.

About 10% of the teaching staff are part-time teachers.

In-service training in not compulsory, but nearly all teachers participate in some form of professional development activity in the course of a school year.

4.2. Higher Preparatory Examination Course *(HF)*

The *HF* is a 2-year course, and the final examination qualifies pupils for further and higher education.

The *HF* course was established in 1967 in order to give young people and adults a 'second chance' in the education system. The *HF* course is taught either at a *Gymnasium* as a full two-year course or at a separate institution (adult education centre) on a single-subject basis over several years.

The formal requirement for admission to these courses is 10 years' school attendance, and the Advanced Leaving Examination of the *Folkeskole* in Danish and the Leaving Examination of the *Folkeskole* in mathematics, English and German.

Education in the full-time courses is free of charge; a small fee is paid by participants in the single-subject courses.

The timetable depends on the subjects chosen by the individual pupil. Teaching extends from mid-August to that time in May when examinations start, with holidays in October, at Christmas and at Easter and from the end of June to mid-August.

Curriculum

The *HF* course is composed of a nucleus of common core subjects and three elective subjects which can be freely combined. The common core subjects are: Danish, religious studies, history, biology, geography, mathematics, English, German, social studies, music, art and physical education/sport. The optional subjects, taught only in the second year (except beginner languages) are: biology, mathematics, German, social studies, music, art, physical education, French/Russian, physics, chemistry, psychology and English.

The *HF* subjects are of a level comparable to the *Gymnasium* subjects, but differ somewhat in content.

The Ministry of Education issues curriculum regulations which lay down the overall aims and content of teaching.

Assessment and qualifications

In order to complete the examination, pupils must pass all the subjects of the common core nucleus, plus some of the elective subjects. Final examinations are held in all subjects (except visual art, physical education and sport and music at common core level) at the end of the year in which instruction in the subjects ends. Both written and oral examinations are held in Danish, English, German/French, mathematics as a common core or an optional subject and in subjects chosen at higher level. Oral examinations only are held in the remaining subjects.

In addition to the written papers and reports, which are handed in on a regular basis in a number of subjects, and a written assignment in Danish and in history in the first year, the pupil must write a major assignment on a chosen subject. This is again written over one week during which there are no lessons. It is assessed by the teacher and an appointed examiner, and the mark given counts towards the overall examination result.

Pupils' performance is graded on a 13-point marking scale. Successful pupils receive a certificate (*Bevis for Hojere Forberedelseseksamen*) indicating their marks for the common core and optional subjects, their mark for the major written assignment and an average mark.

At each *HF* course there are one or more educational **guidance** officers who give pupils educational and vocational guidance.

Most *HF* pupils go on to short or medium-length further education; about two-thirds of *HF* pupils have been away from the education system for more than a year after completing the 10th year of the *Folkeskole*.

Teachers

See *Gymnasium*.

Statistics 1993/94

Gymnasium and *HF**	
Pupils	74,128
Teachers	8,987
Schools (all establishments offering the full course)	152

* includes *Studenterkurser* and single-subject courses.

Average teacher/pupil ratio is 1: 25.

5. Initial vocational training

Initial vocational training in Denmark is provided in three main forms following completion of the *Folkeskole*:

- basic vocational education and training;

- higher commercial courses (*HHX*);

- higher technical courses (*HTX*).

5.1 Basic vocational education and training

Since January 1991, the basic vocational education and training system has changed noticeably. The statutory basis for vocational education primarily consists of Law 210 of 1989 on vocational schools and Law 211 of 1989 on vocational education and training.

The Law on vocational education and training replaces the Law of 1956 on apprentices and the Law of 1977 on *EFG (Erhvervsfaglige Grunduddannelser* – basic vocational training), and forms the overall framework for the vocational education and training sector, which had hitherto included the apprenticeship courses, the *EFG* courses, and the basic technician training courses (e.g. laboratory technician and technical assistant). A common set of rules now exists for all these training courses.

One combined system has thus been established for all basic vocational education and training courses at the commercial schools and the technical schools. These schools receive approximately two-thirds (some 50,000) of a typical year group of young people.

There are now about 85 courses (as against close to 300 before), with more than 200 different specializations. With the exception of one course only, they are all organized as alternance (sandwich) education and training courses, in which theoretical education at a vocational school alternates with practical training in a firm. The limitation of admissions has in principle been abolished, and pupils/trainees and companies have a free choice of school. All vocational education and training courses lead to a skilled-worker certificate.

The training courses consist of a 1st part and a 2nd part, both of which include practical work experience and schooling. An entire training course does not generally last longer than 4 years. The duration of the school periods cannot normally exceed 80 weeks. The more detailed structure of courses, such as the allocation of time between school and in-firm training, is determined by the trade committees. A prerequisite is that there should be more interaction between school education and in-firm training than before.

Courses are generally intended for 16- to 19/20-year-olds.

To be admitted to a vocational education and training course, pupils must have completed compulsory education (normally 9 years' schooling). Admission does not take place on the basis of leaving certificates.

There are two routes into vocational education and training, namely the school-route and the practical training-route. The two admission routes meet at the start of the second school period, after which the pupils/trainees receive the same education and training. Whether the pupils choose the school admission-route or start with a practical training period in a firm, the duration and content of training is the same.

Pupils who choose the school-route normally start with the first school period, which lasts 20 weeks. They try out several different training areas and receive individual and collective guidance on jobs and training. Workshop instruction occupies a central position and is supplemented by instruction in theoretical subjects.

One-third of teaching time is set aside for optional subjects – in preparation for an examination – and subjects of a more general and creative nature. After the first school period, pupils select their training course and continue with the second school period. After the second school period, pupils must have a training contract with a firm before they can begin their in-firm training. Pupils receive their first pay as from the day on which they commence practical work experience.

In just under one-third of the vocational training courses it is not possible for pupils to start training with the first school period; they go straight into the second school period (the first school period is not compulsory).

Trainees who start with a practical training period of 20 weeks in a firm must have a training contract. They receive pay throughout their education and training period, which is partly subsidized by allocations from a collective employers' levy fund (the *AER*) intended to cover wage costs during the trainees' school periods.

In 1991, about 75% of young people admitted to technical schools chose the school route, this percentage was even higher at the commercial schools.

School education

The periods at a commercial or a technical school are not aimed solely at imparting technical and vocational competence within a narrow framework. In addition to vocational skills, the vocational education and training courses are intended to give general knowledge, to strengthen pupils' personal development and to give them an understanding of the structure and development of society. Each school is therefore committed to offering a broad range of optional subjects, to which one-sixth of the total teaching time is allocated.

The principal objective of vocational education and training policy is the broad youth education-character of vocational training, and the youth training courses should provide genuine opportunities for continued training. They must also contribute to the aim that not only young persons who choose youth education in the upper

secondary school or on a course preparing for the higher preparatory examination (*HF*), but also those who choose youth training in a trade, should have general education which, besides being important for their participation in working life is also important for the other aspects of their life.

The subject structure underpins this objective, and with management-by-objectives as the new governing principle completely new opportunities have been created for the decentralized modernization of teaching.

Curriculum

The school part of all vocational education and training courses comprises the four types of practical and theoretical subjects: basic subjects (*Grundfag*), area subjects (*Områdefag*), special subjects (*Specialefag*) and optional subjects (*Valgfag*). Basic subjects and area subjects each represent one-third of the course, whereas special subjects and optional subjects each represent one-sixth.

Whilst the schools decide which optional subjects they must offer, the trade committees have decisive influence with regard to basic subjects, area subjects and special subjects.

The basic subjects combine general and vocational aspects; they are meant to provide a broad-based vocational foundation and are therefore normally common for several areas. They are furthermore meant to support the pupils' personal development, give them an understanding of society and its development, and qualify them for further studies within their vocational field.

The area subjects are particular to the individual course and contribute to giving the pupils a general and specific vocational qualification.

The special subjects in particular contribute to giving the pupils a specific vocational qualification.

Optional subjects are of importance for further education and training and for admission to higher education. Electives are offered which take into account the skills needs and employment prospects in the local area of the school.

Assessment

See below.

Educational and vocational **guidance** at commercial and technical schools is provided by counsellors/guidance officers who have been appointed from among the teachers of the school.

On-the-Job Training

As already mentioned, the basic structure of vocational training is an alternance training course, in which practical training in a firm accounts for about two-thirds of the total training time.

Practical on-the-job training takes place in one or more firms which have been approved by the relevant trade committee as a place for practical work experience for the course concerned, and on the basis of a training contract between trainee and firm.

As from 1 January 1991, the vocational schools have taken over procurement of on-the-job training places; this had hitherto been done by the Employment Service. At the same time, the existing rules have been relaxed, improving the opportunities for the conclusion of combination agreements between several highly specialized enterprises in order to increase the supply of training places.

When the trainee has found an on-the-job training place, a training contract must be concluded between the trainee and the firm. The contract covers the whole of the alternating school-firm course – school periods, practical training periods and any final apprenticeship examination. The training contract is always in writing, and it must be made out on a special form approved by the Minister. Trainees who have not yet become of age must have their parents' consent for them to enter into a training contract.

Pay and conditions are regulated through collective bargaining agreements, the rules of which apply even if neither party to the contract is unionized.

Vocational schools and firms providing practical work experience are bound to exchange information which can benefit the pupil's training. The trade committees must still ensure that the trainees receive a good, all-round training.

Assessment

The work and achievement of trainees is assessed, depending on the subject, by oral or written examinations – sometimes with centrally drawn up assignments – or by continuous assessment of the class work by the teacher. Marks are given according to the 13-point marking scale or another scale approved by the Minister.

Assessment and/or examinations are carried out when the school instruction ends, and the school issues certificates if requirements have been fulfilled. When the pupil has carried out the on-the-job training in accordance with the rules on practical work experience, the firm issues the certificates for this. The Ministry of Education draws up assessment plans for individual training courses. The examination is controlled by the Ministry of Education and the relevant trade committees jointly, with shared roles and responsibilities.

Most vocational education and training courses are subject to a final examination. Depending on the course which has been followed, this may take the form of a journeyman's test, an examination or a combination of the two.

5.2 Vocational Education within the Upper Secondary School System (*HTX* and *HHX*)

In addition to the basic vocational training courses, technical and commercial schools provide courses leading to the higher technical examination (*Højere Teknisk Eksamen – HTX*) and the higher commercial examination (*Højere Handelseksamen – HHX*) respectively. Both courses are purely school-based and end with an examination; they also qualify pupils both for employment and for admission to higher education.

Although the *HHX* courses at the commercial schools and the *HTX* courses at the technical schools have several points in common with the general upper secondary courses, they have clearly retained their special profile and are aimed primarily at employment in the private sector. The courses provide access to the higher education courses at universities, to advanced commercial schools and to engineering diploma courses.

The social partners exert influence upon *HHX* and *HTX*; the Vocational Advisory Council has appointed separate committees for *HHX* and *HTX* to advise the Minister of Education on the content and objectives of the vocational upper secondary courses.

In 1990, Parliament passed the Law concerning *HHX* and *HTX*. The vocationally oriented courses within the upper secondary school system have thereby been combined in one single law with an independent statutory basis. The Law is a consequence of, and an adaptation to, the reform of vocational training, but represents at the same time a strengthening of vocational upper secondary education, which has several features in common with general upper secondary education, both structurally and in content.

Admission to the *HHX* and *HTX* courses has been changed so that suitable pupils can be admitted directly from the *Folkeskole*. At the same time, the admission routes are coordinated with the new introductory parts of the vocational education and training courses. It is possible to change over from basic vocational education courses to *HTX* and *HHX* courses and vice versa – if the school considers the pupil to be suitable. Courses are free of charge.

The courses leading to the *HHX* and *HTX* both last three years and are generally intended for 16- to 19-year-olds. They are divided into two blocks. The first year is vocational training/education – which pupils often take along with the first year pupils following the basic vocational training course – while the following two years are theoretical.

In 1994, a new Act pertaining to the *HHX* and *HTX* was adopted by Parliament; this will be implemented in 1995. The main effect of this Act will be to make the introductory year in both courses more theoretical than it is now.

Curriculum

In the *HHX* courses, pupils learn to work in areas with direct application to business administration and management. Compulsory subjects include: Danish, foreign languages, accountancy, finance, commercial law, data processing, mathematics and economics.

Compulsory subjects in the *HTX* course include: Danish, foreign languages, technology and natural sciences. In addition to its theoretical content, this course also includes industrial workshop and laboratory practice.

Approximately two-thirds of the course consists of compulsory subjects, and one-third of optional subjects.

Assessment

Courses lead to a final examination.

The Ministry of Education decides each year which examinations are to be held. Each pupil normally takes a minimum of 10 and a maximum of 12 examinations. Examinations can be written, oral or in the form of project work. The assessment is expressed by marks given according to the 13-point marking scale.

Teachers

Vocational teacher training in Denmark is basically a pedagogical course supplementing the technical skills and practical work experience of skilled workers who want to become teachers. Teachers of general subjects must have qualifications corresponding to those required at the lower/upper secondary educational level (see page 75).

Initial vocational teacher training takes place at the state institute for the training of vocational teachers (*Statens Erhvervspaedagogiske Laereruddannelse – SEL*) and has a total duration of 500 hours of instruction. Including individual studies and work on the final project, the duration is about 600 hours. Normally, the whole course runs for 12 months.

Teachers are recruited directly by the vocational schools and start teaching before going on a teacher training course. The pedagogical course is alternance-based, and much of the training takes place at the trainee's school as on-the-job training supervised by a counsellor. Within the first two years, teacher trainees must pass the pedagogical examination. Certification is administered by *SEL*.

Vocational teachers are employed full-time, and they have a status like civil servants.

They are obliged to maintain and extend their qualifications, but not necessarily through in-service training courses. (The development of teachers is seen as part of a total competence building strategy in most of the schools. It is considered that learning results from many other activities than participation in courses or formal education.)

Formal requirements for the training of instructors providing on-the-job instruction in firms do not exist.

Statistics 1992/93

Pupils/students	
– Initial vocational education	51,118
– Vocational education and training (incl. *HHX* and *HTX*)	116,572
Vocational teachers (incl. agricultural schools)	16,700 full-time equivalents
Vocational schools	115

5.3 Other basic vocational education and training courses

In addition to the courses mentioned above, there are a number of other basic vocational education and training courses, e.g. the agricultural education and training course, the basic social and health training programmes, and the marine engineering courses.

To complete the picture of the Danish vocational education and training system, there follows a brief description of the social and health training programmes.

The aim of these programmes, which are conducted in special social and health schools run by the 14 counties and under separate legislation, is to train qualified staff in the welfare, health care and nursing areas for broad-based job functions.

The basic social and health training programmes are sandwich-type programmes, where practical training (two-thirds) alternates with theoretical education (one-third). The practical training takes place in the municipalities – in the homes of the clients and in nursing homes.

5.4 Production schools

Under the Law of 6 June 1985, production schools are established at the initiative of municipal and county authorities and set up as independent institutions. Their role is to provide combined education and production programmes which put participants, aged 16 to 19, in a better position to either get a job or start a qualifying training course.

Pupils usually stay in a production school for around 12 months but can leave at any time if they have found a training place or a job.

The main characteristics of the production schools are the flexibility of their curriculum and teaching methods, and their links with market-oriented activities. Educational activities are built upon the needs arising from practical situations; there are therefore no fixed subjects, but tuition in Danish, social sciences, mathematics and contemporary studies is available in all production schools.

Agriculture, gardening, forestry, fish-farming, textiles, solar panels, carpentry and cabinet-making, and souvenirs are the most common sectors covered by the production schools. They are chosen in cooperation with local industry.

5.5 Other courses

Among the various training courses set up to combat unemployment, *EIFU* courses (*Erhvervsintroducerende kurser for unge* – introductory vocational courses for young people) are aimed at providing a broad vocational introduction to the labour market. They combine school-based training of an average duration of 8 to 10 weeks and a period of work experience of 4 weeks. Courses are held at the schools for semi-skilled workers.

As a result of the work of the Social Commission appointed by the Minister of Social Affairs, a new Act on *EGU* courses (*Erhvervsgrunduddannelser* – Basic Vocational Courses) came into effect on 1 August 1993.

The *EGU* course differs from the other vocational education and training courses in that it is a combination course. It has thus not been decided in advance what the course is to lead to, and what the content is to be. The Act on the *EGU* is a framework Act, which makes it possible for courses to be organized according to the wishes and abilities of the individual student. *EGU* courses take two years, and the individual course mainly consists of practical training – only 20-40 weeks are spent on theoretical education.

The practical training takes place mainly in private and public enterprises. It is the aim of the *EGU* to give young people qualifications which may lead to studies in mainstream technical or commercial education and training and create the basis for employment in the labour market.

The *EGU* courses are run by the municipalities; the social partners do not take part in the scheme.

6. Higher education

Higher education institutions may be divided into universities, university centres and other institutions of higher education. There is a great variety of choice. More than 130 institutions offer study programmes of varying lengths and levels. Choice has been further increased by the significant development of non-academic higher education within the field of vocational (technical and commercial) education.

Universities and university centres offer courses and carry out research in traditional university subjects.

The other higher education institutions in the university sector offer courses and carry out research within such fields as engineering, veterinary science, pharmacy, architecture, music, art and various business studies.

The colleges of education train teachers for the *Folkeskole* and have their own independent research institution, the Royal Danish School of Educational Studies.

The non-academic institutions offer medium-length or short courses in particular in the fields of technology, education, social work and health. Further technical education courses are offered at technical schools for students aged 19 +; and these are mainly aimed at employment.

Admission

The entrance qualifications for **higher education** are the Upper Secondary School Leaving Examination (*Studentereksamen*), the Higher Preparatory Examination (*Højere Forberedelseseksamen*), the Higher Commercial Examination (*Højere Handelseksamen*) and the Higher Technical Examination (*Højere Teknisk Eksamen*). Certain non-academic institutions may, however, admit students without these qualifications; alternative requirements include 9-10 years of school attendance, followed by work experience, an entrance examination or a supplementary examination. There is restricted admission to all Danish higher education courses (numerus clausus). Students apply to individual institutions (usually eight) on a centralized application form.

In 1992, approximately 40,000 young people were admitted to higher education (roughly 43% of a year group).

In order to be admitted to one of the **further technical education** courses, students must have completed a vocational education and training course within a field that is relevant to the chosen course.

Admission requirements for **further commercial education** vary from one of the upper secondary level qualifying examinations to completion of a relevant vocational education and training course and/or *Højere Handelseksamen*.

Fees/Student finance

There are no registration/tuition fees in higher education. Student support in the form of state grants and loans is provided to cover living costs and the purchase of books and other teaching materials.

Academic year

As a rule, the academic year is divided into two semesters: from September to December and from January/February to May/June. Students have a week's holiday in October, at Christmas and at Easter. Some courses have two annual intakes.

Courses/Qualifications

As a rule, Bachelor's degrees can now be obtained within all of the **universities'** main areas (BA in theology, social sciences, humanities, BSc in natural sciences and health sciences) after three years of study. A further two years of study leads to the award of a Master's degree (*cand.mag., cand.scient., cand.theol., cand.med.*, etc.).

In the humanities, there are also 4-year degree courses (*cand.phil.*) and a special 6-year Master's degree course (*mag.art.*).

Most courses leading to the award of a Master's degree are prescribed to take five years, but some students take longer.

Degree courses offered by the university centres begin with a one or two-year basic course of an interdisciplinary, problem-oriented nature, which qualifies students for a number of further courses of study.

Further technical education courses are organized as a continuation of basic vocational education and training. Teaching is mainly theoretical and general subjects are linked closely to vocational topics in such a way as to emphasize application rather than pure theory. There are about 25 different further technical education courses, usually lasting from one to two years. In most cases, courses are completed by a state-controlled examination leading to the award of a diploma.

Further technical/commercial education courses are offered in cooperation between technical and commercial schools. An example of such a course is the export technician's course. This lasts four years and is structured in eight 6-month periods, alternating between theoretical education at school and practical training in a firm. It is completed with a major written assignment, and successful students are awarded a diploma.

Further commercial education courses are relatively new and are few, including a 2½-year school-based vocationally-oriented course in computer science and a 2-year course in market economics.

There is a wide range of **medium-length non-university** courses lasting three to 4 years, including 4-year courses in engineering and journalism and 3-year courses in social work, midwifery, occupational therapy, physiotherapy and hospital laboratory work.

Assessment

In general, students on post-secondary courses are assessed through examinations. These take the form either of internal examinations assessed by the examiner(s), or by the examiner(s) and one or more 'external' examiners appointed from among the teachers of the institution, or of external examinations assessed by the teacher-examiner(s) and one or more external examiners appointed by the Ministry of Education.

Assessment is expressed by marks given according to a 13-point scale (10-13 correspond to 'excellent', 7-9 to 'good', 6 to 'satisfactory', 0-5 to 'poor').

Assessment of up to one-third of the course can be expressed by 'pass/fail'. The most essential parts of the course must be assessed through external examinations.

Germany

FEDERAL REPUBLIC OF GERMANY

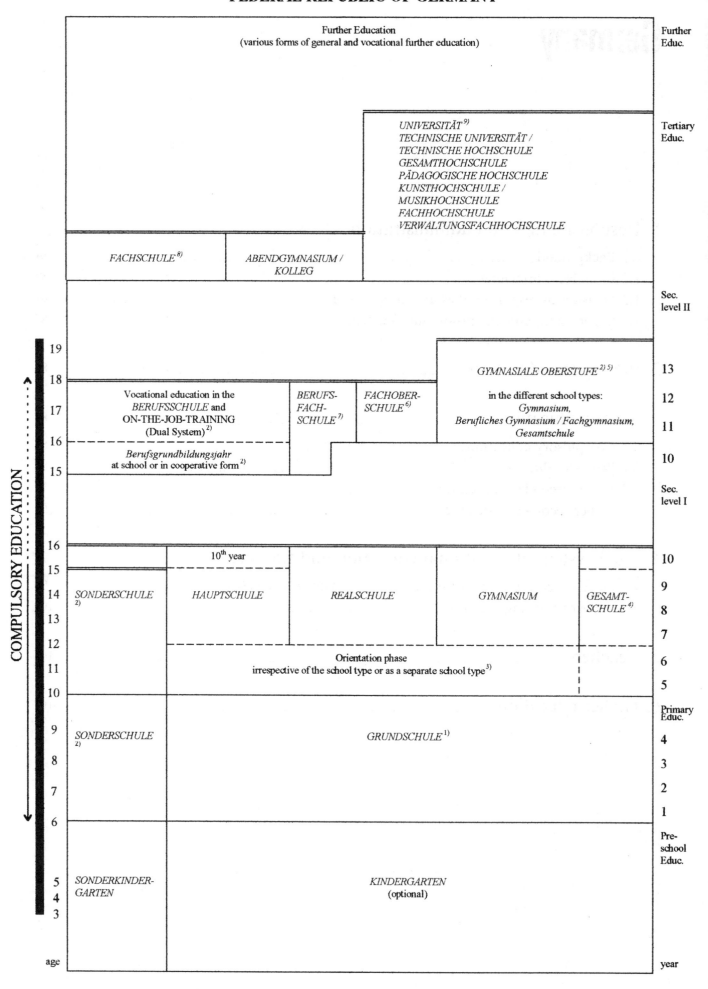

Further Education
(various forms of general and vocational further education)

Further Educ.

UNIVERSITÄT [9]
TECHNISCHE UNIVERSITÄT /
TECHNISCHE HOCHSCHULE
GESAMTHOCHSCHULE
PÄDAGOGISCHE HOCHSCHULE
KUNSTHOCHSCHULE /
MUSIKHOCHSCHULE
FACHHOCHSCHULE
VERWALTUNGSFACHHOCHSCHULE

Tertiary Educ.

FACHSCHULE [8]

ABENDGYMNASIUM /
KOLLEG

Sec. level II

GYMNASIALE OBERSTUFE [2) 5)]

in the different school types:
Gymnasium,
Berufliches Gymnasium / Fachgymnasium,
Gesamtschule

Vocational education in the
BERUFSSCHULE and
ON-THE-JOB-TRAINING
(Dual System) [2]

BERUFS-
FACH-
SCHULE [7]

FACHOBER-
SCHULE [6]

Berufsgrundbildungsjahr
at school or in cooperative form [2]

Sec. level I

19				13
18				12
17				11
16				10
15				

10th year

16						10
15						9
14	*SONDERSCHULE* [2]	*HAUPTSCHULE*	*REALSCHULE*	*GYMNASIUM*	*GESAMT-SCHULE* [4]	8
13						7
12						6
11						5

Orientation phase
irrespective of the school type or as a separate school type [3]

10		Primary Educ.
9	*SONDERSCHULE* [2]	*GRUNDSCHULE* [1]	4
8		3
7		2
6		1

Pre-school Educ.

5	*SONDERKINDER-GARTEN*	*KINDERGARTEN* (optional)
4		
3		

COMPULSORY EDUCATION

age | year

Diagram of the basic structure of the education system. Secondary level I is portrayed in line with the distribution of the school population in 1993: *Hauptschule* 25.6%, *Realschule* 26.1%, *Gymnasium* 31.4%, *integrierte Gesamtschule* 8.9%. Unlike the basic structure presented here, the provision of schools at secondary level I – with the exception of *Sonderschulen* – varying in the different *Länder* includes:

— separate schools which prepare pupils for one of the three school-leaving qualifications, namely the *Hauptschule*, *Realschule* or *Gymnasium* and offered in most *Länder*;

— unified schools which prepare pupils for any one of the three school-leaving qualifications such as in the *kooperative Gesamtschule* and the *Schulzentrum* (a school complex in Bremen), where the *Hauptschule, Realschule and Gymnasium* are united into a single administrative unit, but pupils are streamed according to their intended final qualification. The *integrierte Gesamtschule* unites the three school types administratively and educationally. Pupils are taught in mixed-ability groups but setting is gradually phased in for some subjects;

— unified schools which prepare pupils for one of two leaving certificates (*Hauptschule* and *Realschule* education) with various names in the different *Länder*, such as the *Mittelschule* (Saxony), the *Regelschule* (Thuringia), the *Sekundarschule* (Saxony-Anhalt, Saarland), the *Integrierte Haupt- und Realschule* (Hamburg), the *Verbundene Haupt- und Realschule* (Hesse) and the *Regionale Schule* (Rhineland-Palatinate).

The ability of pupils to transfer between school types and the recognition of school-leaving qualifications is basically guaranteed if the preconditions agreed between the *Länder* are fulfilled. The duration of full-time compulsory education (general compulsory education) is 9 years (10 years in four of the *Länder*) and the subsequent period of part-time compulsory education (compulsory vocational education) is 3 years.

1. In some *Länder* there are special types of transition from *Kindergarten* to primary education (*Vorklassen, Schulkindergärten*). In Berlin and Brandenburg the primary school comprises 6 years.

2. The disabled attend special forms of general education and vocational school types (in some cases integrated with non-handicapped pupils) depending on the type of disability in question. Designation of schools varies according to the law of each *Land* (*Sonderschule, Schule für Behinderte, Förderschule*).

3. Irrespective of school type, years 5 and 6 constitute a phase of particular support, supervision and orientation with regard to the pupil's future educational path and its particular focuses. The orientation stage is organized as a separate organizational unit independent of the standard school types in some *Länder*.

4. The *Gesamtschule* is generally provided in accordance with the respective educational laws of the *Länder* as a standard school type or as a special kind of school.

5. Admission to the *Gymnasiale Oberstufe* requires a formal entrance qualification, which can generally be obtained after year 10. Saxony-Anhalt and Thuringia have ruled that the formal entrance qualification can be awarded after year 9 at the *Gymnasium*. The *Gymnasiale Oberstufe* can generally be completed after 13 school years, in four *Länder* (Saxony, Saxony-Anhalt, Thuringia, Mecklenburg-Western Pomerania), for a transitional period, after 12 years of schooling.

6. The *Fachoberschule* is a school type lasting two years (11th and 12th years) which takes pupils who have completed the *Realschule* and qualifies them for *Fachhochschule*. School leavers from the *Berufsaufbauschule* who have acquired concurrently a *Fachschule* qualification during or following initial vocational education can enter the 12th year directly. Pupils who have successfully completed *Realschule* and have been through initial vocational training can also enter the 12th year of the *Fachoberschule* directly. Alternative routes for acquiring the *Fachhochschulreife* are, for example, the *Berufsfachschule* and *Fachschule*.

7. Full-time vocational schools differing in terms of entrance requirements, duration and leaving certificates. Certain two-year *Berufsfachschulen* requiring a *Realschule* certificate for admission lead to a state-recognized qualification as a technical assistant (*staatlich geprüfter Assistent*), and one-year courses at *Berufsfachschule* offer basic vocational training.

8. *Fachschulen* are schools at secondary level II offering courses of between one and three years duration.

9. Including institutions of higher education offering particular disciplines at university level (e.g. theology, philosophy, medicine, administration studies, sport).

Glossary

BERUFSSCHULE: Part-time vocational school at the upper level of secondary education providing general and vocational education for pupils in initial vocational training; special attention is paid to the requirements of training in the dual system (part-time school and on-the-job training).

FACHGYMNASIUM: See *Berufliches Gymnasium*.

FACHHOCHSCHULE: Institution of higher education offering degree programmes, particularly in engineering, economics, administration, social work, agriculture and design. Preparation for employment on the basis of application-oriented teaching and research is the specific training purpose of the *Fachhochschulen*.

FACHOBERSCHULE: Technical secondary school (years 11 to 12) specialized in various areas and providing access to *Fachhochschulen*.

FACHSCHULE: Technical school providing advanced vocational training.

GESAMTHOCHSCHULE-UNIVERSITÄT: Institution of higher education existing in two *Länder* combining functions of the universities, *Fachhochschulen* and, in some cases, colleges of art and music. They offer courses of study of varying duration and leading to different degrees.

GESAMTSCHULE: Comprehensive school existing in two forms: the cooperative comprehensive school combines the schools of the traditional tripartite system under one roof and harmonizes the curricula in order to facilitate the transfer of pupils between the different coexisting types; the integrated comprehensive school admits all pupils of a certain age without differentiating between the traditional school types. A number of the integrated comprehensive schools also have the upper secondary level, organized as the *Gymnasiale Oberstufe*.

GRUNDSCHULE: Primary school marks the beginning of compulsory education, to which all children go together once they have reached the age of six (in general years 1-4). The aim of the primary school is to provide its pupils with the basis for their subsequent education at the lower level of secondary education.

GYMNASIALE OBERSTUFE: Upper level of the *Gymnasium* (normally years 11, 12, 13) providing pupils who pass the final examination (*Abiturprüfung*) with the general university entrance qualification.

GYMNASIUM: Secondary school (normally years 5 to 13) providing intensified general education and conferring the general university entrance qualification. See also *Allgemeine Hochschulreife*.

HAUPTSCHULE: Secondary school – lower level – providing fundamental general education.

KOLLEG: Institution of general education offering day school courses for adults with work experience and the possibility to acquire the *allgemeine Hochschulreife*.

KUNSTHOCHSCHULE: College of art.

MUSIKHOCHSCHULE: College of music.

PÄDAGOGISCHE HOCHSCHULE: Teacher training college which still exists in two *Länder* where teachers are trained for careers in primary and lower secondary as well as in special education. In the other *Länder* courses for the above-mentioned teaching careers are offered by universities, *Universitäten-Gesamthochschulen* and colleges of art and music.

REALSCHULE: Secondary school – lower level, normally years 5-10 – providing extended general education and giving access to upper secondary education where a higher education entrance qualification or a vocational qualification may be obtained.

SONDERSCHULE: Special schools for children with learning disabilities, schools for the blind and visually handicapped, schools for the deaf and hard of hearing, schools for children with speech handicaps, schools for the physically handicapped, schools for mentally handicapped children, schools for children with behavioural problems and schools for sick pupils.

TECHNISCHE UNIVERSITÄT / TECHNISCHE HOCHSCHULE: Technical university.

VERWALTUNGSFACHHOCHSCHULE: Special type of *Fachhochschule* offering degree programmes in public administration which include periods of on-the-job training for future civil servants at the middle level in federal, *Land* or local authorities.

1. Responsibilities and administration

1.1 Background

The Federal Republic of Germany has a population of 81,338,000 (1993) in a territory of 357,000 square kilometres, the size having increased on 3 October 1990 as a result of German unification through a Treaty between the Federal Republic of Germany and the German Democratic Republic.

Under the *Grundgesetz* (Basic Law), the *Bundestag* (Federal German Parliament) and *Bundesrat* (composed of members of government in the *Länder*) are the legislative bodies. Executive functions in the field of home and foreign affairs are carried out mainly by the Federal Government insofar as the Federation enjoys relevant competence for these fields of policy under the Basic Law. The Federal Government, headed by the Federal Chancellor, is composed of 16 ministers (1994). The administation of justice is exercised by the Federal Constitutional Court (*Bundesverfassungsgericht*) and by other courts of the Federation and the *Länder*. The Federal Constitutional Court is the supreme judiciary body at the constitutional level and examines legislation enacted at Federal and *Land* level to ensure that it is compatible with the Basic Law. The Federal President is the Head of State and is elected for a five-year term.

The Federal Republic is made up of 16 *Länder* (states), including five which were reintroduced in the former German Democratic Republic on the basis of the Establishment of *Länder* Act of July 1990. Each *Land* has its own constitution and government. The Basic Law stipulates that the *Länder* have the right to legislate insofar as the Basic Law does not confer legislative power on the Federation. In the 16 *Länder* there are also 29 administrative areas, 543 counties and 16,043 communes (1992).

In 1993, the labour force was divided between the following sectors: agriculture 3.2%; industry 36.8%; and services 60%. The unemployment rate was 8.9%.

1.2 Basic legal principles

According to the Basic Law, the Federal Republic of Germany is a republic, a democracy, a federal, constitutional and socially responsible State. As far as education is concerned the Basic Law guarantees among other things the freedom of art and science, research and teaching, freedom of creed, conscience and to profess a religion, the freedom to choose one's occupation and place of study or training, equality before the law and the natural right of parents to care for and bring up their children.

1.3 Division of responsibilities and cooperation

The responsibility for education in the Federal Republic of Germany is determined by the federal structure of government. The federal Constitution is the Basic Law (*Grundgesetz*) which stipulates that the State's rights and duties fall to the *Länder*, insofar as the Basic Law does not specify or permit otherwise. The *Länder* are thus entitled to pass legislation where the Basic Law does not confer legislative power on the Federation (*Bund*). Educational legislation and administration of the education system are therefore primarily the responsibility of the *Länder*. This is especially true of the school system, higher education, and adult and continuing education.

The Basic Law defines the number and scope of the **Federation's responsibilities** in the field of education. These apply especially to the following areas in education and science: the regulation of in-company initial and further vocational training in the framework of economic and labour law, the regulation of financial assistance for pupils in schools and students in higher education institutions, the promotion of scientific and academic research, the legal protection of participants in distance-learning courses, and the passing of framework legislation on the general principles of higher education. The Federation is also responsible for legal framework provisions on civil service employment generally and for the payment of salaries and benefits to civil servants (e.g. teachers and professors). The *Länder* then make these provisions more concrete by creating and implementing the relevant *Land* legislation.

In addition to defining the division of responsibilities as described above, the Basic Law also makes provisions for the **Federation to cooperate with the *Länder***, as in the joint task of construction and expansion of higher education institutions and university clinics. In order to coordinate this properly, the Federal Government and the governments of the *Länder* form a planning committee for the construction of higher education institutions, chaired by the **Federal Minister of Education, Science, Research and Technology** and also involving the Federal Minister of Finance and one Minister from each of the *Länder*. The Federation can also enter into agreements with the *Länder* to cooperate on educational planning and on the funding of academic and scientific research institutions and projects of supraregional significance. The forum for this cooperative activity is the *Bund-Länder* Commission for Educational Planning and Research Promotion, in which the Federal Government and the governments of all *Länder* are represented. In-company vocational training and vocational education in schools fall under separate jurisdictions. The Federal Government is responsible for the formulation of training regulations, while the *Länder* create framework curricula. The 'Common Result Protocol' (*Gemeinsames Ergebnisprotokoll*) of 1972 provides the basis for the necessary coordination between the Federation and *Länder* governments.

In addition to cooperation with the Federation, the ***Länder* governments also cooperate amongst themselves**, both in those areas of education for which responsibility falls to the *Länder* and in areas regulated by federal laws insofar as *Land* law is needed for their implementation and application. The Ministers and Senators responsible for education and training, higher education institutions, research, and cultural affairs in the *Länder* work together in the Standing Conference of the Ministers of Education and Cultural Affairs of the *Länder* in the Federal Republic of Germany (*Ständige Konferenz der Kultusminister der Länder in der Bundesrepublik Deutschland*). This Conference of Ministers was established by an agreement among the *Länder* and deals with cultural and educational issues of supraregional significance with a view to reaching a joint position and attending to matters of common interest. Cultural policy is interpreted broadly to include the areas of education, higher education, research, cultural affairs and sport. This cooperation has led to joint and comparable developments in broad areas.

An agreement between the *Länder* of 1964, last amended in 1971, guarantees a uniform fundamental structure of the school system in Germany. Among other things, the agreement covers the beginning and duration of full-time compulsory education, the dates for the start and end of the school year, the duration of school holidays, the designation and organization of the various types of educational institutions, the basic guarantee that pupils can transfer from one school type to another if certain preconditions are fulfilled, the beginning of foreign language courses and the sequence in which languages are learned, the recognition of leaving certificates and teaching qualifications, and the description of the marking system used for school reports and teacher training examinations. In subsequent resolutions, the Standing Conference has defined additional common features of the school system and contributed to the mutual recognition of qualifications in all the *Länder*.

In the area of higher education, the *Länder* have concluded an agreement on the standardization of the *Fachhochschulen* system and have reached numerous further agreements concerning other higher education institutions. Cooperation between the Standing Conference of Ministers and the association of higher education institutions, as represented by their rectors and presidents (*Hochschulrektorenkonferenz*), has created a link between the government bodies which administer higher education in the *Länder*, on the one hand, and the self-administration of the institutions themselves, on the other. This cooperation has taken concrete form in agreements on the content and organization of state examinations (*Staatsprüfungen*) and academic examinations (*Hochschulprüfungen*).

Following the restoration of the unity of Germany as a State on 3 October 1990, education policy in the Federal Republic has focused on bringing together the eleven old and five new *Länder* in the fields of education, science, culture, and sport. Internal unity calls for political and organizational efforts aimed at establishing a common and comparable basic structure for education, especially for the school system, and a common though differentiated higher education and scientific landscape in the Federal Republic of Germany.

1.4 Supervision, administration and financing

Pre-school education

Pre-school education mainly comes under child and youth welfare services. In most *Länder*, government supervision of *Kindergärten* is exercised by the Social Ministries, although in some *Länder* it is performed by the Ministries of Education and Cultural Affairs. The local Youth Welfare Offices (*Jugendämter*) are responsible for administration. Only *Vorklassen* (pre-school classes) for five-year-olds who have not yet reached compulsory schooling age, and *Schulkindergärten* (school kindergartens) for those six-year-olds who have not yet attained a sufficient level to attend school are supervised by the school authorities.

About 70% of all *Kindergärten* are run by voluntary bodies of the child and youth welfare services (mainly churches and welfare associations), while the remaining 30% are maintained by local public authorities (*Gemeinden*). *Kindergärten* run by voluntary bodies are also subject to supervision and are supported financially by the *Länder* and the communes. Despite the allocation of major public

subsidies for this purpose (and of church tax revenues in the case of church run *Kindergärten*), parents of pre-school children are required to pay fees of different amounts, which in some cases depend on their income. The local Youth Welfare Office (*Jugendamt*) pays such charges on behalf of the children of parents of low-income groups. Thus, unlike the school and higher education system, pre-school education is not provided free of charge.

Schools

According to the Basic Law and *Länder* constitutions, the entire school system comes under the supervision and responsibility of the State. The *Länder* Ministries of Education and Cultural Affairs have ultimate authority in the supervision and administration of institutions providing general and vocational education. School supervision includes the mandate to plan and organize the entire school system. The authority of the *Länder* extends not only to the organization of the schools themselves, the content of the courses and teaching objectives, but also to supervising the performance of teachers and other teaching staff. The educational goals set down in school laws are given concrete form in curricula, for which the *Länder* Ministries of Education and Cultural Affairs are responsible. The competent *Länder* ministries establish curricula for the subjects taught at the different types and levels of school. These curricula are usually developed in special curriculum planning commissions by teachers who are assisted by other specialists. Before a curriculum is implemented, there is a procedure which assures the participation of associations and representatives of parents, pupils and teachers.

In order to implement the curricula for the various subjects in the different types of school the respective textbooks are used as learning material in the classroom. These books must be approved by the Ministries of Education and Cultural Affairs and a list of approved books is published regularly.

The administration of schools generally has a three-tiered structure, in which the Ministries of Education and Cultural Affairs of the *Länder* form the upper tier, the school departments of regional governments or independent upper level schools' offices (*Oberschulämter*) the middle tier, and the schools' offices (*Schulämter*) at the local, city, or commune level the lower tier. In some *Länder* and in the city-states, school administration is based on a two-tiered system, and in the city-states it sometimes has only one tier. Here, it is either the middle or the lower tier which is eliminated. *Gymnasien* (lower and upper secondary schools providing intensified general education), comprehensive schools, vocational schools (*berufliche Schulen*) and, in most cases, *Realschulen* (lower secondary schools providing extended general education) are usually supervised by middle-level authorities (regional governments) or by the highest authority (Ministries of Education and Cultural Affairs) directly. The much more numerous *Grundschulen* (primary schools), *Hauptschulen* (lower secondary schools providing fundamental general education), certain special schools and, in some *Länder*, the *Realschulen* as well, are still supervised by the lower school authority.

As a rule, public sector schools are run by local authorities. This means that the local authorities are responsible for setting up, organizing and administering schools, which they must also fund. State responsibility for running schools (i.e. the responsibility of a *Land*) is, with some exceptions, limited to schools whose catchment area and significance stretches beyond the commune, for example, schools with a particular emphasis on training in the arts or sport, certain technical schools (*Fachschulen*), institutions of general education preparing adults for higher education (*Kollegs*) and special schools run under the auspices of the *Land*. In addition to their responsibility for the schools' organization and material needs, the providing body is responsible for administrative staff (i.e. non-teaching staff), while the *Länder* are generally responsible for the teaching staff.

Schools run by voluntary bodies are also subject to state supervision. For their school-leaving certificates to be recognized, these schools must comply with the relevant state regulations concerning the courses taught, teacher qualifications, and examinations. Regulations of the *Länder* governing these schools take their special educational concerns into account.

In principle, attendance at all public sector schools is free of charge. The learning materials pupils need at school are either provided free of charge or can be borrowed from the school. In cases where pupils are given material to keep, parents may sometimes be required to pay some of the costs, depending on their income.

On the basis of legal provisions of the Federation, from year 10 pupils in general and vocational schools may obtain financial assistance in the form of a grant if they have no other source of maintenance or funds (especially from parental income) to meet training requirements. For certain types of school, financial assistance for pupils depends on how easily the place of training can be reached from the parental home or whether the pupil has to live away from home. Training assistance (*Ausbildungsförderung*) is awarded for the pupil's maintenance and training; the pupil's own income and savings and those of his/her parents and spouse, if any, are taken into account in what can be a very complicated process in calculating a pupil's requirements. In addition, most *Länder* have regulations whereby pupils at upper secondary level who are not entitled to financial assistance under the *Bundesausbildungsförderungsgesetz* (Federal Training Assistance Act) can, under certain circumstances, be awarded financial assistance from the *Land*'s own means.

In-company vocational training

Vocational education in schools is the exclusive responsibility of the *Länder*, while the Federal Government is responsible for in-company vocational training. Companies and vocational schools do not provide education and training in isolation from one another. The courses they offer are coordinated in terms of content and organization within the framework of the dual system of vocational education and training. This cooperation, in which business and industry – including both employees and employers through their public-law self-administered organizations – also participate in vocational education and training, is institutionalized by law at the federal, *Land*, regional, and company levels.

At the federal level, the Federal Minister for Education, Science, Research and Technology is responsible for coordination in the domain of in-company vocational training. Representatives of employer's associations, trade unions, *Länder* governments, and the Federal Government work together on an equal footing in the Federal Institute of Vocational Training (*Bundesinstitut für Berufsbildung*). The Institute advises the Federal Government on matters relating to vocational training. It also prepares training regulations for the in-company part of vocational training to be approved by the Federal Government. The Federation and the *Länder* coordinate the training regulations with the framework curricula for the vocational school (*Berufsschule*). At *Land* level, committees consisting of representatives of employers, trade unions, and *Länder* ministries are formed to deal with vocational education and training. They advise *Land* governments in matters regarding vocational education. At regional level, the organizations for business self-administration (chambers of industry and commerce, chambers of handicrafts, chambers of agriculture, chambers of independent professions) are responsible for advising, supervising, and recognizing in-company vocational training within the region on the basis of relevant legislation. In firms providing training, elected labour representatives have the right to participate in planning and implementing in-company vocational training and in the appointment of trainers (*Ausbilder*).

Higher education

As a rule, institutions of higher education have the status of a body corporate and are public institutions under the authority of the *Länder*. They have the right of self-administration within the framework of legal provisions. The higher education institutions draw up their own statutes which then require the approval of the *Land*. Within the *Länder* governments, responsibility for higher education institutions falls to the ministries concerned with science and research. In addition to the usual higher education institutions that are open to all, the Federation and the *Länder* are also responsible for special higher education institutions which only admit certain groups. Among these institutions are the universities of the Federal Armed Forces (*Universitäten der Bundeswehr*) and those *Fachhochschulen* which train Federation and *Länder* civil servants. In addition, there are several

church run institutions of higher education, with the status of a body corporate, and some privately run higher education institutions.

The Higher Education Framework Act (*Hochschulrahmengesetz*) sets out the general principles governing the organization and administration of higher education institutions, academic and artistic staff, and the cooperation of all members of the institutions in their self-administration. The *Länder* define the organizational and administrative details of higher education institutions in their areas of jurisdiction on this basis and in the context of the *Länder* laws governing higher education.

In administrative matters there is a cooperative relationship between the responsible *Land* ministry and the higher education institution. Within a unitary administration the latter's functions include both academic matters and governmental matters such as personnel, economic, budgetary and financial administration. Independent of this, the responsible *Land* minister or government retains legal control (to some extent also academic control), the power to establish and organize institutions, and the final authority in financial and personnel matters.

As regards supervision, institutions of higher education establish curricula for all study courses, which must be submitted to the responsible *Land* ministry. Examination procedures are handled in different ways: for courses leading to a state examination (*Staatsprüfung*), examinations are set by the minister responsible for the subject area. For regulations governing examinations set by the higher education institutions (*Hochschulprüfungen*), the institutions themselves issue the examination regulations as in the case of study regulations. These examination regulations then have to be approved by the competent *Land* ministry.

2. Pre-school education

Pre-school education refers to all institutions of the non-public and public youth welfare services which cater for children from the time they reach the age of three until they begin school. Pre-school education comes before the start of compulsory education, and is therefore not a part of the statutory school system. In Germany, attendance of pre-school institutions is entirely voluntary.

Kindergarten is the traditional form of institutionalized pre-school education for children between the ages of three and six. Under the Child and Youth Welfare Act of 1990, institutions providing pre-school education are called upon to encourage the child's development into an individually responsible and socially competent person. Their function includes the care, education and general up-bringing of the child. *Kindergärten* are responsible for supporting and supplementing the education provided in the family and for compensating for developmental deficiencies in order to provide children with the best possible opportunity for development and education. Children are encouraged through play and other activities suited to their age to develop their physical and mental faculties, to learn to live in society and in the *Kindergarten* group, and to become used to following a regular daily routine and basic rules of hygiene. *Kindergärten* also have the function of assisting children's access to school by ensuring an appropriate level of development. Groups are of mixed ages for children of 3 to 6 years. As a rule, supervision is provided in the morning 5 days a week; in some cases *Kindergärten* are also open in the afternoon.

For children aged five, who are not yet of school age and whose parents wish to provide them with special assistance and preparation for primary school (*Grundschule*), preparatory classes (*Vorklassen* or *Vorschulklassen*) are provided in some *Länder*. Attendance at *Vorklassen* in *Grundschulen* is voluntary for these five-year-olds. The objective of *Vorklassen* is to encourage the children to learn by playing, but without anticipating the subject matter taught in the first year of *Grundschule*.

For children who have reached compulsory school age but whose level of development does not yet allow them to cope with the challenges of the *Grundschule*, institutions of various names – school kindergardens (*Schulkindergärten*) in some *Länder* and pre-school classes (*Vorklassen, or Vorschul-, Vorbereitungs-, or Förderklassen*) in others – have been established. In most *Länder*, the school authorities are authorized by law to require that six-year-olds attend *Schulkindergarten* or pre-school classes. These institutions, like the *Vorklassen* for five-year-olds, have organizational links to *Grundschulen*. The objective of these school-kindergartens is to create and improve the conditions for the healthy mental, emotional, and motivational development of children by promoting – as far as possible on an individual basis – the children's own ability to learn and express themselves through exercises and the handling of materials designed to stimulate and develop their concentration. These establishments work towards achieving a readiness for school enrolment by channelling the children's natural urge to play and engage in activity without anticipating the subject matter taught at school.

Staff

Children in institutions of pre-school education are looked after by trained educational and auxiliary staff. The trained staff include state-recognized *Sozialpädagogen* (qualified youth and community workers) and state-recognized *Erzieher* (qualified youth or child care workers). The auxiliary staff mainly consists of *Kinderpflegerinnen* (children's nurses).

The trained educational staff in the pre-school sector in Germany are not teachers, but mainly state-recognized *Erzieher/Erzieherinnen*. They are trained in *Fachschulen für Sozialpädagogik* (technical schools providing specialized vocational training for professions in educational social work) at upper secondary level. Those wishing to enter this training course must hold at least the *Realschulabschluß* or equivalent, and have completed a relevant vocational training course of at least two years' duration and/or at least two years of work experience. Training covers three years in total: two years' full-time training at the *Fachschule*, and one practical year in a pre-school education institution, supervised by the *Fachschule*.

Statistics

Children enrolled in *Kindergärten*, 1993 – number and percentage of the population of the same age.

	3 years old	4 years old	5 years old	6 years old	total
number	383,000	659,000	753,000	601,000	2,396,000
rates	42.3%	73.4%	82.8%	67.4%	66.4%

Source: Federal Statistical Office 1994.

Pupils and teachers in *Vorklassen* and *Schulkindergärten*, 1992 and 1993.

Type of School	Pupils		Teachers*		Institutions	
	1992	1993	1992	1993	1992	1993
Vorklassen	39,082	41,141	2,048	2,139	1,315	**
Schulkindergärten	41,113	43,691	3,638	3,723	2,621	**

* The statistics included in this report consider 'full-time equivalents' as individual teachers. These equivalents can be either:
  – individual full-time teachers;
  – full-time equivalents made up of teaching hours provided by part-time teachers and calculated in terms of the number of hours required in the particular type of school.
** Complete data are not available for all *Länder*.

Source: Statistical Publication of the Standing Conference of the Ministers of Education and Cultural Affairs, N° 129, and Federal Statistical Office 1994.

Pupils enrolled in *Vorklassen* and *Schulkindergärten*, 1992/93 – percentage of the population of the same age.

Vorklassen		*Schulkindergärten*	
5 years old	6 years old	5 years old	6 years old
1.8%	2.5%	0.2%	3.1%

Source: Federal Statistical Office 1994.

3. School education

3.1 Compulsory education

Compulsory schooling begins for all children at age six. It usually lasts 12 years, consisting of nine years of full-time schooling (in Berlin, Brandenburg, Bremen and North Rhine-Westphalia, 10 years) and three years of part-time schooling, or more, according to the duration of training in a recognized

trainee occupation. For young people, who neither attend a school to continue their general education nor enter into the dual system of vocational training, individual *Länder* impose regulations to prolong their compulsory schooling in some type of full-time vocational school. Moreover, most *Länder* allow pupils who opt for a voluntary 10th year of education to acquire a secondary school qualification giving them access to further full-time courses in the secondary sector.

3.2 Primary education

Primary education is provided at primary schools (*Grundschulen*) for the first to the fourth school year (in Berlin and Brandenburg, the first to the sixth year). In the context of compulsory schooling, all children attend *Grundschule* together. Children are enrolled in the first year at age six and usually transfer to a secondary school after the fourth year. The tasks and objectives of the *Grundschule* are determined by its position in the school system. The *Grundschule* is meant to carry children forward from learning by playing at pre-school level to more systematic forms of school learning, and seeks to adapt the subject matter taught and methods employed to the pupils' requirements and capabilities. The *Grundschule* lays the foundations for secondary education. It endeavours to provide pupils with a structured understanding of the impressions they gain from the world around them and to develop their psychomotor abilities and patterns of social behaviour.

Teaching provision in schools is usually based on classes organized by age group. The children usually have only one teacher during the first two years, but from the third year pupils are increasingly taught by other subject teachers, in order to prepare pupils for secondary school where they will have a different teacher for each subject.

The number of weekly class hours increases at rates which vary, depending on the *Land*, from 17-23 hours in the first year to 23-27 hours per week in the fourth year. One lesson comprises 45 minutes. The school year begins on 1 August and ends on 31 July in the following year. The actual beginning and end depend on the dates of the summer holidays. The total annual duration of school holidays is 75 working days, plus about 10 public or religious holidays. Teaching takes place five days a week, Monday to Friday, in the morning. On the basis of a five-day week, there are on average 188 school days in a school year. Since there are lessons on two or three Saturdays a month in some *Länder*, the actual number of school days will increase accordingly. The total number of weekly lessons, however, will be the same with a five or six-day week.

Curriculum

The acquisition of reading, writing, and arithmetic skills plays a central role in initial teaching at *Grundschulen*. Education is provided both in lessons focused on particular disciplines and subject areas and in interdisciplinary lessons. The subjects taught at this level include German, mathematics and *Sachunterricht* (which provides an introduction to social studies, history, geography, biology, physics and chemistry, which the children will encounter as separate subjects later in their school life). Art, music, sport, and religion are taught as separate subjects. Increasingly, an opportunity for a first encounter with a foreign language is offered from the third year. These first steps in the learning of a foreign language are characterized primarily by learning through play. Priority is given to the spoken use of language and there is no assessment of achievement.

Assessment

At all types of schools and at all levels, each pupil's achievement is continuously monitored by means of written tests and an assessment of his or her oral and practical work. A summary of each pupil's achievement is evaluated in the form of mid-year and year-end reports. Before moving up to the next year, a pupil must fulfil certain minimum requirements in all relevant subjects. A marking system is used to assess achievement.

The Standing Conference of the Ministers of Education and Cultural Affairs has agreed to define the marks as follows:

– *sehr gut* (1) The mark *sehr gut* (very good) should be given for performance which is well above the required standard.

– *gut* (2) The mark *gut* (good) should be given for performance which fully meets the required standard.

– *befriedigend* (3) The mark *befriedigend* (satisfactory) should be given for performance which generally meets the required standard.

– *ausreichend* (4) The mark *ausreichend* (adequate) should be given for performance which, although showing deficiencies, on the whole still meets the required standard.

– *mangelhaft* (5) The mark *mangelhaft* (poor) should be given for performance which does not meet the required standard, but suggests that the basic knowledge is there and that the deficiencies could be made up in a reasonable period of time.

– *ungenügend* (6) The mark *ungenügend* (very poor) should be given for performance which does not meet the required standard and where even the basic skills are so incomplete that the deficiencies could not be made up in a reasonable period of time.

During the first two years of *Grundschule*, pupils are assessed on the basis of a report in which the pupil's progress, strengths and weaknesses in each subject area are described in detail. From the end of the second year at the earliest, pupils receive certificates with marks, which allow the pupil's performance to be measured against the class average and therefore permits a comparative assessment. There are also clear signs of a growing trend towards assessing learning and performance in report form in the third and fourth years. All children progress automatically from the first to the second year. From the second year of *Grundschule*, however, pupils are usually placed in the class appropriate to their level of attainment by being promoted to the next class or asked to repeat.

The transfer to one of the different lower secondary school types where pupils remain at least until the completion of their full-time compulsory education (generally until age 15), is dealt with differently depending on *Land* legislation. Decisions regarding the pupil's future school career are taken on the basis of the recommendation of the school which the pupil is leaving. This is accompanied by detailed consultations with the parents. The final decision is either taken by the parents or by the school or school supervisory authority.

Teachers

Training for teaching careers at *Grundschulen* is divided into two training phases (see 5.). The first phase comprises a six- to eight-semester course of study which emphasizes both educational science and practical teaching experience. Specifically, students must study primary school didactics or two subjects with an optional or specialized subject (including didactics). Possible options and specializations are determined by the *Länder*.

Statistics

Pupils, teachers and schools in the primary sector, 1992/93.

Grundschulen	Pupils	Teachers*	Schools
1992	3,419,497	171,360	17,941
1993	3,475,156	169,842	17,911

* Full-time equivalents.

Source: Statistical Publication of the Standing Conference of the Ministers of Education and Cultural Affairs, N° 129, and Federal Statistical Office 1995.

Primary schools are attended by all children in the relevant age group. The average number of pupils in each *Grundschule* class for all of the Federal Republic came to 22.2 in 1993. The pupil/teacher ratio in the former territory of the Federal Republic came to 20.5 pupils per teacher in 1993.

3.3 Lower secondary education

General lower secondary schools build on the primary education provided at *Grundschulen*. In most *Länder*, these are the *Hauptschule, Realschule, Gymnasium,* and *Gesamtschule*. In recent years, some *Länder* have introduced new types of school with different names depending on the *Land*. These new school types combine the educational paths of the *Hauptschule* and the *Realschule* in one organizational and educational unit. Depending on the *Land* they are called either the *Mittelschule,* the *Sekundarschule,* the *Regelschule,* the *Integrierte Haupt- und Realschule,* the *Verbundene Haupt- und Realschule* and the *Regionale Schule*.

The principle underlying the different types of lower secondary school and the courses they teach is to give pupils a basic general education, combined with an element of individual specialization in line with the support and advancement of the pupil according to his performance and interests. In the fifth and sixth years, regardless of how the school is organized, there is a phase of particular support, observation and orientation towards a further choice of educational path with its own subject specializations. In some *Länder*, this orientation phase in the fifth and sixth years is established as a separate stage independent of the different school types. From the seventh year, the different types of schools and educational paths are increasingly differentiated in terms of which subject areas are offered, what is required in terms of specialization, and which certificates are sought. In more advanced classes, the form each educational path takes and the acquisition of the proper skills for a particular certificate become increasingly important in shaping the individual pupil's school career.

Teaching provision in schools is usually based on classes organized by age group. In certain subjects and types of school offering more than one educational path, lessons can also take place in courses on the basis of ability – especially in years 7 to 10.

As a rule, pupils attend a total of 28 hours of lessons in compulsory subjects and compulsory options in years 5 to 6, and 30 hours in years 7 to 10 irrespective of school type. The length of the school year and the school week as well as the duration of one lesson are the same as in primary education (see 3.2).

3.3.1 School types offering one educational path

School types offering one educational path are the *Hauptschule*, the *Realschule* and the *Gymnasium*.

3.3.1.1 Hauptschule

The *Hauptschule* provides pupils with a fundamental general education. It generally comprises the fifth to the ninth year (in *Länder* with an orientation stage independent of the type of school, from the seventh year, and in *Länder* with ten years of compulsory schooling, from the fifth or seventh to the tenth year).

In most *Länder* where compulsory education covers 9 years, pupils have the option of attending a voluntary tenth year at the *Hauptschule* to acquire a further qualification (e.g. the extended *Hauptschulabschluß*). The *Hauptschule* also offers particularly able pupils the possibility, under certain conditions, of attaining the *Mittlerer Schulabschluß* via this tenth year.

Curriculum

Subjects taught at the *Hauptschule* include German, a foreign language, mathematics, physics,

chemistry, biology, geography, history, *Arbeitslehre* (work orientation) and social studies, music, art, sport, religion and, in some *Länder*, domestic science and economics. Mathematics and foreign language (usually English) courses are frequently taught in sets according to the pupil's aptitude. The aim of this is to better accommodate differences in pupil learning ability, to make it possible for more pupils to gain a further qualification (e.g. the qualified or extended *Hauptschulabschluß*), as well as to facilitate their transition to other types of secondary school.

3.3.1.2 Realschule

The *Realschule* offers pupils an extended general education. The normal form of *Realschule* covers the fifth to tenth year of school (in *Länder* with an orientation stage independent of the type of school, the seventh to tenth year). In Bavaria, Berlin, Brandenburg and Hamburg, the normal form of *Realschule* only has four years, i.e. it only begins in the sixth year. In addition, there is a three- or four-year *Realschule* course for pupils who, after the sixth or seventh year at a *Hauptschule*, wish to transfer to *Realschule*.

The *Realschule* leaving certificate permits a transition to training courses resulting directly in vocational qualifications or to school types providing a higher education entrance qualification, which are described below within the context of the different school-leaving qualifications awarded at the end of lower secondary school (see 3.3.3).

In three *Länder* (Saxony, Saxony-Anhalt, and Thuringia), the *Realschule* as such is not offered in the lower secondary school system, but the *Realschule* leaving certificate can be chosen alongside the Hauptschule leaving certificate at *Mittelschulen* (in Saxony), *Sekundarschulen* (in Saxony-Anhalt), and *Regelschulen* (in Thuringia).

Curriculum

Subjects at *Realschulen* include German, foreign language (usually English), mathematics, physics, chemistry, biology, geography, history, politics, music, art, sport, and religion. In the seventh or eighth year, pupils must take from three to six hours per week of optional courses in addition to the compulsory subjects. According to their personal inclination or aptitude, pupils can choose optional courses to strengthen their knowledge of certain compulsory subjects or can choose new subjects, such as a second foreign language (usually French).

3.3.1.3   *Gymnasium*

Gymnasien offer pupils an intensified general secondary education. *Gymnasien* normally cover the 5th to the 13th year, or – where *Grundschule* lasts for six years and where there is an orientation stage independent of the school type – the 7th to the 13th year. In four *Länder* (Mecklenburg-West Pomerania, Saxony, Saxony-Anhalt, and Thuringia), *Gymnasien* were introduced during the 1990/91 school year to cover the 5th to the 12th year. By passing the *Abitur* examination at the end of the 13th year (or the 12th year in four *Länder*), pupils obtain the general higher education entrance qualification (*allgemeine Hochschulreife*).

In addition to the *Gymnasien* of the normal type, there are extension schools (*Aufbaugymnasien*) to which pupils at *Hauptschule* can transfer at the end of the seventh year, as well as types for particularly gifted leavers of *Realschulen* and vocational schools.

At the end of the tenth year of *Gymnasium*, pupils who have achieved at least pass marks in all subjects are promoted to the upper level of *Gymnasium* (*gymnasiale Oberstufe*).

Curriculum

Subjects at *Gymnasium* in the fifth to ninth or tenth years of *Gymnasium* – which form part of lower secondary education – include German, at least two foreign languages, mathematics, physics, chemistry, biology, geography, history, politics, music, art, sport and religion.

3.3.2   School types offering more than one educational path

School types offering more than one educational path are the *Gesamtschule*, the *Schulzentrum*, the *Mittelschule*, the *Regelschule*, the *Sekundarschule*, the *Verbundende Haupt- und Realschule*, the *Integrierte Haupt- und Realschule* and the *Regionale Schule*. Below, the *Gesamtschule* is described and also, as examples, the three school types which have recently been created in the new *Länder*.

3.3.2.1   *Gesamtschule*

The *kooperative Gesamtschule* (cooperative type) and the *Schulzentrum* (a school complex in Bremen) combine *Hauptschule*, *Realschule* and *Gymnasium* education in one organizational and educational unit. Pupils are streamed according to their intended final qualification (*Hauptschulabschluß*, *Mittlerer Schulabschluß*, entitlement to proceed to the *gymnasiale Oberstufe*).

Integrierte Gesamtschulen (integrated type) constitute an educational and organizational entity. In some subjects setting is gradually phased in, and pupils are taught in courses on at least two different levels which are defined with reference to the curriculum of the chosen course.

Curriculum

In the *integrierte Gesamtschule* teaching on the basis of different ability levels begins in mathematics and first foreign language in year 7, in German usually in year 8 or, at the latest, in year 9 and in at least one science subject (physics or chemistry) in year 9 at the latest. In social science subjects, art, music, sport and religious instruction pupils are usually taught in mixed-ability groups.

At the end of years 9 and 10, all lower secondary leaving certificates may be obtained at the *Gesamtschule*, whether of the cooperative or integrated type, as described in 3.3.3.

3.3.2.2   *Mittelschule*

The *Mittelschule* is a lower secondary school type in **Saxony,** which offers differentiation with general and vocationally-oriented courses and provides the prerequisites for later vocational qualifications. The subjects taught are referred to in the description of the *Hauptschule* and the *Realschule*. Years 5 and 6 are organized as an orientation stage. As from the beginning of year 7, different paths are followed with a view to qualifications and performance development. Teaching at different levels, depending on performance and qualifications aimed at, is received in a fixed set of main subjects (mathematics, first foreign language, German, physics or chemistry). In addition to this, at the beginning of year 7 pupils are required to choose specific options. These options (technical, economic, social/home economics, language, music, sport) occupy 4 or 5 teaching hours a week.

After the successful completion of year 9 pupils acquire the *Hauptschulabschluß*, and if they perform particularly well they may be awarded the *qualifizierende Hauptschulabschluß* (qualifying *Hauptschule* leaving certificate). Upon successful completion of year 10 and the final examination the pupil acquires the *Realschulabschluß*.

3.3.2.3 *Sekundarschule*

In the **Saarland**, the *Sekundarschule* exists alongside the *Hauptschule*, *Realschule*, *Gymnasium* and *Gesamtschule* and is thus one of the standard school types at the lower secondary level. The subjects taught are referred to in the description of the *Hauptschule* and the *Realschule*. During the first two years all subjects are taught in mixed-ability groups. From year 7 onwards, teaching is tailored to a particular qualification (*Hauptschulabschluß*, *Mittlerer Schulabschluß*) and is structured according to ability. At first this differentiation is only applied to certain subjects but by year 9 covers all subjects. Pupils who wish to gain the *Mittlerer Schulabschluß* have the opportunity of choosing a second foreign language from year 7. Year 10 concludes with a leaving qualification procedure.

In **Saxony-Anhalt**, the *Sekundarschule* is also one of the standard types of school, alongside the *Gymnasium*. In the first two years, teaching in some subjects takes place in groups which are classified according to ability. From year 7 pupils receive either *Hauptschule*-type education (years 7-9) to provide them with a basic general education or *Realschule*-type education (years 7-10) to provide them with a general and vocationally-oriented education. The *Hauptschule*-type education is completed at the end of year 9 and the *Realschule*-type education is completed with a final examination at the end of year 10.

3.3.2.4 *Regelschule*

In **Thuringia**, the *Regelschule* offers general education and pre-vocational education and prepares pupils for subsequent training leading to vocational qualifications. The subjects taught are referred to in the description of the *Hauptschule* and the *Realschule*. In the fifth and sixth years, all pupils follow a common curriculum in all subject areas. In some compulsory subjects from the seventh year and in additional subjects from the ninth year, teaching is offered at two levels of difficulty, corresponding to the demands of the *Hauptschule*

and *Realschule* respectively. Pupils seeking a *Realschule* leaving certificate are required to choose from a number of options (e.g. a second foreign language) beginning in the seventh year.

3.3.3 Assessment and qualifications for all lower secondary schools

The organization of assessment for all lower secondary schools is the same as at primary level.

Qualification at the end of year 9

At the end of year 9 pupils in all *Länder* have the option of acquiring a first general qualification, called a *Hauptschulabschluß* (*Hauptschule* leaving certificate) in most *Länder*. As a rule this certificate is granted after year 9 if a sufficient standard has been reached in all relevant subjects. In the types of school in lower secondary education where courses are organized over more than 9 years, a corresponding qualification can be obtained in most of the *Länder* if the pupil has reached a certain standard. This first general qualification is primarily used as a basis for vocational training in the dual system. In addition, under certain circumstances it is the requirement for admission to *Berufsfachschulen* and to the *Berufsgrundbildungsjahr* (basic vocational training year). It is, moreover, the requirement for later admission to certain *Fachschulen* (technical schools providing advanced vocational training) and to institutions offering secondary education for adults, in day or evening classes, leading to university entrance qualifications.

Qualification at the end of year 10

The so-called *Mittlere Schulabschluß* can be obtained in all *Länder* at the end of year 10. This qualification is called the *Realschulabschluß* (*Realschule* leaving certificate) in most *Länder*. This leaving certificate can be obtained at the *Realschule* (and at the *Wirtschaftsschule* in Bavaria) if pupils have achieved a sufficient standard in all subjects at the end of the 10th year. Subject to the satisfaction of certain performance criteria, the *Mittlerer Schulabschluß* can also be obtained at the end of year 10 at other lower secondary schools and, given appropriate records and marks, at the *Berufsschule*. It entitles the holder to proceed to further full-time courses in upper secondary education, e.g. special *Berufsfachschulen* and the *Fachoberschule*.

Entitlement to proceed to the *gymnasiale Oberstufe*

Pupils at *Gymnasien* or at *Gesamtschulen* who have followed a *Gymnasium*-type course are entitled to proceed to the *gymnasiale Oberstufe* if they attain a certain standard in all subjects at the end of the 10th year of the *Gymnasium* (or, in two of the *Länder*, at the end of year 9 at the *Gymnasium*) or of the *Gesamtschule*. An entrance qualification required for transfer to the *gymnasiale Oberstufe* can, however, also be obtained by way of a *Mittlerer Schulabschluß* (*Realschulabschluß*) of a certain merit or via qualifications from *Berufsaufbauschulen* (vocational extension schools), *Berufsfachschulen* (full-time vocational schools) or *Fachschulen* (technical schools).

Teachers

Teacher training for a teaching career in lower secondary schools is provided, as for all teaching careers, in two training phases (see 5.). The first phase usually comprises a six- to ten-semester course of study at an institution of higher education, including at least two subject areas, educational sciences and subject-oriented didactics. In addition, students must participate in practical training periods lasting several weeks.

Statistics

Pupils, teachers and schools in the lower secondary sector, 1993.

Lower secondary education	Pupils	Teachers*	Schools
Orientation stage, independent of school type	375,369	23,220	2,401
Hauptschule	1,102,222	75,684	6,184
Integrated classes for *Haupt-* and *Realschule* pupils	375,926	24,335	1,380
Realschule	1,105,453	65,410	3,527
Gymnasium	1,529,484	92,489	3,143
Integrated *Gesamtschule*	403,165	30,837	798

* Full-time equivalents.

Source: Statistical Publication of the Standing Conference of the Ministers of Education and Cultural Affairs, N° 129, and Federal Statistical Office 1995.

The following overview shows the proportion of pupils in the eighth year in each of the various types of general lower secondary school existing in the majority of *Länder* in 1993:

Hauptschulen	25.6%
Integrated classes for *Haupt-* and *Realschule* pupils	7.4%
Realschulen	26.1%
Gymnasien	31.4%
Integrated *Gesamtschulen*	8.9%

Following the unification of Germany in 1990, the proportion of pupils attending integrated *Gesamtschulen* has grown and the number of pupils attending *Hauptschulen* has fallen the most.

3.4 Upper secondary education

The education available for 16- to 19-year-olds at upper secondary level includes:

– general education;

– courses of vocational education and training;

– mixed general and vocational education courses.

Most young people attending the upper secondary level follow vocational education and training courses, and most of these through the dual system of vocational training which is described in 4.

In the context of developing general education at this level, the *gymnasiale Oberstufe* has been reorganized, based on an agreement of the Standing Conference of Ministers of Education and Cultural Affairs reached in 1972. The underlying educational principle of this reform was to encourage pupils to engage in independent learning and scientific propaedeutic work and to foster their character development. The 1972 Agreement, as amended in 1988, and subsequent relevant resolutions of the Ministers' Conference on further development have upheld the principle that the *Abitur* examination grants access to all subject areas at universities and higher education institutions (*allgemeine Hochschulreife* – general higher education entrance qualification).

The agreements reached also provide for courses within a *Gymnasium*-type education leading to double qualifications, i.e. the right to pursue higher education (*Hochschulreife* or *Fachhochschulreife*) and a vocational qualification. Such courses are held mainly at the upper level of the *Gymnasium* with a technical bias (*berufliche Gymnasien* or *Fachgymnasien*) and lead both to the *Abitur* and to a final vocational examination after four years.

In the area of vocational education and training, the 1991 and 1992 framework agreements between the *Länder* make it possible that, alongside the vocational qualification, pupils can acquire an entitlement to proceed to a higher level within the education system. In this respect the *Mittlerer Schulabschluß* and the *Hochschulreife* are of primary importance. The purpose of such measures is to put vocational education on a par with general education.

3.4.1 *Gymnasiale Oberstufe*

The *gymnasiale Oberstufe* covers years 11-13 (or 10-12 or 11-12 in four *Länder*). Admission to this level requires a qualification entitling holders to enter the *gymnasiale Oberstufe*, which may normally be acquired at the end of the 10th year of the *Gymnasium* or through comparable qualifications acquired at other types of lower secondary schools. Building on lessons taught in lower secondary education, after a transitional period in year 10 or 11 pupils are grouped into courses in the qualification phase to replace the former process of unitary class teaching. Although the pupil is still obliged to study certain subjects or subject groups, he/she now has considerable opportunity to make an individual decision concerning what topics to concentrate on due to the extended range of courses on offer. Related school subjects are grouped together into three main areas:

– language, literature and arts;

– social sciences;

– mathematics, natural sciences and technology.

Each of these three subject areas must be represented in the school record of each pupil until the end of the upper secondary level of the *Gymnasium* and in the *Abitur* examination. Religious education and sport are usually added to the compulsory subjects.

Courses are categorized as basic or advanced according to level (*Grundkurse* and *Leistungskurse* respectively). Basic courses (usually 3 teaching hours a week) are designed to ensure that all pupils acquire a broad general education; advanced courses (5 or 6 teaching hours a week) are designed to offer additional, intensified knowledge and to serve as an in-depth introduction to academic study. Up to two-thirds of the courses are at the basic level. Pupils are required to choose at least two advanced courses, one of which must be either German, continuation of a foreign language, mathematics, or a natural science. If German is the first advanced course, mathematics or a foreign language must be included among the four subjects taken in the *Abitur* examination. New subjects offered at the upper level of the *Gymnasium,* among them foreign languages and vocational subjects, may be offered as the second advanced course. Some *Länder* restrict the choice of advanced courses to certain subject combinations.

In some *Länder*, integrated comprehensive schools (*integrierte Gesamtschulen*) include the 11th to 13th years in addition to lower secondary school which are organized along the same lines as the *gymnasiale Oberstufe*.

Assessment and qualifications

At the *gymnasiale Oberstufe,* performance is assessed using a points system, which in turn corresponds to the conventional six-mark scale (see 3.2).

Mark 1 corresponds to 15/14/13 points, depending on the trend of marks.
Mark 2 corresponds to 12/11/10 points, depending on the trend of marks.
Mark 3 corresponds to 9/8/7 points, depending on the trend of marks.
Mark 4 corresponds to 6/5/4 points, depending on the trend of marks.
Mark 5 corresponds to 3/2/1 points, depending on the trend of marks.
Mark 6 corresponds to 0 points.

The upper level of the *Gymnasium* ends with the *Abitur* examination. Candidates are examined in four subjects, namely the two advanced ones and another in which they take written and, in some cases, oral examinations, as well as a fourth subject which is examined only orally. All three subject areas must be represented. Candidates who are successful in the *Abitur* after 13 years at school are awarded a general higher education entrance qualification (*allgemeine Hochschulreife*). The *allgemeine Hochschulreife*, which until the year 2000 can still be obtained after 12 years at school in four *Länder*, also entitles the holder to commence any course of study at an institution of higher education. The various certificates and qualifications granting their holders access to higher education are described in detail in 6.2 dealing with admission to higher education.

3.4.2 Vocational training at full-time vocational schools

3.4.2.1 *Berufsfachschule* (Full-time vocational school)

Berufsfachschulen are full-time schools which prepare pupils for employment or provide them with vocational education at the same time as continuing their general education. They offer a very wide range of courses. There are *Berufsfachschulen*, amongst others, for business occupations, occupations specialized in foreign languages, crafts industry occupations, home-economics-related and social-work-related occupations, artistic occupations, health sector occupations, etc. In cases where such schools do not provide a full career qualification, the period of attendance may – under certain conditions – be recognized as equivalent to the first year of vocational training in the dual system for the training in a recognized occupation.

Depending on the training objective, *Berufsfachschulen* require their pupils to have a *Hauptschule* or *Realschule* leaving certificate or a *Mittlerer Schulabschluß*. The duration of education at *Berufsfachschulen* varies, depending on the intended career specialization. It takes at least one school year and normally leads to a final examination. *Berufsfachschulen* which have courses lasting at least two years and to which pupils are admitted with *Hauptschule* leaving qualifications also offer an opportunity to obtain a leaving certificate equivalent to the *Realschule* certificate, the so-called *Mittlerer Schulabschluß*. The two-year *Berufsfachschulen* requiring a *Realschule* leaving certificate offer courses in a variety of subject areas leading to a qualification as *Staatlich geprüfter technischer Assistent* (state-certified technical assistant), specializing in e.g. biochemistry, garment making, information technology, mechanical engineering, or *Staatlich geprüfter kaufmännischer Assistent* (state-certified business assistant),

specializing in data processing, foreign languages and secretarial skills. A pupil's weekly timetable at these two-year *Berufsfachschulen* (*Berufskollegs* in Baden-Württemberg and Saxony) amounts to at least 32 periods.

3.4.2.2 *Berufsaufbauschule* (Vocational extension school)

The pupils who attend *Berufsaufbauschulen* already have vocational training or several years' employment. They can also be attended by pupils still in vocational training on a part-time basis. They aim to provide a broader and more profound general and vocational education leading to the acquisition of a qualification for some form of further study. The *Berufsaufbauschule* may be divided into sections such as technology, economics, domestic science and social work, and agriculture. Pupils are required to undergo a total of at least 1,200 periods of instruction in general and vocational subjects. German, foreign language, mathematics and natural science lessons add up to at least 600 periods out of this total. Other courses include social studies with politics and social sciences as well as at least one vocational subject. Instruction related to the chosen specialization lasts for not less than 160 periods. In its full-time form, this type of education takes at least one year and ends with an examination at which successful candidates obtain a qualification equivalent to the *Realschule* leaving certificate (*Mittlerer Schulabschluß*), this being a school entry requirement for certain vocational schools (*Berufsfachschule*, *Fachoberschule* and *berufliches Gymnasium/Fachgymnasium*).

3.4.2.3 *Fachoberschule* (Technical secondary school)

The *Fachoberschule* covers the 11th and 12th years and requires a *Realschule* leaving certificate or a qualification recognized as equivalent (*Mittlerer Schulabschluß*). It equips its pupils with general and specialized theoretical and practical knowledge and skills and leads to the *Fachhochschulreife*. There are *Fachoberschulen* for technology, business and administration, nutrition and domestic science, agriculture, social work, design, nautics, etc. Practical training in the subject of specialization takes place in the 11th year, i.e. in the first year of this school type, on four days a week for the whole year. Alongside this, pupils are expected to spend at least eight periods per week in class. Completed relevant vocational training can serve as a substitute for the 11th year of the *Fachoberschule*, so that pupils with such qualifications can proceed directly to the 12th year. The 12th year (second year of the *Fachoberschule*) comprises at least 30 periods per week of general and specialization-related instruction. The compulsory subjects are German, social studies, mathematics, natural sciences, one foreign language and physical education. At least three-fifths of compulsory classes are taken up with general subjects, which are the same for all pupils.

3.4.2.4 *Berufliches Gymnasium/ Fachgymnasium* (Upper level of the *Gymnasium* with a technical bias)

This type of school is called *Berufliches Gymnasium* in some *Länder* and *Fachgymnasium* in others. Unlike the *Gymnasium*, which as a rule provides continuous education from the 5th to the 12th or 13th year, the *Gymnasium* with a technical bias offers no lower or intermediate level. In some *Länder*, this kind of school takes the form of a *gymnasiale Oberstufe* (upper level of the *Gymnasium*) with career-oriented specializations and offers a three-year course of education. Requiring a *Realschule* leaving certificate at a level which entitles the pupil to attend the *gymnasiale Oberstufe*, or an equivalent qualification, the *berufliches Gymnasium* or *Fachgymnasium* with career-oriented specializations usually leads to a qualification granting access to higher education (*allgemeine Hochschulreife*). Apart from the subjects offered in general education *Gymnasien*, these schools have career-oriented subjects and specializations such as business and engineering (e.g. electrical, metal and construction engineering) which can be chosen in place of general subjects as the second advanced course and as subjects in the *Abitur* examination.

As mentioned above in 3.4, in the *Berufliches Gymnasium* or *Fachgymnasium* it is possible to acquire more than one qualification at the same time (double qualification courses). This is usually a combination of a certificate qualifying for entry to higher education (*Hochschulreife/ Fachhochschulreife*) and a vocational qualification (e.g. for assistant occupations or vocational qualifications in a range of state-recognized occupations requiring formal training). A vocational education of this kind may also be obtained at institutions combining *Gymnasien* and vocational schools (e.g. *Berufsfachschulen*, *Oberstufenzentren*) or in a particular type of school, such as the *Kollegschule* in North Rhine-Westphalia. The courses for double qualifications which lead to the *Hochschulreife* take four years. They involve two separate examinations (the *Abitur* examination and a final examination for a vocational qualification).

3.4.2.5 *Fachschule* (Technical school providing advanced vocational training)

Advanced vocational training at *Fachschulen* is designed to enable specialized experienced personnel to carry out functions with a medium level of responsibility, i.e. to manage enterprises independently in their chosen fields (e.g. agriculture or domestic science), to train junior personnel, or to assume major responsibilities within clearly defined areas. Those who successfully complete *Fachschule* courses perform functions on a level between tasks carried out by graduates and those performed by staff trained in the dual system of vocational training. In order to be admitted to the *Fachschule*, pupils must normally have completed pertinent vocational training in a state-recognized occupation and have practical work experience in the field.

Fachschulen offer one, two and three-year courses. Two-year courses are offered in about 90 different specializations from the fields of technology, business and design and lead to a final examination recognized by the State. The most strongly represented subjects include electrical engineering, mechanical engineering, business management, construction engineering and chemical engineering. Depending on the area of study, persons who have successfully completed courses at *Fachschulen* are entitled to use a professional title such as *Staatlich geprüfter Techniker* (state-certified engineer), *Staatlich geprüfter Betriebswirt* (state-certified business manager), etc. There are also other two-year *Fachschulen* for domestic science and for geriatric nursing, as well as one-year *Fachschulen* (e.g. providing training as a *Staatlich geprüfter Wirtschafter*, a state-certified manager in agriculture) and a three-year course at *Fachschulen für Sozialpädagogik* (technical schools for educational social work), at which *Staatlich anerkannte Erzieher* (state-recognized youth and child care workers) are trained, amongst others, for *Kindergärten*.

Teachers

Training for teaching careers in general education subjects at the upper secondary level or at *Gymnasien* is provided, as for all teaching careers, in two training phases (see 5.). The first phase comprises an 8- to 10-semester (in an artistic subject area, sometimes 12-semester) study course including at least two subject areas. Subject-area studies, including subject-oriented didactics, are supplemented by courses in educational science and practical placements in schools lasting several weeks, and by at least one subject-specific teaching placement during the study course in at least one of the two teaching subjects.

Teacher training incorporating a teaching qualification for vocational school subject areas for teaching subject-related theory and general education subjects comprises an 8- to 10-semester course of study. The requirements are:

- subject-related practical training for at least 12 months in relevant companies;

- an educational sciences component, usually an advanced course in a subject area of vocational education, and a course in a primarily general education subject;

- a practical placement lasting several weeks at a vocational school and, where possible, an additional placement in social work.

In order to take into account the special needs of the various *Länder*, training for teaching careers at vocational schools sometimes takes very different forms. This is true, for example, of the subject areas (and combinations) permitted, the practical placements, and other framework conditions affecting the content and duration of courses.

Statistics

In 1993, approximately 25.9% of all pupils were engaged in education at the upper secondary level. Of these, about 21% attended a school providing general education, 21% a full-time vocational school and 58% a part-time vocational school. The distribution of pupils among the various types of school in 1993 was as follows:

Pupils, teachers and schools in the upper secondary sector during 1993.

Upper secondary education	Pupils	Teachers*	Schools
General education schools:	662,943	60,236	
Gymnasien	586,281	53,063	**
Integrierte Gesamtschulen	34,905	3,352	**
Vocational schools	2,446,961	104,156	9,068
Berufsschulen	1,614,022	44,598	1,843
Berufsgrundbildungsjahr	94,940	5,445	1,484
Berufsfachschulen	284,369	22,145	2,627
Berufsaufbauschulen	5,622	447	211
Fachoberschule	76,898	5,133	787
Berufliche Gymnasien /Fachgymnasien	81,666	6,931	511
*Kollegschulen****	76,795	3,158	39
Fachschulen	153,196	10,174	1,446

* Full-time equivalents.
** Data not available.
*** Only in North-Rhine Westphalia.

Source: Statistical Publication of the Standing Conference of the Ministers of Education and Cultural Affairs, N° 129, and Federal Statistical Office 1995.

4. Dual system of vocational education and training

Following full-time compulsory education, the majority of young people in Germany go on to gain vocational qualifications through the dual system. The system is described as a 'dual' system because training is carried out in two places of learning, i.e. at the workplace and in the *Berufsschule*. Each year around 600,000 young people, two-thirds of those leaving general education schools, commence training within the dual system. The aim of the dual system is to provide a broadly-based basic vocational education and the necessary skills and knowledge required to practise an occupation in a properly structured course of training. Those successfully completing the training are entitled to practise their occupation as a qualified employee in one of the state-recognized occupations for which formal training is required.

Initial training in the workplace is governed primarily by the relevant regulations of the Federation (the *Berufsbildungsgesetz* and *Handwerksordnung*). Training is provided on the basis of a civil-law contract between the business providing training and the young person concerned. The vocational training contract covers all important aspects of the vocational training. In particular it defines the training objective (skills profile for the respective occupation), the duration of training, the amount of time devoted to training every day, the mode and level of payment of the trainee wage and the duties of trainee and trainer (training business). This includes, for example, the duty of the trainee to learn, both in the workplace and the *Berufsschule*, and the duty of the business to provide training. Under the terms of the contract, the business must provide training materials and trainers free of charge, allow the trainee time from work to attend the *Berufsschule* and monitor attendance at the *Berufsschule*.

Both places of learning jointly fulfil the educational assignment of the system of dual vocational training. Before beginning training, the compulsory period of full-time education must have been completed. Other than this, however, there are no other admission requirements for dual vocational training. Those who have completed education at a general education school and those who have completed education at a *Berufsfachschule* are accepted on equal terms. Usually, the trainees spend three days a week at the workplace and two days a week at the *Berufsschule*. The businesses pay trainees a wage, which is subject to a contractual collective bargaining agreement. The wages rise with each year of the traineeship. Training at the *Berufsschule* is financed using public funds, usually from the *Land* or the local authority.

On the basis of consultations with all those responsible for vocational training and, in particular, with the involvement of employers and trade unions, **training regulations** are drawn up which establish minimum course content for around 370 recognized trades and occupations. These regulations apply to the whole country. Thus, there is a proper procedure for drawing on the experience from occupational practice, the findings of labour-market and occupational research and the results of pilot projects and tests carried out by the Federal Institute for Vocational Training (*Bundesinstitut für Berufsbildung*). This allows the training regulations to be brought up to date whenever this is necessitated by changes to the economic structure, to the organization of labour or in technology.

The skills and knowledge which are to be gained in the course of training in the workplace are laid down in a list of requirements for the trade or occupation and the structure, in terms of time and content, in a framework plan. The training business then incorporates this into its own individual training plan. The occupational subject matter to be taught at the *Berufsschule* for each training trade or occupation is stipulated in a **framework curriculum**. The framework curriculum and the training regulations complement each other. The *Länder* either adopt the framework curriculum as it is or convert its provisions into their own curricula.

At the end of vocational training the trainees sit the **final examination** at the 'authorities responsible for vocational training' (regional and sectoral self-governing organizations from the various branches of industry and commerce, e.g. the chambers of industry and commerce, the chambers of crafts and trades, the chambers of the independent professions or of agriculture, all of whom perform functions on behalf of the State in the area of vocational training). The final examination consists of a practical (oral) section and a theoretical (written) section. The examination committees include representatives from the businesses themselves and their staff and also teachers from the *Berufsschule*. By passing the final examination, trainees prove that they have achieved the objective of the dual training in the workplace and at the *Berufsschule*. This entitles them to practise their occupation immediately and thus any period of job orientation or initial on-the-job training can be dispensed with. Successful examination candidates are awarded a certificate showing proficiency as a skilled worker (*Facharbeiterbrief*), commercial assistant (*Kaufmannsgehilfenbrief*) or journeyman (*Gesellenbrief*).

4.1 Place of learning – part-time vocational school *(Berufsschule)*

In the context of the dual system of vocational education and training the *Berufsschule* is an autonomous place of learning. It collaborates on an equal footing with the others engaged in vocational training. Its function is to provide pupils with general and vocational education, giving special attention to meeting the requirements of vocational training. *Berufsschulen* are also expected to offer courses preparing for vocational education or accompanying occupational activities. Depending on the arrangements in the *Länder*, they may also be involved in further and continuing vocational education. *Berufsschulen* provide their pupils with a basic and specialized vocational training, while permitting them to continue their general education. Its purpose is to enable them to carry out their occupational duties and to help shape the world of work and society as a whole by giving them a sense of social and ecological responsibility.

The *Berufsschule* is attended by pupils who have concluded a relevant training contract (*Ausbildungsvertrag*) with a company and also by those pupils who have left the *Hauptschule* or another school upon completion of their full-time compulsory schooling, and have started work, but are still required to attend compulsory vocational education.

The framework curricula for career-related courses at *Berufsschulen* and the training regulations for vocational training in the various state-recognized occupations are worked out jointly by federal and *Länder* authorities in a coordinated procedure which also involves the agreement of the employers and trade unions. About a third of total teaching time at the *Berufsschule* is taken up with general education subjects, namely German, social studies, economics, religion and sport. Foreign languages are included in vocational education when they are likely to be of importance in the pupils' future occupation, e.g. office jobs.

Pupils attend the *Berufsschule* on a part-time basis and usually have at least 12 lessons per week. In some cases instruction takes the form of coherent blocks. *Berufsschule* leavers receive a leaving certificate, if their performance meets the required criteria, which will be recognized as a *Hauptschule* or *Realschule* leaving certificate. Together with the certificate proving that they have successfully completed the requisite vocational training in a company and have appropriate professional experience, the leaving certificate issued by *Berufsschulen* entitle their holders to admission to advanced vocational training at a *Fachschule*.

It is also possible to receive basic vocational training in a separate first stage, either in the form of a year's full-time schooling or through a dual system arrangement. In accordance with a resolution adopted by the Standing Conference of the Ministers of Education and Cultural Affairs, this is known as the basic vocational training year (*Berufsgrundbildungsjahr*). Its purpose is to provide general knowledge and skills, not limited to one specific career area, as well as theoretical and practical education within the scope of a given career area. For the specific recognized occupations for which training and career qualifications are available and which come under one of the career areas offered, it forms a basis for subsequent specialized career training. Pupils are expected to choose one of the 13 currently existing career areas (business and administration; metallurgical engineering; electrical engineering; construction engineering; woodworking techniques; textiles and garment making; chemistry, physics and biology; printing technology; paint technology; interior design; physical hygiene; health, nutrition and home economics; agronomy). Successful completion of the *Berufsgrundbildungsjahr* (basic vocational training year) is counted as the first year of vocational training in the specific recognized occupation associated with the chosen career area.

4.2 Place of learning – company

At the end of 1992, approximately 1.7 million young people were in dual vocational training. Training places are provided in industry and the public service sector, in independent professions and in private households. Some 600,000 training businesses provide around DM 30 billion annually for the places they offer. Under the *Arbeitsförderungsgesetz* (Promotion of Employment Act), public funds are only available to support the training of those young people who are socially disadvantaged due to learning difficulties, or the training of foreigners who, because of insufficient proficiency in German, require special help to start and successfully complete a course of training.

Within the dual system there are around 370 recognized occupations for which formal training is required. These cover a broad spectrum of skilled occupations in industry, commerce, crafts, the independent professions, public service, agriculture and shipping.

On the basis of training regulations, the businesses teach specialist and general qualifications tailored to occupational practice. The specialized theoretical knowledge acquired from the *Berufsschule* is combined with occupational practice and applied in concrete situations. Since adherence to the training regulations is obligatory, a uniform national standard is guaranteed which meets the requirements of each occupation, so that trainees will not be tied to the immediate needs of a particular business. Training may only take place in businesses which are able to provide training personnel with proven capabilities who can pass on the skills required under the training regulations. The suitability of the training businesses and their training personnel is ascertained and constantly monitored by the competent self-governing bodies of industry (the chambers). The chambers also check that the proper training is being given.

In order to maintain the available number of training places those businesses which, either due to their size, structure or facilities, are less able to provide all the required training elements can still be involved in the training scheme thanks to the provision of complementary training measures at supra-company training centres (*überbetriebliche Berufsbildungsstätten*). With their modern facilities, these inter-company training centres are able to cover those aspects of training which small businesses are not usually able to provide for reasons of cost or lack of capacity.

Due to the restructuring problems still facing industry in the new *Länder*, young people there who are unable to find a training place in a business can receive occupational vocational training at a vocational training centre not attached to any business (*außerbetriebliche Berufsbildungsstätte*). The practical aspects of training programmes normally covered in a business are covered in training workshops and learning offices set up by the bodies responsible for training. The connection with occupational practice is provided by periods of work experience.

5. Teachers

Teacher training for all school types and teaching careers is organized in two phases:

- A study programme at a higher education institution, e.g. university, technical university (*Technische Hochschule / Technische Universität*), comprehensive university (*Universität-Gesamthochschule*), teacher training college (*Pädagogische Hochschule*), college of art or music (*Kunsthochschule, Musikhochschule*), which is geared to the requirements of the teaching profession and the required certificates, and includes student-teacher practical training components as an integrated part of the course.

- A pedagogical-practical training programme in the form of a *Vorbereitungsdienst* (preparatory service) at seminars for teacher training and training schools.

This course of study leads to the First State Examination (*Erste Staatsprüfung*) which serves as an entrance qualification for the preparatory service. Depending on laws specific to each *Land*, appropriate diploma examinations can take the place of the First State Examination in some cases (e.g. for teachers in certain subjects areas at vocational schools).

Representing the second phase of teacher training, the preparatory service serves as practical teacher training. Depending on the *Land* and type of teaching career, the duration of this training varies from 18 to 24 months. The *Vorbereitungsdienst* consists of sitting in on lectures (*Hospitation*), guided and independent teaching at training schools, and participation in general or subject-specific seminars where the experience gained in practical situations is discussed and analysed in greater detail. This training period leads to the Second State Examination (*Zweite Staatsprüfung*) for teachers, which is the prerequisite – but not a guarantee – for finally obtaining a teaching position.

Teachers at public sector schools in the Federal Republic of Germany are usually civil servants. Their legal status is defined by the Civil Service Code in the particular *Land*, which are in turn based on the Civil Service Framework Act (*Beamtenrechtsrahmengesetz*). In the new *Länder*, teachers currently have the status of employees. Although they have not yet been made civil servants, this is planned as soon as a suitable legal assessment has been made of the salary levels of teachers who received their training in the former *GDR*.

All teachers are required to undergo in-service training, the intention being to ensure that teachers keep abreast of developments in their fields and to offer them an opportunity to obtain additional qualifications. The Further Training Institutes for the Teaching Profession established by the Ministries of Education and Cultural Affairs offer a wide range of courses which address problems specific to individual types of school and class levels, as well as those of more general significance, including legal matters and school administration.

6. Higher education

6.1 Types of higher education institutions

6.1.1 Universities

The universities and equivalent higher education institutions (*Technische Universitäten / Technische Hochschulen, Universitäten-Gesamthochschulen* and institutions which only offer certain university departments) are responsible for conducting research, teaching and studies as well as for promoting highly qualified young scientists and academics. Universities and equivalent higher education institutions are entitled to award doctorates (*Promotionsrecht*) and to certify additional academic achievements in research and teaching of a specific discipline (*Habilitationsrecht*). They usually offer a range of subjects from theology and the humanities to law, economic and social sciences, natural sciences, engineering, agriculture and medicine.

The *Universitäten-Gesamthochschulen* (comprehensive universities in Hessen and North Rhine-Westphalia) bring together under one roof research, teaching and study functions otherwise carried out by universities, *Fachhochschulen* and sometimes also *Kunsthochschulen* and *Musikhochschulen* (colleges of art and music). The distinguishing feature of *Universitäten-Gesamthochschulen* is that they offer integrated study programmes (*integrierte Studiengänge*) combining, within a tiered system in terms of content and duration, the educational objectives of university courses and the degree programmes of *Fachhochschulen*. The *Universitäten-Gesamthochschulen* run study programmes of varying durations leading to different degrees.

Universities which only offer certain departments include institutions specializing in medicine, veterinary medicine, administration and sports sciences as well as two *Bundeswehr* universities for officers in the federal armed forces. Apart from the theological departments/faculties at public universities, the churches maintain a number of institutions of higher education and departments/faculties of their own for the training of their theologians.

Some university study programmes lead to academic examinations (*Hochschulprüfungen*: *Diplomprüfung, Magisterprüfung,* or *Promotion*); others lead to state examinations (*Staatsprüfungen*) or in theology also to church examinations (*kirchliche Prüfungen*). For further details see 6.5.

6.1.2 *Pädagogische Hochschulen* (teacher training colleges)

Pädagogische Hochschulen train teachers for *Grundschulen* and certain types of lower-level secondary school as well as *Sonderschulen* (special schools). There is also a course leading to a *Diplom* in education sciences (*Diplom-Pädagoge*). All other types of teachers are trained at universities, *Technische Universitäten/Technische Hochschulen, Universitäten-Gesamthochschulen* as well as *Kunsthochschulen* and *Musikhochschulen* (colleges of art and music). In the 1970s, most of the *Pädagogische Hochschulen* became part of universities. Today they exist as institutions in their own right in only two *Länder* (Baden-Württemberg and Thuringia).

Students at *Pädagogische Hochschulen* study for at least three or four years before taking the First State Examination (*Erste Staatsprüfung*) and continuing with their *Vorbereitungsdienst* (preparatory service) leading to the Second State Examination (*Zweite*

Staatsprüfung). As is the case for the graduates of university teacher training courses, the graduates of teacher training colleges can be employed as teachers at the relevant schools only after having completed the preparatory service.

6.1.3 Colleges of art and music

Kunsthochschulen and *Musikhochschulen* offer courses of study in the visual, design and performing arts and in musical disciplines, some of them even in the related scientific disciplines (science of art, history of art, musicology, history of music, music education).

It is one of the main distinguishing features of a *Kunsthochschule* or *Musikhochschule* that the artistic training takes the form of individual instruction or instruction in small groups (classes). Art and music courses lead to a *Diplom* (first degree), nomination as a *Meisterschüler* (master pupil), the *künstlerische Reifeprüfung* (artistic final examination) or the *Konzertexamen* (concert examination).

Apart from the above-mentioned courses for artistic training, the colleges of art and music also offer teacher training courses entitling graduates to start a career as an art or music teacher at school after having passed the relevant *Staatsprüfung* and completed the *Vorbereitungsdienst*.

6.1.4 *Fachhochschulen*

Fachhochschulen serve a specific purpose of their own in the context of the task, common to all higher education institutions, of providing an academic education. The bulk of their courses of study are in the engineering sciences, economics and business studies, agricultural science, social sciences, library science, documentation and information science, and design. The courses of study themselves and the organization of teaching and study are particularly application-oriented and geared to the demands of professional practice. The research and development work carried out at the *Fachhochschulen* is similarly aimed at specific applications and is complemented by scientific consultancy work and organized technology transfer activities.

Courses at *Fachhochschulen* lead to an examination for a diploma (*Diplomprüfung*). Degrees granted by *Fachhochschulen* include the abbreviation *FH* (*Fachhochschule*).

6.1.5 Distance study courses

Apart from higher education institutions which require the presence of the student, there are others offering correspondence courses. The *Fernuniversität-Gesamthochschule* in Hagen, for instance, runs university-level courses leading both to *Diplom* and *Magister* degrees. Study centres have been set up in several cities throughout the Federal Republic of Germany and abroad to provide local academic advice services and to carry out various activities requiring the presence of students. Several institutions of higher education in the new *Länder* also offer distance study courses leading to vocational qualifications. In recent years, a growing number of institutions of higher education, particularly in the new *Länder*, have been offering further educational studies through distance learning.

6.2 Admission

Pupils who have attended general or vocational secondary schools, have chosen the appropriate courses, and have passed the necessary leaving examinations are entitled to attend higher education institutions.

A school leaving certificate qualifying pupils for higher education (*Hochschulreife* or *Fachhochschulreife*), is required for admission to any course of study at this level. There are three different types of qualifications for admission to higher education:

– the general higher education entrance qualification (*allgemeine Hochschulreife*) entitles its holder to study at any higher education institution without restriction as to the subjects or subject areas;

– the subject-restricted higher education entrance qualification (*fachgebundene Hochschulreife*) gives its holder access to specific courses of study at universities or equivalent institutions of higher education, and usually at *Fachhochschulen*;

– the *Fachhochschule* entrance qualification (*Fachhochschulreife*) allows its holder to enrol at a *Fachhochschule* and for integrated courses of study at *Universitäten-Gesamthochschulen* (comprehensive universities).

The *allgemeine Hochschulreife* or *fachgebundene Hochschulreife* (general or subject-restricted *Hochschulreife*) is generally obtained on completion of the 13th year at school at the end of the *gymnasiale Oberstufe,* or at the end of vocational upper secondary courses also leading to general *Hochschulreife.* The general higher education entrance qualifications which can be obtained after 12 years in certain *Länder* (Mecklenburg-Western Pomerania, Saxony, Saxony-Anhalt, Thuringia) until the year 2000, also entitle the holder to enter higher education without restrictions with regard to subjects or subject-areas.

Night school courses at *Abendgymnasien* for those in employment and day school courses for pupils with work experience at *Kollegs* also lead to the general higher education entrance qualification. Additional opportunities are offered for 'non-pupils' wanting to acquire the *Abitur* in the form of the *Nichtschülerprüfung* and of the *Begabtenprüfung* leading to higher education admission for gifted applicants who are in work.

The *Fachhochschulreife* is normally awarded at a *Fachoberschule* after 12 consecutive years of schooling. It is also possible to obtain the *Fachhochschulreife* through special additional courses offered, for instance, at *Berufsfachschulen* and *Fachschulen*, which primarily lead to vocational qualifications.

In certain *Länder*, pupils who hold a vocational qualification but do not have the entrance qualification for higher education have several options if they still wish to pursue their studies. They must demonstrate the knowledge and the ability necessary for their studies under an entrance procedure (e.g. by enrolling temporarily on a trial basis) or by passing an entrance examination of an institution of higher education (ranking examination, aptitude test and interview).

Prospective students at *Kunsthochschulen* and *Musikhochschulen* (art and music colleges) are not only expected to have the requisite formal qualifications (*Hochschulreife*) but also to demonstrate their artistic aptitude. In most of the *Länder*, exclusively artistic courses of study (i.e. not those courses qualifying candidates for the teaching profession) also accept students without *Hochschulreife*, as long as they can demonstrate exceptional artistic talent. Another exception are the practical aptitude tests for sport study programmes. These tests, however, are not required by all institutions offering training as a sports instructor or sports scientist. In addition to this, in some *Länder* candidates are required to take an aptitude test before being accepted for particular courses of study at *Fachhochschulen* (e.g. design, architecture).

Applicants for various courses of study, in particular the technical ones, are required to meet additional requirements, such as having completed subject-related practicals before starting their course of study, alongside the qualifications entitling them to admission to an institution of higher education.

Article 12 of the Basic Law guarantees the right in the Federal Republic of Germany for all Germans to freely choose their occupation or profession, their place of employment and their place of study or training. In principle, anyone with the *allgemeine Hochschulreife* or *fachgebundene Hochschulreife* (general or subject-restricted higher education entrance qualification) is entitled to embark on a course of higher education. As a result of the high numbers of applicants and the insufficient number of study places, there are currently (winter semester 1994/95) restrictions throughout Germany on admission to university courses in the following subject areas: architecture, business administration, biology, forestry, food and home economics, food chemistry, medicine, pharmacy, psychology, law, veterinary medicine, economics, and dentistry. The places available to students in these subjects are allocated in a central selection procedure. The courses included in the nationwide selection procedure may vary from semester to semester. There are no restrictions on admission to the vast majority of courses. Several higher education institutions also restrict admission locally, or in particular subject areas that are not included in the nationwide selection procedure. In these cases, the institution decides whether or not to admit a candidate. Selection, both in the central and the local selection procedures, is based primarily on the average marks received by the applicant in the *Abitur* and the length of time between taking the *Abitur* and applying to the higher education institution. Further criteria are applied in assessing applications to study medicine (e.g. a test and an interview).

6.3 Fees/Student finance

German and foreign students attending higher education institutions in the Federal Republic of Germany (with the exception of some private institutions) are generally not required to pay any application, tuition or examination fees. Instead, students are required to pay a *Sozialbeitrag* (social contribution) or a *Studentenwerksbeitrag* (contribution to the student administration) for the use of the social facilities. If the institution in question has an *Allgemeiner Studentenausschuß* (*AStA* – general student committee) as a student self-governing body, students also have to pay a *Studentenschaftsbeitrag* (contribution to the student body) which is either included in the *Sozialbeitrag* or paid separately.

Students who have no other means (mainly from parents' income) of maintenance and finance for a course of study in higher education can receive financial assistance under the terms of the Federal Training Assistance Act (*Bundesausbildungsförderungsgesetz – BAföG*). The duration for which assistance is payable under *BAföG* varies according to the study course taken and the longest period of assistance allowed under the respective regulations. The monthly amount depends on the students' own income and personal circumstances as well as those of their parents and other relatives required to support them. Half of the assistance is provided as a grant or interest-free loan. The schedule for loan repayment takes into account the student's social status and income.

6.4 Academic year

The academic year is divided into semesters. At universities, the summer semester runs from April to September (at *Fachhochschulen* from March to August) and the winter semester from October to March (at *Fachhochschulen* from September to February). Lectures in the winter semester at universities and *Fachhochschulen* are usually held from late September/early October until mid/late February. In the summer semester, lectures at universities are from mid-April to mid-July and at *Fachhochschulen* from mid-March to mid-July. A period of three months without lectures at *Fachhochschulen* and five months at other higher education institutions allows students time for individual study and time to prepare for lectures

and seminars, complete assignments, undergo practical training and sit examinations.

6.5 Courses/Assessment/ Qualifications

Students may receive instruction in the form of lectures, introductory and advanced seminars (*Proseminare, Hauptseminare*), exercises, practicals, or excursions. Lectures are designed first and foremost to provide students with the general and background knowledge they need for their courses. Seminars provide an opportunity to investigate a defined topic more intensively. Topics are generally chosen because they are the focus of considerable research in the field or by the department. To acquire achievement certificates (*Scheine*), students are required to do oral or written work. These certificates are required for admission to examinations and are the basis for assessing the students' performance during the course of study. In the experimental sciences, the practical exercises students carry out in connection with lectures, notably compulsory laboratory work, provide a basis for continuous assessment of performance.

Studies at institutions of higher education are generally divided into a first stage, with the *Grundstudium* (at university, usually four semesters) leading to an intermediate examination, and a second stage or *Hauptstudium* ending with the final degree examination.

For every course of studies, the examination regulations establish guidelines for the time in which the course and the corresponding examination can be completed. For university courses this guideline period (*Regelstudienzeit*) is between eight and ten semesters; the usual period of time required to study medicine is six years and three months. At *Fachhochschulen*, the guideline period is at least eight semesters, including practical semesters. The actual amount of time spent studying at a university is, in many cases, one to two-and-a-half years longer on average than the period of time in the guidelines, and at *Fachhochschulen* about one year longer.

One must distinguish between academic qualifications, state examinations and church examinations. Success in the final examination usually qualifies the candidate for a particular profession.

Higher education institutions are authorized by law to hold academic examinations (*Hochschulprüfungen*). These examinations, on the basis of which academic degrees are conferred, include:

- the *Diplomprüfung* (*Diplom* examination), which leads to the *Diplomgrad* (*Diplom* degree), e.g. *Diplom-Ingenieur* (awarded by a university), or *Diplom-Ingenieur (FH)* (awarded by a *Fachhochschule*);

- the *Magisterprüfung* (*Magister* examination), leading to the *Magistergrad* (*Magister* degree), e.g. *Magister Artium*;

- the *Promotion* (doctorate), leading to the *Doktorgrad* (doctoral degree), e.g. *Doctor philosophiae*.

Some courses leading to professions in which there is a particular public interest end with a *Staatsprüfung* (state examination). This is especially the case for courses in medicine, dentistry, veterinary medicine, pharmacy, law, food chemistry, and for teacher training courses. The standard of performance required for the *Staatsprüfung* is the same as that for the *Hochschulprüfung*. For the most part, there is only a formal difference between the two kinds of examination. Representatives of the state examining authorities (*Staatliche Prüfungsämter*) in the *Länder* participate alongside professors as examiners in state examinations.

Law students and future teachers who have passed the First State Examination (*Erste Staatsprüfung*) move on to a preparatory service (*Vorbereitungsdienst*), leading to a Second State Examination (*Zweite Staatsprüfung*). They must pass this second examination to qualify as a judge or a teacher.

Greece

GREECE

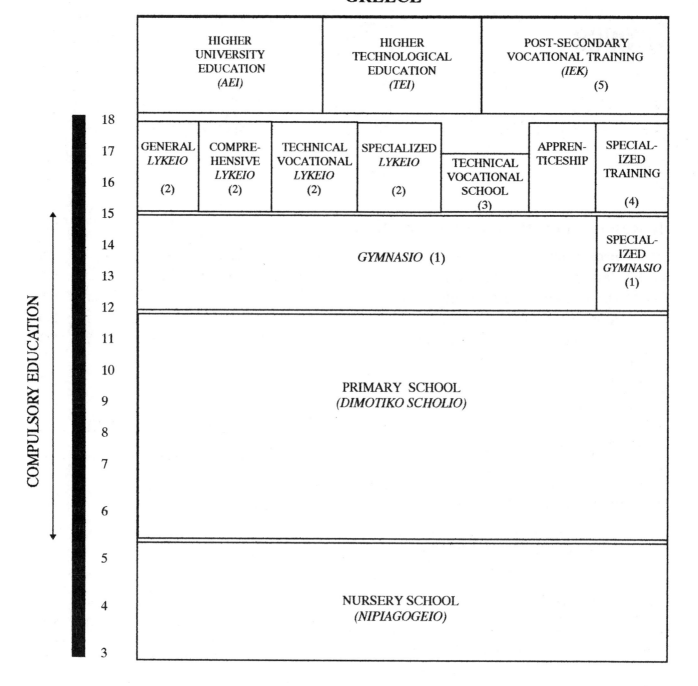

1.The *Gymnasio* provides general education at lower secondary level with the leaving certificate *(Apolytirio Gymnasiou)* providing access to the *Lykeio*. Evening *Gymnasia* provide equivalent education for employed persons 14 years of age or over. There are specialized Ecclesiastical and Music *Gymnasia* and *Gymnasio* Sports Departments.

2.The *Lykeio* provides education at upper secondary level with the leaving certificate *(Apolytirio Lykeiou)* providing access to the general university entrance examinations. General *Lykeia* provide general secondary education, Technical-Vocational *Lykeia* combine general education with vocational training, Comprehensive *Lykeia* aim to link general and technical-vocational education. There are specialized Classical, Ecclesiastical and Music *Lykeia* and *Lykeio* Sports Departments. Evening *Lykeia* provide equivalent education, lasting 4 years, for employed persons.

3.The Technical-Vocational School *(TES)* provides up to 2 years of technical-vocational education at upper secondary level leading to employment. Evening *TES* provide courses of up to 3 years for employed persons.

4.Specialized training of various lengths, in particular the courses run by the *OAED* (Manpower Employment Organization).

5.Post-secondary vocational training is provided in Institutes of Vocational Training *(IEK)* which do not correspond to a specific level of education.

1. Responsibilities and administration

1.1 Background

Greece covers a total area of 131,990 square kilometres and has a population of around 10,264,156 (1991). The official language is Greek.

According to the 1975 Constitution, amended in 1986, Greece is a Presidential Democracy headed by the President. Legislative power is exercised by Parliament and the President. There are 300 MPs, elected every four years by universal secret ballot. The President is elected by Parliament for a five-year term which can be renewed once.

Executive power is exercised, in accordance with the Constitution, by the President and the Government. The ruling party, following elections in October 1993, is the Socialist Party (*PASOK*).

Greece is divided into 13 regions and 54 prefectures which include municipalities and communes. The head of each prefecture is the Prefect, who, in accordance with new legislation (Law 2218/1994) is elected for four years by direct universal and secret ballot. The heads of the municipalities and the communes are also elected for four years.

The predominant religion in Greece (97.6%) is Eastern Orthodox.

In 1993, the unemployment rate was 9.67% (National Statistical Office). There were 3,720,180 employed, divided between the sectors as follows: primary 21.34%; secondary 24.19%; and tertiary 54.47%.

1.2 Basic principles: education

Education is a basic mission of the State, and its aim is to provide moral, intellectual, vocational and physical instruction for the Greeks, to promote national and religious awareness and to develop free, responsible citizens. All Greeks have the right to free education, at all levels of education in state education institutions which operate with financial support from the State.

Every citizen has equal educational opportunities irrespective of family background, origin and sex.

1.3 Distribution of responsibilities

The Greek education system is governed by national laws passed by Parliament, and by executive acts (decrees, ministerial decisions). Overall responsibility for education rests with the Ministry of National Education and Religious Affairs.

The administration and management of primary and secondary education is the responsibility of the 108 Directorates of Primary and Secondary Education in the 54 prefectures, which report directly to the Ministry. In prefectures with a large school population, there are also Education Offices.

Higher education institutions (*AEIs*/universities and *TEIs*/institutions of technological education) are autonomous according to the Constitution, but are funded and supervised by the Ministry of National Education and Religious Affairs.

Responsibilities concerning vocational education and training for young people are shared by the Ministry of National Education and Religious Affairs and the Ministry of Labour. The Ministry of National Education and Religious Affairs is responsible for the provision of vocational education in post-compulsory secondary education. The Organization for Vocational Education and Training (*OEEK*), which has total responsibility for the recently created vocational training institutes (*IEKs*) is also under the auspices of this Ministry.

The Ministry of Labour, through the Manpower Employment Organization (*OAED*), runs technical-vocational schools as Apprenticeship Schools (*Scholes Mathiteias*) and operates parallel programmes of vocational training for adults in Centres for Vocational Training (*KEK*) under the responsibility of various bodies. Other ministries, such as the Ministry of Agriculture, run vocational schools for training in the sectors of agriculture and animal husbandry.

1.4 Administration

Central level

Responsibility for national education policy lies with the **Ministry of National Education and Religious Affairs**. The basic functions and responsibilities of this Ministry consist in defining, evaluating and creating the conditions for meeting educational needs. In particular, it proposes legislation in the field of education, and is responsible for implementing the laws and the associated administrative decisions. It coordinates and evaluates the regional services and schools and provides financial support for educational activities.

Some functions and responsibilities have been delegated to public organizations and other bodies which report directly to the Ministry.

More specifically, these organizations and bodies are:

- **The Pedagogical Institute.** This is an autonomous public body operating under the supervision of the Ministry of National Education and Religious Affairs. It is responsible for the formulation of guidelines, the preparation of timetables and curricula, the commissioning and approval of textbooks, the application of vocational guidance, the introduction of new subjects, the application of new teaching methods, the provision of in-service training for teachers, etc.

- **School Advisers of Primary and Secondary Education.** These have a minimum of fifteen years' educational experience and a significant

number hold postgraduate degrees. In secondary education, each School Adviser is responsible for a group of teachers who teach the same discipline(s). Thus, there are School Advisers responsible for language teachers, science teachers, etc. School Advisers provide in-service training and pedagogical support for teachers.

- **The School Buildings Organization (*OSK*).** This is a self-governing organization responsible for the construction of school buildings and for their equipment.

- **The Textbook Publishing Organization (*OEDV*).** This is a self-governing organization responsible for the publication of school books and other educational books, and for their free distribution to schools.

- **The Organization for Vocational Education and Training (*OEEK*).** This is a self-governing body, established by Law 2009/14.2.1992, for the organization and running of state Institutes of Vocational Education and Training (*IEKs*) which are the responsibility of the Ministry of National Education and Religious Affairs. It also supervises private *IEKs*. Its tasks also include: studying and assessing the requirements for specialized personnel in each sector of the economy, in collaboration with other competent bodies; recognizing and accrediting the education and training provided by the *IEKs*; recognizing the certificates awarded by other Greek organizations responsible for vocational education and training and the equivalence of corresponding foreign certificates; defining professional rights at all levels of vocational education and training, in collaboration with the ministries which are competent in each case, and with the social partners; managing all the EU funds intended for technical and vocational education and training under the responsibility of the Ministry of National Education and Religious Affairs; and carrying out research, making surveys, keeping statistics and documentation in connection with vocational education and training.

The *OEEK's* Administration Board comprises representatives from the Ministry of National Education and Religious Affairs, the Ministry of Labour, the Ministry of National Economy, the Ministry of Finance, and the social partners (employers – employees).

- **The State Grants Foundation** (*IKY*). This is the national grants body. Its purposes are: to issue grants, loans and awards to Greek expatriates and foreign nationals; to issue grants and financial support within the framework of European cooperation programmes; to gather and distribute information on all the grants and financial support offered to Greek citizens and to carry out, or to commission out to third parties, the research, studies and publishing relevant to its purposes.

- **The Interuniversity Centre for the Recognition of Foreign Qualifications** (*DIKATSA*). This is a self-governing legal entity of public law, whose functions are: to recognize foreign universities and the qualifications they award as equivalent to Greek ones; and to recognize qualifications from foreign universities as equivalent to qualifications from Greek universities in cases where there is no corresponding specialization in Greece.

- **The National Youth Foundation** (*EIN*). This is a legal entity of private law of the broader public sector, self-governing and supervised by the Ministry of National Education and Religious Affairs. It founds university and other students' halls of residence, pupils' halls of residence and pupils' centres, promotes cultural events, excursions, camping programmes, and implements special programmes of the General Secretariat of Youth.

Prefecture level

The basic duties and responsibilities of the Directors of primary and secondary education in each prefecture are: coordination of the Education Offices in their prefecture; supervision of the school head teachers and coordination of the schools functioning in their prefecture; supervision and coordination of the maintenance of school buildings and the improvement of school equipment and workshops; allocation of teaching staff to schools; supervision of private schools; submission of proposals both to the Prefect of their prefecture and to the Ministry of National Education and Religious Affairs for the improvement of educational activities in their prefecture. The administrative tasks and responsibilities of the Heads of Education Offices are similar to those of the Directors of education in the prefecture.

In addition, issues concerning teachers' status are dealt with by a **Regional Council** in each prefecture and by a **Central Council** in the Ministry of National Education and Religious Affairs at national level. The Councils consist of five members. The President of the Regional Council is the head of the Directorate of Education in the prefecture, two members are heads of Education Offices or, if there are none, teachers with the highest grade in the career structure (A grade), and two further members are elected representatives of teachers.

The Central Council comprises three heads of Directorates of Education with corresponding alternates and two elected representatives of teachers.

Institutional level

The school head teacher, supported by the deputy head teacher, and the Teachers' Council are involved in the administration of each **school**. The basic tasks and responsibilities of the school head teacher are: coordination of all school activities in accordance with the legal regulations; supervision of the teaching staff; maintenance of teachers' records and financial management of the school.

The Teachers' Council is responsible for the implementation of legal regulations concerning the curricula, pupil attendance, the management of discipline problems, the supervision of activities undertaken by the Pupils' Communities and all other events taking place in the school.

Universities (*AEI*) are fully self-governing legal entities of public law. Each university is governed by collective bodies which are set up and which operate in accordance with specific legislation. These bodies are the Senate, the Rector's Board and the Rector. The members of these bodies are exclusively members of the university community of each university. The organization of the universities is implemented by Presidential Decree or Ministerial Decision following a proposal of the university bodies and an opinion of the University Education Council (*SAP*). Members of the research-teaching staff are appointed by the Rector. The General Meeting of each university department is responsible for drawing up the curriculum for that department. The department also issues degrees, the name of which is established in advance by Presidential Decree.

Institutions of technological education (*TEI*) are also fully self-governing legal entities of public law, governed by collective bodies, with the general meeting of each department determining the curriculum and the department issuing degrees.

1.5 Inspection

There is no inspectorate as such in Greece. Certain supervisory tasks are carried out by the Directorates and Offices of Education in the prefectures. The guidance of teachers is carried out by School Advisers.

1.6 Financing

Public schools are built by the State. The operating expenses of nursery, primary and secondary schools are covered by credits from the Ministry of the Interior. By decisions of this Ministry these credits are distributed to the Prefecture Councils which then, on the basis of proposals of the Directors of Education, distribute credits to the local authorities which allocate them to School Committees. Schools' rent costs are met by credits paid into the prefecture budget.

Higher education institutions (universities/*AEI* and institutions of technological education/*TEI*) are funded by the Ministry of National Education and Religious Affairs but they can have their own sources of funds. The assets of each university are administered by a legal entity of public law specially set up for this purpose by the university and supervised by the Ministry. The provision of equipment and materials is at the charge of the universities themselves.

1.7 Private schools

Private primary and secondary schools operate under the same legislation as public schools. They have the same curriculum as public schools. If a private school develops an initiative relating to the curriculum, the approval of the Ministry of

National Education and Religious Affairs is required.

The conditions for the employment of teaching staff, the equivalence of certificates and the rules of operation are regulated by laws and decisions of the Ministry of National Education and Religious Affairs.

No private school receives funding from the State. Pupils pay tuition fees, but textbooks are provided free. Private technical and vocational schools cannot receive grants and are funded by fees.

1.8 Participatory and advisory bodies

The **National Education Council** (*ESYP*) makes proposals to the Government on matters of education policy for all levels of education, continuing education and adult education. It consists of the Directors of the Ministry and representatives from other Ministries, the Pedagogical Institute, the political parties, the Orthodox Church, the National Federation of Local Government, teaching and research staff in higher education, the Confederation of Parents, the National Students Union, the federations of Primary and Secondary Teachers, the national federations from the world of production and the General Secretariats of Youth and Adult Education.

The following advisory bodies make proposals to the Minister of National Education and Religious Affairs relating to the organization, development, founding, funding, etc. of universities (*AEI*):

– The **National Academy of Letters and Sciences** (*EAGE*) (not yet in operation), comprising representatives of social and university bodies, ministries and political parties.

– The **University Education Council** (*SAP*), consisting of the rectors of all the universities, and also representatives of all the country's political, productive and social bodies.

– The **Interuniversity Research Council** (*DSE*), which deals with research matters and is composed of academic researchers of international repute.

– The **Committee for the Evaluation of University Work,** which evaluates the teaching, research and administrative work of each university, and is also composed of rectors and members of teaching-research staff.

The following bodies make proposals to the Minister of Education and Religious Affairs relating to the organization, development, founding, funding, etc. of institutions of technological education (*TEI*):

– The **Technological Education Council** (*STE*), which consists of the Minister of National Education and Religious Affairs or his representative as chairman, one representative of the other ministries, the political parties in the Greek Parliament, representatives of the productive strata (Chambers of Commerce, Association of Greek Industries, etc.) and trade union bodies.

– The **Technological Education Institute** (*ITE*), which consists of seven Counsellors and 10 Advisers who are appointed by the Minister of National Education and Religious Affairs for a three-year term of office, following an announcement and an opinion from the *STE*.

– The **Regional Council for Technological Education** (*PSTE*), which consists of the Prefect or his representative as chairman, the *TEI* Council, and representatives of local government, the local social and productive bodies, and students.

At the level of the prefecture, the following bodies are in operation:

– The **Prefectural or Sub-Prefectural Education Committee**, which operates in the capital of each prefecture or sub-prefecture. It comprises the Prefect (*Nomarchis*), Sub-Prefect (*Eparchos*), or their representative, representatives of the School Advisers, the educational administration, the parents' federation and academic and productive bodies. It makes proposals to the Prefect or Sub-Prefect on matters of education.

– The **Municipal or Communal Education Committee**, which operates in each municipality or commune. It consists of representatives of the municipality or of the commune, of the parents' association, head teachers of schools, and a representative of local productive strata and

bodies. It makes proposals to the Mayor or the President of the commune or to the municipal or communal council on measures to improve the organization and functioning of the local schools.

At the level of the schools, the following bodies are in operation:

– The **School Council**, which consists of the Teachers' Association, the Administrative Board of the Parents' Association, a representative of local government and, especially in the case of School Councils in secondary schools, a representative of the Pupils' Communities. The task of the School Council is to ensure the smooth running of the school in every appropriate way, to establish means of communication between teachers and the pupils' families, and to ensure that the pupils and the school environment are healthy.

– The **School Committee**, which consists of a representative of the municipality or the commune, a representative of the Parents' Association, of the pupils of the school, the head teacher of the school and in secondary schools a representative of the Pupils' Communities. The task of the School Committee is to manage the credits for the operational costs of the school, and to deal with any problem regarding the operation of the school.

– The **Parents' Association** of each school, which participates in the School Council and, through their representatives, in the other participatory and advisory bodies.

– The **Pupils' Communities**, which give the pupils the opportunity to take initiatives and to contribute to the smooth running of the school.

– **Environmental Education Centres,** which are intended to provide scientific and technical assistance for environmental education programmes which operate mainly in secondary schools.

– **Young People's Advisory Centres,** whose purpose is to support educational programmes which deal with the development of health education in schools, in particular, to provide information on the prevention of drug dependence.

2. Pre-school education

Pre-school education is optional and is intended for children aged from 3½ to 5½ years; it is of two years' duration. It is provided in nursery schools (*nipiagogia*) which operate either independently or in primary schools.

Most are organized by the State but a few are organized by the private sector. In the former, priority for admission is given to children living in the area where the school is located.

State schools are free of charge. In private schools, pupils' families pay fixed fees, reviewed annually by the Minister of Trade.

In 1990/91, the percentage of children attending nursery schools was 59%. Most children – around 95% – attend state schools.

There are one-teacher (*monothesia*) and two-teacher (*dithesia*) nursery schools. The former have from 7 to 30 children, the latter have from 31 to 60 children. The sections are mixed and organized independently of the age of the children, but there are work groups formed according to age.

They operate for roughly 172 days a year, and the timetable is 3½ hours daily, either in the morning (8.30 a.m. to 12.30 p.m.) or in the afternoon (2.00 p.m. to 5.00 p.m.).

The purpose of the nursery school is to assist in the all-round, harmonious and balanced development of the children, their psychomotor, social, emotional, moral and religious development, the cultivation of skills, and mental and aesthetic development, in a climate of freedom, security and mental stimulation.

Curriculum and assessment

Since 1989, a new curriculum, defined in Presidential Decree 486/1989 A, has been in application in pre-school establishments.

Recommendations for daily activities provide for both time for play in small groups in activity corners and periods of activity whose aims and objectives are established in advance by the teacher; the latter may arise out of spontaneous or planned activities.

When organizing activities, the teacher, taking into account the curriculum guidelines and the level of development of the children, chooses one or more areas of development out of those mentioned above and one or more aims. Teachers then assess the results of their educational activity.

Teachers

See 3.1.

Statistics 1993/94

	Pupils	Teachers	Schools
State	128,835	7,859	5,424
Private	5,487	235	135

Of the total number of nursery schools, 875 (15.7%) operate in the Athens area, with 33,307 pupils (24.8%) and 1,537 nursery teachers (18.9%).

Source: National Statistical Office.

3. Compulsory education

In Greece, compulsory education lasts for 9 years (from the year in which the child reaches 5½ years old until he/she reaches 15), of which the first 6 years are spent at primary school (*Dimotiko Scholio*) and the last 3 years at lower secondary school (*Gymnasio*).

3.1 Primary education (*Dimotiko scholio*)

Primary education is intended for pupils aged 5 1/2 to 12 years.

The aim of primary education is, generally, the pupils' all-round mental and physical development. In particular, the primary school helps the pupils:

- to broaden and readjust the relationship between their creative activity and the programmes, situations and phenomena which they are studying;

- to build up the mechanisms which contribute to the assimilation of knowledge, to develop physically, to improve their physical and mental well-being, and to develop their motor skills;

- to grasp the essence of the fundamental concepts and gradually acquire the ability to proceed from the data of the senses to the field of abstract thought;

- to familiarize themselves gradually with moral, religious, national, humanitarian and other values and to organize them into a system of values;

- to cultivate their aesthetic judgment so that they can appreciate works of art and express themselves correspondingly through their own artistic creations.

Primary schools (*Dimotika Scholia*) may be state or private. The choice of state or private school is the parents' decision. If state school is chosen, the child must attend the school nearest to his/her place of permanent residence. There are state primary schools throughout the country, even in remote and inaccessible areas.

State education is provided free of charge. Books are also provided free of charge.

According to the number of permanent teaching posts, primary schools are divided into one-post, two-post, etc., up to six- or twelve-post. Pupils are assigned to classes by age. Most subjects in the primary school curriculum are taught by the class teacher, who may change group or class every year. The foreign language, physical education and arts subjects are taught by specialist teachers.

Primary schools operate five days a week, with 5-6 hours of teaching per day according to the class. The weekly teaching hours vary between 25 and 30, according to the class and whether or not teaching includes a foreign language, music, etc. The school timetable runs from 8.15 a.m. to 1.30 p.m., and where there are different schools sharing the same building, there is also an afternoon and evening timetable from 2.00 p.m. to 7.00 p.m. The school year lasts 175 days, from 11 September to 15 June.

Curriculum

The subjects taught in the first and second classes are: modern Greek language, mathematics, environmental studies, physical education, art education and school life. In the third and fourth classes, the curriculum includes: modern Greek language, mathematics, environmental studies, religion, history, physical education, art education and, in the fourth class, 3 hours' foreign language teaching per week, and one hour's teaching of school life and culture per week, and music. In the fifth and sixth classes, the curriculum includes:

modern Greek language, mathematics, geography, the natural world, religion, history, social and political education, physical education, art education, music, foreign language and school life.

The detailed curricula and timetables are drawn up by the Pedagogical Institute which is also responsible for school textbooks; there is no choice of textbooks.

In addition to the ordinary curriculum, there are remedial teaching programmes for less able pupils, mainly in language and mathematics. There are also creative activity programmes (*PDAMET*) attended by children of working parents after school hours, programmes for special social groups (the illiterate, gypsies), and induction classes for children of returning nationals and foreigners.

Assessment

The assessment of pupils in primary school is based on daily oral tests and pupils' overall participation in the learning process, on the results of their achievement in relation to the assessment criteria, which can refer to more than one unit of teaching, and on the results of work done at school or at home.

During the first term, pupils in the last two classes write a brief project on various topics, which is completed with the assistance of the teacher and presented to the class.

In all classes there is a descriptive assessment of pupils, which allows teachers to provide detailed information to pupils and their parents on the results of their efforts at school, their abilities and talents and any shortcomings and weaknesses they have in particular fields. The class teacher keeps a school register where more analytical data on the descriptive assessment of pupils is recorded for school use.

In addition to the descriptive assessment, in the 3rd and 4th classes a marking scale is used: Excellent (A), Very good (B), Good (C), Quite good (D). In the 5th and 6th classes the following scale is used: Excellent (9,10), Very good (7,8), Good (5,6), Quite good.

The results of pupils' assessment are discussed at a special meeting of the Teachers' Association. Pupils' parents and guardians are then invited to a special meeting with the class teacher where they are informed of and discuss pupils' performance and any learning difficulties and receive their 'progress report'.

At the end of the school year, pupils in classes 1,2,3,4 and 5 are awarded a 'progress certificate' and pupils in the 6th class are given a 'study certificate' for use when enrolling at a *Gymnasio*. The word 'promoted' is written on the progress certificate for class 1,2,3, and 4.

Apart from the word 'promoted' or 'released' as appropriate, the progress certificate of class 5 or the study certificate of class 6 contains the descriptive mark and its numeric equivalent, which comprises the final average mark for the year.

Pupils are automatically promoted to the next class. A pupil must repeat a class only when he/she has attended school for less than half the school year.

Teachers

Most nursery and primary school teachers already in post have been trained at the Colleges of Nursery and Primary Education respectively, where studies lasted two years.

In accordance with Law 1268 of 1982, University Departments of Nursery and Primary Education have been created, where studies last four years. The first such University Departments began to operate from the 1984/85 academic year, with the first nursery and primary teachers graduating in 1988.

Before taking up their post, nursery and primary teachers must follow a three-month introductory teacher training course in a Regional Training Centre (*PEK*).

Teachers who have between 5 and 25 years of teaching experience are invited every five or six years to follow three months' compulsory in-service training (that is, three or four times during their career).

Nursery and primary teachers who are appointed in state education are civil servants. They complete a two-year probationary period before becoming permanent.

Statistics 1993/94

	Pupils	Teachers	Schools
State	690,201	37,214	6,967
Private	54,341	2,607	411

Of the total number of primary schools, 1,032 schools (13.7%) operate in the Athens area, with 227,008 pupils (29.1%) and 10,059 teachers (25.9%).

Source: National Statistical Office.

3.2 Lower secondary education *(Gymnasio)*

The *Gymnasio* constitutes the lower level of secondary education. Attendance at a *Gymnasio* is compulsory. It lasts 3 years and is intended for pupils aged 12 to 15 years. There are state and private *Gymnasia*.

The purpose of the *Gymnasio* is to promote the pupils' all-round development in relation to the abilities which they have at this age, and the corresponding demands of life. In particular, it helps the pupils:

- to broaden their values (moral, religious, national, humanitarian and others) so that they can regulate their behaviour and control and direct their emotions towards creative goals and humanitarian actions;

- to supplement and combine the acquisition of knowledge with the corresponding social concerns;

- to cultivate their powers of verbal expression;

- to achieve normal physical development and cultivate their physical aptitudes and abilities;

- to familiarize themselves with the various forms of art and to develop aesthetic judgment for their own artistic expression;

- to become aware of their capabilities and skills and to gain knowledge of the various occupations, so that they can develop in a balanced manner as people and as future working men and women, understanding the equally valuable contributions of intellectual and manual work to social progress and development.

The *Gymnasia* provide a general education in all classes. There are day schools and evening schools (attended by working pupils over 14 years old). Also in operation are: *Gymnasia* with a special curriculum covering the needs of children of Greeks returning from abroad; music *Gymnasia; Gymnasia* with sports departments; and special schools or special sections in ordinary schools, for children with special educational needs.

Primary school leavers are automatically admitted to the first class without examination. Attendance is free of charge, and school books are also supplied free of charge to pupils and teachers by the Ministry of National Education and Religious Affairs.

Gymnasia are coeducational schools. The classes, 1st, 2nd and 3rd, are organized according to the children's age. Teachers may stay with the same classes for one, two or three years, but there is no general rule in this matter.

In many cases, *Gymnasia* are housed in the same buildings as primary schools or *Lykeia* (upper secondary schools). Consequently, these schools operate alternately with a morning or an afternoon and evening timetable. The school building can be used outside school hours by the pupils themselves, or by the parents' associations or other local bodies.

Gymnasia operate five days a week, and their timetable varies between 33 and 35 'hours' (40-45 minutes) a week. The total number of teaching days is about 175 per year and the school year runs from 1 September to 30 June.

Curriculum

The curriculum is the same for all pupils and includes: religion, ancient Greek literature, modern Greek language and literature, mathematics, physics-chemistry, history, geography, biology, physical education, art education, computer science-technology, foreign languages (English/ French and German), school careers guidance, domestic science, social education, according to the class and in conformity with Law 1566/85 and subsequent modifications.

Assessment and qualifications

The teaching year is divided into three terms. Each term, the teachers assess the pupils' performance through oral and written tests (a one-hour test in the first and the second term). In addition, there are 15-minute written tests to assess whether pupils have understood a specific lesson.

The system of assessment also includes one revision examination (June), which the pupils sit when they have assimilated and structured three-fifths of the material taught from the beginning until the end of the school year.

The final mark of each pupil is based on his/her average mark for oral assessment and the marks in the written examinations at the end of the year.

Pupils are promoted to the next class if their final mark in all subjects is on average at least 10 out of a possible 20. If this mark is not achieved in one to four subjects, the pupil is entered to resit examinations in September. If the mark is below 10 in more than four subjects, the pupil repeats the same class. Pupils also remain in the same class if they have exceeded the stipulated limit for absences from school (50 unjustified and up to 150 justified). If, in spite of exceeding the limit for absences, pupils have an average mark of at least 15 and their conduct is excellent, they are referred for examination in all subjects in September.

In order to be awarded the leaving certificate (*Apolytirio Gymnasiou*) a pupil must as a rule have an average of 10 out of a possible 20 in all subjects and must not have exceeded the permitted number of absences from school.

The decision as to whether a pupil moves up to the next class or is awarded the leaving certificate at the end of the three years of study is taken by the Teachers' Association.

When the teachers consider that they require extra help, pupils who are behind in language, mathematics, physics, chemistry and foreign language attend the remedial teaching course. This begins at the start of the second term and covers 1-2 teaching hours per day and a total of up to 10 hours per week, according to the number of pupils.

Every term, the pupils' parents or guardians are given a progress report. In the first class, details of the pupil's performance are entered in his/her personal report book; entries continue to be made until completion of the *Gymnasio*.

At the end of each year, if requested by the pupil's parent or guardian, a study certificate can be issued for use outside the school, or a school certificate for use when enrolling the pupil in a foreign school abroad. The *Gymnasio* leaving certificate can be used for enrolment in a school or as a 'testimonial' for non-school use.

Teachers

The teachers teach the subject of their specialization. They are university graduates and have followed four years of study in the subject concerned. The majority of them are civil servants with permanent posts. However, there are also deputies and teachers on hourly wages who are appointed to cover certain educational needs. Compulsory introductory and in-service training is organized in the same way as for nursery and primary teachers.

Statistics 1993/94

	Pupils	Teachers	Schools
State	425,937	28,176	1,776
Private	18,102	1,320	90

Source: National Statistical Office.

Music *Gymnasia*

Music *Gymnasia* were established in 1988 for the purpose of providing not only general but also specialized musical knowledge to talented pupils who wish to pursue music studies. Primary school leavers are admitted to these schools after taking entrance examinations in music. The daily timetable consists of two cycles: the morning cycle in which pupils attend lessons in general education; and the afternoon cycle in which they attend individual lessons, musical instrument practice, etc. The timetable covers 46 hours per week. Pupils who complete the Music *Gymnasio* can then continue at the corresponding *Lykeio*. There are 15 Music *Gymnasia* and 2 Music *Lykeia*.

Gymnasio Sports Departments

These departments were set up for the first time in the school year 1988/89 by Ministerial Decision G4/902/29.9.1988, ratified by Law 1894/90.

Sports Departments are now operating in 80 *Gymnasia* around the country.

In these departments, the physical education lesson is replaced with two hours per day of sports coaching by physical education teachers specializing in a particular sport; all other subjects are taught as in the general departments. In each department, two to five sports are taught by various teachers. Pupils are selected through special tests in each sport, and they follow the sport for which they have been selected.

4. Post-compulsory secondary education (Upper secondary education)

The institutions of upper secondary education are the *Lykeia* and the Technical-Vocational Schools (*TES*). Pupils who have completed the *Gymnasio* can enrol in any upper secondary institution. There are no entrance examinations.

4.1 *Lykeia*

Lykeia can be state or private education institutions. There are both day schools and evening schools. The evening schools are attended by working pupils. The course of study lasts three years, except in evening schools where it lasts four years. At state *Lykeia*, attendance is free of charge and school books are distributed free of charge to the pupils by the State.

The existing types of *Lykeio* are: the General *Lykeio*, the Technical – Vocational *Lykeio*, the Comprehensive (*Polikladiko*) *Lykeio*, the Classical *Lykeio*, the Ecclesiastical *Lykeio* and the Music *Lykeio*. There are also *Lykeio* Sports Departments.

General *Lykeio (Geniko Lykeio)*

This aims to build the character and personality of the pupils so that they are able to contribute to the social, economic and cultural development of the country, gain an understanding of society, and make correct choices for their further studies and careers. Pupils must attend daily for three years; there are 30 teaching hours per week in all three classes. In class 3, the subjects are divided into A (general education) and B (preparatory studies for university and *TEI*).

Curriculum

The curriculum of the common course of general education in the first two years includes: religion, modern Greek, ancient Greek, history, mathematics, physics, chemistry, geology, foreign languages (English-French-German), physical education, art-music, school vocational guidance, psychology, cosmography, biology, depending on the class and in accordance with Law 309/1976 and subsequent modifications.

The curriculum of the third year includes a common core of general subjects (religion, philosophy, history, rudiments of political science – democratic citizenship, foreign languages, physical education) and the following preparatory subjects depending on the option stream (*desmi*):

Preparatory subject	Option stream			
	1	2	3	4
Modern Greek language and literature	X	X	X	X
Mathematics	X	X		X
Physics	X	X		
Chemistry	X	X		
Biology – Anthropology		X		
Ancient Greek language and literature			X	
Latin			X	
History			X	X
Sociology				X
Political Economy				X

Each option stream is designed to prepare pupils to enter certain faculties of higher education.

The year following the one in which he or she leaves a *Lykeio*, a pupil can, if he or she wishes, apply to faculties prepared for in another option stream, and then study the necessary subjects outside school without needing to attend a *Lykeio*.

The Technical-Vocational *Lykeio* (*Tecniko-Epagelmatiko Lykeio – TEL*)

The aim of this *Lykeio*, in addition to those mentioned under the General *Lykeio,* is to give pupils the necessary technical and vocational knowledge to enable them to develop their skills, so that after leaving school they can successfully work in a specific technical or vocational field. There are 34 hours of tuition per week.

Curriculum

In the 1st class, all pupils follow a common curriculum. There are 21 hours of general subjects (religion, modern Greek, history, mathematics, physics, chemistry, foreign language, physical education, principles of democracy) and 13 hours of orientation subjects in a technical-vocational field

(school vocational guidance, design, mechanics, principles of electricity, principles of economics, agriculture and development, principles of medicine). These form the basis for the sectors of specialization which distinguish the 2nd and 3rd classes, but also make it possible for pupils in the 3rd class to take one of the three option streams – 1, 2 and 4 – of the General *Lykeio*.

In the 2nd class, there are 19 hours of general subjects and 15 hours of vocational subjects. The latter hours include workshop experience in one of the following sectors: engineering, electricity and electronics, construction, chemistry and metallurgy, textiles, applied arts, informatics, economics and administration and geotechnical sector.

Pupils in the 3rd class take a core of general education subjects. In addition, they take one of the option streams mentioned above or follow a course in a specialization department aimed at employment.

If they want to take up one of the places set aside for *TEL* leavers at an Institution of Technological Education (*TEI*), pupils who complete courses in specialization departments at the end of the 1994/95 school year will submit an application and then be selected on the basis of their marks for the final class of the *TEL*. As from 1996, such pupils will take entrance examinations in subjects to be determined shortly.

The Comprehensive *Lykeio* (*Enaio Polykladiko Lykeio – EPL*)

The Comprehensive *Lykeio* (*EPL*) is a new type of school (first introduced in 1984) which is qualitatively different; it is the outcome of combining general and technical education. *EPL* pupils have the option of following whatever course of study they wish: either vocational training leading to a technical occupation or general education preparing for entry to higher education.

In the 1st class, all pupils follow a common curriculum of 31 hours of tuition per week and 3 hours of elective subjects. The 2nd class is divided into six 'cycles' of study which form the starting-point for a group of related occupations or for study at a University or *TEI*. Pupils follow a common curriculum of 16 hours per week, 2 hours of elective subjects and 16 hours of 'cycle' subjects. In the 3rd year, there are 14 hours of common curriculum subjects. In addition, pupils select one of the four option streams if they wish to enter higher education, or further specialize for employment. In the latter case they take the subjects in one of the 17 specialized branches which are an extension of the 'cycle' subjects in the second year.

The common curriculum includes: religion, modern Greek, ancient Greek, history, mathematics, information technology-computers, physics, chemistry, man and society, technology and production, ecology and environment, elements of economics, physical education, foreign languages and careers education.

The 6 'cycles' of study are:

– Man and society;

– Health, natural sciences and social welfare;

– Economics and administration;

– Mechanical Technology;

– Electrical Engineering and Electronic Technology;

– Chemical Technology and Primary Sector Technology.

The 17 branches to which the 'cycles' lead are:

– Option stream C;

– Administrative services – secretaries;

– Librarians;

– Computer science;

– Option stream B;

– Medical Laboratories;

– Social Welfare;

– Option Stream D;

– Economics;

– Applied Arts;

– Option stream A;

– Structural Works;

– Engineering;

– Electricity;

– Electronics;

– Chemistry;

– Agriculture.

After successfully completing the 3rd class, pupils can attend one of the *EPL* (specialization departments) for a further school year.

A series of optional subjects are taught in the afternoon to cultivate pupils' special talents and interests. These subjects relate to the following sectors: music and dance, arts, sports, foreign languages, theatre and cinema, journalism, modern technology and the social sector.

The Classical *Lykeio*

In addition to functioning as a General *Lykeio*, this *Lykeio* aims to broaden pupils' knowledge in the field of classical studies.

The common curriculum, taught for 30 hours in the 1st and 2nd classes, includes, in addition to the subjects studied in the General *Lykeio*, Latin and German. In the 3rd year, there are 10 hours of general education subjects and 20 hours of subjects in the 3rd and 4th option streams.

There are 12 Classical *Lykeia*.

The Ecclesiastical *Lykeio*

This *Lykeio* only admits boys. Its structure is the same as that in the General *Lykeio*, but all pupils must choose the 3rd option stream and more time is devoted to theology. It aims to allow those boys who wish to do so to acquire the qualifications and appropriate behaviour to enter the clergy.

There are 16 Ecclesiastical *Lykeia*.

The Music *Lykeio*

This aims to prepare and train young people who want to pursue a career in the field of music without disregarding their general education, in case they eventually choose another field. There are two Music *Lykeia*.

Lykeio Sports Departments

The establishment of these departments is covered by the same Ministerial Decision as the *Gymnasio* departments. The first *Lykeio* Sports Departments have been in operation experimentally since the 1992/93 school year. They are operating experimentally during the current school year, because there are to be changes in secondary education. There are Sports Departments in 15 *Lykeia* around the country.

In these departments, all the subjects in the *Lykeio* curriculum are taught, including physical education but, in addition, there are two hours of sports training every day. The pupils attending these departments have preferentially been selected from among members of national teams or groups of trainees for national teams, school leavers from *Gymnasio* Sports Departments, and outstanding athletes from local sports clubs.

Assessment and qualifications

Each term teachers assess pupils by means of oral and written tests as in the *Gymnasio*. In addition, at the end of each school year, in June, pupils sit official written examinations in each subject to determine whether they move up to the next year and whether they receive the leaving certificate (*Apolytirio Lykeiou*).

The final mark of each pupil is based on his/her average mark for oral assessment and the marks in the written examinations at the end of the year.

The Teachers' Association makes the final decision on promotion to the next class and on the award of certificates.

4.2 Technical-Vocational School *(TES)*

These are technical schools with a two-year course of study in the case of day schools, and a three-year course of study in the case of evening schools.

At the *TES*, 30 hours of tuition are provided each week in classes 1 and 2, of which 6 hours cover general subjects (modern Greek, mathematics, physics, foreign language, rudiments of democracy)

and 24 hours cover specialization subjects and workshop training.

The procedures for assessing pupils are the same as those in *Lykeia*. Pupils successfully completing the course are awarded a certificate (*Ptychio*) in various specializations (car mechanics, refrigerator technicians, etc.). They can seek employment or enter the first year of all types of *Lykeio* or the 2nd year of the Technical-Vocational or Comprehensive *Lykeio*.

4.3 Teachers

Upper secondary school teachers are university graduates; they have followed four years of university studies in their specialized subject.

Graduates from the institutions of technological education (*TEI*), where studies last three years, may also be appointed in technical vocational *Lykeia* (*TEL*), comprehensive *Lykeia* (*EPL*) and technical vocational schools (*TES*). They teach subjects of a technical nature and have followed a one-year teacher training course in the College of Technical Education (*PATES*). They are also civil servants.

Compulsory introductory and in-service training is organized in the same way as for other levels.

4.4 Statistics 1993/94

		Pupils	Teachers	Schools
General *Lykeia*	State	241,596	16,635	1,099
	Private	13,988	1,094	71
Comprehensive *Lykeia*	State	22,084	1,878	25
Technical Vocational *Lykeia*	State	99,075	6,876	273
	Private	15,592	1,760	80
Ecclesiastical *Lykeia*	State	1,045	102	14
	Private	86	11	1
Technical Vocational Schools *(TES)*	State	35,902	2,882	56
	Private	4,701	650	209

Source: National Statistical Office.

5. Initial vocational training

Law 2009/14.2.1992 established the National System of Vocational Education and Training, with the following aims: the organization, development and provision of vocational training; the formal certification of vocational training; the integration of secondary school leavers into levels of training stipulated in the above law and in Directive 92/51 of the European Union; and the implementation of all kinds of national or Community programmes of vocational education and training.

5.1 Institutes of Vocational Training (IEK)

The Institutes of Vocational Training (IEK) do not correspond to a specific level of education.

Their aim is to deliver every type of vocational training, whether initial or continuing, in order to provide trainees with corresponding qualifications, through the teaching of scientific, technical, vocational and practical subjects; and to enable them to develop corresponding skills, so as to facilitate their vocational integration into society and ensure their adaptation to the changing needs of the production process.

Training takes place both in education institutions – which are either state or private – and in firms and industries in the area where the IEK operates. The student's average amount of practice in real working conditions varies according to the specialization. It is estimated that the practical part of training varies between 25% and 50%.

Considerable efforts have also been made to enable IEK students, towards the end of their course, to be placed in firms.

The various departments of the IEK, in accordance with Law 2009/1992, admit school leavers from Gymnasia, Technical-Vocational Schools, OAED courses and all types of Lykeio, and adults with all levels of education. The Law has been implemented as regards Lykeio leavers; this means that General Lykeia leavers are provided with initial vocational training (which gives young people who have not entered higher education the opportunity to acquire the necessary skills to be integrated into the labour market), while leavers from Technical-Vocational Lykeia (TEL) and Comprehensive Lykeia (EPL) are given the opportunity to supplement their technical knowledge.

There are no tuition fees in IEK. Students are accepted to IEK on the basis of certain conditions such as:

– leaving certificate mark;

– knowledge of foreign languages (for some specializations);

– work experience, taking into account certain social criteria.

The public IEK are housed in the school buildings of existing TEL or EPL or on hired premises.

The school year comprises two separate semesters: winter and spring. The winter semester begins on 1 October and ends on 14 February, and the spring semester begins on 15 February and ends on 30 June.

Training lasts 4 semesters for trainees with the leaving certificate (Apolytirio) of the General Lykeio, the TEL or the EPL. For TEL leavers who continue to specialize in the sector they have studied at the TEL, training lasts 2 semesters and for EPL leavers who continue to specialize in the specialization department they have studied at the EPL, training lasts 1 semester.

At present there are 79 specializations in the state and private IEK.

Trainees must attend theoretical, practical and mixed lessons. During training, assessment takes the form of revision examinations twice a semester; there are final examinations at the end.

Those completing training are awarded a Certificate of Vocational Training (*Vevaiosi epagelmatikis katartisis*) mentioning the specialization and the duration of training. This gives them the right to take part in the final qualifying examinations leading to the award of a Diploma.

The teachers at *IEK* come from the labour market and higher and secondary technical education, and are selected on the basis of their qualifications. For their selection, according to the internal operating regulation of the *IEK*, a committee is set up in the *IEK* in different areas, which is made up of the Director and Deputy Director of the *IEK* and a representative of the Organization for Vocational Education and Training (*OEEK*). In future it is planned that in-service training will be provided periodically.

Statistics 1993/94

	Pupils	Teachers	Schools
State *IEK*	12,926	4,250	57

Source: *OEEK*.

5.2 The Organization for Manpower Employment (OAED)

One of the main activities of the Organization for Manpower Employment (*OAED*) is the provision of technical and vocational training for young people and adults in various technical specializations, in traditional or modern occupations, under the system of initial vocational training – apprenticeship.

The apprenticeship system combines training in the *OAED's* Apprenticeship Schools with practical work, i.e. employment in public or private firms.

The central administration at the *OAED* supervises all of its schools, which exist in all the prefectures of the country. The bodies taking part in the administration are the Ministry of Labour and the General Confederation of Workers of Greece

(*GSEE*) and the Association of Greek Industries (*SEV*). Training provided by the *OAED* is financed by the state budget and the European Union.

Attendance of the training courses is compulsory and free of charge.

The apprenticeship system is intended for unemployed young people aged between 15 and 18, and in exceptional cases up to the age of 23. *Gymnasio* school leavers are accepted.

The apprenticeship course lasts three years. In the first year, the apprentices attend classes at the school every day. In the second and third years, the apprentices attend classes at the school one day a week, and spend the remaining four days doing practical work with the employer.

The content of the curriculum refers to compulsory subjects, not elective or optional subjects. The ratio of theoretical to practical subjects is 75% to 25%.

The apprentices are assessed through final examinations in all sectors. Those who pass are awarded diplomas (*Ptychia*) issued by the *OAED*. These are equivalent to the certificates of the Technical-Vocational Schools (*TES*).

Teachers

The teachers' basic training and their qualifications vary according to the specialization that they are appointed to teach. This means that teachers in *OAED* schools are technical experts – construction site managers, technologists, mechanical engineers, engineers, teachers of general subjects and computing, etc.

According to their official status, permanent teachers make up 35% of the total number of teachers; teachers under contract represent the remaining 65%.

There is no compulsory in-service training, but from time to time the *OAED* organizes various training seminars, either in Greece or abroad, for the in-service training of permanent teachers.

Statistics

About 14,000 to 15,000 trainees attend Apprenticeship Schools each year. There are about 700 *OAED* permanent teachers, and about 1,300 teachers on a works contract each year.

6. Higher education

6.1 Universities *(AEI)*

In accordance with Article 16 paragraph 5 of the Constitution, university education is provided by the State at institutions which are fully self-governing legal entities of public law. State supervision is carried out by the Minister of National Education and Religious Affairs.

There are 18 universities throughout the country, and the newly established Open University in Athens, which is not yet in operation. The universities consist of faculties; these are divided into departments, and the departments into sections. The department is the basic functional academic unit and covers the subject matter of a discipline. The curriculum of the department leads to a uniform Degree (*Ptychio*).

Admission

Candidates must first obtain a *Lykeio* leaving certificate and then take the general entrance examinations which are held every year in the second fortnight of June.

The general examinations include general assessment subjects which lead to the corresponding departments of higher education. Each candidate is examined in four subjects. These subjects are taught during the final class of the *Lykeio*, so candidates tell their school at the beginning of the school year what option stream they aim to follow.

Each candidate can retake examinations an unlimited number of times in all four subjects. During the 2 years following his/her first attempt, the candidate can retake examinations in at least one subject, while marks in the remaining (three) subjects are unchanged.

For some sections, in addition to the general examinations in general assessment subjects, the candidates are also examined in special subjects: e.g. for architectural sections, they are also examined in free-hand sketching and line drawing; for foreign language sections, in the relevant foreign language; for the music studies section, in music subjects, etc.

The number of entrants is restricted throughout the range of higher education (numerus clausus).

Fees/Student finance

Attendance at universities is free of charge. Textbooks are issued free of charge to all students. Food is also provided free of charge, but not to all students; it depends on the student's personal or his/her family's finances.

Academic year

The academic year begins on 1 September and ends on 31 August the following year. Each academic year is organized in two semesters.

Courses

Teaching in individual subject areas is organized along the lines of a study programme, including a list of compulsory subjects and a list from which a choice of subjects must be made.

In most faculties courses last a total of eight semesters; they last 10 semesters in the Polytechnic Schools and the Dental School, and 12 in the Medical School. Each semester includes 13 full weeks for teaching and two to three weeks for examinations.

Assessment/Qualifications

The student's grade in each subject is determined by the professor teaching the course, who is obliged to organize, according to his/her judgment, written and oral examinations. The grade can be based on course material and practical exercises.

Students who fail compulsory subjects are required to repeat that subject the following semester.

Qualifications are issued by the departments; they therefore constitute the Degree (*Ptychio*) of the department concerned.

6.2 Higher technological education *(TEI)*

Higher technological education is provided by institutions which are self-governing legal entities of public law within the scope of Law 1404/83, called Institutions of Technological Education (*TEI*). They are also supervised by the Minister of National Education and Religious Affairs.

TEI are clearly differentiated – in terms of their role and their own and their graduates' orientation, and in terms of subject matter and degrees – from the universities. In particular, they are expected:

- to provide theoretical and practical education suited to the application of scientific, technical, artistic or other knowledge and professional skills;
- to contribute towards forming responsible citizens who are capable of contributing, as executives within the framework of democratic planning, to the economic, social and cultural development of the country;
- to implement the right of all Greek citizens to free education according to their aptitudes and as stipulated by the relevant laws.

There are 14 *TEI* throughout the country, plus 6 *TEI* branches in the same number of towns. The *TEI* comprise departments grouped in faculties covering the main areas of study. The faculties are:

- Graphic Arts and Art Studies;
- Management and Economics;
- Health and Caring Professions;
- Agricultural Technology;
- Applied Technology;
- Food Technology and Nutrition.

Admission

Candidates must have completed the 12 years of general education and must take the general entrance examinations, as mentioned under university education.

Fees/Student finance

Education and books are provided free of charge in *TEI*, and also board and lodging under certain conditions. Students are also entitled to medical care and reduced fares on public transport.

Academic year

The academic year starts on 1 September and ends on 5 July. It is divided into two semesters.

Courses/Assessment/Qualifications

Study courses at *TEI* are based on specialized classes and lectures. Attendance is compulsory. Courses cover a period of six or seven teaching semesters, and one semester of practical training. The duration of each teaching semester is 15 weeks, and each week includes 30-32 teaching hours.

The students are assessed by the teacher of the subject on the basis of tests and assignments to determine their progress, and their performance in the final examinations of each semester.

In order to graduate, each student is required a) to have successfully completed all the courses, b) to have prepared his degree assignment, the grade of which is taken into account when determining the grade of the degree, and c) to have successfully completed practical training in the relevant profession.

TEI graduates are awarded the Degree (*Ptychio*) of the department which they have attended.

Spain

SPAIN (PRE-REFORM)

	UNIVERSITY LEVEL EDUCATION	NON-UNIVERSITY LEVEL EDUCATION	OCCUPATIONAL TRAINING PROGRAMMES (FPO) — WORKSHOP SCHOOLS — SKILLED CRAFT CENTRES (5)
19			
18	UNIVERSITY ORIENTATION COURSE (*COU*) (3)	VOCATIONAL TRAINING (*FPII*) (4)	
17			
16	INTEGRATED SECONDARY EDUCATION (*BUP*) (2)		
15		VOCATIONAL TRAINING (*FPI*) (4)	
14			
13			
12	UPPER CYCLE		
11			
10	**BASIC GENERAL EDUCATION (1)**		
9	**(*EGB*)**		
	INTERMEDIATE CYCLE		
8			
7			
	LOWER CYCLE		
6			
5	NURSERY SCHOOL (*ESCUELA DE PARVULOS*)		
4	**PRE-SCHOOL EDUCATION**		
3			
2	KINDERGARTEN (*JARDIN DE INFANCIA*)		

COMPULSORY EDUCATION (covers ages 6 to 14)

1. *EGB* (*Educación General Básica*) or basic general education covers the 8 years (6 to 14 years) of compulsory education. There is no division between primary and lower secondary education. *EGB* leads to upper secondary education or to lower level vocational training.

2. *BUP* (*Bachillerato Unificado Polivalente*) comprises general education at upper secondary level, preparing for access to university.

3. *COU* (*Curso de Orientación Universitaria*) comprises a one-year university orientation course.

4. *FPI* (*Formación Profesional I*) comprises 2 years of general education and vocational training leading to *FPII*, the second year of *BUP*, or employment. *FPII* comprises 3 years of general education and vocational training leading to certain related university courses, or employment. Evening courses in *FP* are available for employed persons over 16 (*FPI*) and 18 (*FPII*).

5. These training courses can be entered at any stage between 16 and 25. The occupational training programmes (*FPO*) last 800 hours, training in the workshop schools lasts 1 to 3 years, and in the skilled craft centres 6 to 12 months.

·········· = division in the level / type of education.

------ = alternative beginning or end of level / type of education.

SPAIN (POST-REFORM)

	UNIVERSITY LEVEL EDUCATION	NON-UNIVERSITY LEVEL EDUCATION	HIGHER VOCATIONAL TRAINING (2)	OCCUPATIONAL TRAINING/FPO WORKSHOP SCHOOLS SKILLED CRAFT CENTRES (3)
18				
17	BACHILLERATO (1)	INTERMEDIATE VOCATIONAL TRAINING (2)		
16	SECONDARY EDUCATION			
15	2ND CYCLE			
14	COMPULSORY SECONDARY			
13	1ST CYCLE	EDUCATION		
12				
11	3RD CYCLE			
10				
9	2ND CYCLE	PRIMARY EDUCATION		
8				
7	1ST CYCLE			
6				
5	2ND CYCLE			
4				
3	INFANT EDUCATION			
2				
1	1ST CYCLE			
0				

COMPULSORY EDUCATION (spanning ages 6 to 16)

1. *Bachillerato* comprises general education at upper secondary level providing access to higher education and to employment.

2. Intermediate and Higher Vocational Training comprises specific vocational training for employment. The diploma obtained at the end of Higher Vocational Training will also give direct access to certain related university courses.

3. These training courses can be entered at any age between 16 and 25. The occupational training programmes (*FPO*) last 800 hours, training in the workshop schools lasts 1 to 3 years, and in skilled craft centres 6 to 12 months.

·········· = division in the level / type of education.

‑ ‑ ‑ ‑ ‑ = alternative beginning or end of level / type of education.

1. Responsibilities and administration

1.1 Background

Spain covers an area of 504,759 square kilometres and has a population of 39,790,055 (1993).

Spain is a parliamentary monarchy. With the first democratic elections in 1977, the Democratic Central Union Party, a centralist party, governed from 1977 to 1982 and the Spanish Workers' Socialist Party, a party of left-wing moderates, has governed since. Legislative power resides in the General Assembly of the Spanish Parliament – the Congress of Deputies and the Senate. Executive power is exercised by the President and his Government.

According to the 1978 Constitution, Spanish territory is organized into Municipalities, Provinces, Autonomous Communities and the State. The seventeen Autonomous Communities can assume certain powers, including responsibility in educational matters, but the State holds sole powers in certain matters.

Castillian is the official state language and all Spaniards have a duty to learn it and the right to use it. Other languages are also official within their respective Autonomous Communities in accordance with their Statutes (*Estatutos*). Official languages within their respective Autonomous Communities are Catalan, Galician, Basque (*Euskera*) and Valencian.

Employment by sectors is as follows: agriculture 5%; industry 39% (of which 29% in manufacturing); services 56%. The overall unemployment rate (16 to 55+) in 1993 was 22.725%.

Spain does not have an official state religion. Public authorities take into account all the religious beliefs in Spanish society and maintain cooperative links with the Catholic Church and other religions.

Under the terms of an agreement with the Holy See regarding the teaching of the Catholic religion, the Spanish State recognizes the fundamental right to religious education and undertakes to guarantee that this right is exercised.

1.2 Basic principles: education

The 1978 Constitution, which contains the basic guidelines that apply to all legislation in the area of education, put forward three fundamental principles: the recognition that education is one of the basic rights that the State must guarantee; other fundamental rights relating to education are recognized; and educational responsibilities are divided between the Central Government and the Autonomous Communities.

1.3 Distribution of responsibilities

The 1978 Constitution determines the distribution of responsibilities between the State and the 17 Autonomous Communities into which the country is territorially divided. In terms of education (pre-school, primary and secondary education, school 'regulated' vocational training and higher education), the Constitution identifies a series of areas over which the State has exclusive competence and others for which the Autonomous Communities may assume responsibility. An Autonomous Community assumes 'full powers' over education when it takes over all the regulatory and executive responsibilities not included within the State's exclusive area of competence.

The seven Spanish Autonomous Communities which at present enjoy full powers over education are: Andalusia, the Basque Country, the Canary

Islands, Catalonia, Galicia, Navarra and Valencia. It is expected that all the Autonomous Communities will gradually acquire these powers, with the result that the Spanish education system will be managed by 17 administrations, under the coordination of the Ministry for Education and Science (*Ministerio de Educación y Ciencia – MEC*). The Autonomous Communities which do not yet have such powers are progressively initiating new educational activities through cooperation agreements with the *MEC*. Spain currently has eight educational administrations, corresponding to those Autonomous Communities with full powers for education and the *MEC* itself.

Both the Ministry and the Autonomous Communities have decentralized provincial or municipal services, with real managerial responsibilities.

Non-school or 'occupational' vocational training is the responsibility of the Ministry of Labour and Social Security in collaboration with its National Employment Institute (*Instituto Nacional de Empleo – INEM*) and the Autonomous Communities with full powers over the administration of vocational training – Andalusia, Galicia, Valencia and Catalonia (as in the education field, transfer of powers to the Autonomous Communities is in progress). Other public and private bodies, the social partners and professional organizations participate in training provision.

All institutions may be state, state-subsidized private and non-state-subsidized private, under the responsibility of the central or autonomous education administrations.

Pre-school establishments may also be set up and managed by the Ministry of Labour and Social Security and the municipalities.

1.4 Administration

State

The Constitution gives the State exclusive responsibility for the following aspects of education, essential for ensuring the basic unity of the system throughout Spain:

– The regulation of conditions to be satisfied so that academic and vocational qualifications are recognized as valid throughout Spain.

– The promulgation and implementation of basic guidelines concerning the fundamental principle of the right to education.

– The general regulation of the education system (the duration of compulsory schooling, the levels, sections (*grados*), specialist subjects, cycles, and the number of academic years corresponding to each; requirements for moving up from one educational level to the next; minimum curriculum and examination requirements and the establishment of the basic characteristics of the official school register (*Libro de Escolaridad*).

– The definition of minimum requirements for education institutions (the qualifications of teaching staff, teacher/pupil ratios, facilities and equipment, and the number of school places).

– The regulation of basic education, guaranteeing the right and duty to learn the Castilian (Spanish) language, notwithstanding the responsibility of each Autonomous Community to develop its own language.

– 'Higher Inspection' of the education system.

– Student grant policy.

– International cooperation in education.

– General planning of investment in education, in accordance with forecasts provided by the Autonomous Communities.

The Central Educational Administration with exclusive national responsibility for education is the *MEC*, which is required to coordinate its activities with those of the Autonomous Educational Administrations (*Administraciones Educativas Autonómas*). Moreover, the *MEC* is responsible for administering education in the ten Autonomous Communities which have not yet had full powers for education devolved to them. The *MEC* is headed by one Minister assisted by a Management Board. The higher authorities through which the *MEC* carries out its functions are:

– the Secretariat of State for Education (*Secretaría de Estado de Educación*), which includes the Directorates-General for Educational Renewal (*Renovación Pedagógica*), Schools (*Centros Escolares*), Regulated Vocational Training and

Educational Promotion (*Formación Profesional Reglada y Promoción Educativa*), Coordination (*Coordinación*) and 'Higher Inspection' (*Alta Inspección*);

- the State Secretariat for Universities and Research (*Secretaría de Estado de Universidades e Investigación*), which includes the Directorates-General for Higher Education (*Enseñanza Superior*) and for Scientific and Technical Research (*Investigación Científica y Técnica*);

- the Higher Council for Sport (*Consejo Superior de Deportes*), which includes the Directorates-General for Sport (*Deportes*) and for Sports Infrastructure (*Infraestructuras Deportivas*);

- the Sub-Secretariat for Education and Science (*Subsecretaría de Educación y Ciencia*), which includes the Technical General Secretariat (*Secretaría General Técnica*) and the Directorates-General for Planning and Investment (*Programación e Inversiones*) and for Staff and Services (*Personal y Servicios*).

Furthermore, in those **Autonomous Communities with full educational powers**, there exists an **Education and Science Office** (*Oficina de Educación y Ciencia*) in each province, responsible for the functions and services which have not been transferred since they form part of the State's responsibilities.

In the **Autonomous Communities without devolved educational powers**, education is administered by the *MEC*'s **Provincial Directorates** (*Direcciones provinciales*). These bodies are responsible for managing staff employment and administration (teaching and other staff), authorizing educational institutions, replacing textbooks and teaching material, organizing individual study grants, organizing transport and catering services, residential holiday centres and residential schools (*Escuelas-Hogar*), as well as maintenance and equipment in non-university institutions. Provincial Directorates comprise a General Secretariat, Educational Programme Units (*Unidades de Programas Educativos*) and Construction and Equipment Units (*Construcciones y Equipamientos*), and the Technical Inspection Service of the province (*Servicio de Inspección Técnica*).

However, educational decentralization does not merely involve redistributing powers amongst the different administrative levels, but also encouraging

social participation. The national advisory bodies responsible for social participation are the State School Council (*Consejo Escolar del Estado*), the General Council for Vocational Training (*Consejo General de la Formación Profesional*) and the University Council (*Consejo de Universidades*) (see 1.8).

Autonomous Communities

It is necessary to differentiate between those Autonomous Communities with full powers and those which continue to be administered by the *MEC*.

The former have their own administrative structures which, in principle, correspond to the organization of the central administration of education and training. For example, a department responsible for education alone or in combination with science, or culture or sport with Directorates-General for the different types of education and training and functions.

Autonomous Communities without devolved powers still have an administrative structure (department) for matters relating to education, albeit in conjunction with other administrative bodies.

The remit of Autonomous Communities with full powers includes responsibility for education institutions (construction, renovation, equipment), teaching staff (provision of places in state education institutions within their own sphere of influence), technical inspection services, as well as the administration and implementation of state provisions for the planning and regulation of levels of education, option streams (*modalidades*), sections and specialisms.

The social participation body in the Autonomous Communities is the Regional School Council (*Consejos Escolares Territoriales*).

Local

The municipal authorities (town councils) are responsible for local education administration. Since their specific educational jurisdiction has not yet been legally established, there is no individual institution common to all town councils. Most have a Municipal Education Department (*Concejalía de*

Educación) which is responsible for the provision and maintenance of school buildings and the management of municipal education-related programmes. Some town councils have created Municipal Education Institutes (*Institutos Municipales de Educación*) to carry out these tasks. The Municipal School Councils (*Consejos Escolares Municipales)* are the local social participation bodies.

Educational institutions

In publicly funded **non-university education** institutions, responsibility for administrative and financial management lies either with individuals (*unipersonales)* or with collegiate bodies (*colegiados)*. 'Individuals' include a head teacher, a secretary and a head of studies (*Jefe de Estudios*), and 'collegiate bodies' include a School Council (*Consejo Escolar*) and a Teachers' Assembly (*Claustro de Profesores*). Publicy financed private institutions (*concertados*) are only required to have a head teacher, a School Council and a Teachers' Assembly. Legislation does not lay down any requirements for organization and participation in completely private institutions.

The body common to all publicly funded institutions is the School Council, consisting of representatives of the teaching staff, parents, pupils, etc. Its responsibilities include electing the head teacher, school discipline, pupil admission and financial management.

The Constitution and the 1983 Law on University Reform (*Ley de Reforma Universitaria – LRU*) confer upon **universities** specific authority to carry out their teaching and research mandate, endowing them with legal status and administrative powers. According to the *LRU*, a minimum requirement is for the statutes of each university to establish a series of collegiate governing bodies – Social Council (*Consejo Social*), University Senate (*Claustro Universitario*), Governing Boards (*Juntas de Gobierno*), Faculty Boards (*Juntas de Facultad*), etc., as well as governing bodies composed of individuals (Rector, Vice-Rectors, General Secretary, Faculty Deans, etc.). These bodies are responsible for administration and financial management. Again, no requirements have been stipulated in legislation concerning organization and participation in private universities.

In state universities, the participation of all sectors involved is two-fold: internal, encompassing the various sectors of the university community, particularly collegiate bodies (professors, students and administrative and service staff), and external, through the Social Council, the university's social participation body. The Social Council includes representatives from the university itself, and from unions and employers' organizations. It is responsible for approving the budgets and supervising the financial activities of the university, as well as for providing services.

It is the institution itself, regardless of whether it is state or private, university or non-university, which is responsible for **pupil/student assessment**, and for awarding the corresponding certificates.

Similarly, at non-university level the institution itself is responsible for the selection of **textbooks and curricular material** from those authorized by the respective educational authorities, which does not prevent teaching staff from introducing other support material into their classrooms. Moreover, groups of teachers may opt to draw up their own curricular material with the purpose of adapting the curriculum to the needs of their pupils. At university level such choice is encompassed within the framework of professorial independence (*libertad de cátedra*).

1.5 Inspection

The inspection of Spanish education takes place at two levels: 'Higher Inspection' and 'Technical Inspection'.

Higher inspection (*Alta Inspección*) is carried out by the *MEC*. Territorial state higher inspection services have been set up in the seven Autonomous Communities that already hold full educational powers. The aim of higher inspection is to ensure that the rules for guaranteeing the structure and organization of the education system are observed. Its functions include: confirming that the plans, curricula and educational guidelines, as well as teaching material, are in line with the provisions laid down by the Central Administration; checking that the requirements determined by the State for the general structure and organization of the respective option streams, levels, cycles, duration of studies, admission requirements, etc. are being fulfilled; verifying that the courses available comply with the provisions laid down by the State with respect to the award of qualifications; ensuring that basic conditions are observed for guaranteeing equality for all Spaniards with regard to linguistic duties and rights; making sure that the award of study grants and subsidies is appropriate, etc.

Technical inspections (*Inspecciones Tecnicas de educación*). Each of the eight educational administrations (*MEC* plus the Communities with full powers), has its own organization which carries out inspections within its own territory. These functions have a dual purpose: both to provide guidance and support for education work and to monitor and evaluate the educational system in order to ensure that its educational objectives are satisfactorily met.

1.6 Financing

Education funding comes from both public and private sources. Public funds are contributed by the *MEC* (although other Ministries also contribute to a certain degree), by the Autonomous Communities and by local authorities. Private funding is provided by families and other entities responsible for paying private educational costs.

Public funds are not only devoted to state education, but are also used to subsidize some private institutions (*centros privados concertados*) (guaranteeing that they remain free of charge during the period of compulsory education), and to pay student grants and allowances.

The greater part of public funds is spent on staffing costs (financing for the salaries of teachers in public and subsidized private institutions initially comes from the Administration), the purchase of goods and services, subsidies for private education institutions and investment. Education institutions receive financing for specific items and must justify the use of such financing to the authorities.

In state universities, students are required to make a contribution towards education costs, through registration fees which are fixed by the Autonomous Communities in which the university is located, or by the *MEC* in those Communities which have not yet assumed full powers over education. However, in private universities, students pay the full costs through corresponding registration fees which each university is entitled to set independently.

Education is free of charge in publicly funded schools.

At all stages of education and in both state and private institutions, families finance extra activities such as meals, school transport, out-of-school activities, as well as textbooks and teaching materials. Public funding, in the form of grants, is available for textbooks, transport, meals and accommodation in certain circumstances (depending on the pupils/students' level of academic achievement and family income). Students awarded grants are exempt from tuition fees.

1.7 Private schools

Private establishments are usually classified by their administrative authority – usually an association, the Catholic Church or other religious group.

Private schools may be divided into subsidized (*centros concertados*) and non-subsidized (*centros no concertados*) establishments, depending on whether they receive public funding.

Non-subsidized private schools are subject to a general approval regime, and enjoy complete freedom of internal organization, choice of teachers, admission requirements, rules of conduct, and financial administration.

However, in order to receive public funding, subsidized private schools must meet the following requirements:

– provide education free of charge and be non-profit-making;

– establish a School Council as the chief management and administrative body;

– observe similar admission criteria to state schools;

– recruit teaching staff by means of a controlled procedure;

– maintain the average pupil/teacher ratio set by the Government;

– comply with the minimum curriculum and examination requirements.

1.8 Advisory bodies

The **State School Council** (*Consejo Escolar del Estado*) is involved in the general planning of education and basic standards, and advises on legislation. The Council comprises a Chairman and Secretary-General (nominated by the Minister of Education), a Vice-Chairman elected by the Council and 80 advisers including teachers from public and private institutions and universities, representatives of education authorities, parents, pupils, administrative and service staff and employers' organizations.

The **General Council for Vocational Training** (*Consejo General de Formacion Profesional*) advises the Government on matters concerning 'regulated' and 'occupational' vocational training and vocational guidance. It also draws up (with Government approval) and monitors the implementation of the National Vocational Training Programme (*Programma Nacional de Formación Profesional*). It comprises 39 members, equal representatives of the social partners and the Ministries of Education and of Labour and Social Security. It is chaired alternately by the Ministers of the latter. Alternately, Vice-Chairmen represent the Ministries and the social partners.

The **University Council** (*Consejo de Universidades*) has the task of administering, coordinating, planning, proposing and advising in matters concerning higher education. It is chaired by the Minister of Education. Members include those responsible for university education in the Autonomous Communities with full powers, rectors of public universities and other prestigious persons from university circles.

1.9 'Occupational' vocational training *(Formación profesional ocupacional)*

Within their respective fields of competence, and in addition to the vocational training provided in schools by the Ministry for Education and Science (*MEC*) and the Autonomous Communities, the National Employment Institute (*Instituto Nacional de Empleo – INEM*) and the Autonomous Communities are responsible for the provision of 'occupational' vocational training. In addition, other public and private bodies, the social partners and professional organizations participate, channelling their contribution via 'Programme Contracts' (*Contratos programas*) and cooperation agreements.

The Ministry of Labour and Social Security is responsible for funding and managing the training institutions, through the *INEM* and the Autonomous Communities with full powers. The criteria for allocating *INEM* resources, subsidies and funding are formulated according to existing needs, programmes, course levels, degree of difficulty in providing training programmes, suitability of institutional facilities, etc.

The curriculum is initially drawn up by the *INEM* and the course is offered to those involved in occupational vocational training (cooperating centres, employers' organizations, the social partners, etc.). This is preceded by a three-year plan of training initiatives to establish the distribution of priority groups at national and Autonomous Community level. A plan for administering the National Training and Professional Insertion Plan (*Plan Nacional de Formación e Inserción Profesional – FIP Plan*) is also drawn up by the *INEM* or, as the case may be, by the Autonomous Communities having full powers. The corresponding committees draw up and submit a report on these plans to the General Council for Vocational Training (*Consejo General de la Formacion Profesional*) (See 1.8).

The *INEM* National Executive Committee (*Comisión Ejecutiva Nacional*), composed of its Director-General and eight committee members (delegates from the most representative employers' and trade union organizations and from the public administration), supervises and monitors the application of agreements adopted by the General Council, identifies in advance any issues to be submitted to the General Council and carries out any tasks which the Council may delegate to it, and proposes measures which are deemed to be necessary in order to better fulfil the aims of the *INEM*.

The Ministry of Labour and Social Security, through the Directorate-General for Employment (*Dirección General de Empleo*), is responsible for trainee assessment and evaluating the results of *FIP Plan* training courses. The competent employment administrations are responsible for delivering the relevant vocational certificates.

Within the Ministry of Labour and Social Security, there is a Directorate-General for Work Inspection and Social Security (*Dirección General de Inspección de Trabajo y Seguridad Social*) and a General Inspectorate for Services (*Inspección General de Servicios*) which participate, like the *INEM* Provincial Departments and the Directorate-General for Employment, in the assessment, selection and guidance process for pupils and training courses, taking into account the objectives defined in the plan and the type of course.

1.10 Recent legislation on education

The three main education Laws concerning the right to education under the provisions of the 1978 Constitution, approved by Parliament are:

- the Basic Law regulating the Right to Education (*Ley Orgánica del Derecho a la Educación – LODE*) of 1985;

- the Basic Law on University Reform (*Ley Orgánica de Reforma Universitaria – LRU*) of 1983;

- the Basic Law on the General Structure and Organization of the Education System (*Ley Orgánica de Ordenación General del Sistema Educativo – LOGSE*) of 1990.

The *LOGSE* has given rise to a complete reform of the non-university education system. This reform will be carried out gradually over a period of nine years, beginning with the 1991/92 academic year. The main objectives of this reform are:

- To extend free compulsory and comprehensive education to the age of 16, which is the minimum legal working age.

- To reorganize the various levels of education as follows:

0-6 years	Infant Education (non-compulsory)
6-12 years	Primary Education (compulsory)
12-16 years	Compulsory secondary education (*Educación Secundaria Obligatoria - ESO*)
16-18 years	*Bachillerato* (non-compulsory)
16+ years	Intermediate and Higher Vocational Training (*Formación Profesional - FP*).

- To establish a new curricular policy according to which the Autonomous Administrations, schools and pupils (through their choice of options) will each play their part in determining the final form of the curriculum, based on a minimum core curriculum established by the Central Administration for the whole State (*Enseñanzas Mínimas*). The term curriculum covers the whole set of aims, content, teaching methods and assessment criteria for each of the levels, stages, cycles, sections and option streams (*modalidades*) in the education system.

- To guarantee the educational and vocational guidance of pupils, especially with respect to the different education options and the transition from school to working life.

The new system is being introduced progressively according to the following timetable:

YEAR	LEVEL OF EDUCATION
1991/92	Infant Education
1992/93	1st and 2nd years of Primary Education
1993/94	3rd and 4th years of Primary Education
1994/95	5th year of Primary Education
1995/96	6th year of Primary Education
1996/97	1st year of *ESO*
1997/98	2nd year of *ESO*
1998/99	3rd year of *ESO* and 1st year of *Bachillerato*
1999/2000	4th year of *ESO*, 2nd year of *Bachillerato* and Intermediate Vocational Training.

Higher Vocational Training will be introduced gradually throughout the whole reform timetable.

Some of the Autonomous Communities are planning to introduce the new system within a shorter period of time. The reform's own driving force may also bring about faster implementation in particular sectors, such as vocational training.

2. Pre-school education

Pre-school education is not compulsory, and the only access requirement is the age of pupils entering education at each level. In public pre-school establishments education is free, and admission criteria may only be applied when demand for places exceeds supply. Priority criteria for public and subsidized private schools include distance from home, annual family income and the presence of brothers or sisters at the school. Private pre-school establishments can set their own admission requirements. The *LOGSE* will guarantee the provision of school places for all children who request post-reform 'infant education' (*Educación Infantil*).

In public establishments, parents of pupils pay certain costs (catering and transport, teaching materials and textbooks), depending on their income. They cover all costs in private centres.

Public institutions are mixed, private ones are only exceptionally single-sex. Class groups are organized according to age. A pupil's intellectual ability or school achievement must not be used as criteria for class grouping.

In pre-school institutions offering the second cycle, the school year runs from the second fortnight of September to the second fortnight of June, covering 175 days or 35 weeks of five days. The overall weekly timetable covers 25 hours. The school day lasts five hours, usually divided into morning and afternoon sessions of three and two hours respectively, with a two-hour interval between the two (9.00/10.00 a.m. to 12.00 a.m./1.00 p.m. and 2.30/3.00 p.m. to 4.30/5.00 p.m.). For the first cycle there may be a more flexible timetable in order for it to fulfil its social function.

It is estimated that in 1994/95, 55.9% of 3-year-olds attend a pre-school institution. The figure is 99.8% for 4- to 5-year-olds.

2.1 Pre-reform pre-school education (*Educación Preescolar*)

The General Education Act (*LGE*) of 1970 for the first time included pre-school education as a specific level of the Spanish education system.

Pre-school education is divided into two stages:

- *Jardín de Infancia* (kindergarten), for children aged two and three years old;

- *Escuela de Párvulos* (nursery school), for children aged four and five years old.

Both kindergarten and nursery schools may be state or privately run.

The schools aim to foster the harmonious development of the children's personalities, both as individuals and as part of a group.

Curriculum and assessment

The main features of the curricula for the two stages of pre-school education are:

- the global nature of this level of education;

- the definition of basic standards (*Niveles Básicos de Referencia*) (targets);

- structuring into subject areas, subdivided into subject blocks and work topics.

Six main subject areas have been established: Spanish language, mathematics, understanding of nature and the social environment, art education, physical education and personal and social relationships.

Religious education is also available depending on parents' wishes. In addition, the Autonomous

Communities of the Balearic Islands, Catalonia, Galicia, Navarre, Valencia and the Basque Country teach their own languages.

The *LGE* underlines the need for teaching to involve a wealth of experience, learning through play, spontaneity and creativity, and the interaction of personalities in a group.

Planning should be coordinated between teachers at pre-school level and those in the first cycle of *EGB* to ensure continuity.

Pupil assessment is continuous and designed purely to provide information to a pupil's own teacher and parents. For each of the subject areas, assessment is based above all on teachers' observations of their pupils.

Teachers can organize additional and support activities for pupils with learning difficulties.

2.2 Post-reform pre-school education: infant education (Educación Infantil)

Under the *LOGSE,* pre-school education is now called infant education (*Educación Infantil*). Infant education becomes an integral part of the education system but will remain optional. It is divided into two cycles: for children from 0 to 3 years old and from 3 to 6 years old.

The public authorities will ensure that a sufficient number of school places are available to all those who require them. Infant schools may offer only the first cycle of pre-school education, only the second, or both. In order to offer both cycles, educational institutions will need to provide a minimum of six units (three for each cycle), and fulfil a set of basic requirements; the minimum number of units needed to offer only one of these cycles is three. Units will contain a maximum of eight pupils of under one year old, 13 of one to two years old, 20 of two to three years old and 25 of three to six years old.

Public establishments offering infant education which are authorized by the *MEC* or Autonomous Communities with full educational powers are called *Escuelas de Educación Infantil.* The *Escuelas de Educación Infantil* under the responsibility of the *MEC* or Autonomous Communities with full

powers usually offer only the second cycle and are attached to schools offering primary education. Those under the responsibility of other Administrations also offer the first cycle.

Private establishments authorized by the *MEC* or Autonomous Communities with full powers are called *Centros de Educación Infantil* and offer only the first or second cycle of infant education, or both.

There are other institutions with a regular intake of children under six years, which do not have administrative authorization as education centres. These are called *Guarderías* or other names and have until the year 2000 to fulfil a set of legal requirements (those mentioned above and others) to become authorized education centres.

The basic aim of this stage is the child's physical, intellectual, emotional, social and spiritual development. However, the *LOGSE* recognizes that it is undoubtedly educational in nature, as opposed to providing supervision and care, which has very often been the case in the past.

Curriculum and assessment

Curricula are centred on three subject areas which relate to the sphere of experience and development of young children: identity and personal independence, the physical and social environment, and communication and representation.

Each of these subject areas has to be handled differently for each of the cycles. The first cycle concentrates on the development of movement, body control, initial expressions of communication and language, the discovery of personal identity and the first elements of social interaction and relationships. In the second cycle, the aim is for children to learn to make use of language, to discover the physical and social characteristics of the environment in which they live, to build a positive and balanced self-image, and to develop behavioural habits which will allow them to achieve basic personal independence.

Again, there must be a global approach to teaching, based on experience, activities and play, in an atmosphere of affection and trust. Similarly, pupil assessment has to be global, continuous and formative. This allows the teacher to ascertain the effect of teaching methods and the goals to be pursued. Assessment techniques include interviews with parents and the direct and systematic observation of children by teaching staff.

The school timetable must be organized in an integrated way and include activities and experiences which respect a child's rhythms of activity, play and rest. No timetables have been fixed at national level. Teachers can organize activities and experiments to foster learning and development and prevent the aggravation of learning difficulties.

Again, infant education must be closely coordinated with primary education, in order to guarantee a smooth transition from one to the other.

2.3 Teachers

Initial training for teachers at pre-school level (and *EGB* level) is provided by University *EGB* Teacher Training Colleges (*Escuelas Universitarias de Profesorado de EGB*), which are intermediate-level university institutions attached to universities. The qualification obtained on successful completion of training is the Diploma in *EGB* Teaching (*Diplomado en Profesorado de EGB*). Courses last three years and students may specialize in philology, human sciences, science, special education and pre-school education.

Initial training for pre-school and primary teachers is now subject to reform and must comply with the provisions of the *LOGSE*. The new qualification of *Maestro* (teacher) replaces that of *EGB* teacher. Training continues to be provided in University Teacher Training Colleges, now called *Escuelas Universitarias de formación del Profesorado*. The three-year concurrent course combines academic training with general pedagogy, including teaching practice. Students may specialize in infant education, primary education, foreign languages, music education, physical education, special education and education for pupils with speech and/or hearing impairments.

In order to teach at pre-school level, *Maestros* must have specialized in infant education. They are qualified to teach all subject areas at this level. During the first cycle, pre-school institutions may employ other teaching staff, such as senior technical specialists in infant education (*Técnicos superiores*

en Educación Infantil) or technical specialists in kindergarten (*Técnicos especialistas en Jardín de Infancia*), who work in the same way as teachers.

Pre-school teachers, as well as those at primary and secondary levels, include two groups: public sector teachers (who work in state institutions and may either be state officials or contract teachers, otherwise known as *interinos* (interim teachers)); and private sector teachers (employed by private or private subsidized institutions, who have the status of company employees).

Access to a permanent state teaching post, whether it be pre-school, primary or secondary, is by means of a competitive examination (*concurso-oposición*) of merit and ability, which is organized by the various education authorities.

Teaching staff in private education are subject to the normal rules which govern employment contracts. Access to a teaching post is negotiated on a commercial basis, and results in a work contract signed by the owner of the school. It can be of variable duration, ranging from one year to an indefinite contract. Teachers in private schools are required to possess the same initial qualifications as teachers in state schools.

The *LOGSE* stipulates that in-service training is a right and an obligation for teachers at all levels of education. Training activities have a specific impact on a teacher's professional career, either leading to success in competitive examinations or competitions, or as a prerequisite for teachers in *MEC* territory who wish to obtain a specific increase in salary. In order to obtain this supplement, teachers need to prove that they have participated in training courses of a total duration of at least 100 hours every six years.

2.4 Statistics 1991/92

	Public	Private
Pupils	635,238	390,509
Teachers*	199,202	83,538
Schools	18,759*	8,509*
	(29,190)**	(14,525)**

* pre-school and *EGB*.
** groups of pre-school pupils.

Source: Ministry of Education and Science (*MEC*).

3. Compulsory education

According to the *LGE*, basic general education (*Educación General Básica – EGB*) lasting eight years, makes up the compulsory education to be taken by all Spaniards between the ages of six and fourteen – equivalent to primary and part of lower secondary education in some other countries, but combined in a single common school.

The *LOGSE* extends compulsory education by two years – to age 16 – and establishes a difference between Primary Education (for pupils aged 6 to 12) and Compulsory Secondary Education (for pupils aged 12 to 16).

4. Primary education

All pupils are accepted in *EGB* and in Primary Education (*Educación Primaria*) as long as they have reached the required age; pupils need not have attended pre-school education. Admission criteria may be applied on the same basis as at pre-school level.

In state schools all levels of compulsory education are completely free. Financial assistance is provided for meals, transport and boarding facilities on the basis of family income. Subsidized private schools must satisfy a series of requirements in order to receive public financing. Completely private schools are financed solely through family contributions.

In both state and private schools, families cover the cost of teaching material and textbooks, but financial assistance is available from the State.

State institutions are mixed, private ones are sometimes single sex. School time is organized in the same way as at pre-school level.

4.1 Pre-reform primary education (*Educación General Básica – EGB*)

State *EGB* schools are mainly set up by the *MEC* and the Autonomous Communities.

EGB comprises three cycles:

– Lower Cycle – 1st and 2nd years, for children aged 6 to 8;

– Intermediate Cycle – 3rd, 4th and 5th years, for children aged 8 to 11;

– Upper Cycle – 6th, 7th and 8th years, for children aged 11 to 14.

The cycle constitutes the basic unit of organization in terms of curriculum, assessment and remedial work. Pupils are assigned to classes by age. Flexibility allows for pupil heterogeneity – pupils are never grouped according to sex or learning ability.

The team of teachers is allotted to each cycle and the same teacher remains with the class throughout a whole cycle. During the upper cycle, teachers are allotted to certain areas and even subjects on the basis of continuity within cycles and subject specialization. Subject specialists teach English, French, music and physical education. Each group is therefore taught by several teachers per year, but one teacher is appointed as the tutor for each group.

The following text covers only the Upper Cycle because the Lower and Intermediate Cycles have now been abolished in accordance with the timetable for the implementation of the reform of the education system.

Curriculum, assessment and qualifications

The curricula and guidelines for the *EGB* are defined by the *MEC*, allowing for adequate flexibility to adjust them to Spain's various geographical regions. The subjects are grouped into areas of knowledge and are taught at the same level to all pupils in the same class.

The curriculum of the upper cycle comprises the following compulsory subject areas: Spanish language (Castilian) and literature, mathematics, modern foreign language, social sciences, natural sciences, arts, basic technology, physical education and sport, and religious education.

At the end of each year in the upper cycle, pupils who have not obtained a positive overall mark must take an examination in the subjects they did not pass if they are to move up to the next year. A pupil who does not receive a positive mark at the end of a year may have to undertake remedial work or (after consulting the pupil's parents) be required to repeat the year.

After eight years of compulsory education, pupils who have been successful in the three cycles of *EGB* receive the School Graduate Certificate (*Graduado Escolar*), which entitles them to enter upper secondary school (*BUP* or *FP*). There is no examination for this certificate. Other pupils may continue their education in institutions of basic general education and sit an examination called *Prueba de Madurez* in the subjects they failed. These examinations are prepared and assessed by teachers in the individual schools. Pupils aged 16, who have still failed to obtain the *Graduado Escolar* certificate, receive the School Attendance Certificate (*Certificado de Escolaridad*), which only entitles them to take up vocational training.

4.2 Post-reform primary education (*Educación Primaria*)

Primary education lasts six years and is divided into three two-year cycles, corresponding to ages 6 to 8 years, 8 to 10 years and 10 to 12 years respectively. The aim of primary education is to provide all children with a common education which allows them to acquire basic cultural skills and knowledge relating to oral expression, reading, writing and arithmetic, and progressive independence within their environment.

Primary education institutions should have at least one class (with a maximum of 25 pupils) for each school year and offer the three above-mentioned cycles.

Pupils are generally assigned to classes by age and remain in the same group throughout primary school. In rural schools, for practical reasons, classes include pupils of different ages.

Each group of pupils is assigned to one class teacher throughout each cycle, who acts as their tutor and is responsible for teaching the majority of subjects. There are specialist teachers for physical education, foreign languages and music.

Curriculum and assessment

The curriculum is organized into areas of knowledge and experience. An annual school timetable has been established by the *MEC* corresponding to the minimum core curriculum requirements (*Enseñanzas Mínimas*) which have to be met nationwide and respect the concept of comprehensive and integrated teaching. These subject areas, compulsory for all pupils, are: knowledge of the natural, social and cultural environment (175 hours in the first cycle and 170 hours in the second and third cycles), artistic education (140 hours, 105 hours), physical education (140 hours, 105 hours), Castilian language and literature (350 hours, 275 hours), mathematics (175 hours, 170 hours), Catholic religion (which schools are obliged to offer but which is optional for pupils) / alternative study activities (105 hours, 105 hours) and foreign languages (170 hours in the second and third cycles).

The Autonomous Communities with two official languages, Castilian and their own language, can devote 10% of the total time allocated to language teaching to the teaching of their own language.

Foreign language learning is compulsory from the first year of the second cycle (i.e. at age eight). This is a significant innovation, since in *EGB* foreign language learning did not begin until 11 years of age.

Assessment is continuous (using various tests) and comprehensive (taking into account the different subject areas), in accordance with pre-defined objectives. It is based on the pupil's achievements throughout the cycle. It falls to the tutor to take the appropriate decisions on completion of the cycle, taking into consideration the reports of the other teachers for the particular group of pupils. In principle, pupils move automatically from one cycle to the next. If a pupil's results are not satisfactory at the end of a cycle, he/she may remain in that cycle for one more year. However, this may only happen in exceptional cases and is permitted only once during this phase. Furthermore, when it is noted that a pupil is not responding to the overall planned objectives, teachers are required to provide appropriate additional teaching and, where necessary, adapt the curriculum.

Educational **guidance** is provided by tutors.

4.3 Teachers

The minimum qualification needed to teach at *EGB* level is the Diploma from University *EGB* Teacher Training Colleges (*Diplomado en las Escuelas Universitarias de Profesorado de EGB*). (See 2.).

Primary education will in future be provided by *Maestros* with specialist training in primary education, which covers all the subject areas at this level, except music, physical education and foreign languages. These subject areas will be provided only by *Maestros* with the corresponding specialist training.

In order to teach in state primary schools, teachers must belong to the Teachers' Association (*Cuerpo de Maestros*) or be an interim teacher. For teachers in the private sector, the same requirements for initial training apply as in the state sector, and contracts are negotiable, as for private pre-school teaching staff.

The status of teachers and in-service training requirements are the same as at pre-school level.

4.4 Statistics 1991/92

	Public	Private
Pupils	3,015,496	1,633,943
Teachers*	199,202	83,538
Schools	18,759*	8,509*
	(127,891)**	(51,399)**

* pre-school and *EGB*.
** groups of *EGB* pupils.

Source: Ministry of Education and Science (*MEC*).

5. Secondary education

5.1 Pre-reform secondary education (*Enseñanzas Medias*)

The Spanish term *Enseñanzas Medias* refers to the level of post-compulsory education following *EGB* and roughly corresponds to what is called in some other countries upper secondary education. According to the Law of 1970, *Enseñanzas Medias* comprises two categories:

- *BUP* – *Bachillerato Unificado Polivalente* (Integrated Upper Secondary Education) which lasts 3 years and normally prepares pupils aged 14 to 17 for access to university; in addition to the 3 years, they must follow a one-year university orientation course – *COU (Curso de Orientación Universitaria)*. It also prepares pupils for employment. The *BUP* was implemented in the 1975/76 school year.

- *FP* – *Formación Profesional* (Vocational Training) which is divided into two levels: *FP*I lasting 2 years (for 14- to 16-year-olds) and *FP*II lasting 3 years (for 16- to 19-year-olds). *FP* aims to enable pupils to exercise the specific techniques of their chosen occupations and also continue their general education. Evening courses in *FP*I are available for employed pupils over 16, and in *FP*II for employed pupils over 18.

In order to be admitted to the *BUP*, pupils must have the School Graduate Certificate (*Graduado Escolar*); the School Attendance Certificate (*Certificado de Escolaridad*) is sufficient for *FP*I. Pupils who have completed *FP*I may enter *FP*II and the second year of the *BUP*. The *COU* is open to pupils who have successfully completed *BUP* or *FP*II.

The *BUP* and *COU* may be followed as day or evening courses either at education institutions or through distance learning. The day regime is the most common, with a full timetable, and studies may be arranged in one of three ways: spread over the morning and the afternoon; as a continuous session in the morning; or as a continuous session in the afternoon. The evening regime is always subject to a reduced timetable. The *FP* can be studied in a day regime, an evening regime or, in the case of *FP*II, as an external pupil. This depends on the institution being available for more than one group of pupils.

BUP/COU schools may be state or privately run. In the case of *Enseñanzas Medias*, the State draws up individual agreements with private schools which were totally or partly state funded at the time the Basic Law regulating the Right to Education was published in 1985. Private schools are classified according to their educational characteristics (material conditions, teachers) as free, semi-recognized and recognized.

Education is free of charge in state schools providing *BUP* and *FP*, although parents must pay for additional services, such as canteens and transport.

Special grants from the *MEC* are available to encourage pupils from low-income families to continue their education at this level, awarded on the basis of family income and the pupil's academic achievement, to cover travelling expenses, teaching materials, etc.

There may be *FP* sections in the same schools as *BUP*, with the same conditions. There are also *FP* schools and polytechnics, private or state run. State schools are mixed, private ones are sometimes single-sex. Classes are organized by age and are taught by different subject specialists.

Organizational and curricular experimentation of different kinds has been carried out in individual *Enseñanzas Medias* institutions in recent years. An evaluation of this experimental reform was taken into account in the reorganization of this level of education under the Basic Law of 1990 (*LOGSE*).

In 1991/92, 62.8% of 14- to 18-year-olds attended *BUP*, *COU* and experimental programmes, and 27.3% of 14- to 18-year-olds attended *FP*.

In *BUP, COU* and *FP*, the school year runs from 1 October to 30 June covering 170 days per year, 5 days per week. There are 29 lessons of 50 minutes per week.

5.1.1 *BUP*

Curriculum

The curriculum for the first and second year of the *BUP* is identical for all pupils.

The curriculum comprises: Spanish language and literature, foreign language, mathematics, physical education and sport, religion/ethics, natural sciences (1st year), history of civilization and art (1st year), music (1st year), drawing (1st year), physics and chemistry (2nd year), human and economic geography (2nd year), Latin (2nd year), technical/vocational course (2nd year).

In the third year of *BUP* there are common and optional subjects.

The common subjects are: foreign language, geography and history (including civics), technical/vocational education and activities, physical education and sport, religion/ethics, philosophy.

Pupils must choose three subjects from either option A (Spanish language and literature, Latin, Greek, mathematics) or B (Spanish language and literature, natural sciences, physics and chemistry and mathematics).

In addition, pupils can study a second foreign language as an optional subject.

Assessment and qualifications

Pupils in state and recognized schools are assessed continuously throughout the year, and at the end of the year receive an overall mark determined by all their teachers. There are two examination periods per year (*convocatoria*) – in June and September. Pupils who fail in any subjects in June may retake these subjects in September. Those who fail in

September in more than two subjects must repeat the year. Those who fail in only one or two subjects progress to the next year but follow remedial classes in the subject(s) concerned. Pupils who complete the three-year course successfully are awarded the *Bachillerato*; there is no final examination. Pupils in semi-recognized schools are assessed by a mixed examining board of teachers from their own and a state school, and pupils in free schools are assessed in state schools. Both the pupils' performance during the year and in the examinations are taken into account.

5.1.2 *COU*

Curriculum

From the 1988/89 school year, the curriculum of the *COU*, first laid down in 1975, has been changed in order to allow greater choice of university studies. This new curriculum comprises the same three common subjects as before but now includes four option streams instead of the previous two. Each option stream comprises two compulsory subjects and four optional subjects from which the pupils must choose two.

The common subjects, which are compulsory for all pupils, are: foreign language, Spanish language and philosophy.

The four option streams are:

Option A (sciences and technology)		Option B (biology and health)
mathematics I physics	compulsory	chemistry biology
chemistry biology geology technical drawing	optional	mathematics I physics geology technical drawing

Option C (social sciences)		Option D (humanities and languages)
mathematics II history of contemporary society	compulsory	literature history of contemporary society
literature Latin Greek art history	optional	Latin Greek art history mathematics II

The common subjects and option stream subjects cover 26 hours per week.

In addition, pupils can study a second foreign language, sport or religion as optional subjects.

Assessment and qualifications

Assessment procedures are the same as for the *BUP*. Pupils who fail in more than three subjects in the second examination session in September must repeat the whole year. Pupils who fail in less than three subjects must re-enrol in the *COU* to follow remedial courses. They may enrol in the *COU* for a maximum of three times.

In order to have access to university education, those pupils who have successfully completed the *COU* must normally also take an entrance examination organized by each university (*Pruebas de Aptitud para el Accesso a la Universidad – PAAU*, commonly known as *Selectividad*).

5.1.3 Vocational Training (*Formación Profesional*)

Curriculum

*FP*I and *FP*II both have two components:

- general education;

- specialist training in a particular branch, which includes practical training in the school workshop or in the workplace.

The general education component of the curriculum covers similar material to that of the *BUP* but in less depth.

*FP*I: Spanish language (Castilian) (1st year only), foreign language, arts (2nd year only), religion/ethics, physical education and sport, civics (2nd year only).

*FP*II: Spanish language (Castilian), foreign language, arts, religion/ethics, physical education and sport, mathematics, physics and chemistry, natural sciences.

*FP*I and *FP*II have 21 specialist branches: administration and commerce, agriculture, graphic arts, automotive engineering, construction, technical drawing, electricity and electronics, community services, hotel and tourism, image and sound, metal, wood, mining, fashion and tailoring, marine and fisheries, hairdressing and beauty treatment, skins and leather, chemistry, health, textiles, glass and ceramics.

*FP*I lasts two years and is divided into three areas of knowledge: Core Training (360 hours each year); Applied Sciences related to the chosen vocational branch (126 hours during the first year and 198 in the second one); Technical Studies and Work Experience specific to the chosen occupation (540 hours each year).

There are two types (*modalidades*) of *FP*II: General and Specialized (*Enseñanzas Especializadas*). The General type lasts two years and is divided into three areas of knowledge: Core Training (216 hours during the first year and 288 in the second one); Technology and Work Experience (792 hours during the first year and 684 during the second one); Business Training (72 hours during the first year and 108 during the second one). The Specialized type lasts three years and is divided into two areas: Basic Training (468 hours during the three years) and Further Studies (612 hours during the three years).

Assessment and qualifications

Pupils are subject to continuous assessment throughout the year by every subject teacher, and receive a mark at the end of each assessment period. If they pass all subjects in a certain field, they receive an overall mark for that. If they have a negative mark in one subject they are required to take remedial courses. The final mark for the year (an average of the different assessments) is based on the marks received in each field. Pupils who do not pass may take examinations during the two examination periods per year, in June and September (the same as in the *BUP*).

Successful pupils in *FP*I receive the assistant technician's certificate (*Técnico Auxiliar*). This gives access to *FP*II, the second year of the *BUP*, or employment. Those who are not successful receive a school attendance certificate (*Certificado de Escolaridad*).

Pupils who are successful in all years of *FP*II obtain a specialist technician's certificate (*Técnico Especialista*). This gives direct access to certain related university courses or employment, or to the *COU*, which leads to university education.

5.2 Post-reform secondary education

Under the reform, compulsory education has been extended to the age of 16 and secondary education has been reorganized as follows:

– Compulsory secondary education for 12- to 16-year-olds;

– *Bachillerato* (post compulsory) for 16- to 18-year-olds;

– Intermediate Vocational Training for 16- to 18-year-olds.

Compulsory secondary education therefore includes the last two years of the pre-reform *EGB* (12- to 14-year-olds) and the first two years of pre-reform *Enseñanzas Medias* (14- to 16-year-olds).

It is intended that the effective extension of compulsory education to 16 years of age will not only broaden the education common to all pupils, but also postpone the choice between academic and vocational studies, eliminate streaming and allow pupils to enter the labour market on its completion.

Given that *FP*I and *FP*II were considered to be too academic and far removed from the world of production, reformed vocational training is designed to provide pupils with the qualifications they need to perform various professional activities successfully.

Vocational training includes both basic vocational training (introduced during compulsory secondary education and in the *Bachillerato*) and specific vocational training (intermediate and higher levels).

5.2.1 Compulsory secondary education (*Educación Secundaria Obligatoria - ESO*)

Compulsory secondary education (*ESO*) is divided into two two-year cycles, corresponding to ages 12 to 14 and 14 to 16. Access to this stage is automatic upon completion of primary education. Its purpose is two-fold: to complete compulsory study and provide access to employment; and to prepare for post-secondary education.

It will be provided by secondary schools which will have to accommodate a minimum of one class for each school year. The maximum number of pupils for each class unit, into which pupils are grouped by age, will be 30. In addition to teaching this stage of education, such schools may also teach the *Bachillerato* and Vocational Training.

Curriculum, assessment and qualifications

The curriculum is organized in a similar way to that of primary education, although at this stage areas of learning tend to cover limited subject matter, and optional subjects are introduced progressively. The goal is to ensure diversity without relinquishing the overall principle of comprehensive education.

Basic vocational training is introduced in the form of general technology education (*Educación Tecnológica*) for all pupils (as a specific subject area). It covers training in different technologies and also awareness of society and employment, and aims to provide pupils with the knowledge and basic skills indispensable for a wide variety of careers.

There are compulsory subject areas with different minimum timetable allocations depending on the cycle, and in accordance with the minimum core curriculum requirements (*Enseñanzas Mínimas*) for the whole of Spain: social sciences, geography and history (140 hours for the first cycle, 160 hours for the second cycle), physical education (70 hours, 70 hours), Castilian language, language of the corresponding Autonomous Community and literature (210 hours, 240 hours), foreign languages (210 hours, 240 hours), mathematics (140 hours, 160 hours), Catholic religion (compulsory provision in schools but optional for pupils) / alternative study activities (105 hours, 105 hours), natural sciences (140 hours, 90 hours), plastic and visual arts (70 hours, 35 hours), music (70 hours, 35 hours), technology (125 hours, 70 hours). In the final year, pupils have to choose two of the last four subject areas. A few school hours are left to allow Autonomous Communities and the *MEC* to extend and adapt the timetable as required.

In the first cycle, optional subjects must constitute approximately 10% of the school timetable. In the second cycle, the structure of the curriculum becomes more complex and optional subjects are increased to cover some 25-35%. Nevertheless, the guiding principle is that the optional subjects chosen should in no way condition or limit future educational choices. It is compulsory for schools to offer a second foreign language and the classics, at least in one year of the second cycle.

The aim is also to improve the match between education and individual needs, with teachers adapting or modifying the general curriculum to suit a pupil or group of pupils.

Pupil assessment is continuous and integrated, but separated into the various areas or subjects. Both in the *MEC* territory, as well as in most of the Autonomous Communities, assessment must be carried out collectively by the team of teachers which is responsible for the same group of pupils, with the coordination of the tutor and advice from the Guidance Department (*Departamento de Orientación*). At the beginning of the *ESO*, teachers will make an initial assessment of every pupil. Teachers will hold at least three assessment meetings during the year. Assessment results will be expressed on the following qualification scale: *Insuficiente, Suficiente, Bien, Notable* and *Sobresaliente*. The last assessment meeting will take place at the end of the school year in June on three occasions during the *ESO*: at the end of the first cycle and at the end of each year of the second cycle.

Pupils are promoted automatically from one year to the next, but in exceptional cases, those who do not achieve the aims of the cycle may be made to repeat a year, at the end of the first cycle or after any of the second cycle years, so they may remain for two additional years in compulsory secondary education.

Pupils who have attained the required objectives at the end of compulsory secondary education will receive a certificate of secondary education (*Graduado en Educación Secundaria*). This qualification will enable the pupil to gain access to the *Bachillerato* and intermediate level specific vocational training. All pupils, whether they achieve the objectives or not, receive an attendance certificate from the school, recording the number of years studied as well as the marks obtained for each of the different subject areas, and giving guidance concerning the pupil's educational or professional future.

Compulsory education can extend to a maximum age of 18. Specific Social Guarantee (*Garantía Social*) programmes are designed for those pupils who do not manage to obtain a certificate. Local administrations may collaborate in these programmes, with the aim of offering pupils a basic minimum vocational training to enable them to enter working life or continue their studies.

5.2.2 *Bachillerato*

The new *Bachillerato* lasts for two years (16 to 18 years of age). Its aim is to foster intellectual and emotional maturity, as well as to provide the knowledge and skills which allow pupils to fulfil their social functions responsibly and competently ('terminal value') and qualify them to enter higher level vocational training or university.

To be accepted for the new *Bachillerato*, to be introduced during 1998/99 (first year), pupils must hold the certificate of secondary education (*Graduado en Educación Secundaria*).

The *Bachillerato* will be offered by secondary schools or exceptionally in schools exclusively for the *Bachillerato*, providing a minimum of four classes. Schools will need to offer at least two *Bachillerato* option streams (*modalidades*), and conditions regarding facilities and premises will vary according to the option streams available. The maximum number of pupils for each teacher/class will be 35.

Curriculum, assessment and qualifications

The *Bachillerato* is diversified (containing various option streams) which allows the pupil to progress in various fields of knowledge or towards working life. The *Bachillerato* has a minimum of four option streams: arts, natural and health sciences, humanities and social sciences, and technology. Basic vocational training continues to be introduced, with the further addition of vocational elements and transition to working life.

The curricular unit for the *Bachillerato* is the subject. Subjects are grouped into common core subjects, subjects which belong to each option stream and optional subjects. The minimum educational requirements (*Enseñanzas Mínimas*) for core subjects, subjects by option stream and optional subjects are established by the *MEC*. The curriculum which is developed on the basis of these is established by the authorities (the *MEC* or the Autonomous Communities).

Option stream subjects are allocated a minimum of 70 hours.

Common core subjects and the minimum timetable requirements for each subject (*Enseñanzas Mínimas*), throughout the two years whether taught over one or two years, are: physical education (35 hours), philosophy (70 hours), history (70 hours), Castilian language and literature (210 hours), foreign language (210 hours), religion/alternative study activities (70 hours). Those Autonomous Communities with their own language are able to devote 10% of the total time for language teaching to this language.

Teaching methods should foster pupils' ability to learn individually, work in a team and apply appropriate methods of research, and should emphasize the relationship between the theoretical aspects of subjects and their practical application.

Pupils should be assessed by subject taking into account the assessment criteria established for every subject and measured in relation to the educational aims of the *Bachillerato*. This will comprise continuous assessment throughout the learning process and final assessment at the end of the school year.

Every year, teachers will hold at least three assessment meetings. The final qualification in the different subjects will be determined at the last meeting. In September an extraordinary assessment meeting will be held for those pupils who have not passed all the subjects in the final year assessment. Teachers are required to consider all the subjects taught in the relevant school year and the academic maturity of pupils in relation to the objectives of the *Bachillerato* and their potential for progressing in further studies.

To move up from the first to the second year, pupils must not fail in more than two subjects. Those who have failed more than three subjects at the end of the second year are obliged to repeat the year. The maximum period a pupil may take to complete the *Bachillerato* is four years. The marking system will be based on a numerical scale of one to ten, without decimals.

Only pupils who have passed in all subjects will receive the *Bachillerato* certificate, entitling them to access to higher level vocational training or university studies (in the latter case, after having passed a university entrance examination – *Pruebas de Aptitud para el Accesso a la Universidad – PAAU*, commonly known as *selectividad*). There is no final examination for the *Bachillerato*.

5.2.3 Specific vocational training

Specific Vocational Training (*Formación Profesional específica – FP*) is structured into two training levels: intermediate level *FP* and higher level *FP* (*Formación profesional de grado medio/de grado superior*). Its objective is to facilitate integration into working life, to contribute towards continuing training for all citizens and to meet the demands of the productive sector for skills.

In principle, in order to gain admittance to intermediate level *FP*, it is necessary to have successfully completed compulsory secondary education. However, access will also be possible by means of a test regulated by the education authorities to ascertain that candidates have sufficient knowledge and skills.

In order to gain access to the higher level *FP*, it will, in principle, be necessary for a candidate to have a *Bachillerato* certificate. Admission requirements may also include having studied specific related subjects in the *Bachillerato*. However, candidates aged 20 years and over without academic requirements may also gain admission through a test, regulated by the education authorities, to confirm that they are sufficiently mature in relation to the objectives of the *Bachillerato* and have the vocational skills required for the respective occupational field (those who can demonstrate that they have work experience directly relevant to the vocational studies they wish to take may be exempt from the last part).

Intermediate level *FP* may be offered by ordinary secondary schools called *Institutos de educación* secundaria (those which teach the *ESO* or the *Bachillerato*) or by institutions devoted exclusively to offering specific *FP*. Higher level *FP* is taught in special institutions or in *Institutos de educación secundaria* which offer the *Bachillerato*. Requirements for facilities and premises vary according to the training cycles offered. The maximum number of pupils per teacher is 30.

Since 1988, Levels II and III of the so-called vocational modules (*Módulos Profesionales* – which correspond to the intermediate and higher level *FP* respectively) have been progressively set up and introduced experimentally.

Curriculum, assessment and qualifications

In the plan for the new *FP* (still under preparation), it is intended to promote especially the participation of social partners to help identify which skills are really required by the productive system and the labour market.

In the plan, a common structure has been established for the academic organization of vocational qualifications and corresponding minimum educational requirements. The basic objective is the acquisition of the vocational skills pertaining to each qualification, which will take the form of an associated occupational profile. This profile is structured into units of ability or ranges of vocational skills.

The cycles (intermediate and higher levels) are divided into vocational modules of theoretical and practical training whose duration is suited to the nature of the corresponding vocational skill. A practical training module which will take place in work centres is to be included, and those who can demonstrate relevant work experience may be exempt. This module will usually last 300-400 hours. Work centres may be firms or institutions offering productive/training posts which complement the vocational skills the pupils have acquired in education establishments.

The modules are grouped in the following families: administration and management; agriculture and stockbreeding; graphic arts; automotion; sales and marketing; construction; electricity and electronics; personal beauty; hotels and tourism; sound and image; wood and furniture; industrial mechanics; chemistry; health; socio-cultural services; textiles.

Teaching methods must encourage pupils to form a global and coordinated view of the productive processes in which they will participate, by integrating the relevant scientific, technological and organizational subject matter.

Pupil assessment should be continuous and by vocational module, and teachers must consider the entire range of modules corresponding to each training cycle when making their assessments. Assessment of the practical training module in work centres will involve the collaboration of the teacher assigned by the corresponding work centre who is responsible for the pupils' training. In order to complete the training cycle successfully, a pupil will need to obtain a positive assessment in each of the modules included in the cycle.

It is planned that periodically, and not less than every five years, the Government will review vocational qualifications in order to adapt them continuously to the evolution in vocational skills.

Upon successful completion of intermediate *FP*, pupils receive the qualification of *Técnico* (technical specialist). Those who obtain this qualification may gain direct access to specific option streams in the *Bachillerato* depending on the corresponding *FP* studies. The qualification of senior technical specialist (*Técnico Superior*) is obtained upon successful completion of higher *FP*; this allows direct access to specific university studies related to the particular vocational training course followed.

As at primary level, one teacher is delegated as the tutor of a particular class and provides educational and vocational **guidance**. In 1987, experimental Guidance Departments were set up in some public upper secondary schools to coordinate the work of tutors and provide counselling (usually a teacher released from normal duties).

As a result of the *LOGSE*, Guidance Departments are being set up in all secondary schools.

5.3 Teachers

Teachers are specialists in one subject and normally teach this subject.

In order to be able to teach at *BUP* and *COU* levels, a teacher must first be a university graduate (*Licenciado*), engineer (*Ingeniero*) or architect (*Arquitecto*), and therefore have completed the first two cycles of university education (4 – 5 years) in university faculties or higher technical schools. Prospective teachers must then follow a course at an Institute of Educational Sciences (*Institutos de Ciencias de la Educación*) leading to the *CAP* (*Certificado de Aptitud Pedagógica*-Teacher Training Certificate), which entitles them to teach at secondary level. Graduates with a degree in education (*Licenciados en Pedagogía*) and those who can demonstrate teaching experience in secondary education (*Enseñanzas Medias*) do not have to fulfil this requirement.

In order to become an *FP* teacher, the minimum requirement is to be a university graduate (*Diplomado Universitario*), technical architect (*Arquitecto Técnico*) or technical engineer (*Ingeniero Técnico*) of university schools, university faculties or higher technical colleges. Workshop tutors (*Maestros de Taller*) who teach practical subjects in *FP*I must have completed at least *FP*II.

Two new developments have appeared with the advent of the *LOGSE*. Firstly, in order to teach any of the specific *FP* option streams, a university degree will normally be necessary (*Licenciado*, *Ingeniero* or *Arquitecto*). And secondly, all teaching staff in secondary education and *FP* will need to follow a teacher training course (with the same exemptions as for the *CAP*) in order to obtain the professional qualification to teach. This course, organized by the universities, will last at least one academic year and include a period of teaching practice.

Once the reform comes into force, a teacher will have to belong to the Association of Teachers in Secondary Education (*Cuerpo de Profesores de Enseñanza Secundaria*) or be an interim teacher in order to teach *ESO*, *Bachillerato* or *FP* in state schools. In addition, only teachers belonging to the Association of Technical *FP* Teachers (*Cuerpo de Profesores Técnicos de FP*) will be able to teach specific *FP*, and in some cases, *ESO* and *Bachillerato*. In addition, for certain areas or

subjects of specific *FP* it will be possible to engage experienced professionals as specialist teachers (part-time).

Teachers in private secondary education are required to possess the same initial qualifications as state-sector teachers, and identical employment conditions apply as to teachers in private pre-school and primary education.

Teachers' status and in-service training requirements are the same as at pre-school level.

5.4 Statistics

	Public	Private
BUP and *COU*		
Pupils	1,080,404	424,744
Experimental *Bachillerato*	104,264	21,965
Teachers*	73,411	26,239
Schools*	1,745	1,401
*FP*I and *FP*II		
Pupils	614,055	261,746
Experimental *FP*		
Modules II	4,768	420
Modules III	7,748	857
Teachers*	53,046	14,946
Schools*	1,212	1,104

* Also includes teachers and schools involved in the experimental *Bachillerato* or *FP*.

Source: Ministry for Education and Science (*MEC*).

Pupils entering post-compulsory education

General Education	*BUP* (1st year *BUP*)	354,475	56,5%
	Experimental *Bachillerato* (1st cycle, 1st year)	59,887	9.5%
	Total General Education	414,362	66.0%
Vocational Training	*FP*I (1st year)	213,402	34.0%
Total (General Education + Vocational Training)		627,764	100%

6. Higher education

Higher education encompasses all post-secondary education. It covers university studies, non-university studies which are officially equivalent, and the remainder of post-secondary education which is recognized by the *MEC* but where qualifications are not equivalent to those delivered in the general mainstream education system.

6.1 University education

Following the 1983 law on university education (*LRU*), the process to reform university qualifications and curricula began. Universities now approve their own curricula, following the general guidelines laid down by the *MEC* for each university qualification. A fundamental element of this reform is the gradual increase in the supply of university courses, especially those in the first cycle. Similarly, the creation of new state and private universities has been established. There are 48 universities, 41 state run and seven under the responsibility of the Roman Catholic Church or a private organization.

University Education is provided in University Faculties (*Facultades Universitarias*), Higher Technical Colleges (*Escuelas Técnicas Superiores*), University Schools (*Escuelas Universitarias*) and University Colleges (*Colegios Universitarios*).

Admission

Access to the university faculties, higher technical colleges and university colleges requires an overall positive assessment in the *COU* and a pass mark in the *PAAU* (*Pruebas de Aptitud para el Acceso a la Universidad* – university entrance examination). This arrangement will remain in force until the current *BUP* is phased out. With the advent of the *LOGSE*, the *COU* will be abolished but the entrance examination will be maintained, which together with the *Bachillerato* qualifications will help to assess the knowledge and maturity of pupils. In order to gain access to university schools, it is necessary to have passed *COU*, *FP*II or the new *Bachillerato*.

Since 1993, the *PAAU* has comprised two tests, one based on common *COU* subjects to assess pupils' general education, the other based on compulsory and optional subjects included in the chosen options. The overall (average) mark together with the average overall mark during *BUP* and *COU* courses determines the final mark for the *PAAU*. The *PAAU* is carried out by the higher education institutions themselves.

Once an applicant fulfils the academic requirements, admission procedures for university institutions depend on the particular institution. Access to these institutions depends on capacity and, where there is excess demand for places, a system of priorities exists. These may be based on factors such as the examination session (*convocatoria*) in which the *PAAU* was passed, the marks obtained in tests, the option or option stream studied in *COU* or in the new *Bachillerato*, the average mark obtained at *BUP* and *COU* or, as the case may be, in the new *Bachillerato* or in *FP*II, etc.

Each year, the University Council, a national body, determines the number of available places in each higher education establishment. 70% of study courses are subject to numerus clausus (1991/92). The student applies directly to the institution at which he/she is interested in enrolling.

Fees/Student Finance

The fees of each university are set by the Autonomous Communities in which the university is located or by the State in those Communities where the authorities have not taken on those powers.

There is a scholarship system administered by the Ministry of Education and Science in collaboration with the Autonomous Communities and the universities themselves.

Academic year

The university academic year begins in the first week of October and ends in the first week of June, with an average of 20 to 30 hours of classes a week, including practical sessions. The legal academic year establishes 220 days as the teaching period for each course, with holiday periods at Christmas and at Easter.

Courses/Qualifications

University education prior to the reform involves two types of study courses: those of one cycle (lasting three years) and those of three cycles (the first being of three years, the second of two and the third corresponding to a Doctorate (*Doctorado*)). Following the reform, these courses will be structured into studies comprising only the first cycle, studies of two cycles without an intermediate qualification, studies of two cycles with an intermediate qualification, and studies of the third cycle.

All three university cycles may be studied at university faculties or at higher technical colleges. The courses at these institutions last at least two cycles, the first for three years, the second for two or three years. On successful completion of the first two cycles, the qualification of *Licenciado* (Master's Degree) is awarded at the faculties, whilst at technical colleges the corresponding qualification is *Arquitecto* or *Ingeniero*. At both types of institution, after passing a third two-year cycle and preparing a doctoral thesis, the qualification of *Doctor* is awarded.

Only first cycle studies lasting three years are offered at university schools, which lead to the qualification of *Diplomado, Arquitecto Técnico* (Technical Architect) or *Ingeniero Técnico* (Technical Engineer).

University colleges offer the first cycle of university studies. Once they have completed this, students may continue the second cycle at the university faculties to which the college is attached.

All of the university institutions mentioned above also provide postgraduate courses oriented towards the professional application of the knowledge acquired, which enable qualifications specific to each university to be obtained.

The *UNED* (*Universidad National de Educación a Distancia* – The National Distance-Learning University), which is both state run and nationwide, offers university education by correspondence. In addition to the official programmes of university studies, the *UNED* also includes Open Distance-Learning Programmes (*Programas de Enseñanza Abierta a Distancia*), structured in short courses which do not require prior qualifications.

Assessment

Each student has the option of sitting a minimum of four and a maximum of six examination sessions (*convocatorias de exámen*) in order to obtain passes in the subjects studied, usually on an annual basis. Students may attend two examination sessions during each academic year, an ordinary session in June and an extraordinary session in September. Some subjects are studied in courses lasting four months from the beginning of the academic year; examinations for these may be taken in February.

First-year students who fail all examinations cannot continue their studies.

6.2 Post-secondary non-university education

There are other courses which, although they are not taught in university institutions, are officially comparable to university level, leading to qualifications which are equivalent to those of *Diplomado* or *Licenciado*.

There is also another group of courses which are authorized and recognized by the *MEC,* but the qualifications they lead to are not comparable with those awarded at any of the other levels of education in the general system.

Higher level specific vocational training (*Formación Profesional específica de Grado Superior*) has been described under 'Specific vocational training' (see 5.2.3).

7. 'Occupational' vocational training (Formación profesional ocupacional)

With the aim of matching vocational training more closely to the needs of the labour market, the National Vocational Training Programme (*Programa Nacional de Formación Profesional*), jointly agreed between the social partners and the public administrations, brings together the two vocational training systems currently in force. These are 'regulated' vocational training (*Formación Profesional reglada*) provided by the education system (see 5.), and 'occupational' vocational training (*Formación profesional ocupacional*) covered by the National Training and Professional Insertion Plan (*FIP Plan – Plan National de Formación e Inserción Profesional*) administered by the *INEM* or the Autonomous Communities with full powers over vocational training.

The aim of the programme is for the education and employment administrations to coordinate their activities in order to achieve maximum coherence in the development of training courses, establishing channels for regulating the comparability or equivalence of 'occupational' vocational training, with its work placements, and of the training provided by the educational administration, with the objective of helping to adapt training to technological change.

One of the aims of 'occupational' vocational training is to provide suitable vocational qualifications for unemployed people wishing to join or rejoin the labour market. This is achieved by means of training courses organized within the framework of the *FIP* Plan, which are regulated by Royal Decree 631/1993 of 3 May.

7.1 Occupational training courses (Formación ocupacional)

The minimum age for admission to occupational training courses is 16 years, and this type of training is available throughout a person's working life. There is a very high level of course attendance, and preference for participating in such courses is given to: unemployed people on unemployment benefit; the long-term unemployed over 25 years old; unemployed people under 25 years old with at least six months' work experience; unemployed persons with difficulties in entering or re-entering the labour market; and those seeking a first job, where they fulfil the necessary requirements.

The training initiatives included in the *FIP* Plan are entirely free of charge. Moreover, the scheme covers trainee accident insurance, teaching equipment, teaching materials, school supplies, transport allowances, maintenance and accommodation. Those who have a right to grants include the disabled, pupils participating in the programme for workshop-schools and skilled craft centres (see below), and young people under 25 years old from rural areas, who have no right to a farm subsidy or who have had the duration of such rights reduced.

The length of courses is determined by the type of course and training needs. Courses can be classified as: broad-based (lasting on average 950 hours), occupational (on average 350 hours) and specialized (on average 250 hours). Courses for the unemployed from rural areas last at least 250 hours and their objective is to provide occupational retraining.

Training is provided by the *INEM*'s occupational training centres, or by centres organized by the Autonomous Communities which have assumed powers for managing the *FIP* Plan, by cooperating centres and firms, and in collaboration with other administrative authorities (Autonomous and local). Courses are predominantly practical in nature. The centres combine the conditions established in the rules governing the *FIP* Plan; they must possess a workshop in which trainees carry out practical work training and have a teacher/pupil ratio no higher than 1:20. In the case of distance training, there may be no fewer than 50 pupils and no more than 75.

Training centres must comply with technical-educational, material and staff requirements in order to have official approval to teach a particular specialist subject, and must also meet the needs of the industrial sector.

Tutors have intermediate and higher level qualifications as well as teaching experience. They fall into the following categories: employees on a temporary contract (not staff teachers), full-time officials employed by the *INEM* and tutors belonging to other bodies which provide courses (cooperating centres, firms). The *INEM* organizes refresher and further training courses, which take the form of technical-vocational training in the specialist subject and training in teaching methods. In 1992, the *INEM* successfully trained 4,109 students in its training course for tutors.

The *INEM* currently includes 28 specialized national centres for occupational groups, in which one of its functions is the development of training schemes for teachers and education experts. Other functions of the *INEM*'s national centres include: the development and updating of studies in specific sectors; updating the Permanent Observatory of Occupations (*Observatorio Permanente de las Ocupaciones*); the formulation, monitoring and assessment of teaching aids; studies to determine the minimum core curriculum and training schedules composed of modules in each special subject, which lead on to the corresponding occupation; and the training of job-seekers.

The competent employment administrations which manage the *FIP* Plan issue *certificados de profesionalidad* (vocational certificates), which are official in character and valid throughout the entire country, to pupils who have received a positive assessment for their respective occupational level.

The Ministry of Employment and Social Security is compiling a national index of vocational certificates (*Repertorio Nacional de Certificados de Profesionalidad*) in coordination with the Ministry of Education and Science's catalogue of vocational certificates (*Catálogo de Títulos Profesionales*), with the aim of establishing a system of comparability and equivalence between 'regulated' vocational training courses and knowledge acquired during 'occupational' training and work experience schemes.

7.2 Workshop-schools (escuelas taller) and skilled craft centres (casas de oficios)

Under the heading of 'occupational' vocational training, it is also appropriate to mention the training carried out by the workshop-schools (*escuelas taller*) and skilled craft centres (*casas de oficio*), which takes the form of public employment-training programmes with the purpose of training the unemployed, especially young people under 25 years of age. Training consists mostly of courses alternating with work and work placements to improve their employment opportunities in occupations related to the restoration or promotion of the artistic, historical, cultural or environmental heritage and to improve living conditions in urban areas. These employment-training programmes are governed by a specific regulation, the Ministerial Decree of 29 March 1988, subsequently amended by the Act of 3 August 1994.

These programmes comprise two phases: an initial training stage which, in the case of workshop-schools, may not be shorter than six months; and another sandwich training stage. In workshop-schools, the programme lasts between one and three years, and in skilled craft centres, for one year. In both cases, the period of sandwich training is subject to an apprenticeship contract. Moreover, on completion of their training courses, pupils receive guidance, counselling, vocational and business information, and technical assistance.

The training programme of workshop-schools includes activities related to the restoration and promotion of Spain's artistic heritage; the rehabilitation of urban areas and the environment; and the restoration and refurbishment of the publicly owned infrastructure which houses business initiative centres (*Centros de Iniciativa Empresarial*). The programme of workshop-schools should form part of integrated employment plans to respond to the requirements of the labour market and stimulate the development of the regions, thereby generating new jobs.

Skilled craft centres serve as centres for training and youth employment, and are principally situated in urban areas which record the highest levels of unemployed young people. The training programme of skilled craft centres includes activities associated with the maintenance and care of urban areas and the environment; the improvement of living conditions in villages and towns by providing social and community services; and other activity which facilitates the entry of young people into working life, while at the same time restoring craft trades, preferably by incorporating new technologies.

Both workshop-schools and skilled craft centres organize specific programmes for pupils who have not completed compulsory secondary education as laid down in the *LOGSE* (*Ley Orgánica de Ordenación General del Sistema Educativo* – basic law on the general structure and organization of the education system). Their purpose is to provide pupils with the basic training which will enable them to enter working life or to continue with 'regulated' education.

The law requires workshop-schools and skilled craft centres to design a training plan by specialist subject in relation to the works or services to be undertaken, in such a way that the training plan establishes a link between the specialist subject and the works or services.

Pupils receive a certificate from the entities sponsoring workshop-schools or skilled craft centres, which states the hours of training, qualification acquired and training modules completed. This certificate may be totally or partially accredited by the *certificado de profesionalidad* provided for in the *FIP* Plan. At the same time, and in accordance with the provisions of the *LOGSE,* this certificate may also serve to accredit specific vocational training modules as provided for in the reform of 'regulated' vocational training.

7.3 Statistics

FIP Plan
Pupils trained by age (with a positive assessment)

Age	Year			
	1990	1991	1992	1993
< 20	53,029	49,716	37,005	16,753
20-24	85,007	84,643	72,515	44,271
25-29	53,559	60,572	57,738	36,621

Source: *INEM*.

Workshop schools and skilled craft centres, 1993

Autonomous Community	Number of workshop and skilled craft centres	Number of pupils
ANDALUCÍA	277	12,616
ARAGON	40	1,132
ASTURIAS	66	2,854
BALEARES	8	292
CANARIAS	26	1,044
CANTABRIA	32	1,277
CASTILLA LA MANCHA	66	2,727
CASTILLA-LEON	106	4,374
CATALUÑA	101	5,081
COMUNIDAD VALENCIANA	50	1,807
EXTREMADURA	62	2,719
GALICIA	74	3,235
MADRID	69	2,823
MURCIA	20	1,096
NAVARRA	5	230
PAÍS VASCO	24	909
LA RIOJA	5	107
CEUTA	2	90
MELILLA	1	35
NATIONAL TOTAL	1,034	44,448

Source: *INEM*.

France

FRANCE

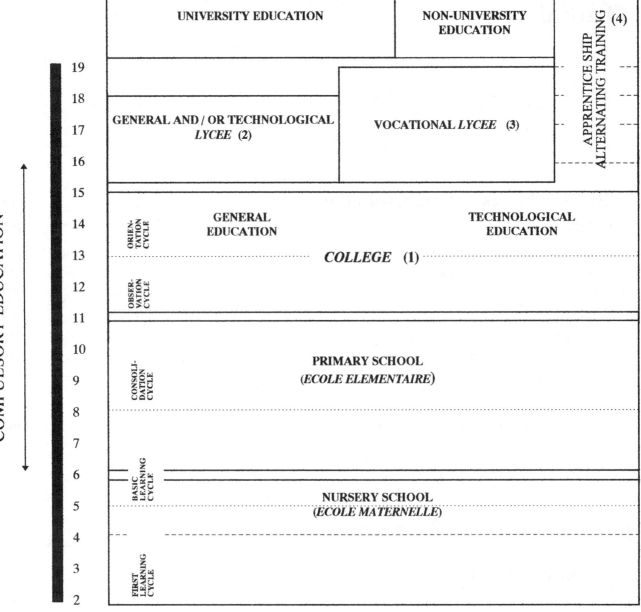

1.The *Collège* provides general education at lower secondary level leading to a national certificate (*Brevet*). The orientation cycle includes both general and technological education.

2.The general and/or technological *Lycée* provides upper secondary education leading to higher education or employment. Pupils prepare for the general *Baccalauréat*, which usually leads to higher education, the technological *Baccalauréat* (*B.Tn*), which leads either to employment or to higher education, or the technical certificate (*brevet de technicien, BT*), which generally leads to employment. The preparatory classes for the *grandes écoles* (*classes préparatoires aux grandes écoles, CPGA*) and the higher technical sections (*sections de techniciens supérieurs, STS*) in *Lycées* provide post-*Baccalauréat* training.

3.The vocational *Lycée* is an institution of secondary education providing young people with general technological and vocational training. It leads after two years to the vocational aptitude certificate (*certificat d'aptitude professionnelle, CAP*) or the vocational studies certificate (*brevet d'études professionnelles, BEP*), and, after two additional years, to the vocational *Baccalauréat*.

4.These courses can be entered between the age of 16 and 25. Apprenticeship training lasts two years. Alternating training: qualification contracts last six months minimum, 24 months maximum; adaptation contracts last six months minimum; and guidance contracts last from three to six months.

·········· = division in the level / type of education

- - - - - = alternative beginning or end of level / type of education

1. Responsibilities and administration

1.1 Background

France is a Republic and its Constitution, adopted in 1958, gives the President of the Republic, who is elected directly by the people, very important powers. He appoints the Prime Minister, who is responsible to him and to Parliament.

France has a population of 57.8 million, which is increasing at the rate of just over 0.3% each year. Population density is 101.7 inhabitants per square kilometre and 73.4% of the population lives in cities. More than 10% of the working age population, or 3.3 million people, are currently unemployed. Foreigners account for 3.6 million inhabitants and a further 1.3 million have recently become French by naturalization.

Metropolitan France is currently divided into 22 regions, each of which contains from 2 to 8 *départements*. There are 96 metropolitan and five overseas *départements*. The official language of the country and of the education system is French.

1.2 Basic principles: education

In France, public education, which caters for more than 80% of pupils, is secular. In the name of freedom of education, private education also exists; this is mainly composed of Catholic establishments which have a contract with the State.

The Framework Law on education nº 89-486 of 10 July 1989 establishes education as the top national priority and sets as its objective 'to educate an entire age group to at least the level of the vocational aptitude certificate (*CAP*) or vocational studies certificate (*BEP*) and 80% of the group to *Baccalauréat* level within ten years'.

The Five-year Law nº 93-1313 concerning work, employment and vocational training recognizes the particular responsibility of the national education service to assure integration into working life, and establishes the principle that 'every young person must be given the opportunity to take up vocational training before he or she leaves the education system, regardless of the level of education he or she has completed'.

1.3 Distribution of responsibilities

The Government is responsible for the definition and implementation of education policy, within the general framework fixed by the legislature which, in accordance with the Constitution, fixes the 'general principles' applying to the education system.

Two ministers are responsible for education policy: the Minister for National Education for matters concerning school education; and the Minister for Higher Education and Research for matters concerning higher education. In addition, the Ministry of Agriculture and Fisheries is responsible for agricultural education; the Ministry of Labour, Employment and Vocational Training plays an important role in vocational training; and the Ministry of Youth and Sport and the Ministry of Culture and of the French Language contribute to the organization of educational activities for young people.

Traditionally, the French education system has been extremely centralized. Since its decision in 1982 to transfer to the local authorities certain powers and responsibilities which had previously been exercised by the State, France has begun the important process of decentralization which has profoundly altered the distribution of powers between the public administrations of the State and those of the local authorities. At the same time, the State continues to guarantee the smooth operation of public services and cohesion within the education system.

The decentralization laws of 1982 and 1983 have significantly increased the role of the regions, *départements* and communes.

Primary schools are organized and administered by the communes; *Collèges* (lower secondary schools) by the *départements*; and *Lycées* (upper secondary schools) by the regions.

The Ministry of Labour and the regions supervise vocational training outside the school system, and regional councils organize annual apprenticeship programmes.

Universities are public education institutions which enjoy administrative, financial and academic autonomy. There are numerous other public or private higher education institutions attached to various ministries.

1.4 Administration

Central authorities

The central administration of the **Ministry of National Education** includes nine educational directorates: Directorate of Schools (*DE*); Directorate of *Lycées* and *Collèges* (*DLC*); Directorate of Teaching Staff in *Lycées* and *Collèges* (*DPELC*); Directorate of General and International Affairs and Cooperation (*DAGIC*); Directorate of Administrative, Maintenance and Service Personnel (*DPAOS*); General Directorate of Finances and Administrative Control (*DGF*); Directorate of Assessment and Planning (*DEP*); Directorate of Inspection and Administrative Personnel (*DPID*); and Directorate of Information and New Technologies (*DITN*).

The General Inspectorates, Financial Control, and the Cabinet Office are attached directly to the Minister's Cabinet.

The central administration of the **Ministry of Higher Education** includes four main directorates: General Directorate of Higher Education; General Directorate of Administration, Human Resources and Financial Affairs; General Directorate of

Research and Technology (to which the Directorate of Innovation, Technology and Regional Activity is attached); and Directorate of Scientific and Technical Information and Libraries. International affairs are dealt with by the Delegation for European and International Relations and for French-speakers.

The State defines educational guidelines and curricula. As in the past, the State oversees the recruitment, training and administration of staff; it establishes statutes and operational rules for the institutions and provides them with the necessary teaching and administrative posts. The Minister for National Education determines the dates of school holidays in each of the three zones in metropolitan France. The school year is established on the basis of 316 half-days of work during the year.

Regional authorities

The **regions** now have the status of territorial authorities. They are administered by an elected Regional Council and have general responsibility for economic, social, sanitary, cultural, and scientific development and town and country planning. The regions are responsible for building and maintaining *Lycées* (upper secondary schools) and for specialized institutions, and they have important powers in the area of vocational training. In cooperation with the *départements*, they must develop an overview of quantitative and qualitative training needs, i.e. of medium-term needs for school facilities at each level and in each type of education.

Départements fulfil a dual function as local authorities represented by an elected assembly, the General Council, and state administrative districts responsible for providing school transport and maintaining and building *Collèges* (lower secondary schools). *Départements* are divided into cantons.

For administrative purposes, nursery and primary schools are placed under the direct control of the **communes**, which establish them and administer their budgets. Decisions affecting these schools are therefore made by local government bodies. However, inasmuch as the State is responsible for new posts and the employment of teachers, the decision to create a new school or class cannot take effect without the approval of the representative of the State. Power is thus in reality divided between the State and the local authorities.

Institutional level

Collèges, general or technological Lycées, and vocational Lycées are local public schools with legal responsibility and financial autonomy. The state representative (prefect of the *département* for *Collèges*, prefect of the region for *Lycées*) establishes schools by decree at the suggestion, depending on the case, of the *département*, the region, or, in certain cases, the commune or group of interested communes.

Institutions include the following bodies:

- the Board of Governors (*Conseil d'administration*), made up of representatives of the local authorities, the administration and staff of the institution, and parents and pupils;

- the Permanent Committee (*Commission permanente*) and the Disciplinary Council (*Conseil de discipline*);

- the Class Council (*Conseil de classe*), which meets at least once each term;

- teaching teams within a cycle whose role is to improve coordination between teachers in developing and implementing the school plan and ensure the continuity and assessment of pupils' work. In each class, the principal teacher ensures coordination between pupils and the other teachers.

The amended decree of 30 August 1985 recognizes the autonomy of *Collèges* and *Lycées* in teaching and educational matters. This autonomy applies to the general organization of the institution and is exercised by developing a school plan according to the procedures set out in the framework law for education of 10 July 1989 and in the ministerial circular of 17 May 1990. This plan must be discussed within the school and then adopted by the board of governors. The plan defines the specific methods by which national objectives and curricula are to be implemented, taking particular account of the characteristics of the local school population and the resources of the socio-cultural and economic environment.

The powers and responsibilities of head teachers are based primarily on their legal and administrative status (which are different at primary and secondary level). At primary level, head teachers, called *'directeurs'*, are teachers appointed to carry out this function. At secondary level, the head teacher, called *'principal'* in *Collèges* and *'proviseur'* in *Lycées*, is an employee of the Ministry. Head teachers are recruited by competitive examination and enjoy a special status in accordance with decree n° 88-343 of 11 April 1988.

The law of 16 January 1984 grants administrative, financial, teaching and academic autonomy to **universities.**

According to the law of 1984, universities form the following statutory bodies: an Administrative Council (*Conseil d'administration*), an Academic Council (*Conseil scientifique*) and a Council of Studies and University Life (*Conseil des études et de la vie universitaire*). These bodies include representatives of teachers, researchers, students, and administrative and technical staff, as well as people from outside the university.

The president of the university is elected by all members of the three statutory bodies. He or she directs the university, presides over the statutory bodies, and supervises revenue and expenditure. The president has authority over the entire staff, appoints boards of examiners, and is responsible for maintaining order.

In the spirit of the law of 26 January 1984, since 1989 the Ministry of Higher Education has entered into a new relationship with higher education institutions. A policy characterized by the negotiation of four-year contracts between the State and the institutions has been substituted for the traditional annual grants of resources and facilities for teaching by the central administration. This contractual policy is designed both to give new and real meaning to the autonomy of the universities and to give the State the means to exercise its responsibility for promoting education and ensuring its coherence. Each institution defines a development plan designed to meet both national goals and local training needs. This plan, which deals with all the institution's activities, is presented to the responsible services in the Ministry and then negotiated with them. These negotiations lead to the signing of a contract obliging the State to grant specific resources (in the form of teaching posts, operational credits, etc.) to the institution for a period of four years.

1.5 Inspection

General inspectorate

In addition to evaluating and stimulating the education system, the general inspectorate provides advice and information to the Minister for National Education. The general inspectorate is made up of general inspectors of national education and general inspectors of administration.

The general inspectorate of national education participates in the supervision of inspection and administrative staff and of teaching and guidance staff. The inspectorate takes part in their training and recruitment (sitting on the examining boards for competitive examinations), the supervision of their activities and the evaluation of the education system as a whole. This evaluation covers school institutions, types of education and training, the content of education, curricula, teaching methods, techniques employed and school results. In its annual report on the state of education, the general inspectorate of national education also makes available information on innovative practices, especially in teaching.

In the context of its responsibilities, **the general inspectorate of administration** provides advice and makes proposals to the Minister for National Education. The inspectorate is charged with examining and assessing the structures of the school network, whether they meet education needs, and equipment plans; the employment of staff; the physical organization and operation of schools; and the administration of funds allocated by the Ministry.

Alongside the general inspectorate of education, the general inspectorate of libraries is responsible for university libraries and for institutions attached to the Ministry of Culture: public information libraries, and *département* and municipal libraries.

Regional and *département* inspectorates

Under the authority of the *recteur* (head of the administrative unit or district, called *académie*) or the *académie* inspector and in cooperation with the competent general inspectors, the regional teaching inspectors are charged with the 'marking' and the appraisal of secondary level teachers of their discipline. The *département* inspectors are responsible for the inspection of primary level institutions and teachers.

Evaluation of higher education

The Law of 26 January 1984 created a National Evaluation Committee (*Comité national d'évaluation* – *CNE*) for higher education. This committee constitutes an independent administrative authority which sets its own projects and enjoys financial autonomy.

The national evaluation committee examines and assesses all the activities of universities, colleges, and institutions under the responsibility of the Ministry of Higher Education. It can also evaluate institutions under the responsibility of other ministries.

The committee examines institutions and not individuals. It assesses the quality of research and teaching, teacher training, continuing training, the administration of staff and services, the academic environment, the admission and supervision of students, local integration, and national and international contacts. To accomplish these tasks, the committee has established a series of operational indicators.

Each year, the national evaluation committee submits a report on its activities and on the state of higher education and research to the President of the Republic.

1.6 Financing

The State covers the salaries of teaching, administrative and guidance staff. However, the local authorities are now responsible for investment and operational expenditure: the regions for upper secondary education institutions – *Lycées*, and regional institutions for special education (*éducation adaptée*) (*EREA*); the *départements* for lower secondary schools (*Collèges*); and the communes for nursery and primary schools. The regions also contribute to the financing of universities, in particular for major investments, together with the State.

The cost of apprenticeship is covered by an apprenticeship levy paid by enterprises, the State and the general councils.

1.7 Private education

The majority of private education institutions are denominational – mainly Catholic – and have signed a contract with the State, which then provides them with significant financial support, including the cost of teachers' salaries and of their initial and in-service training. Institutions under contract must adhere to the timetables and curricula applied in public education and are subject to state supervision.

Approximately 17% of pupils from nursery to upper secondary level currently attend private schools. In this sector, families must pay school fees which vary from school to school.

1.8 Advisory bodies

The Minister for National Education is assisted by several advisory bodies whose role is to provide information, formulate proposals or give advice.

The principal advisory bodies are:

- The Higher Council for Education (*Conseil supérieur de l'éducation – CSE*), with 95 members, representing staff in public education (48 members); users – parents, pupils and students (19 members); and territorial authorities, associations for out-of-school activities, and educational interest groups (28 members). This Council provides advice on all educational issues (such as objectives and operation, regulations, etc.).

- The National Curriculum Council (*Conseil national des programmes – CNP*). Created by the

framework law of July 1989, the council 'advises and submits proposals (to the competent ministers) on the general conception of education, important objectives to be reached, the adaptation of curricula and subject areas to achieve these objectives, and their adjustment to developments in knowledge'.

- Joint committees, made up of an equal number of representatives from the administration and staff. They include Joint Technical Committees (*Comités techniques paritaires – CTP*), National Joint Administrative Committees (*Commissions administratives paritaires nationales – CAPN*), and vocational advisory committees.

In the field of higher education, there is the National Council for Higher Education and Research (*Conseil national de l'enseignement supérieur et de la recherche – CNESER*), which comprises 61 members, representing staff (29), students (11) and the main national educational, cultural, scientific, economic and social interest groups (21). This provides advice to the Minister on the main orientations for higher education: draft reforms, types of education, distribution of financing between institutions, etc.

There are eight further national public institutions providing education-related services under the direct responsibility of the Ministry of National Education and/or the Ministry of Higher Education and Research: the National Institute for Educational Research (*INRP*), the National Centre for Educational Documentation (*CNDP*), the National Centre for Distance Education (*CNED*), the National Centre for University and School Life (*CNOUS*), the National Office for Information on Studies and Professions (*ONISEP*), the Centre for Studies and Research on Qualifications (*CEREQ*), the International Centre for Educational Studies (*CIEP*), and the Union of Groupings of Public Purchases (*UGAP*).

2. Pre-school education (Enseignement préélémentaire)

Pre-school education is optional and is available to children between the ages of two and five. Children who have reached two by the first day of the school year can be admitted to nursery schools (écoles maternelles) and infant classes (classes enfantines) if space is available. An effort is made to give priority to nursery school places in socially-disadvantaged areas. At age three, every child should be able to attend a nursery school or an infant class at the request of his/her family.

In the absence of a nursery school or an infant class, children aged five, for whom parents request school admission, are admitted to the infant section in a primary school (école élémentaire) and enter the basic learning cycle.

France has a long tradition of providing pre-school education, and for this reason more than 99% of children aged three attend school. The attendance rate for two-year-olds has reached 35.2%.

Attendance at public nursery schools is free of charge. In private nursery schools, parents pay school fees.

The school area of public schools is fixed by the municipal authorities. The framework law for education of 10 July 1989 reflects developments that had been taking place since 1975 by stating that: 'It must be possible for every child at the age of three to be admitted to a nursery school or an infant class as close as possible to his or her home, at the request of his/her family'.

Decree n° 90-788 of 6 September 1990 concerning the organization and operation of nursery and primary schools stipulates that the general objective of nursery education is to develop the children's full potential in order to permit them to shape their own personality and to give them the best possible chance to succeed in school and life by preparing them for further learning.

The services of a specialized person recruited by the communal authorities are available to all nursery classes. To compensate for the effect of nursery school closures due to the decline in the number of children, especially in rural or mountainous areas, there are sometimes intercommunal nursery schools which serve children from several communes, or part-time classes and peripatetic classes (classes ambulantes) in areas with a very low population density.

The children are generally divided by age into three sections: 'lower', 'middle' and 'upper'. This division is flexible in order to take into account the different learning rhythms and maturity of each child and the skills he or she has acquired. The teaching team, in consultation with parents, can choose to place a child in the section which best suits his or her needs, even if it does not precisely correspond to the child's age. The three sections correspond to the first learning cycle, while the upper section, along with the first two years of primary school, corresponds to the basic learning cycle. Multi-year cycles with objectives to be attained over a period longer than a single school year have been implemented in response to the desire to adapt schools better to children's needs.

Children have 26 hours of lessons per week.

Curriculum and assessment

The main educational activities contribute to the children's general development and prepare them for primary school. They cover physical, scientific, and technical activities and activities promoting communication and oral and written expression. Games play an important role in nursery school, but this does not mean that rigour and effort are excluded.

The national education inspector (*IEN*) responsible for the district supervises the administrative and educational operation of the institutions. The school council meets at least once each term; it votes on the school's internal regulations and establishes the plan for the school week.

The organization of teaching into cycles makes it easier for the team of teachers to adapt teaching activities to the learning rhythm and progress of each child. The provisions put in place in each cycle take into account the particular difficulties and learning rhythm of each child. The teacher or the team is responsible for regularly assessing the achievement of each pupil and for recommending whether he/she should move up to primary school or be kept back within pre-school education.

Teachers

As nursery school constitutes an integral part of the education system, teachers in nursery schools receive the same training as primary school teachers: after three years of post-secondary education (usually at university) leading to a diploma, they spend one or two years (the first year is optional) at a university teacher training institute (*Institut universitaire de formation des maîtres – IUFM*). On completion of the second year of the *IUFM*, successful students are designated 'school teachers' (*professeurs des écoles*).

As officials of the public education system or as contractors in a private school under contract, nursery school teachers have the same rights, responsibilities and duties as teachers in primary schools (their careers follow the same paths, they are required to spend the same amount of time at school – 316 half-days – and they have the same right to in-service training).

Statistics 1992/93

	Public	Private
Pupils		
Nursery schools	1,895,547	36,793
Infant classes	336,950	280,348
Teachers	279,078*	
Nursery Schools	18,646	395
Pupil-teacher ratio	27.5	27.3

* Nursery and Primary
   (301,300 including special education).

3. Compulsory education

School attendance is compulsory between the ages of 6 and 16. This requirement includes both the primary school (*école élémentaire*) and the *Collège*. On average, pupils leaving the *Collège* (which lasts four years, unless they have repeated a year) are 15 years of age. In theory, pupils must therefore still attend school full-time for at least one more year to satisfy the compulsory schooling requirement, either in a general or technological *Lycée* or in a vocational *Lycée*.

4. Primary education (Enseignement élémentaire)

Primary education is governed by the Framework Law for Education of 10 July 1989. Decree nº 90-788 of 6 September 1990 defines its organization and operation.

Attendance at primary school is free of charge and is compulsory for all children from the age of six. Primary education lasts five years or up to the age of 11. As a rule, parents are required to enrol their children in the school area in which they live, but exceptions can be granted allowing them to send their children to another school of their choice.

Primary school provides pupils with the basic elements and tools of knowledge: oral and written expression, reading and mathematics. It allows pupils to make use of and develop their intelligence, sensitivity and manual, physical and artistic abilities. School permits pupils to extend their awareness of time, space, the objects of the modern world and their own body. It permits the gradual acquisition of methodological skills and provides pupils with a solid preparation for further schooling at a *Collège*.

The organization of primary education presents particular problems in sparsely-populated zones such as rural and mountainous areas. Schools have therefore been restructured in these areas (pupils from several communes have been grouped together or the different levels of education have been redistributed and regrouped).

Primary school includes five classes divided into two cycles: the basic learning cycle which begins in the upper section of nursery school and continues in the first two years of primary school; and the consolidation cycle which covers the final three years (*CE2, CM1* and *CM2*) before admission to the *Collège*.

The basic unit of organization is the group/class. To make it easier for all children to succeed, this structure can vary: one teacher can follow a group of pupils throughout an entire cycle; classes can cover several courses; and the teachers' services can be decompartmentalized or specialized.

Since 1 January 1992, there have been 26 hours of lessons per week. Schools usually close on Wednesdays and on Saturday afternoons as well as on Sundays.

Sports and artistic and cultural activities are frequently offered in addition to the 26 hours of teaching. These extracurricular activities are organized by local organizations or associations.

In most schools, a cafeteria is organized by the local authorities or an association. A supervised or directed study service, usually provided by teachers, is also available for children whose parents work.

Curriculum

National curricula and an official text establish the skills to be acquired in the course of each cycle. The overall timetable is flexible within the compulsory subject areas set by the curriculum and within the optional courses such as foreign languages; the latter have been introduced in certain schools on an experimental basis since 1989.

Basic Learning Cycle

Compulsory subject areas	Minimum	Maximum
French, history, geography and civics	9.5 hours	13.5 hours
Mathematics, science and technology	5.5 hours	9.5 hours
Physical education and sports, art	6 hours	8 hours
Total		26 hours

Consolidation Cycle
(with or without a foreign language)

Compulsory subject areas	Minimum	Maximum
French, history, geography and civics	8.5 hours	12.5 hours
Mathematics, science and technology	6.5 hours	10.5 hours
Physical education and sports, art	6 hours	8 hours
Total		26 hours

Since public schools in France are secular, religion is not taught – except in the Upper-Rhine, Lower Rhine and Moselle *départements,* which have retained a special status since their return to France in 1918.

The timetables will be subject to a new regulation at the beginning of the 1995/96 school year.

The curricula and instructions for primary school were supplemented in January 1991 by a document entitled 'Cycles in Primary Education'. This document sets out the broad lines of education policy for primary schools and the skills which pupils should acquire in the course of each cycle.

There are no prescribed teaching methods or materials. Teachers in each school agree on the particular materials they wish to use from the range available from private publishers. Teaching materials are usually published for use nationwide. Local or regional associations and documentation centres in the regions or *départements* sometimes produce teaching materials as a local supplement to those published for national use.

Assessment

The Teachers' Council of each cycle promotes pupils within the cycle on the recommendation of their teacher. Parents must be informed regularly of their child's progress.

A national test has been organized at the beginning of each school year since 1989 to assess the reading, writing and mathematical skills of all pupils entering the consolidation cycle (and in the 6th class in *Collèges*). The primary goal of this test is to provide teachers with a tool to gauge their pupils' progress in these three basic areas. This assessment should assist teachers in choosing the teaching activities most suited to the pupils.

To adapt to the learning rhythms of each child, the amount of time spent in each cycle can be extended or reduced by one year. Each child's situation is assessed by the Teachers' Council of the cycle, in some cases at the parents' request. A written proposal is sent to parents, who can accept it or challenge it by appealing to a higher authority (which then takes the final decision).

Each child has a report book (*livret scolaire*), which is shown regularly to parents and constitutes a method of communication between teacher and family. This report book indicates the results of periodic assessment and provides information on the skills acquired by the pupil. It informs parents of proposals by the Teachers' Council of the cycle concerning the child's promotion to a higher class or cycle and of the final decisions taken.

Children who complete normal school attendance or have difficulties that are not covered by special education are promoted automatically from primary school to the first class of secondary school. As is the case in primary school, parents are expected (unless an exception is made) to enrol their children in an institution in their own school area.

Teachers

Teachers are assigned to particular classes. One teacher is responsible for each class, although the teachers concerned can agree that for certain subject areas pupils are grouped by subject area.

First level (pre-school and primary) teachers are recruited on the basis of the same academic competitive examination and receive identical initial training. At the end of this training, new teachers are assigned to the pre-school or the primary level on the basis partly of their preference and partly of the availability of posts in the *département*.

Since 1992, first level teachers (*professeurs des écoles*) have been recruited from among holders of a diploma confirming completion of at least three years of post-secondary education. Candidates are admitted to a university teacher training institute (*IUFM*) on the basis of an examination of their dossier and in some cases an interview.

The *IUFM* are higher education institutions which have replaced the previous training structures for teachers in the first and second levels (*écoles normales d'instituteurs, centres pédagogiques régionaux, écoles normales nationales d'apprentissage).* At the end of the first year (optional) of theoretical and practical training at an *IUFM*, candidates for the first level take the competitive recruitment examination. Successful students become trainee teachers and are remunerated for their work. They then complete a second year of training, at the end of which they are appointed to positions as school teachers.

Circular n° 26 of 14 November 1994 defines the national framework for the content and certification of training organized by the *IUFM*. The structure of this training is based on the link between theoretical and practical training throughout the programme.

The qualification received at the end of the second year is based on the work accomplished during the eight-week period of teaching practice, the subjects studied at the *IUFM*, and a thesis dealing with a practical aspect of education. It grants teachers official status and gives them the right to a teaching position.

Qualified first level teachers may devote 36 weeks to in-service training during their career, but this training is not compulsory.

Statistics 1992/93

	Public	Private
Pupils*	3,462,791	597,617
Teachers	279,078**	
Schools	36,489	5,746

* Including special education
** Nursery and Primary
(301,300 including special education).

5. Secondary education

Secondary education begins in the *Collège*, the only institution admitting all pupils for the first four years of secondary education, and continues in a general and technological *Lycée* or a vocational *Lycée*.

5.1 *Collèges*

Collèges were created by the law of 11 July 1975. Education lasts four years – 6th, 5th, 4th and 3rd classes (i.e. 1st, 2nd, 3rd and 4th years respectively). A variety of routes ensures that all pupils reach the 3rd class.

Even when preparing pupils for vocational education, *Collèges* provide secondary education of a general nature within the framework of compulsory education. As a result, all children who complete the consolidation cycle of primary school are admitted to a *Collège* at the latest at the age of 12.

Collèges have the status of local public institutions with legal responsibility and financial autonomy. School life is governed by internal regulations voted on annually by the Board of Governors and brought to the attention of all, especially the parents. The head teacher, called '*principal*', performs administrative and teaching duties.

Collèges serve the dual objective of preparing all pupils for social integration and for school success, which means that each institution must organize assistance for pupils experiencing difficulties.

In order to provide the best possible conditions for all pupils up to the 3rd class, at the beginning of the 1992/93 school year 3rd classes preparing pupils for integration into working life were created. The purpose of these classes, which offer a link to the world of work, is to provide a positive framework for pupils whose primary goal is to gain admission to vocational training.

In addition to this 3rd 'integration' class, where the number of pupils is reduced to 15, some *Collèges* have established special sections, such as music classes with specially arranged timetables and sports studies, as well as bilingual, international, and European sections.

Education in *Collèges* is organized in two cycles of two years each:

- the observation cycle, comprising the 6th and 5th classes, consolidates and completes primary education, while providing the first elements of secondary education, and is identical for all pupils;

- the orientation cycle, comprising the 4th and 3rd classes of general and technological education.

By ministerial decision the organization of education will change as from the beginning of the 1995/96 school year. There will be three cycles: the 6th class will constitute the cycle of observation and adaptation; the 5th and 4th classes will become the consolidation cycle; and the 3rd class will be the orientation cycle.

General and technological education offer the same orientation opportunities at the end of the 3rd class, but they differ in the teaching materials and methods employed. Subject areas taught in general education allow pupils to learn to think logically, to master means of expression and to develop personal working habits. In technological classes, knowledge is approached by studying technical and technological projects developed by the teaching team as a whole and designed to lead pupils to specific accomplishments.

Each *Collège* organizes the school week in its own way. Subject areas should be distributed evenly with teaching spread over five (sometimes six) mornings

and two to four afternoons. No teaching is provided on Wednesday and Saturday afternoons.

Class hours usually include 55 minutes of teaching and a five-minute break between classes. Pupils are admitted to the school ten minutes before the beginning of classes. Two facilities provide supervision outside class hours: supervised study, which allows pupils to work or read under the guidance of supervisory staff (*surveillants d'externat*) or qualified teaching staff (*maîtres d'internat*), and documentation and information centres (*CDI*).

The *CDI* are directed by a documentalist, who makes educational materials available to pupils and teachers and provides technical assistance, such as audiovisual and copy services. Pupils can carry out documentary research in the *CDI*, which allows them gradually to become more independent.

Curriculum

Observation Cycle: 6th and 5th classes

The weekly timetable is as follows:

French	4.5 hours
Mathematics	3 hours
1st modern foreign language	3 hours
History, geography and an introduction to economics	2.5 hours
Civics	1 hour
Biology and geology	1.5 hours
Plastic arts	1 hour
Music	1 hour
Technology	2 hours
Physical education and sport	3 hours
Total	22.5 hours

As from the observation cycle, a contingent timetable, calculated on the basis of three hours per week for each division of the 6th and 5th classes, makes it possible for each school to increase the number of hours indicated in the above table to provide support teaching to pupils experiencing difficulties.

Orientation Cycle: 4th and 3rd classes of general education

Pupils promoted from the 5th class to the 4th class of general education are distributed among undifferentiated classes. In the common subject areas, the weekly timetable is as follows:

French	4.5 hours
Mathematics	4 hours
1st modern foreign language	3 hours
History, geography and an introduction to economics	2.5 hours
Civics	1 hour
Biology and geology	1.5 hours
Physics and chemistry	2 hours
Plastic arts	1 hour
Music	1 hour
Technology	1.5 hours
Physical education and sport	3 hours
Total	25 hours

In addition to these common subject areas, pupils must select one optional course. They can also choose a second optional course if they wish. The hours for the various options are as follows:

Latin	3 hours
Greek	3 hours
2nd modern foreign language	3 hours
Intensified study of 1st modern foreign language	2 hours
Total:	27 or 28 hours, depending on the compulsory option

As in the 6th and 5th classes, *Collèges* organize differentiated educational activities to meet the needs of pupils, especially those experiencing difficulties.

Orientation Cycle: 4th and 3rd classes of technological education

Technological education combines technological training and general education. The weekly timetable is as follows:

French	4.5 hours
Mathematics	4 hours
1st modern foreign language	3 hours
History, geography and civics	3 hours
Technology	7 hours
Physical sciences	1 hour
Biology	1 hour
Art	2 hours
Physical education and sport	3 hours
Total	28.5 hours

As from the 4th class, pupils may choose to study a second modern foreign language in addition to the above compulsory courses.

The decree of 9 March 1993, which established these timetables, specifies that 'all subject areas must contribute wherever possible to the technological aspect of education', and that for French, mathematics and physical sciences 'a considerable part of the compulsory timetable must in any case be devoted to this end'.

Technological education itself, for which seven hours have been set aside each week, is provided as integrated technology in *Collèges* and is organized around three main areas: mechanics and automation; electronics and industrial computer science; and economics and management including the use of computer science and knowledge of the work environment.

Official guidelines do not prescribe specific teaching methods, but the curricula defined by the Ministry must be respected. As in primary education, teachers in a particular subject area select teaching materials from the range offered by educational publishers.

Assessment and qualifications

During his or her years in a *Collège*, each pupil is assessed in a way which will determine his or her orientation.

Families are informed of the work done by their children by means of:

- a termly report which contains the pupil's results and teachers' comments in each subject area, general comments, and advice from the head teacher;

- a book (*carnet*) for marks and correspondence which provides a link between parents and teachers. This includes a class timetable, pages reserved for correspondence (such as requests for appointments and meeting dates), and sometimes a summary of marks received;

- contacts and meetings with class teachers and especially with the principal teacher and guidance counsellor;

- regular parent-teacher meetings.

There are currently no regulations on the marking of pupils attending *Collèges*. In practice, pupils' results first take the form of a series of marks noted in the report submitted each term to parents by the school management. These marks concern class work or personal work, the weekly amount of which is determined by the Teachers' Council. Marks in each subject area are accompanied by detailed comments by the teacher on the work and progress achieved by the pupil.

Finally, the pupil's results in the 4th and 3rd classes are noted on a school report card which is taken into account for the award of the national certificate (*diplôme national du brevet*). This is a general education certificate and does not determine the pupil's future orientation. The certificate is awarded on the basis of marks achieved in the examination at the end of the 3rd class and of the results during the 4th and 3rd classes.

Guidance is an educational activity, the purpose of which is to assist each pupil throughout his or her school career to make reasoned educational and vocational choices. Guidance is one of the school's primary functions.

The Framework Law on Education of 10 July 1989 states in article 8 that 'the right to guidance counselling and information concerning courses and occupations is part of the right to education'.

Decree n° 90-484 of 14 June 1990 defines the principles and forms of guidance for pupils.

At the end of the 4th class, three options can be considered in discussions with the family, depending on the pupil's achievements and personal goals:

– repetition of a general or technological 4th class;

– promotion to a general or technological 3rd class;

– promotion to a 3rd 'integration' class to prepare for a qualifying vocational training programme.

The 3rd class, the final year of *Collège* and of the orientation cycle, constitutes the key period in guidance. Three options are possible:

– the 2nd general or technological class which leads to a general or technological *Baccalauréat*;

– the 2nd vocational class which leads to a vocational studies certificate (*brevet d'études professionnelles – BEP*). This option allows pupils to advance ultimately to a vocational or technological *Baccalauréat*, after they have received an initial vocational qualification;

– the first year of preparation for the vocational aptitude certificate (*certificat d'aptitude professionnelle – CAP*).

The Class Council proposes an option based on the wishes expressed by the pupil and his or her family. The proposal is submitted to the family which can accept it or appeal to a committee.

5.2. General or technological *Lycées* (*Lycées d'enseignement général et technologique*)

General or technological *Lycées* are coeducational secondary schools which prepare pupils in three years (2nd, 1st and terminal classes) for the following certificates: the general *Baccalauréat*, the technological *Baccalauréat*, and the technical certificate (*brevet de technicien*).

Preparatory classes for *grandes écoles* (*CPGA*) and higher technical sections (*STS*) established within *Lycées* offer post-*Baccalauréat* training.

Collège leavers usually attend *Lycées* in their own school districts, unless their family opts for private education, or the specialization chosen (for example, a foreign language not included at the local school, a European section, etc.) involves attending an institution further away.

Pupils coming from a private institution under contract will be admitted to public secondary education on the basis of the option proposed by the private institution concerned. Pupils may also transfer from a public institution to a private institution under contract, in which case that school is required to respect measures taken by the public institution which affect the education and orientation of the pupils.

The financial and administrative organization, the decision-making and consultation structures, and the provisions concerning the organization of the school day are the same as in *Collèges*.

Curriculum

2nd class

The 2nd class includes the following common courses, for which there is a common timetable and identical curriculum for all pupils:

French	4 hours
Mathematics	3.5 hours
Physics and chemistry	3.5 hours
Life and earth sciences	2 hours
Technology of automated systems	3 hours
Modern foreign language	2.5 hours
History and geography	3 hours
Physical education and sport	2 hours

In addition, pupils follow 3 hours of compulsory education per week in the form of modules – group work in addition to the normal timetable in the following subject areas: French, mathematics, history-geography, modern foreign language (45 minutes per week for each subject area). This new type of teaching is designed to allow teachers to address the heterogeneity of their pupils by using diversified teaching activities and reorganizing pupils in groups smaller than the class itself.

In addition to the common courses, pupils are required to choose two options, which allows them to test their preferences and aptitudes with regard to the type of *Baccalauréat* for which they would study in the 1st and the terminal classes.

Pupils may also attend an optional course in the practical workshops made available in their *Lycée* within the context of its own educational projects.

There are also specific 2nd classes in preparation for a specific qualification. For example, the section leading to the *Baccalauréat* F 11 Music and the sections leading to certain technical certificates (*brevets de technicien*), such as printing, mirror-glass production, clothing, the hotel trade, graphics industries and music.

The timetables established by the decree of 17 January 1992 range between 29.5 and 31.5 hours per week, depending on the options selected.

1st and Terminal Classes

The reform of the *Lycées* has led to a reorganization of the 1st and terminal classes, characterized by a reduction in the number of types of courses and corresponding *Baccalauréats*.

At the end of the 2nd general or technological class, pupils have a choice between:

- Three types of general *Baccalauréat*: L (literary), ES (economic and social), and S (scientific).

- Four types of technological *Baccalauréat*: STT (sciences and tertiary technologies), STI (sciences and industrial technologies), STL (sciences and laboratory technologies), SMS (medico-social sciences).

- Specific technological *Baccalauréats* (being revised): for the hotel trade, applied arts, music, and dance.

The types of courses that prepare for the various *Baccalauréats* are very different but usually include common, elective and optional courses.

- The technical certificate (*brevet de technicien*). This provides a qualification as a technician specialized in a specific area and includes common and compulsory general courses: French, introduction to the modern world, a modern foreign language, mathematics, and physical education and sport; specific courses according to the specialization chosen; and technological and vocational courses. Pupils who have been awarded a technical certificate can:

  - enter employment by taking up a position corresponding to their specialization;

  - continue their studies, primarily in higher technical sections (*STS*) or in a university institute of technology (*IUT*).

Some technical certificates can be obtained immediately after the 3rd class by attending a specific 2nd class (*seconde spécifique*). Others can be obtained after a 2nd class for pupils who have followed a specific option (*seconde de détermination*).

Agricultural *Lycées* offer agricultural technical certificates (*brevet de technicien agricole – BTA*) after a specific 2nd class. These certificates qualify pupils to become agricultural technicians.

The Ministry of National Education establishes curricula which teachers are required to respect for these levels, as it does for all other levels of education. Teachers are free to choose their teaching methods and materials. As upper secondary education is not included in compulsory education, families must pay for supplies and school books.

Assessment and qualifications

Pupils are required to do independent and written work at home and in class. The Teachers' Council determines the importance of and adjusts the length of these assignments. In class, pupils take timed tests. Families are informed of their children's results by means of:

- a term report containing the results of and comments on pupil's work in each subject area, general comments, and advice from the head teacher;

- a book (*carnet*) for marks and correspondence which provides a link between parents and teachers;

- contacts and meetings with class teachers;

- parent-teacher meetings.

The 2nd class plays an important role in the pupil's orientation. At the beginning of the 2nd class, all pupils are assessed in the basic disciplines: French, mathematics and a modern foreign language.

In the second term, the pupil and his or her parents make a provisional statement on their preferences with regard to future courses. During the third term, the family expresses in writing its choices concerning the types of courses the pupil would take in the 1st class, ranked in order of preference.

On the basis of these statements and of the pupils' school results and all other assessments, the Class Council drafts proposals concerning which types of courses the pupil will attend in the 1st class. The family can appeal if they do not agree with the decision of the Class Council.

Studies completed in *Lycées* of general and/or technological education lead to a general or technological *Baccalauréat* examination.

The *Baccalauréat*

The *Baccalauréat* is the equivalent to the first year of university. It is the key to admission to higher education. It is organized to reflect the types of courses offered in the 1st class and includes both compulsory and optional examinations.

The examinations relate to the official curricula of the terminal classes in *Lycées*. Only one examination session is organized each year on a date set by the Minister for National Education. The Minister appoints a *recteur* to select the examination subjects.

An examination session is organized under the same conditions in September for candidates who were unable, for reasons beyond their control, to sit the examination at the end of the previous school year.

Pupils who do not pass the *Baccalauréat* examination but have on average received marks equivalent to at least 8/20 can obtain a secondary school leaving certificate (*certificat de fin d'études secondaires*). This certificate, awarded by the *recteur*, states that the pupil has completed secondary education in its entirety, but it does not entitle the pupil to enter higher education.

5.3. Vocational *Lycées* (*Lycées professionnels*)

The vocational *Lycées* prepare for examinations for which the following certificates are awarded:

- the vocational aptitude certificate (*certificat d'aptitude professionnelle – CAP*);

- the vocational studies certificate (*brevet d'études professionnelles – BEP*);

- the vocational *Baccalauréat*.

Vocational aptitude certificate (*CAP*)

The vocational aptitude certificate (*CAP*) is designed to provide a qualification to exercise an occupation.

Preparation involves:

- General education (14.5 to 16 hours per week, depending on the *CAP*): French, mathematics, history and geography, economics, civics, a modern foreign language, art education, home and social economics, and physical education. Education is intended to provide pupils with basic general knowledge focused on the modern world, but it is also adapted to vocational needs.

- Technological and vocational education (12 to 17 hours per week depending on the *CAP*). This takes the form of theoretical courses, practical exercises, and on-the-job training in workshops and offices, and provides the vocational knowledge and skills required for the occupation concerned.

- Varying periods of on-the-job training.

After the *CAP*, some pupils continue their studies and prepare for a vocational studies certificate (*BEP*).

Vocational studies certificate (*BEP*)

The vocational studies certificate (*BEP*) confers the vocational qualification of skilled worker or employee. The certificate requires more extensive training in a vocational field than the *CAP*. Vocational *Lycées* prepare pupils who have completed the 3rd class of *Collège* for the *BEP* in two years.

Courses include:

- General education (14 to 22 hours). Most of the general education subject areas taught in *Collèges* continue to be taught in vocational *Lycées*. They are oriented more directly towards vocational needs. General education is important for success in vocational examinations and enables pupils to continue their studies in preparation for a vocational or technological *Baccalauréat*.

- Technological education (16 to 20 hours). This differs according to the specialization chosen, but always includes a common curriculum for several specializations that are similar or belong to the same vocational sector, and specialized or specific training linked directly to the exercise of the occupation concerned.

Both the theoretical and the practical timetables are heavier than in the *Collège* (33 to 36 hours, depending on the specialization), but the distribution of hours is different and there is less work to be done at home.

- Periods of on-the-job training. Since the beginning of the 1992/93 school year, periods of on-the-job training leading to an examination are being introduced gradually into the preparation of the different *BEP*. Priority is being given to the construction sector, the hotel trade, and graphics industries.

Pupils holding a *BEP* can either enter working life or continue their studies in preparation for a vocational or technological *Baccalauréat*, which requires two further years of schooling (1st and terminal classes). In the case of the technological *Baccalauréat*, holders of a *BEP* can improve their chances of success in technological studies at *Baccalauréat* level and beyond by following an 'adapted' 1st class (*première d'adaptation*) beforehand.

Vocational *Baccalauréat*

The vocational *Baccalauréat* is prepared during the two years which constitute the final cycle in the vocational route (1st and terminal vocational classes). Unlike the technological *Baccalauréat*, the vocational *Baccalauréat* is primarily a vocational integration certificate leading directly to the exercise of an occupation, although it also entitles holders to enter university studies.

The vocational *Baccalauréat* provides qualifying training for a particular occupation and admits candidates holding a *BEP* (or a *CAP* prepared in two years after the 3rd class) corresponding to the vocational *Baccalauréat* concerned.

The creation of this diploma in 1985 had a dual objective:

- To respond to the growing demand from businesses for highly qualified production and maintenance workers having qualifications between those of advanced technicians – who hold an advanced technical certificate (*BTS*) or technological university diploma (*DUT*) – and qualified workers – who hold a *CAP* or *BEP*. The level of the latter appeared increasingly insufficient to keep up with the development of new technologies in the production of all goods and services (such as computer-assisted design and manufacturing, robotics, office automation, automated production techniques, and computer science for industrial and management applications).

- To respond to the development of new maintenance techniques for personal electronic and computer equipment (such as video recorders, personal computers, and video disks).

The vocational *Baccalauréats* were created in close collaboration with employers and take into account specific vocational requirements in order to lead directly to employment. They differ from technological *Baccalauréats*, inasmuch as they are targeted on specific occupations, whereas the technological *Baccalauréats* are much broader in scope (electronics, mechanics, etc.).

The 30 hours of lessons per week are distributed as follows:

- Vocational, technological, and scientific education (16 to 18 hours).

- General education:

  - French, with an emphasis on expression and awareness of the world (3 to 4 hours);

  - a modern foreign language (2 to 3 hours);

  - knowledge of the contemporary world through history, geography, and civics (2 hours);

  - physical education and sport (2 hours);

  - art (2 hours).

In addition, 3 to 6 hours are set aside for individual projects.

- On-the-job training, the distinguishing feature of which is the length of time spent on the job: 16 to 20 weeks over two years.

Assessment

The principles for the assessment and guidance of pupils are the same as in the general and technological *Lycées*.

Teachers

As for teachers at primary level, candidates who wish to teach at secondary level must have acquired at least a *Licence* (university degree obtained after a 3-year course) or another diploma reflecting at least three years of post-secondary study in one of the Member States of the European Union or four years in another country. After recruitment, on the basis of a dossier or interview, future teachers must indicate when they enter a university teacher training institute (*IUFM*) that they wish to teach at secondary level, as this will require more extensive study of the subject they wish to teach.

At the end of the first year at an *IUFM*, candidates for teaching positions at secondary level sit a national competitive examination leading to one of the following certificates:

- *CAPES* (the certificate of aptitude for teaching at secondary level), organized by subject area (with the exception of physical education and sport);

- *CAPEPS* (the certificate of aptitude for teaching physical education and sport);

- *CAPET* (the certificate of aptitude for teaching technical education);

- *CAPLP2* (the certificate of aptitude for teaching in a vocational *Lycée*), organized by subject area in general and vocational education;

- *agrégation*, also organized by subject area, for candidates holding a *maîtrise* (Master's degree obtained after 4 years' study), an equivalent diploma, or one of the certificates of aptitude for teaching mentioned above.

Students who pass these competitive examinations become trainee teachers (*professeurs-stagiaires*) for one year and are paid as such.

The Minister for National Education announces the formal appointment of candidates passed by the academic boards of examiners. As public sector teachers are civil servants, they belong to one of the three groups of teachers with a career path marked by 11 stages: *professeurs des écoles, professeurs certifiés, professeurs agrégés*. They all have a credit of 36 weeks for in-service teacher training.

Like teachers in the public sector, teachers in the private sector under contract to the State are usually recruited from among holders of a *Licence* or other diploma awarded after at least three years of post-secondary study.

Statistics 1992/93

	Public	Private
Pupils		
Collèges	2,560,500	667,800
Vocational *Lycées*	524,100	153,600
General and Technological *Lycées*	1,224,800	328,000
Teachers	355,306*	86,617*
Schools		
Collèges	4,811	
Vocational *Lycées*	1,248	3,758*
General and Technological *Lycées*	1,337	

* *Collèges*, Vocational *Lycées* + General/Technological *Lycées*.

6. Initial vocational training

The Minister for National Education is traditionally responsible for initial vocational training, that is, for pupils and students not in employment.

The Five-year Law of 20 December 1993 on work, employment and vocational training recognizes that the national education service has particular responsibility for the vocational integration of young people; article 54 stipulates that 'every young person must be offered vocational training before leaving the education system whatever level of education he or she has completed'.

This law introduces regional plans for the development of vocational training for young people, covering all training preparing young people for employment: initial training (school and apprenticeship), integration contracts and continuing vocational training. These plans will be drawn up after consultation with the *Académie* Councils of the national education service, and then approved by the Regional Councils after consultation with the educational authorities concerned: the annual agreements defining, for the State and the region, the planning and financing of training will be co-signed by the educational authorities concerned.

Implemented as a measure to combat unemployment, training for 'initial integration into working life' includes **apprenticeship** and **training measures** for young people between the ages of 16 and 25. Apprenticeship, defined in the law of 1971, is a special route in initial vocational training, while training measures for young people between the ages of 16 and 25, developed since 1983 at the initiative of the social partners, are based on the general system of continuing training.

6.1 Apprenticeship

Apprenticeship is a form of alternating initial vocational training under an employment contract. It combines the acquisition of know-how in a firm with theoretical education in an apprentice training centre (*centre de formation d'apprentis – CFA*) and

leads to a certificate of vocational or technological education or another recognized certificate.

The apprenticeship contract is a particular type of contract available to any young person between 16 and 25 years of age. It lasts from one to three years. During the contract period, the apprentice receives a salary which varies according to his/her age and progress; the apprentice is covered by employment legislation. Employers must be recognized as apprenticeship masters by the Prefect of the *département*; this procedure was simplified as of 1994.

Training takes place at the same time in the enterprise and in the *CFA*. Employers are required to provide apprentices with practical training and to enrol them in a *CFA* providing instruction corresponding to the training called for in the contract.

The *CFA* are institutions created by agreement between the managing body and the State or the region. They must offer a minimum of 400 hours of training per year on average and at least 1,500 hours if they are preparing trainees for a vocational *Baccalauréat* or higher technical certificate (*brevet technique supérieur*). In this latter case, the *CFA* may delegate some of the theoretical training to an educational institution and some of the practical technological training to an enterprise. The *CFA* are supervised by the Ministry of National Education.

Apprenticeships are financed from two sources: an apprenticeship levy equivalent to 0.5% of the gross annual salary costs of enterprises (the liberal and agricultural professions are exempted from this requirement) and the regional apprenticeship fund. The latter is funded by state transfers and by the regional council's own resources.

6.2 Alternating training measures for 16- to 25-year-olds

These measures are based on three types of integration contracts: guidance contracts qualification contracts and adaptation contracts.

Guidance contracts (*contrats d'orientation*) are offered to people aged up to 21 years who do not hold a technical or vocational education certificate and who have not completed secondary general education. This contract should lead to integration into working life by means of vocational guidance gained through in-company work experience. The contract, which can be extended to young people up to the age of 26, lasts for three to six months and is not renewable. It includes vocational guidance actions such as pre-training modules and on- or off-the-job training linked to an enterprise. The acquisition of skills is assessed in agreement with the trainee. Trainees under contract are paid by various means.

Qualification contracts (*contrats de qualification*) are offered to young people under the age of 26 who wish to complete their initial training with a vocational training course. This contract, which is concluded with an approved firm, lasts between 6 and 24 months. Employers undertake to provide the young people with employment and vocational training leading to a qualification or certificate. At least 25% of the total time of the contract must be used for general, vocational or technological training provided during working time. While under contract, the young person receives a salary and is protected by all legislation applying to employees.

Adaptation contracts (*contrats d'adaptation*) are employment contracts between a firm and a young unemployed person under the age of 26 and may be of limited or unlimited duration. As the name indicates, these contracts are designed to provide training allowing the trainee to adapt to a specific kind of employment. These contracts are a form of alternating training, linking general, vocational and technological training and the acquisition of vocational skills during working time. Under this contract, 200 hours of training must be provided. While under contract, the young person receives a salary and is protected by all legislation applying to employees.

These contracts may be reorganized within the framework of a draft law presented in the autumn of 1994.

Regardless of the type of contract, the employer must appoint a tutor from among the employees to assist trainees on a voluntary basis. Each tutor supervises the activities of a maximum of three trainees and liaises between the young people and the other employees in the firm. Tutors are trained for this activity.

All enterprises must use or pay a further 0.1% in addition to the apprenticeship levy, and all enterprises employing ten or more people must use or allocate 0.3% of their gross annual salary costs to fund alternating training programmes.

In addition to the contracts described above, the following are available:

- Individualized training credit (*crédit formation individualisé*) for young people. This was established in 1991 and gives young people without qualifications the right to attend a personalized training course leading to certification. Training credit has three purposes: to provide young people with qualifications; to encourage training bodies to individualize the training they provide; and to establish an administrative organization capable of stimulating the system: the training zone. It is essentially a composite system, as it can make use of other existing structures and measures.

- Solidarity employment contracts (*contrats emploi solidarité*). These were created in 1990 for 18- to 25-year-olds with a qualification equivalent to a vocational *Baccalauréat* or a technical certificate having difficulty in finding employment. This type of contract enables trainees to work half-time under a part-time employment contract. It is not a measure leading to a qualification and can only be concluded for up to three periods of 3 to 12 months. Trainees work for 20 hours a week and receive pay equivalent to the index-linked minimum wage (*SMIC*). During the contract, training can be organized for the young person during his or her free time, but such training is unpaid.

Since 1 July 1994, responsibility for qualifying training for young people has been transferred from the State to the regions. As regards the transfer of responsibility for pre-qualification activities and assistance, information and guidance, each region must sign an agreement with the State before 31 December 1998.

6.3 Guidance

In the school environment, guidance is provided through the mediation of the National Office for Information on Studies and Occupations (*ONISEP*) and Centres for Information and Guidance (*CIO*). Although *CIO* operate primarily in the school environment, these centres are open to all groups. In this way, *CIO* counsel job seekers and provide various services: assistance, information, documentation and individual meetings with a guidance counsellor. They have developed a system of self-documentation for occupations and training programmes.

In addition, since 1986 the Ministry of National Education has been developing its own system for the integration of young people (*DIJEN*) who leave the education system before receiving a *Baccalauréat*. It was designed to care for and guide young people, and to encourage them to renew contact with the school system. Guidance provided for young people outside the school environment is one of the major developments of the 1980s. Since 1982, permanent centres for information and guidance (*PAIO*) have been open to young people between the ages of 16 and 25 to provide information concerning available training programmes. Local agencies (*missions locales*) are also available to young people between the ages of 16 and 25 who have left school without an employment or apprenticeship contract. They deal with a wide range of problems including vocational integration, accommodation and health.

There are currently 450 *PAIO* and 238 local agencies with 5,000 employees.

PAIO and local agencies received and assisted 750,000 young people in 1993. In addition, there is the Information and Documentation Centre for Young People (*CIDJ*) with its 25 regional centres (*CRIJ*) which receive young people and provide information on all areas of daily life.

6.4 Statistics

Apprenticeship 1993/94

In France, there are almost 600 apprentice training centres; of these, about 450 lead to diplomas awarded by the Ministry of Education and 150 to those in the agriculture sector.

CFA are managed by private organizations (around 45% of apprentices), Chambers of occupations (around 30%), Chambers of commerce and industry (around 10%), public education institutions (around 7.5%) or territorial authorities, etc.

Apprentices	
Ministry of National Education	218,354*
Agriculture sector	11,600**

* 6,370 increase on 1992/93.
** 15,770 increase on 1992/93.

Distribution by type of certificate (Ministry of National Education)		
Voc. aptitude certificate (*CAP*)	162,297	+0.5
Voc. studies certificate (*BEP*)	19,395	+32.7
Additional endorsements	5,135	+9.9
Voc. certificate (*Brévet professionnel*)	15,005	+16.2
Voc. *Baccalauréat*	8,693	+26.3
Adv. technical certificate (*BTS*)	4,621	+41.3
Other level III certificates	1,276	+59.8
Level I & II certificates	1,932	+133.3

Source: Ministry of National Education.

56.5% of apprentices followed training in the secondary sector and 43.5% in the tertiary sector.

Alternating training programmes

Year	*SIVP*	*CA*	*CQ*	Total
1985	49,854	21,226	3,031	74,111
1986	175,112	172,825	19,247	367,184
1987	323,268	250,629	38,566	612,453
1988	289,405	99,431	65,373	454,209
1989	90,660	118,131	92,375	301,166
1990	51,983	113,022	101,706	266,711

SIVP – introductory courses to working life, replaced in 1991 by the guidance contract.
CA – adaptation contract.
CQ – qualification contract.

Source: Ministry of Labour.

7. Higher education

The law of 26 January 1984, called the Savary Law, defines higher education as a public service including all post-secondary education attached to the different ministerial departments. The tasks of higher education include:

– providing initial and continuing education;

– conducting scientific and technological research and using the results;

– spreading culture and disseminating scientific and technical information;

– promoting international cooperation.

This law defines the basic principles applying to higher education courses under the responsibility of the Ministry of Higher Education and Research, and also establishes the principles governing the organization and operation of higher education institutions, including universities, colleges and institutes outside universities, teacher training colleges (*écoles normales supérieures*), French colleges abroad and the '*grandes écoles*'.

Higher education is characterized by a great variety of institutions. Organization and admission procedures vary according to the type of institution and the purpose of the education provided.

Higher education institutions include:

– universities, which are public institutions admitting (in principal without selection procedures except in the fields of medicine and pharmacy) all applicants who hold a *Baccalauréat* (or other qualification judged to be equivalent) and wish to enrol for short (two years after the *Baccalauréat*) or long (three or more years after the *Baccalauréat*) courses of study. Universities cater for a large number of students and provide a wide variety of study programmes, including basic and practical education. Students who will be permitted to continue their education are gradually selected in the course of succeeding cycles of study;

– public or private colleges and institutes, which provide higher vocational education under the supervision of various ministries. This takes the form of:

– short courses: technological, commercial, or paramedical training, etc.;

– long courses (three or more years after the *Baccalauréat*): advanced training in political science, engineering, commerce and management, veterinary science, notarial skills, architecture, telecommunications and art.

These institutions select students from among applicants holding a *Baccalauréat* on the basis of a competitive examination or the assessment of dossiers by a board of examiners. Subject to the conditions established by decree nº 86-906 of 23 August 1985, applicants can also be admitted to the various levels of post-*Baccalauréat* training in an institution attached to the Ministry of Higher Education – a university, institute or public college – on the basis of an assessment of past studies, work experience or personal skills.

7.1 Universities

The law of 26 January 1984 on higher education defines universities as public institutions with a scientific, cultural, and vocational character. They have administrative, financial, pedagogical and academic autonomy.

Universities are multi-disciplinary: each is made up of education and research units focused on a particular discipline but sharing common objectives. Universities can also include institutes and colleges created by decree, and departments, laboratories, and research centres created by the administrative council of the university. Each university body defines its own statutes and structures.

Admission

To enrol at a university, applicants must hold a *Baccalauréat* or certificate judged equivalent or must have the national diploma providing access to university studies (*diplôme d'accès aux études universitaires – DAEU*). The latter is awarded by universities qualified to do so at the end of a one-year course corresponding to at least 225 hours of education.

Fees/Student finance

The registration fees for public institutions of higher education are determined each year by ministerial decree. Fees are not high in public institutions under the Minister for Higher Education.

Students are eligible for financial assistance; there are higher education grants provided on the basis of social criteria, grants provided on the basis of universities' own criteria (for the preparation of the *DEA*, the *DESS*, the *agrégation* or certain civil service recruitment examinations) and interest-free loans to be reimbursed not later than ten years after completion of studies.

Courses/Qualifications

Long university courses are organized in three successive cycles, each of which leads to national qualifications.

The **first cycle** is an extension of education leading up to the *Baccalauréat* and prepares students to continue studies in the second cycle or in a vocational integration programme. It lasts two years and leads to a certificate of general university studies (*diplôme d'études universitaires générales – DEUG*).

With the exception of law and economics, study programmes are organized in the form of modules (coherent groups of courses) for which credits are awarded to make it easier to change orientation, to interrupt and renew studies, and to study part-time.

Students are required to study at least one modern foreign language in all programmes.

In the case of programmes in the health fields (medicine, dentistry, pharmacy and human biology), students are selected on the basis of performance at the end of the first year. The number of students to be admitted to the second year is determined each year by a joint decree of the Ministry of Higher Education and the Ministry of Health.

The **second cycle** is a consolidation cycle of advanced general, scientific and technical education leading to the exercise of professional responsibilities. This cycle lasts two to three years. There are several types of education:

- basic, professional, and/or specialized education leading to the degrees of *licence* (*DEUG* + 1 year) and *maîtrise* (*licence* + 1 year);

- professional education leading to a scientific or technical *maîtrise* in two years (*DEUG* + 2 years) or to a *maîtrise* in computer methodology applied to management (*DEUG* + 2 years);

- 3-year study courses leading to an engineering degree (*maîtrise* + 1 year, or *DEUG* + 3 years);

- study courses at university institutes of professional education (*IUP*), which accept students who have completed a first year of higher education (first year of *DEUG* or of a preparatory class for the *grandes écoles*). Three-year university and professional courses lead to a *maîtrise* (*Baccalauréat* + 4 years);

- study courses at university teacher training institutes (*IUFM*), which accept students who have completed three years of post-secondary education. University and professional training courses last two years and provide access to the teaching professions.

In addition to national degrees recognized by the Ministry of Higher Education and Research, universities can offer certificates on their own authority (certificates of the university or institution).

The **third cycle** offers highly specialized education and training in research. Students are selected from among applicants holding a *maîtrise*, an engineering degree, or a certificate judged equivalent.

Provisions affecting the third cycle are found in the interministerial decree of 30 March 1992, published in the *Journal officiel* of 3 April 1992.

There are two types of education:

– professional education of one year, with a compulsory period of in-company training, leading to a certificate of advanced specialized studies (*diplôme d'études supérieures spécialisées – DESS*);

– training in (and through) research, leading at the end of the first year to an advanced studies certificate (*diplôme d'études approfondies – DEA*) and then to the preparation over three or four years of a doctorate (defence of a thesis or presentation of a collection of work).

Those who have obtained a doctorate may apply for a certificate recognizing their ability to conduct advanced original research and to train young researchers. The ultimate purpose of this certificate is to entitle the holder to become a university professor.

In addition, master engineers and student engineers in their final year of engineering college can prepare a technological research certificate (*diplôme de recherche technologique - DRT*), a third cycle certificate awarded at the end of a study programme in innovation through technological research in the industrial or tertiary sectors.

Training in the health fields is also organized in three cycles. The total length of training depends on the discipline chosen:

– eight years to obtain the state degree of doctor in general medicine;

– 10 to 11 years (depending on the specialization) for the state degree of doctor in specialized medicine;

– five years for the degree of doctor in dentistry;

– six years for the degree of doctor in pharmacy.

Assessment

Procedures for assessing students are fixed by the universities themselves. Qualifications are almost always awarded on the basis of written and oral examinations. Universities usually also organize a continuous assessment of the knowledge acquired by students which allows them to take into account their performance throughout the year.

7.2 Other higher education

There are two types of other higher education: short and long courses.

Short courses

These mainly concern the industrial and tertiary sectors. Following two and sometimes three years of study, a certificate of professional education is awarded. Courses are offered in:

– University institutes of technology (*institut universitaire de technologie – IUT*) attached to universities. Training leads to a university technology certificate (*diplôme universitaire de technologie – DUT*), which entitles the holder to take on a managerial position in the secondary and tertiary sectors. Admission to an *IUT* is subject to selection.

– Higher technical sections (*sections de techniciens supérieurs – STS*) set up within general and technological *Lycées*: studies, which last two years, differ from those offered in *IUT* as they are more highly specialized and relate to very precise needs. Training leads to an advanced technical certificate (*brevet de technicien supérieur – BTS*). Admission to an *STS* is based on the applicant's dossier.

– Universities, where students can prepare a certificate of scientific and technical university studies (*diplôme d'études universitaires scientifiques et techniques – DEUST*) in two years, entitling them to enter employment directly.

– Universities and colleges attached to the Ministry of Health for paramedical training. Admission to these courses is very selective and is decided at the time of the *Baccalauréat* on the basis of a competitive examination, a normal examination, test or interview. Studies can last up to four years.

Long courses

The law of 12 July 1875 established the principle of the freedom of higher education making it possible to create private higher education institutions through a legal declaration of establishment. These very diverse institutions have highly selective entrance procedures in common. A *Baccalauréat* is required but is not enough to secure a place.

There are:

- engineering colleges (*écoles d'ingénieurs*);

- the *grandes écoles* of commerce and management;

- *Ecole des hautes études commerciales (HEC)*;

- *Ecole supérieure des sciences économiques et commerciales (ESSEC)*;

- *Ecole supérieure de commerce de Paris (Sup de Co)*;

- *Ecole supérieure de commerce de Lyon*;

- *Ecoles supérieures de commerce et d'administration des entreprises (ESCAE)*, of which there are 18;

- *Ecoles* or *Instituts supérieurs de sciences commerciales*, of which there are 17;

- 'Catholic colleges', private institutions recognized by the Ministry of Higher Education and Research, which provide both university and college courses. Students attending these institutions take examinations before university examination boards. The five Catholic colleges are located in Paris, Lille, Lyons, Angers, and Toulouse.

All private institutions can request state recognition.

The Minister for Higher Education grants recognition by decree. Recognized institutions are entitled to receive state subsidies and their students can receive public education grants. Recognized institutions are subject to inspection, and the appointment of their directors and teaching staff is subject to approval by the *recteur* of the *académie*.

The Minister for Higher Education can, by decree, grant institutions that have been recognized by the State for at least five years the right to award official certificates ('*revêtus du visa officiel*' in current jargon). The criteria for awarding this right are the same as for recognition, but include additional requirements concerning the level and quality of education.

In the public sector only, there are:

- Nine political science colleges (*instituts d'études politiques - IEP*). The one in Paris ('*Sciences-po*') accepts candidates holding a *Baccalauréat* to the first year after a very rigorous selection examination. Holders of a certificate equivalent to at least a *licence* can be admitted to the second year after an interview.

IEP award a certificate after three years of study. They also offer their graduates advanced courses lasting one to two years within the framework of third cycle studies.

- Colleges of natural science (*grandes écoles scientifiques*) under the Ministry of Higher Education (such as the *Ecole Centrale des Arts et Manufactures, Ecole Centrale de Lyon, Ecole nationale supérieure des Arts et Industries textiles*, and E*cole nationale supérieure d'Arts et Métiers*). Students are admitted on the basis of a highly selective competitive entrance examination. Students can prepare for the entrance examination in a two-year course following the *Baccalauréat* in the scientific preparatory classes in *Lycées*, in the first cycle of university or, sometimes, in the colleges themselves. After admission, studies take between two and five years depending on the college. The colleges award an engineering degree approved by the committee on diplomas and certificates (*commission des titres*) attached to the Ministry of Higher Education and Research.

- Four teacher training colleges (*écoles normales supérieures – ENS*) in Paris, Fontenay/Saint-Cloud, Lyons, and Cachan. These schools set similarly high admission requirements. A highly selective competitive entrance examination prepared in scientific preparatory classes for two years following the *Baccalauréat* (particularly in 'advanced mathematics' and then 'special mathematics' classes) or in literary preparatory classes ('advanced literature' and 'first-higher' classes). These lead to national university certificates and to the competitive examination for the recruitment of teachers (*certificat d'aptitude au professorat de l'enseignement secondaire/CAPES* and *agrégation*).

- Certain higher education colleges attached to other ministries, in particular:

  - The *Ecole nationale d'administration (ENA)* which is under the responsibility of the Prime Minister and trains civil servants destined to occupy senior administrative posts.

  - Military training institutions attached to the Ministry of Defence, including schools for the army, navy and air force. Admission to the most prestigious colleges (including the *école polytechnique*, the *école spéciale militaire de Saint-Cyr*, the *école navale*, and the *école de l'air de Salon-de-Provence*) is on the basis of competitive examinations at the end of the scientific preparatory classes.

  - Mining colleges under the Ministry of Industry accept students on the basis of a competitive examination or of the applicant's qualifications (depending on the case: *Baccalauréat* + 1 year, *Baccalauréat* + 2 years or *Baccalauréat* + 4 years). These colleges award an engineering degree at the end of three or four years.

- The *école nationale des Ponts et Chaussées* under the Ministry of Development, doyen of the *grandes écoles,* recruits students by competitive examination at the end of the scientific preparatory classes or on the basis of qualifications. The college awards an engineering degree at the end of three or four years.

- Institutions of advanced agricultural training under the Ministry of Agriculture.

- National colleges of veterinary medicine under the Ministry of Health.

- Art colleges under the Ministry of Culture.

- Architecture colleges under the Ministry of Development.

Ireland

IRELAND

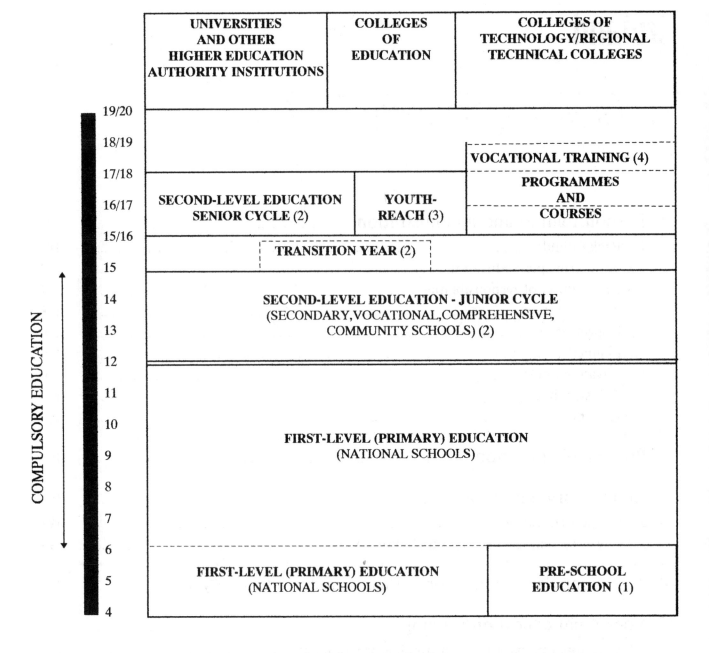

	UNIVERSITIES AND OTHER HIGHER EDUCATION AUTHORITY INSTITUTIONS	COLLEGES OF EDUCATION	COLLEGES OF TECHNOLOGY/REGIONAL TECHNICAL COLLEGES
19/20			
18/19			VOCATIONAL TRAINING (4)
17/18	SECOND-LEVEL EDUCATION SENIOR CYCLE (2)	YOUTH-REACH (3)	PROGRAMMES AND COURSES
16/17			
15/16			
15	TRANSITION YEAR (2)		
14	SECOND-LEVEL EDUCATION - JUNIOR CYCLE (SECONDARY, VOCATIONAL, COMPREHENSIVE, COMMUNITY SCHOOLS) (2)		
13			
12			
11	FIRST-LEVEL (PRIMARY) EDUCATION (NATIONAL SCHOOLS)		
10			
9			
8			
7			
6			
5	FIRST-LEVEL (PRIMARY) EDUCATION (NATIONAL SCHOOLS)		PRE-SCHOOL EDUCATION (1)
4			

COMPULSORY EDUCATION

1. There is no national system of pre-school education in Ireland. However, primary *(National)* schools may accept pupils on or after their 4th birthday. Existing pre-school services are mainly private and not part of the formal education system. The average age for starting school is five years.

2. Second-level schools cover lower and upper secondary education - Junior and Senior Cycles. The four main types - Secondary, Vocational, Comprehensive and Community - all now offer a comprehensive curriculum combining academic and vocational subjects. The Transition Year is a one-year interdisciplinary programme, either at the end of full-time schooling or in preparation for the Senior Cycle. The Junior Cycle leads to the new Junior Certificate providing access to the Senior Cycle.

At Senior Cycle, the main courses are the 2-year Leaving Certificate leading to higher education or employment, and the Vocational Preparation and Training Programmes which prepare for working life.

3. Youthreach is an education and training programme available to young people who have left school with no formal qualification. It lasts 2 years (a Foundation year and a Progression year).

It is run jointly by the education authorities (Vocational Education Committees - VEC) and the Vocational Training and Employment Authority *(FAS)*.

4. Training courses of various lengths are provided by *FAS* for unemployed young people: Community Training Workshops, Travellers Training Workshops.

------- = alternative beginning or end of level/type of education

1. Responsibilities and administration

1.1 Background

Ireland is a parliamentary democracy. The National Parliament (*Oireachtas*) consists of the President (*Uachtaran*) and a House of Representatives (*Dail Eireann*) and a Senate (*Seanad*). The Prime Minister (*Taoiseach*) is the Head of the Government. As of December 1994, the Government comprises a coalition between the Labour Party, Democratic Left and Fine Gael.

At the local level, the elected authorities are the county councils (27), county boroughs and borough corporations (5), borough corporations (6), urban district councils (49) and boards of town commissioners (30).

Under the Constitution (*Bunreacht na hEireann*) freedom of conscience and freedom to profess and practise religion is guaranteed, subject to public order and morality. The majority of Irish people are Roman Catholic (91.5% according to the 1991 census).

The Constitution states that the Irish language (*Gaeilge*), the national language, is the first official language, and recognizes English, the mother tongue of the majority of the population, as second official language. Irish is spoken in the *Gaeltacht* areas.

1.2 Basic principles: education

The Constitution recognizes the right and duty of parents to provide for their children's education, and guarantees parents the freedom to decide where education should take place, i.e. 'in their homes or in private schools or in schools recognized or established by the State'. The State is obliged by the Constitution to ensure that children receive a certain minimum education, to provide for free first-level education and to supplement and to aid private and corporate initiatives when the public good requires it.

The historical background to these constitutional provisions is that in the nineteenth century and earlier, the State encouraged the development of a primary school system based on voluntary local initiatives and under local control and management. The State did not undertake to provide schools but would aid their provision in response to local initiatives. These local initiatives were mostly taken by the various Churches with the result that the system of primary education became denominational in character.

In parallel with the system of primary education, secondary schools were established mainly on the initiative of various religious orders involved in education and, starting in the late eighteenth century, without public endowment. There was initially no Government involvement in the establishment or operation of these schools.

1.3 Distribution of responsibilities

The overall responsibility for education in Ireland lies with the Minister for Education who is a member of the Irish Government and responsible to the National Parliament. In practice, the administration of education in Ireland is conducted from the Department of Education. Thus, the system of administration is a centralized one, although there are elements of localized management at first and second levels. Higher education institutions are autonomous statutory bodies. The Green Paper published in June 1992 envisages a major shift of responsibility for day-to-day administration from the Department to the individual school level.

The Minister for Education and the Minister for Enterprise and Employment (through the Training and Employment Authority – *Foras Aiseanna Soathair* or *FAS*) have specific responsibilities in the area of vocational education and training generally, while the Minister for Agriculture and Food has responsibility for training in the agriculture sector. The Minister for Tourism and Trade has responsibility for training for the hotel and catering industry, in conjunction with the Minister for Education. The Minister for Health has some responsibility for pre-school child care.

1.4 Administration

Central level

The Minister for Education is responsible for the introduction of legislation relating to education and the legislation is implemented by the Department of Education. Very little legislation exists in the area of education. The system largely operates under Ministerial regulations which reflect the provisions of the Constitution relating to education.

The Department of Education sets the general regulations for the recognition of schools, effectively controls the curriculum and the public examination system and establishes rules and regulations for the management, resourcing and staffing of schools, and negotiates teachers' salary scales.

The Department also exercises a detailed control function, particulary in budgetary matters, within the vocational sector (Vocational Education Committees). In addition, it has an overview function in relation to certain higher-level institutions and is directly responsible for negotiating overall funding levels for designated institutions under the Higher Education Authority.

The Higher Education Authority (HEA) has statutory responsibility for furthering the development of higher education and assisting in the coordination of state investment in higher education and preparing proposals for such investment.

In addition, the Authority advises the Minister for Education on the need or otherwise for the establishment of new institutions of higher education, on the nature and form of those institutions and on the legislative measures required in relation to their establishment or in relation to any existing institution of higher education. It is also required to maintain a continuous review of the demand and need for higher education.

The National Council for Educational Awards (NCEA) has statutory responsibility for the validation of courses and the award of qualifications in the Regional Technical Colleges and other non-university institutions. It also sets and monitors standards in the colleges and, through it, a transfer network operates. Qualifications awarded by the NCEA are internationally recognized by academic, professional, trade and craft bodies.

The National Council for Vocational Awards (NCVA) was established in 1991 to develop a comprehensive system of assessment and certification for a wide range of vocational training programmes with particular reference to those provided in the education sector: e.g. all Vocational Preparation and Training programmes in schools other than those included within the Senior Cycle; vocational training modules in relation to the Leaving Certificate and the Senior Certificate Programmes; and the Vocational Training Opportunities Scheme (VTOS).

Local level

At **primary school level**, Boards of Management are responsible for the day-to-day government of the schools subject to the regulations laid down by the Department of Education. The Patron (e.g. bishop, moderator, chief rabbi or a committee in multi-denominational schools) of the school is responsible for initiating the steps necessary to establish the Board of Management, appointing the elected representatives to the Board and for nominating the Chairperson of the Board. The Chairperson has specific functions for ensuring that the Rules for National Schools are being adhered to. The Board comprises members appointed by the Patron and parents, and the school principal. It includes a teacher in schools of seven or more teachers.

At **second level**, there are private Secondary Schools and public Community, Comprehensive and Vocational Schools and Community Colleges.

Most Secondary Schools are owned and managed by Catholic religious orders and congregations and diocesan authorities. A small number of Secondary Schools are under Protestant management. Due to a decline in religious vocations, there has been an increase in the number of lay people assuming the post of school principal and in some areas, religious orders have surrendered control and, indeed, ownership of schools.

Secondary Schools are managed by Boards representative of the owners or trustees; parents and teachers are appointed to Boards and the head teacher or principal is also a member of the Board. The Association of Management of Catholic Secondary Schools (AMCSS) represents the management of all Secondary Schools, whether religious, clerical or lay at regional level. At national level, there is the Council of Management of Catholic Secondary Schools (CMCSS).

Community Colleges and Community and Comprehensive Schools are owned and funded by the State but are locally managed. The Boards of Management of Comprehensive Schools include at least one nominee each of the Minister for Education (an Inspector), the local Vocational Education Committee (VEC) and the diocesan authority. The Boards of Management of Community Schools consist of three nominees of the VEC, three of the relevant religious order or congregation, two elected parent representatives, two elected teacher representatives and the school principal.

Vocational schools are managed either directly by the Vocational Education Committee (VEC) of the area in which each school is located or by a subcommittee of the VEC. All Community Colleges have management Boards which are subcommittees of the local VEC. Typically, the composition of the Board is similar to that for a Community school.

There are 38 Vocational Education Committees, each of which has responsibility for continuing and technical education in its area. Each VEC appoints a Chief Executive Officer (CEO) who directs the organization and administration of the system in its area. Vocational teachers are appointed to a VEC area and may, in principle, be assigned to serve anywhere within the geographical area under the control of the VEC.

Universities and other **higher education institutions** are autonomous statutory bodies. The Regional Technical Colleges, formerly administered by the VEC, became autonomous statutory bodies when the College Act came into force in 1993. However, the State reserves itself the right to participate in the permanent planning and budgetary management of higher education.

1.5 Inspection

The Inspectorate is part of the Department of Education and is headed by a Chief Inspector, assisted by two Deputy Chief Inspectors; one for primary level and one for post-primary level.

The Inspectorate is composed of three independent sections with the Chief Inspector as the sole coordinating authority under the Secretary and the Minister:

– primary (for first level and special education);

– post-primary (for second level);

– psychological service (mainly for second level).

Responsibilities are assigned to individuals on both a geographical and a specialization basis. In broad terms, and with exceptions, primary inspectors are assigned duties on a geographical basis and post-primary inspectors on a specialization basis.

The Inspectors are the main liaison between the schools and the Department of Education. Their duties include the inspection and evaluation of teachers, counselling and demonstrating, the planning of curricula and the administration of tests and examinations, the organization of and participation in in-service training courses, liaison with Colleges of Education, the interviewing of teachers for some posts and acting as information officers on behalf of the Department of Education. At senior level, inspectors have a policy advisory role.

1.6 Financing

Most of the capital costs of primary schools – 85% or more – are met by state funding, the remainder by local contributions. Per capita grants are paid to

Boards of Management to help with running costs, and the State pays the salaries of teachers in full. Parishes contribute a per capita payment for each child to the National School attended by the child. Many National School Boards of Management find it necessary to raise additional funds for the effective running of the schools, and seek 'voluntary contributions' from parents.

95% of Secondary Schools participate in a scheme of free education, which seeks to ensure equality of educational opportunity for all young people regardless of family circumstances.

Although privately managed, Secondary Schools receive considerable financial assistance from the Department of Education – payment almost in full of teachers' salaries and allowances, 90% of the cost of approved building and equipment, capitation grants for each eligible pupil, payment of grants in lieu of tuition fees to schools participating in the free education scheme. In addition, most of these schools seek 'voluntary contributions' from parents.

Over 90% of funding for Vocational Schools and Community Colleges is provided by the State and the salaries of teachers in these institutions are paid by the State.

Community and Comprehensive Schools are owned and funded entirely by the State through the Department of Education.

Most institutions of higher education are supported substantially by the State – e.g. universities and teaching colleges receive about 70% of their income from the State. Since its founding in 1968, the Higher Education Authority (HEA) has acted as the budgetary agency for the Department of Education (see above).

1.7 Private schools

Private non-aided education is not significantly developed at primary level. Those private primary schools that exist are autonomous in ownership and administration. Normally, teachers in such schools are fully qualified. The schools are funded by parents' fees, donations, fund-raising or other private means.

Legally, all voluntary Secondary Schools are private in ownership, but they receive considerable financial assistance from the Department of Education. In fee-paying schools the State pays almost all the salaries of recognized teachers. In non-fee-paying schools the State pays, in addition, capitation grants and certain other grants. To ensure state recognition, all Secondary Schools must operate in accordance with the Rules and Programmes for Secondary Schools, set by the Department.

1.8 Advisory bodies

In November 1987, the National Council for Curriculum and Assessment (NCCA) was established by the Minister for Education. The brief given to the Council can be summarized under four main headings:

– to advise the Minister on the curriculum at first and second levels;

– to advise the Minister on appropriate modes and techniques of assessment;

– to coordinate research and development;

– to monitor standards of pupil performance in the public examinations.

The NCCA replaced the former interim Curriculum and Examinations Board.

1.9 Reform

The Government published a Green Paper in June, 1992 entitled 'Education for a Changing World'. The document outlined the Government's proposals and was intended to generate discussion leading, it is hoped, to a consensus among the various interests involved as to the direction Irish education should take for the rest of the decade and into the next century.

Currently, the Department of Education is preparing a White Paper on Education which will, *inter alia*, pave the way for an Education Act to give legislative effect to the measures required. It is hoped that the White Paper will be published before the end of 1994.

2. Pre-school education

There is no national system of pre-school institutions or nurseries in Ireland. However, National Schools (primary schools) may accept pupils on or after their fourth birthday – 4- to 5-year-olds in the Junior Infants class and 5- to 6-year-olds in the Senior Infants class. Children are enrolled subject to availability of accommodation. Although the statutory age for National School entry is 6 years, in 1991 approximately 55% of 4-year-olds and almost 99% of 5-year-olds were in full-time attendance at school. Education in National Schools is free and the schools are recognized under the rules of the Department of Education.

Infant classes vary significantly in size and many combine Junior and Senior Infants. They are open on the same days as other classes in National Schools, but normally operate from 9.15 a.m. until between 1.00 and 2.15 p.m.

The programme of instruction followed during the two years of pre-compulsory schooling is part of an integrated programme extending over the eight years of first-level schooling. The role of infant classes is to initiate children in formal learning.

In addition to religious instruction, these classes are required to provide three hours of secular instruction each day. Teachers monitor pupils' progress through continuous observation.

A limited scheme of pre-school education, funded by the Department of Education, exists for certain groups of children under four years. This includes some 53 pre-school units for approximately 600 travellers' children and 8 pre-school units for some 400 children from disadvantaged families in special inner-city projects under the 'Early Start' programme.

The remaining pre-school educational services which do exist have developed mainly on a voluntary private basis. Provision of this kind is not normally aided by the Department of Education, and is not part of the formal education system. These include playgroups, Irish medium playgroups (naíonraí) and day care centres. The latter usually receive financial assistance from the Department of Health. Parents are required to contribute towards the cost of sending their children to playgroups and day care centres.

In 1993/94, 1,704 pre-school playgroups were registered with the Irish Pre-School Playgroups Association. These catered for 19,757 infants between 2 and 5 years of age. There were 245 national naíonraí catering for children aged 3 to 4 years.

Staff/Teachers

The teachers of infant classes are primary teachers, with the same training and the same status and pay. Pre-school units for travellers' children are staffed jointly by teachers and child care workers.

Playgroup staff do not usually have any special training. In the naíonraí, An Comhchoiste Reamhscolaíochta provides training courses. Staff in day care centres hold either a national certificate awarded after two years of training or have other kinds of private training.

3. Compulsory education

The period of compulsory education is governed by the School Attendance Act, 1926. The law requires that children attend school between the ages of 6 and 15 years. It is very rare for parents to invoke their Constitutional right to educate their children at home. Full-time compulsory education is therefore of nine years' duration. The last three years of compulsory education are usually spent in the Junior Cycle of second-level education.

3.1 Primary education

As mentioned above, the vast majority of primary schools (also known as National Schools) are, in effect, state-aided parish schools established under diocesan patronage, and the State gives explicit recognition to their denominational character. The State finances thirteen multi-denominational schools on the same basis as other primary schools. These were established in response to parental demand. Schools may also be established where parents wish their children to be educated through the medium of the Irish language. Outside of the *Gaeltacht* (Irish-speaking area), there are 78 such schools providing primary education.

Primary education in Ireland covers a period of eight years (from 4 years of age – see 2.), after which the majority of pupils transfer to secondary schools at approximately 12 years of age. The State provides for free first-level education in National Schools, which are attended by over 98% of children to age 12 +. Private primary schools charging fees are not entitled to receive state support, but they offer a broadly similar type of education. Normally, no defined catchment area is imposed on parents in the National School system. School transport services give accessibility where needed.

Of the 3,300 National Schools throughout the country, 372 are single sex boys' schools and 204 are single sex girls' schools. The remainder are coeducational. Up to half of all National Schools have fewer than 100 pupils (and hence 3 or fewer teachers). With very few exceptions, all schools have fewer than 800 pupils. In the main, school buildings are used for one set of pupils per day. The typical National School divides pupils by age into eight year-groups. More than half the classes in National Schools are single-grade classes. Some are multi-grade classes and almost a quarter are consecutive-grade classes or classes where two age groups are combined.

Department of Education regulations require that primary schools should be open not later than 9.30 a.m. but in practice, especially in urban areas, schools tend to begin classes at 9.00 a.m. and finish at 3.00 p.m. In addition to religious instruction, primary classes are required to provide four hours of secular instruction each day. National Schools are required to be open from Monday to Friday, for 184 days each year, spread over three terms from 1 September to 30 June.

Curriculum

The present National School curriculum, which came into force in 1971, is child-centred rather than subject-centred and allows for flexibility in timetabling and teaching methods. The main components taught are: Irish language, English language, mathematics, social and environmental studies (history, geography, civics and elementary science), art and crafts, music, physical education and religious instruction.

A reform of all aspects of the National School curriculum is at present being undertaken by the National Council for Curriculum and Assessment (NCCA).

Assessment

There is no formal examination at the end of the first-level education cycle. National School teachers in Ireland carry out their own assessment of pupils' performance, through either standardized tests or their own tests based on areas of the curriculum. End-of-year tests are given in most classes. Reports (normally in writing) are provided for parents. A formal report card is completed by each teacher about each pupil at the end of primary education. These cards are sent to the pupil's secondary school and are not given to parents.

Most pupils advance to the next higher class at the end of each year. In certain circumstances a pupil may repeat a year, but this is not usual. There are special measures to cater for those in need of remedial education and from disadvantaged areas. There are 160 special classes for children of travellers in National Schools.

Teachers

Basic staffing levels for primary schools are governed by the number of pupils in the schools and the manner in which these numbers fall within the enrolment ranges specified by the Department of Education in the schedule of enrolments for the appointment and retention of teachers.

The initial training of teachers for National Schools takes place in five Colleges of Education. Courses are normally of three years' duration. For Colleges affiliated to the University of Dublin, however, pass degree courses last three years, while honours courses are of four years' duration. The study of the theory and methodology of education is combined with periods of teaching practice in all years. Students also take two or three academic subjects in the first year and one academic subject in subsequent years. On successful completion of the courses, students are awarded the degree of Bachelor of Education by the relevant university.

Following graduation, students may apply for teaching posts which are normally advertised in the national press by the Boards of Management. Depending on the nature of the post advertised, employment may be of a temporary or permanent nature. However, because of a surplus of trained teachers, a large proportion of newly-trained teachers now enter the profession as temporary teachers, mainly as replacements for teachers on career breaks and maternity leave.

In-service training is not compulsory.

Statistics 1992/93

	State-Aided	Private
Pupils	521,531	8,280
Teachers	20,761	
Schools	3,326*	79

* includes 117 special schools.

The pupil/teacher ratio was 25.1:1.

3.2 Lower second-level education *(Junior Cycle)*

The last three years of compulsory education (for pupils aged 12 to 15 years) usually take place in the Junior Cycle of one of the main types of second-level schools: Secondary, Vocational, Comprehensive, Community Schools or Community College. Parents are free to choose the second-level school. Schools that do not have places for all applicants operate various methods of selection. Until 1994, some Secondary Schools had entrance examinations.

60% of pupils attend Secondary Schools, 30% attend Vocational Schools, 2% attend Comprehensive Schools and 6% attend Community Schools.

Education is free of charge in the latter three types of schools and also in those Secondary Schools participating in the scheme of free education mentioned above. The remaining Secondary Schools (about 5%) charge fees.

The Secondary School (sometimes referred to as Voluntary Secondary School) is the largest category, comprising approximately two-thirds of all second-level schools. A small proportion of these schools cater for boarders. Traditionally, these schools provided an academic (or grammar school) type of education. In recent years, however, they have been increasingly influenced by the practical and technical content of vocational education, the innovatory thrust of an extensive range of development projects, and the example and outcomes of major initiatives in the area of transition to adult and working life. In the same period, a broad consensus has emerged that every second-level school should attempt to offer a comprehensive curriculum, providing a broad balance between academic and vocational subjects.

Initially, the main thrust of the Vocational Schools was the inculcation of manual skills and the preparation of young people for trades. Nowadays, however, the full range of second-level courses is available in these schools.

Comprehensive Schools were first established in 1966 in areas where existing second-level provision was inadequate or non-existent. Fifteen such schools were established between 1966 and 1972. They combine academic and vocational subjects in a wide curriculum. It was also intended that they would have an experimental function.

Community Schools and Community Colleges are similar in many ways to Comprehensive Schools but differ in management structure. The first such schools were established in 1972/73. As in the Comprehensive Schools, these schools provide a broad curriculum, embracing both practical and academic subjects for all the children of their areas in the second-level age range.

Many Community Schools and Community Colleges had their origins in the amalgamation of Secondary and Vocational Schools due for replacement or renovation. They are also seen as meeting a demand in newly developed urban areas formerly supplied through separate Secondary and Vocational Schools. Apart from the provision of comprehensive facilities to cater for the varying aptitudes and abilities of all children irrespective of family means, it was envisaged that these schools and colleges would achieve the optimum utilization of teachers, buildings and equipment, as well as being the focal point for community activities.

With minor exceptions, Vocational, Comprehensive and Community Schools and Community Colleges are coeducational. Many secondary schools are, however, single sex. Of the 467 secondary schools in the country, 129 are single sex boys' schools, 168 are single sex girls' schools and 170 are coeducational.

The majority of second-level schools have an enrolment of between 300 and 800 pupils. As a rule, pupils in each year of Junior Cycle are grouped by age. Teachers are subject specialists and generally stay with their subject classes throughout the cycle.

Almost all second-level schools are open for five days (they may operate a six-day week). Most schools operate for 30 hours per week, or 6 hours per day, usually between 9.00 a.m. and 3.30 or 4.00 p.m. All boy's schools and most coeducational schools have a half-day of classes on Wednesday. Class periods tend to be of 35 to 40 minutes' duration. The school year is organized over three terms, with schools usually open for 180 days, including the days of public examinations, from 1 September to the end of May.

Curriculum, assessment and qualifications

A broad consensus has emerged that every second-level school should attempt to offer a comprehensive curriculum providing a balance between academic and vocational subjects. Recognized schools, public and private, must conform to state requirements with regard to educational standards and the general structure of the system. The courses prescribed for the Certificate Examinations, which are centrally devised and administered by the Department of Education, are followed by most pupils and class groups.

The programme for Secondary Schools must include the following subjects: Irish and English, history, geography, mathematics, civics, science, languages (classical and modern European), business studies and home economics.

Provision is also made for physical education and singing.

The curricula of the Community, Comprehensive and Vocational Schools as well as of the Community Colleges tend, in practice, to approximate to those in Secondary Schools, though with differences of emphasis.

As a rule, pupils in Junior Cycle study from eight to ten subjects for the Junior Certificate Examinations.

In order to allow for differences in the needs, abilities and aptitudes of young people within the

Junior Certificate programme, subjects are offered at two levels: Ordinary and Higher. Mathematics, Irish and English are offered at three levels: Foundation, Ordinary and Higher. These three subjects, together with history, geography and civics, constitute a core group of subjects which must be taken, together with at least two subjects from a list that includes languages, science, home economics, business studies, art, music and craft and design.

The Junior Certificate examination is taken at the end of the third year of second-level education, wherein individual attainment is assessed. Each subject is examined individually by means of a written examination. Apart from modern languages, oral examinations are not a feature of the Irish education system at this level. Account is not taken of assessments carried out during the year. Grades are awarded, based on the candidate's performance, ranging from A (over 85%) to F (10%-15%), and NG (less than 10%).

In addition, all schools organize tests, usually pre-Christmas and in May and towards the end of the school year. These school based examinations are usually formal and set by the subject teachers. Reports are normally sent to parents. Many teachers also give regular tests within class periods to stimulate the learning process. The majority of schools also organize formal tests a few months prior to the Junior Certificate examinations to assess the performance levels of pupils.

Teachers

See 4.

Statistics – Lower second-level 1992/93

	Pupils*	Teachers**	Schools***
Secondary Schools	132,150	12,250	467
Vocational Schools and Community Colleges	47,830	5,005	248
Community Schools	22,402	2,043	54
Comprehensive Schools	5,522	509	16

  * Junior Cycle
 ** Full-time teachers, Junior and Senior Cycle
*** Junior and Senior Cycle.

4. Post compulsory education – Upper second-level *(Senior Cycle)*

All pupils who commenced their second-level education in September 1991 and after may remain for three years in the Senior Cycle. Pupils have a variety of options to choose from.

Most pupils remain at school after age 15: over 90% of age 16, 75% of age 17 and about 50% of age 18 are in full-time schooling. Approximately 77% of the age group complete second-level education.

At the end of compulsory schooling, pupils may follow a two-year course at Senior Cycle at a second-level school leading to the Leaving Certificate examination. This examination has as its stated aim 'to prepare pupils for immediate entry into open society or for proceeding to further education'. It is used for a variety of purposes: for example, as an entry qualification for a range of third-level institutions, including the universities and as a selection test for entry to many kinds of employment. This variety of use makes the Leaving Certificate a dominant influence upon much of the work of second-level schools, affecting curriculum, methodology, assessment and organization.

Curriculum, assessment and qualifications

The approved course for recognized senior pupils must include not less than five subjects of which one should be Irish. In the Rules for Secondary Schools of the Department of Education, the subjects approved are grouped as follows:

Language Group: Irish, English, French, German, Italian, Spanish, Latin, Greek, Hebrew studies, classical studies.

Science Group: mathematics, physics, chemistry, physics and chemistry, biology, applied mathematics.

Business Studies Group: accounting, business organization, economics, economic history.

Applied Science Group: engineering, technical drawing, construction studies, physics and chemistry, agricultural science, agricultural economics, home economics (scientific and social), home economics (general).

Social Studies Group: history, geography, art (including crafts), music, home economics (general).

It is recommended that each pupil should take at least three subjects from the group of subjects for which he/she is best fitted, and at least two subjects from outside that group.

Separate Ordinary Level and Higher Level Leaving Certificate papers are set in all subjects.

Assessment and certification procedures are the same as for the Junior Certificate examination.

Transition Year

From the beginning of the 1994/95 school year, a Transition Year was recognized as the first year of a three-year Senior Cycle. The Transition Year offers pupils a broad educational experience with a view to the attainment of increased maturity before proceeding to further study and/or vocational preparation. It provides a bridge to help pupils make the transition from a highly structured environment to one where they will take greater responsibility for their own learning and decision-making.

Pupils participate in learning strategies which are active and experiential and which help them to develop a range of transferable critical thinking and creative problem-solving skills. The Transition Year also provides an opportunity for pupils to reflect on and develop an awareness of the value of education and training in preparing them for the demands of the adult world of work and relationships, in the absence of examination pressure. Work experience is also an important component of this programme.

Schools are obliged to ensure that there is a clear distinction between the Transition Year programme and the corresponding Leaving Certificate syllabus.

The content of the Transition Year programme includes elements of the following: social education, moral education, education for living (including homecrafts and education for parenthood, employment and leisure), philosophy and applied logic, music and the arts, Irish studies, European languages, visual education, media education and communications skills.

More than 460 second-level schools are now providing a Transition Year – approximately 60% of the total number of schools.

The Department of Education does not provide formal certification on completion of the Transition Year programme. However, schools continue to develop appropriate forms of certification to suit their pupils.

Second-level Teachers

Teachers in second-level schools are usually trained in a university postgraduate course of one year leading to the Higher Diploma in Education (HDE). They generally already have a BA, BSc or B Comm. The teacher training course is devoted to professional studies and includes at least 100 hours' teaching practice.

Teachers of practical subjects, such as Home Economics, Woodwork, Metalwork, Rural Science and Art, follow four-year concurrent programmes of academic studies and professional training leading to the award of a degree. More time is devoted to educational studies in these courses than in the HDE courses.

All teachers are employed by their individual school managements but are classified as public servants.

In-service training is not compulsory. Courses range from one-day seminars to courses of up to four weeks' duration.

Statistics – Upper second-level 1992/93

	Pupils*	Teachers**	Schools***
Secondary Schools	79,375	12,250	467
Vocational Schools and Community Colleges	25,285	5,005	248
Community Schools	11,782	2,043	54
Comprehensive Schools	3,055	509	16

  * Senior Cycle
 ** Full-time teachers, Junior and Senior Cycle
*** Junior and Senior Cycle.

5. Vocational education/training

A wide range of vocational education and training programmes is provided to meet the specific needs of individual pupils and the manpower needs of the economy – from actions to prevent early school leaving to the application of knowledge at post-graduate level. The main objectives of these programmes are:

– to improve the responsiveness and flexibility of the education and training system to meet educational, social and economic needs;

– to maintain and enhance participation rates in vocational education or training at all levels in order to promote equity and enhance industrial competitiveness;

– to equip enterprises and workers with the skills and competences needed to cope with occupational, structural and technological change;

– to ensure the competitiveness of Irish industry through the supply of skilled manpower at a variety of levels.

The main programmes in this category are:

– the Vocational Preparation and Training Programmes;

– the Leaving Certificate Vocational Programme;

– the Leaving Certificate Applied Programme;

– Youthreach;

– the Vocational Training Opportunities Scheme;

– Community Training Workshops;

– Travellers' Training Workshops.

5.1 Vocational Preparation and Training Programmes

The primary aim of these programmes is to prepare young people for working life. There are two programmes – Vocational Preparation and Training 1 (VPT 1) and Vocational Preparation and Training 2 (VPT 2). VPT 1 is intended for young persons who will leave school at 15 to 16 years of age with few, if any, formal educational qualifications and who are proposing to enter the labour market.

The VPT 1 programme consists of 800 hours' full-time training and work experience of at least 200 hours. It is structured into three main components:

– Vocational Studies;

– Preparation for Working Life;

– General Studies (i.e. communications, social mathematics and education for living).

Training in new technologies is an important feature of the overall programme.

VPT 2 is for young persons who have completed VPT 1 or an equivalent programme or who have formal qualifications but lack vocational training or experience. It is a self-contained one-year programme of vocational training designed to provide successful participants with specific vocational skills in order to enhance their prospects of securing lasting full-time employment. The structure of VPT 2 is broadly similar to that of VPT 1: clearly at this stage, the component parts of the programme are taken at a higher level.

During the 1994/95 school year, there were approximately 25,500 pupils on these programmes which are provided in second-level schools.

5.2 Leaving Certificate Vocational Programme

This programme lasts two years. It is also provided in second-level schools and is intended for pupils aged 15 to 16 who have just completed the Junior Cycle and are about to begin the Senior Cycle. They follow the Leaving Certificate Programme in at least five subjects including Irish and at least two subjects from construction studies, engineering and technical drawing.

The Leaving Certificate Vocational Programme is at present undergoing modification and expansion. The objective of the restructured programme is the enhancement of the vocational dimension within the Leaving Certificate Higher and Ordinary levels. This is to be achieved by providing a greater range of vocational subject groupings and also by the introduction of mandatory link modules between subjects within the Leaving Certificate Vocational Programme. The three mandatory link modules are:

Enterprise Education: in general this module is designed to integrate closely with the vocational subject groupings followed by a pupil. The module will include skill and knowledge based areas such as active learning skills through industry-linked projects, practical business skills, information technology skills and communications and interpersonal skills.

Preparation for Work: this will provide pupils with opportunities for a structured interaction with the workplace environment through visits and case-studies of local and national enterprises.

Work Experience: the work experience module will comprise two weeks or 80 hours over the two years of the programme.

The restructured programme will provide for a greater number of pupils and will also ensure greater access by girls.

5.3 Leaving Certificate Applied Programme

The Leaving Certificate Applied Programme will be available from September 1995. It will be a self-contained two-year programme replacing and expanding on the existing Senior Certificate and Vocational Preparation and Training 1 (see above). The new programme may not be taken in conjunction with Leaving Certificate subjects at Ordinary or Foundation levels. It is intended that the programme will allow for adaptation to the particular needs and circumstances of the local environment.

The programme will be an option for those who do not wish to proceed directly to third-level education or for those pupils whose needs, aspirations, aptitudes or abilities are not adequately provided for by the other Leaving Certificate programmes. Pupils who successfully complete the programme can proceed to post-Leaving Certificate courses, subject to any special entry requirements for specific courses.

5.4 Youthreach

The purpose of this programme is to provide two years of education, training and work experience/placement for young people who leave school without any formal educational qualifications. The programme is operated jointly by the local education and training authorities, principally Vocational Education Committees (VEC) and the National Employment Authority (*FAS*). There are approximately 2,000 places in the education system and an additional 900 places in the *FAS* element of the programme.

The Foundation Year provides basic skills training, practical work training and general education, together with guidance and counselling. It is based on VEC and *FAS* programmes specially extended and adapted. All programmes are full-time, 35 hours per week, and available on a year-round basis.

The Progression Year, under the responsibility of *FAS*, provides a series of options such as specific skills training courses, temporary employment schemes, community youth training programmes, subsidized private sector job or training contracts, full-time or part-time programmes of further education, etc.

5.5 Vocational Training Opportunities Scheme

The Vocational Training Opportunities Scheme (VTOS) provides an opportunity for the long-term unemployed over 21 years of age to return to full-time education and training. The basic aim of the scheme is to address a structural problem in the labour market where more than 80% of the long-term unemployed have left school before completing the Leaving Certificate and more than 50% have had no schooling beyond primary level. The scheme is operated by Vocational Education Committees and is jointly funded by the Departments of Education and of Social Welfare. The number participating at present is approximately 3,500.

Courses are of up to two years' duration and focus on the development of employment related skills, including technological and business skills and socio-personal development. There is also a strong emphasis on the core skills of literacy, numeracy and communication.

Because of the high profile of the Leaving Certificate with employers in Ireland, trainees on VTOS are encouraged to take Leaving Certificate subjects or to acquire a portfolio of certification with qualifications from the Leaving and Junior Certificate.

5.6 Community Training Workshops

The Community Training Workshops Programme is run jointly by the Department of Education and the National Training Authority (*FAS*) and is designed to provide training for young people in the 16 to 25 year age group who are at risk due to poor educational attainment, literacy/numeracy difficulties and low self-esteem and who, accordingly, cannot avail of the more mainstream training and employment programmes. The Department of Education's input is the provision of instruction hours through the Vocational Education Committees. The 500 people on the programme at present receive a training allowance from the National Employment Authority (*FAS*).

5.7 Travellers Training Workshops

In the Irish context, travellers are groups of people who do not have a permanent residence. The Training Workshops are run jointly by the Department of Education and *FAS* to help travellers develop to their full potential, to break the cycle of illiteracy and social deprivation in which they are trapped and to enable them to become self-reliant and self-supporting members of society. The Department of Eduction provides instruction hours through the Vocational Education Committees (VEC) within the workshops to promote literacy and numeracy instruction. The VECs also provide the funding of overheads and material costs in these centres. The 1,100 participants receive a training allowance from the National Training Authority (*FAS*).

6. Higher education

Traditionally, the third-level education system in Ireland has comprised the university sector, the technical/technological colleges and the colleges of education – all of which are substantially funded by the State and are autonomous and self-governing.

In addition, particularly in recent years, a number of independent private colleges have developed, offering a range of mainly business-related courses conferring professional qualifications and, in some instances, recognized diplomas and degrees.

Admission

With very few exceptions, entrance to third-level education in Ireland is only possible following successful completion of the Leaving Certificate examination or equivalent. Application for admission to all institutions of higher education is made to a Central Applications Office (*CAO*) which offers places based on the points awarded to the student for results in not more than six subjects taken at the Leaving Certificate. Other equivalent examinations are accepted for students educated outside the State. Competition for places, particularly at the universities, is very keen and for this reason, students who make application to the Central Applications Office are asked to list the courses they wish to pursue in order of their individual preferences.

Fees/Student finance

There are tuition fees for all courses of higher education.

A scheme of higher education grants based, *inter alia*, on the means testing of parents' income is administered by the Local Authorities (County Councils and County Borough Corporations). The eligibility criteria for these grants are laid down by the Department of Education, which also arbitrates on appeals and questions of interpretation. The grants are designed to cover the cost of tuition at third-level institutions and they also include a maintenance element. The amounts expended by the local authorities on the higher education grants scheme are reimbursed to them from central exchequer funds.

Academic year

The main academic year commences in early October and finishes at the end of May. It is generally organized into three terms.

Depending on the course involved, examinations may take place in May, June or September, but lectures and workshops occur normally between October and May.

6.1 Universities

There are four Universities in Ireland – the National University of Ireland, the University of Dublin (Trinity College), the University of Limerick and Dublin City University.

The National University of Ireland (NUI) is organized on a federal basis but the constituent colleges in Dublin, Cork and Galway enjoy a large measure of autonomy. A further three colleges – St Patrick's College, Maynooth, the Royal College of Surgeons and St Angela's College of Education for Home Economics – are recognized colleges of the NUI.

In addition to undertaking research in a wide range of disciplines, the Universities and University Colleges offer degree programmes at Bachelor, Master's and Doctorate levels – in the humanities, in the scientific, technical and social sciences, and in the medical area. A range of undergraduate and postgraduate diplomas is also offered and the universities have continuing and distance education programmes.

Courses/Qualifications

The Irish university system has set programmes leading to a Bachelor's degree at the end of three or four years, depending on the course followed. First degree courses in Architecture and Veterinary Medicine take five years; in Dentistry they take five or six years and in Medicine they take six years. Typically, teaching at undergraduate level is by way of a set programme of lectures supplemented by tutorials and, where appropriate, practical demonstration and laboratory work. Master's degrees, which require another one to three years of study, are usually taken by coursework, research work or some combination of both. For the most part doctoral degrees are awarded on the basis of research.

To an increasing extent, undergraduate courses are being modularized or 'unitized' to allow greater flexibility in course structure and student choice.

Universities award their own degrees using external examiners to ensure consistence of standards.

Assessment

As a general rule, higher education courses include end-of-year examinations. Success in these is necessary for advancement; opportunities for students who fail to repeat examinations are widely available. Many university and college courses also include ongoing assessment of assignments, projects, extended essays, research work and field work.

6.2 Colleges of Technology

Regional Technical Colleges (RTCs), which were introduced in the 1970s to provide for further technical education needs, have over the years become an integral part of the Irish third-level system.

There are now eleven Regional Technical Colleges offering training courses for trade and industry over a broad spectrum of occupations and levels, including Business Studies, Engineering and Technology, and Science and Paramedical Studies.

There are two-year Certificate courses, three-year Diploma courses and in a limited number of areas, four-year programmes leading to a Degree awarded by the National Council for Educational Awards (NCEA). Students can move from Certificate to Diploma to Degree level depending on examination performance.

In addition to the Regional Technical Colleges, there are a number of other specialist colleges offering courses at third-level.

The Dublin Institute of Technology (DIT) is now a single institution comprising the former Colleges of Technology in Dublin, the Dublin College of Catering and the Colleges of Marketing and Design, of Commerce and of Music. The DIT offers a broad range of courses covering Certificate, Diploma/Degree and Professional Awards. The NCEA validates certain courses at the Certificate and Diploma level. Graduates of some professional or degree-level courses are eligible for the award of the degrees of the University of Dublin. A substantial number of courses lead solely to DIT awards. Others lead to awards by organizations such as the London City and Guilds, the Department of Education and a variety of professional bodies.

In 1992, legislation was enacted which gave a statutory basis to the DIT and the RTCs as independent self-governing institutions. This legislation gave a statutory remit to these institutions in relation to the provision of services to industry and recognized the regional role of the RTCs.

6.3 Colleges of Education

The training of teachers for primary schools (first level) is provided in specialized teacher training colleges which are denominational and privately managed but largely financed by the State. There are four colleges in Dublin (St Patrick's College, Drumcondra, Church of Ireland Training College, Rathmines, St Mary's, Marino and the Froebel College, Sion Hill). A fifth College, (Mary Immaculate College of Education) is located in Limerick.

St Patrick's College in Dublin and Mary Immaculate College in Limerick are by far the largest colleges, training some 85% of all first-level teachers. All first-level teachers are now awarded a university degree on successful completion of their studies.

Statistics – Higher education 1993/94

Type of Institution	Number of Students
Universities and Teacher Training Colleges	49,739
Colleges of Technology (including Regional Technical Colleges)	34,458

Italy

ITALY

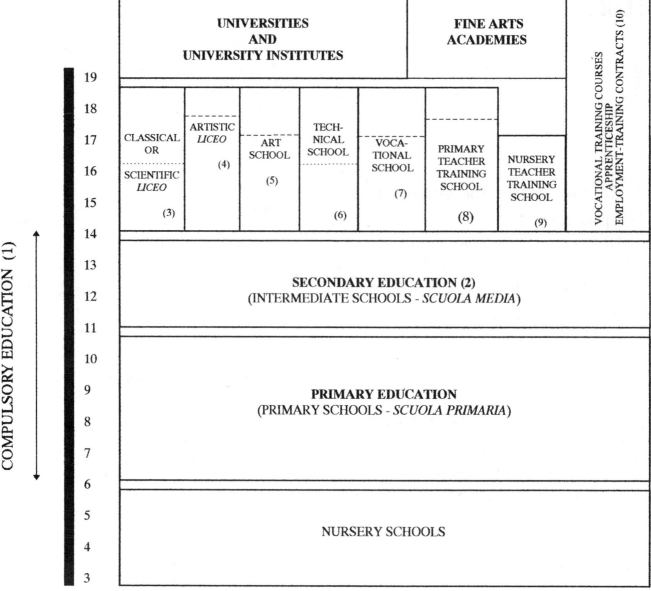

1. The Government has proposed to extend compulsory education from 8 to 10 years, that is, until 16.

2. *Scuola Media* (intermediate schools) provide comprehensive general lower secondary education with the school leaving certificate providing access to upper secondary schools.

3. 5-year upper secondary general and classical or scientific course with the school leaving certificate (*Maturità*) providing access to all university education.

4. 4-year general and artistic course leading to higher level courses. 5th complementary year leads to the upper secondary school leaving certificate providing access to all university education.

5. 3-year general and artistic course leading to employment. A further 2-year course has been established experimentally in certain schools leading to the applied arts upper secondary school leaving certificate which provides access to higher level artistic schools.

6. 5-year general and technical course leading to the technical school leaving certificate providing access to employment or higher or university education (*Maturità tecnica*).

7. 3-year general and vocational course leading to a "qualification certificate" and employment. 5-year experimental courses lead to the vocational school leaving certificate which is equivalent to the technical school leaving certificate.

8. 4-year course of general and teacher education for primary school teachers also providing access to further study at university faculties of education. 5th complementary year provides access to certain university faculties.

9. 3-year course of general and teacher education for nursery school teachers.

10. These courses can be entered at any age between 15 and 25 (and sometimes beyond).

------ = alternative beginning or end of level / type of education.

.... = division in the level/type of education

1. Responsibilities and administration

1.1 Background

Italy has a population of 57,576,429 and covers an area of 301,377 square kilometres. It is a Parliamentary Republic headed by a President and a Parliament which consists of the Chamber of Deputies and the Senate.

For administrative purposes Italy is divided into 20 autonomous territorial areas, regions, with their own legislative, administrative and financial powers. (Legislative powers are conferred on the Regional Councils; the Regional Commission is the executive body). The regions are divided into provinces, which group together a number of communes linked to an urban centre or capital. At both provincial and communal levels, administration is in the hands of elected councils.

Italian is the official language, although in some areas the use of the local language is officially authorized for local authority documents and for education. These areas have a special form of autonomy and are known as 'Special Status Regions'. The country's most widespread religion, Roman Catholicism, is not a state religion.

In 1992, the main employment sectors were agriculture (8.2%) and industry (31.9%); the other 59.9% of the working population were employed in other activities. The unemployment rate was 11.5%.

1.2 Basic principles: education

The basic principles relating to education, laid down in the Italian Constitution, include: freedom of education; the State's duty to provide a network of education establishments of every type and level, open to everyone without distinction; the right of private individuals to set up schools at no cost to the State; and the duty of parents to educate their children for at least eight years (corresponding to primary and lower secondary education, which is free of charge in state schools). Appropriate measures have to be taken to enable capable and deserving students to enter higher levels of education even if they lack financial resources.

1.3 Distribution of responsibilities

Education in Italy has traditionally been centrally administered. Since the end of the 1950s responsibilities and services have gradually been decentralized; in 1972 many of the State's administrative powers over education were transferred to the local authorities – regions, provinces and communes. Education policy, however, remains centralized, and all schools – state, non-state public (e.g. run by cities and communes) or private – must conform to national laws and decrees and regulations if they wish to be legally authorized.

The overall responsibility for education is in the hands of two ministries: the Ministry for Public Education (*MPI*) which covers all pre-school, primary and secondary education; and the Ministry for Universities and Scientific Research, to which powers over all higher education were transferred from the *MPI* in 1989.

Close links exist between the two Ministries on certain issues, and with the Budget, Treasury, and Finance Ministries on all questions related to funding, and with the Labour and Social Security Ministry for links between schools and the world of work.

Central power is executed by Ministerial delegations and branches at regional and provincial level. Individual schools have certain administrative autonomy. All universities have teaching, scientific, organizational, financial and accounting autonomy.

Since 1975, the regions have had legal and administrative responsibility for vocational training offered to young people outside the education system, with the Ministry of Labour playing a role of guidance and coordination.

1.4 Administration

Ministry of Public Education (*MPI*)

Within the Ministry of Public Education (*MPI*) at **national level**, the Minister is assisted by one or more under-secretaries. There are organizational units within the *MPI* dealing with the different levels and types of schools, teacher training, cultural exchanges, non-state education, the administration of personnel and of the *MPI*'s central and peripheral offices. There is a special service for pre-school education, and three inspectorates are responsible respectively for physical education and sports, artistic education and pensions.

As mentioned above, the *MPI* has general responsibility for the supervision and coordination of all educational activities, and issues legislation to this effect. It is involved in the planning, study and promotion of education, and the general supervision of all educational institutions. It issues general guidelines on curricula and assessment and sets the final examinations at upper secondary and non-university higher education levels. It promotes curriculum and syllabus changes and authorizes experimentation affecting the curriculum and teaching hours. It directly administers arrangements concerning the budget and the recruitment and mobility of staff and promotes in-service teacher training. It also controls the automation and mechanization of services.

The *MPI* is represented at **local level** by regional and provincial education offices which implement centrally-defined political and administrative directives and establish contact with local authorities in order to harmonize activities and services.

In each of the 20 regions, there is a Regional Education Superintendency (*Sovrintendenza Scolastica Regionale*) managed by a Superintendent; and in the provinces there is a Provincial Directorate of Education (*Provveditorato agli Studi*) managed by a Provincial Director of Education. The regional Superintendencies were created in 1963 when local authorities at regional level began to operate, and at first were almost exclusively involved in the development and rationalization of school buildings and the establishment of new primary and secondary schools in cooperation with the regional authorities. They are now above all involved in upper secondary school teacher recruitment, through the organization and administration of competitions for teaching posts (*concorsi*), and the determination of the school year. They also act as a forum for the Provincial School Offices.

The Provincial Directorates of Education are like local branches of the central administration and are of considerable importance. Their main task is to ensure the enforcement of centrally-issued directives applicable to education institutions at primary and secondary level, be they private or state. They are concerned with the recruitment of teaching staff in primary and lower secondary schools, personnel management and the general management of schools in their province. Head teachers and teachers in primary and secondary schools are directly responsible to the Provincial Directors of Education.

The Provincial Directors of Education consult the Provincial Schools Councils and the District Schools Councils. The former also advise the regional authorities; the latter also make proposals to Central Government and to all the local authorities.

The Provincial Schools Council (*Consiglio Scolastico Provinciale*) comprises elected representatives of the head teachers of state and legally recognized schools, teaching and non-teaching staff, parents, the administrative staff of the Provincial Directorate and of the communes in the province, and of the social partners. The Provincial Director, the Education Inspector of the provincial authorities and a representative of the Regional Council are ex-officio members. The Provincial Council gives advice on the establishment and distribution of schools, educational guidance, the right to study, the use of school premises for educational purposes by public and private bodies and the distribution of funds to be allocated to schools.

The Educational District corresponds to a portion of regional territory with uniform social, cultural and economic characteristics, making it possible to define an overall education policy. The District Schools Councils (*Consiglio Scolastico Distrettuale*) are made up of elected representatives of head teachers of state and non-state schools in its territory, representatives of teachers and parents from schools of all levels and, in the case of upper secondary schools, pupils, trade union representatives and persons representing local economic and cultural interests. They plan experimental teaching, extracurricular and inter-school activities, educational and vocational guidance services and medical services for schools.

Ministry of Universities and Scientific and Technological Research

The Ministry of Universities and Scientific and Technological Research was established in May 1989 to help bring about changes in the running of universities and the organization of studies, following the Law of 1990 on the reform of the education system. The Ministry's tasks are: to plan and promote scientific and technological research; to draw up the university development plan every three years; to distribute the funds in the Ministry's budget for universities, on the basis of objective criteria defined by law; and to coordinate Italian participation in international programmes involving universities and/or scientific research.

Institutions

In recent years, administrative powers have gradually been decentralized from the *MPI*'s provincial offices to individual **schools** and **colleges**, which all have administrative autonomy as regards administrative, operating and teaching expenses covered by funds allocated annually. In each institution, administrative functions are carried out by the School Council (*Consiglio di istituto*) and the principal (*Preside*) or head teacher (*Direttore didattico*).

The School Council is responsible for budgetary matters and for the organization and planning of non-educational school activities. Within the limits of the budget and law, it deliberates the purchase, renewal and maintenance of school equipment and teaching materials and decides on the use of premises and equipment, on extracurricular and sports activities, on remedial and support courses and on cooperation with other schools. The School Council is made up of representatives elected by teaching and non-teaching staff, parents and, in upper secondary schools, pupils. The principal or head teacher is an ex-officio member. A chairman is elected from parents' representatives. The Council also elects its own Executive Board, chaired by the principal or head teacher.

Head teachers or principals are responsible for representing the school in the outside world and for management, supervision and discipline within the school. They coordinate all school activities and are responsible for compliance with legislative provisions; they implement the decisions of the School Council, organize the school internally, i.e. timetable, formation of classes, allocation of teachers, and decide on disciplinary measures for pupils; they promote or coordinate training activities for teaching and non-teaching staff. They are also responsible for drawing up administrative documents relating to the pay and career advancement of teaching and non-teaching staff and the granting of leave and the recruitment of temporary teachers for less than one academic year. Head teachers are assisted in their duties by one or more colleagues from the teaching staff depending on the size of the school, and are directly responsible to the Provincial Directors of Education.

Teaching and educational activity is the joint responsibility of the head teacher or principal and the Teachers' Assembly (*Collegio dei docenti*) and the Interclass Council (*Consiglio d'interclasse*) in primary schools, and the Class Council (*Consiglio di classe*) in secondary schools. Schools have teaching and educational autonomy within the limits of the curricula formulated at national level and the regulations issued by Central Government.

The Teachers' Assembly is composed of all the permanent and temporary teachers of each primary school group or individual primary or secondary school, and is chaired by the principal or head teacher. It formulates teaching and educational plans for each school year, taking into account specific local requirements, national guidelines and state legislation, and decides on types of interdisciplinary coordination while respecting the freedom of teaching of each teacher. It periodically evaluates teaching to check that it conforms to the planned objectives and proposes improvements when necessary. It also selects textbooks and teaching materials, in consultation with the Class Councils, and makes proposals concerning the organization of the school and in-service teacher training.

The Class Council is composed of teachers of the same class and four elected parents' representatives, two of whom are replaced by two pupils' representatives at upper secondary level. The Inter-Class Council consists of the teachers of all the parallel classes and one elected parent for each class. It also formulates educational and teaching plans for the class, checks the progress of teaching and discipline in the class, organizes supplementary and extramural activities and carries out the periodical and final assesment of pupils (there are no external examinations).

Universities are legally represented by the Rector who is chosen by the professors from among their own ranks. The Rector undertakes to carry out the decisions made by the *Senato Accademico*, a collegiate body with decision-making responsibilities as regards educational-scientific subjects and questions of general interest, and by the *Consiglio di Amministrazione*, the board responsible for the administrative, economic and financial management of the university. Each university is divided into a certain number of faculties which carry out administrative and scientific-educational activities, administer examinations and issue one or more degrees or diplomas, corresponding to the various courses of study they provide. The departments, established by a Presidential Decree of 1980, promote research activities in a set field of study; they have their own structure and financial and managerial autonomy.

The Faculty Committee, consisting of the Dean and all the permanent professors and researchers, carries out programming and coordinating functions. When the subjects discussed concern their interests more closely, student representatives may also take part in the meetings. The Department Committee, chaired by the Department Head, is made up of professors and researchers, representatives of the non-teaching staff, and

doctoral and other students. This Committee makes decisions regarding research and teaching activities.

Local authorities (Regions, Provinces and Communes)

There are special-statute **regions** and ordinary-statute regions. The statutes of the former limit the powers of the state authorities. For example, with regard to the *MPI*, they allow for regional offices to be set up either to collaborate with the *MPI's* local offices or to replace them. All regions have their own legislative and administrative responsibilities within the general guidelines set out in state laws. In collaboration with other local authorities, they plan the establishment and construction of new schools or improvements to existing structures and administer funds received from the State for this purpose. They organize medical and psychological support services for pupils and measures to make it possible for all pupils to complete compulsory education and, as appropriate, continue their studies. The regions are responsible for vocational education, training and guidance outside upper secondary schools and universities, including the supervision of private activities in these areas. Regions may use the premises and equipment of state schools. Day-to-day management may be delegated to the communes.

The **provinces** ensure the provision of premises, equipment, services and non-teaching staff to some upper secondary schools: scientific *lycea* and technical schools.

The **communes**, often representing small residential communities and limited areas, have their own or regionally or provincially-delegated responsibilities for the services needed to run schools and ensure that young people can attend compulsory education, upper secondary education or vocational training, whatever their financial or physical circumstances. Support services include free school transport, the organization of school meals in or out of school, which are free or subsidized, depending on family circumstances, and the award of purchase vouchers for textbooks and financial grants.

In order to improve the management of services, small communes often join together as consortia or associations of communes.

1.5 Inspection

The Technical Inspectorate provides the Minister of Education with technical advice and supervises the education system as a whole. Inspectors are answerable to the Minister who appoints the Central and Regional Coordinators.

Some inspectors work at the *MPI* and some work at regional level, divided up according to types of schools or subject areas, on the basis of programmes defined annually at the national and regional service conferences. An annual report on the activities carried out is drawn up by the Central Coordinator. The duties of inspectors include: technical assistance to schools carrying out experimental projects; technical and educational advice to schools on planning, organization and research activities; collaborating in defining proposals for renewing teaching programmes and examinations; ensuring the implementation of Ministerial Directives and the appropriate use of human and material resources; and collaborating in defining in-service training plans for school staff and giving advice during their implementation.

1.6 Financing

With regard to public education, the state funds the central and local offices of the Ministry of Education (*MPI*), the salaries and the initial and in-service training of teaching and non-teaching staff in compulsory education and most upper secondary schools, and the management of schools' teaching materials. Most funds are transferred to the provincial offices of the *MPI* or to individual schools. The School Council decides on the purchase, renewal and maintenance of school equipment and teaching materials, library endowments and consumer materials for classes. The preliminary budget and final accounts for school expenditure are drawn up by an Executive Board, elected by the School Council and chaired by the head teacher. The school secretary, with clerical assistance, is responsible for accounting matters within the school and is an ex-officio member of the Executive Board.

Technical and vocational schools use funds allocated directly by the *MPI* for necessary expenditure and purchases, investment and the collection of funds needed for operating agricultural schools, laboratories and facilities attached to these schools. The School Council and school secretary have additional accounting responsibilities.

Regions have particular powers as regards school buildings, vocational education, training and guidance, school transport, school meals and the supply of textbooks free of charge, but these powers are usually delegated to the provinces and communes. The provincial authorities cover the cost of building schools of primary and lower secondary education, and technical and scientific upper secondary schools. The communal authorities cover the building costs of classical upper secondary schools.

The Ministry of Universities and Scientific and Technological Research distributes available funds amongst state universities and those private universities which have conformed to the structure of the public sector and have obtained authorization to issue legally recognized qualifications. Private universities also receive financial resources from local organizations, associations or foundations. In the context of university autonomy, state universities are allowed to accept financing and contributions for research and for activities for different users. Additional income comes from student fees for services such as laboratories and libraries.

1.7 Private Education

At all levels of education there are completely private institutions (*scuole private*) administered by private individuals or bodies corporate, charging fees and issuing qualifications that are not legally recognized. At primary level, their creation requires the authorization of the *MPI*; at secondary level they do not require such approval but must comply with public order, hygiene and health regulations.

There are also officially recognized private schools. At primary level, these are subsidized schools (*scuole sussidiate*), established after they have the approval of the Provincial Director of Education, or state authorized schools (*scuole parificate*), opened only by corporations, associations or organizations on the basis of an agreement with the Provincial Director after they have the approval of the *MPI*. At secondary level, they are legally recognized schools (*scuole legalmente riconosciute*) or state authorized schools (*scuole pareggiate*) according to Ministerial Decree. The former may be administered by public bodies or individuals, the latter by non-state or religious public bodies.

In recognized schools, the curricula, pupil assessment and teachers' qualifications must be similar to those in state schools. No fees are charged in recognized primary schools; and whilst recognized secondary schools do charge fees, they must provide free places to secondary level pupils receiving local authority scholarships.

The State rarely provides aid to private schools and then only in the form of subsidies or grants to institutions which cater for educational or social needs that state education does not meet.

1.8 Advisory/Consultative/ Participatory bodies

The National Education Council (*Consiglio Nazionale della Pubblica Istruzione*) assists the Minister of Education with the planning and supervision of education policy. It is made up of 71 members representing teaching staff and head teachers from education institutions at all levels, both state run and legally recognized, technical inspectors and personnel from central and local education authorities, the world of work (and the economy) and universities. It is chaired by the Minister. It elects supervisory committees for technical inspection staff, administrative staff in state schools and institutes, and permanent and supply teaching staff in state upper secondary and art schools.

The main advisory body for university education is the National University Council (*CUN*), in which the representatives of the various categories of university staff and students participate. On the subject of the right to study, the Minister asks the opinion of the National Council for the Right to University Studies, while the National Council for Science and Technology is the body through which the scientific community contributes to the definition of policies concerning scientific and technological research.

2. Pre-school education (Scuola dell'infanzia)

The present system of state nursery schools (*Scuola materna*) was established by legislation of 1968; this provided for funding for non-state (local or private) nursery schools. Before 1968, nursery schools were established and run by cities, communes and private or religious bodies. The overall responsibility for state pre-school establishments, for children aged 3 to 6 years, lies with the Ministry of Public Education (*MPI*), with the administration of the majority of nursery schools delegated to local education authorities. The establishment of state nursery schools has led to an expansion in provision, but the State does not, however, cover all requirements. Non-state schools receive funding from the State provided that certain conditions, considered essential, are observed.

Private pre-school establishments usually charge fees; others do not, but parents may contribute to the cost of transport and school meals provided by the communes. On average, 91.1% of 3- to 6-year-olds attend pre-school classes (1991/92 figures), roughly 50% in the non-state sector and 50% in state schools.

Under the *MPI*'s guidelines on education in state nursery schools in the Decree of June 1991, pre-school education, although it is not compulsory, has been recognized as the first rung of the educational ladder. The aims of pre-school education, set out in the guidelines, are to strengthen children's physical, intellectual and psychodynamic characteristics, to gradually help them to achieve independence and to develop their sensorial, perceptive, motor, linguistic and intellectual abilities.

Schools are coeducational and structured into groups or sections. Typically, a school has three sections comprising children of the same age (3, 4 and 5 years), but sections may also be composed of mixed age groups. In smaller locations, a school may be composed of only one mixed-age section. Each section must have a minimum of 14 and a maximum of 28 children, with two teachers per section; it must have from 10 to 20 children when there are children with handicaps. Whilst there is no legislation to this effect, teachers usually stay with the same section for the whole three years.

School activities normally last a minimum of 7 hours a day, 4 hours in the morning and 3 hours in the afternoon, but can be increased to 9 or 10 hours, usually on 5 or sometimes 6 (including Saturdays) days a week, depending on the needs of individual families. In certain cases the sections may operate in the mornings only, with one teacher.

The school year starts in September, on a date varying according to the region, and ends on 30 June. There are holidays of around 9 weeks in the summer, 2 weeks at Christmas and one week at Easter. Teaching must be provided for at least 10 months and may be extended to 11 months at parents' request. In July and August, communes may run educational and recreational services with different staff.

Curriculum

Since many activities are shared between the sections it is not possible to specify precise lesson times, subjects or play times, as all these interact. The *MPI*'s guidelines of June 1991 suggest that teachers organize activities in accordance with the age, maturity and environment of the pupils, to incorporate the following: body and movement; speech and words; space, order and measure; objects, time and nature; messages, forms and media; the self and others.

Assessment

The *MPI*'s guidelines prescribe that the teacher's initial assessment of the child's ability on admission be followed by other checks throughout the school year, making it possible to continually adjust educational methods and content to the child's abilities. A final assessment of skills is made before the child enters primary school. Specific programmes to prepare pupils for the transition to primary school are frequently organized, as well as information meetings for parents to discuss the transition procedure.

Teachers

Until now, nursery school teachers have been trained at upper secondary school level (*Scuola Magistrale*) through a three-year concurrent academic and teacher training course, including teaching practice. Under recent legislation (November 1990), nursery school teachers will gradually, from 1994/95, be trained through a four-year concurrent university course of academic and teacher training. After gaining a qualification, teachers must pass the examination (*concorso*) to acquire permanent teacher status.

Teachers of pre-school age children do not specialize in specific subjects. They may work full-time or part-time and those in state schools are civil servants. Those in legally recognized private schools must also have the qualifications stipulated for state pre-school teachers.

Teachers are not legally required to follow in-service training.

Statistics 1992/93

Pupils	1,569,811
Teachers	75,601*
Schools	27,274

State and non-state / private.
* State schools only.

Sources: Annuario ISTAT 1993. Istruzione e Cultura.
Ministero della Pubblica Istruzione. Servizio Statistico (1993).

3. Compulsory education

Compulsory education begins at the age of six years and continues up to the age of 14, including five years of primary and three years of lower secondary education. There is a longstanding proposal by the Government to extend compulsory education from eight to ten years, that is, until 16 years of age.

Compulsory education may be completed by attending state or non-state schools or through education at home.

Compulsory schooling is governed by national laws and regulations, which apply throughout the country in both state and officially recognized private institutions. The latter may obtain state funding if the service they offer replaces or integrates with that offered by the State.

3.1 Primary education (Scuola primaria)

Between 1985 and 1990 primary education underwent a process of renewal with new programmes (curricula) and a new structure set out in legislation. The educational aims and programmes of primary schools (*Scuola primaria*) are defined and set out on a national basis.

Under the terms of the legislation of February 1985, primary school education is aimed at promoting initial cultural literacy and the full development of the individual pupil, with an emphasis on interaction with families and the broader social community. The law of 1990 also indicates how educational activities at primary level should be linked with those at pre-school and lower secondary levels.

Children spend 5 years of primary education, from age 6 to 11, in primary schools.

Primary education is provided in state and officially recognized private schools and is free of charge; the number of completely private schools is very small. Children normally attend the school closest to their home. Schools must be established in locations where there are at least 10 children of compulsory school age in a 2-kilometre radius. In small schools all ages and abilities may be combined in one group.

Classes comprise no more than 25 pupils, and no more than 20 if there is a handicapped child requiring special education.

Primary education is divided into two stages, one of two years (cycle 1) and one of three years (cycle 2). Pupils automatically pass from cycle 1 to cycle 2 and move freely within each cycle. In cycle 1, teaching is multidisciplinary and the class teacher plays a predominant role, although the same class group or groups of pupils from different classes may be organized in an open class system and taught by several teachers. The planning of these activities is the responsibility of the Teachers' Assembly (*Collegio dei docenti*). In cycle 2, different teachers are used and teaching is divided into subject areas.

Since 1990, teachers have no longer been allocated to a class but to 'modules' comprising two classes with three teachers or three classes with four teachers. Teachers are not subject specialists, but on the basis of their specific competences they are responsible for one of the three subject areas covered by each module (see Curriculum). Teachers remain in the same module for a whole cycle.

The school year starts in September and ends on 30 June, with holidays at Christmas, at Easter and in the summer (see Pre-school education). It covers a minimum of 200 school days per year.

In the first year, the timetable covers 27 hours a week; this increases to 30 hours in the second year. It may be spread over five days from 8.30 a.m. to 4.30

p.m. with a lunch break, six mornings from 8.30 a.m. to 1.00 p.m., or five/six mornings and one, two or three afternoons a week. Based on parents' choices, extracurricular activities may be provided by schools in the afternoon, as long as the total number of hours does not exceed 37 per week, including lunch breaks. The length of each lesson is flexible and decided by the teachers.

Curriculum

The Law of June 1990 reformed the primary school system and allowed the new curricula, approved in legislation of February 1985, to be fully implemented. Subjects set out in the ministerial curricula are: Italian language, foreign language (introduced from the 3rd year in the 1992/93 school year under the Decree of June 1991), mathematics, sciences, history, geography, social studies, art education, education in sound and music, physical education and Catholic religion (optional).

Teaching in the first two years (cycle 1) is through an overall pre-disciplinary approach. Differentiation between subjects develops gradually in the third to fifth years (cycle 2).

Teaching is divided into modules comprising three areas where subjects are grouped together (linguistic-expressive, scientific-logical-mathematical and historic-geographical-social). Teachers are responsible for one of the three areas and coordinate their own teaching activities with those of the other teachers in the module to ensure coherence and uniformity of teaching.

The choice of textbooks is left to the individual teachers.

Assessment

Pupils' progress and maturity are assessed throughout the school year on the basis of individual teachers' observations of written and oral classwork and homework by the Inter-Class Council (*Consiglio d'interclasse*), an assembly of teachers of all the parallel classes. For the purposes of assessment, the school year is divided into periods of three or four months and a report (*scheda*) is sent to parents at the end of each period. Assessments are not expressed in the form of numerical marks; the reports show the overall

development and formation of the pupil's personality and his or her commitment to learn. Parents may meet teachers for an explanation of the reports.

There is a final assessment, based on the year's work, at the end of the year for admission to the following year; non-admission only takes place in exceptional cases at the recommendation of the Inter-Class Council.

At the end of the fifth year, pupils take the primary school leaving certificate examinations (*Licenza elementare*) to gain access to lower secondary school (*scuola media*). This consists of two written papers, relating respectively to language and expression and logic and mathematics, and one oral examination covering all subjects together. The examiners are the class teachers and two teachers nominated by the Teachers' Assembly. Should a pupil fail this examination, which is extremely unusual, he/she may repeat the year and retake it.

Teachers

Until now, primary school teachers have been trained at upper secondary school level (*Istituto Magistrale*) through four-year concurrent academic and teacher training courses, including teaching practice. Under the legislation of November 1990, primary school teachers, like nursery school teachers, will eventually be trained through a four-year university course.

After gaining a qualification, teachers must pass the examination (*concorso*) to acquire permanent teacher status.

Primary school teachers may work full-time or part-time and those in state schools are civil servants. Those teaching in officially recognized private schools must have the same qualifications as those in state schools.

Teachers are not legally required to follow in-service training.

Statistics 1992/93

Pupils	2,959,564
Teachers	264,615*
Schools	22,710

State and non-state / private.
* State schools only.

Sources: Annuario ISTAT 1993. Istruzione e Cultura.
       Ministero della Pubblica Istruzione. Servizio Statistico (1993).

3.2 Lower secondary education (Scuola media)

The last three years of compulsory schooling, for pupils aged 11 to 14, take place in lower secondary schools (scuola media). Access is dependent on passing the primary school leaving certificate examinations. Pupils may remain longer than the compulsory three years if they have to repeat years; some drop out before taking the lower secondary school leaving certificate examination (5.6% in 1991).

Lower secondary schools are fully comprehensive and provide free education (according to a common curriculum) to all children in the appropriate age range, regardless of their origin or social status. Their aim is as much to train pupils for adulthood and citizenship as for further study. They must be set up in communes with at least 3,000 inhabitants or wherever there is a need for such a school, according to the law of December 1962. No school may have more than 24 classes and no class may contain more than 25 pupils. Pupils are grouped according to age.

Teachers are specialized in individual subjects but interact with each other. Each teacher is assigned to a class but teaches his/her specialized subject to his/her own or other classes. Teachers normally stay with the same classes for the three years.

There are still a few private lower secondary schools; they account for less than 10% of pupils at lower secondary level.

The school year starts in mid-September (no earlier than 10) and ends on 30 June, covering a minimum of 200 school days per year. The compulsory timetable consists of 30 hours of lessons per week (five hours for each morning from Monday to Saturday), distributed amongst the various subjects in periods of 60 minutes. There must be a ten-minute break after the second or third hour.

At the request of a sufficient number of families (enough to allow for the formation of one or more classes), a school may decide to extend the school timetable to 36-40 hours a week (plus school lunch breaks). These additional hours are used for extra-curricular or subsidiary studies.

Curriculum

The general outline of the curriculum is laid down by the Ministry of Education, and is adapted to local and environmental circumstances by each school. The new teaching programmes, outlined in the law of February 1979, underline that the school's aim is to prepare pupils for life and careers and stipulate that individual subjects should be taught separately, by specialized teachers, but be linked with other subjects through cooperation between the teachers and interdisciplinary activities.

The subjects taught in all three years are: Italian, history, civics, geography, foreign language, sciences (mathematics, physics, chemistry and natural sciences), technical education, art, music, physical education and religion (optional).

There are no prescribed **textbooks**; the Teachers' Assembly in collaboration with subject teachers chooses one or more commercially produced textbook per subject.

Assessment and qualifications

In accordance with the Law of August 1977, the traditional grading system based on marks of one to 10 assigned by the individual teachers has been abolished, as have remedial examinations. Now, each teacher enters in a personal record (scheda personale) systematic comments on the learning progress and the level of maturity of each pupil; this is based on all oral and written classwork and homework, attitudes and behaviour. For the purposes of assessment, the school year is divided into three or four-month periods. At the end of each period, an analytical written assessment based on the information in the personal record is submitted by each subject teacher to the Class Council (*Consiglio di classe*), composed of all the teachers, which then formulates an overall written assessment. The written assessments and the personal record are sent to parents with explanatory notes. At its final overall assessment meeting of the year, the Class Council decides whether pupils should be promoted to the following year.

At the end of the third year, pupils take the examination for the lower secondary school leaving certificate (*Diploma di Licenza Media*), which is necessary for entry to upper secondary schools. This is administered by the teachers and an outside chairman. The examination consists of three written tests (Italian, mathematics and a foreign language) and a multidisciplinary oral test. The marks for each test are used as a basis for determining an overall mark of 'excellent', 'very good', 'good', or 'adequate' (pass marks) or 'fail'. For pupils passing the examination, advice and suggestions regarding further education are appended to the certificate.

Each pupil receives an attestation of completion of compulsory education, which contains the final overall assessment of the Class Council; it is attached to the personal record.

Teachers

Teachers are required to have obtained a university degree or a diploma from an institution of higher education in their specialist subject. University courses last between four and six years, while those in higher education institutions last between three and four years. Prospective teachers must then pass specific aptitude tests to have access to a probationary year of teaching. During this year, the teacher must follow training seminars and then pass the examination (*concorsi*) to acquire permanent teacher status. Under the law of November 1990, specialization courses will be organized for prospective secondary school teachers at postgraduate schools. These will lead to a diploma qualifying for the teaching profession and required for admission to examinations for permanent posts in secondary schools.

Teachers in state schools are civil servants. Since 1989 it has been possible to work part-time, usually for 50% of normal working hours.

Teachers are not legally required to follow in-service training.

Statistics 1992/93

Pupils	2,059,044
Teachers	233,034*
Schools	9,857

State and non-state / private.
* State schools only.

Sources: Annuario ISTAT 1993. Istruzione e Cultura.
Ministero della Pubblica Istruzione. Servizio Statistico (1993).

4. Post-compulsory education (Upper secondary education)

Upper secondary education is intended for young people between the ages of 14 and 19 years. After completing compulsory education (lower secondary school) they can follow courses lasting three, four or five years, after which they have the choice of entering higher education or employment at middle-management level or as specialized workers.

All post-compulsory schools belong to upper secondary education which consists of the following categories:

– classical and scientific (classical type);

– artistic;

– technical;

– vocational.

Until the full implementation of the law of November 1990 reforming university arrangements, schools of nursery and primary teacher training continue to be included in the classical category of upper secondary education.

In 1993, 31.6% of the age group entered classical and scientific education, 3.5% artistic, 35.8% technical and 19.5% vocational.

Upper secondary education remains the only level of education that has not changed its structure for several decades. However, a Presidential Decree of 1974 allows schools to carry out innovative projects, in particular to increase the number and type of courses and introduce new subjects. (Over 63% of schools are involved in such projects.)

Under a general reform of upper secondary education the Ministry of Education has been examining the possibility of extending compulsory education to 16 years of age. At present, 25% of pupils in this category of education leave school during the first two years.

As mentioned, to be granted access to upper secondary schools, pupils must hold the lower secondary school leaving certificate (*Diploma di Licenza Media*). On the basis of the guidance from lower secondary teachers, appended to the certificate, pupils and their families choose which upper secondary school they wish to attend. The only real limitation is the physical capacity of the school.

Most upper secondary schools are state schools; a small number, about 9%, are private.

All upper secondary schools charge tuition fees but, in accordance with the constitutional 'right to study', pupils in state schools may be exempt from fees (or receive financial support), on the basis of family income and/or their (achievement in the) assessment at the end of each year. All pupils pay for textbooks.

Pupils are normally grouped according to age, taking account of the cycle and the subjects studied. Within the same classes, subjects are taught at the same level to all. Pupils in difficulty may receive help from subject teachers. Teachers normally stay with the same classes throughout each cycle.

The school year begins in mid-September and ends on 30 June, covering a minimum of 200 school days including assessment periods (except the final upper secondary examination which may be held in July). It is divided into three terms with long holidays in the summer and shorter breaks at Christmas and at Easter.

4.1 Classical type education

Classical *Liceo (Liceo classico)*

The aim of the Classical *Liceo* is to prepare pupils for university and other forms of higher education.

In 1991, 70% of schools in the classical category took part in innovative projects which have led to changes in their structure and content, particularly in the field of linguistic and educational-social specializations.

Studies take five years and consist of two cycles:

- the lower cycle, the 4th and 5th *Ginnasio* classes, so called because they constitute the last two years of the old five-year *Ginnasio* (the first three years of the *Ginnasio* have been absorbed into the lower secondary school);

- and the upper cycle, the 1st, 2nd and 3rd *Liceo* classes. (The examinations for passage from the *Ginnasio* to the *Liceo* were abolished in the 1960s.)

The number of lessons per 6-day week varies from 27 to 29, each of 60 minutes' duration.

Curriculum

The compulsory subjects are:

Ginnasio: Italian language and literature, Latin language, Greek language, foreign modern language and literature, history, geography, mathematics and physical education.

Liceo: Italian language and literature, Latin language and literature, Greek language and literature, history, philosophy, natural sciences, chemistry and geography, mathematics and physics, history of art and physical education.

Religion is optional.

Scientific *Liceo (Liceo scientifico)*

The Scientific *Liceo* aims to develop and deepen the education of pupils intending to follow university studies in science, medicine and surgery. Since 1968, this *Liceo* has permitted access to all types of university training or higher education. It consists of a five-year course, divided into an initial period of two years, followed by a period of three years, without intermediate examinations. The two cycles are separated solely for the purpose of structuring teaching programmes and subdividing teaching posts.

The timetable is made up of 25 to 30 lessons per week, each of 60 minutes' duration, spread over a 6-day week.

Curriculum

The compulsory subjects are: Italian language and literature, Latin language and literature, foreign language and literature, history, philosophy, geography (in the first year), natural sciences, chemistry and astronomical geography (in the last years), mathematics and physics, drawing and physical education.

Religion is optional.

Primary Teacher Training School *(Istituto Magistrale)*

The Primary Teacher Training School trains primary school teachers and provides access to further study at the university faculty of education. This school offers a four-year course which can, however, be completed by a fifth year, at the end of which pupils have access to certain university faculties related to the studies followed during this fifth year.

The school week covers five days with three hours of classes per day.

Curriculum

The compulsory subjects are: Italian language and literature, Latin language and literature, foreign language (only in the 1st and 2nd years), philosophy, education and teaching practice and psychology, history, civics, geography (only in the 1st and 2nd years), natural sciences, chemistry and geography, mathematics and physics, drawing and history of art, choral singing, physical education.

Religion and a musical instrument are optional.

Nursery Teacher Training School *(Scuola Magistrale)*

The Nursery Teacher Training School trains teachers for nursery schools and consists of a three-year course. There are 30 hours of classes spread over a 6-day week.

Curriculum

The compulsory subjects are: Italian language and literature, education, history and geography, accountancy, mathematics and natural sciences, hygiene and paediatrics, music and choral singing, home economics, theory and application of physical education, handicrafts and drawing, teaching practice.

Religion is optional.

Assessment and qualifications (all classical type education)

For the purposes of assessment, the school year is again divided into periods of three or four months, depending on the Teachers' Assembly of each school. At the end of each period, the Class Council discusses and assesses each pupil's work. This is based on the grades received by the pupil in oral and written tests taken in all subjects during the year, which teachers of each subject enter in the class register. Information provided by all the teachers as to the regular attendance and participation of the pupil in all subjects, the initial level of the pupil and his/her subsequent progress and other useful information obtained from contacts with the pupil's family are all taken into account. At the meeting of the Class Council, which takes place at the end of the final period of the year, a final assessment of the commitment and progress of each pupil throughout the school year is given. This is expressed by a mark out of 10. Pupils must achieve at least 6 out of 10 for each subject and 8 for behaviour. Those with lower grades for some subjects must pass a 'repeat' examination in September before entering the following year.

At the end of the upper secondary school, pupils take the examination for the upper secondary school leaving certificate (*Maturità*). Only those with a positive assessment for the previous year are admitted to this examination; in fact, nearly 100% of pupils take it. The examination comprises two written tests and one oral test, set by the Ministry of Education. They are marked by a board of examiners comprising a teacher from the school and

teachers from other schools appointed by the Ministry of Education. In the first written test pupils must answer one of four questions, which are intended to discover their expressive and critical abilities. The second written test relates to the content of a subject studied during the final year. The oral test covers two subjects selected respectively by the candidate and the examining board and includes discussion of the written tests. The final assessment is in the form of a mark out of 60. Guidance on further studies is submitted in writing at the request of those interested. The certificate is specific to the type of school (*Diploma di Maturita classica, scientifica*, etc.).

Teachers

See Lower secondary education.

Statistics 1992/93

	Pupils	Teachers	Schools
Classical *Liceo*	231,064		753
Scientific *Liceo*	472,950		1,038
Primary teacher training school	159,518	57,370*	641
Nursery teacher training school	21,522		165

State and non-state / private.
* State schools only. Figures by type of school are not available.

Sources: Annuario ISTAT 1993. Istruzione e Cultura.
Ministero della Pubblica Istruzione. Servizio Statistico (1993).

4.2 Artistic type education

Artistic *Liceo (Liceo Artistico)*

The aim of the Artistic *Liceo* is to provide pupils with specialist education in painting, sculpture, stage design and architecture. The course lasts for four years and is divided into two sections: one for the study of figurative arts and stage design; and the other for the study of architecture. The first two-year cycle is identical in both sections; in the second cycle the number of hours for artistic subjects differs. The first section provides access to higher-level courses at the Fine Arts Academy (*Academia di*

Belle arti), the second to the university faculties of architecture. By following a fifth year, pupils can take examinations to obtain the artistic upper secondary school leaving certificate (*Diploma di Maturità Artistica*), which provides access to all university faculties.

There are 31-38 lessons per 6-day week to allow extra time for artistic subjects.

Curriculum

The compulsory subjects are:

General subjects: Italian language and literature and history, history of art, mathematics and physics, natural sciences, chemistry and physical geography, physical education.

Artistic subjects: Life drawing, still life, figure modelling, ornamental modelling, geometric drawing, perspective, elements of architecture and anatomy for artists.

Religion is optional.

Art Schools *(Istituti d'Arte)*

The aim of the Art Schools is to prepare pupils for traditional types of work and artistic output in industry, using the raw materials of the region. The study programmes of these schools cover a total of 34 sections (the arts of ceramics, gold, textiles, coral, alabaster, printing, wood, mosaics, glass, etc).

Courses initially last three years and lead to the final examination for obtaining the master of art diploma (*Diploma di Maestro d'Arte Applicata*). A further two-year course has been established experimentally in some schools, making it possible for pupils to obtain the applied arts upper secondary school leaving certificate (*Diploma Maturità di Arte Applicata*), which allows them to continue studying at higher-level art schools.

There are 31 – 38 lessons per week to allow extra time for artistic subjects.

Curriculum

The compulsory subjects are:

General subjects: Italian language and literature, history and civics, history of art and of applied arts, mathematics and physics, natural sciences, chemistry and geography.

Artistic subjects: Geometric and architectural drawing, life drawing, plastic arts.

Religion is optional.

These basic subjects, common to all options, are supplemented by different technologies and practical work depending on the type of craft industry for which the course is a preparation.

Assessment and qualifications

See Classical type education.

Teachers

See Lower secondary education.

Statistics 1992/93

	Pupils	Teachers	Schools
Artistic *Liceo*	36,652	3,458*	135
Art School	61,618	6,662*	165

State and non-state / private.
* State schools only.

Sources: Annuario ISTAT 1993. Istruzione e Cultura.
Ministero della Pubblica Istruzione. Servizio Statistico (1993).

4.3 Technical education

The purpose of technical education is to prepare pupils between the age of 14 and 19 years for work in particular occupations or to undertake technical or administrative duties in the areas of agriculture, industry and commerce. There are nine different types of Technical School (*Istituto Tecnico*): for agriculture, commerce, business with foreign languages, tourism, surveying, industry, foreign trade, naval and 'female' occupations. The latter are open to both female and male pupils despite their name. The courses are divided into two cycles, one of two years and one of three years. In the first two-year cycle all pupils study the same subjects, the only difference being the practical work carried out in the laboratories and workshops specific to certain departments. In the following three-year cycle, the subjects relating to the specialist option predominate, with considerable scope for related practical work.

The timetable for practical and theoretical lessons over the 6-day week varies between 31 and 38 hours of lessons, normally lasting 60 minutes, but sometimes 50 or 55 minutes depending on the teacher's decision.

Curriculum

Generally, the curriculum of the technical school during the first two-year cycle comprises the following subjects common to all departments and specializations: Italian language and literature, history and civics, geography, foreign languages, mathematics, physics, natural sciences and chemistry, drawing, physical education, religion (optional).

The only difference lies in the practical exercises which are carried out in the different departments.

In the following three-year period, general subjects such as Italian literature, history and civics and physical education are common to all; the other disciplines are related to the specific department or specialization, with much of the programme devoted to specifically-oriented practical exercises.

Assessment and qualifications

See Vocational education.

Teachers

See Lower secondary education.

Statistics 1992/93

Pupils	1,273,682
Teachers	111,334*
Schools	2,962

State and non-state / private.
* State schools only.

Sources: Annuario ISTAT 1993. Istruzione e Cultura.
Ministero della Pubblica Istruzione. Servizio Statistico (1993).

4.4 Vocational education

Vocational education offers a three-year course to pupils aged 14 to 17, with an extension for those who follow the five-year experimental courses to 19 years of age.

The purpose of the Vocational School (*Istituto Professionale*) is to train skilled workers, with particular attention to the local labour market.

There are five types of vocational schools: for agriculture, trade and industry, commerce, the hotel industry and 'female' occupations. Again, the latter are open to both female and male pupils despite their name.

Each school comprises different qualification sections matched to profiles required by the labour market. There are about 180 qualification sections in all, though not more than 60 per school.

There are a minimum of 31 and a maximum of 40 practical and theoretical lessons of 60 minutes per week. Sometimes these are reduced to 50 or 55 minutes due to the large number of courses to be scheduled.

Curriculum

The curricula in the Vocational Schools are more flexible than in the Technical Schools. There are no fixed patterns regarding the subjects taught and the timetables. Ministerial decrees establish the vocational profiles and the subjects common to all sections.

Qualification examinations may be taken at the end of the two or three-year courses.

Since 1969, experimental five-year courses have been set up in these schools with the purpose of providing a more general and applied education. Courses lead to the labour market or higher education. In the five-year course more time is devoted to general subjects in the first two years. It is also possible for those pupils on the shorter, two or three-year vocational courses to join the five-year course in the fourth year, once they have passed their qualification examinations, or to join a two-year integration course set up to complement a three-year course.

The five-year course may also be set up in Technical Schools to test new vocational profiles.

The timetables and curricula are organized in the same way as for the short courses.

Subjects common to all sections are: Italian language and literature, history, civics, physical education and religion (optional). In addition, there are subjects specific to each specialization and its related technologies.

Assessment and qualifications (technical and vocational education)

Pupils in technical and vocational education are assessed in the same way as those in other schools of upper secondary education.

On completion of the basic courses offered by Technical Schools, the five-year experimental courses, or the two-year complementary courses for Vocational Schools, pupils who have received a positive assessment for the previous year are admitted to the vocational or technical school

leaving certificate examinations in the specialization chosen during their studies. The examination procedure is the same as for other types of upper secondary schools.

Teachers

See Lower secondary education.

Statistics 1992/93

Pupils	534,044
Teachers	51,852*
Schools	1,702

State and non-state / private.
* State schools only.

Sources: Annuario ISTAT 1993. Istruzione e Cultura.
Ministero della Pubblica Istruzione. Servizio Statistico (1993).

5. Higher education

The legal foundations for the present-day higher education system in Italy are set out in Article 33 of the Constitution, which recognizes the right of universities and academies to act autonomously within the limits set by the law. Both public and private organizations have the right to establish schools and educational institutes; therefore higher education is divided into state and non-state establishments. There is also a distinction between universities and non-university higher education, the latter mainly comprising establishments offering education in the arts.

5.1 Universities

This category not only includes universities but also the Higher Institutes of Physical Education, higher institutions with special statutes, such as the Oriental Institute of Naples, the Higher Naval Institute of Naples and the College of Education of Pisa, schools of postgraduate and specialist studies and other higher institutions at university level.

Admission

The candidates for entry to university must possess an upper secondary leaving certificate (*Maturità*), gained after a five-year course of study. There is a numerus clausus at national level for dentistry and orthodontics; for these subjects an entrance examination is set by the appropriate faculty. In the final assessment of candidates for these faculties the marks obtained in the *Maturità* count for 30% and those of the entrance examination for 70%. An allocation of student places (*numero programmato*), caused by bottlenecks in student capacity, has also been introduced in a few universities for certain programmes: medicine and surgery, veterinary medicine, international studies and environmental sciences. For other faculties there is normally no limitation on student numbers.

Students apply directly to the institution at which they are interested in enrolling.

Fees/Student finance

Registration fees, centrally established in state universities, must be paid by all students. They must also pay special contribution fees laid down by the individual universities. Individual institutions may also exempt students from the payment of fees. Students may receive financial assistance in the form of state grants and interest-free loans guaranteed by the regions. They may also find a part-time job.

Academic year

The academic year normally starts on 5 November at the latest and ends on 15 June, not including the end-of-year examination session. The start and the end may vary by region by up to 15 days. Depending on the university, the year may be divided into semesters.

Courses/Qualifications

The various degree (*diploma di laurea*) courses are grouped as follows: scientific, medical, engineering, agriculture, economic, political-social, law, literary. For each degree course there is a chart which sets out the compulsory and the optional subjects, the number of examinations students must take and the educational modules. These rules, which are currently being reformed, will enable the faculties to propose alternative courses of study.

There is a limit on the number of subjects a student may take and on the overall length of the course, but students choose the components of their course themselves, subject to the approval of the faculty concerned. For example, the political science course lasts four years and comprises 21 examinations, whereas the agricultural science course lasts five years and comprises 38 examinations. The actual average for most courses is from four to six years.

Since 1990, there has been a two- to three-year course, providing students with the knowledge and expertise needed to find work in specific professional areas, which leads to a university diploma.

Assessment

Students must sit (and pass) examinations in each subject included in their study plan, some every year, as well as the final degree examination. Examinations in specific subjects test the maturity of candidates and their general knowledge of the subject.

An examining board appointed by the head of the faculty awards the marks. This board is composed of a teacher of the specific subject, a teacher of a similar subject and a subject expert. Marks of 0 to 10 are awarded by each board member, with a maximum mark of 30. The minimum mark for passing the examination is 18. Students may take the examination when they wish and may resit at any number of further examination sessions if they fail. This means that the total length of studies is usually prolonged.

For the final degree assessment students also have to carry out research under the supervision of a professor and the results of this are described in a degree thesis. This is then discussed by an eleven-member examining board. The final mark takes account of the average of the marks awarded for preceding examinations and the quality of the thesis. The minimum pass mark is 66. A 'first class' degree is awarded for a maximum mark of 110 (cum laude).

The law stipulates that examinations must take place in at least two sessions a year, one immediately after the end of the academic year and the other one month prior to the start of the academic year.

5.2 Higher non-university education

Non-university education establishments are under the jurisdiction of the Ministry of Education and include the following institutions providing education in the arts:

- Academies of Fine Arts (*Academia di belle arti*);

- Higher Institutes for Art Industries (*Istituto superiore per le industrie artistiche*);

- National Academy of Dramatic Art (*Academia di Arte Drammatica*);

- National Academy of Dance (*Academia di Danza*);

- Academies of Music (*Conservatoria di Musica*).

The initial courses of the latter two institutions are open to pupils who have the primary school leaving certificate, and pupils therefore follow normal secondary education in parallel. Pupils may also enter music academies at the end of lower secondary education. Fees are payable in all institutions. The State provides financial assistance to students from poorer families and to students with good marks.

The 19 **Fine Arts Academies** are intended to train students as artists. Access is by entrance examination. Students who already possess the artistic upper secondary school leaving certificate (*Maturità*) are exempt from this examination. All courses last four years and are specialized in painting, sculpture, decoration or stage design. Attendance is compulsory and students sit annual examinations for promotion to the following year. These examinations cover academic subjects; marks for art subjects are based on work carried out during the academic year. The final examination at the end of the course consists of a dissertation on a history of art subject and examinations in all the other academic subjects, together with an exhibition

of the best work the student has done during the whole course. An examining board asks the student questions on the technique and spirit of the work exhibited. A diploma mentioning the student's specialization is issued to students who pass these examinations. The academic year lasts from 4/5 November until 15 June.

The five **Higher Institutes for Art Industries** offer four-year courses in industrial design and graphic design. Access is by entrance examination, for students with the upper secondary school leaving certificate (*Maturita*). The academic year lasts from 5 November until 31 May. Attendance is compulsory and students sit annual examinations for promotion to the following year. At the end of the course, students sit an examination consisting in the presentation and discussion of a work project, and are awarded a diploma on a par with that obtained at the Academy of Fine Arts.

The **National Academy of Dramatic Art** offers two four-year courses, one specializing in acting, the other in directing. Applicants must have an upper secondary school leaving certificate. Admission to the acting course, open to students between 18 and 23 years of age, is by means of practical and written tests. For the directing course, open to students between 23 and 28 years of age, there are similar entrance tests, with a more detailed interview covering art, literature and culture. Attendance is compulsory. The academic year lasts from November to June, with examinations in June and October. At the end of the third year students sit the final diploma examination.

The **National Academy of Dance** offers:

- a normal eight-year course, entered on completion of primary school, divided into two three-year periods and a final two-year period;

- a subsequent three-year advanced course for soloists, choreographers or teachers.

In addition to possessing the primary leaving certificate, candidates for the normal course must take an aptitude test. There is an age limit of 10 to 12 for girls and 11 to 14 for boys. On the normal course, pupils take completion examinations at the end of each period (written, oral or practical) and may obtain a first certificate after the final period. This certificate, together with an upper secondary school certificate makes students eligible for the advanced course. On the advanced courses, promotion from year to year takes place by examination. The examination for the advanced diploma includes practical, written and oral tests in the various disciplines set out in the curriculum and in the student's own specialization. The academic year lasts from 1 October until 20 May.

Music Conservatories also admit students on the basis of an aptitude test. Teaching is structured in sections, depending on the type of studies being followed: composition, conducting, singing, instrumental. The curriculum is divided into two or three periods: lower and upper, or lower, intermediate and upper. Studies last for five or ten years from the end of primary education, depending on the section. In addition to their chosen subject students study solfege and specific academic subjects. Attendance is compulsory and students sit annual examinations for promotion to the following year. A certificate is issued at the end of the lower and intermediate periods, and a diploma in the discipline concerned is awarded at the end of the upper period. The academic year lasts from November to June, with examinations in June and October.

6. Initial vocational training

The Law of December 1978, 'Outline law on vocational training', provided the first complete regulation of the national vocational training system and defined the tasks of the State, the regions, the local authorities, both sides of industry, enterprises and their consortia and agencies with vocational training as their main objective. The Law states that training is an instrument of education and advancement and 'takes place in keeping with economic planning objectives and is intended to promote employment, production and the development of labour organization in line with scientific and technological progress'.

Initial vocational training is offered to young people who have completed their compulsory schooling and who wish to prepare for a specific vocational certificate.

This training is provided by the regional authorities in both multi-annual and one-year courses. Multi-annual courses are specifically targeted to meet regional, political and economic goals. One-year courses have a more operational character and are offered in proportion to the resources allocated for specific training projects.

Courses are offered throughout the country in approximately 2,790 vocational training centres administered by the regional governments and by centres belonging to organizations under contract to the regions, which are private non-profit making organizations. In terms of the number of courses and the type of activities offered, the most important organizations are: *ENAIP (Ente Nazionale Istruzione Professionale)*, *ACLI (Associazione Cattolica Lavoratori Italiani)*, *CNOS (Centro Nazionale Opere Salesiane)*, *IAL-CISL (Istituto Addestramento Lavoratori-Confederazione Italiana Sindacati Lavoratori)*, *ENFAP-UIL (Ente Nazionale Formazione Addestramento Professionale dell'Unione Italiana Lavoratori)*.

Initial training courses

Initial training, which covers agriculture, industries and crafts and the services sector, includes the following types of courses:

- Courses leading to a first certificate;

- 'integration' courses completing secondary school education;

- post-certification courses, organized by the regional education authorities for students who obtained 'weak' certificates (for example, from primary or nursery teacher training schools), and for students requiring further and specialized courses leading to specific certificates;

- courses and post-certification activities offered in schools, but organized and financed by the regional authorities;

- 'level two' courses, which offer further education after a first certificate.

The first category, which lasts for a minimum of one or a maximum of two years, leads to a basic certificate and is intended for young people who have completed compulsory education. These courses constitute 37% of the regional authorities' training activities.

The second category is intended for students who have completed vocational training and wish to return to secondary school, and for students in upper secondary school, and lead to a specialized certificate for those who complete the final classes (*classi terminali*) of secondary school. These courses are complementary to the school curriculum and are taken in addition to the general national curriculum.

An important part of the third category is the large number of hours of work placements and classes led by experts active in working life. These constitute 1.1% of the courses administerd by the regional vocational training programme. In addition to their growing number, these courses are important because they represent the only time when school, vocational training and the workplace interact at institutional level.

The last two categories, called 'level two' or 'post certification' courses, offer preparation for mid-level qualifications and constitute 16% of the regional authorities activities.

Initial vocational training, which in the past attracted students who, for the most part, had obtained the weakest marks in their lower secondary school certificate, or had abandoned upper secondary education, has in recent years shifted its emphasis to attract students who have performed better at school.

There are approximately 19,000 teachers, of whom one-third teach in public centres and two-thirds in centres under contract to the regional governments.

Apprenticeship *(Apprendistato)*

Apprenticeship is regulated by Law n° 25 of 1955, which represents an important step forward in the promotion of certified training.

Apprenticeship is based on a contract according to which the employer must teach, or ensure that the apprentice is taught in his enterprise, the necessary technical skills to become a skilled worker. The employer pays the apprentice a salary for his work.

An apprenticeship contract is available to young people between 15 and 26 years of age.

The apprentice must work 32 hours per week and attend theoretical courses for 8 hours per week (not necessarily all together). Theoretical courses last an average of 150 hours per year.

At the end of the apprenticeship contract, the apprentice must take an examination organized in a similar way to those in the regional vocational training system. The examination leads to the qualification agreed in the apprenticeship contract, which is equivalent to the qualifications awarded on completion of the regional courses.

The apprenticeship system involves around 605,000 young people each year. 53% of these young people are apprenticed in the crafts sector, but there are a considerable number of apprentices in other sectors. 80% are apprenticed in enterprises in northern and central Italy.

Trainers are usually employees of the enterprise concerned.

Employment-Training Contracts (Contratti di formazione-lavoro)

Employment-Training Contracts (*CFL*) are covered by the Law of 1983 which supplements existing legislation on the development of youth employment. Under the *CFL*, employers hire young people between 15 and 29 years of age for a period of one year on a fixed-term training contract.

Following agreements between the social partners and the Government, the continuing unemployment of young people led to the adoption of Law 863/84, which changes the nature of the employment-training contract.

The new law provides for public and private companies and their consortia to take on young people of their choice between 15 and 32 years of age for a period of 24 months. At the end of the initial contract period, companies can renew or terminate the contract.

There are no legal provisions regarding the division of time between training and work. Enterprises must only submit training plans when they request financial support from the region.

Information on young people's integration into the labour market shows how important this type of training is; it involves about 500,000 young people each year. By 1990, six years after the above-mentioned new law was adopted, 2,500,000 young people had been involved in a *CFL* in order to enter the world of work.

According to *ISFOL (Instituto per lo sviluppo della formazione professionale dei lavoratori* – Institute for the development of vocational training), there has been a trend towards more 15- to 18-year-olds taking part in *CFL*. Two-thirds of participants have only a compulsory school leaving certificate, which confirms that the *CFL* involve young people with low-level qualifications. The industrial sector hires about half of the workers-trainees, followed by the tertiary sector; there are few contracts in the primary sector. The central role of small firms (with less than 50 employees) is also confirmed; 70% of participants are contracted to these.

The trainers are employees of the enterprise signing the contract.

Luxembourg

LUXEMBOURG

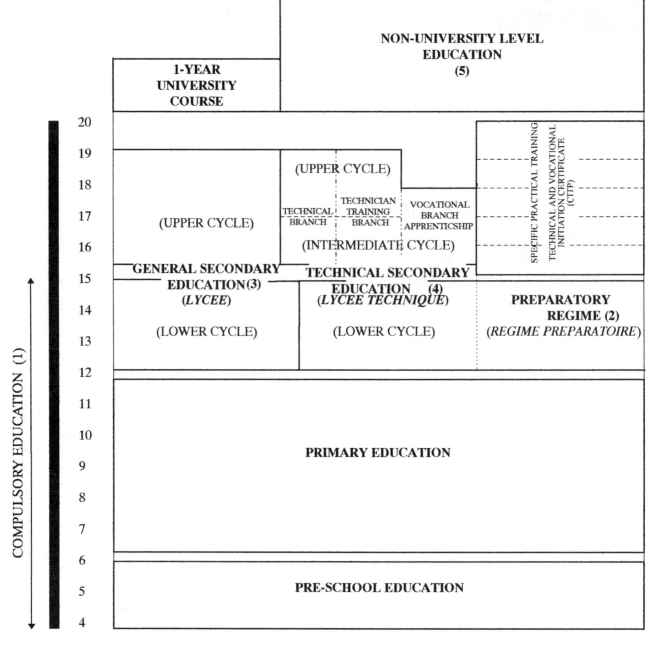

1. Compulsory education includes two years of pre-school education.

2. The preparatory regime (*régime préparatoire*) of technical secondary education (formerly complementary education /*enseignement complémentaire*) provides a 3-year course in general and practically-oriented subjects for pupils aged 12 to 15 who have completed 6 years at primary school but who are not allowed to transfer to secondary education (i.e. they have not passed the entrance examination). The preparatory regime prepares pupils for a vocational qualification.

3. General secondary education covers seven years of study divided into a lower cycle (completing compulsory education) and an upper cycle. The lower cycle leads to a certificate attesting the completion of compulsory education. The upper cycle leads to a secondary school leaving certificate which provides access to university education.

4. Technical secondary education covers six or seven years of study divided into two or three cycles respectively. The lower cycle leads to a certificate attesting the completion of compulsory education. The intermediate cycle comprises a technical branch and technician's training branch which lead to the upper cycle, and a vocational branch which includes parallel apprenticeship training in a firm leading to the certificate of technical and vocational proficiency providing access to employment. The upper cycle leads either to a technical secondary education leaving certificate providing access to higher education or to a technician's certificate.

5. 2- to 3-year courses.

- - - - - - = alternative beginning or end of level/type of education

1. Responsibilities and administration

1.1 Background

Luxembourg is officially a trilingual country. The Law of 24 February 1984 on the languages regime stipulates that the national language of Luxembourg is Luxembourgish (*Letzeburgesch* – a Frankish-Moselle dialect which is the vernacular for the entire indigenous population of Luxembourg). The two official languages are French and German (which are used as languages of communication with non-Luxembourgers and as written languages for legislation and administration). The three traditional languages have now been joined by the languages of immigration.

Luxembourg has a population of 385,317, almost 27% of which is the resident foreign population. With an urbanization rate of around 70% and an economy based on the services sector for more than 60% of GDP and employment, Luxembourg belongs to the post-industrial countries of Europe. The unemployment rate is traditionally very low, normally around 2.4% (25% of the unemployed are young people in the 16- to 25-year age group).

Luxembourg is a Constitutional Monarchy. Executive power is exercised by the Grand Duke, who devolves this power to the Government. The exercise of legislative power is shared by the Grand Duke and the Chamber of Deputies (Parliament). Since the 1984 election, the Government has been a coalition of the Christian Social and Socialist Workers Parties; they were re-elected in the 1989 election.

Luxembourg is a small country (2,586 square kilometres), with no provinces and no departments; the local authority (the commune) is the only element of territorial decentralization. There are 118 communes.

1.2 Basic principles: education

According to Article 23 of the Constitution, 'the State shall ensure that all Luxembourgers receive primary education, which shall be compulsory and free of charge. The State shall set up the requisite secondary school establishments and higher education courses, and shall also set up vocational training courses to be provided free of charge'.

There is no separation betwen Church and State and this link is reflected in the education system. However, pupils who do not want to attend the religious education course may choose a non-denominational ethics course (*morale laïque*).

1.3 Distribution of responsibilities

The Ministry of National Education and Vocational Training (*Ministère de l'Education Nationale et de la Formation Professionnelle*) is reponsible for the whole of education and training, from pre-school education to university courses. As regards vocational training, it is responsible for both the school-based part and the part provided in enterprises, without prejudice to the responsibilities of the professional chambers.

All sections of education are governed by Grand Ducal and ministerial laws and regulations drawn up and executed by the one Ministry of National Education and Vocational Training and voted on by Parliament.

The commune is the partner of the Ministry of National Education and Vocational Training at pre-school and primary levels and for certain aspects of adult education. Post-primary establishments (secondary and higher education) are run by the Ministry with the assistance of their respective head teachers or directors.

The social partners, through professional chambers, are consulted on certain matters concerning technical secondary education and vocational training. They have wide-ranging legal responsibilities regarding the apprenticeship system.

The vast majority of pre-school, primary and secondary schools in Luxembourg are public. There are, however, private schools established as bodies corporate; these are almost all administered by the Catholic Church.

1.4 Administration

Ministry of National Education and Vocational Training

The administrative system can reasonably be said to be centralized; with the main points being decided at national level. Legislation and the broad lines of all levels of education and training in terms of curriculum, general objectives, methods (to be applied very generally), assessment, the organization of time and holidays are decided at ministerial level.

Curricula and school textbooks are proposed by ad hoc committees and approved by the Ministry of National Education and Vocational Training. These committees comprise specialist teachers and representatives of the Ministry. Vocational training programmes are drawn up in collaboration with professional chambers, and committees may also include representatives of other Ministries. Final examinations are organized by the Ministry of National Education and Vocational Training.

The Ministry of National Education and Vocational Training also approves the establishment of all education and training institutions. With regard to public post-primary education the Ministry actually establishes institutions, is responsible for the appointment of head teachers and, directly or through the head teachers, supervises curricula, methodology, assessment and the organization of time.

The Ministry of National Education and Vocational Training is under the political responsibility of one Minister of Education and Vocational Training. The Ministry's various departments are:

- staff and administration;

- pre-school and primary education;

- general secondary education;

- technical secondary education;

- vocational training;

- higher and university education;

- adult education;

- special education (*éducation différenciée*);

- research;

- informatics and statistics;

- publications;

- budget, school buildings and materials;

- educational psychology and guidance centre (*Centre de psychologie et d'orientation scolaires*);

- pedagogical and technological research and innovation department (*Service de Coordination de la Recherche et de l'Innovation Pédagogique et Technologique*);

- Eurydice.

Not all officials in the Ministry of National Education and Vocational Training are civil servants in the proper sense of the word. A certain number of posts are filled by teachers of primary education (*instituteurs attachés*) and teachers of secondary education (*professeurs attachés*).

Communes

In the communes, power is wielded by the Local Council, acting through the Local Education Committee (*commission scolaire*). This comprises the Mayor, a member of the clergy (appointed by the Minister of Education and Vocational Training on the proposal of the Archbishop) and three lay members (appointed by the Local Council), or five lay members in communes with 3,000 or more inhabitants, including parents of schoolchildren. The Local Education Committee is responsible in the area under its jurisdiction for implementing laws and regulations.

Communes establish public pre-school and primary institutions and are responsible for their management and administration. Through the Local Education Committee, they are responsible for pre-school and primary infrastructure, i.e. buildings, furniture and teaching materials, and take the decisions with regard to the admission of children and the appointment of new teachers (the appointment then has to be approved by the Minister). It is also up to the local education committee to monitor the school curriculum and timetable and school attendance.

Educational institutions

Establishments of **pre-school and primary education** have no head teachers. Teachers work under the direction of the inspectorate of primary education. There is no hierarchy within schools, although a partial administrative remit may be entrusted to one of the teachers.

Institutions of **secondary and secondary technical education** and of **further and higher education** are run by the national authorities and their respective head teachers or directors.

Secondary and secondary technical establishments are run by a head teacher (*directeur/trice*) and one or more assistants. The teaching body is collegial, although in addition to established teachers there may be teachers who are engaged for a limited period only. Each school also has its own administrative and technical staff who report to the head teacher. The head teacher is responsible for the proper functioning of the school. He or she is generally in charge of teaching, staff matters and pupils. More particularly, the head teacher is responsible for inspection duties, and is the hierarchical superior of all the teaching, administrative and technical staff. The head teacher is appointed by the Grand Duke.

Each general secondary and technical secondary school has an Education Council (*conseil d'éducation*), comprising nine full and nine alternate members – the head teacher, and teachers', parents' and pupils' representatives. *Inter alia*, the Education Council is responsible for the establishment project (*projet d'établissement*) of the school; this is an autonomous project which aims to

promote educational initiatives and organize activities to ease access to vocational training and the transition to adult and working life.

Social partners

The social partners are consulted on all legislation regarding technical secondary education, apprenticeship and other vocational training courses. Together with the Ministry of National Education and Vocational Training and the Ministry of Labour, they determine the occupations subject to apprenticeship and the firms eligible to train apprentices, establish theoretical and practical training programmes and final examinations, and award qualifications.

1.5 Inspection

At primary level, inspection lies with ministerial inspectors (all former school teachers). As mentioned above, at post-primary level (secondary and higher education and vocational training) the head teachers of the individual institutions are responsible for inspection.

There are 16 inspectors who have a geographical area to cover; they report to the Inspector-General, who in turn reports to the Minister. The Inspector-General is particularly responsible for teaching staff, whilst inspectors ensure that the laws and regulations pertaining to primary education are observed.

Tasks include the monitoring of both curricula and textbooks which, as mentioned above, are centrally prescribed by the Ministry, and controlling the work of pre-school and primary school teachers. Private institutions are also subject to state inspection.

1.6 Financing

The bulk of the cost of education is assumed by the Central Government budget. However, one-third of pre-school and primary school teachers' salaries are paid by the communes, along with the cost of the maintenance of buildings, furniture and materials. Secondary and higher education and teacher training are paid for entirely by Central

Government directly from the Ministry of National Education and Vocational Training. In-firm vocational training is financed by the firm concerned, which receives a subsidy from Central Government.

To cover their expenditure, local authorities have access to income from their property and from the product of local taxes and levies. They also receive Central Government subsidies and funds and may take up loans.

Pupils and students do not pay fees. Textbooks and other materials are completely free at primary level but pupils/students may have to purchase some textbooks and materials at post-primary level. However, needy pupils/students can apply for financial support from the Ministry of National Education and Vocational Training to cover purchase costs.

During their in-firm training, apprentices receive an indemnity from their employer, fixed by the Ministry of National Education and Vocational Training on the proposal of the professional chambers.

1.7 Private schools

There are very few private schools of pre-school and primary education and a small number of private schools of secondary education. At primary level, there are four denominational private schools and one non-denominational private school. There is also a difference between those private establishments subsidized by the State and those which are not. The latter are limited to specialized training (for example, the tertiary banking sector).

Subsidized private establishments mainly offer post-primary education (two establishments also cover primary education), both general secondary and technical secondary. They receive a state subsidy towards their running costs on condition that curricula, timetables, teaching methods and teaching staff correspond to those in state schools.

Parents pay a contribution towards the running costs of private schools *pro rata* to their family income.

Pupils from private schools must sit the same final examinations as those in state schools to obtain certificates recognized by the State.

1.8 Advisory bodies

For advice on the management and planning of the whole education system, the Minister of Education and Vocational Training may consult the Higher Advisory Committee on Education (*Conseil Supérieur de l'Education Nationale*), whose task it is to study general problems related to education and teaching, to comment on questions and problems submitted by the Minister and to make its own proposals, suggestions and comments on educational matters.

The Committee is composed of a maximum of 42 members, appointed by the Minister of Education and Vocational Training for a renewable period of two years, representing other Ministries (sports, health, family affairs, etc.), the clergy, teachers, parents, industry, etc. The Committee works through an executive of ten of its members, also appointed by the Minister of Education and Vocational Training.

As mentioned above, at municipal level, Local Education Committees represent the commune authorities, the Church and the local population with regard to pre-school and primary education. Teachers are not allowed to sit on the Local Education Committee.

For both general secondary and technical secondary education there are national colleges of head teachers (meeting separately), which give opinions on any draft legislation, regulation or administative provision submitted to them by the Minister of Education and Vocational Training.

Parents' associations may be set up and invited to help teachers, but they have no legal basis and are of a purely advisory nature.

2. Compulsory education

Compulsory education in Luxembourg lasts 11 years, comprising nine years in the formal school education system (six years of primary and three years of secondary education) and two years of pre-school education. Compulsory education starts at the age of four and is usually completed at the age of 15. Schooling is compulsory; in rare cases, primary education can take place at home.

3. Pre-school education (Education préscolaire)

The provision of pre-school education in Luxembourg differs slightly from that in other Member States as it is compulsory. The Grand-Ducal Regulation of 22 October 1976 made pre-school education compulsory for five-year-olds and optional for four-year-olds. The Grand-Ducal Regulation of 2 September 1992 made it compulsory for children aged four. This decision was made on the basis that children need longer to reach the expected standards, given the fact that the whole school system (and beyond) is bilingual. Pre-school education itself is usually in Luxembourgish. Thus, pre-school education lasts for two years and is intended for children from four to six years of age. It is normally provided in nursery schools (*jardins d'enfants*).

In principle, all children fulfilling the age and residence conditions are admitted to the school nearest their home. Certain local authorities run infant classes (*classes d'éducation préscolaire*) for children who were not four years of age by 1 September and, therefore, did not qualify for entry to the pre-school system.

There are pre-school units throughout the country. In the rural and less densely populated regions, local authorities have set up centralized pre-school units with free transport organized for children from outlying areas.

The attendance rate in pre-school establishments is extremely high: practically 100%.

Pre-school establishments are under the authority of the Ministry of National Education and Vocational Training, which finances about two-thirds of teachers' salaries. The administration and maintenance of most pre-school establishments come under the responsibility of the communes. Parents are not required to pay for pre-school education.

Pre-school establishments are usually attached to primary school buildings, but offer a programme suited to the age of the children concerned, with two classes on average. Theoretically, a class comprises one class teacher and between 18 and 22 pupils.

The pre-school units are open 212 days per year, from 8.00 a.m. to 11.45 a.m. from Monday to Friday and from 2.00 p.m. to 4.00 p.m. on Monday, Wednesday and Friday. In most local authority areas, there are no pre-school sessions on Saturdays. In around 10 local authority areas, there are continuous sessions offering child care facilities from 7.30 a.m. to 6.00 p.m. The school year commences on 15 September and runs until 15 July. The first term finishes at Christmas, the second at Easter and the third in July. At the end of the first two terms, children have two weeks' holiday.

Curriculum

Despite the fact that two years of pre-school education are compulsory, there is no formal teaching. Pre-school education is expected to foster the physical, intellectual and moral development of the children and to prepare them for entry to primary school. An outline plan was drawn up by the Ministry in 1991, laying down general objectives, course content and methods. Certain activities are listed as being particularly conducive to the development of pre-school children:

- physical activities (games, dance, sport, balancing activities, swimming, etc.);
- musical activities (songs from a variety of national and cultural traditions, rhythmic work, dance, the use of instruments);
- artistic activities (drawing, painting, modelling, printing, etc.);
- logical and mathematical activities;
- language activities;
- science activities.

In the Ministerial Circular of April 1990, teachers are also asked to pay particular attention to organizing regular teaching sessions in order to develop the teaching of Luxembourgish.

Teachers enjoy quite a broad measure of liberty in respect of play methods and teaching proper (pre-school teaching as such is not compulsory). Methods and materials are not prescribed by the Ministry at this level.

There is no fixed weekly timetable. Where particular cognitive activities are in progress (pre-reading, pre-writing, etc.), these should not, in principle, exceed 30 minutes.

Assessment

Children undergo no assessment during their two pre-school years.

Where a child has failed to reach the requisite level of physical or psychological development at the end of the pre-school period, the teacher must inform the inspector and the parents accordingly. A consensus is then reached, and sometimes the child does a third year at pre-school level or is admitted to one of the French-speaking *classes d'accueil* (reception classes) or into a *classe d'attente* (where the programme of the first year is spread over two years). Assessment is the responsibility of the teacher, except in difficult cases where the inspector is also involved.

The transition from pre-school to primary school is normally no problem, except for children who have not yet reached the required proficiency in Luxembourgish.

Teachers

Each class has a full-time teacher and no assistants. There are no specially trained teachers for different subjects, but there are specially trained monitors for courses such as swimming and physical activities.

From 1983/84, initial training takes place at one institute of higher education, the teacher training institute (*Institut Supérieur d'Etudes et de Recherches Pédagogiques – ISERP*). It lasts for three years and leads to the certificate of educational studies, pre-school option (*Certificat d'études pédagogiques, option préscolaire*). At present, pre-school and primary teachers are central government civil servants.

In-service training is in general optional; one-day training sessions (*journées d'échanges pédagogiques*) are organized by the Ministry of Education and Vocational Training which can make participation in these sessions compulsory.

(Up to four years old, children can attend day care centres (*foyers du jour*) which are the responsibility of the Ministry of the Family and Solidarity.)

Statistics 1992/93

	Public	Private
Pupils	7,803	38
Teachers	467	not available
Schools	not available	1

4. Primary education (Enseignement primaire)

Primary education covers a period of six years and is intended for 6- to 12-year-olds.

Public primary schools (*écoles primaires*) are run by the local authorities. They do not charge tuition fees. The requisite school material and textbooks are provided by 116 of the 118 local authorities, with the other two (with very tight budgetary constraints) requiring parents to bear some of the cost.

Only very few primary schools are maintained by private bodies or institutions. Private schools charge fees.

Any child who has completed six years of age by 1 September may be admitted to the school in his or her particular area. There is a 100% attendance rate.

The size of schools differs from one commune to another depending on the number of inhabitants. The average class size is 17 or 18 children. According to a Ministerial Circular of 1990, the Minister of Education and Vocational Training intends to increase class sizes to between 18 and 22 pupils. Schools generally assign pupils to classes by age.

One teacher presents all basic subjects. There may be specialized teachers in subjects such as physical education, music, religion and art. In most communes, the same teacher remains with the same group/class for two years.

Within the primary schools a distinction is made between the three levels: the lower level (first two years), the intermediate level (third and fourth years), and the upper level (final two years).

There are 30 lessons of 50 or 55 minutes per week. Teaching is spread over the whole week: six morning sessions (Monday to Saturday) with four lessons each and three afternoon sessions (Monday, Wednesday and Friday) with two lessons each.

Schools are open 212 days per year, from 8.00 a.m. to 11.45 a.m. and from 2.00 p.m. to 4.00 p.m. The school year is the same as at pre-school level.

Midday care centres have recently been set up in around 12 local authority areas for children whose parents go out to work. Salary and operational costs are borne 50% by Central Government and 50% by local authorities. Parents pay for the cost of meals taken at school.

The purpose of primary school is to ensure that everyone receives a basic education, which is indispensable for any new skill and any subsequent course of training, and enables people to cope with changing situations. Whilst it is true that certain elementary cultural techniques, such as reading, writing and arithmetic, are a priority concern, equal importance must be attached to developing thought processes, the ability to solve problems and communication techniques. This basic education also needs to develop attitudes and behavioural patterns in respect of society, the natural and cultural environment, technology and oneself.

Curriculum

Since compulsory education is governed by national laws, primary school curricula are set out by the Ministry of National Education and Vocational Training and apply throughout the country.

Although the aims and programmes of primary education in Luxembourg are not really different from that in other Member States (teaching of reading, writing, arithmetic, artistic and physical activities, study of the local environment, development of social behaviour, etc.), both teaching methods and procedures are unique because of the linguistic peculiarity of the country, where three languages are used on equal terms.

Teaching in primary schools starts off in Luxembourgish which the vast majority of children speak at home. Reading begins in German, a language which becomes the teaching language for practically all subjects. French, which is taught as a foreign language, starts towards the middle of the second school year. Luxembourgish continues to be used in parallel to German and French.

The current curriculum has been in force since 1989 and includes: religious education, Luxembourgish, French (from the second half of the second year), German, arithmetic, introduction to science (first four years), history (last two years), geography (last two years), natural sciences (last two years), art, crafts, music, physical education and sport, options and other subjects (first four years) and 'supervised activity' (first year).

'Options and other subjects' includes occasional lessons on road safety, technology, consumer affairs, etc.

Proposals and suggestions are made to teachers regarding **teaching methods**, but they are not required to follow them. There are **textbooks** prescribed by the Ministry, and teachers usually use these.

Due to the workload created by the use of different languages, there is a certain rate of failure at school; this has prompted the Minister of Education and Vocational Training to introduce a set of **reforms** designed to reduce this workload. Textbooks are being rewritten and a wider range of teaching material is to be provided for teachers, with teaching methods being adapted to the specific needs of children in the various age groups.

Assessment

Pupils are assessed continuously by the teacher. From the first year, there are periodic written tests called school exercises (*devoirs scolaires*) in each subject, but they do not constitute formal examinations. Three times a year, the pupils receive a report card based on the assessment of their work during the term.

The decision as to whether a pupil should be promoted from one class to the next is made at the end of each year by the teacher, on the basis of the marks gained during the year for written work, homework and oral participation. At the end of each year, the pupil receives a report card which indicates whether he or she has passed the year and may be admitted to the next class. In order to move up to the next class, a child must have obtained the minimum number of points (30 out of 60) in two of the three main subjects (German, French and arithmetic); if not, he or she must repeat the class.

There are no examinations between the three levels of primary education. At the end of the sixth year, there is an examination designed to establish whether children should go to a general secondary school or a technical secondary school. The medium and long-term aim is to replace this examination by continuous assessment schemes; it will be retained only in cases where continuous assessment is disputed. There is no final examination or leaving certificate.

The educational psychology and guidance centre (*Centre de psychologie et d'orientation scolaires – CPOS*) collaborates in the **guidance** of pupils in the sixth year.

For pupils who are weak in one or two subjects, there are remedial classes (*cours d'appui*) during the school year in certain communes. Running parallel to the primary school classes, there are also *classes spéciales* (special classes) and *classes d'attente* for children with serious learning difficulties.

Teachers
(also partially for the preparatory regime of technical secondary education)

From 1983/84, initial training takes place at the one institute of higher education for teacher training (*Institut Supérieur d'Etudes et de Recherches Pédagogiques – ISERP*); it lasts three years, and leads to the certificate of educational studies, primary option (*Certificat d'études pédagogiques, option primaire*).

Teachers are central government civil servants. They may work full-time or part-time.

In general, in-service training is optional; one-day training sessions (*journées d'échanges pédagogiques*) organized by the Ministry of Education and Vocational Training may be declared compulsory.

Statistics 1992/93

	Public	Private
Pupils	24,619	353
Teachers	1,851	not available
Schools	not available	2

Preparatory regime of technical secondary education
(formerly complementary education (*enseignement complémentaire*))

After the six years of compulsory primary education, a preparatory regime has been created to cater for pupils who have completed six years at primary school but who are not allowed to transfer to secondary education.

At present, 9 of the 14 technical *lycées* organize a preparatory regime.

There are no admission requirements for the preparatory regime; pupils who have not taken or have not passed the examination held at the end of the sixth year of primary education can be admitted to the seventh class (*classe de 7e*) of the preparatory regime.

Pupils fall within the age range 12 to 15, but age differences in one class may be considerable as a result of frequent repetitions of classes at primary level. There are 12 to 18 pupils per class.

The preparatory regime aims to prepare pupils either for vocational training or for the transition to adult and working life.

Pupils continue to be taught general subjects but, in addition, they have lessons in practically-oriented subjects like metalwork, woodwork or home economics. Pupil assessment and promotion are also broadly the same as at primary school.

Statistics 1993/94

	Public	Private
Pupils	1,086	173
Teachers	263	20
Schools	12	3

5. Secondary education *(Enseignement secondaire)*

Pupils must attend some form of full-time secondary education for at least three years after completing six years of primary education, covering the age range 12 to 15.

As mentioned above, to be admitted to the first year of secondary education, pupils must sit a national entrance examination; this comprises tests in French and German (dictation and language exercises) and arithmetic. There are separate examinations for admission to general secondary schools and technical secondary schools, organized throughout the country; pupils can take both.

After this entrance examination, and depending on their abilities, preferences and examination results, pupils are oriented to one of the two main categories of post-primary education:

– general secondary education;

– technical secondary education.

5.1 General secondary education *(Enseignement secondaire général)*

General secondary education is provided in *Lycées*. It covers seven years of study (for pupils aged 12 to 19) and is divided into two cycles – lower and upper. The lower cycle lasts three years and completes compulsory education.

The Law of 10 May 1968 reformed secondary education. It introduced coeducational schools and stipulated that general secondary education, on the basis of a detailed general education, was intended essentially to prepare both boys and girls for university-level studies. *Lycées* vary in size, often depending on whether they are located in urban or rural areas. They do not all offer the same range of optional subjects.

In accordance with the Law of 22 June 1989, general secondary education is divided into three levels:

- the lower cycle (classes 7 (orientation class), 6 and 5 – *classes de 7e, 6e et 5e*);

- the comprehensive cycle of the upper cycle (classes 4 and 3 – *classes de 4e et 3e*);

- the specialization cycle of the upper cycle (classes 2 and 1 – *classes de 2e et 1e*).

As from class 6, pupils choose between classical education and modern education. Education is then divided into branches from class 5. Pupils must choose between the arts branch and the sciences branch. Finally, in class 2 pupils opt for a specific section. From this moment, the direction of studies is totally irreversible.

Subjects are taught at the same level to all pupils in the same class.

There are 30 lessons of 50 minutes per week. Teaching is spread over the whole week: six morning sessions (Monday to Saturday) with four lessons each and three afternoon sessions (Monday, Wednesday and Friday) with two lessons each. Schools are open 216 days per year, in principle, from 8.00 a.m. to 11.45 a.m. and from 2.00 p.m. to 4.00 p.m.

The school year commences on 15 September and runs until 15 July. The first term finishes at Christmas, the second at Easter and the third in July. At the end of the first two terms, pupils have two weeks' holiday.

Lower cycle

Curriculum

The curriculum includes: religious education and ethics, French, German and English, history, philosophy, political economics, civics, mathematics, biology, geography, physics, chemistry, art, music, physical education and the new information technologies.

In the orientation class (class 7 – *classe de 7e*), the curriculum is the same for all pupils. Language teaching covers Luxembourgish, French and German. At the beginning of class 6, pupils choose between classical education including the study of Latin, and modern education including the study of English.

For languages, teaching is essentially in the language itself, but for other subjects the vehicular/teaching language is German in the lower stages of secondary education and French in the upper stages, except for mathematics which is always taught in French.

Assessment and qualifications

There are no end-of-year examinations. Pupils are regularly assessed by teachers on the basis of continuous assessment throughout the three years. There are periodic written tests (*devoirs scolaires*) in each subject. At the end of each term (three) pupils receive a report card based on the assessment of their work during the term. At the end of each year, the pupil receives a report card which indicates whether he or she has passed the year and may be admitted to the next class. Pupils are marked out of 60. Reference is made to: grades achieved in the relevant subjects; the sum total for coefficients for inadequate grades; and the annual weighted average. These criteria allow for a certain degree of compensation where one or two grades are not quite of the required level, provided that the pupil has a general average of at least 35. The Class Council decides, at the end of each school year, which children should move up to the next year.

Pupils who have successfully completed the nine years of compulsory education receive a certificate indicating that they have completed compulsory education and with what degree of success.

Pupils who have successfully completed class 5 may continue to the four years of the upper cycle leading to a secondary school leaving certificate, which gives access to higher and university education.

Upper cycle

Curriculum

According to Article 47 of the Act of 22 June 1989, at the beginning of the comprehensive cycle (classes 4 and 3) of upper secondary education, pupils choose either the arts branch or the sciences branch; the main difference is the mathematics course. Within the two general branches, pupils choose between pre-specialization options. Pupils in classical education (with Latin) can study a fourth language from class 4, in which case they can opt for shorter Latin studies.

At the beginning of the specialization cycle (classes 2 and 1) of upper secondary education, pupils opt for one of the following sections:

Classical education

- arts branch
  Latin – languages (A1);
  Latin – human and social sciences (A2);
  Latin – art;
  Latin – music.

- sciences branch
  Latin – mathematics – physical sciences (B);
  Latin – mathematics – natural sciences (C);
  Latin – mathematics – economic sciences (D).

Modern education

- arts branch
  foreign languages (A1);
  foreign languages – human and social sciences (A2);
  foreign languages – arts (E);
  foreign languages – music (F).

- sciences branch
  foreign languages – mathematics – physical sciences (B);
  foreign languages – mathematics – natural sciences (C);
  foreign languages – mathematics – economic sciences (D).

When the number of lessons per week by section is below 30, pupils have to choose one or several additional optional courses of 1 to 2 lessons per week to reach a minimum of 30 and a maximum of 31 lessons per week.

The curriculum of classical and modern secondary education includes the following (all years):

- religious and moral education, moral and social training;

- French language and literature;

- German language and literature;

- English language and literature;

- a fourth foreign language;

- history;

- philosophy;

- civics;

- mathematics;

- new information and communication technologies;

- biology;

- geography;

- physics;

- art;

- music;

- physical education.

Classical secondary education also includes Latin language and literature.

Assessment and qualifications

There are no end-of-year examinations during the first three years of the upper cycle; again, pupils are judged on the basis of continuous assessment (see lower cycle). At the end of each year, the pupil receives a report card which indicates whether or not he or she has passed the year and may be admitted to the next class.

However, at the end of the final year of secondary education, pupils have to take the secondary school leaving examination (*examen de fin d'études secondaires*). Candidates take tests and examinations in all the subjects studied during their final year in the secondary school. The examination is organized nationally.

Successful candidates are awarded the secondary school leaving certificate (*diplôme de fin d'études secondaires*), issued by the State. In 1990, there was an 80% success rate.

A reform of the secondary school leaving examination has recently taken place. The first stage provides for a compensatory system for grades within the examination subjects. The second provides for account to be taken of grades achieved during the course of the year, the weighting being one-third continuous assessment and two-thirds examination results. Finally, the third stage provides for the introduction of an oral examination.

Lycées have a **guidance** and psychology service under the aegis of the educational psychology and guidance centre; teachers and psychologists provide information and advice to pupils, parents and teachers.

Teachers

General secondary teachers (*professeurs de l'enseignement secondaire*) are subject specialists. They are qualified in at least one subject, but may teach more than one.

In order to qualify, teachers must have completed an academic course lasting at least four years at a foreign university (and obtained a degree), plus three years' theoretical and practical teacher training under the Luxembourg University Centre, including five terms of teaching practice in a school.

Teachers are civil servants and may work full-time or part-time. In general, in-service training is optional.

5.2 Technical secondary education *(Enseignement secondaire technique)*

Article 1 of the Law of 4 September 1990 stipulates that 'Technical secondary education, which is the same for both boys and girls, prepares pupils, in close cooperation with the business world, for working life by providing them with general, social, technical and vocational education. It also prepares them for higher education'.

Technical education is provided in technical *lycées* (*lycées techniques*) and covers the age range 12 to 19. The number of years followed beyond the lower cycle (which completes compulsory schooling) depends on the course chosen.

Technical secondary education is divided into three cycles:

- the lower cycle of three years, which begins after the sixth year of primary education (7th, 8th and 9th class);

- the intermediate cycle, which comprises:

    - a vocational branch where courses usually last three years;

    - a technician's training branch where courses usually last two years; and

    - a technical branch where courses usually last two years;

- the upper cycle, which comprises:

    - a technician's training branch where courses usually last two years; and

    - a technical branch where courses usually last two years.

Pupils are grouped according to their ability and their performance in examinations.

The school year is exactly the same as in general secondary education.

Lower cycle

The objectives of the lower cycle are to broaden and enhance basic knowledge; to orient pupils towards future training and to prepare them to continue their studies in the different branches of the intermediate cycle; and to facilitate the transition from school to working life.

The lower cycle covers three years:

- a seventh year of observation, which provides pupils with a common programme of general training and builds on the knowledge acquired earlier;

- an eighth year of orientation, which deepens the basic general training and prepares pupils for future academic and vocational orientation (pupils choose between two streams: technical and general);

- a ninth year of determination, which prepares pupils for learning and further study in the various branches and divisions of the intermediate cycle (pupils choose between three streams: technical, general and vocational).

Curriculum

The curriculum in the lower cycle focuses mainly on general education, which encompasses the following subject areas:

- languages;

- mathematics;

- natural sciences;

- social sciences;

- technological education;

- artistic education;

- musical education;

- physical and sports education;

- religious instruction, moral and social education.

The curriculum also includes practical and manual work for orientation purposes, as well as activities to facilitate the transition to working life.

Studies in the eighth and ninth years are organized along flexible lines so that the disciplines, curricula, levels of instruction, teaching methods, number of weekly lessons per discipline and the criteria for pupil promotion may vary between the different streams.

In the 9th class, the curriculum includes optional subjects (commerce, natural sciences, chemistry, crafts, electricity and mechanics), which allows pupils to choose studies in line with their preferences and abilities in view of the different branches of the intermediate cycle. Pupils also follow an introductory course in new information technologies.

Support courses may be offered to provide links between the streams.

It may be necessary for a pupil to change school after the lower cycle, depending on what subjects are on offer at the various schools.

Assessment and qualifications

There are no end-of-year examinations. Pupils are regularly assessed by teachers on the basis of continuous assessment throughout the three years (see lower cycle of general secondary education). If a pupil fails the third year (9th class), he or she can either repeat the year or transfer to certain vocational training courses. Pupils successfully completing the technical stream have access to all intermediate cycle branches; those from the general stream may enter the technician's training and vocational branches; and those in the vocational stream may only enter the vocational branch.

All pupils who have fulfilled their obligation to attend school receive a certificate to this effect. For pupils who successfully complete the ninth class, the certificate recognizes their successful completion of the lower cycle.

Intermediate cycle

The purpose of the intermediate cycle is to teach pupils a trade or occupation and to prepare them for upper-cycle studies.

The intermediate cycle lasts for two or three years, comprising the 10th and 11th classes and, depending on the branch chosen, the 12th class. The latter consists basically of practical training, and ends with the end-of-apprenticeship examination, for which the certificate of technical and vocational proficiency (*Certificat d'aptitude technique et professionelle – CATP*) is awarded.

The intermediate cycle has three branches:

- vocational branch;

- technician's training branch;

- technical branch.

The **vocational branch** takes the form of an apprenticeship and usually includes practical training, lasting around 32 hours per week, in a firm under an apprenticeship contract parallel to a minimum of eight lessons per week in concomitant vocational courses (general and vocational subjects) in a technical *lycée*.

The vocational branch is divided into the following divisions:

- agriculture;

- arts and crafts;

- commerce and administration;

- hotel and tourism;

- industrial training;

- domestic science;

- paramedical and social studies.

The details of vocational training courses (length, number of weekly lessons in classes, curriculum) are determined by the competent professional chambers. As mentioned above, most apprenticeships involve three years' practical training with theoretical training in a technical *lycée*. Training for certain occupations (such as assistant accountant, restaurateur, horticulturalist or farmer) may involve a combination of full-time vocational studies in a technical *lycée* for one or two years followed by one or two years of practical training and concomitant courses. A small number of occupations require three years of training entirely in school.

The **technician's training branch** in the intermediate cycle prepares pupils for technician's training in the upper cycle. Technician's training in the intermediate cycle lasts two years (the 10th and 11th classes) full-time.

The technician's training branch may include the following divisions:

- administration and commerce;

- agriculture;

- art;

- biology;

- chemistry;

- electrotechnology;

- civil engineering;

- hotel and tourism;

- mechanics.

The **technical branch** of the intermediate cycle also lasts two years (the 10th and 11th classes) full-time, and leads to the upper cycle course for the technical secondary education leaving certificate (*diplôme de fin d'études secondaires techniques*).

The technical branch of the intermediate cycle may comprise the following divisions:

- administration and commerce;

- paramedical and social studies;

- general technical studies.

Curriculum

Curricula for the classes of the technician's training and technical branches include:

- general education course (religious or moral education, English, French, a third language, mathematics, chemistry, physics, knowledge of the modern world, physical education);

- vocational course (which varies according to the section);

- practical course (which varies according to the section).

There are between 30 and 32 lessons of 50 to 55 minutes per week.

Upper cycle

The objective of the upper cycle is to provide pupils with a vocational qualification (technician's training branch) to help them enter the labour market, or to provide them with the requisite knowledge for higher or university education (technical branch, technical secondary education leaving certificate).

The upper cycle comprises two years of full-time study in the 12th and 13th classes and encompasses two branches: technician's training and technical.

The **technician's training branch** may include the following divisions:

- administration and commerce;

- agriculture;

- art;

- biology;

- chemistry;

- electrotechnology;

- civil engineering;

- hotel and tourism;

- mechanics;

- computer science.

The **technical branch** may include the following divisions:

- administration and commerce;

- paramedical and social studies;

- general technical studies.

Curriculum

The curricula of the classes of the upper cycle include:

- administrative division
  - general education course (German, English, French, knowledge of the modern world);
  - scientific and economic course (including mathematics, economics and law);
  - technical course;
  - physical education course;
  - optional course (religion or ethics).

- general technical division
  - general education course (German, English, French, economics and social sciences, civics);
  - scientific course (mathematics, computer science, physics, chemistry, general mechanics, electricity);
  - technical and practical course;
  - physical education course;
  - optional course (religion or ethics).

- technician's training division
  - general education course (German, English, French, knowledge of the modern world, economics and social sciences, civics, physical education);
  - scientific and technical course (which varies according to the section);
  - practical course (which varies according to the section).

There is generally a maximum of 32 lessons per week.

Assessment and qualifications
(Intermediate and Upper Cycles)

Except in the case of pupils in the 13th class of the upper cycle and the 12th, basically practical, classes of the intermediate cycle (leading to the *CATP*), the Class Council decides at the end of the school year whether to allow pupils who have sat tests in each of the disciplines in the curriculum to move up to the next class.

Promotion decisions are based on results for the entire school year, consisting of:

- marks in the various relevant disciplines;

- the sum of the coefficients of unsatisfactory marks (each discipline is assigned a coefficient between 1 and 4);

- the weighted annual average.

Pupils move up from the lower cycle to the intermediate cycle on the basis of a guidance profile indicating the divisions and sections to which they can be admitted. This is based on the marks obtained, weighted to take account of educational and vocational guidance and accompanied by the opinion of the Class Council and the psychological and guidance service (under the aegis of the educational psychology and guidance centre, teachers and psychologists provide information and advice to pupils, parents and teachers).

Studies in the **vocational branch of the intermediate cycle** lead to an end-of-apprenticeship examination at the end of the final year of studies, for which successful candidates are awarded the *CATP*. The end-of-apprenticeship examination is a national examination. It includes a theoretical and a practical section, normally at the end of the 11th and 12th classes respectively. Marks in theoretical and practical work during the end-of-apprenticeship year may be taken into account. The *CATP* is delivered jointly by the Ministry of National Education and Vocational Training and the professional chambers. It is a final diploma, but holders may also be admitted to the 12th class of technical secondary education (technician's training branch). They can also follow studies leading to the *brevet de maitrise* (see below) in their specialization.

For pupils who need longer to learn the theoretical part of apprenticeship training there is a two-cycle apprenticeship scheme providing basic vocational training. It caters in particular for pupils who have not been allowed to enter a 10th class of the intermediate cycle as described above, or who are failing in an intermediate cycle class. The first cycle comprises a two-year course which may be completed in up to four years, depending on the pupil's aptitude. At the end of the first cycle of two years, the candidate is awarded a certificate of technical and vocational initiation (*certificat d'initiation technique et professionelle – CITP).* The certificate of manual competence (*certificat de capacité manuelle – CCM*) is given to pupils who only complete practical training. Pupils may continue their studies in the second cycle, which ends with the end-of-apprenticeship examination (*CATP*).

The **upper cycle technician's training branch** leads to a national examination. Pupils who pass this examination receive a technician's certificate (*diplôme de technicien*) specifying the division and disciplines in which they have been examined and mentioning that they have the requisite knowledge for higher technical studies.

The **upper cycle technical branch** also leads to a national examination. Pupils who pass this examination receive a technical secondary education leaving certificate (*diplôme de fin d'études secondaires techniques*) specifying the division, the section if appropriate, and the disciplines in which the candidates have been examined and mentioning that they have the requisite knowledge for higher studies (including university studies).

In terms of access to the regulated occupations and admission to public-sector jobs, the certificates awarded for the technician's training course and the technical course confer the same rights as the secondary school leaving certificate.

Teachers

Teachers in technical secondary education are generally subject specialists. They are qualified in at least one subject, but may teach more than one. There are various categories of teachers, including general secondary teachers (see 5.1) who teach general subjects in technical secondary education.

Teachers in engineering sciences (*professeurs-ingénieurs*) and science teachers (*professeurs de*

sciences de l'enseignement secondaire technique) are subject specialists. They must have completed at least four years at a foreign university. Technical education teachers (*professeurs d'enseignement technique*) must have completed three years at a foreign university. Instructors of special subjects (*maître de cours spéciaux*) must have completed two years of studies at non-university higher level in the subject concerned. Instructors of technical subjects (*maître de cours pratiques*) must have completed a master craftman's course (*brevet de maîtrise*) in his/her trade and have three years' professional experience. They all then follow three years of theoretical and practical teacher training under the Luxembourg University Centre, including five terms of teaching practice in schools.

Teachers are civil servants and may work full-time or part-time. In general, in-service training is optional, but all or part of courses organized by *ISERP* may be declared compulsory by the Ministry of National Education and Vocational Training.

Statistics 1991/92

	Public	Private
Pupils (general)	8,420	953
(technical)	12,397	1,911
Teachers	856	not available
Schools (general)	9	5
(technical)	14	6
CATP awarded (1993)		
– *CATP* arts and crafts		221
– *CCM* arts and crafts		101
– *CATP* industrial/ commerce/hotel		559
– *CATP/CCM* agriculture		38

6. Initial vocational training

Vocational orientation and initiation courses (*COIP*) are offered to young job-seekers without qualifications, who were not admitted to technical secondary education. These courses stress personal development, information, orientation, motivation to follow a training course and job-seeking techniques. The *COIP* may include practical training in an enterprise.

The number of young people in this situation is currently decreasing, since opportunities for continuing studies to obtain the *CITP* (*certificat d'initiation technique et professionelle*) are increasing. The main objective of these centres is to enable young people to enter or re-enter technical secondary education.

Specific training courses are run in collaboration with German training organizations. These courses vary in length depending on the activity concerned: assistant storekeeper – 621 hours, 240 of which in a firm; engine drivers – 22 weeks; nature and environmental protection – 45 weeks; robotics – 45 weeks; waste recovery and water treatment – 24 months. All training courses comprise a theoretical and a practical part (on the spot or in a firm) divided between the continuing training centre in Luxembourg and the German training centre. The courses are set up specifically in connection with the requirements of the firms on either side of the border. Some tens of young people are involved each year.

The continuing training centres also provide eight hours of training each month for young people on training courses in firms, comprising: civics and social education, work psychology, introduction to new technologies, relations with the authorities.

Another type of specific vocational training is the course leading to the **brevet de maîtrise**, a certificate pertaining to a particular trade or occupation.

Maîtrise courses follow on from the certificate of technical and vocational proficiency (*CATP)* and are intended to prepare pupils for the final *maîtrise* examination. Courses are staggered over three years and concern only the theoretical and practical branches relating to a trade or occupation. They are held mainly at weekends, and are open to holders of a *CATP* in the particular trade or occupation or an associated trade or occupation.

This type of training may be considered very specific, since its main objective is to give holders of the *maîtrise* certificate the right of establishment, i.e. the right to create their own enterprise or the right to train apprentices.

The *maîtrise* examination consists of a theoretical part covering the theory of business management and professional theory, and a practical part involving tests of manual skill.

The *Chambre des métiers* is responsible for the organization of training and awards the certificate. This body alone is authorized to award a particular certificate, determining the trades or occupations for which a *maîtrise* certificate is required for the exercise of the occupation, and setting the conditions of access and the procedures (duration, content, examination methods) for obtaining the certificate.

The certificate is recognized by the State; the departments concerned are the Ministry of National Education and Vocational Training (as the organizer of courses), the Ministry of Labour (which supervises the *Chambre des métiers*) and the Ministry of the Independent Professions (*Ministère des Classes moyennes*), the ministry responsible for the right of establishment.

The rights associated with the possession of this certificate (the right of establishment and the right to train apprentices) are limited to the world of work; the certificate does not provide access to studies (either technical secondary or post-secondary). However, as mentioned above, the holder of a *maîtrise* certificate may, upon passing a qualification examination and completing the competitive recruitment examination, qualify as an instructor of technical subjects in technical secondary education.

238 *brevets de maîtrise* were awarded in 1993.

7. Higher education

Higher education currently encompasses only a very limited number of courses and institutions. Applications for enrolment are made directly to the institution concerned. There are no tuition fees. The Government can grant financial assistance in the form of a scholarship, and/or a loan with a low interest rate.

7.1 University education

University education is restricted to a first year of studies provided within the framework of the Luxembourg University Centre (*Centre Universitaire de Luxembourg*). The courses offered include: Classics, Romance language and literature, German language and literature, English language and literature, philosophy, history, geography (Department of Arts and Social Sciences), law and economics (Department of Law and Economics), chemistry and biology, mathematics and physics with an engineering subsection, medicine and pharmacy (Department of Sciences).

Admission

Persons holding the Luxembourg general or technical secondary school leaving certificate may enrol in all sections. Holders of the technician's certificate are admitted to the sub-section for student engineers in the Department of Sciences, and the short course (*cycle court*) of management studies (see below).

It is up to the administrator of the department concerned to decide whether to admit students who fulfil the normal admission conditions or others who are thought to have the requisite knowledge to follow the course successfully.

Academic year

The academic year lasts from the first week of October until the middle of the following July, divided into two semesters.

Courses/Assessment/Qualifications

A Grand-Ducal Decree determines the academic structure of the courses, the curricula and the examination procedures. Instruction consists of compulsory and optional subjects and is given in the form of lectures and tutorials.

Students have to write the papers and take the written and oral tests required of them by their teachers. An examination is held at the end of the year. Marks are given at the end of the semester or year on a scale from 0 to 20.

Students who successfully complete the one-year course receive a certificate (*certificat d'études*) detailing the subject matter covered. They may continue their studies in the second year at a foreign university under any of the numerous equivalency agreements between the *Centre Universitaire* and foreign universities, including institutions in Belgium, France, Germany and the UK.

7.2 Non-university higher education

Non-university higher education is provided in various institutions.

The *Institut Supérieur de Technologie* (*IST*), established in 1979, provides a higher technological training course lasting three years. This covers civil engineering, electrical engineering (electronics and industrial engineering), mechanical engineering and applied informatics.

Holders of a technical secondary school leaving certificate may be admitted directly to the first year. Holders of a general secondary school leaving certificate and technician's certificate are admitted on the basis of their file.

The academic year runs from mid-September to the end of June, divided into two semesters.

The course includes general, scientific and technological education.

There is an examination at the end of the third year, leading to the award of a diploma and the title of engineer-technician. Whilst it is a final qualification, graduates may continue their higher education studies abroad in order to become graduate engineers.

The *Institut Supérieur d'Etudes et de Recherches Pédagogiques* (*ISERP*) trains teachers for pre-school and primary education in conjunction with the University Centre, and the *Institut d'Etudes Educatives et Sociales* (*IEES*) trains graduate teachers for special education. Both courses last three years.

To be admitted to either course, applicants must hold a secondary school leaving certificate. Each year the Government determines the number of students to be admitted to the first year of the *ISERP*.

The course comprises theoretical and practical training, the latter including teaching exercises and teaching practice in a school for seven weeks each year. At the end of the first year, there is an examination relating to all course subjects taught at *ISERP* and at the University Centre. Successful students move up to the second year. Students who successfully complete the final examination at the end of the third year are issued a teaching certificate (pre-school or primary option) by the Ministry of Education and Vocational Training.

Since the 1983/84 academic year, the **Department of Law and Economics of the University Centre** has been offering a short course in management studies. This lasts two years, and trains managers for the services sector: data processing in industry and administration; commerce and banking; and business management.

Enrolment in the first year is open to all persons holding the general or technical secondary school leaving certificate or a technician's certificate.

An examination is held at the end of each academic year. Students move up from the first to the second year provided they pass the examination held at the end of the first year. A certificate is issued to all those who do so. At the end of the second year, there is a final examination comprising written and oral tests in the subject matter covered in the course. Students must obtain at least 10 points out of 20 in all subjects. Two examination sessions are organized each year, one in June/July, the other in September/October. Candidates who fail in a limited number of subjects may resit the examination at the next session. Overall failure means that the entire examination has to be resat. Candidates who fail a second time may not resit again. Successful students are issued a diploma of higher management studies, mentioning the relevant subsection and annotated 'very good', 'good' or with no special remarks.

Certain **technical secondary schools** provide post-secondary training leading to the higher technician's certificate (*brevet de technicien supérieur – BTS*). Training lasts two years. Applicants must hold either a technician's certificate, a general or technical secondary school leaving certificate or, under certain conditions, a *CATP*.

It covers executive secretarial studies, management/accounting, marketing/international trade and cartoon animation, and includes various periods of practical training in a firm. Students are awarded the certificate on successful completion of the second year.

Netherlands

NETHERLANDS

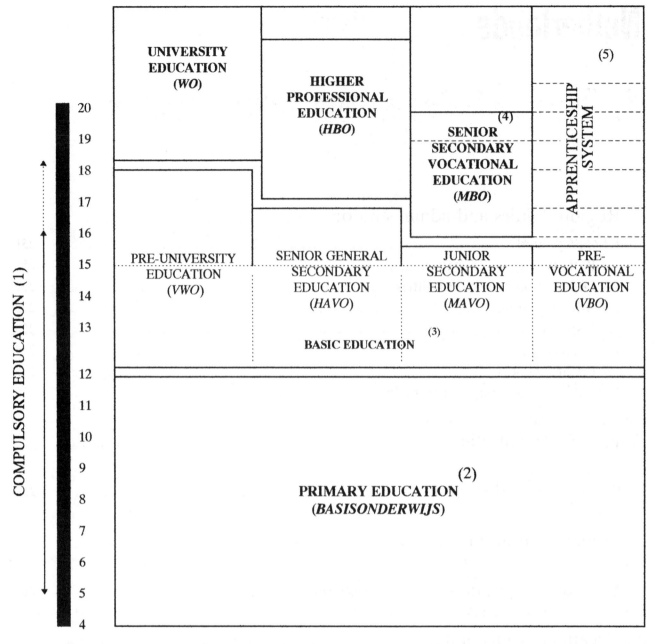

1. Compulsory education lasts either 12 years full-time (5 to 17) or full-time from 5 until the end of the school year in which the pupil has reached the age of 16 followed by part-time compulsory education until the age of 18.

2. Separate pre-school education does not exist formally in the Netherlands. Primary education lasts for eight years - 4 to 12 (compulsory from 5). Provision for children below four is the responsibility of the Ministry of Welfare, Health and Cultural Affairs.

3. As from the 1993/94 school year, all types of secondary education begin with a three-year period of basic education (*basisvorming*), offering broad-based general teaching in which no strict distinction is made between general and technical subjects.

4. Depending on the course chosen, it may last up to 4 years. *MBO* is designed for pupils aged around 16-19.

5. Apprenticeship training lasts 2 to 3 years and advanced apprenticeship 1 to 3 years.

················· = division in the level/type of education

– – – – – – – – · = alternative beginning or end of level/type of education

1. Responsibilities and administration

1.1 Background

The Netherlands is a Constitutional Monarchy with a parliamentary system. The Parliament (States General) together with the Sovereign and Government Ministers forms the legislature and the Sovereign and Ministers form the executive. There are two Houses of Parliament. The main political parties are the Christian Democrats, the Socialists and the Liberals. Until 1994, the Government was formed by a coalition of the first two; in 1994, a coalition of Socialists and Liberals has been formed.

The Dutch Constitution guarantees freedom of religion; the Roman Catholics form the largest single group (33%). 39% of the Dutch population practise no religion (1992).

The national language is Dutch. In the province of Friesland, Frisian is spoken and is the official language of the provincial and local councils (schools teach both in Dutch and in Frisian).

In 1993, the population of the Netherlands was over 15 million, living in an area of some 41,000 square kilometres. The birthrate has dropped by about 25% since the end of the sixties. 5% of the Dutch population consists of immigrants of other nationalities.

Of the 6½ million workforce (1993), 415,000 were registered as unemployed. 50% of GNP comes from the export of products and services. In 1992, the division of employment sectors was: agriculture (5%), industry/utilities (19%), construction industry (7%), commercial service industry (27%), government/defence/education (13%), other sectors (29%).

1.2 Basic principles: education

One of the key features of the Dutch education system, laid down in Article 23 of the Constitution, is freedom of education, which includes:

- the freedom to set up schools in accordance with religious or ideological principles;

- financial equality between public and private education;

- the requirement for municipal authorities to provide a suitable form of public education.

The freedom to set up schools in accordance with religious or ideological principles has led to a wide variety of education establishments, in particular, the parallel existence of public (*openbare scholen*) and private (*bijzondere scholen*) schools, to which all statutes apply equally. Some 70% of pupils attend private schools.

Freedom of education is restricted by the requirements laid down in the Compulsory Education Act. This law stipulates that children must attend an education establishment full-time until the end of the year in which they reach the age of 16 or have completed at least 12 full years. After full-time compulsory education it is compulsory to attend school at least part-time until the age of 18.

The freedom of privately run schools is also constrained by funding conditions.

1.3 Distribution of responsibilities

The Dutch education system combines a unified education system, regulated by central laws, with the decentralized administration and management of schools. Overall responsibility for the public-private education system lies with the State, represented by the Minister of Education, Culture and Science, and the legislative power of the Dutch Parliament. The administration and management of schools of primary and secondary general and vocational education is locally organized. The municipal authorities are the local authorities for all schools in the area. The municipal authorities are the competent authority for publicly run schools, while foundations or associations are the competent authorities for private schools.

The apprenticeship system is coordinated by 31 national independent professional/sectorial associations or foundations. The theoretical part of the apprenticeship is the responsibility of the Ministry of Education, Culture and Science, while the practical part is the responsibility of the employer.

There are around 70 colleges for higher professional education. Furthermore, there are ten publicly run universities and three private ones.

Organized pre-school child care facilities are funded by the Ministry of Health, Welfare and Sport.

1.4 Administration

Central authorities

The Ministry of Education, Culture and Science is headed by the Minister of Education, Culture and Science. One or two State Secretaries (junior ministers) of Education, Culture and Science may also be appointed.

Central Government controls education by means of laws and regulations in accordance with the provisions laid down in the Constitution. The prime responsibilities of the Ministry of Education, Culture and Science relate to the structuring and funding of the system, the management of publicly run institutions, inspection and examination procedures and financial aid to students. Control may be exercised by imposing qualitative or quantitative standards for the educational process

in schools and/or for the results they produce, and by means of arrangements for the allocation of financial and other resources, and the imposition of conditions to be met by schools.

The Ministry of Education, Culture and Science lays down conditions, especially in primary and secondary education, relating to the types of schools that can exist, the length of courses, compulsory and optional school subjects, the minimum and maximum number of lessons to be given and their length, the norms for class division, the examination syllabus and national examinations, and standards of competence, salaries, status and teaching hours of teaching staff. The Ministry does not set up schools, but does determine norms for their establishment. These conditions apply to both public and private education.

Provinces

The provinces have a limited role to play when it comes to managing education and its content. They are required to perform supervisory and jurisdictional duties. This includes tasks relating to supervising the sufficient provision of public and private primary and secondary education, and organizing training and adult education activities.

Local authorities (municipalities)

The municipal authorities have a dual role: they are both the local authorities for all schools in the area (whether publicly or privately run) and at the same time the competent authorities – in effect the school boards – for the publicly run schools. They also ensure compliance with the Compulsory Education Act.

At primary level, their tasks include planning and coordinating accommodation, facilities and material provision, and appointing additional staff. At secondary level, the municipalities have a statutory responsibility to ensure maximum use of buildings; furthermore, they act in this area almost exclusively as competent authorities.

The Municipal Council sets up public schools and approves the establishment of private schools.

Competent authority

The competent authority (or school board) assumes the responsibilities involved in running a **school** insofar as based on statutory provisions; the day-to-day management of primary and secondary schools may be delegated to the head teacher (rector in schools providing pre-university education, central management team in *MBO* schools), but ultimate responsibility still rests with the competent authority itself.

As mentioned above, the municipal authorities act as the competent authority for public education, whereas the competent authorities for private schools are the administration boards, associations or institutions responsible for setting up the schools. There are approximately 6,300 competent authorities in the Dutch education system.

The tasks and responsibilities of the boards of public and private schools are very similar. They include decisions with regard to the curriculum, the choice of teaching materials, the establishment of the school plan, timetable (lessons per compulsory or optional subject), the appointment and dismissal of head teachers, teachers and non-teaching staff, the admission and expulsion of pupils, the use of school buildings, school hours and the management of financial resources and arrangements for their administration.

Linked to the specific function of public-authority education, in addition, the boards of publicly run schools have to ensure the provision of enough schools, comply with statutory rules (as well as with funding provisions), ensure that pupils are not refused admission because of their beliefs, and be accountable to the Municipal Council for management activities.

The Government lays down a framework within which **HBO institutions** have to operate, but it is the responsibility of the competent authority to expand on the Government framework within the teaching and examination regulations. In their education and examination regulation, *HBO* colleges are required to specify the teaching programme, the main subjects and the content and form of the different examinations.

For the **universities** the same legal framework is applied as for the *HBO* institutions. The day-to-day management of a university is handled by the Executive Board and the University Council. The Executive Boards, comprising three members, including the rector, is accountable to the Minister of Education, Culture and Science and to the University Council. The University Council comprises up to thirty representatives of the academic staff, students and the support and administrative staff.

National Apprenticeship Agencies

Each business sector has its own national agency (a total of 31), whose board includes representatives from employer's associations, trade union organizations and schools. As part of general efforts to scale up activities (as is taking place in the *MBO* sector), plans are under way to consolidate the 31 national agencies into 13 specialized national centres.

The duties of the agencies are to advise on attainment targets, to organize examinations and to provide support for apprentices in the workplace. This is carried out by a counsellor who is the contact person between school and work, and provides guidance to pupils.

The final attainment levels for the *MBO* system are established by the Business Sector Consultation between Education and Industry (*BOOB*), an advisory body, and approved by the Ministry.

1.5 Inspection

The monitoring of both **public and private education** systems is performed by the Inspectorate for Education, as defined in Article 23 of the Constitution. The inspection procedure is set out in detail in education Acts. The Ministry of Education, Culture and Science provides the funding for the inspectorate, whose staff members enjoy the status of civil servants. The Minister is entitled to issue instructions as regards the implementation of the inspectorate's tasks, be kept fully informed about the inspectorate's activities, and assess the inspectorate's annual workplan.

The Inspectorate Council is in charge of the inspectorate and is responsible for the management of the organization. Members of the Inspectorate Council include the Inspector General. In addition to the management headquarters, there are 13 regional offices.

Agricultural training is supervised by the Minister of Agriculture, Nature Management and Fisheries through six regional offices.

The responsibilities of the inspectorate are:

- to ensure compliance with statutory regulations;

- to keep up to date with the educational situation by visiting schools;

- to promote the development of consultations on education with the competent authorities, the staff of schools and the regional or local authorities;

- to report to and advise the Minister.

The inspectorate reports on the impressions gained during school visits and publishes a yearly report on its findings.

The Minister of Education, Culture and Science aims to turn the inspectorate into an independent body, within the terms of existing legislation and with funding by the Ministry.

In **higher education** (*HBO* institutions as well as universities), a system of internal quality control is coupled with periodical external quality controls by so-called visiting committees.

1.6 Financing

Funding for all levels and types of education comes, in principle, entirely out of central government funds. The Ministry of Education, Culture and Science administers almost all central government expenditure on education, while the Ministry of Agriculture, Nature Management and Fisheries funds agricultural education. Funding is provided to public and private establishments according to the same criteria.

Primary schools and schools for special education (primary and secondary) receive funding to cover staffing costs, operation and accommodation. Within this government funding several funding systems exist to create a large measure of institutional autonomy:

- the Londo system, which is designed as a way of funding the provision of buildings, teaching materials and maintenance on the basis of pre-determined norms;

- the staff establishment budget system, which gives a great amount of autonomy with regard to the use of staff resources;

- lump-sum funding, which gives schools a degree of discretion as to how the annual budget is spent on staffing and operation costs.

While the Londo system and the staff establishment budget system are for specified items, the lump-sum funding provides budgets for all forms of expenditure.

Public and private **secondary schools** receive government funding to cover the costs of staffing, operation, establishment and equipment. Like primary and special education, the staff establishment budget system and lump-sum funding are used in secondary education as systems of funding.

Most costs are paid directly to the competent authority; primary accommodation costs are paid to the local authority.

The Central Government provides lump-sum grants to the *MBO* **schools** to spend as they see fit on staff costs or on upgrading facilities. The schools are free to choose between these two items. Under the funding rules, schools are required to keep accounts. The schools are entitled to keep any revenue earned from activities contracted with third parties. Members of school staff may also perform activities on a contractual basis within their regular terms of employment.

The national bodies coordinating the **apprenticeship system** receive central government funding (28 from the Ministry of Education, Culture and Science and 3 from the Ministry of Agriculture, Nature Management and Fisheries) and there may be additional funding from the particular industry concerned. Funding is based to a large extent on the number of apprenticeship contracts concluded. The cost of the theoretical part of apprenticeships is the responsibility of the Ministry of Education, Culture and Science, the cost of the practical part is borne by the employers, who receive contributions from the Ministry of Social Affairs and Employment.

In August 1993, the Higher Education and Research Act granted institutions of **higher**

education considerable autonomy regarding financial policy.

New funding systems have been introduced for university and higher professional education. With the exception of the Open University, this comprises lump-sum funding based on criteria for the number of students and study performance, with only two prices for courses. Central Government pays up to 90% of higher education costs.

Education is free for all pupils up to the age of 16, although there may be costs to cover the purchase of books and teaching materials and travel. Pupils of 16 and over have to pay annual tuition fees (including apprentices). All students from 18 to 27 enrolled in full-time secondary or higher education are entitled to a basic grant and, depending on parental income, a supplementary grant or interest-bearing loan. Pupils aged 12 to 17 attending mainstream education may be entitled to study costs allowances, depending on parental income.

The Ministry of Health, Welfare and Sport funds organized child care via the municipalities. The latter decide whether and how to devote the resources to child care.

1.7 Private schools

Private schools are established upon private initiative and are run by a board of governors, an association or foundation. Under the terms of the Constitution, all schools – public and private – are funded on an equal basis. In other words, the Government funds both public and private schools in the same way. Central Government pays teachers in public and private schools; they have the same salary scales and terms of employment and enjoy the status of public servants.

In order to receive state financing, schools must observe certain conditions set out in specific government laws and regulations.

Private schools are free to establish curricular content according to their own principles, to choose their own teaching methods and appoint members of staff who agree with the school's religious or ideological tenets. The private education system consists of different types of schools: Roman Catholic schools, Protestant schools and general private schools, the latter being based on specific ideological or pedagogical principles.

1.8 Advisory and consultative bodies

A great many advisory and consultative bodies exist in the Netherlands and they are entitled to make recommendations on education policy.

Advisory bodies

The **Education Council** (*Onderwijsraad – OR*) is a permanent advisory body established in 1919, whose task is to ensure continuing equal financial treatment for public and private education, the coherence of education policy and legislation and continuing freedom of education.

The **Advisory Council for Education** (*Adviesraad voor Onderwijs – ARO*), set up in 1991 reports on any social trends of importance to education and gives advice on how education policy can respond to these trends.

The Royal Dutch Academy of Sciences (*Koninklijke Nederlandse Akademie van Wetenschappen – KNAW*) and the Advisory Council on Science and Technology Policy (*Advisieraad voor het Wetenschaps- en Technologiebeleid – AWT*) give advice on science and science policy respectively. Advisory bodies that offer advice not only on education are the Socio-Economic Council (*Sociaal Economische Raad – SER*), the Advisory Council on Government Policy (*Wetenschappelijke Raad voor het Regeringsbeleid – WRR*), the Equal Opportunities Council (*Emancipatieraad*) and the Youth Policy Council (*Raad voor het Jeugdbeleid*).

Consultative bodies

With regard to primary and secondary education the Minister of Education, Culture and Science consults within the Central Committee for Educational Consultation with representatives of parents, teachers and school boards. There is also a Secondary Education Consultative Committee whose membership includes, in addition, representatives of employers and trade unions. For matters relating to higher education, the Minister consults within the Higher Education Consultative Body with the administrations of higher professional education institutions and universities and student organizations.

On matters concerning working conditions for staff in the education sector, the Minister consults with the Boards Organizations Committee, representing school boards, and the Consultative Committee for Education and Science, representing civil servants and teachers unions.

Support structure

Support services for schools are either general support services, for example, the school counselling services, or specialized support organizations. The three specialized support organizations are the national education advisory centres: the Foundation for Educational Research (*SVO*), the National Institute for Educational Measurement (examinations) (*CITO*), and the National Institute for Curriculum Development (*SLO*).

Participation councils

Every primary and secondary school is required to set up a participation council representing staff and parents/pupils.

Parental participation can also take place through the parents' council. Staff can set up staff councils. Pupils can set up a pupils' council. The latter can all make recommendations to the participation council and/or head teacher.

Participation in higher education is defined in the Higher Education and Research Act (*WHW*). Every institution of higher professional education has a participation council representing staff and students. Its powers vary from one college to another. At universities students participate in the University Council and in subject committees.

2. Pre-school education

Separate nursery schools no longer exist in the Netherlands, as primary education has been extended to cover 4- to 6-year-olds. For 4- and 5-year-olds who do not attend a primary school the most common child care facilities are coeducational playgroups (*Peuterspeelzaal*) and day care centres (*Kinderdagverblijven*). Their aim is to stimulate the cognitive, social and emotional development of children through play.

Playgroups are for children aged 2 to 4, and are usually open three days a week for two-and-a-half to four hours a day. They are partly funded by the State through the local authorities, but may also be privately funded. Parents are required to make a contribution. Group size is limited to a maximum of 12 to 14 children. Some 35% of all children aged 2 and 3 go to a playgroup (50% of all 3-year-olds). Only some playgroups employ professional staff.

Day care centres are for children aged from six weeks to four or five years old. Children may go to

day care centres five days a week, from about 7.00 a.m. to 6.00 p.m., or for just part of the week. Funding for these types of child care facilities is channelled through the local authorities by the Ministry of Health, Welfare and Sport. Parents are required to pay an income-related contribution. Day care centres may also be funded by private resources. There must be two full-time or three part-time monitors per group. There is no statutory limit on the number of children in a group, but it normally has 8 to 16 children. Roughly 1% of children in the 0 to 4 age bracket go to a day care centre.

Monitors are required to hold an *MBO* certificate at the very least, or an *HBO* certificate.

At the end of 1992, 3,766 playgroups accommodated some 191,000 children. There were 1,155 full-time day care facilities (56,700 children) and 153 part-time ones (3,600 children).

3. Compulsory education

Compulsory education is laid down in the Compulsory Education Act. Every child must attend school full-time from the first school day of the month following his/her fifth birthday; however, nearly all children attend school from the age of four.

Compulsory schooling lasts either 12 years full-time (5 to 17), or full-time from five until the end of the school year in which the pupil reaches the age of 16 followed by part-time compulsory schooling until the age of 18 (majority).

4. Primary education (Basisonderwijs)

Primary education lasts for eight years, for children aged four to 12. It is provided in primary schools (*Basisschool*) which are subject to the Primary Education Act. This Act sets out the educational objectives, the rules on organizing education and the position of teaching staff, pupils and parents.

The Primary Education Act came into operation in 1985, replacing both the Nursery Education Act of 1956 and the Primary Education Act of 1920. Up to 1985, there were separate nursery schools for 4- to 6-year-olds with old-style primary schools catering for 6- to 12-year-olds.

As mentioned above, although children are obliged by law to attend school when they are five years old, almost all children start primary school at four (i.e. the first year is optional). For subsequent years, there is a 100% attendance rate.

The aim of primary education is to provide eight years of uninterrupted education as a foundation for secondary education. Primary education is oriented towards the emotional and intellectual development of the child, the development of creativity, the learning of knowledge and the acquisition of social, cultural and physical skills.

Primary education is provided in public and private schools. Some 65% of primary schools belong to the private education system. Parents can choose between publicly or privately run schools. For the purposes of public authority education, most municipalities are divided into catchment areas in order to ensure an efficient spread of pupils. Pupils must attend a publicly run school in the catchment area designated by the local authority (usually that in which the pupil lives), although exemption from this rule is possible. The rule does not apply to private education. Primary education is free of charge. School books are supplied by the school.

Primary schools are coeducational, separate school units. The establishment and closure of schools is based on the pupil density within a municipality: the number of children aged 4 to 12 per square kilometre. The minimum school size varies with the size of the municipality and is established by the Government.

Most primary schools are divided into eight classes, each containing one age-group. However, as schools are free to decide on organizational matters themselves, it is possible for classes to contain more than one age-group. The first four years are referred to as the junior classes and the last four as senior classes. Pupils may also be grouped by different levels of achievement, with possible mobility between the groups.

The same teacher is responsible for teaching a class all subjects during a school year. A specialized teacher may take certain subjects such as physical education. It is up to the schools to decide whether to assign a different teacher to a class at the end of each year.

The number of teachers allocated to a school depends on the number of pupils. Pupils with a mental or physical handicap and/or from low socio-economic background count for more than 1 pupil; their 'weight' is established in accordance with regulations from the Ministry of Education, Culture and Science.

Primary schools may make use of the facilities of school **guidance** services, most of which are organized at local and regional level. The school counselling services provide support to schools as a whole and give guidance to individual pupils.

The school year runs from 1 August to 31 July. The date for the six-week summer holiday and its duration are laid down by government authorities. They are staggered over the three large regions into which the country is divided for this purpose. Other holidays are determined by the competent authorities.

The minimum number of hours that a pupil must attend school during each academic year is established by law. Pupils receive at least 3,520 hours of teaching over the first four school years and at least 4,000 hours over the last four school years. During the first four years, there are at least 22 hours of lessons per week and after that at least 25 hours of lessons per week. Pupils receive a maximum of 5.5 hours of lessons a day. No rules are applied as regards the length of lessons, but in general they last for 60 minutes. The minimum number of school days per year is 200 and a school week is made up of five days. The school day lasts from 8.30/9.00 a.m. to 3.00/3.30 p.m. with a lunch break lasting an average of an hour to an hour-and-a-half. Wednesday afternoon is usually free. The competent authorities are responsible for determining school hours.

Children are allowed to remain at school during the break at midday. The Primary Education Act imposes a duty on the competent authority of the school to enable pupils to stay in the school buildings and grounds, if the parents so wish. The competent authority may organize the necessary supervision or this may be left up to the parents, who are required to pay for the supervisory services.

Curriculum

The Primary Education Act lists subjects that must always be taught to all pupils in primary school, if possible in an interdisciplinary form:

– sensory coordination and physical exercise;

– Dutch;

– arithmetic and mathematics;

– English;

– a number of factual subject areas: geography, history, science (including biology), social studies (including civics), intellectual and religious movements;

– expressive activities: developing the use of language, drawing, music, handicrafts, play and movement;

– social and life skills, such as road safety;

– health education.

Schools in the province of Friesland must also teach Frisian, and may conduct some lessons in that language.

The curriculum for each school is drawn up in a school plan featuring teaching and development objectives, the subjects, teaching methods, school organization and the means used to assess pupils' achievement. Provision may be made for pupils without a Dutch background. Each year, the two-year school plan is developed into a plan of activities which sets out the pupils' activities for the year in question, the duties of the teaching staff as well as the teaching time, holidays and other free days. The school plan and the activity plan must be submitted to the inspectorate for approval.

In January 1994, the Primary Education Evaluation Committee (*CEB*) published its report on the state of primary education. The Committee concludes that there are too many subjects included in the curriculum, which leads to an overloaded programme within the teaching time available. There is currently an investigation into which measures are to be taken.

Primary schools are free to choose their **teaching methods** and curricular content. Primary schools are also free to choose which **teaching materials** to use. They are not prescribed by Central Government but are the subject of commercial activity.

Assessment

The assessment of pupils' academic performance in all subjects is continuous; it is carried out at regular intervals (usually twice during the year and once at the end of it) by the teacher on the basis of all (oral and written) work accomplished during the school year. A scale of 1-10 is used for awarding marks. A score of 1 is extremely poor, while 10 is given for excellence. Pupils' individual progress is recorded in school reports.

Each school decides on measures to accommodate weaker pupils (different groups, support teachers or repeating). The teacher(s) and the school authority decide on whether a pupil moves up to the next class. Although it is possible for pupils to repeat every year, it is rare for a pupil to have to repeat a class or a year (1 to 2% do so each year). In principle, all pupils complete primary education.

No certificates or diplomas are awarded to primary school leavers, but pupils do receive a school report, which the head teacher draws up in consultation with the teachers. This describes their individual level of achievement and potential and advises on further study. Parents receive a copy of the report, but are not obliged to follow the advice on further study.

However, national tests organized by *CITO* (Central Institute for Test Development) have been developed for the final year of primary education and are used in some 60% of schools. These are aimed at guaging pupils' knowledge and understanding with regard to entry to the different types of secondary education, and may be taken into consideration in the school report.

Teachers

Primary school teachers have a primary school teacher diploma (*diploma leraar basisonderwijs*), obtained on completion of a primary teacher training course at an *HBO* (higher professional education) institution. They are fully qualified to teach all primary school subjects to all age groups. Full-time training courses last for four years and part-time courses from four to six years.

In addition to general subjects, students training to be a primary school teacher are also taught a specialist subject, chosen from among such subjects as physical education, drawing, music, handicrafts and Frisian. Specialist teachers working in primary schools sometimes teach nothing but their specialist subject. One-quarter of the training is made up of teaching practice.

Teachers in public and private schools enjoy the status of civil servants and may work full-time or part-time.

In-service teacher training is regulated by law, but no in-service training is compulsory. When completed successfully, it leads to a certificate.

Statistics 1991/92

Pupils	1,519,800	1,484,400
Teachers	89,300	90,900
Schools	9,420	9,370

5. Secondary education (Voortgezet onderwijs)

After completing primary education, pupils move on to secondary education. Secondary education is attended by 12- to 16/18-year-olds and is governed by the Secondary Education Act (*Wet op het voortgezet onderwijs*), in force since 1968.

Secondary education is divided into the following types:

- pre-university education (*Voorbereidend Wetenschappelijk Onderwijs – VWO*) for 12- to 18-year-olds;

- senior general secondary education (*Hoger Algemeen Voortgezet Onderwijs – HAVO*) for 12- to 17-year-olds;

- junior general secondary education (*Middelbaar Algemeen Voortgezet Onderwijs – MAVO*) for 12- to 16-year-olds;

- pre-vocational education (*Voorbereidend Beroepsonderwijs – VBO*) for 12- to 16-year-olds.

In *VBO* schools, lessons are given in general and vocational subjects. In *VWO, HAVO* and *MAVO* schools, education is primarily of a general nature.

According to the Basic Education 1993-1998 Decree, as from the 1993/94 school year, all types of secondary education begin with a three-year period of **basic education** (*basisvorming*), offering broad-based general teaching in which no strict distinction is made between general and technical subjects. The aim is to delay the choice of studies and modernize the curricula.

There had previously been a one-year transition class at the beginning of secondary education which facilitated progression to the second year of more than one type of school.

Pre-university education (*VWO*) lasts six years (including basic education) and prepares pupils for university education. However, pupils who have completed *VWO* can also go on to higher professional education. *VWO* is provided at three types of schools: the *Atheneum* (no classical languages), the *Gymnasium* (classical languages are compulsory) and the *Lyceum* (classical languages are optional).

Senior general secondary education (*HAVO*) lasts five years (including basic education) and prepares pupils for higher professional education, but many pupils go on to a *VWO* or a senior secondary vocational school (*MBO*).

Junior general secondary education (*MAVO*) lasts four years (including basic education). On completion of a *MAVO* school, pupils may go on to senior secondary vocational education (*MBO*), or they may decide to attend *HAVO* courses or enter the apprenticeship system.

Pre-vocational education (*VBO*) lasts four years (including basic education) and leads to senior secondary vocational education (*MBO*) and the apprenticeship system. *VBO* covers technical courses, home economics and domestic science, tradespeople's courses, commercial and administration courses, and agricultural courses. It is not a final stage in education but provides the basis for further vocational courses. *VBO* was begun in 1992 for pupils in the first year.

Up to that date, initial vocational education was provided in the form of junior secondary vocational education (*Lager Beroepsonderwijs – LBO*). Pupils already in *LBO* will continue until the end of their courses.

Secondary education is provided in both public and private schools. Roughly 70% of general secondary schools are private and some 90% of *VBO* (and *MBO*) schools are private. Tuition is free for all pupils up to 16, although books and teaching materials may have to be purchased. Pupils aged 16 and over must pay annual tuition fees, but parents can apply for allowances.

Secondary schools are coeducational. The type and name of a school is determined by the type of secondary education it provides. Some secondary schools may form part of a combined school embracing a number of different types of secondary education. Sizes vary greatly, from less than 300 to over 1,000. According to ministerial policy, the intention is to increase the number of secondary schools offering *VWO, HAVO, MAVO* and *VBO* courses within the same institution.

Pupils are admitted to secondary education if they have completed primary education (at an average age of 12 years old). Entry is decided by an admissions committee on the basis of the report from the pupil's primary school. For admission to *MAVO, HAVO* and *VWO*, pupils must have been assessed to establish their suitability. Where a *MAVO* school shares a common first year with a *VBO* school, there are no conditions for admission; there are no conditions for admission to *VBO*.

It is common for classes to be arranged according to age groups. Classes may, however, contain pupils of one level or school type, or of mixed levels/school types (for example *VBO/MAVO, MAVO/HAVO, HAVO/VWO*). Within combined schools the pupils are sometimes all mixed during the first year (a transition period).

The number of teachers allocated to a school is established every year, based on the number of pupils. If a school has different kinds of teachers (full qualification, qualification for lower secondary education, physical education), the number of teachers is established for each level separately.

The school year runs from 1 August to 31 July. There were 195 school days per year; there are now 200 during basic education (as from the 1993/94 school year). The maximum time which may be allocated to pupil holidays is 60 school days. The summer holidays last for 7 weeks in July and August, staggered over the three large regions into which the country is divided for this purpose. The dates and length of the summer holidays are prescribed by Central Government, (except in the case of *MBO* courses). The dates of the Christmas and the May holidays are the same throughout the country. The competent authority decides on the dates and length of the remaining holidays, although Central Government does recommend two periods for the autumn and spring breaks. Schools operate five days per week.

The school board and the competent authority are required to establish a school plan giving an overview of the organization and content of teaching and a lesson timetable, and submit it for approval by the inspectorate. No requirements are laid down for subject matter, methodology or teaching methods, but examinations are subject to certain conditions.

Curriculum

The recommended timetable for basic education contains 15 compulsory subjects: Dutch, English, second foreign language (French, German), mathematics, biology, physics and chemistry, computer and information literacy, history and civics, geography, economics, technology, social and life skills, visual arts/ music/ dance/ drama (at least two of these), physical education. In addition, 20% of the total curriculum is made up of optional subjects (Latin, religious instruction, mother tongue teaching, pre-vocational subjects, subjects from the basic curriculum, individual lessons or study or careers **guidance**). The time need not be used in the same way for every pupil and its extent may vary from one course year to the next.

National attainment targets are being set for the subjects in the basic curriculum. They are compulsory minimum standards for schools to achieve by the end of the period of basic education. There are two different achievement levels for basic education and pupils are grouped by level of achievement in such a way that it is possible for certain pupils to finish basic education in two years instead of three, while others may take four years.

The timetable gives a guide for the minimum number of lessons per subject. There is no obligation to adhere to the timetable except in the case of the number of hours set for social and life skills, physical education and art subjects. For *VBO* there is also a prescribed minimum number of hours for directly vocational subjects. During the first three years of *VWO* and *HAVO* courses, it is compulsory to take a third modern language (French, German, sometimes Spanish), and the curriculum for *Gymnasium* pupils must also include Latin or Greek during the first three years.

After the second year of the course, *VBO* schools can provide fewer than 1,000 lessons in the subjects prescribed for the basic curriculum, and replace these with vocationally oriented subjects. This is on condition that a total of at least 3,000 lessons are provided in the subjects of the basic curriculum over the three years.

Timetables also exist for the years following the basic education period. The recommended timetable for the whole period of all types of secondary education includes: Dutch, English, French and German language, history and civics, geography, mathematics, physics and chemistry, biology, music, drawing, handicrafts, dance, drama, physical education, technology, social and life skills, computer and information literacy, economics, and individual lessons. The main difference between the different types of secondary education is the level at which the subjects are studied and the number of lessons devoted to different subjects over the whole period of a particular type of education.

The recommended timetable for *VWO* and *HAVO* also includes literature in the languages already mentioned. In addition, pupils in the *Gymnasium* must also study Latin and Greek language and literature. A good deal of the recommended timetable for *VBO* is also devoted to vocationally oriented subjects.

Optional subjects for *VWO, HAVO* and *MAVO* are: Frisian, other modern foreign languages, Esperanto, biblical studies, history of Christianity, religious knowledge, astronomy, philosophy, film, theatre, performing arts, history of art, health care and care of the home, nutrition and clothing. In addition, pupils in *VWO* can study Hebrew language, those in the *Gymnasium* can study economic science and law, and those in the *Atheneum* can study Latin and an introduction to the culture of the ancient world. There are to be more detailed rules for individualized *VBO*.

There is one achievement level for each type of secondary education after basic education, and mobility between the different types is possible.

The minimum number of lessons to be provided per year is given in the recommended timetables for each type of school. During the first three years of secondary education, pupils receive a minimum of 1,280 lessons of 50 minutes per year. During the period of basic education, a minimum of 1,000 lessons are in the subjects of the basic curriculum. Tuition can be provided in periods longer or shorter than 50 minutes.

This means that the average school week will consist of 32 lessons of 50 minutes each. All schools will be required to devote 25 hours to the compulsory subjects making up basic education. The remaining seven hours may be devoted to subjects of the schools own choosing.

The Ministry does not prescribe **textbooks**; teachers are free to choose teaching materials.

Schools are not legally bound to provide educational and vocational **guidance**, but there is often a teacher who does so.

Assessment and qualifications

As at primary level, the assessment of pupils' academic performance in all subjects is continuous; it is carried out at regular intervals (usually twice during the year and once at the end of it) by the teacher, and is recorded in school reports. In the final year, the last assessment before the final examinations is made at Christmas. Marks are awarded on a scale of 1 to 10; a score of 1 is extremely poor, 10 is given for excellence, and 6 is the pass mark.

Pupils move up to the next class if thay have received the mark 'sufficient' (6) at the end of the year for the majority of subjects. Pupils can repeat the year once; if their marks are not deemed sufficient at the end of this year, they must change to another type of education. The 15 compulsory subjects studied during the basic education period culminate in final tests for each subject, with the exception of physical education. The tests will be determined by the attainment targets and will be taken in each subject or combination of subjects. Interim testing may also take place where subjects are not taught throughout the entire period of basic education. The final test may not, however, be completed before the end of the second year of the course. Schools may supplement the tests with their own examinations and can decide when and in what order tests are taken. The first final tests will be taken in the 1994/95 school year. Pupils successfully completing basic education will be awarded a certificate (*getuigschrift basisvorming*).

At the end of the second year, the competent authority will provide pupils with a recommendation as to their further course of study. Pupils unable to achieve all the core attainment targets may qualify for exemption from the attainment targets or from one or more subjects in the basic curriculum. A committee appointed by the school board will decide on such exemptions.

The maximum period pupils may take to complete the first stage of secondary education (the 4-year courses of *VBO* and *MAVO*, the first three years of *HAVO* and *VWO*) is five years.

VWO, *HAVO*, *MAVO* and *VBO* courses culminate in a final examination comprising a school examination and a national examination. The school examination is prepared by the individual school and is taken in the final school year. It consists of two or more oral and/or written tests (per subject). The national examination is the same for all schools of a certain type and is taken at the same time. The final grade is the average of the marks for the school and national examinations.

The *VWO* final examination contains seven subjects. Dutch and one other modern language (French, German or English) are compulsory subjects. At a *Gymnasium*, Latin and Greek are also compulsory subjects. The other subjects are of the candidate's own choice. Physical education is not an examination subject. It is possible to sit examinations in more than seven subjects. The *VWO* certificate distinguishes between an *Atheneum* and a *Gymnasium* certificate.

The *HAVO* final examination features six subjects. Dutch and one other modern language (French, German, English or Spanish) are compulsory subjects. The other examination subjects are of the candidate's own choice. Physical education is not an examination subject. It is possible to sit the examination in seven subjects.

The *MAVO* leaving examination covers six subjects. Dutch and one other modern language (French, German, English or Spanish) are compulsory subjects. The other subjects are of the candidate's own choice. Physical education is not an

examination subject. Examinations may be sat at C or D level. At least three subjects must be done at D level, which is the most demanding.

The *VBO* leaving examination is composed of six or seven subjects, both general and vocational subjects. At least two vocational subjects must be chosen for the examinations. The general subjects are taken at A, B, C, or D level, whilst the vocational subjects are taken at A, B or C level. For subjects taken at A or B level, examinations will consist entirely of internal school tests set by the competent authority. Physical education is not an examination subject. New C and D level examination syllabuses for the vocationally oriented *VBO* subjects will be in operation from 1994.

Pupils who pass one of the different leaving examinations are awarded a certificate (*Diploma*) which takes the same form throughout the country for the different types of school.

Teachers

Teachers are subject specialists. Those trained under the previous teacher training system were specialized in two subjects; those under the present system specialize in one subject, but may teach two. It is up to the schools to decide whether teachers change classes at the end of each year.

Teachers in **secondary schools** are of two kinds: those with a full teaching qualification (*leraar voortgezet onderwijs eerstegraads*) and those with a lower secondary teaching qualification (*leraar voortgezet onderwijs tweedegraads*). Fully qualified teachers are entitled to give lessons in all secondary schools, whereas teachers with a lower secondary qualification may only give lessons in the first three years of *VWO* and *HAVO* schools and in all years of *MAVO*, *VBO* and *MBO* schools. These qualifications are obtained through teacher training courses provided by universities (*WO*) and institutions of higher professional education (*HBO*).

HBO provides teacher training courses leading to a qualification in one subject. Courses last four years full-time or part-time for a lower secondary teaching qualification and three successive years part-time for a full teaching qualification in general subjects.

Courses for a full teaching qualification in physical education (*leraar voortgezet onderwijs eerstegraads*) last four years full-time.

Universities provide teacher training courses (one year full-time) leading to a full teaching qualification in one of the *HAVO* and *VWO* examination subjects. This training may be followed upon completion of *HBO* or university studies.

Teaching practice is a vital component of all teacher training courses. All teacher training leads to a certificate indicating the field of study and the level of attainment.

All teaching staff in public and private schools enjoy the status of civil servants and may work full-time or part-time.

In-service teacher training is regulated by law, but is not compulsory. When completed successfully, it leads to a certificate.

Statistics 1990/91

	Full-time	Part-time
Pupils	683,662	87,817
Teachers	89,370*	
Schools	1,242	78

* *VWO, HAVO, MAVO, LBO and MBO.*

Pupils and schools by type of course, 1991/92

	Pupils	Schools
Mixed class *AVO*	154,122	1,189
Middenschool/ basisvorming	11,599	28
MAVO	203,805	974
HAVO	141,377	488
VWO	162,689	504

6. Vocational education

Vocational education covers the following:

– Senior secondary vocational education (*MBO*);

– Apprenticeship;

– Training provided in the context of schemes for the unemployed.

Vocational education is at present undergoing significant changes. Reform began in 1987 with the Sector Restructuring and Modernization Act (*Wet Sectorvorming en Vernieuwing – SVM-wet*) for senior secondary vocational education (*MBO*). The two fixed requirements (*MBO* schools must have at least 600 pupils and no separate schools for short *MBO* courses) led to the 382 old *MBO* schools being

transformed into about 140 new-style schools. Some included mergers with establishments for apprentices and part-time *MBO* courses. The reform was completed for the *MBO* in 1991.

On 1 August 1993, the Part-time Vocational Courses Act (*Wet op het Cursorisch Beroepsonderwijs – WCBO*) came into effect, establishing regulations for the apprenticeship system, part-time senior secondary vocational education and training for specific occupations.

The aim of the Act is to introduce a flexible system of retraining and refresher courses, to align education with the labour market and to utilize the educational infrastructure for the benefit of the employed and unemployed. The *WCBO* forms the legal premise for implementing and funding training activities through the regional employment services (*Regionale Bureaus Arbeidsvoorziening*). At the same time, steps have been taken to broaden the tasks and field of action for secondary schools. In addition to the regular funding from Central Government, they are also entitled to resources from the employment service organization responsible for running vocational courses for job-seekers. Schools may also become involved in self-financing courses, for example, in response to requests from companies.

A new law on vocational education and adult education should come into effect in 1996 (*Wet educatie beroepsonderwijs – WEB*). This Bill replaces existing legislation: *SVM-wet, WCBO, KVE* and *VAVO*. The aim of the Bill is to make vocational education and adult education more effective.

The decision to create regional bodies for the apprenticeship system (*Regionale Opleidingscentra – ROC*), for vocational education and adult education represents a major step towards the integration of the various sorts of vocational training, as intended in the *WEB*. The *ROC* provide the following types of training: adult basic education, general secondary adult education, apprenticeship system, senior secondary vocational education (*MBO*) and local non-formal education.

28 Regional Service Centres (*RDC*) were set up in 1993, amalgamating the Regional Bodies for the apprenticeship system, the subsidized private agencies for educational and vocational guidance and the contact centres for education and the labour market. The *RDC* are independent organizations providing educational and vocational guidance and acting as an interface between education and the labour market. They are funded by the Ministry of Education, Culture and Science.

Efforts are also being made to create a national structure of qualifications for each sector of industry: a system of training with related final attainment levels, certification units, examinations and diplomas and the rights that go with them. A major step in this direction is the decision to integrate the Business Sector Consultations between Education and Industry (*Bedrijfstakgewijs Overleg Onderwijs Bedrijfsleven – BOOB*), which sets the final attainment level(s) for *MBO* courses,

and the national training agencies, which set the level(s) for the apprenticeship system.

6.1 Senior secondary vocational education (*Middelbaar beroepsonderwijs – MBO*)

Depending on the course chosen, *MBO* may last up to 4 years. It is designed for pupils aged around 16 to 19.

Part-time *MBO* comes under the Part-time Vocational Courses Act while full-time courses come under the Secondary Education Act. Part-time *MBO* courses are taught in the evening and sometimes partially during the day. They last two to three years, depending on the type of course. For some courses, pupils have to be in relevant employment. There are tuition fees for full-time and part-time *MBO* courses.

There are 144 *MBO* schools providing full-time education and 459 offering training on a part-time basis (1991/92).

MBO covers four training sectors:

– technical (technical, laboratory and nautical education);

– social services and health care (nine options);

– economics and administration (including tourism and leisure);

– agriculture.

MBO is provided at schools specifically designed for this type of education; every school has at least one sector and these sectors are divided into sections in which there are a number of different training courses. A good many *MBO* schools spread their activities over several sectors. Agricultural education is alone in being sector specific. It falls within the competence of the Ministry of Agriculture, Nature Management and Fisheries and is undergoing a merger process between *MBO* courses, short *MBO* courses and secondary-level agricultural education. There are 25 agricultural training centres (*AOC*). *MBO* schools offer education for middle management activities in industry, the social services and the civil service.

The various alternative requirements for admission to senior secondary vocational education are: a *VBO* qualification; a *MAVO* qualification; proof of promotion to the fourth year of *HAVO* or *VWO*; a qualification from a short course; any other qualification designated by the Minister. These requirements apply to short, intermediate or long courses; for admission to the first year of the intermediate and full-length courses, however, additional requirements may be set as to the number of examination subjects taken at B or C level. In addition to the minimum requirements, schools may themselves have additional preferences with regard to such matters as combinations of subjects studied, the level of achievement in final examination subjects and the applicant's aptitude and motivation for the particular course of study. Admission to the one-year guidance and transition programmes is not dependent on previous qualifications. For each type of training, the prior training is indicated, as well as the level of attainment.

Long courses, lasting three to four years, are directly accessible to pupils who have completed *MAVO* or *LBO (VBO)* courses with at least three subjects at C level, or the first three years of *HAVO*. Pupils with a certificate from an intermediate course, a short course or a guidance or transition programme can also move on to the full-length course. They lead to middle-management activities (EC level I). Pupils may also move on from the long courses to higher professional training (*HBO*).

Intermediate courses are directly accessible to pupils who have completed *MAVO* or *VBO (LBO)* courses with at least three subjects at B level. Training provides the skills needed for the exercise of an independent profession or trade (EC level III). Intermediate courses are for the time being run on an experimental basis and are limited to three options: electrical engineering, mechanical engineering and the hotel and catering trade; and last at most three years.

Short courses are directly accessible to pupils who have completed *VBO (LBO)* and *MAVO* courses (no requirements as to levels). Training provides the skills necessary for the exercise of a trade or occupation at starting level (EC level II), or to move on to a full-length *MBO* course (the final level of short *MBO* courses is comparable to the elementary level of the apprenticeship system).

One year **guidance and transition programmes** are aimed at providing guidance for pupils in their choice of vocational training and providing opportunities for progressing towards long and intermediate training courses.

Curriculum

All *MBO* schools offer general and vocational training. Compulsory on-the-job training occupies an important place in *MBO* courses. A formal contract is signed between the competent authority, the pupil and the provider of the placement. No provision is made for a minimum timetable of lessons.

MBO schools have the opportunity to draw up the curricula themselves in accordance with the final attainment levels established by the Minister of Education, Culture and Science. Final attainment levels stipulate the sort of knowledge, understanding, skills and professional attitudes that pupils must acquire. The levels of attainment are integrated into vocational training profiles which themselves are based on job profiles.

Each year, *MBO* schools are required to set down in a school plan a description and justification of education provision. They establish an examination syllabus (based on the attainment levels) for each section and decide on the leaving examination. In the case of components where the leaving examinations are set nationally, it is the Ministry of Education, Culture and Science which sets the examination syllabus.

All of the new *MBO* courses have a modular structure. They are made up of a certain number of certificate units, some compulsory others optional. Each certificate unit comprises one or more modules. Most courses include two compulsory on-the-job training periods: 100 days during the course and 100 days at the end of it. A certificate is also awarded for the on-the-job training.

Assessment and qualifications

At present, the examinations are governed by a large number of institutional decisions, but in future the *MBO* schools will to a large extent set the examinations themselves. Work is being done on harmonizing the different examination regulations so as to form one regulation for the entire reformed

MBO system. There are two types of examinations: an internal examination and a national examination. The national examination applies solely to subjects/examination components/certificate units that are covered by statutory regulations. Each year the Minister establishes for every sector a national examination board which prepares the nationwide examination syllabus on the basis of advice offered by education and business associations. The Minister makes the final decision. The competent authorities of *MBO* schools present the inspectorate with an examination regulation and an annual programme of testing and assessment. The national examination and the internal examination procedures are prepared under the responsibility of the competent authority. The form of standard diplomas and lists of grades are decided by the Minister of Education, Culture and Science and are identical throughout the country.

In the new *MBO* courses assessment takes place at the end of each module. On completion of a certain number of modules trainees are awarded a certificate. If they obtain all the compulsory certificates they are awarded a diploma.

Teachers

In order to teach all classes at *MBO* schools, teachers need a full or lower secondary teaching qualification, obtained through a course of higher professional training at an *HBO* college. The trainee teachers are taught general subjects, technical subjects and physical education.

All teaching staff in public and private schools enjoy the status of civil servants and may work full-time or part-time.

6.2 Apprenticeship

The apprenticeship system is governed by the Part-time Vocational Courses Act. Up to August 1993, the apprenticeship system had its own separate legislation. The apprenticeship system development plan (1990) contains plans for the reform of the training courses.

Apprenticeship takes the form of a two-tier system, whereby on-the-job training is linked with theoretical training, which means that the apprentice enjoys both trainee and employee status. There are tuition fees for the theoretical training.

The theoretical aspects of the chosen occupation are taught on a day-release basis at a regional apprenticeship training institute (*Streekscholen*) or other school, while the practical work is done either in industry or in trainee workshops. In the first case an apprenticeship contract is entered into with the employer, whereby the firm undertakes to give the pupil a sound training. In the second, pupils practise skills under the supervision of a practical teacher in trainee workshops set up by firms. Sometimes these workshops are used in addition to training in industry, and sometimes they take its place.

The responsibility for organizing the practical training lies with the employer, who appoints a training instructor for this purpose. Support is given by a consultant from the national agency responsible for the apprenticeship system.

The company provides the trainee-cum-employee with the opportunity of attending additional day-release courses, two-thirds of which consist of vocationally oriented instruction and one-third of general subjects. Training is given at a variety of levels:

- transition courses for trainees who have too low a level of training (for example, immigrants, the long-term unemployed and women returning to a career after having a family);

- training providing skills to become a craftsman/woman at beginner's level;

- training to become a fully-qualified craftsman/woman;

- specialized training for self-employed entrepreneurs.

The apprenticeship system is available to young people over 16 who have completed their full-time compulsory schooling. It lasts between one and three years, depending on the level. Where previous education is inadequate, training is usually one year longer.

There are three different levels of apprenticeship training:

Elementary courses (comparable with short *MBO* courses), lasting two or three years, and leading to the exercise of an occupation or trade at beginner's level (basic training, EC level II). Applicants must have *LBO (VBO)* or *MAVO* certificates or three years of *HAVO/VWO* training.

Advanced courses (comparable with intermediate *MBO* courses), lasting one or two years, and leading to the exercise of an independent trade or profession (middle-level training, EC level III). Applicants must have completed basic training or a short *MBO* course.

Tertiary courses (comparable with but narrower than full-length *MBO* courses), lasting one or two years, and leading to the exercise of a specialized profession or trade (higher-level training, EC level IV). Applicants must have completed intermediate training or an intermediate *MBO* course.

Curriculum

The content of practical training depends on the employer. The day-release course (*beroepsbegeleidend onderwijs*) comprises general and vocationally-oriented training and is intended to complement the practical training. There are roughly 400 training courses available.

Apprentices attend day-release courses at an apprenticeship training institute on one or two days a week and for the rest of the week are employed in companies. Each day at the training institute consists of 8 or 9 lessons, 6 of which are theoretical vocational education and 3 are general education.

The Minister of Education, Culture and Science is responsible for establishing the overall curriculum (*totaal programma*), which is broken down into two parts: an indicative teaching programme and a practical programme. There are also entry requirements, conditions governing the amount of practical training and requirements to be met as regards the practical and theoretical parts of the examination.

Assessment and qualifications

The examination syllabus is established by the national agency for the apprenticeship system. The Ministry of Education, Culture and Science confines itself to establishing the final attainment levels and the related breakdown into certificate units. At the end of practical training, the national agency allows an examination to be taken. This examination, made up of practical and theoretical parts, is administered by a committee constituted by the Minister of Education, Culture and Science, acting on the proposal of the national agency. Courses lead to a nationally recognized vocational diploma awarded by the national body for the particular field.

Teachers

See *MBO* with regard to teachers of theoretical training.

The practical training sessions are given by a trainer, who, depending on the size of the firm, will be either the head of the firm or a qualified employee. Larger firms usually have a separate department where training is provided by instructors appointed for this purpose. These trainers enjoy the same rights as other employees, not those of teachers in the apprenticeship system.

6.3 Training in the context of employment policy

Training in the context of employment policy lies within the competence of the Central Manpower Services Board (*Centraal Bestuur voor de Arbeidsvoorziening – CBA*), which is a division of the Ministry of Social Affairs and Employment. With the introduction of the Employment Policy Act of 1991, this matter became the joint responsibility of Central Government, employers' associations and trade union organizations. The *CBA* prepares a long-term national policy framework that acts as a guide for the 28 Regional Manpower Services Boards (*Regionale Besturen Arbeidsvoorziening – RBA*). Their task is to establish the number of unemployed people who need training as well as the training institutions and training initiatives required. The most significant of these are:

1. Vocational Training Centres

2. Vocational Guidance and Vocational Training Centres

3. Vocational Schools for Women

4. Basic Vocationally-Oriented Education for Adults

5. Training Framework Branch Training.

1, 2 and 3 are training establishments, whilst 4 and 5 are training initiatives.

Statistics 1991/92
VBO and *MBO*

	Pupils	Schools
VBO	220,935	445 (34 combined with *MBO*)
MBO	284,404	110

7. Higher education

Higher education includes higher (non-university) professional education (*Hoger beroepsonderwijs – HBO*), university education (*Wetenschappelijk onderwijs – WO*) and the Open University (OU, distance learning at higher education level). Higher education caters for students roughly 18 years old and over and comes under the Higher Education and Scientific Research Act of 1993. This new law replaces some 16 laws and orders in Council, including the University Education Act and the Open University Act. Until 1986, higher professional education was covered by the provisions of the Secondary Education Act and since then by separate legislation, the Higher Vocational Education Act. As from 1984, the level of *HBO* was scaled up from secondary to higher education and many institutions were merged.

Both higher professional education and university education provide teacher training.

Institutions have a tradition of academic freedom and autonomy. They assume responsibility for the content of degree programmes. They receive an annual budget from the State, dependent, among other factors, on the number of students registered. In higher education a system of internal quality control is coupled with periodical external quality controls by so-called visiting committees.

7.1 Higher professional education

Higher professional education (*HBO*) provides both theoretical and practical training for occupations which require a higher professional qualification. *HBO* courses are almost always closely linked to a particular field of employment and most include a compulsory work placement.

This type of education is available in 70 *HBO* colleges of which roughly 30% are public and some 70% are private.

HBO covers seven training sectors: agriculture, education (teacher training), technology, economics, social and cultural welfare, health care and art. *HBO* establishments generally encompass several different sectors.

There are both short and full-length courses. The normal courses last four years, with a maximum enrolment period of six years. For part-time courses, there is a maximum enrolment period (i.e. to complete the course) of nine years.

Admission

In order to enrol on an *HBO* course, pupils must hold either the *HAVO, VWO* or MBO certificate (three or four-year course). In addition to these admission requirements, the institutions may themselves impose further requirements and standards with regard to the combination of subjects studied.

The Government has the power to impose an admissions quota (numerus clausus), depending on the labour market.

Fees/Student finance

Students in the *HBO* system pay an annual fee. All students receive a basic higher education grant and may apply for a supplementary grant and interest-bearing loan in addition.

Academic year

Each academic year comprises 42 weeks. Lectures start in the first week of September.

Courses

Each course comprises 168 credits (four years). One credit is equivalent to one week of study (40 hours), made up of lectures, laboratory work (where applicable) and independent study. The first part of the course is called the 'propaedeutic stage' and covers general topics. Of the maximum total length of six years, two may be spent on this stage. In each course year, there is a period of up to ten weeks in which no teaching is provided and no examinations set. Following the propadeutic stage, students specialize in a specific field. They also undertake practical exercises outside the institution itself. The time spent on these depends on the course and varies between several months and one year. The final section of training mostly consists of a written paper in the student's subject area.

As from 1992, a number of *HBO* institutions have been providing an experimental form of education termed 'cooperative education', whereby periods of study alternate regularly with periods of work in a relevant full-time job. During the work periods the student is not regarded as formally enrolled and these periods do not count towards the maximum permitted duration of study.

Assessment/Qualifications

At the end of the first year, a 'propaedeutic' or foundation course examination is set that has to be passed within two years. The final examination is taken after the fourth year. There are interim examinations (*tentamens*) in each subject, usually every two or three months.

Pupils abandoning the course before the final examination receive a declaration of how far they have got in the course and what interim examinations they have sat.

Pupils who pass the examination are awarded a higher education degree (*getuigschrift van HBO*) listing the subjects examined, and may be given a title, such as *ingenieur* (graduate engineer) for graduates of technology and agriculture and natural environment courses or *baccalaureus* (bachelor) for graduates of other types of courses.

7.2 University education

University education (*WO*) is provided in 13 universities and the Open University system for distance learning at higher education level. Nine universities provide teaching over a broad range of disciplines, while the three technical universities and the agricultural university concentrate on subjects within their particular specialized fields. In all, there are almost 100 different courses available.

There are ten public universities and three private ones.

Admission

Those seeking to enter university must possess a *VWO* certificate, sit an *HBO* foundation course examination or take an entrance examination (*colloquium doctum*).

There is a centralized admissions system for distributing places at the various universities.

Decisions are made annually by the institutions or the Minister of Education, Culture and Science as to which courses are to be subject to an admissions' quota (numerus clausus).

Fees/Student finance

University students pay an annual fee equal to that paid by *HBO* students. All students receive a basic higher education grant and may apply for a supplementary grant and interest-bearing loan in addition.

Academic year

Each academic year comprises 42 weeks. Lectures start in the first week of September.

Courses

University education covers both theoretical studies and specialized training, such as for the legal and medical professions. Degree courses (*doctoraalprogrammas*) officially last four years (168 credits), but because many students do not manage to complete them in four years, they may take up to six years. Medical studies can take 5 to 6 years. Every university course includes a propaedeutic or foundation stage which gives the student a general introduction to the subject with specialization increasing throughout the course.

The study load of courses is expressed in terms of credits (one credit equals one week's work – 40 hours), made up of lectures, laboratory work (where applicable) and independent study. There are also courses with a lighter study load.

On completion of the degree course, a training course may be followed for a period ranging from one to four years, for example, a teacher training course or a medical training course. It is also possible to become a trainee researcher at a university.

Assessment/Qualifications

At the end of the first year, a 'propaedeutic' or foundation course examination is set that has to be passed within two years. The final examination is taken after the fourth year. There are interim examinations (*tentamens*) in each subject, usually every two or three months.

Students abandoning the course before the final examination receive an official declaration of how far they have got in the course and what interim examinations they have sat.

When the student passes the final examination, he or she is awarded a certificate listing the different parts of the examination and mentioning the degree obtained, and granted the title of *doctorandus, meester* or *ingenieur* (Master, M.). The latter is used by graduates from the technical universities and the agricultural university.

Statistics 1992/93

	Students
Higher professional training (*HBO*)	261,000*
University education *(WO)*	162,000
Open University	67,900 (1992)

* including part-time students.

Source: Facts and Figures 1993 - 's-Gravenhage, SDU/DOP, 1993.

Austria

AUSTRIA

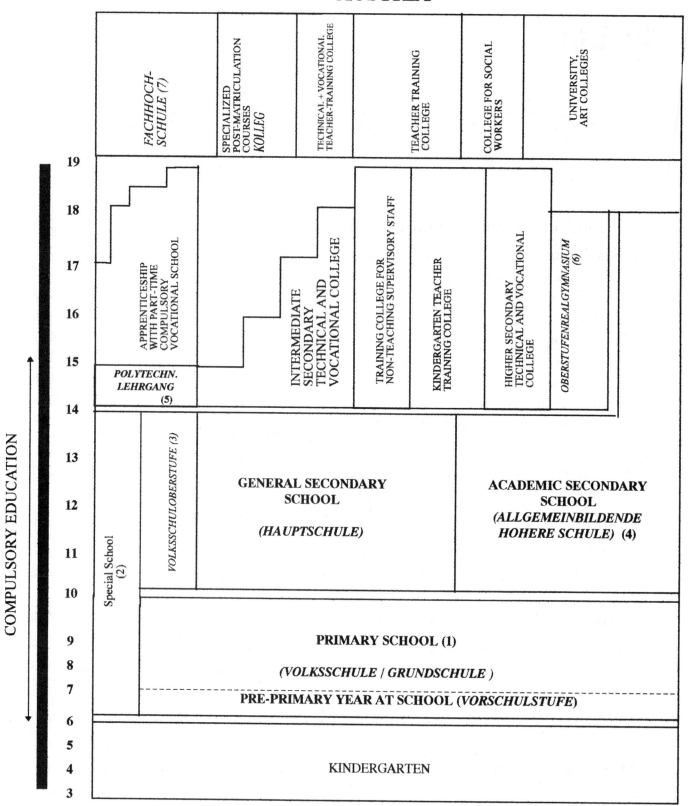

1. The pre-primary year precedes primary school, and is for children of compulsory school age who are not yet mature enough to attend primary school proper.

2. Special schools are not described in the text.

3. The Upper Level of Primary School. It is one of the school types at the lower level of secondary education, but the number of pupils now attending such schools is negligible.

4. The academic secondary school comprises four years at the lower level and four years at the upper level.

5. Pre-vocational year. This mainly concerns 14- to 15-year-olds wishing to learn an occupation immediately after the completion of compulsory schooling.

6. Separate upper-level type of academic secondary school, entered on completion of eight years of general education.

7. Post-secondary special-subject colleges. These have been established from the academic year 1994/95 as an alternative to existing university studies.

1. Responsibilities and administration

1.1 Background

Austria is a federal State with a total area of 83,855 square kilometres, consisting of nine provinces (*Länder*). The population is 7,795,786 (1991) and Vienna, the capital, has 1,539,848 inhabitants. 59% of the population live in urban areas.

Austria, a monarchy up to 1918, is now a parliamentary democracy with a Constitution, established in 1920/1929, based on republican, democratic, federal and legal principles, as well the principle of the division of legislative and executive power and the separation of justice and administration.

The Federal President is the supreme representative of State, elected directly by the people for a 6-year term. The National and Federal Chambers are the legislative bodies of the Republic, the National Chamber being the most important. The members of the Federal Chamber come from the parliaments of the *Länder* ('diets'). The Government is formed by the Federal Chancellor, Vice-Chancellor and Federal Ministers. Each *Land* has a regional government and administration.

The municipalities are not part of the general state administration but are bodies with an independent right of administration. They have an elected Municipal Council led by the Mayor.

In Austria there is an organizational and institutional division between Church and State. Religion is taught in schools. The predominant religion is Roman Catholicism.

The official language is German. The rights of local Slovenian and Croatian groups are recognized under Article 7 of the State Treaty of 1955. In some primary schools (*Volksschule/Grundschule*), Croatian and German are used on an equal basis in the first three years. The same is true for the Hungarian communities in the province of Burgenland.

In 1992, the percentage of the working population in each employment sector was as follows: primary sector 3.3%, secondary sector 39.4%, tertiary sector 57.3%. The unemployment rate was 4.3% (1993).

1.2 Basic principles: education

According to the School Organization Act of 25 July 1962 'it shall be the task of the Austrian school to foster the development of the talents and potential abilities of young persons in accordance with ethical, religious and social values and the appreciation of that which is true, good and beautiful, by giving them an education corresponding to their respective courses of studies. It shall give young people the knowledge and skills required for their future lives and occupations and train them to acquire knowledge on their own initiative.'

The Austrian Constitution guarantees general access to public schools without distinction of birth, gender, race, status, class, language or religion. Private sector schools, in contrast, may select pupils according to religion, language or gender, although this is rarely applied.

1.3 Distribution of responsibilities

In Austria, education has always been a most sensitive area, heavily disputed among political decision-makers. This explains the pragmatic distribution of responsibilities between different bodies and entities. The existing legal framework therefore renders attempts at amending education laws very difficult.

The Federal Ministry of Education and the Arts (*Bundesministerium für Unterricht und Kunst*) has overall responsibility for primary and secondary education, including intermediate and higher secondary technical and vocational colleges, training colleges for kindergarten teachers and non-teaching supervisory staff, and part-time compulsory vocational schools.

The work experience part of initial vocational training is the responsibility of the Federal Ministry of Economic Affairs.

Non-university higher education also falls under the responsibility of the Federal Ministry of Education and the Arts, while the Ministry of Science and Research is responsible for the universities and the *Fachhochschulen*.

As is the case with governmental administration in general, responsibilities are divided between legislation and implementation. Four areas should be distinguished:

- **The Federation has exclusive responsibility for legislation and implementation** with regard to the entire field of academic secondary schooling, intermediate and higher technical and vocational education and training for kindergarten teaching and non-teaching staff, and with regard to the conditions of service and staff representation rights of teachers at these schools.

- **The Federation is responsible for legislation, and individual *Länder* are responsible for implementation** with regard to the conditions of service and staff representation rights of teachers at public sector schools of compulsory education.

- **The Federation is responsible for basic legislation, and the *Länder* are responsible for the issuing of implementing laws and their implementation** with regard to the organizational structure of federal education authorities in the *Länder* and the external organization of public sector schools of compulsory education. All basic legislation has a framework character and is expressed through implementing laws promulgated by the 'diets', the legislative bodies at provincial level.

- **The *Länder* are responsible for legislation and implementation** with regard to nursery schools (*kindergarten*).

1.4 Administration

Federal Authorities

Separate federal bodies have been established wherever the Federation is responsible for implementation. These are:

- **District School Boards** at the level of the political 'districts';

- **Provincial School Boards** at the level of the *Länder*; and

- the **Federal Ministry of Education and the Arts** for the entire territory.

The District and Provincial School Boards are the federal school authorities in the *Länder* and – apart from the right to consultation in important matters – are not involved in the implementation of matters under the responsibility of the individual *Länder*. The Austrian system of administration is characterized by a two-tier hierarchy. Provincial School Boards have designated jurisdiction in matters referred to a District School Board, while the Federal Ministry of Education and the Arts deals with cases referred to Provincial School Boards in the first instance.

Federal Ministry of Education

In general, the Federal Government introduces draft laws, known as government bills, in the National Council. Drawn up by the Federal Ministry of Education and the Arts, these drafts have first been submitted to the Collegiate Councils in the District and Provincial School Boards for an expert opinion. Basic laws enacted by the Federation will normally prescribe a deadline by which the *Länder* must issue pertinent implementing laws (6 months to one year). Implementing laws are passed by the 'diets'. More detailed provisions are contained in the individual constitutions of the *Länder*.

The Federal Minister of Education and the Arts promulgates curricula on the basis of the School Organization Act. It also endorses textbook lists for every subject. While there is no ban on selecting non-listed textbooks, these will not be made available free of charge.

The preparatory groundwork for curricular development has been entrusted to teachers' working groups set up for virtually all subjects. Teachers' working groups work on an informal basis. Textbooks are selected by the Teachers' Conferences, which are established by law. They belong to the decision-making bodies within a school.

Provincial School Boards

Provincial School Boards are directed by the Provincial Governor (as chairman of the Provincial School Board); for all practical purposes he is assisted in the fulfilment of his duties by an Executive Chairman. The central body within a Provincial School Board is the Collegiate Council, made up of voting members and members with consultative status. Voting members are represented on the Collegiate Council in accordance with the balance of power held by the political parties in the provincial 'diet'. They are mostly pupils' parents and teachers' representatives.

It is one of the major tasks of the Collegiate Council to submit proposals for the appointment of teachers and head teachers at intermediate and higher secondary schools. The Federal Minister selects one of three candidates suggested, who will then be appointed by the Federal President. Collegiate Councils also issue general directives on existing laws and ordinances (e.g. curricula) and submit expert opinions on draft laws and regulations.

District School Boards

District School Boards are headed by the District Governor. The Collegiate Councils at district level are structured and set up on the same basis as those at provincial level.

The Collegiate Council at district level issues general directives and submits expert opinions on draft laws and regulations, and on curricula.

Offices of the Provincial Government

The implementation of matters falling under the responsibility of the individual *Länder* is carried out by executive authorities at provincial level – the so-called Offices of the Provincial Government (*Amt der Landesregierung*).

Their most important task is the maintenance of public sector schools of general compulsory education and the appointment of teachers and head teachers at these schools. However, in all those matters not set down in law the District and Provincial School Boards have to be consulted.

School autonomy

From the school year 1993/94, the 14th amendment to the School Organization Act empowers schools to issue their own curricular regulations autonomously by a two-thirds vote of the School Committee or the School Forum. The former consists of teachers', pupils' and parents' representatives, while in the latter, which is established in compulsory schools, only teachers and parents are involved. General secondary schools have 16 units (lessons) spread over 4 years, and academic secondary schools have 8 lessons within the first four years to use as they wish. Schools may also – within certain limits – determine the number of pupils required to establish or divide a class.

Intermediate and higher secondary technical and vocational colleges also enjoy some degree of autonomy with regard to the curriculum (each college is free to decide on at least two hours from the list of compulsory subjects), and the provision of specialized study courses.

All Austrian schools have some financial autonomy. For intermediate and higher secondary technical and vocational colleges this kind of autonomy serves the procurement of computers and technical equipment. This makes occupation-oriented, project-based forms of education (e.g. 'company practice') easier to implement.

1.5 Inspection

Austria's education system is characterized by a long tradition of school inspection, headed by provincial school inspectors responsible for an entire *Land*. At compulsory school level, provincial school inspectors are assisted by district school inspectors, and in intermediate and higher secondary education by subject inspectors.

Inspection of the compulsory schools and intermediate secondary schools in the fields of agriculture and forestry – with the exception of a few federal schools – is carried out by the provinces.

There are a few schools (e.g. the higher secondary schools in the fields of agriculture and forestry, one intermediate school in the field of forestry, a number of higher secondary industrial schools in Vienna, etc.) which come directly under the Federal Ministry of Education and the Arts.

1.6 Financing

Schools of compulsory education (primary schools, general secondary schools, special schools, pre-vocational schools and vocational schools) are maintained by the *Länder*, by municipalities or municipal associations.

While most of the schools in general compulsory education are maintained by municipalities or municipal associations, part-time compulsory vocational schools are maintained by the *Länder*.

Maintaining and operating a school includes its establishment, maintenance and repair of the school buildings, payment of overheads, purchase of equipment and teaching aids, and the employment of the necessary auxiliary staff (caretakers, maintenance staff, etc.). The employment of teachers at compulsory schools is exclusively the responsibility of a *Land*. Teachers in public sector schools of compulsory education are employed by the *Land*, which pays the cost of their salaries. However, the *Land* is fully compensated for this cost by the Federation in the process of fiscal adjustment. (The sole exception being teachers at compulsory vocational schools, where this refund is granted only up to 50%.)

Public sector schools of compulsory education are not allowed to charge tuition fees. Transport to and from school using public transport facilities is free. Textbooks are provided to pupils free of charge, and they are entitled to keep them.

Intermediate and higher secondary schools are established and maintained by the Federation, which bears the full cost, including teachers' salaries. Teachers do not enter into an employment

contract with the school, but with the Federation. As in compulsory education, intermediate and higher schools may not charge tuition fees and textbooks and transport are free.

Austrian schools have relatively few funds of their own to administer. Reforms are under way to increase their financial autonomy.

All **Universities and Art Colleges** have been established by the State (there are no private universities) and are predominately financed from the state budget.

1.7 Private schools

The Austrian Constitution provides the right to establish private schools. Most private schools are run by the churches or special interest groups (chambers). There are two basic types of private schools: those which teach the official curriculum, and those which have their own curriculum.

Many private schools are subsidized by the State (infrastructure and other expenses). Those run by an officially recognized church can claim to have their teaching staff paid by the State. These teachers remain federal employees (at intermediate and higher secondary schools) or provincial employees (in compulsory education). Private schools which are not run by an officially recognized church cannot claim to have their teaching staff paid by the State. On the basis of a private contract, these schools may be treated in the same way as those run by an officially recognized church.

All private schools may apply to the Federal Ministry of Education and the Arts for a subsidy for extraordinary expenses, on the basis of a private contract, for example, for building costs.

1.8 Advisory bodies

The following advisory bodies have been set up and attached to the Federal Ministry of Education and the Arts, mainly to advise the Federal Minister:

– School Reform Commission: this is composed of members delegated by the political parties represented in the National Council, the Provincial School Boards, and the lobbies, as well as university professors of education.

- The Centre for Educational Development: this consists of four departments. Each department specializes in certain fields. Department I is concerned with groundwork, the development of the primary school and the integration of handicapped children; Department II concentrates on evaluation and educational research; Department III concentrates on basic principles and concepts for modern language teaching for all types of schools; and Department IV specializes in upper secondary education, vocational education and school development.

- Commission for Consultation in Matters of Compulsory Vocational Schooling (questions concerning part-time schools for the training of apprentices): this consists of representatives of the Federal Ministry of Education and the Arts, the Federal Ministry of Economic Affairs (responsible for the in-company part of training in the dual-system), the Federal Ministry of Labour and Social Affairs (responsible for labour-market policy), as well as representatives of the Austrian Chamber of Commerce, the Association of Austrian Industrialists, the Austrian Federal Youth Ring (the central organization of Austrian youth associations), and of the 'vocational school teachers' section of the Austrian Trades Union Congress.

- Parents' Advisory Board: this consists of representatives of the main associations of parents and related organizations. It usually meets five times in the course of a school year under the chairmanship of the Federal Minister of Education and the Arts or an official nominated by him.

- Pupils' Advisory Board: this consists of pupils' representatives and representatives of youth organizations. It usually meets three times in the course of a school year, in each case for a period of at least two days, under the chairmanship of the Federal Minister of Education and the Arts or an official nominated by him.

1.9 Educational and careers guidance

Approximately 2,500 school guidance counsellors and educational consultants provide counselling services at all Austrian schools (with the exception of primary schools). Full-time teachers are partially released from their normal activities to provide counselling. Guidance counsellors receive on-going training through the Federal Ministry of Education and the Arts.

Their work focuses on providing:

- information on the educational options offered at their particular school;

- information on educational options offered by the education system as a whole.

In addition, there is close cooperation with the Labour Exchanges, which fulfil an important role in providing vocational/careers guidance at school.

Presentations at parents' evenings and one-to-one counselling during consultation hours also form part of the services offered.

2. Pre-school education (Vorschulerziehung)

Nursery school (*kindergarten*) is the traditional form of pre-school education for children aged 3 to 6 in Austria. However, it does not form part of the education system. Nursery school is optional and children attend at their parents' initiative.

In 1991/92, 85.6% of all children in Austria from five to six years old attended nursery schools (in 1960/61 the corresponding figure was only 23.5%). There are striking regional differences in the degree of nursery school provision.

Anyone wishing to open a nursery school has to comply with a number of conditions to ensure that the educational mandate of nursery school is observed. There are public kindergartens (established and maintained by the Federation, the *Länder* or the municipalities) and private kindergartens. Some of the private kindergartens are administered by educators and parents as autonomous groups. The majority of kindergartens have been set up by the municipalities (almost 75%).

Staff and operational costs are generally borne by the administering body. The contributions made by the *Länder* to the cost of the establishment and operation of a kindergarten vary considerably; this is true in particular for private kindergartens.

Private kindergartens which are run by associations, churches or religious orders receive grants towards meeting the cost of staff and overheads on certain conditions, either on a discretionary basis, or according to a fixed percentage rate in accordance with the applicable Nursery School Act. Private kindergartens run by other bodies than the above-mentioned generally do not receive any financial support.

Some kindergartens do not charge any fees at all, while many municipalities charge a kindergarten attendance fee according to a graded scheme adjusted to net family income. Private kindergartens similarly charge varying amounts.

Nursery education focuses on developing the child's personality as a whole and is not primarily concerned with preparing children for school.

To achieve this objective, kindergartens are run in small, generally coeducational, groups (either age groups or so called 'family groups' – 3-, 4- and 5-year-olds mixed up) taking individual styles and approaches into account and systematically providing different games and materials. First and foremost a child at nursery school should have the chance of gaining experiences through appropriate play activities without the pressure of time or achievement.

Nursery schooling is either full-day or half-day. Half-day kindergarten lasts from at least 7.00 a.m. to 12.00 a.m., with the possibility of lunch. Full-day kindergarten lasts from 7.00 a.m. to 7.00 p.m. and includes lunch. Parents may pick up their children whenever they want. Many kindergartens are open throughout the year.

Staff

Kindergarten staff are either trained in special schools at upper secondary level or in special training colleges at post-secondary level. The latter consist of a two-year teacher training course for those who have passed a matriculation examination; they will also be open to those who have not passed such an examination but have worked in related occupational fields. The latter have to pass a special entrance examination. These colleges constitute a major reform in the kindergarten sector.

Statistics 1993/94

Children aged three to five in public kindergartens	
Children	196,204
Staff*	15,733
Kindergarten	4,100

* excluding technical cleaning and kitchen staff.

Source: Die Kindergärten (Kindertagesheime), Berichtsjahr 1993/94, Beiträge zur Österreichischen Statistik, (ed.) Austrian Central Statistical Office, Volume 1,139, Vienna 1994.

3. Compulsory education

Compulsory schooling in Austria lasts for nine years. It applies to all children permanently residing in Austria, regardless of their nationality. Compulsory school age starts on 1 September following the child's sixth birthday and ends at the age of 15 (nine years).

Public schools in Austria are free. Parents are obliged to register their child at the appropriate school – in most cases the school nearest to the place of residence – and to make sure that he/she attends on a regular basis. If a child has his/her 6th birthday between 1 September and 31 December, and provided he/she is physically and mentally mature enough to attend classes, he/she may – at the discretion of the head teacher – be admitted early to the first grade of primary school.

The nine years of compulsory schooling can be completed in either of the following ways:

- Years 1 to 4
  primary school;
  special school (1).

- Years 5 to 8
  general secondary school;
  years 1 to 4 of academic secondary school;
  upper level of primary school (1);
  upper level of special school (1).

- Year 9
  a pre-vocational year;
  continuation of primary school, general secondary school or special school (2);
  year 1 of an intermediate or higher secondary vocational and technical college;
  year 1 of a kindergarten teacher training college or a training college for non-teaching supervisory staff;
  year 5 of an academic secondary school.

(1) These schools are attended by a small fraction of each age level only.

(2) For pupils who have had to repeat one or several years.

There is no certificate marking the end of compulsory education, but in the annual report at the end of year 9 it is mentioned that the pupil has completed compulsory education.

School time

Depending on the *Land*, the school year starts on the first or second Monday in September and ends on the Friday between June 27 and July 3, or July 4 and 10 respectively. There are two semesters, separated by a one-week holiday, the last week of January or one of the first three weeks in February. The main summer holidays are the months of July and August. Other holidays are at Christmas and at Easter.

Head teachers are responsible for ensuring that the total number of weekly lessons as laid down in the curriculum is evenly spread over the days of the week. Primary schools have a five- or six-day week, secondary schools generally have a six-day week. On the basis of a six-day week there are about 215 school days per year. In general, classes must not begin before 8.00 a.m. or last longer than six hours in the morning (if the afternoon is free) or five hours (if there are afternoon classes). A lesson lasts for 50 minutes. Sufficient breaks of at least 5 minutes, but no longer than 20 minutes, are to intersperse the lessons.

3.1 Primary education (*Primarbereich*)

Primary education covers four years (1 to 4) and is provided at primary schools (*Volksschule/Grundschule*).

While primary schools actually extend beyond the primary level (years 1 to 8, including the upper level of primary school), they are currently represented almost exclusively by primary school proper (years 1 to 4), as the upper level, covering secondary level, has been more or less abolished. Primary schools also offer a pre-primary year (*Vorschulstufe*) to some 6-year-olds, who then will have spent five years at primary level.

3.1.1 Pre-primary year at school

The pre-primary year precedes primary school and is designed to foster the development of children of compulsory school age who are not yet mature enough to attend primary school proper. However, unlike nursery school, the pre-primary year is part of the school system.

The decision on whether or not a child should enter a pre-primary class is taken when the child is registered by his/her parents to enter compulsory schooling. At the time of registration, the head teacher of the primary school assesses the child's maturity by means of a series of simple questions, such as counting objects, naming colours and providing his/her name and address. Children who have already been admitted to the first year of primary school may be deferred to the next school year if they later prove not to be mature enough. This decision has to be taken before 31 December.

The number of children determines whether the pre-primary course is run as a class or as a group. Pre-primary classes are run with more than 10 children (20 weekly units/lessons); less than 10 children form a pre-primary group (8 – 10 weekly lessons).

The educational content of the pre-primary year comprises compulsory practical exercises in the following subjects, totalling 20 weekly lessons:

– religious instruction

– local history, geography, biology

– road safety

– language and oral expression

– early mathematics

– singing and music-making

– exercises in rhythm

– drawing

– crafts

– physical education

– playing.

In the pre-primary year there is no assessment of achievement; the annual report is a certificate of attendance.

3.1.2 Primary school

It is the objective of primary school to provide a common basic education for all pupils.

Classes are coeducational. The maximum number of pupils per class is 30, and each primary school grade corresponds to one class. If the number of pupils in each year is too small, several years may be combined in one class. Teachers are class teachers, and spend the four years with the same class of children.

Pre-school classes are often accommodated in a primary school, which might be located in the same building as, or in a building adjacent to, a general secondary school, depending on the local situation.

Curriculum

At present, two slightly varying sets of approved subject hours for primary schools exist.

One is as follows:

Compulsory subjects	Years and number of weekly lessons			
	1st	2nd	3rd	4th
Religious instruction	2	2	2	2
Local history, geography, biology	3	3	3	3
German, reading, writing	7	7	–	–
German, reading	–	–	7	7
Mathematics	4	4	4	4
Music	1	1	1	1
Drawing	1	1	–	–
Drawing, writing	–	–	2	2
Handicraft	1	1	2	2
Physical education	2	2	3	3

Compulsory practical exercises				
Modern foreign language	–	–	1	1
Road safety [1]	×	×	×	×
Total number of weekly lessons	21	21	25	25

[1] Ten annual lessons for each year to be considered during the overall planning of lessons for individual subjects.

The teaching of a modern foreign language (English, French, Italian, Croatian, Slovenian, Hungarian, Czech or Slovak) starts as early as the 3rd year as a compulsory practical exercise (no assessment of achievement). However, in most schools it is English. Compulsory subjects and compulsory practical exercises are taught to mixed-ability groups. Optional exercises may be chosen on a voluntary basis.

Teachers are free to decide on the **teaching methods** and **materials** they use. However, the form and contents of the latter must comply with the curriculum for the particular year and be suited to children of that age. Both head teachers and school inspectors are entitled to issue directives to teachers on this matter.

Assessment

General Provisions

As far as assessment procedures, marking, the repetition of years and reports are concerned, a distinction has to be made between general provisions, applying to all schools, and specific regulations that refer to certain types of schools only.

As a general rule, performance assessment should be evenly spread over the school year.

Performance is determined by:

- assessing the active participation of pupils in class work;

- oral assessment;

- written assessment (class assignments, tests, dictations);

- practical assessment;

- graphic assessment (e.g. in subjects like descriptive geometry).

Teachers are responsible for all assessments; they generally assess individual skills and capabilities in individual subjects. Marks range from 1 to 5.

Compulsory and optional subjects are both graded. School reports are a summary of pupils' achievements. Schools issue termly reports (at the end of the first semester), annual reports (at the end of the year) and certificates (after successful completion of a particular type of school).

The annual report considers pupils' achievement during the entire year, but particular weight is given to the most recent assessment. Pupils are graded as follows: very good (1), good (2), satisfactory (3), sufficient (4), insufficient (5).

As a general rule, pupils are entitled to enter the next year if they have been assessed in all compulsory subjects and never rated 'insufficient', although the law in fact provides for the possibility of teachers allowing pupils to progress to the next year with one 'insufficient' rating. This, however, is the exception. Pupils who are rated 'insufficient' in no more than two subjects must usually sit a repeat test at the beginning of the following school year. If they fail or if they have more then two 'insufficient' ratings, they have to repeat the year.

Specific Regulations for Primary Schools

In primary schools, achievement is determined by assessing pupil's participation in class work, and in the 4th year by school tests (written assessment). There is no oral assessment.

Primary schools issue termly reports and annual reports.

The first two years of primary education are one cycle. The first-years are entitled to enter the second year regardless of their assessment in the annual report. Pupils who are not entitled to pass to the next year may repeat the year they have failed. In contrast to secondary schooling, there is no repeat examination.

Children whose mother tongue is not German receive remedial teaching, mainly in the German language, either separately or as part of classroom teaching. There are:

- remedial language lessons to improve German-language skills,

- remedial teachers who concentrate particularly on children with poor German-language skills, etc.

In addition, teachers can decide that supplementary teaching of a general nature should be given to any pupils needing remedial teaching in German or mathematics.

In the course of the fourth year, either towards the end of the first term or at the beginning of the second term of the school year, parents or guardians are informed about the further educational possibilities for their child on the basis of his/her interests and past achievements.

3.1.3 Teachers

Teachers for the pre-primary year and primary school and teachers in special schools are trained at non-university level Teacher Training Colleges (*Pädagogische Akademien*).

Candidates for teacher training colleges must have passed their matriculation examination at an academic secondary or a higher secondary technical and vocational school, or must have passed a special entrance examination (*Studien-berechtigungsprüfung*).

The training course lasts at least six semesters (three years) and is completed by a teaching qualification examination.

Prospective primary school teachers acquire the whole range of skills necessary for teaching all subjects in primary and pre-primary education. There may be specialized teachers for religion, crafts and foreign languages.

Primary school teachers are provincial employees (i.e. civil servants) under either a private-law or a public-law contract (tenured service). Part-time employment is possible in some cases.

The law comprising the rights and duties of teachers is very vague on the subject of compulsory in-service training and primarily refers to personal initiative; participation is not compulsory. One-third of in-service training activities are attended during the holidays, two-thirds during the school year.

3.1.4 Statistics 1993/94

Primary schools (including pre-primary schools)	
Pupils	382,204
Teachers*	30,807
Schools	3,384
Pupil/teacher ratio	12.4
Pupil/class ratio	19.7

* In this and all further tables teachers are counted by heads, both full-time and part-time.

Pre-primary education at primary schools	
Pupils	9,699
Pre-primary classes and groups	913

Source: Austrian School Statistics 93/94, (ed.) Federal Ministry of Education and the Arts in cooperation with the Austrian Central Statistical Office, Vienna 1994.

3.2 Secondary education: lower level

The first division into separately organized school types occurs at the lower level of secondary education, that is:

– General secondary school (*Hauptschule*);

– Academic secondary school – lower level; (*Allgemeinbildende Höhere Schule, AHS-Unterstufe*);

– Upper level of primary school (*Volksschuloberstufe*).

About 30% of all primary school leavers in Austria attend academic secondary school, while about 70% go to general secondary school. The number going into the upper level of primary school is negligible.

Pupils must have successfully completed the fourth year of primary school to be admitted to general secondary school. In order to be admitted to an academic secondary school, they must have been rated 'very good' or 'good' in German, reading and mathematics. Pupils who do not meet these standards have to pass an admission test.

3.2.1 General secondary school

General secondary school covers years 5 to 8 (10- to 14-year-olds), and provides general education in coeducational classes.

It prepares pupils for employment and for the transition to intermediate and higher secondary schools. The size of general secondary schools varies for regional and demographic reasons. They are often accommodated in the same building as or one adjacent to a primary school. They are maintained by a municipality or municipal association.

General secondary classes are organized as follows:

– Pupils are allocated to one of three ability groups in German, mathematics and the modern foreign language after an observation period (generally 8 to 10 weeks). The educational requirements and aims in the top ability group correspond to those of the academic secondary school. Within one ability group pupils generally have approximately the same level of ability; however, internal differentiation is possible.

- In all other subjects there is mixed ability teaching within established classes.

- Pupils may be transferred to the next higher or next lower ability group at two dates in year 1, and at three dates in years 2 to 4.

- Compulsory preparatory/remedial teaching is provided to pupils upgraded to a higher group or those facing downgrading.

- Pupils with good results in a general secondary school may transfer directly to an academic secondary school.

Curriculum

The approved number of hours per subject at general secondary schools are usually as follows (schools drawing up their own curricula within the framework of school autonomy are entitled to alter subject hours within certain limits):

Compulsory subjects	Years and weekly lessons				Total
	1st	2nd	3rd	4th	
Religious instruction	2	2	2	2	8
German	5	5	4	4	18
Modern foreign language	5	4	3	3	15
History and social studies	–	3	2	2	7
Geography and economics	2	2	2	2	8
Mathematics	5	4	4	4	17
Geometry	–	–	1.5	1.5	3
Biology and environmental education	3	2	2	2	9
Physics and chemistry	–	2	2	4	8
Music	2	2	2	1	7
Drawing, writing	2	2	2	2	8
Handicraft	2	2	–	–	4
Elementary technical work ('technology')[1]	–	–	2	2	4
Textile work[1]	–	–	2	2	4
Home economics	–	–	1.5	1.5	3
Physical education	4	4	3	3	14
Total weekly lessons	32	34	33	34	133

[1] alternative compulsory subject.

There are also optional subjects and practical exercises. Home economics and the alternative compulsory subjects 'technology' and 'textile work' must be taught in coeducational groups, if chosen by both girls and boys. In principle, general secondary schools teach English as a modern foreign language; some offer French or Italian.

Teachers are free to decide on the **teaching methods** and **materials** they use. However, the form and contents of the latter must comply with the curriculum for the particular year and be suited to children of that age. Both head teachers and school inspectors are entitled to issue directives to teachers on this matter.

Assessment and qualifications

The general rules for assessment procedures, marking and reports are the same as described under 'General Provisions' in 3.1.2.

Pupils are generally allowed to move to the next year if they have been assessed in all compulsory subjects and are not rated 'insufficient' in their annual report. The following distinctions have to be made between 'insufficient' ratings in the annual report:

- 'Insufficient' rating in an ability group subject (1st and 2nd ability group). There is no repeat examination; the pupils are allowed to move to the next year where they have to attend the lower ability group.

- 'Insufficient' rating in an ability group subject (3rd ability group) and/or in one or two other compulsory subjects. The pupils have to sit a repeat examination. Such an examination cannot be taken in more than two subjects. In some cases, however, which are referred to in the relevant law, it is possible to move to the next year with **one** 'insufficient' rating.

Pupils who have successfully completed general secondary school (without repeating years) may be admitted to the pre-vocational year to complete compulsory education (see 3.2.3). They may also choose to go to an intermediate or higher secondary technical and vocational college, most of which operate admission tests (see 4.1.2 and 4.1.3), or to an academic secondary school. At the end of the general secondary school a certificate (*Hauptschulabschlußzeugnis*) is issued.

For transition to the fifth year of academic secondary school, without an admission test, pupils must have been assessed 'sufficient' in German, mathematics and the modern foreign language if they were in the first ability group, and rated at least 'good' in the second ability group; and have been assessed at least 'satisfactory' in all other compulsory subjects.

Pupils have to sit admission tests in compulsory subjects for which they have received lower grades than these. Additional admission examinations are held in subjects which general secondary schools either do not teach at all, or teach at a much lower standard than the lower level of academic secondary school.

There are no such additional admission examinations for the *Oberstufenrealgymnasium* (a separate upper-level form of the academic secondary school), which builds on the curriculum of the general secondary school (see 4.1.1).

Pupils who have completed their compulsory education at the end of general secondary school may seek employment or take up apprenticeship training (see 5.).

Teachers

General secondary school and pre-vocational year teachers, like primary and special school teachers, follow post-matriculation training at Teacher Training Colleges.

The training course lasts at least six semesters (three years) and ends with a teaching qualification examination.

Teachers for general secondary schools and the pre-vocational year are qualified in two subjects (subject teacher system). They teach their subjects in various classes and, provided that it is one of the ability group subjects, in various ability groups. In general secondary school, teachers often teach their subjects to the same class for all four years, although changes may be necessary for various reasons (e.g. maternity leave). From the pedagogical point of view continuity is recommended.

As regards employment and in-service training, the situation is the same as for primary education *mutatis mutandis*.

Statistics 1993/94

General secondary schools	
Pupils	267,359
Teachers	34,239
Schools	1,179
Pupil/teacher ratio	7.8
Pupil/class ratio	23.3

Source: Austrian School Statistics 93/94, (ed.) Federal Ministry of Education and the Arts in cooperation with the Austrian Central Statistical Office, Vienna 1994.

3.2.2 Academic secondary school/lower level (Allgemeinbildende höhere Schule, AHS – Unterstufe)

Academic secondary school comprises four years at the lower level (10- to 14-year-olds) and four years at the upper level (14- to 18-year-olds).

This chapter on the lower level of secondary education deals with the lower level of academic secondary school (*AHS – Unterstufe*).

The lower level of the two-level *AHS* is organized in coeducational classes according to age, and provides a comprehensive and in-depth general education. It has a dual function, since it both prepares pupils for the corresponding *AHS* upper level and also enables them to transfer to vocational schools.

The size of each *AHS* varies for regional and demographic reasons. The number of schools is considerably lower than that of general secondary schools. Pupils must sometimes travel long distances to school or attend boarding schools. Academic secondary schools are less integrated in the local communities than primary or general secondary schools.

The first two years of the lower level are uniformly organized, run according to a common curriculum and serve as a period of observation and orientation. The curriculum corresponds to that of general secondary schools. A modern foreign language is taught from the first year onwards.

In the third year a division into three types takes place:

– *Gymnasium* (including Latin);

– *Realgymnasium* (with geometry and an emphasis on mathematics and handicrafts); and

– *Wirtschaftskundliches Realgymnasium* (with an emphasis on chemistry and handicrafts).

There is no ability grouping.

Curriculum

The approved number of hours per subject at the lower level of academic secondary school are as follows (the differences in years three and four between the *Gymnasium* and the other two types are marked in brackets, first for the *Realgymnasium*, then for the *Wirtschaftskundliches Realgymnasium*):

Compulsory subjects	Years and weekly lessons			
	1st	2nd	3rd	4th
Religious instruction	2	2	2	2
German	5	5	4	4
Modern foreign language	5	4	3	3
Latin	–	–	5(-,-)	5(-,-)
History and social studies	–	3	2	2
Geography and economics	2	2	2	2
Mathematics	5	4	3(4,3)	3(4,3)
Geometry	–	–	–(2,-)	–(2,-)
Biology and environmental education	3	2	2	2
Chemistry	–	–	–(2,-)	2
Physics	–	2	2	2
Music	2	2	2	–(1,2)
Arts	2	2	2	2
Handicraft	2	2	–	–
Technology/Textile Work*)	–	–	–(2,3)	–(2,4)
Physical education	4	4	4	3
Total weekly lessons	32	34	33	33

* alternative compulsory subject.

There are also optional subjects and practical exercises.

Teachers are free to decide on the **teaching methods** and **materials** they use. However, the form and contents of the latter must comply with the curriculum for the particular year and be suited to children of that age. Both head teachers and school inspectors are entitled to issue directives to teachers on this matter.

Assessment

The general rules for assessment procedures, marking and reports are the same as described under 'General Provisions' in 3.1.2.

Pupils are generally allowed to move to the next year, if assessed in all compulsory subjects and not rated 'insufficient' in the annual report. Pupils with an 'insufficient' rating in one or two compulsory subjects may sit a repeat examination at the beginning of the next school year and provided they pass may move on to the next year. (In some cases, referred to in the relevant law, it is possible to move to the next year with **one** 'insufficient' rating). Pupils

not entitled to move to the next year may repeat the year they failed provided that the maximum number of years allowed for attending the eight forms of *AHS* (10 years) is not exceeded.

Pupils with temporary difficulties in a subject may, on the recommendation of a teacher, attend remedial teaching on a voluntary basis in German, foreign languages, mathematics and geometry. Remedial teaching is provided in two weekly lessons for a duration of eight weeks at the most.

Teachers

Teachers at academic secondary schools are trained at universities or fine arts colleges. Courses for qualifying as a teacher are defined as diploma studies. They last nine semesters (four-and-a-half years). Students must pass two diploma examinations and submit a diploma paper in order to graduate with an academic degree (*Magister*). Studies include academic training, generally in two subjects, pedagogical training in the last 5 semesters, and a *Schulpraktikum* comprising a 4-week introductory phase and 8 weeks of teaching practice.

The *Magister* diploma does not automatically entitle candidates to a permanent teaching post. Prior to being permanently employed, graduates have to successfully complete both a year of teaching in a school and additional courses (*Unterrichtspraktikum*).

Teachers at academic secondary schools are federal employees, under either a private-law contract or a public-law contract (tenured service). Part-time employment is possible, but not usual.

As regards in-service teacher training, the situation is the same as at primary level.

Statistics 1993/94

Lower and upper level of academic secondary school	
Pupils	172,437
Teachers	18,934
Schools	312
Pupil/teacher ratio	9.1
Pupil/class ratio	24.6

Source: Austrian School Statistics 93/94, (ed.) Federal Ministry of Education and the Arts in cooperation with the Austrian Central Statistical Office, Vienna 1994.

3.2.3 Pre-vocational year (Polytechnischer Lehrgang)

The pre-vocational year mainly concerns the 14 to 15 age-group, i.e. pupils in the ninth year wishing to learn an occupation immediately after the completion of compulsory schooling. The pre-vocational year complements young people's basic education, leading to working life by preparing them for a specific occupation.

By providing a wide selection of information and by familiarizing pupils with different working methods and the local work environment (vocational guidance), the pre-vocational year facilitates career choice.

Compulsory subjects (33.5 weekly lessons) are differentiated according to the occupation concerned, allowing pupils to select 9 weekly lessons of elective compulsory subjects from fields such as technology, industry and commerce, social studies and biology or agriculture. Pupils may furthermore enrol for 6 weekly lessons of optional subjects and optional exercises. German, English and mathematics are taught as compulsory subjects in three ability groups. Company visits and all-day practicals in trainee workshops, vocational schools or companies familiarize pupils with the work environment. All pupils in the pre-vocational year learn how to use a computer for practical and vocational purposes, in particular as part of the elective compulsory subjects.

Depending on the local situation, the pre-vocational year is run either in a separate school or in conjunction with a school of general compulsory education.

Statistics 1993/94

Pre-vocational year	
Pupils	18,174
Teachers	(1,649*)
Schools	
Pupil/teacher ratio	figures not available
Pupil/class ratio	21.0

* Teachers at separately organized pre-vocational schools.

Source: Austrian School Statistics 93/94, (ed.) Federal Ministry of Education and the Arts in cooperation with the Austrian Central Statistical Office, Vienna 1994.

3.2.4 Options after completion of lower secondary schooling

The critical time for selecting further education is one year before the completion of compulsory education. At this point, almost 100% of all pupils attend general secondary school (more than two-thirds) or the lower level of academic secondary school (less than one-third).

Of the **general secondary school leavers**:

– 44% opt for the pre-vocational year or apprenticeship training;

– 45% opt for an intermediate or higher secondary technical or vocational college;

– approximately 5% attend the upper level of academic secondary school;

– another 5% repeat the last year or leave school.

Of the **lower-level academic secondary school leavers**:

– more than 60% continue to the upper level of academic secondary school;

– more than 30% opt for an intermediate or (in most cases) higher secondary technical or vocational college;

– all others take up apprenticeship training, repeat a year, or leave school.

100% of all pupils who are capable of schooling complete compulsory education, in whichever school type. Approximately 99% of pupils opt for further education or apprenticeship training after completion of compulsory schooling. Since 1970, the percentage of young people not opting for any further education or apprenticeship training immediately after completion of compulsory schooling has fallen from 18% to approximately one percent.

4. Post-compulsory education

4.1 Secondary education: upper level

At upper secondary level the differentiation in the school system becomes more marked due to the more clearly discernible interests and talents of pupils, as well as the requirements of society for different forms of vocational qualifications.

Besides academic secondary schools, years 9 to 13 (14- to 19-year-olds) are also provided in secondary technical and vocational schools.

The upper level of secondary education therefore comprises the following school types:

- pre-vocational year (see 3.2.3);

- upper level of academic secondary school (years 9 to 12);

- vocational school (years 10 to 13 maximum) – parallel to in-company vocational training ('dual system') (see 5.);

- intermediate technical and vocational colleges (years 9 to 12 maximum);

- higher technical and vocational colleges (years 9 to 13);

- Kindergarten Teacher Training College (years 9 to 13);

- Training College for Non-Teaching Supervisory Staff (years 9 to 13).

Academic secondary schools, higher technical and vocational schools, and the training colleges for kindergarten teachers and non-teaching supervisory staff lead to the matriculation examination certificate, which entitles the holder to university studies.

The principles of the organization of school time are the same as in compulsory education (see 3.).

Classes are coeducational and generally made up of pupils of the same age group. There is no ability grouping in the upper level of secondary education.

4.1.1 Academic secondary school/ upper level (Allgemeinbildende höhere Schule, AHS – Oberstufe)

It is the task of the upper level of *AHS* to give pupils a comprehensive and in-depth general education and to prepare them for university studies. The upper level comprises 4 years (9 to 12) for 14- to 18-year-olds, and builds on the 4 years (5 to 8) of the lower level.

General information on the academic secondary school is in section 3.2.2.

The upper level comprises the same three types as years 3 and 4 at the lower level: *Gymnasium, Realgymnasium and Wirtschaftskundliches Realgymnasium*, but they are characterized as follows:

- *Gymnasium:* in addition to Latin, pupils from the 5th year onwards learn either a second modern foreign language or Greek;

- *Realgymnasium:* more mathematics from the 5th year onwards, as well as Latin or a second modern foreign language; also geometry or more biology and environmental education, chemistry and physics;

- *Wirtschaftskundliches Realgymnasium:* from the 5th year onwards, a second modern foreign language or Latin; also home economics and nutrition, more geography and economics, biology and environmental education, psychology and philosophy.

There is also a separate upper-level type of academic school (years 5 to 8), the *Oberstufenrealgymnasium*, entered on completion of eight years of general education. Pupils learn a second modern foreign language or Latin from the 5th year onwards. They may choose between three orientations: musical instrument playing, design and crafts, or more biology and environmental science, chemistry and physics. This type of school has made the upper level of secondary education accessible to pupils from regions where other upper secondary schools do not exist (in particular for general secondary school leavers).

Curriculum

The common curriculum covers most of the compulsory subjects in the curriculum for the lower level.

In all three types, as well as in the *Oberstufenrealgymnasium*, elective compulsory subjects amounting to 8 weekly lessons (*Gymnasium, Oberstufenrealgymnasium*), 10 weekly lessons (*Realgymnasium*) and 12 weekly lessons (*Wirtschaftskundliches Realgymnasium*) must be chosen in years 6 to 8. Computer science is taught as a compulsory subject (2 weekly lessons) in the fifth year of all types.

Assessment and qualifications

The general rules for assessment procedures, marking and reports are described under 'General Provisions' in 3.1.2.

Academic secondary school, like all other upper secondary schools, ends with a matriculation examination (*Matura*). Students who have passed this examination and obtained the matriculation examination certificate (*Reifeprüfungszeugnis*) are called 'Maturanten' (upper secondary school leavers). The matriculation examination certificate provides access to university studies. All candidates who have completed the last year successfully are entitled to sit the matriculation examination at the main examination date. It is also possible to do so with just one 'insufficient' rating.

As of the school year 1992/93, the matriculation examination was reformed. The new leaving examination at academic secondary schools now comprises two equivalent *Matura* options:

- seven examinations (some written, some oral) in at least four different subject areas; or

- the submission of a paper on a specialized field of study (*Fachbereichsarbeit*), instead of one of the written examinations, which must be finished during the first semester of the 8th year.

4.1.2 Intermediate secondary technical and vocational colleges *(Berufsbildende mittlere Schulen – BMS)*

Intermediate secondary technical and vocational colleges provide not only a thorough general education but also practical vocational training for specific occupations. They are full-time schools (except for the colleges for working adults).

Pupils are generally accepted after successful completion of the 8th year (i.e. at the age of 14) and after passing an aptitude test. Depending on the sector they cover, these schools have courses lasting from one to four years.

Courses focus on practical training in school workshops, laboratories and practical rooms. Pupils must take part in compulsory practical training in companies or enterprises during their summer holidays (the number and duration of these training periods is laid down in the curriculum; in the commercial and trade schools summer work placements are voluntary).

The conditions for moving to the next year are laid down by law (see also 3.2.2 Assessment).

After completion of this type of school pupils may take the matriculation examination by attending supplementary bridging courses. These courses (4 to 6 semesters) are organized on request, for some sectors only, and not in all parts of the country.

Pupils successfully completing at least three years at an intermediate secondary technical or vocational college have access to the regulated trades.

Intermediate secondary technical and vocational colleges cover the following major sectors:

- agriculture and forestry;

- industry and trade (combination of training in commerce and tourism);

- commerce

  * secretarial and administrative

  * business (intermediate commercial schools);

- industrial, technical, arts and crafts

  * industrial and technical

  * textile industry

  * tourism

  * arts and crafts;

- social work;

- nursing professions (governed by the Nursing Act);

- medico-technical professions (governed by the Nursing Act).

Since 1984/85, the number of pupils at intermediate secondary technical and vocational colleges, especially at commercial colleges, has been falling by some 4% annually. This is explained by a trend towards the higher secondary technical and vocational colleges, which lead to the matriculation examination.

4.1.3 Higher secondary technical and vocational colleges (Berufsbildende höhere Schulen – BHS)

To be admitted to a higher secondary technical and vocational college pupils must have successfully completed the 8th year and passed an aptitude test.

Higher secondary technical and vocational colleges provide general and vocational education (**double qualification**), and lead both to the exercise of an occupation and to university (matriculation examination). Education is full-time and lasts 5 years.

The curriculum is divided into three equal parts: general education, vocational theory and vocational practice (in school workshops, laboratories, kitchens and other practical rooms).

Pupils at higher secondary technical and vocational schools must take part in compulsory practical training in business and industry during the summer holidays (the number and duration of these training periods is laid down in the curriculum; in commercial schools practical training periods are voluntary).

Pupils successfully completing higher secondary technical and vocational colleges are entitled to practise their own trade after three years of professional experience. They may also have access to the regulated trades.

After these three years of professional experience in their field, those who have completed higher secondary technical colleges and higher secondary colleges of agriculture and forestry may be called 'Ingenieur'.

The most important higher secondary technical and vocational colleges are:

- higher secondary technical college (branches: mechanical engineering, electrical engineering, electronic engineering, electronic data processing and organization, civil engineering and construction, chemistry, textile engineering, business engineering, etc.);

- higher secondary college for fashion and garment technology;

- higher secondary college for tourism;

- higher secondary college for commerce (Handelsakademie);

- higher secondary college for industry and trade;

- higher secondary college for agriculture and forestry (branches: agriculture, horticulture, viticulture, fruit farming, forestry, dairy farming, etc.).

There are some 50% more pupils at higher secondary technical and vocational colleges than in the upper level of academic secondary schools.

Teachers

Teachers are subject specialists. Training courses entitle teachers to teach their subjects at both technical and vocational colleges (which are frequently part of the same building). The nature of training courses and admission requirements depend on the subjects to be taught.

The training of teachers of general subjects in intermediate and higher technical and vocational colleges is the same as that of academic secondary school teachers (see 3.2.2).

Teachers of business and management are also trained at university for a minimum of 4½ years (9 semesters). The course comprises academic and pedagogical training (education sciences, pedagogy and methodology in the last 5 semesters and 1 semester of teaching practice) and leads to a *Magister* degree and Teaching Diploma. To obtain a teaching contract, 2 years of experience in the profession concerned is also required.

Teachers of engineering and law must hold a university degree (*Magister*) in the fields of specialization and have 4 years of professional experience. They follow 6 weeks of training during the first 2 years of their teaching contract at an in-service teacher training college (*Pädagogisches Institut*). This covers education sciences, pedagogy and methodology, the relevant field and school legislation, and leads to a teaching certificate.

Teachers of vocational practice (word-processing, shorthand, etc.) must hold a matriculation examination certificate and have 1 or 2 years of professional experience. They then complete two years of full-time studies at a Technical and Vocational Teacher Training College, covering education sciences, pedagogy and methodology, the relevant subject areas and school legislation, leading to a Teaching Diploma.

Domestic science teachers must also hold a matriculation examination certificate and follow a 2- to 3-year course at a Technical and Vocational Teacher Training College, leading to a Teaching Diploma. To be eligible for a teaching contract, they must have 1 year of professional experience.

All teachers are public employees. As regards in-service training, the situation is the same as at primary level.

4.1.4 Training Colleges for Non-Teaching Supervisory Staff, Kindergarten Teacher Training Colleges

The **Training College for Non-Teaching Supervisory Staff** trains supervisory staff for day care centres and boarding establishments for children and adolescents, as well as for supervision outside school hours.

Admission is conditional upon the successful completion of the 8th year and passing an aptitude test. The courses at this college last 5 years and end with a matriculation examination and a professional qualification, entitling the student to study at a university or academy.

A two-year course is offered to upper secondary school leavers.

The admission criteria and the prescribed duration of studies for the **Kindergarten Teacher Training College** are identical to those for Training Colleges for Non-teaching Supervisory Staff. Courses again end with a matriculation examination and a professional qualification, entitling the student to enrol in university studies.

The establishment of a two-year course for upper secondary school leavers is under way.

The curriculum for both colleges comprises general education, such as German, a modern foreign language, history, geography, mathematics, physics, chemistry, biology, music and physical education, and also job-oriented subjects. The theoretical part takes place at the colleges, while the practical part is in normal nursery schools, or in day care centres or boarding establishments respectively. Students practise under the supervision of specially trained nursery school teachers, or non-teaching supervisory staff.

4.1.5 Statistics 1993/94

Upper level of academic secondary schools and intermediate and higher technical and vocational colleges

	academic secondary schools – upper level	intermediate technical + vocational colleges	higher technical + vocational colleges
Pupils	69,272	53,613	99,971
Teachers	not available	not available	not available
Schools	310	502	265
Pupil/teacher ratio	not available	not available	not available
Pupil/class ratio	21.8	21.4	22.8

Source: Austrian School Statistics 93/94, (ed.) Federal Ministry of Education and the Arts in cooperation with the Austrian Central Statistical Office, Vienna 1994.

4.2 Higher non-university education

There are few non-university higher education options in Austria. However, a *Fachhochschule* study course (in post-secondary special-subject colleges) will be established in 1994/95 (see 6.). The following options are currently available:

- Teacher Training Colleges, Training Colleges for Religious Education Teachers, Technical and Vocational Teacher Training Colleges;

- Colleges for Social Workers;

- Paramedical Colleges;

- Specialized post-matriculation courses for technical and commercial professions.

As mentioned above, Teacher Training Colleges train teachers for primary school, general secondary school, special schools and for the pre-vocational year. Separate teacher training colleges train religious education teachers.

As also mentioned above, Technical and Vocational Teacher Training Colleges train vocational teachers for some fields of instruction in intermediate and higher secondary technical and vocational colleges.

Colleges for Social Workers train social workers; the course lasts 6 semesters.

Non-university training at Paramedical Colleges is divided into seven different branches. The minimum length of training is two years.

These forms of post-secondary education cater primarily for upper secondary school leavers, but admission is also possible via preparatory courses or aptitude tests.

Academic secondary school leavers may receive vocational training in specialized post-matriculation courses (of 4 to 6 semesters) in commerce, crafts, trade and tourism. Higher technical and vocational college leavers studying at these post-secondary colleges may obtain an additional vocational qualification (e.g. higher technical colleges leavers may attend a post-secondary commercial college). In some disciplines, specialized post-matriculation colleges have been introduced to provide ongoing professional training for secondary vocational and technical college leavers.

Statistics 1993/94

	Students
Teacher training college	7,083
Training college for religious education teachers	789
Technical and vocational teacher training college	575
Colleges for social workers	1,262

Source: Austrian School Statistics 93/94, (ed.) Federal Ministry of Education and the Arts in cooperation with the Austrian Central Statistical Office, Vienna 1994.

5. Initial vocational training

In addition to training at intermediate and higher secondary technical and vocational colleges (see 4.1.3 and 4.1.4) a considerable amount of initial vocational training is provided by apprenticeship training schemes ('dual system').

Apprenticeship training has always been characterized by the dual system of training in business or industry, combined with a theoretical course at a compulsory vocational school. Whilst apprenticeship is based on an apprenticeship contract under labour law, apprentices are still considered to be in compulsory education because they must enrol in a part-time vocational school.

50% of all young people aged 15 to 18 are prepared for their future occupation within the dual apprenticeship training scheme.

More than 60,000 enterprises and companies take part in the apprenticeship training scheme, especially small and medium-sized companies in the fields of commerce and trade, crafts and tourism, which train approximately 80% of all apprentices. Industrial enterprises and their state-of-the-art training workshops also make a significant contribution to the training of young people.

At present, a total of 220 occupations and trades are covered by the apprenticeship scheme. The most popular ones with female apprentices are sales, hairdressing, clerical work, waitress/cook; male apprentices prefer such occupations as car mechanic, joiner and carpenter, plumber and electrician, bricklayer and machine operator.

Part-time compulsory vocational school (*Berufsschule*)

All apprentices attend a part-time compulsory vocational school from the time they enter their apprenticeship until it is completed, i.e. until the successful completion of the last year provided in the vocational school in question. Apprenticeship training and thus part-time compulsory schooling lasts at least two years, but no longer than four years; most apprenticeships last three years.

In order to be admitted to apprenticeship training, young people must have completed nine years of compulsory education; apprentices are therefore at least 15 years of age.

Compulsory part-time vocational schools provide basic and specialized education. Their general aim is to promote and complement the apprenticeship training provided in business and industry and to provide general education. A number of specialized theoretical and practical compulsory subjects are taught in two ability groups.

The **curriculum** for general education in all part-time vocational schools comprises politics, German and communication, economics and correspondence, accounting and an occupation-related foreign language (English, French).

The theoretical and practical subjects differ depending on the chosen apprenticeship.

Apprentices attend compulsory vocational school at least one 9-hour day each five- or six-day week during the school year, or in blocks ('course design') covering at least eight to ten weeks of each school year, 9 hours a day, five or six days a week.

Seasonal compulsory vocational schools provide courses during a particular season of the year.

The general regulations for **assessment** procedures, marking and reports are the same as described under 'General Provisions' in 3.1.2.

Apprenticeship training ends with an end-of-apprenticeship examination before a board of examiners set up by the legally established interest groups (social partners). In addition, fully-trained apprentices are awarded a leaving certificate by the part-time compulsory vocational school (*Abschlußzeugnis der Berufsschule*).

Teachers of general education, business and management, wordprocessing, etc. and technical theory must have the matriculation examination certificate and 2 years of professional experience. They initially follow 6 weeks' training during the first 2 years of their teaching contract at an in-service teacher training college (*Pädagogisches Institut*) leading to a Teaching Diploma. They are later released from their teaching duties to follow a 1-year (2 semesters) training course at a Vocational Teacher Training College. Workshop training is provided by skilled workers with 6 years of relevant professional experience and a master craftman's qualification.

Statistics 1992/93

Part-time compulsory vocational school	
Pupils	140,070
Teachers	4,711
Schools	230
Pupil/teacher ratio	29.7
Pupil/class ratio	23.9

Source: Austrian School Statistics 93/94, (ed.) Federal Ministry of Education and the Arts in cooperation with the Austrian Central Statistical Office, Vienna 1994.

6. Higher education

Admission

Austria has 12 universities and 6 art colleges, all of which are autonomous, offering a total of 430 study programmes and more than 600 different study options.

To be admitted to a normal course of study, students must have the matriculation examination certificate. Students apply to a particular university for a course. They then have to enrol on the chosen course each semester. In some cases, they may be required to take supplementary examinations; students who do not meet some of the formal admission requirements for the chosen course of study have to take supplementary examinations either before matriculation (e.g. Latin for the study of medicine) or within the first two semesters of the course (e.g. accounting for the study of industrial management). The study laws define the formal requirements to be met for the different courses of study. The fine arts colleges require the matriculation examination only for some of their courses. Admission is subject to an entrance examination in which artistic talent is assessed. Candidates who have not passed the matriculation examination may sit a special university entrance examination (*Studienberechtigungsprüfung*) which provides access to university studies (or in some cases studies at an art college) in a limited range of subjects. There is no numerus clausus in Austria.

Fees/Student finance

There are no tuition fees for Austrian nationals at universities and colleges of higher education. Needy students receive a grant.

Academic year

The academic year lasts from October to the end of June. It is divided into two semesters.

Courses/Qualifications

University study courses, which are primarily aimed at providing an academic education to young people in conjunction with career preparation, lead to an academic degree. A number of short profession-oriented study programmes do not lead to an academic degree. A distinction is made between first degree studies, doctoral studies, additional and supplementary study courses (*Erweiterungs- und Aufbaustudien*).

The structure of courses leading to a teaching qualification have already been described in 3.2.2.

Studies leading to a first degree (*Magister, Mag.; Diplomingenieur, Dipl.Ing.; or Dipl.Tierarzt*) are divided into two stages, both ending with a degree examination. Before the second degree examination students must submit a degree paper. Students who have obtained a first degree are admitted to doctoral studies in their specialized, or a related, field of study. Doctoral studies include a thesis and an oral examination in several fields. Medical studies consist of three stages and lead directly to a doctorate.

The minimum length of all courses is defined by law. Most last from 8 to 10 semesters (four to five academic years). Doctoral studies take at least another two semesters. The minimum duration of medical studies is 12 semesters. However, the actual length is generally longer. Only 6% of all students complete their studies within the prescribed minimum time.

Most of the courses at fine arts colleges lead to an academic degree (*Magister*); the structure of art college courses is similar to those at universities. Diploma courses last from three to six years.

Graduates of short study courses receive a professional title, but not an academic degree. The minimum length of short courses is less than that of study courses leading to academic degrees (5 or 6 semesters at university, 4 to 8 at art colleges).

Graduates of architecture at an art college are awarded the title of *Mag.arch*; *Mag.art* is awarded to graduates of teacher training courses and all other diploma studies.

Assessment

Students are assessed by oral or written examinations for lecture courses. Final examinations are held by a board of examiners. Diploma papers and doctoral theses are also considered for assessment.

The different types of examination are generally defined by law. The laws and ordinances governing the different study courses prescribe how many examinations and which type (oral, written, single examination, board of examiners, etc.) have to be passed during the course of studies. The lecturer decides when, how often during the semester and by which of the prescribed methods students are assessed.

Statistics

In 1992, approximately 200,000 regular students were enrolled at universities and art colleges, 20,000 of whom (10%) were non-Austrians. There were more than 16,000 teaching staff.

Fachhochschulen
(post-secondary special-subject college)

In accordance with the relevant law, enacted in May 1993 by the Austrian Parliament, *Fachhochschulen* have been established in Austria from the academic year 1994/95 onwards as an alternative to existing university studies. They offer scientifically-based, practically-oriented vocational training courses lasting a minimum of six semesters and covering a minimum of 1,950 lessons.

Admission is not restricted to persons with a matriculation examination certificate; these colleges also cater for persons with the required professional vocational skills. Graduates of vocational schools, who have already acquired specialized knowledge and skills, will receive special credits towards their particular study programme in order to reduce its total duration.

Graduates of *Fachhochschulen* will be entitled to enrol in doctoral studies in their field at a university.

Funding is provided by the Government and by private bodies. Fees are not charged at *Fachhochschulen*.

The various institutions offer specialized courses in fields such as engineering, business and social and health matters. Some courses are already running, while others are still being designed.

Portugal

PORTUGAL

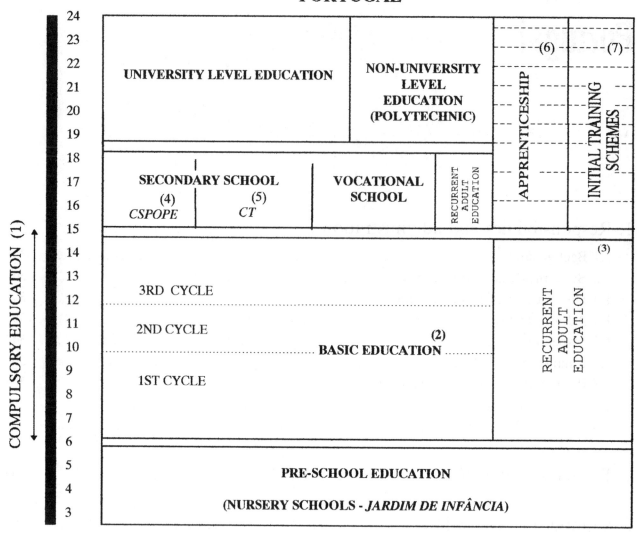

1.Until 1987, compulsory education in Portugal lasted 6 years, whilst compulsory attendance lasted until 14 years of age (i.e. 8 years). The Comprehensive Law on the Education System of October 1986 extended compulsory education to 9 years - applicable to pupils enrolled in the first year of basic education for the 1987/88 school year and for subsequent school years.

2. Basic Education comprises compulsory education of 9 years, consisting of three consecutive cycles of 4, 2 and 3 years respectively, and is roughly equivalent to primary and lower secondary level.

3. 3-year evening courses of general or technical education for early school leavers and adults.

4. Secondary courses predominantly leading to further studies (*Cursos Secundários Predominantemente Orientados para o Prosseguimento de Estudos - CSPOPE,*) or general courses;

5. Secondary courses predominantly oriented towards working life, or technological courses (*Cursos Tecnológicos - CT*).

6. Apprenticeship is accessible to young people aged 14 to 24. It lasts 1 to 4 years.

7. Initial training schemes in various employment sectors, of various lengths.

················· = division in the level/type of education

– – – – – – – – · = alternative beginning or end of level/type of education

1. Responsibilities and administration

1.1 Background

Portugal covers a total area of 91,985 square kilometres and has a resident population of 9,853 million (1991). Portuguese is the language spoken throughout the country. The dominant religion is Catholicism.

In accordance with the Constitution, Portugal is a Democratic Republic. The Head of State is the President of the Republic; legislative power is vested in the Assembly of the Republic. Both are elected by direct universal suffrage. The head of the Government is the Prime Minister.

The islands of the Azores and Madeira are Autonomous Regions with Governments and Regional Legislative Assemblies with considerable powers. Throughout Portugal there are local authorities (*autarquias locais*), either the municipality or the *freguesia* (parish).

The gross domestic product (GDP) per sector of activity in 1990 was: services – 55%; extracting and processing industries – 27.6%; construction – 7.4%; agriculture, forestry, hunting and fisheries – 6.7%; electricity, gas and water – 3.3%. In 1993, the unemployment rate, with respect to the working age population, was 5.5%.

1.2 Basic principles: education

The Comprehensive Law on the Education System of 14 October 1986 (46/86) established the general framework for the reorganization of the Portuguese education system.

The education system comprises a set of facilities that ensure the right to education and guarantee equal opportunities to both access to school and success at school.

The State is responsible for the democratization of education; it is not entitled to direct education and culture on any particular philosophical, aesthetic, political or religious lines. State education is non-denominational, but the right to found private and cooperative schools is guaranteed.

1.3 Distribution of responsibilities

Education in general is the sole responsibility of the Ministry of Education, apart from some education establishments that are either jointly supervised with, or fall under the administration of, other Ministries.

The central authorities ensure the implementation of laws passed and decisions taken by the Government and Parliament, and develop additional decisions, instructions and notifications. The administration of all levels of education is in the process of being reformed and the Ministry's regional services are being restructured with a view to decentralization. The decision-making powers of local (and regional) authorities are also increasing, and educational institutions themselves have increasing autonomy.

The financing of public education is basically provided by Central Government, the Ministry of Education and others, although local authorities have some responsibility.

Public universities and polytechnics have administrative, financial, academic and pedagogical autonomy.

The Ministry of Employment and Social Security (*MESS*), through its Institute of Employment and

Vocational Training (*IEFP*) and in collaboration with the social partners, is responsible for apprenticeships and centres of employment and vocational training. It also has joint responsibility, with the Ministry of Education, for vocational schools and runs some pre-school establishments.

1.4 Administration

Ministry of Education

The Ministry of Education (*Ministério da Educação – ME*) is responsible for defining national policy on education and sport. Its duties are to promote the development and modernization of the education system, strengthen the link between education and research, science, technology and culture, preserve and spread the Portuguese language and promote the development of an integrated sports policy.

The Ministry of Education comprises central and regional services. In April 1993, the Ministry was restructured, making the regional services stronger and the central structure more flexible. The Minister of Education is responsible for the political direction of the Ministry, assisted by the Secretaries of State for Higher Education and for Education and Sport, the Under-Secretary of State (who is the Minister of Education's deputy) and the directors of the various departments and services of the Ministry of Education. The **central services** of the Ministry of Education are as follows:

– Department of Planning and Financial Management;

– Department of Higher Education;

– Department of Secondary Education;

– Department of Basic Education;

– Department of Educational Resource Management;

– General Inspectorate of Education;

– Cabinet for the Implementation and Monitoring of the School Year;

– General Secretariat.

The central services essentially deal with the design, development, coordination, evaluation and inspection of education and training.

The Ministry of Education makes decisions with regard to the establishment and general organization of schools and school time and the employment of staff, and issues guidelines on the content of pre-school education and the curricula for basic and secondary education. Together with the *MESS*, it approves curricula for the vocational schools.

The **regional services** are the five Regional Directorates of Education (*direcções regionais de educação*), decentralized services that carry out the tasks of the Ministry of Education at regional level with regard to the guidance, coordination and support of non-higher education establishments, the management of human, financial and material resources, school social support and support for young children. In cooperation with the Department for Higher Education, they also coordinate and implement measures on admission to higher education.

There are also **three services** which operate under the supervision of the Minister of Education:

– the Camoes Institute, which, among other tasks, promotes and supports the teaching of the Portuguese language and culture abroad;

– the Institute for Educational Innovation, which aims to promote scientific and technical research, with regard to curricular development and the organizational development of the education system, to contribute to increasing educational innovation, and to design and produce means of evaluating the education system and methods of assessing pupils, monitor their implementation and study their results;

– the Sports Institute, which supports and promotes sports and plays a major role in the field of school sports and physical education.

In the autonomous regions of the Azores and Madeira, the administration of education is the responsibility of the regional governments, through their respective Regional Secretariats of Education. They adapt national education policy to the region and also undertake the management of human, material and financial resources.

Institutional level

With regard to the administration of **public non-higher education establishments**, the reform provides for a new system for the direction, administration and management of schools. This gives the schools a more participatory and decisive role in the system, and allows them cultural, pedagogical, administrative and financial independence. The new management bodies will be responsible either for a school or for a school area (where the size and location of schools does not justify them having their own separate management bodies).

The School Council or School Area Council (*conselho de escola*) is responsible for appointing an executive director (*director executivo*) and for guiding activities, including the approval of various documents submitted by the Pedagogical Council (*conselho pedagógico*). It comprises representatives of teaching and non-teaching staff, parents, the municipal council and, as ex-officio members, the executive director and chairman of the Pedagogical Council. Pupils are also represented in schools where secondary education is provided.

The Pedagogical Council is responsible for drawing up various documents on the pedagogical aspects of school activities – the school plan, the staff training plan, the internal regulations and the plan of activities, proposals and reports on curricular management and extracurricular programmes and activities, pupil guidance, support and assessment. It comprises representatives of teachers, parents, the executive director, and the psychology and guidance services. In establishments providing the second and third cycle of basic education and secondary education, it also consists of pupil representatives and the heads of curricular and training departments.

The Administrative Council (*conselho administrativo*), composed of the executive director, an assistant and the head of the school administration services, is responsible for administrative and financial management.

There is no single management model for **universities**, but the management bodies of the faculties or equivalent units must include a representative assembly, a school board, a pedagogical council and an academic council. The organizing bodies of public universities are: the University Assembly, which elects the Vice-Chancellor and approves the statutes; the University Senate, which makes final decisions on the creation of university structures, development plans and budgets; and the Vice-Chancellor, who superintends the university's academic, administrative and financial management. The University Assembly and the Senate consist of an equal number of representatives of teaching staff and students, in addition to representatives of researchers and non-teaching staff.

Universities also create, in their statutes, councils of an advisory nature which ensure the link with the local economic, social and cultural community.

The administrative bodies of **polytechnics** are: the Chairman, who superintends the institution's academic, administrative and financial management; the General Council, which approves the plan of activities and the proposals for the creation, alteration or closure of organizational units; the Administrative Council, which prepares and allocates the budget.

Within the scope of financial autonomy, higher education institutions are free to manage the annual funds the State grants them and to collect and manage their own funds.

1.5 Inspection

The General Inspectorate of Education (*Inspecção Geral da Educação – IGE*) is responsible for the educational and technical supervision and monitoring of all education establishments. With regard to public higher education, the Inspectorate is also responsible for verifying compliance with the legal provisions governing fees and support for students. In addition, the Inspectorate has the task of monitoring the financial and administrative efficiency of the education system as a whole.

The Inspectorate is run by an Inspector General who is assisted by two Sub-Inspector Generals. It exercises its authority at central level through five coordination units covering the following areas:

- technical and pedagogical inspection of pre-school, basic and secondary education;

- administrative and financial inspection of pre-school, basic and secondary education;

- inspection of private and cooperative schools outside higher education, and of vocational schools;

- inspection of public, private and cooperative higher education;

- technical and legal assistance.

The Inspectorate also has regional delegations, which are responsible in terms of hierarchy and function to the Inspector General. These are decentralized services whose territory coincides with that of the five Regional Directorates of Education. The regional delegations are responsible for the pedagogical, administrative and financial supervision of the education system in their respective areas.

1.6 Financing

State education is essentially financed by the Ministry of Education, although the financing of some institutions is shared with other Ministries (e.g. the Military Academy or the Naval School, which are under the supervision of the Ministry of Defence and the Ministry of Education).

The Ministry of Education finances central and regional services through the allocation of funds, and finances private and cooperative education by means of budgetary transfers.

The regional administration of the autonomous regions of the Azores and Madeira finance, with their own resources and with state budgetary transfers, educational services and establishments.

The co-financing provided by the *PRODEP* (*Programa de Desenvolvimento Educativo para Portugal*, or Programme of Educational Development for Portugal), resulting from the European Community Decision of 18 June 1990, should also be mentioned. The programme deals with financing and resources within the field of training and innovation and the modernization of educational infrastructure (construction and equipment of new classrooms, vocational education, higher education).

The municipalities are partly responsible for educational finance and expenses. They cover the construction, maintenance, equipment and certain operational expenses of schools of pre-school education and the first cycle of basic education, and

provide complementary funding for school transport and extracurricular and leisure activities.

Compulsory education is free as regards fees and other payments related to enrolment, school attendance and certificates. In certain cases, pupils are also entitled to free use of books, school material, transport, meals and accommodation. However, pupils and their families do make an important financial contribution to education through the payment of enrolment and tuition fees and the purchase of books for both secondary and higher education (there are only token tuition fees in secondary education).

1.7 Private and cooperative schools

Private and cooperative schools are set up and managed by private individuals acting individually or collectively.

Private and cooperative schools which provide collective instruction in keeping with the objectives of the national education system are eligible for the same benefits as public schools.

1.8 Consultative bodies

There are five consultative bodies:

- The National Council for Education (*CNE*), an independent higher advisory body of the Ministry, set up in 1992, which has autonomous administrative and financial powers. It is, on its own initiative or upon request, responsible for issuing opinions, reports and recommendations on all education issues, and particularly for ensuring the enforcement and development of the provisions set out in the Comprehensive Law on the Education System of 1986. It consists of approximately 55 members who represent the different organizations directly involved in educational, political and social sectors.

- The Council for Private and Cooperative Education (*CCEPC*), which advises the Minister of Education on measures to be taken to allow establishments of private and cooperative education to be included in the education system.

- The Council for Higher Education – Industry Cooperation (*CESE*), whose purpose is to develop cooperation between industry and centres of knowledge, namely universities and official research and development organizations, and to improve the technological base and the technical training of the labour force.

- The Higher Sports Council (*CSD*), which is responsible for following the progress of sport and for studying and issuing reports on the guidelines established by the public administration in the area of sports policy. Private and public entities who play a role in sports are, among others, represented in this council.

- The National School Sports Council (*CNDE*), which participates in the definition of the general guidelines and proposes activities, actions and projects to develop school sports.

1.9 Vocational training

The Ministry of Employment and Social Security (*Ministério do Emprego e da Segurança Social – MESS*) is responsible for defining and pursuing policies relating to employment and vocational training, and social security. Its central structure, for the areas of employment and vocational training, incorporates the Directorate-General of Employment and Vocational Training (*Direcção-Geral do Emprego e Formação Profissional – DGEFP*) and the Institute of Employment and Vocational Training (*Instituto do Emprego e Formação Profissional – IEFP*), and its Regional Directorates.

Since 1980, the Inter-Ministerial Commission for Employment (*Comissão Interministerial para o Emprego – CIME*), attached to the Minister of Employment and Social Security, has been working on proposals to establish a global policy for employment and coordinates all vocational training actions, whatever the level of training.

The *DGEFP* is responsible for innovation and technical and legislative support in the fields of employment and vocational training.

The *IEFP* is responsible for implementing the measures relating to employment and vocational training policy, particularly those resulting from programmes run within the European Community Support Framework (*Quadro Comunitário de Apoio – QCA*) and the new vocational certification system.

A tripartite executive committee is responsible for the management of the *IEFP*. The Government and the social partners are also represented in the consultative committees and the regional bodies of the *IEFP*. The *IEFP*'s Department of Vocational Training is responsible for curricular development, designing and preparing training programmes, defining training profiles, trainers' training, apprenticeship and the technical coordination of vocational training centres. Within the context of apprenticeship, the *IEFP* runs the national apprenticeship committee (*Comissão Nacional de Aprendizagem – CNA*), composed of representatives of several ministries and the social partners. The *CNA* has an overall role in recommending legislative and governmental measures and in coordinating the work of the regional committees.

Following the development of a permanent link and cooperation between vocational training within the education system and vocational training at the labour market level, a permanent monitoring group (*Grupo de Acompanhamento Permanente*), coordinated by a representative of the Ministry of Education and a representative of the Ministry of Employment and Social Security, was set up in May 1992.

In addition to the establishment of the legal system for the certification of training in the labour market by Decree Law 95/92 of 23 May, a Standing Committee for Vocational Certification (*Comissão Permanente de Certificação*) was set up.

2. Pre-school education (Educação pré-escolar)

Pre-school education is seen as forming an integral part of the state education system, as laid down in the Law of July 1975, which defines its objectives and sets up state nursery teacher training colleges.

Also in the 1970s, the various nursery education services, which were then divided among several bodies, were coordinated and centralized under the Ministry of Education and the Ministry of Employment and Social Security (*Ministério do Emprego e da Segurança Social – MESS*).

Pre-school education is optional and is provided for children between the ages of three and six, the legal age for commencing basic education. Children of this age-group generally attend nursery school (*Jardim de Infância*).

Under the supervision of the Ministry of Education, there is a state network and a private and cooperative network of nursery schools whose administration and operation are coordinated and monitored by the Regional Directorates of Education.

The network of pre-school institutions run by the *MESS* through Regional Social Security Centres also includes state and private nursery schools. The latter fall under the auspices of various other bodies, such as the Private Social Solidarity Institutions (*Instituições Privadas de Solidariedade Social – IPPS*), cooperatives, autarchies and companies. Most of the state and private institutions under the supervision of the *MESS* offer creches for children from birth to age three. The two types of services (nursery schools and creches) may operate in the same building or separately.

Although there has been a very rapid growth in the state network of the Ministry of Education over the last decade, it represents less than half of the total capacity of nursery schools. Of the other institutions, most are under Private Social Solidarity Institutions or are private or cooperative schools. In 1992, approximately 49.9% of 3- to 6-year-olds attended a nursery school – around 40% of these were in state nursery schools under the Ministry of Education, 15% were in private or cooperative schools and 45% were in establishments under the *MESS*.

In schools under the Ministry of Education, priority access is given to children who will be attending compulsory education as from the following year and whose parents or legal guardians reside or work in the *freguesia* (parish) where the nursery school is located. Whenever the number of places available is lower than the number of applicants, priority is given to older children; for this purpose their age is counted in years, months and days successively.

In schools under the *MESS*, priority is given to children whose families lack the necessary social and financial means.

Attendance is free at nursery schools run by the Ministry of Education, while at those run by the *MESS*, parents share the costs, according to their family income (in public and private non-profit-making establishments).

In accordance with the 1986 Comprehensive Law on the Education System, the overall objectives of pre-school education are to develop the child's emotional stability, social, intellectual and motor skills and health habits and to deal with the child's inadequacies, handicaps or precocious behaviour. Pre-school education should complement the education provided by the family with which it must cooperate closely.

Although these objectives are common to all pre-school institutions, in nursery schools under the Ministry of Education education is predominant, whereas those under the *MESS* also provide social assistance. Often integrated in social services centres, the latter are established in larger buildings with larger numbers of children and staff, provide meals and benefit from other health services.

Whenever nursery school size and attendance so permit, the groups of children are organized in rooms according to their age. At nursery schools run by the Ministry of Education, no more than 25 children can be assigned to one teacher, and for homogeneous groups of three-year-olds, no more than 15. Teachers usually change groups each year. At institutions under the *MESS*, the teacher/child ratio is around 1:27. There are around 75 children in each institution. At both types of establishment, groups are mixed.

Nursery schools under the Ministry of Education provide educational activities for five hours a day, divided into two periods, five days each week. The timetable may be increased by non-academic hours. The school holidays comprise 45 days in the summer and one week at Christmas and at Easter.

Nursery schools under the *MESS* are open for 10 – 12 hours a day, five days a week, and most close for one month a year in the summer.

Curriculum

In general, pre-school education consists of a series of activities based on the objectives and guidelines (non-compulsory) laid down by the Ministry of Education.

These guidelines relate to the role to be played at nursery schools by expression through movement, and dramatic, visual and musical expression, learning the mother tongue and mathematics. The activities recommended, whether for individuals or in groups, comprise art, painting, modelling, story-telling and playing at 'Let's pretend', and are aimed at developing the child's independence, creativeness and social skills. In some cases, pre-reading and pre-writing activities may be undertaken.

Assessment

Throughout the year, at the end of each phase, the teacher assesses: whether the objectives defined for

the phase have been accomplished; what development the children have made and what competences they have acquired; and whether the plan of activities needs to be reformulated so as to better ensure the emotional, social, psychomotor, perceptive, cognitive and moral development of the children.

Children move on to basic education at the beginning of the school year in which they have their sixth birthday. In the event of duly proven special educational needs, it may be recommended for a child to stay on at nursery school beyond the legal age.

Teachers

Nursery teachers have a degree *(Bacharelato),* obtained after three years' training at non-university institutions of higher education (*Escolas superiores de educação*).

In establishments under both Ministries, auxiliaries may be provided. Auxiliary staff may have various types of training, but they must have completed compulsory schooling.

The in-service training requirements for nursery teachers are the same as those for basic and secondary education teachers.

Teachers in state schools are civil servants.

Statistics 1993/94

Ministry of Education			
	State	Private	Total
Pupils	72,345	29,382	101,727
Nursery teachers	4,305	1,604	5,909
Schools	3,249	967	4,216

Ministry of Employment and Social Security	
	State & Private
Pupils	83,000
Nursery teachers	3,120
Schools	1,191

3. Compulsory education

According to the Comprehensive Law on the Education System of October 1986, compulsory education lasts nine years, for six- to fifteen-year-olds – applicable to pupils enrolled in the first year of compulsory education for the 1987/88 school year and for subsequent school years. It is provided by Basic Education.

Until 1987, compulsory education lasted six years and comprised two cycles: primary education lasting four years (6- to 10-year-olds) and preparatory education lasting two years (10- to 12-year-olds). Compulsory school attendance, however, lasted eight years, until 14 years of age; pupils who could not progress further would attend preparatory education until 14 years of age.

4. Basic education (Ensino básico)

Basic education is compulsory for all children who have reached the age of six by 15 September of the first school year and lasts 9 years.

Basic education, where part of compulsory state education, is free of charge. There are no entrance or enrolment fees, or payments with regard to school attendance, report cards, school insurance and complementary support in the fields of educational guidance and psychology, school social support and school health.

General support for education (school meals, school transport, and accommodation schemes) is given to more needy pupils as a priority. School books and other school materials, together with direct financial assistance, are provided exclusively to the most needy pupils. Depending on the family's socio-economic situation, this support is free or subject to a contribution. The expenses of support schemes in private and cooperative schools may be borne by the State.

The objectives of basic education, set out in the 1986 Comprehensive Law on the Education System, are: to provide a general education for all pupils; to ensure that theoretical and practical knowledge, schooling and everyday life are interrelated; to provide physical and motor development, encourage manual activities and promote artistic education; to teach a first foreign language and begin a second; to provide the basic knowledge that will enable pupils to continue their studies or to be accepted on vocational training courses; to develop knowledge and appreciation of the specific values of Portuguese identity, language, history and culture; to develop independent attitudes; to provide children with specific educational needs with suitable conditions for their development; and to create conditions that will encourage the school and educational success of all pupils.

Basic education is divided into three consecutive cycles:

– first cycle, which lasts for four years (6- to 10-year-olds);

– second cycle, which lasts for two years (10- to 12-year-olds);

– third cycle, which lasts for three years (12- to 15-year-olds).

4.1 First cycle

This cycle is provided by mixed primary schools (*escolas primarias*) in the state, private and cooperative sectors. As mentioned above, children who are six years old by 15 September – and, as an exception, those reaching that age by 31 December – may begin this cycle. Priority is given to older children when filling school vacancies.

The 1986 Comprehensive Law on the Education System defines the specific objectives for the first cycle as: the development of oral language and the introduction and progressive mastery of reading and writing, the basic concepts of arithmetic and calculus, knowledge of the physical and social environment, and visual, dramatic, musical and motor expression.

Classes are organized by age. Teaching is of a global nature and a given class of pupils is taught by a single teacher throughout. Other teachers may assist in specific areas.

There is no set organization of class time (duration of a lesson and allocation of time to subject areas). Teaching time is managed by the teacher, taking into account the characteristics of the group, the school timetable and the breaks agreed by the School Council (*conselho de escola*).

The timetable depends on the availability of space in school buildings. One of the two weekly 25-hour schemes (including break times) may be adopted,

from Monday to Friday. In the normal scheme (always compulsory, except when there is a shortage of premises), morning courses usually start at 9.00 a.m. and finish at 12.00 a.m. In the afternoon, courses usually start at 2.00 p.m. and finish at 4.00 p.m.

In the two-shift scheme (only adopted for those classes that cannot be held under the normal scheme), courses start at 8.00 a.m. and finish at 1.00 p.m. in the morning session. In the afternoon session, courses start at 1.15 p.m. and finish at 6.15 p.m.

The duration of the school year is fixed annually by the Ministry of Education. The 1993/94 school year lasted for 184 days from Monday to Friday. After the summer holidays (around 10 weeks), schools in Portugal reopen around the second fortnight of September. The school year generally ends around the end of June.

Curriculum

The new curricular plans and programmes for the first cycle, which were introduced experimentally in the 1989/90 school year, are now in general application – except for the programmes of the fourth year, which will be introduced in 1994/95.

The curriculum is composed of the following compulsory subject areas:

– Expression and education: physical/motor, musical, dramatic and visual arts;

– Study of the environment;

– Portuguese language;

– Mathematics;

– Personal and social development or moral and religious education (Catholic or other denominations);

– School area: an area of the curriculum whose objectives relate to the acquisition of knowledge through multidisciplinary activities and projects. This is achieved by establishing a connection between the school and the environment and the personal and social development of pupils.

In addition, there are extracurricular activities organized by the schools, which are optional and are predominantly games-oriented and cultural in nature, aimed at the creative and formative use of pupils' free time, including school sports.

All of these subjects are included in the curriculum in each year of this cycle, but at varying levels.

Depending on the resources available, schools may begin teaching a foreign language, either orally or in a 'games' context.

School **textbooks** are produced commercially, but the Ministry of Education may be involved in the publication of compulsory course materials. Textbooks are valid for a minimum of four years during the first cycle.

Assessment and qualifications

See below.

Teachers

See 6.

Statistics 1993/94

	State	Private	Total
Pupils	541,865	42,622	584,487
Teachers	39,738	1,300	41,038
Schools	9,638	673	10,311

4.2 Second cycle

The second cycle of basic education is provided in State or private education establishments (preparatory schools and preparatory/secondary schools – *escolas preparatórias, escolas preparatórias/secundárias*) and in centres for basic distance education. The latter operate in areas which have a low pupil population and are less accessible geographically.

Pupils who have successfully completed the first cycle, at a minimum age of nine and a maximum age of 14, are admitted to the second cycle of basic education. They have to attend the educational establishment in the area in which they live.

The objectives for this cycle relate to the teaching of the humanities, art, sports, science and technology and moral and civic education: the aim is to enable pupils to assimilate and interpret information creatively and critically so as to equip them with the methods, means and knowledge to pursue their education. This should also enable pupils' development to lead to an awareness of the community and its problems.

The Pedagogical Council (*conselho pedagógico*) takes into account the specific conditions of the school and the individual needs of pupils when deciding on the organization of classes. In general, classes are mixed and comprise pupils aged 10 to 12 and 12 to 14. Care is taken to maintain the group/class of the previous school year, provided the Class Council does not advise otherwise. Pupils repeating their studies have to be integrated into classes of the same, or nearest, age level. The number of pupils per class varies depending on the size of the classroom, with an average of 30. Up to four pupils with physical or mental disabilities can be integrated into each class, but these classes cannot then have more than 20 pupils.

The second cycle operates on a multi-teacher system, with one teacher for each subject or combination of two subjects. It is desirable, but not compulsory, for pupils to be taught the same subject by the same teacher throughout the cycle.

The weekly timetable comprises 31 lessons of 50 minutes each. The school timetable is organized between Monday and Friday, or Saturday if the School Board so decides. The 1993/94 school year was the same as in the first cycle for schools open from Monday to Friday. It lasted 220 days for schools open from Monday to Saturday. The annual total number of hours of teaching is, however, the same under the 5-day and 6-day week systems, as the teaching not given on Saturdays is distributed over the other days of the week.

Curriculum

The curriculum, compulsory for all pupils, is organized into five multidisciplinary areas and one non-subject curricular area – the 'school area'.

The multidisciplinary areas are:

- language and social studies: Portuguese language, Portuguese history and geography, and a foreign language (German, French or English);

- exact and natural sciences: mathematics and natural sciences;

- artistic and technological education: visual and technological education and musical education;

- physical education;

- personal and social education: personal and social development or moral and religious education (Catholic or other denominations).

The 'school area' comprises multidisciplinary activities and projects which aim to enhance learning, to make pupils aware of the connection between the school and the environment and to contribute to their personal and social development. It lasts for 95-110 hours per year, is run independently by the schools and is organized according to the corresponding reduction in lesson hours devoted to the subjects involved in each project.

In addition, there are extracurricular activities which are optional and predominantly games-oriented and cultural in nature, aimed at the creative and formative use of pupils' free time. School sports are included these activities.

Textbooks are valid for a minimum of four years.

Assessment and qualifications

See below.

Teachers

See 6.

Statistics 1993/94

	State	Private	Total
Pupils	300,477 (day)	25,686 (day)	326,163 (day)
	5,250 (evening)	373 (evening)	5,623 (evening)
Teachers*	91,925	9,420	101,345
Schools**	679	239	918

* This includes teachers in the 2nd and 3rd cycles of basic education and in secondary education, day and evening classes.
** This includes institutions which provide education at more than one level and have been counted at each level.

4.3 Third cycle

The third cycle of basic education comprises three years of study, the final year constituting the end of the nine years of compulsory basic education (for pupils who enrolled for their first year of schooling in the school year 1987/88 or after).

It is taught in preparatory/secondary schools and in secondary schools. Evening courses are also offered, but they follow the model prior to the reform, the general unified course.

Pupils who have completed the second cycle or its equivalent can enter the third cycle of basic education. They have to attend the educational establishment in the area in which they live.

This cycle has the following specific objectives:

- the systematic and differentiated acquisition of modern culture, in its humanistic, literary, artistic, physical, sports and technological aspects, all of which are essential for entering working life and for continuing studies;

- educational and vocational guidance, to facilitate the choice between further education or entering working life, respecting individual achievement.

This cycle is organized according to the same general criteria as the second cycle. It operates on a multi-teacher system, with one teacher for each subject. The classes are mixed.

The pupils' weekly timetable comprises 31 lessons. Each lesson lasts 50 minutes.

The school year is the same as in the 2nd cycle.

Curriculum

The curriculum for the third cycle includes subjects and multidisciplinary subject areas.

The subjects are: Portuguese language; foreign language (continuation of the foreign language started in the second cycle); human and social sciences (history and geography); mathematics, physical and natural sciences (physics and chemistry, natural sciences); visual education; and physical education.

The multidisciplinary areas, allowing pupils a choice, are:

- Personal and social education, with a choice between personal and social development and moral and religious education (Catholic or other denominations);

- Optional area, with a choice between a second foreign language, music education and technological education.

There is also a school area, which lasts for 95-110 hours a year in this cycle, run independently by the schools and organized according to the corresponding reduction in lesson hours devoted to the subjects involved in each project. In this cycle, the school area includes civics education (participation in democratic institutions). Each pupil's assessment in this subject is taken into consideration for the award of the basic education certificate.

In addition, there are extracurricular activities which are optional and predominantly games-oriented and cultural in nature, aimed at the creative and formative use of pupils' free time. School sports are incorporated into these activities.

Textbooks are valid for a minimum of three years.

Assessment and qualifications

See below.

Teachers

See 6.

Statistics 1993/94

	State	Private	Total
Pupils	405,882 (day)	36,980 (day)	442,862 (day)
	47,633 (evening)	5,131 (evening)	52,764 (evening)
Teachers*	91,925	9,420	101,345
Schools**	971	202	1,173

* This includes teachers in the 2nd and 3rd cycles of basic education and in secondary education, day and evening classes.
** This includes institutions which provide education at more than one level and have been counted at each level.

4.4 Assessment and qualifications

As it is a factor governing educational practice, assessment is systematic and continuous and focuses on the achievement of the general objectives of each of the cycles and the specific objectives of each subject or subject area.

In addition to the school bodies, pupils and parents, the following services participate in the assessment process: psychological and guidance services; special education services; and other services at the request of the Pedagogical or School Council.

Pupils in basic education are subject to formative, summative and specialized assessment.

Formative assessment is the joint responsibility of the teachers who actually teach the pupils concerned and the other teachers. In the second and third cycles, the class director (a teacher chosen by the executive director from among the teachers of a particular class) is responsible for coordinating the assessment, ensuring its global and integrated nature.

Formative assessment is descriptive and qualitative in nature, and is based on comprehensive information gathered by teachers relating to the various areas of learning. It is intended to inform pupils, parents, their teachers and others concerned of the quality of the teaching and learning processes and the extent to which curriculum objectives have been achieved. It is also intended to help teachers in their choice of methods and materials. The formal decision on formative assessment is taken at the end of each school term, at an ordinary meeting of the

School Council in the first cycle or of the Class Council in the second and third cycles.

Summative assessment is the responsibility of all teachers and educational experts forming the School Council or Class Council, who refer to general criteria defined by the School Council in the first cycle or by the Pedagogical Council in the other cycles. It is also made at a meeting of the School Council in the first cycle or by the Class Council in the second and third cycles, enabling decisions to be taken on educational assistance and support. It is usually made at the end of each school term and at the end of each cycle, but cannot be made before the end of the second year at school. At the end of each cycle, this assessment aims to compare the pupil's overall development with the overall objectives of the school cycle (the minimum national curriculum objectives laid down by the Minister of Education and the objectives set by each establishment).

The summative assessment made in the first cycle is descriptive and, in the second and third cycles, it is expressed by marks on a scale from 1 to 5, accompanied by a summary of the descriptive comments entered in the school records as a result of the formative assessment process. For the purpose of moving from one class to the next, the summative assessment made at the end of each year is expressed by pass or fail. In the latter case, the pupil repeats. Pupils may repeat the entire year or follow a specific support plan incorporating the subjects or subject areas in which they have not achieved the minimum objectives.

At the end of the second term of any school year, the competent assessment bodies may make an extraordinary summative assessment of pupils retained that year. This provides for a recovery plan for the pupil through educational support measures.

A **specialized assessment** is necessary during the course of a summative assessment when a pupil who has already been kept back in any school year does not have the necessary capacity to continue. It is used at the request of the School Council (first cycle) or the Class Council (second and third cycles) by teachers and other education experts, after consultation with the pupil's parents, and should lead to a specific educational support plan to be implemented during the following school year.

Pupils who obtain a pass in the final summative assessment in the third cycle are deemed to have completed basic education and are awarded a basic education certificate (*diploma do ensino básico*) by the administrative body of the school attended, without any final examination (state or equivalent private or cooperative).

Pupils who have reached the age limit for compulsory schooling (15 years) without completing the third cycle may receive a certificate of completion of compulsory schooling. Such pupils can apply for the basic education certificate by sitting examinations held by schools for external pupils *(aluno auto-proposto);* the school provides specific support whenever possible.

Guidance is provided by the counselling and guidance services, specialist educational support units incorporated into the school network, which perform their tasks in the schools or the school areas. In the first and second cycles, guidance is predominantly psycho-pedagogical, while in the third cycle it includes educational and vocational guidance.

5. Secondary education (Ensino secundario)

On completion of compulsory schooling, pupils may opt for one of three different types of courses:

- **Secondary school courses,** part of the normal *(regular)* education system;

- **Vocational school courses,** an alternative to normal education;

- **Art education courses.**

5.1 Secondary school courses

The new model for the organization of normal secondary education was first applied in some schools, on the basis of the teaching experience acquired, in 1990/91 and was generalized as from the 1993/94 school year.

This type of education lasts for three years (15- to 18-year-olds) and is organized in a single study cycle covering the 10th, 11th and 12th years of schooling.

Pupils who have successfully completed basic education or the equivalent (9th year of schooling) have access to any secondary school course. Pupils normally enrol at a school in the area where they live.

In terms of general objectives, normal secondary education aims to consolidate and deepen the knowledge acquired in basic education and to prepare young people both for further studies and for employment.

On the basis of this objective, two different types of courses are organized:

- Secondary courses predominantly leading to further studies (*Cursos Secundários Predominantemente Orientados para o Prosseguimento de Estudos – CSPOPE*), or general courses;

- Secondary courses predominantly oriented towards working life, or technological courses (*Cursos Tecnológicos – CT*).

All courses include the same components of general, specific and technical education, the general education being common to both types of courses. Pupils can change from one type to another. Both types of courses are compulsory in all schools, although one of them may predominate.

Technological education is reinforced in this new model, with the extension of the technological courses to all secondary schools and technological education to all *CSPOPE* pupils. It is up to the schools to choose the *CSPOPE* technical education subjects and the technological courses to be provided each year from among those offered nationally.

The duration of the school year, which begins in the second fortnight of September and ends at the end of the second week of June, is defined by an Order published annually by the Ministry of Education. The 1993/94 school year consisted of 220 school days for schools open from Monday to Saturday and of 184 days for those open from Monday to Friday.

The number of lesson hours per week is as follows, depending on the courses and the year of schooling:

	Courses leading to further studies	Technological courses
10th and 11th years:	29-33 hours	30-32 hours
12th year:	27-35 hours	28-32 hours

As in basic education, classes are organized by age group, taking into account the need to maintain the group/class from the previous school year, to ensure a numerical balance of the sexes and to integrate up to four pupils with special needs. Teachers usually change classes each year.

Curriculum

With regard to content, secondary school courses (*CSPOPE* and *CT*) are organized into four subject groups, according to the different branches of study:

- Scientific and natural;

- Arts;

- Economic and social;

- Humanities.

Each of these main branches includes a course primarily leading to further studies (*CSPOPE*) and various technological courses (*CT*) representing major technological areas. In 1992/93, there were 11 *CT* – Chemistry, Civil construction, Electrotechnical/electronics, Mechanics, Computing, Design, Arts and Crafts, Administration, Communication, Commercial services, Social activity (*Animação Social*).

As mentioned above, the curriculum for the two types of courses comprises:

- general education;

- specific education;

- technical education;

- school area.

General education is common to all *CSPOPE* and *CT* and is compulsory for all pupils.

It covers the following subjects: Portuguese, introduction to philosophy, foreign language I or II, physical education, personal and social development or moral and religious education (Catholic or other denominations).

The weekly timetable varies, depending on the course: from 12 to 15 hours in the 10th and 11th years and from 6 to 9 hours in the 12th year in *CSPOPE;* and from 12 to 13 hours in the 10th and 11th years and from 6 to 7 hours in the 12th year in *CT*.

Specific education includes two or three compulsory subjects which are common within the same branch of the *CSPOPE* or the *CT*. These core curricula ensure interchange between the two courses and enable pupils wishing to continue their studies to do so. In the *CSPOPE*, pupils may choose additional subjects, up to the limit of the time available.

The weekly timetable for the *CSPOPE* in the 10th and 11th years varies from 11 to 13 hours and in the 12th year from 15 to 22 hours. 7 to 9 hours are allocated to specific education in the *CT* throughout the three years of secondary education.

The aim of **technical education**, particularly in the *CT*, is the acquisition of skills that will enable young people to gain access to a wide range of vocational activities and sectors.

In the *CSPOPE*, it lasts for six hours a week each year, divided into one or two technological or art subjects from which pupils are free to choose, solely depending on what each school offers. In the *CT*, technical education covers a group of four subjects, closely linked with the specific education component, according to the qualification objectives of each course.

It is planned that the schools themselves will organize different procedures at the end of this component: seminars, work experience and training courses.

The weekly timetable is the same in the 10th and 11th years (10 to 11 hours) and increases in the 12th year (15 to 17 hours).

The **school area** is again an interdisciplinary area organized and run by the schools, and is compulsory.

In addition to the curricular activities, education establishments have to organize extracurricular games-oriented and cultural activities, which are predominantly held outside school time and are optional.

The curricular programmes and corresponding school **textbooks** are valid for at least three years. Textbooks are produced commercially but the Ministry of Education may be involved. Although the pupils' and teachers' right to resort to other sources of information is respected, textbooks for each subject are selected by the Pedagogical Council of each school.

Assessment and qualifications

Within the context of the gradual generalization of the curricular reform, a new assessment system is being implemented. Assessment is systematic and continuous, and both formative and summative.

Formative assessment is the responsibility of the teachers in collaboration with the school counselling and guidance bodies, and aims to inform pupils, their parents and teachers and others concerned of the quality and development of the education process. This form of assessment is descriptive and qualitative and must contribute to the establishment of intermediate targets, the adoption of remedial teaching measures and guidance for pupils regarding their curricular options.

Summative assessment is both internal and external.

The internal assessment is the responsibility of the teachers forming the Class Council, and aims to inform pupils and their parents about their achievement in relation to the objectives of the curriculum and to substantiate any decisions with regard to their school career.

There is a general written test administered by the schools in every subject at the end of the 10th and 11th years, and in practical subjects studied in the 12th year which are not subject to final examination. The end-of-year marks for each subject are the weighted average of the results of continuous assessment (obtained in the last term) and of the general test. On the basis of these marks, the Class Council decides whether the pupil should be promoted to the next class or should repeat; the Class Council must furnish recommendations regarding remedial teaching measures in cases where this is justified.

The external assessment, for which the Ministry is responsible, aims to promote the homogeneity of the grading system in secondary schooling at national level, allowing comparable final marks to be awarded at the end of this level of schooling.

This assessment consists of final written examinations in the 12th year in most of the subjects included in the two types of courses. Final marks in the subjects covered by the national examination are computed from the weighted average of the marks obtained in the internal assessment, for the year(s) in which the subjects were taught, and those marks obtained in the final examination. In order to pass, pupils must receive pass marks in all the subjects of their respective course.

The current system also provides for a comparative assessment, aimed at monitoring the quality of the school system at local, regional and national level by the Ministry of Education.

Pupils who successfully complete secondary education receive a certificate (*diploma de estudos secundários*) specifying the courses completed and the final marks obtained. Those completing technological courses also receive a level III vocational qualification certificate (*diploma de qualificação profissional*).

Guidance

Educational and vocational guidance is provided by the secondary school psychology and guidance services through the following activities:

- educational and vocational information measures;

- planning and monitoring of study visits, training courses or other forms of contact pupils have with the environment and with the world of work;

- individual or group support for pupils in the selection of options and career planning.

These services operate in the schools where they are based.

With regard to state post-secondary education, there are no studies or training at a non-higher level and all the options for continuing studies are included within the framework of university higher education or polytechnic higher education.

Access to either of these forms of education depends on the results obtained in secondary education (10/11th and 12th years, plus the aptitude test – *prova de aferição*) and the marks obtained in specific tests chosen by the higher education institutions.

5.2 Vocational school courses

The vocational schools, set up in 1989, constitute an alternative to the normal education system and prepare pupils for working life and strengthen the links between school and work. They aim primarily to meet local and regional needs, through diversified courses within each area of training. These schools are for both adolescents and adults.

The minimum requirements for admission vary according to the nature of the course, but for most courses, they correspond to completion of the 9th year of schooling.

In the current phase of transition to a 9-year period of basic education, pupils who have completed the 2nd cycle of basic education (6th year of schooling) or who have failed to complete the 3rd cycle have access to 3-year courses equivalent to the last 3 years of the nine years of schooling.

Most courses last 3 years. Each school year lasts 40 weeks, with a weekly timetable of 30 hours.

Vocational schools have administrative, financial and pedagogical autonomy; in this context it is the individual school which is responsible for the organization of classes.

Curriculum

Courses include socio-cultural, scientific, and technical/technological and practical training in varying proportions according to the starting level of the pupil and the vocational qualification aimed at. They are usually organized in the form of modules.

The socio-cultural component includes three subjects: Portuguese, a foreign language and social integration. 100 hours per school year are allocated to each of these subjects, in a total of 25% of the yearly timetable.

The scientific component also covers 25% of the yearly timetable and includes between two and four basic subjects, which are adjusted to the basic nature of the various branches. These subjects must correspond to education at secondary level, and also be linked to the technical applications of technical-vocational training, within the scope of the specific purpose of each course.

The technical, technological and practical component covers 50% of the yearly timetable and includes between four and six technical subjects, some of a predominantly practical nature. The latter can be taught in a simulated environment – in the laboratory or the workshop – or in a real work environment.

Assessment and qualifications

In vocational school courses, assessment is predominantly of a practical and continuous nature, and is based on what is learnt in each module, set of modules or subjects.

In addition to being assessed for each module, pupils are assessed both qualitatively and quantitatively at four different times during the school year. These assessments are carried out by the Class Council, and each school may establish the most appropriate form for pupils to participate in this process.

When the pupils do not obtain sufficient grades to pass a module, training component or subject, the Pedagogical Council of the school must provide the pupils with extra teaching support. It may also suggest that the pupil repeat modules, training components or subjects.

At the end of the period of work experience, the pupil submits a self-assessment training report; his/her support teacher also presents a report in which the pupil's performance in the work environment is described and qualitatively assessed.

This course also includes a vocational aptitude test, in the form of an interdisciplinary project. Pupils who obtain a grade of 10 or more pass the test.

The final grade in the course is calculated by taking the sum of the grade obtained in the vocational aptitude test and the simple arithmetical average of the grades obtained in all the subjects, and dividing it by two.

Pupils who have passed in all the subjects in the socio-cultural and scientific components, and who have failed in only one subject of the technical component, are awarded a secondary school leaving certificate (*diploma de estudos secundários*).

A vocational qualification certificate (*certificado de qualificação profissional*) is awarded to pupils who have passed the vocational aptitude test.

5.3 Art education courses

There are various types of training in the field of art provided at secondary schools, vocational schools and specialist art schools.

Secondary school courses

Secondary schools providing normal education offer three art courses.

One of the courses (*CSPOPE*) is intended for young people who wish to continue their studies; the other two are technological courses ('design' and 'arts and crafts') which lead to a level III vocational qualification, in addition to the secondary school leaving certificate.

All the courses last for three years.

Vocational school courses

These schools offer training in various fields of art, in particular, graphic arts, textiles, pottery, jewellery, fashion, cinema, audiovisual, dance, drama and music.

They last for three years and lead to the same certificate as the other vocational courses.

Courses in specialist art schools

These art courses have their own curricula and are intended for young people who wish to continue their studies or enter employment.

In the fields of dance and music, specialist training is provided for pupils with recognized aptitudes and talents in these areas. They can continue studies of this kind after finishing basic education if they have previous experience. These training courses are held in conservatories, music schools and academies, and dance schools, which offer an education incorporating or connected with that in normal secondary schools.

In the field of visual arts, specialist courses are run in schools in Lisbon and Oporto.

Teachers

See 6.

Statistics 1993/94

All secondary courses with the exception of vocational schools.

	State	Private	Total
Teachers*	91,925	9,420	101,345
Schools**	485	146	631

* This includes teachers in the 2nd and 3rd cycles of basic education and in secondary education, day and evening classes.
** This includes institutions which provide education at more than one level and have been counted at each level.

CSPOPE and academic education corresponding to the previous model (11th and 12th years).

	State	Private	Total
Pupils	291,566	21,117	312,683

CT and Technical – Vocational Education corresponding to the previous model (11th and 12th years).

	State	Private	Total
Pupils	28,216	2,842	31,058

Evening courses (being phased out).

	State	Private	Total
Pupils	62,829	8,603	71,432

Vocational schools.

	State	Private	Total
Pupils	231	21,931	22,162
Teachers	58	5,482	5,540
Schools	3	211	214

6. Teachers of basic and secondary education

All teachers in basic and secondary education are subject specialists.

According to the 1986 Comprehensive Law on the Education System, the initial training of teachers of the first and second cycles of basic education can be provided in non-university institutions of higher education *(escolas superiores de educação)* or in universities, whereas the training of teachers of the third cycle of basic education and of secondary education takes place solely in universities. Whilst training for teachers of the different cycles of basic education varies, courses are organized in such a way that teachers of the second and third cycles also gain qualifications to teach the preceding cycle.

Courses for first cycle teachers last three years and lead to the *Bacharelato* degree.

Courses for second cycle teachers last four or five years – the first three years leading to the *Bacharelato* degree, the last one or two leading to a specialized higher education diploma. Second cycle teachers may alternatively have a *Licenciatura* degree obtained after 5 years.

Courses for third cycle and secondary teachers last five or six years and lead to a *Licenciatura* degree.

All courses include academic and pedagogical training and teaching practice.

Some teachers in the second and third cycles of basic education and secondary education have been appointed without initial teacher training; they have purely academic *Licenciatura* degrees. Those with less than 6 years' teaching experience follow a 2-year course at a higher education institution; those with more than 6 years' experience may follow a 1-year course provided by the Open University.

State teachers are civil servants. Teachers have access to the profession on the basis of their qualifications and experience.

The number of in-service training units considered to be a minimum requirement for career progress is equal to the number of years the teacher is required to remain at each salary scale. The annual average number is four credit units, each corresponding to a minimum of six hours.

7. Higher education

State higher education

State higher education consists of both university higher education and polytechnic higher education. The former is more theory-oriented. The creation of polytechnic higher education schools began in 1979, although most of the schools set up only came into operation as of 1985/86. This specifically vocational education is provided in strategic areas for the economic and social development of the country at basically regional education establishments.

University education aims to ensure a sound scientific and cultural preparation and provide technical training enabling students to carry out vocational and cultural activities, fostering the development of abilities related to thinking, innovation and critical analysis.

Polytechnic education aims to provide sound cultural and technical training at a higher level, to develop ability for innovation and critical analysis and to provide theoretical and practical education in the sciences and their application to professional activities.

Private and cooperative higher education

Private and cooperative higher education is based on legal statutes which establish the conditions for setting up institutions and courses, recognize the respective academic degrees and define state supervision with regard to the quality of education provided and the possibility of financial support.

Private and cooperative higher education has increased since 1986, when the establishment of several universities and a large number of private higher education establishments was authorized. By the 1991/92 academic year, four private and cooperative universities and 68 higher education establishments had been set up.

Education dependent on other Ministries

Some higher education is dependent on the Armed and Police Forces, provided by the Military Academy, the Air Force Academy, the Naval School and the Higher Police School. These state higher education institutions are all under the responsibility of various Ministries and are normally the subject of dual supervision: general supervision by the Ministry on which they are administratively dependent, and academic supervision by this Ministry and by the Ministry of Education.

The Military Academy, Air Force Academy and Naval School award *licenciado* degrees (higher education qualification) in their respective areas of specialization.

Admission

In 1992/93, in accordance with Decree 189 of September 1992, a new system for admission to state, private and cooperative higher education (universities and polytechnics) came into force.

Access to higher education establishments and courses is subject to numerus clausus. The number of places in state higher education supervised by the Ministry of Education is established annually by the respective management bodies. In private and cooperative higher education, the task of establishing the number of places is the responsibility of the Minister of Education, based on the proposals of the higher education institutions concerned.

Applicants must have successfully completed the 12th year in secondary education or hold legally equivalent qualifications, and have sat an aptitude test (*Prova de Aferição*) and the specific tests (*Provas específicas*) set for each course by the relevant higher education institutions. The aptitude test consists of a non-eliminatory written national examination in the subjects studied in secondary education. This is held after completion of the 12th year of schooling and has no influence on the award of the secondary school leaving certificate.

There is a centralized general admissions procedure. Applicants have to indicate, at national level through the Ministry of Education's *Nucleo de Acesso ao Ensino Superior*, in decreasing order of preference, up to six higher education establishments/courses they would like to attend. The order of applicants for each course is determined at each education establishment by an application mark, calculated on the basis of the various tests and secondary education marks.

The rules for access to the *Universidade Católica Portuguesa* (Portuguese Catholic University) are an exception to the above system and are set out in legislation passed in 1990.

Fees/Student finance

Students in state higher education pay fees which vary from institution to institution. The amount is fixed by the institution itself depending on the respective average cost per student. This system enables students to be exempted from or pay reduced fees in accordance with the per capita annual income of their families. Students from low-income families may also be entitled to a grant to cover subsistence, transport and study costs. Loans also exist, but are rare. Students awarded grants are exempt from tuition fees.

Academic year

There is no fixed date at national level for the beginning of the academic year in higher education institutions, as each School Board is responsible for its calendar. However, the year generally begins on October 15 and ends on July 31. Most institutions divide the academic year into two semesters, although certain subjects may be given throughout the year.

The academic year normally lasts for 15 to 16 weeks per semester, and the students usually have an average of 25/26 to 32 weekly class hours.

Courses/Qualifications

Within the scope of **state higher education**, the universities offer courses in all fields of study (humanities, social and behavioural sciences, business and management training, law, natural and exact sciences, mathematics and computer science, engineering sciences and technology, medical sciences, agriculture, forestry and fisheries, architecture and town planning and physical education). These courses may last for four, five or six years and lead to *licenciado* degrees.

The polytechnic higher education schools cover study areas such as agriculture, education, technology and/or management, accountancy and administration, engineering, art, nursing, sailing, conservation and restoration. Courses last for three or four years and lead to *bacharel* or *licenciado* degrees respectively.

Polytechnic higher education also leads to diplomas in specialist higher studies providing scientific, technical and cultural training in fields specializing in one activity and, after two years' study, the *bacharel* degree can be converted into a *licenciado* degree for vocational and academic purposes.

Private and cooperative higher education offers a wide range of courses from law, social sciences, humanities, fine arts, architecture and town planning, mathematics, computer science, business and company administration, engineering sciences and technology to dentistry. These courses last for three or four/five years, depending on whether they lead to *bacharel* or *licenciado* degrees.

Assessment

Students are assessed in each subject in their course. Assessment procedures depend on the institution or faculty concerned, but usually take the form of examinations. Students may retake examinations they have failed.

Statistics 1993/94

	State	Private	Total
Students	170,027	83,526	253,553
Teachers	16,450	7,432	23,882
Institutions	158	103	261

8. Initial vocational training

Within the framework of the Economic and Social Agreement established between the Government and the social partners at the end of 1990, a consensus was reached on the need to dynamize training by developing conditions for its generalization and quantitative and qualitative intensification, an objective that has been consolidated during the 1990-93 period.

The dividing line between the education and training systems is becoming less and less apparent, since both play decisive roles in initial and continuing training.

In 1992, within the scope of the technical-vocational education system, 27 Joint Decrees of the Ministry of Education and the Ministry of Employment and Social Security (MESS) set up some 80 new courses in the most diverse areas throughout the country, aiming to satisfy new concerns and arouse new interest among young people.

8.1 Apprenticeship system

The apprenticeship system comprises apprenticeship and pre-apprenticeship courses.

Apprenticeship

Apprenticeship (Decree-Law 102/84 of 25 March and 436/88 of 23 November) is based on cooperation between education, training and the labour market, with the aim of integrating young people into working life and developing human resources in companies.

Apprenticeship is intended for young people between 14 and 24 years of age, who have completed at least six years of compulsory education. Those who have not completed compulsory education (entering the normal education system before 1987) have access to pre-apprenticeship courses.

Apprenticeship is formalized in an apprenticeship contract, in which a recognized and qualified company undertakes to provide vocational training in cooperation with a training centre (centro de formação). The MESS, through the Institute of Employment and Vocational Training (IEFP), is responsible for checking the training capacity of each company and fixing the number of apprentices.

Apprenticeship lasts from one to four years, and comprises three parts:

– general training, provided in vocational training centres, for 25% of the time, including Portuguese, the contemporary world and a foreign language;

– technological training, also provided in vocational training centres, for 45% of the time. This varies according to the vocational sector and integrates basic sciences as support in technological fields, and activities simulating work situations;

– practical training, provided in an enterprise for 10% of the time in the 1st year, 25% of the time in the 2nd year, and 45% of the time in the 3rd and 4th years.

Throughout the course there should be a formative and continuous **assessment** of trainees in all aspects of the curriculum by means of tests and examinations in the three parts: general, technological and practical training.

Marks ranging from 0 to 20 are awarded for each aspect or part of the course. Ten points are considered the average minimum mark necessary to pass in each of the parts. However, in one of general or technological training a mark not lower than eight points is acceptable. Each year, the trainee is awarded final marks based on the arithmetical average of the marks obtained in the three parts of training. In order to move from one year to the next, trainees must receive pass marks in all three parts of training; a year may still be repeated in exceptional and duly justified cases.

Trainees who pass the final year of their course can be admitted to an examination of vocational aptitude.

All elements of assessment must be included in the trainee's report card which is presented to the examining board to be taken into account when they make the final assessment for the course.

The examining boards for the tests include at least three representatives from the respective technological area: one representative of the *IEFP*, who will chair the board; a trainer in the area of simulated practice or technological training; and a monitor of practical training.

The examining board for the vocational aptitude examination includes at least one representative from the Ministry of Education, the *IEFP* who will chair the board, and the social partners.

Trainees passing their apprenticeship receive a *Certificado de Aptidão Profissional* (certificate of vocational aptitude), which is important for the purposes of issuing professional documents and may lead to a certificate recognized as equivalent to school education.

The regulations for each occupation or group of occupations is defined in proposals issued by the *Comissão Nacional de Aprendizagem – CNA* (National Apprenticeship Committee), and adopted by joint decrees of the Ministers of Education and of Employment and Social Security.

Pre-apprenticeship

Pre-apprenticeship, established in Decree-Law 383/91, aims to complete compulsory education and, at the same time, to establish other conditions for access to apprenticeship in a skilled occupation.

It is intended for young people aged between 15 and 21 who, on the date of registration, have not completed compulsory education, or attended any school or course run by the Ministry of Education and have entered the education system before 1987 (commencement of nine years' compulsory

education as laid down by the Comprehensive Law on the Education System of 14 October 1986).

Pre-apprenticeship comprises general training (16 hours a week) and vocational training (19 hours a week) in a specific area, incorporating a practical component in which young people gain on-the-job experience (20% of the total time allocation).

General training is provided by state, private or cooperative education teachers. Vocational training is undertaken by training officers or monitors. State, private or cooperative bodies may establish these courses, concluding agreements between the parties involved (training centres, education establishments, employers and union organizations, local authorities, etc.).

The *IEFP* awards transport, personal accident insurance, subsistence and accommodation allowances and a monthly training grant.

The **assessment** of trainees on pre-apprenticeship courses is also both formative and continuous, but results in a general qualitative description of the trainee – either 'Able' or 'Not yet able'. Those trainees who are described 'Able' on completion of all areas of general and vocational training are considered to have passed their pre-apprenticeship course. Trainees described 'Not able' may repeat the year.

```
        *
      *   *
```

Thus, in accordance with the European Union qualification level to which it leads, the apprenticeship system is as follows:

Certification (level)	Minimum schooling required	Schooling equivalent	Duration
I (Pre-apprentice-ship)	1st cycle of basic education (4th year of schooling)	2nd cycle of basic education (6th year of schooling)	1-2 years
II	2nd cycle of basic education (6th year of schooling)	3rd cycle of basic education (9th year of schooling)	3-4 years
	3rd cycle of basic education (9th year of schooling)	Capitalization of secondary education modules	1-3 years
III	3rd cycle of basic education (9th year of schooling)	Secondary education (12th year of schooling)	3-4 years

Apprenticeship is provided in 27 training areas: agro-food; fisheries; automobile industry;

footwear; ceramics and glass; civil construction; cork; electricity; electronics; energy; cooling and air-conditioning; casting; mining; graphics and paper-making; timber and furniture; metallurgy and metal engineering; jewellery; chemicals; textiles; banking and insurance; communications; hotel, catering and tourism; computer industry; health; services; transport; and quality management.

There were 17,901 trainees involved in the apprenticeship system in 1992 and 20,320 in 1993.

In 1991, the number of trainees increased by some 36%. Most of these trainees followed Level II courses. However, this percentage fell from 87% to 74% compared with the previous year. Level III courses, launched in 1991, involved some 24% of the trainees in 1992 (compared with 11% in 1991). Level I courses were attended by some 3% of the total trainees (compared with 2% in 1991). There was an overall pass rate of 88.3%.

In 1992, the programme involved 10,356 trainers (compared with 10,006 in 1991), of whom around 50% were monitors/tutors supervising trainees during their on-the-job-training.

There has traditionally been a high number of trainers in comparison with the number of trainees in the apprenticeship system, due in part to the diversity of training courses available, the specific nature of multidisciplinary courses and the maximum limit of five young people per trainer in practical on-the-job training. In addition, apprenticeship is spread throughout Portugal and relies, in most cases, on external trainers whose involvement in the training process is both occasional and secondary. However, the regions have tried to reverse this trend by developing efforts to select a more stable group of trainers.

8.2 Initial training schemes

With a view to integrating young people into working life, other schemes – in addition to the apprenticeship system – were developed under the responsibility of state departments and public organizations, which were also incorporated into operational programmes *(Programas Operacionais – PO)* run by the Institute of Employment and Vocational Training *(Instituto do Emprego e Formação Profissional – IEFP)*, under the auspices

of the European Community Support Framework *(Quadro Comunitario de Apoio – QCA)*. These include the Programme for the Integration of Young People into Working Life *(Programa de Inserção de Jovens na Vida Profissional – IJOVIP)* and the Programme for the Training and Integration of Executives *((Programa de Formação – Integração de Quadros – FIQ)* which ran from 1989 until April 1993.

From 9 April 1993 until the end of the current year, new regulations have come into force (Ruling 52/93) with regard to training schemes promoted by the *IEFP*, taking into account the Vocational Training Policy Agreement, which aims to promote vocational training leading to qualifications and lasting at least one year.

The new measures aim to prepare young people and executives better for employment, helping them to obtain vocational and employment qualifications, and to provide employers with skilled workers.

These measures are aimed at:

- young unemployed people registered at job centres, aged between 18 and 25, who have followed compulsory schooling as a minimum requirement and are not attending school (apart from those who have registered for evening courses);

- young people under 25, registered at job centres, who hold a university degree or the equivalent, or who have followed a technical-vocational course or the 12th year of schooling.

On-the-job-training schemes and training courses provided in a work context (enterprises, public and private bodies, professional organizations), lasting one year, are carried out in two stages:

- 90 working days of general theory and technological training, six hours a day;

- 150 working days of practical training, seven hours a day.

State, private or cooperative bodies which are interested in the training and recruitment of workers and meet the requirements for receiving trainees on their premises may apply to the *IEFP* to become organizing bodies.

A standard training contract will be drawn up between the organizing bodies and the trainees, establishing the relations between the parties. The training scheme and training course for trainees will be established after the cooperation agreement has been drawn up between the *IEFP* and the organizing bodies.

The *IEFP* provides trainees with a training grant on a monthly basis and, as appropriate, may pay an accommodation allowance and travel expenses.

In the framework of initial training for young people, training is also provided in the areas of agriculture, fisheries, industry, tourism, health and services (banking, insurance).

The major objectives for the implementation of a strategic approach to the new employment and vocational training programme for the period 1994-1999 have been established, bearing in mind the current situation and the future prospects of the labour market. One of the main objectives will be to expand and examine carefully the initial training of young people, both through qualifying subsystems of long-term training and through initial training schemes of at least one year's duration before commencing working life, and by taking measures with a view to integrating young people into the labour market.

Finland

FINLAND

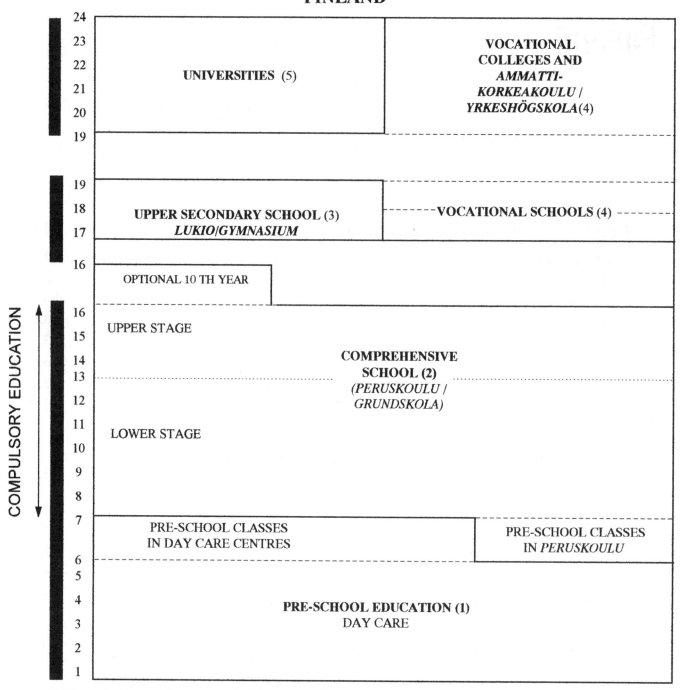

1. The main forms of day care are the kindergarten/day care centres (*Päiväkoti/Daghem*) for children up to the age of 6, and family day care. 6- to 7-year-olds can follow pre-school education in day care centres or in comprehensive schools.

2. *Peruskoulu,* the comprehensive school, lasts nine years, but can also provide pre-school education for six-year-olds and an optional tenth year for those who have completed their compulsory education.

3. *Lukio,* the upper secondary school, provides three years of general education leading to the national matriculation examination.

4. Basic vocational training (2-3 years) is given in multidisciplinary or specialized vocational schools. Higher vocational education (3-5 years) is usually given at specialized colleges which can be entered either after comprehensive school or (usually) after completed secondary level studies. Apprenticeship is provided as an alternative route to these qualifications. *Ammattikorkeakoulu* is a new *Fachhochschule*-type institution of higher vocational education whose 3- to 4- year programmes lead to an academic degree.

5. The basic university degree (Master's degree) consists of three stages and takes 5-6 years to complete.

······ = division in the level/type of education

– – – – = alternative beginning or end of level / type of education.

1. Responsibilities and administration

1.1 Background

Finland has a land area of 338,000 square kilometres. Its population is just over five million, about 60% of whom live in cities and built-up areas. The population of the capital, Helsinki, is about 500,000.

There are two official languages in Finland, Finnish and Swedish, with 94% of the population speaking Finnish as their mother tongue and 6% Swedish. Finnish citizens are entitled to receive public services, including education, in their mother tongue. Sámi speakers, about 0.03% of the population, are entitled to receive education in their mother tongue. The state religions are Lutheran (87%) and Orthodox (1%). About 10% of the population do not belong to any religious denomination.

Finland is a parliamentary republic. The 200 members of the unicameral Parliament are elected by General Election for a four-year term. Parliament enacts all legislation, and the Government must enjoy the confidence of Parliament. The President of the Republic is elected by direct popular vote for a six-year term. Local government is exercised by 12 provinces and 440 municipalities.

The employment sectors are distributed as follows: services 60%, industry 30%, agriculture 10%. In May 1994, the unemployment rate was 18.1%. In 1991, it was 7.5%.

1.2 Basic principles: education

The Constitution Act of Finland (1919) stipulates that general compulsory education and a folk school free of charge must be enacted by law. It also charges the Government with maintaining or subsidizing vocational education, general education, higher education in applied arts and sciences and university education. The Constitution Act further stipulates that the right to found private schools and reformatories shall be enacted by law and that home tuition shall not be supervised by the authorities.

In the post-war period, the main aim of Finland's education policy has been to raise the level of education and to offer equal education opportunities to all citizens regardless of their place of residence, wealth, mother tongue or sex. This aim has largely been attained. The network of schools and institutions covers the entire country, and there are enough pupil places to satisfy demand.

The focus of education policy has shifted from creating the infrastructure to improving quality. The present stage involves improving the efficiency of the education system, enhancing its capacity for meeting demand, increasing the number of choices available to pupils and transferring to schools the power to make decisions about the curriculum and its implementation. Educational institutions are encouraged to cooperate with each other and with the surrounding community. The aim is to produce a simple and clear, internationally compatible education structure and a study environment sensitive to the pupils individual wishes and to the needs of society.

In June 1993, the Council of State made a decision in principle on the development of the Finnish education system in the 1990s. According to this decision, the role of education and scientific research in the national development strategy will be reinforced. The main aims of education and science policy are: to maintain a high and wide-ranging level of education; to promote the spiritual growth of the nation; to encourage initiative and enterprise; to improve the quality of education and research; to expand the industrial base and consolidate the innovation process; to harmonize work, education and changing life situations; to develop professional skills and increase employment.

1.3 Distribution of responsibilities

The Ministry of Education is the highest education authority in Finland. Nearly all publicly subsidized education is subordinate to or supervised by the Ministry.

The most important sectors of education falling outside the purview of the Ministry of Education are: children's day care (Ministry of Social Affairs and Health); military training (Ministry of Defence); and police, border guard and fire training (Ministry of the Interior).

The provinces and municipalities also have certain responsibilities. Under recent legislation, regions, comprising several municipalities, will be responsible for administration at regional/local level and provincial involvement will decrease.

1.4 Administration

Central

The legislative framework for and general principles of education policy are enacted by Parliament. The Government, the Ministry of Education and the National Board of Education are responsible for implementing this policy at the central administration level.

The Ministry of Education prepares education legislation and makes the necessary decisions for submission to the Government. The purview of the Ministry of Education includes education and research: comprehensive school, upper secondary school, vocational schools and colleges, and universities. The Ministry is also responsible for culture, church, youth and sports affairs. The Ministry of Education has two ministers: the Minister of Education, responsible for education

and science; and the Minister of Culture, responsible for culture, church, youth and sports affairs. The Ministry of Education is divided into an education and science policy section, a culture section and administrative and staff functions.

The National Board of Education is an expert agency responsible for the development of education aims, content and methods in comprehensive school, upper secondary school, vocational training and adult education. It draws up and approves the national guidelines for curriculum design and is responsible for evaluating the Finnish education system. It also assists the Ministry of Education in preparing education policy decisions. The National Board of Education is managed by a Board of Directors, whose members are education experts, representatives of the social partners, municipal officials and teachers. The National Board of Education is divided into a general education section, a vocational education section, an adult education section, a Swedish-speaking education section, a planning group and administrative and service functions.

There are no other central administrative units in the education sector in Finland. National guidance of the education system is at the discretion of the Government and the Ministry of Education regarding the founding of secondary and higher education institutions and the scaling (setting quotas for different sectors and regions) of vocational education. Educational institutions are guided operatively through the aims enacted by legislation and through the national guidelines for curriculum design. Feedback on the work of the education system is collected through statistics and targeted evaluations. This information in itself has a steering effect on teaching.

Regional/local/institutional

For the purposes of regional administration, Finland is divided into twelve provinces. Each province has a provincial government headed by a governor, and a state department or unit for the administration of schools and culture. In the past few years, the duties of the provincial governments have decreased; they now manage only the national student selection system within the province, allocate vocational training student capacity among the colleges in the province and allocate certain extraordinary Government subsidies. Provincial involvement in education administration continues to decrease; the aim is to create a two-tier administration system involving only the state central administration and local authorities. New legislation (1994) has shifted regional planning and development to the regions themselves, managed by Regional Councils whose authority is based on the municipalities which make up their respective regions. In other words, regional development is being transferred from the national parliamentary decision-making process to the municipal level. The division of responsibility between the provinces and the Regional Councils is in a state of transition at present and subject to political debate.

Local administration is managed by the municipalities, which are self-governing and have the right to levy taxes. There are about 440 municipalities in Finland. Decision-making power in a municipality rests with the elected Municipal Council. The Council appoints the municipal executive board and several advisory boards.

Each municipality has at least one School Board appointed by the Municipal Council. Most upper secondary schools and comprehensive schools are maintained by the municipalities. The municipal school authority can also be responsible for adult training centres, night schools and vocational institutions. State owned and privately owned schools do not come within the sphere of the municipal authority, but are directly subordinate to the central administration.

In Finland, a municipality is obliged to organize comprehensive school education for all children living within its borders or to ensure that children of school age can receive comparable teaching in some other manner. Upper secondary schools, vocational schools and colleges can be maintained by municipalities, intermunicipal authorities (cooperation between municipalities for certain schools), or private organizations or foundations, subject to government approval.

There are only 24 private comprehensive schools in Finland (0.5%). These are mainly maintained by internationally recognized educational organizations. Only one school is maintained by a religious organization. About 54% of all vocational institutions are maintained by municipalities (usually by two or more municipalities jointly); 34% are state owned and 12% are private.

Each school can and usually does have a managing board where teachers, non-teaching staff, pupils/ students and parents are represented. The main tasks of the managing board are developing the work of the school and promoting cooperation inside the school and between the school, parents and the local community. In each school there is also a pupils/students' union which, among other things, elects the pupil/student representatives to the managing board. Each municipal authority decides on the distribution of responsibilities between the municipal administration and the managing board of a particular school. Moreover, municipalities can cooperate in school administration and two or more schools can have a managing board in common.

Vocational schools and higher vocational education institutions usually have similar managing boards (parents are not represented), but they tend to be more independent and powerful. State and privately run vocational schools always have one. In addition to managing boards, as a rule vocational institutions have one or more advisory boards to promote training and cooperation between school and working life. These boards consist of representatives from the school, its teachers, the main social partners in the relevant fields and other experts.

Curricula for comprehensive school, upper secondary school and vocational institutions are drawn up locally. Every school must have a curriculum decided upon by those maintaining the school or an organ appointed by them, usually the municipality or the School Board. Curricula are based on the national guidelines for curriculum design issued by the National Board of Education. Curriculum design in universities and polytechnics is guided solely by legislation. Teaching materials are not inspected or defined in advance in Finland. The decision for choosing teaching material usually rests with individual teachers.

The teachers and institutions themselves are responsible for assessing student performance and for issuing reports. Only the matriculation examination, which concludes upper secondary school, is organized and marked by a national examination committee appointed by the Ministry of Education.

All universities are maintained by the State. They enjoy a high degree of autonomy in organizing teaching, research and other internal matters. At university level it falls within their autonomy to found advisory bodies. The decision-making bodies are regulated in Acts and Decrees and there is separate legislation about each university. The legislation varies from university to university but there are generally decision-making bodies at three levels: central administration, faculty (by science) and institute (by subject) levels. At each level at least professors, other personnel and students are represented.

1.5 Inspection

There is no separate school inspectorate. National guidance of the education system is at the discretion of the Government and the Ministry of Education.

1.6 Financing

Responsibility for education provision, construction and financing is divided between the State and local authorities; universities are financed directly from the state budget. A separate Act stipulates the distribution of financial responsibility for comprehensive schools, upper secondary schools and vocational education. The principles of public financing are the same irrespective of the owner of the school or institution.

Local authorities and other parties maintaining schools and institutions are entitled to government grants for the founding and operating costs of educational institutions in addition to their own funding. Government subsidies are calculated to cover from 25% to 70% of founding costs and 45% to 60% of operating costs. The main factors affecting government subsidies are the number of pupils and the financial capacity of the municipalities concerned. Government subsidies are not earmarked for any particular costs.

Teachers' salaries are paid by the school or the owner of the school, usually the municipality.

Comprehensive school is completely free for pupils, inclusive of tuition, teaching materials, school meals and transport. In general, tuition is free at other levels, too. At secondary level, school meals are free and transport can be free, but pupils are usually required to pay for teaching materials.

The Government supports secondary and university-level students through grants, study loan guarantees and interest subsidies.

1.7 Private education

Non-subsidized private education is practically non-existent in Finland. The general principles of government subsidies and curricular guidance also apply to privately maintained schools.

1.8 Advisory bodies

The Ministry of Education is assisted by three major advisory bodies. The Council for Higher Education deals with and prepares matters of principle concerning the planning and development of higher education. The Advisory Council for Adult Education examines questions relating to the development of continuing education. The Advisory Council for Educational Planning deals with the quantitative development of all post-compulsory education and forecasts educational needs.

The National Board of Education is assisted by a number of advisory boards representing the relevant social partners and expertise in the different sectors of vocational education.

2. Pre-school education: Day care and pre-school classes (Päivähoito/Dagvård, Esikoulu/Förskola)

Day care is governed by the Act and Decree on children's day care. The day care system is administered by the Ministry of Social Affairs and Health. Responsibility for organizing day care rests with the social services of the local authorities. By law, a municipality must provide for sufficient day care to cover needs. The day care service is a social service subject to a fee, determined by parental income and the size of the family.

All children under the age of three are entitled to day care if their parents so desire. Instead of a day care place, parents can opt for the municipal child care allowance with which they can organize day care for their child as they please.

The supply of day care places for children over three does not always meet demand. If there are not enough places, priority must be given to children who require day care for social or educational reasons.

The main forms of day care are the kindergarten/ day care centre (*Päiväkoti/Daghem*) and family day care. Day care can also involve guided play, for example, playground activities.

The aim of day care is to support the parents in bringing up the child and to promote the balanced growth and learning of the child. Day care can be full-time or part-time. The maximum daily times for full-time and part-time day care are ten and five hours respectively. Day care centres are usually open for 5 days per week, but can be open for 6 or 7 days, throughout the whole year. They are usually open between 6.30 a.m. and 5.30 p.m., but other arrangements can be made according to need.

Day care centres are institutions for the day care of children up to the age of six/seven. They are usually organized by age group (e.g. under-threes and threes-to-sixes). In large day care centres, six-year-olds have a separate pre-school class. The size of day care centres and of groups of children is not regulated. However, there are regulations concerning the minimum number of staff per group, according to the number and age of the children. In practice, most day care centres have 20 to 100 places.

Family day care takes place in the home of the carer or in another private home. The advantages of this form of day care are the home-like conditions and small groups. One carer is allowed a maximum of four children below school age, plus one part-time day care child who is in school or pre-school. Training for private carers varies. Each municipality has a family day care counsellor who coordinates the work of the private carers.

33% of the 0 to 6 year age group attend one of the main forms of day care full-time and 7.5% part-time. Day care centres also provide voluntary pre-school teaching for six-year-olds who will start school the following year. About 59% of all six-year-olds (34,360 children) participate in pre-school teaching.

In sparsely populated areas, pre-school teaching is organized at schools, in which case it comes under the administration of the Ministry of Education. This form of pre-school provision is attended by only about 2% (1,950 children) of each age group. It complements the day care system and ensures equal education opportunities for all children under school age nationwide. Apart from the publicly provided services, the Church and some voluntary organizations provide various pre-school teaching services.

Teaching for six-year-olds is based on the curriculum guidelines for day care centres and comprehensive schools, which have been issued jointly by the National Board of Education and the National Research and Development Centre for Welfare and Health. The basic principles are the child's individuality and initiative in learning, playing and his/her relationship with the community, culture and the natural environment. Teaching is not organized by subject but by thematic projects in which the various subjects are naturally connected to things children do. The curriculum guidelines include, for reference only, the following subjects: language and communication, nature and the environment, mathematics, art, music, handicrafts, physical education, and ethical and religious instruction.

Teachers/Staff

The teaching and guidance staff in day care centres consist of kindergarten teachers, who have educational responsibility, child day care workers, paediatric nurses and other child care professionals.

Kindergarten teachers have completed three years of teacher training at a specialized institution of higher vocational education. Child day care workers have completed two-and-a-half years of

vocational training at upper-secondary level. Child day care and pre-school workers must follow further education or in-service training every five years. Training for family day care childminders lasts a minimum of 260 hours.

In 1995, the education of kindergarten teachers is being transferred to universities. The programme will comprise 120 credits leading to a lower university degree (see page 345).

Statistics 1992/93

	Day care centre	Family day care
Children		
Full-time	88,600	57,600
Part-time	23,900	8,900
Teachers/Staff	50,150	
Centres/families	2,087	16,550
Pupil/Staff ratio	5.4	2.9

3. Compulsory education

All Finnish citizens are obliged to obtain education for a period of ten years, beginning in the year in which they have their seventh birthday. The obligation expires in the year they are seventeen years old or when they have completed the comprehensive school curriculum, whichever occurs first. Compulsory education does not mean compulsory school attendance; pupils are free to acquire the equivalent skills and knowledge from some other source. In practice, however, nearly all Finns attend the nine-year comprehensive school.

Comprehensive school (Peruskoulu/Grundskola)

The comprehensive school provides general education for the whole age group, and is free of charge for all citizens. It is governed by the Act and Decree on the Comprehensive School (1983). The comprehensive school is intended for children from 7 to 16 years of age and lasts nine years. There are no entrance requirements. Children are invited to attend school in the year in which they have their seventh birthday. A pupil is free, within certain limits, to choose his/her comprehensive school within his/her home municipality. If it is impossible for a pupil to attend school, for health or some other reason, the home municipality of the pupil is obliged to provide comparable teaching in some other form. In practice, almost 100% of all children attend comprehensive school and obtain a leaving certificate. In the 1991/92 school year, 78 pupils dropped out of comprehensive school (0.1% of the age group).

The comprehensive school is divided into the lower stage (years 1 to 6) and upper stage (years 7 to 9). Comprehensive school can also provide pre-school education for six-year-olds and an extra tenth year for those who have completed their compulsory education. However, the entire nine-year school is considered a single entity enacted by law. Since nearly all comprehensive schools and most upper secondary schools operate under municipal jurisdiction, their administrative organization varies: lower stage comprehensive schools, upper stage comprehensive schools and upper secondary schools can function as separate units or in various combinations.

Finnish children are provided with teaching in their mother tongue, that is, Finnish, Swedish or Sami. Each school usually employs only one language. Special arrangements exist for immigrants and refugees. All schools are coeducational.

The aims of the comprehensive school are to promote the development of pupils' personalities, to support their attainment of the skills and knowledge required for further study or employment, and to ensure their growth and cooperation by taking individual differences into account.

All pupils who complete the comprehensive school are equally qualified to continue their studies at upper secondary school or vocational school. After leaving comprehensive school, pupils can choose any educational institution in the country to continue their studies. This is possible since pupils' home municipality is obliged to cover upper secondary or vocational education costs not covered by government subsidies.

The school year begins in August and ends in the 22nd week of the following calendar year and is divided into two semesters. The school year consists of 190 working days; the number of hours of lessons of an individual pupil range from 19 to 32 per 5-day week, depending on the form and the number of optional subjects.

Curriculum

Teaching in comprehensive schools is provided according to the school curriculum, which is drawn up by the local education authorities and schools on the basis of the national guidelines on curriculum design drawn up by the National Board of Education. Municipalities and schools have significant powers in deciding on the curriculum to ensure that teaching meets local needs. The guidelines essentially contain the general aims of the comprehensive school, the aims and central content of the various subjects and the principles for pupil assessment. The subjects included in the curriculum are stipulated in the Comprehensive School Act and Decree. The distribution of hours is decided by the Council of State. In the main, all pupils at the lower stage receive the same teaching, but schools are free to vary the weight and grouping of individual subjects by allocating teaching resources within the general framework of government financing. The curriculum for the upper stage includes common subjects and elective subjects, as well as practical work experience and courses embracing several subjects.

The distribution of hours at the lower stage of the comprehensive schools is as follows:

Subject	Minimum curriculum hours over six years
Finnish/Swedish (mother tongue)	32
Language beginning at the lower stage (foreign language or second national language) (A language)	8
Optional language	4
Mathematics	22
Environment and nature study	15
Religion or ethics	8
History	3
Arts and skills of which	44
Music	6
Art	6
Handcrafts	8
Physical education	12

Curriculum hours are the cumulative weekly hours taught over the entire six-year lower stage. Thus, the 32 hours of Finnish/Swedish work out at an average of $5^{1}/_3$ hours per week for six years. The municipality or school can decide how to distribute these hours per year. The municipality or school can also decide to allocate a higher number of hours to compulsory subjects; the total minimum is 132 hours, while the total maximum is 144 hours.

The distribution of hours at the upper stage of the comprehensive schools is as follows:

Subject	Minimum curriculum hours over three years
Finnish/Swedish (mother tongue)	8
Foreign language beginning at the lower stage (A language)	8
Foreign language beginning at the upper stage (B language)	6
Mathematics	9
Biology, geography	7
Physics, chemistry	6
Religion or ethics	3
History, social studies	6
Music	1
Art	2
Home economics	3
Handicrafts, technical work, textile work	3
Physical education	6
Pupil guidance	2
General education subjects –minimum total	70
Elective subjects – maximum total	20

The above figures are the weekly curriculum taught over the entire three-year upper stage. Thus, the 8 hours of Finnish/Swedish work out at an average of $2^{2}/_3$ hours per week for three years. The municipality or school can decide how to distribute the hours per year.

Elective subjects are no longer stipulated by decree, with the exception of Sámi, which must be provided as an option in areas with a Sámi-speaking population. The number, type and form of elective subjects can be decided by the municipality or school.

At the lower stage of the comprehensive school pupil **guidance** is integrated (no separate hours) and concentrates on learning skills and methods. At the upper stage it takes the form of individual guidance, small group or class instruction or discussions on further studies and careers. There are usually also study visits to work places, upper secondary and vocational schools.

Assessment

The purpose of assessment is to encourage the pupil in a positive way to set his/her own goals, plan his/her work and make independent choices. For this reason, assessment is an ongoing part of the daily activities at school. Each pupil is given a report in writing at the end of the school year and at least once during the school year. After completing the comprehensive school, the pupil is given a leaving certificate. The reports may be descriptive in the first four years. The numerical grades range from 4 (fail) to 10 (excellent). Assessment is based on continuous achievement (competence) in classwork and homework and tests organized by teachers; assessment is relative to the aims of the curriculum. A pupil can be required to repeat a class in comprehensive school, but this is not very common. In 1992, 0.4% of all pupils were required to repeat a class and 0.1% left school without a leaving certificate.

Teachers

There are four kinds of teacher in comprehensive schools:

- class teachers, who teach all of the lower stage subjects;

- subject teachers, who teach one or two subjects at the upper stage and, in some cases, at the lower stage, too;

- special teachers, who teach children suffering from speaking, reading or writing disorders or other problems in normal comprehensive schools, in special classes in normal comprehensive schools or in special schools for severely disabled pupils;

- counsellors, who provide educational and vocational guidance at the upper stage.

The qualification requirements for teaching posts are stipulated by decree. The class teacher training programme consists of 160 credits (4 years) and leads to an academic degree, its main subject being pedagogics. Class teacher studies also include basic studies in several subjects, specialization in one or two teaching subjects and a period of practical teacher training.

A subject teacher must have an academic degree from the faculty to which his subject belongs. A subject teacher's degree must include studies in pedagogics and a period of practical teacher training.

Most teachers (94%) are employed full-time as municipal civil servants. Comprehensive school teachers must participate in in-service training at least three days a year.

Reform

The comprehensive school reform was begun in 1971 and implemented by stages over the following ten years. The main substance of the reform was to create a nine-year school system for all children of compulsory education age. Before this, a system had been used whereby pupils were divided at the age of eleven into two streams: those aiming at vocational training and employment on the one hand and those aiming at further studies on the other.

Comprehensive school has remained structurally more or less the same since the 1970s. However, the authority of the local authority and the school has been systematically augmented through partial reform and through developing the distribution of hours; at the same time, the degree of central control has been decreased. The national guidelines for curriculum design were introduced in 1985, leaving the local authorities and schools to draw up their own curricula. Since 1991, government financing

has been computational, and local decision-making has been further enhanced. The 1993 decision on the distribution of hours in comprehensive school will significantly increase the opportunities for local authorities and schools to profile teaching according to local and pupil needs. Placing the subjects in different years was wholly delegated to the local level. The decision on distributing hours stipulates the minimum number of hours in any given subject, but this figure can be raised by a local decision. The local curriculum also determines which elective subjects will be offered at each school.

Statistics 1992-Comprehensive Schools

Schools by teaching language	Finnish	4,406
	Swedish	321
	Other	3
	Total	4,730
Pupils	Finnish	561,005
	Swedish	30,650
	Total	591,655
Teachers (full-time)	Finnish	41,752
	Swedish	2,679
	Total	44,431

4. Upper secondary school (Lukio/Gymnasium)

Education policy principles

Post-compulsory education is provided mainly by upper secondary schools, vocational schools and vocational colleges. Those wishing to enter upper secondary schools or vocational institutions must possess the comprehensive school leaving certificate.

One of the main principles of Finnish education policy is to make post-compulsory education available to the entire age group. Over half (54%) of comprehensive school leavers continue their studies at upper secondary schools, and slightly under half (40%) go on to vocational institutions. The remaining 6% either enter the optional 10th year or the labour market.

Upper secondary education is progressing towards a highly decentralized system. The responsibility for teaching arrangements, course content and the selection of teaching material have been passed to the local level, giving upper secondary schools and vocational institutions the opportunity to cooperate with each other and to increase the educational resources needed in their respective areas and meet the pupils' individual needs. Vocational education and training are described in 5.

Upper secondary school (Lukio/Gymnasium)

The upper secondary school provides three years of general education for pupils aged 16 to 19. It continues the teaching functions of the comprehensive school and qualifies the pupil for all higher level studies. The upper secondary school leads to the national matriculation examination.

Several regulations govern upper secondary schools; these regulations were thoroughly revised in 1991. Maintenance of an upper secondary school is subject to approval by the Council of State. The maintaining body can be a municipality, an intermunicipal authority or a private body. Previously, the supply of upper secondary schools was regulated by decisions concerning pupil numbers, but this principle was abandoned in 1993, and pupil numbers now follow demand. There are 481 upper secondary schools in all in Finland, of which 18 are night schools. The main purpose of the latter is to provide people with an opportunity to complete upper secondary school while working. There is an average of 224 pupils per school, with an average of 30 pupils per group.

Traditionally, classes have been organized by age with pupils allocated on the basis of their subject choices each year. Since 1982, teaching in upper secondary schools has been organized into courses, each course consisting of 38 lessons of 45 minutes each. The usual practice is to divide the school year into sections of five or six periods each. Each section has a different study plan and concentrates on a selection of subjects. It is completely up to the individual school how teaching is distributed; even the traditional practice of teaching all subjects throughout the school year can be followed.

An experiment was begun in 1987 to dispense with form progression in upper secondary schools, leaving the order and placement of courses for the schools and pupils to decide. As a result, a system dispensing with forms was implemented nationwide as of 1994.

This choice, too, will be made by the school: it can if it prefers opt to continue as a three-form school with pupils progressing from one form to the next year by year. If the school chooses to dispense with forms, the pupils can opt to extend their studies over three or four years.

The school year in upper secondary school begins in August and ends in the 22nd week of the following calendar year. In a three-form school the first two years have 190 days of teaching and the third year at least 120. The end of the spring term is used for final examinations and the oral and written matriculation examination. Schools operate five days per week. Opening hours are not regulated and vary from school to school.

Curriculum

The subjects and subject groups in the upper secondary school curriculum are defined in the Upper Secondary School Act and Decree. The Council of State decides on the minimum number of courses in each subject. The National Board of Education decides on the guidelines for drawing up the curriculum at individual schools. Within the national guidelines, schools draw up their own curriculum, or the schools of a municipality may cooperate in drawing up a curriculum.

Upper secondary school studies consist of compulsory studies, advanced studies and applied studies. Every pupil must complete the compulsory studies. The school must provide the advanced studies for the pupil to choose from. The pupil is responsible for taking a sufficient number of courses. The applied studies can be further studies in existing subjects or new subjects. Each school can decide on these independently. These courses can also be offered by arrangement with other institutions, such as vocational institutions or private music schools.

The distribution of hours in upper secondary school (number of courses x 38 lessons of 45 minutes) is as follows:

Subject or subject group	Compulsory studies	Advanced courses – minimum offered by the school
Finnish/Swedish	6	2
Foreign languages		
Language begun in lower stage of comprehensive school (A language)	6	2
Language begun in upper stage of comprehensive school (B language)	5	2
Other languages		16
Mathematics		
Basic course	6	2
Advanced course	10	3
Environment and natural sciences		
Biology	2	2
Geography	2	2
Physics	1	7
Chemistry	1	3
Moral subjects		
Religion/ethics	3	2
Philosophy	1	2
Psychology		5
History, Social Studies	5	3
Arts	3	
Music (1-2)		3
Art (1-2)		3
Physical education, Health education	3	3
Pupil counselling	1	
Compulsory subjects	45-49	
Advanced courses minimum (from those offered)	10	
Applied studies courses (to make up the total minimum)		
Total minimum	75	

Assessment and qualifications

The purpose of pupil assessment is to give pupils feedback on the progress of their studies and on their achievement both during and when concluding upper secondary school.

Assessment is based on aims defined in the curriculum. As mentioned above, studies in upper secondary school are divided into courses of 38 'hours' each on average. The performance of the pupil is assessed by the teacher at the end of each course. This assessment is based on any written tests and the continuous assessment of the learning process and work of the pupil.

Results can be expressed by numerical marks (4 to 10) or, for example, by pass/fail or a description. The assessment method is set down in the school curriculum; this also defines how the assessment for each subject is carried out on the basis of the course assessments. Nevertheless, only numerical marks are used in reports and certificates.

Pupils are deemed to have completed upper secondary school when they have satisfactorily completed the required number of courses in all subjects in their study programmes, in accordance with the minimum requirements given above. They are then awarded a leaving certificate.

At the end of the third year, pupils take the matriculation examination. It comprises four compulsory subjects and optional subjects. The compulsory subjects are mother tongue (Finnish, Swedish or Sámi, depending on which is the teaching language at the school), the second official language (Finnish or Swedish), one foreign language and either mathematics or science and humanities. The latter comprises questions in several subjects; the pupil is free to choose any combination of questions and subjects: religion and ethics, psychology and philosophy, history and civics, physics, chemistry, biology and geography.

The matriculation examination is set and assessed nationally, at the same time countrywide, by a committee appointed by the Ministry of Education. A separate certificate is given for passing the matriculation examination. Each subject is awarded a grade on a scale consisting of laudatur (7), eximia cum laude approbatur (6), magna cum laude approbatur (5), cum laude approbatur (4), lubenter approbatur (3), approbatur (2) and improbatur (0).

Of the pupils matriculating from upper secondary school, about one-third go on to university, while two-thirds continue at vocational institutions or the new higher-level institutions (*Ammattikorkeakoulut*).

Teachers

Upper secondary school teachers usually have an academic degree like comprehensive school subject teachers (see above). As subject teachers, they usually teach one or two subjects. The majority have full-time posts and are local government officials.

Upper secondary school teachers are obliged to devote three days a year to in-service training.

A teaching post can be shared with another educational institution, such as a comprehensive school or vocational institution. The Nordic countries have entered an agreement on a common job market in all five Nordic countries for teachers of general, aesthetic and practical subjects in comprehensive school, upper secondary school and vocational institutions.

Statistics 1992/93

General Upper Secondary Education	
Schools	
Finnish	428
Swedish	32
Other	3
Total	463
Pupils	
Finnish	93,448
Swedish	5,688
Total	99,136
Teachers	
Finnish	5,965
Swedish	410
Total	6,375

5. Vocational education and training

The Finnish vocational education system is a combination of various disciplines, institution types and levels of education. It is governed by the Act on Vocational Institutions (1987) and separate decrees for each type of institution. Vocational education is offered at three distinct levels, and students can at present enter all of them either after leaving comprehensive school or after passing the matriculation examination. Students entering from comprehensive school can obtain a school-level qualification after 2 to 3 years of study (ISCED level 3), a college-level qualification after 2 to 5 years (ISCED level 5), and a higher-level qualification after 4 to 5 years (ISCED level 6). Upper secondary school leavers can complete each level in less time – six months to 1 year less – than comprehensive school leavers, since they are credited for their upper secondary school studies. The two groups basically have separate curricula, but they study for the same qualifications. Significant changes are currently being implemented in the structure of vocational education in order, for instance, to clarify the distinction between levels.

Under the existing structure, teaching is organized into 26 basic programmes that cover all branches of working life. These basic programmes are further sub-divided into about 220 occupation-oriented specialization courses. Students who enter vocational education directly from the comprehensive school choose one of the basic programmes in the first year but do not decide whether to take a school-level or college-level specialization course until the second year. In each of the 26 basic programmes, the first-year studies consist of the general and vocational subjects that the school-level and college-level qualifications have in common. After the first year, the students choose specialization courses, some of which are at the secondary level, some at the college or higher-level. There are exceptions to the rule. In practice, most people studying for college-level or higher-level qualifications already have a secondary-level vocational certificate or have passed the matriculation examination. The study programmes for students who have passed the matriculation examination are organized separately; these students go directly to the specialization courses. The final qualifications are the same regardless of prior studies. About 17% of the school-level study programmes are based on the matriculation examination; the corresponding figure for college-level and higher-level studies is 60%.

Eight basic programmes out of 26 have been made into consecutive rather than parallel programmes; thus, a secondary-level qualification is required for admission to college-level studies.

The entire system will change over to the consecutive model in 1995. The vocational education system will be reformed, and college level and vocational higher level education will only be entered by students who have completed either general upper secondary school or vocational secondary education. Simultaneously, the whole system of basic programmes will be dismantled, and education will be reorganized into more extensive entities and programmes based on sectors and fields.

A vocational school leaving certificate qualifies the student for further studies in the same field at a vocational college or higher-level institution; the student can qualify for university studies by passing the matriculation examination. Completed college-level and higher-level studies qualify the student for university studies.

Vocational education is usually given in institutions which are specialized by occupational sector and offer both secondary and post-secondary education. For industrial occupations, secondary level vocational education is usually given at multidisciplinary vocational schools and post-secondary level education at technical institutions.

Apprenticeship is provided as an alternative to school-form vocational studies, but this only involves about 3 to 4% of all vocational education students.

There are 13 basic programmes for industrial occupations. The most common courses are engineering and metallurgy, electronics, automobile industry and transport, construction and textile industry.

Maritime institutes provide tuition at both the secondary and post-secondary levels.

There are specialized institutes for handicrafts, applied art and communications. Students completing courses at these institutes usually work in small craft businesses or in the applied arts sector.

Commercial institutes qualify students for many occupations in business, trade, public administration and information technology. Tuition is given at both the secondary and post-secondary levels.

Hotel and restaurant training is available at specialized hotel and restaurant institutes, multidisciplinary vocational schools and certain maritime institutes. Some institutes specialize in home and institutional economics.

Health and social affairs training is given at specialized institutes at both the secondary and post-secondary levels. There are also specialized institutes for cosmetology, hairdressing, art, music and physical education.

Agricultural institutes provide secondary level and post-secondary level tuition in agriculture, horticulture and fishing.

Forestry institutes provide tuition at the secondary and post-secondary levels. Forestry studies include a great deal of practical training.

Nearly all agricultural and forestry institutes and about half of the home economics institutes are boarding schools.

The school year is divided into two semesters. The autumn semester begins in August and ends in December. The spring semester begins in January and ends in May. The number of working days in a school year is usually 190, and students have a maximum of 35 hours of lessons per week.

Curriculum

The curricula for vocational education are based on the national guidelines for curriculum design. Institutions draw up their own curricula within the national framework. They can allocate a maximum of 30% of total teaching time to local and regional training needs.

The National Board of Education draws up, approves and maintains the guidelines for curriculum design. New curricula will be introduced in all sectors in 1995. The guidelines are outlined in cooperation with experts representing the labour market, research institutes and educational institutions.

At the moment, the curricula include occupation-oriented vocational studies and common compulsory subjects. All vocational studies include, in addition to the general and theoretical subjects, practical training. Most of the studies are conducted at the vocational institution, although some of the practical work in the curriculum can be organized on-the-job. Contrary to the usual apprenticeship practice, the student and employer do not usually have a contractual relationship. The employer is paid for the instruction he provides. This mainly involves periods of one to five months.

Common compulsory subjects in secondary level studies are Finnish and Swedish (one of which is taught as the mother tongue), a foreign language, mathematics, physics, chemistry, information technology, social studies, physical education and health, and art appreciation.

Assessment

A student's performance is assessed on a scale of 1-5: excellent (5), good (4-3) and satisfactory (2-1). A student must pass all subjects in his/her study programme with at least the grade 'satisfactory' in order to obtain a leaving certificate. Assessment is based on aims defined in the curriculum and is carried out by the teachers in each subject. The grades indicated on the leaving certificate are decided upon by all teachers at a staff meeting.

Apprenticeship

Apprenticeship is a special contract in which the employer undertakes to give a specified type of instruction and the student commits himself to work in return for this training. Apprenticeship training is governed by law. The employer is entitled to compensation from public funds for costs incurred by the training. Both the firm willing to take apprentices and the contracts are to be approved by a local apprenticeship authority.

Apprenticeship training follows the training programme guidelines approved by the National Board of Education, defined for nearly all sectors, and the detailed programme which is included in each individual contract. The duration of an apprenticeship ranges from one to four years. The

on-the-job training, which takes up 60% to 90% of the training time, is supplemented by theoretical courses at vocational institutions or adult education centres.

Teachers

Vocational education teachers must have a higher vocational qualification or university degree in their field and also appropriate work experience. In addition, they are required to complete pedagogical studies. Teachers at technical institutions and institutions providing training in the arts and media sectors are not required to have completed pedagogical training before being appointed to a post; they can follow training over two to three years on the job.

Pedagogical studies comprise 40 credits and are conceived as a one-year course, although they can be spread over two years. The studies include general studies, general and occupation-oriented pedagogical studies, practical training and a final paper (thesis). These studies are provided by vocational teacher training colleges and universities.

Teachers at vocational institutions are required to undergo an average of five days of in-service training annually to improve their professional skills.

Teachers are generally employed full-time by the authority that maintains the institution, hires the teachers and pays their salaries.

Reform

Vocational education in Finland is to be fundamentally reformed in the near future. A broadly based study structure will replace the earlier basic programmes and specialization courses. Students will have more alternatives and options. They will be able to select modules from different fields, such as trade and industry or social affairs and health. Experiments in such combinations have been going on for several years in all vocational sectors at both secondary and post-secondary levels.

Separate legislation has been enacted concerning these experiments, which applies to both secondary and post-secondary education (see 6.). New experiments can be launched up to the year 1999. The main purpose of the experiments is to investigate cooperation between vocational institutions and upper secondary schools and to provide students with a choice of studies from several institutions. Under these experiments, students can obtain a new-style qualification based on a combination of upper secondary and vocational studies. The duration of studies is flexible, from two to four years. The experiments currently involve 139 secondary-level institutions and about 35,000 students.

Although the experiments will continue for some years yet, many changes have been made to permanent legislation in the light of experience. Obstacles to inter-institutional cooperation in particular have been removed, and the students' right to have courses from other institutions recognized in their qualification has been improved. In terms of structure, it has been decided that secondary and post-secondary studies will no longer be parallel. As of 1995, higher vocational studies will only be accessible to students who already have a secondary level qualification awarded by an upper secondary school or vocational institution.

Statistics 1992/93

Vocational Education and Training	
Institutions, by owner	
State	166
Municipality	267
Private	57
Total	490
(50 of these teach through the medium of Swedish)	
Students, by owner of school	
State	54,601
Municipality	90,215
Private	12,754
Total	157,570
Teachers, by owner of school	
State	7,319
Municipality	9,577
Private	1,669
Total	18,565

Some key figures (1991)

Type of institution	Number	Average teaching group size	Students per teacher
Multidisciplinary vocational institution	118	13	9
Hotel and restaurant institute	13	15	10
Commercial institute	70	25	14
Home and institutional economics institute	50	15	8
Arts institute	6	12	9
Handicrafts and industrial arts institute	44	10	7
Agricultural institute	59	15	8
Maritime institute	3	16	6
Forestry institute	25	14	5
Social welfare institute	27	18	9
Technical institute	31	23	15
Health institute	48	17	10
Total/Overall average	494	16	10

6. Higher education

6.1 *Ammattikorkeakoulu/ Yrkeshögskola*

New legislation was passed in 1991 which initiated an educational reform aimed at simplifying the entire vocational education system and setting up a distinct non-university sector of higher education. The Government has given 22 experimental *Ammattikorkeakoulut*, combining 85 former vocational institutions, permission to operate. Of these, 16 are multidisciplinary and/or made up of more than one institution. Six consist of a single institution. Such experiments are in progress in all of Finland's provinces.

During the academic year 1992/93, there were 6,400 places available for new students in the *Ammattikorkeakoulut*. The number of places per unit ranges from 50 to 720, the average being 290. When the experiment reaches its full scope, the size of the units will range from 1,000 to 3,000 students.

The main disciplines are technology (37% of all starting places), commerce (36%) and health care (10%). The experiment will cover 84% of all current college-level and vocational higher education study programmes.

The *Ammattikorkeakoulut* operate in parallel with the universities, awarding new types of degrees. These are legally defined as higher education degrees, but have a more pronounced vocational emphasis than academic degrees.

In 1992/93, the *Ammattikorkeakoulut* offered 48 degree programmes and a total of 180 specializations. The nature and scope of the degree programmes are subject to approval by the Ministry of Education. The programmes consist of basic studies, professional studies, degree work and practical training. A compulsory on-the-job training period equivalent to a minimum of 20 credits is an integral part of the degree programme.

Degree programmes are expressed in credits ('study weeks'). One credit corresponds to approximately 40 hours of study; an academic year is equivalent to 40 credits. The programmes consist of between 120 and 160 credits, corresponding to 3-4 years of study, depending on the discipline.

Young people can apply for entry to an *Ammattikorkeakoulu* after completing their secondary education. The required qualifications are school-level vocational studies, the matriculation examination or equivalent studies abroad. Applicants who have taken the matriculation examination or have completed upper secondary school or higher-level vocational education qualify for all *Ammattikorkeakoulu* studies; those with school-level vocational studies are eligible only for studies in the same discipline.

Legislation to regularize the situation of the *Ammattikorkeakoulut* is in preparation and is intended to come into force during 1995.

6.2 Universities *(Yliopisto/Universitet, Korkeakoulu/Högskola)*

There are 22 institutions of higher education in Finland, with a combined student population of 126,000. Ten of these institutions are traditional multidisciplinary universities (*Yliopisto*) and twelve are specialized institutions (*Korkeakoulu*). The latter comprise three schools of economics and business administration, three universities of technology and architecture, a college of veterinary medicine, a university of industrial arts, an academy of fine arts, one music academy, one theatre academy and the National Defence College. All 22 institutions of higher education are publicly financed state bodies enjoying autonomy in respect of their internal affairs. The Ministry of Education is responsible for the general development of the higher education system.

Each institution is governed by an Act of Parliament. The aims and scope of basic degrees and the structure of advanced degrees are defined by decree. The close connection between research and teaching is a characteristic feature of the Finnish university system. All institutions of higher education provide both basic and advanced studies up to doctorate level, and are expected to engage in research. The institutions also offer continuing training, vocational courses and open university courses.

Admission

A student who passes the Finnish matriculation examination is eligible for higher education. Since 1991, college and higher vocational level diplomas awarded by vocational institutions also provide the same eligibility. The universities decide upon their own entrance requirements. The selection criteria and application deadlines vary between the institutions, the fields of study, and even between the disciplines in the same field of study. Admission is based on an entrance examination or on school certificates, usually on both. Entrance examinations are compulsory in nearly all fields of study.

The number of students admitted to the universities is determined by the institutions themselves on the basis of a framework fixed by the Government. The annual number of newly-enrolled students has been 16,000-17,000 in recent years.

Fees/Student finance

Students at Finnish universities do not have to pay for tuition or for taking a degree. Students can apply for financial assistance from public funds. The granting of assistance is coordinated by the Social Insurance Institution (*KELA*).

Three forms of financial assistance are available to university students: grants, housing allowances and loans. There are also a variety of scholarships available, but these are limited. Study grants and housing allowances (which are paid to students to compensate living costs) do not have to be repaid. Student loans are granted by banks and guaranteed by the State. Over a period of time, the proportion of grants and accommodation allowances relative to repayable loans has increased.

Financial assistance is guaranteed for one academic year at a time. Students can receive assistance for a maximum of 70 months, 55 of these for studies toward a higher degree and the remainder for further studies. In the academic year 1992/93, 70,000 university students – 58% of those enrolled – were granted financial assistance for education.

Academic year

The academic year usually begins in September and ends in May. It is divided into two semesters. Most universities are active throughout the year and offer different summer courses and extra examinations.

Courses/Qualifications

The basic degree corresponds to a Master's degree. Studies are divided into twenty fields and over 160 study programmes. The basic degree consists of three stages: general studies, subject studies and advanced studies. The advanced studies involve independent research and a final paper (thesis). It takes 5-6 years to complete the basic degree.

In some fields, it has been possible to sit a lower examination, corresponding to a Bachelor's degree. Studies for these examinations take from three to three-and-a-half years to complete. From the beginning of 1994, the lower university degree was extended to almost all fields of study.

The amount of time taken to complete postgraduate degrees varies greatly, even though planning work is based on the assumption that a licentiate degree would take two to three years and a doctorate about four years after completion of the basic degree.

About 9,000 Master's degrees and over 1,000 licentiate degrees/doctorates are completed annually.

Assessment

Students are subject to continuous assessment. Student assessment varies between universities and faculties. In most cases, the student's progress is assessed on the basis of written examinations taken at the end of lecture series or courses or larger study units. The examination can be based on lectures the student has attended or books read. In addition, oral examinations can be required. Grades are entered into the university computer register. As part of the advanced studies, students must write a thesis. In universities of art, the thesis can take the form of a work of art, such as a concert, a performance or an artistic study.

Separate credits are usually examined by teachers of the course in question, but the final responsibility for assessment remains with the professor of the subject. The final examinations and thesis are usually assessed by two or more impartial examiners appointed by the faculty.

Open university education

Open university education offers people the possibility to participate in university education regardless of the level of education they have completed. As its name implies, this is a system of study with no formal admission requirements. Students can follow studies included in the degree programmes of universities, as well as other, separately organized studies.

Sweden

SWEDEN

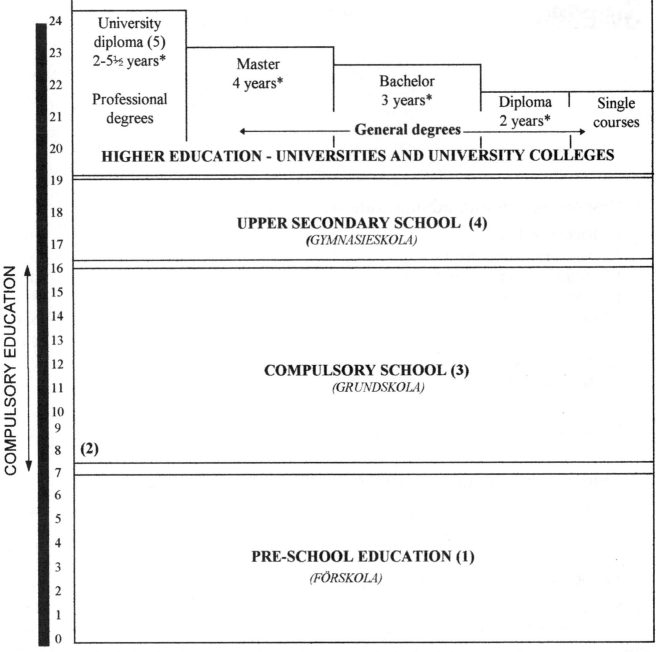

1. In pre-school education there are several institutions catering for the 0 to 6/7 age range: day care centres (*daghem*), part-time groups (*deltidsgrupper*) and open pre-school institutions (*öppen förskola*).

2. Since 1991, children have the right to start compulsory school at the age of six years, if their parents so desire, and if the municipality has the capacity to provide this opportunity. This option should be available in all municipalities by the school year 1997/98.

3. The compulsory school is attended by children aged 6/7 to 16 years. It is a comprehensive coeducational school designed to accommodate all members of the young generation.

4. In the new comprehensive upper secondary school, introduced in 1992 and to be fully implemented at the beginning of the school year 1995/96, all education is organized in study programmes of three years' duration. There are to be 16 nationally determined programmes, 14 of which are primarily vocationally oriented and two preparing primarily for university studies.

5. The professional degrees awarded at universities and university colleges (*högskola*) are obtained upon completion of programmes of varying length (2 to 5 1/2 years). The programmes lead to specific professions, e.g. University Diploma in Medicine or in Education (for Upper Secondary School).

1. Responsibilities and administration

1.1 Background

Sweden covers a total area of 450,000 square kilometres and has a population of 8.7 million. The national language is Swedish. For many centuries, Sweden was ethnically and linguistically very homogeneous with two exceptions – the Finnish-speaking population of the north-east and the Sámi (Lapps). Today, approximately one million of Sweden's total population are immigrants or have at least one immigrant parent; immigrants include citizens from other Nordic countries.

Sweden is a Constitutional Monarchy with a parliamentary form of government; the King has only ceremonial functions as Head of State and the formal power of governmental decision rests with the Cabinet. Parliament (the *Riksdag*) is the country's highest decision-making body. Since 1971, it has had one chamber with 349 members, who are chosen by direct election. As from 1994, the Parliament will be elected every fourth year. With the exception of six years of non-socialist rule (1976-1982), the Social Democrats were in power from 1932 to 1991, either alone or in coalition with other parties. At the 1991 elections, the non-socialist parties together won a majority and ruled for three years. At the 1994 elections, the Social Democrats came back into power.

Local government is exercised through the 24 County Councils and 286 municipalities.

Around 95% of the population belong to the official Lutheran State Church.

In 1993, employment by sectors was as follows: agriculture, forestry 3.5%; trade, transport, banking 30%; mining, manufacturing 20%; building, construction 6%; public sector 40.5%. In September 1994, the unemployment rate was 7.3 %.

1.2 Basic principles: education

One fundamental principle of the Swedish education system is that everybody must have access to equivalent education, regardless of ethnic and social background and of place of residence. Compulsory school and upper secondary school are both comprehensive, designed to accommodate all members of the young generation; and all schools are coeducational. The curricula for compulsory and upper secondary education are valid nationwide.

Adult education in Sweden has a long history and options for further and continuing education are available in many different forms throughout the country. Education for adults equivalent to the education provided by the compulsory and upper secondary school is part of the public school system.

1.3 Distribution of responsibilities

Overall responsibility for education in Sweden is borne by Parliament and the Government. With the exception of the University of Agricultural Sciences, which comes under the Ministry of Agriculture, and employment training, which is the responsibility of the Ministry of Labour, all education and vocational training comes under the jurisdiction of the Ministry of Education and Science. Overall responsibility for pre-school provision, which does not belong to the education sector, is borne by the Ministry of Health and Social Affairs.

A characteristic feature of the Swedish administrative system is the division of tasks between ministries and central administrative agencies. The ministries are rather small units, each consisting of not more than 150 persons. They are mainly concerned with preparing the Government's bills for Parliament and issuing laws and regulations and general rules for the administrative agencies. The enforcement of laws and government decisions is entrusted to 100 or so relatively independent administrative agencies.

Those responsible for the provision of education under the Ministry of Education and Science are the State, the County Councils, the municipalities and private school organizers. (The regional level of educational administration was abolished in 1992).

Education in Sweden has traditionally been organized within the public sector. For many years, the control of activities within the education system was heavily centralized. Through legislation, regulations and curricula the State issued detailed instructions and rules on educational activities and on the spending of state grants. The education system has, however, undergone fundamental changes in recent years, which have limited the role of the State.

The main principle for the distribution of responsibilities in the Swedish education system at present is that Parliament and the Government should control educational activities by defining national objectives, while national and local education authorities and the organizers of the different institutions are responsible for ensuring that activities are implemented in line with these national objectives and achieve the necessary results.

1.4 Administration

Central level

Legislation is passed by Parliament which also decides on the funding of government appropriations to the education system. The Government issues the ordinances and general guidelines applying to the various types of education and decides on the distribution of government appropriations. The Government also lays down the curricula and syllabi for the school system.

The State is responsible for ensuring that all educational activities are monitored and evaluated and for the central development and improvement of the education system. The State is also responsible for providing financial assistance to students. Subject to the authority of Parliament and the Government, these state functions are performed by central government agencies immediately subordinate to the Ministry of Education and Science.

The main central authority responsible for the supervision of the school system is the **National Agency for Education**. Its foremost responsibilities include the national monitoring, evaluation and supervision of all school activities, and central development work within the school sector. The Agency is also responsible for ensuring that research is undertaken and that in-service training is arranged for teachers. The Agency itself arranges basic training for school managers and some in-service training for teachers.

Responsibility for the evaluation of higher education is borne by the **Chancellor's Office for Swedish Universities**, which coordinates the assessment and evaluation of the institutions of higher education. The Chancellor's Office is also responsible for examining whether an institution of higher education has the right to award degrees. Monitoring of the activities of universities and university colleges at national level is entrusted to the **National Agency for Higher Education**, which also provides different kinds of services for the institutions of higher education (e.g. coordination of the admission of students) and information on higher education in Sweden and other countries.

The **National Board of Student Aid** is responsible for the administration, observation and evaluation of financial assistance to students for post-compulsory studies in Sweden and abroad.

The national agencies submit annual reports and budget proposals to the Government. In addition, at three-year intervals or longer, they are to provide Parliament and the Government with a comprehensive picture of the situation within their field of responsibility, together with data for the long-term national development of the education sector.

Local level

The local authorities (County Councils and municipalities) are bound by law and regulations to provide a number of basic services for which, however, they receive subsidies from the national Government. In addition, they have the right to levy income taxes and they also charge fees for various services. Practically all education in Sweden below university level is operated by the local authorities.

Responsibility for teaching staff was transferred from the State to the municipalities with effect from 1 January 1991, and on 1 July 1991 municipalities were given undivided responsibility for organizing and implementing school activities.

Each Municipal Council and County Council appoints one or more committees which have the responsibility to ensure that educational activities are conducted in compliance with state regulations and guidelines and that the external conditions of education are as appropriate and favourable as possible. The committee or committees responsible for schools are obliged to ensure, *inter alia*, that schools are built and sufficient facilities are provided, that the activities of schools in the municipality are coordinated, that qualified teaching and non-teaching staff are hired and receive in-service training, that municipal funds are allocated for school activities, that it is made possible to achieve the objectives laid down in the curricula and that the general guidelines are complied with. In practice, it is the responsibility of the local committees to ensure that Swedish schools uphold equivalent standards all over the country. Every municipality is required to set out the general objectives for its schools in a school plan, adopted by the Municipal Council.

The municipality is obliged to monitor and evaluate the school plan and to provide the State with reports on facts and circumstances of relevance for the evaluation of educational activities. In addition, every school has to devise a work plan, based on the curriculum and local priorities. The work plan is also to be monitored and evaluated.

The organization of administration within a municipality, such as the inclusion of one or more schools in a head teacher's school management district or the allocation of responsibilities and financing, varies from one municipality to another.

Institutional level

On 1 July 1993, there was a radical reform of the **higher education** system, including the introduction of a new Higher Education Act and a new system for the allocation of resources to universities and university colleges. The role of the State was limited. The universities and university colleges are now much more autonomous and are free to decide on matters which were earlier determined by Parliament and the Government, *inter alia*, the organization of study, the admission of students, the use of available resources and the institutional structure.

1.5 Inspection

There is no inspectorate as such in Sweden. However, now that the administration of the education system is based on objectives and results, the State and local authorities, as well as individual schools and institutions of higher education, are required to systematically monitor and evaluate educational activities in relation to the objectives and conditions applying to them. As mentioned above, the National Agency for Education and the Chancellor's Office for Swedish Universities monitor and evaluate the system at national level.

1.6 Financing

With effect from 1 January 1993, state subsidies to municipalities take the form of a general equalization grant. The state grant provides a supplement to the tax revenues of every municipality and is also aimed at equalizing differences between municipalities. State funding, then, is not directly linked to school organization; the municipalities are free to use the grant for the educational services or activities they choose. In a growing number of municipalities the committee(s) entrusts to each school an overall budget for salaries, the costs of teaching materials and equipment, rents and income from, for example, letting school premises. However, if a municipality seriously disregards its obligations under the Education Act, or under regulations issued on the basis of the Act, the Government has the right to intervene. In addition, there are special state grants for research and development, in-service training for school staff and measures for mentally handicapped pupils, and for a number of independent upper secondary schools.

Teaching materials and school meals in compulsory school are free of charge to the individual pupil; in most municipalities, this also applies to upper secondary pupils. The municipalities are obliged to provide free school transport for compulsory school pupils, but not for pupils who choose to attend a school different from that proposed by the municipality.

All pupils between 16 and 20 years of age who are attending upper secondary education receive state study assistance. This also applies to pupils attending private schools if their studies come under state supervision. Study assistance at upper secondary level comprises a general study grant, representing a continuation of child allowance, payable to all pupils from the age of 16, and a means-tested grant to be used towards the cost of studies and daily travel.

Higher education is financed directly from the State. For many years, the allocation of resources for undergraduate education was based on the number of first-year students. On 1 July 1993, a new resource allocation system for undergraduate education was introduced. Appropriations for universities and university colleges are now based on proposals from the Government and made out as lump sums directly from Parliament to each institution. The basic principles of the allocation system is that appropriations are made as a remuneration for results achieved. Results refer to the number of credit points earned by students (about 60%) and the number of full-time equivalent students taught at the institution (about 40%). The total amount of money that can be allocated to a university or university college is based on an education task contract for a three-year period.

Higher education institutions operated by local authorities, i.e. Colleges of Health Sciences, obtain state subsidies. Each County Council and municipality is responsible for the remaining costs.

1.7 Private institutions

A guiding principle of the education policy implemented after the change of Government in Autumn 1991 has been to create scope for diversity within the education system and freedom for individual pupils and students to choose between different types of schools and institutions of higher education and between study routes. New possibilities have thus been opened up for private school organizers to operate within the system; the percentage of private compulsory and upper secondary schools is now 1.5%. Nearly half of these have a specific pedagogical orientation, such as the Montessori or Rudolf Steiner methods; others are denominational or have a more general pedagogical approach.

The municipalities are obliged to compensate the **independent compulsory schools** that are approved by the National Agency for Education for pupils who choose this type of school. The municipal grant equals, per pupil, not less than 85% of the average cost per pupil in municipal compulsory schools. The new Government has announced that this percentage will be lowered in the near future. Starting from the school year 1994/95, the municipalities will also be obliged to give **independent upper secondary schools** a grant per pupil, providing the school fulfils certain requirements. Independent schools are able to charge a reasonable fee to cover certain costs which are not covered by state grants.

As from the school year 1993/94, municipalities and County Councils also have the opportunity of contracting private school organizers to provide tuition in particular subjects in the upper secondary school.

There are few private institutions within **higher education**, the only one with a research function being the Stockholm School of Economics. However, in accordance with a decision in Parliament in the spring of 1993, two of the state institutions were transformed into independent foundations on 1 July 1994: the University College of Jönköping and Chalmers University of Technology. The State also subsidizes a number of institutions run by private organizers, and private institutions of higher education have also been given the opportunity to operate within a regulatory framework defining their relationship with the State. Recognition by the Government now implies placement in one of two categories: those given the right to award degrees, and those given the same right but, in addition, receiving state subsidies to assist with operational costs. Students at an independent university or college with the right to award degrees have the right to receive study assistance.

1.8 Advisory bodies

Teachers' organizations and other employees' organizations are entitled, under the Co-determination Act, to receive information on and to influence impending decisions. Pupils' rights are enshrined in the Education Act, but their practical implementation is decided locally. In the compulsory school, it is the head teacher's duty (usually performed by the teachers) to provide information to and consult pupils and parents on matters which are of importance to the pupils and concern the entire school. Parents are organized in parents' or parent-teacher associations and are able to influence school work in this way. At national level, the National School and Home Union is consulted.

2. Pre-school education

Pre-school education in Sweden belongs to the public child care sector and is regulated under the Social Services Act of 1980. The aims and capacity of public child care are decided by Parliament, whereas the Ministry of Health and Social Affairs is responsible for the preparation of laws and proposals related to child care. The National Board of Health and Welfare and the county administrations are together responsible for supervising the pre-school institutions and other forms of child care nationwide.

It is aimed that public child care should be available to all children whose parents so wish. Since 1975, all children aged 6 and over, as well as handicapped children from the age of four, have been eligible for pre-school education for a minimum of one year. Attendance is optional for the child, but provision is mandatory for the municipal authorities.

Public child care is jointly financed by the municipal budget and fees paid by parents. Only pre-school education for 6-year-olds is free of charge to parents. All public child care is coeducational.

In 1985, Parliament decided that public child care should be expanded so that by 1991 all pre-school children over the age of eighteen months would be provided for. In some municipalities this objective has not yet been achieved. Where there are insufficient places, children in need of special support for their development, e.g. children who are physically or mentally handicapped, are given priority in the allocation of pre-school places. In December 1993, Parliament decided to amend the Social Services Act so that the municipalities will be obliged to offer all children aged 1 to 12 years, whose parents are gainfully employed or studying, a place in public or private child care, starting on 1 January 1995.

About 50% of all children aged 0 to 6 years and about 30% of all children aged 7 to 12 take part in public child care.

Child care services take the following forms:

- **Day care centres** (*daghem*), for children aged 1 to 6 years, whose parents are gainfully employed or studying. Day care centres are usually open between 6.30 a.m. and 6.00 p.m., Monday to Friday, all year round.

- **Part-time groups** (*deltidsgrupper*), for children aged 4 to 6 years. These groups operate during the school year and meet for three hours daily, morning or afternoon.

- **Open pre-school institutions** (*öppen förskola*), for pre-school age children without any other kind of pre-school place. The children attend a few times a week in the company of a parent or family child minder.

- **After-school centres** (*fritidshem*), for children aged 6/7 to 12 years. The purpose of these centres, which are open before and after school, and during school holidays, is to provide after-school activities and learning options in addition to the school curriculum.

The term pre-school institution (*förskola*) is used to denote day care services, part-time groups and open pre-school institutions.

In day care centres, children are usually divided into mixed-age groups. These groups are made up of either small children up to the age of three, sibling groups (usually children aged 3 to 6 years), or extended sibling groups, which can include children of all pre-school ages as well as younger schoolchildren. The average day care centre has four groups or sections, each with some 15-18 children.

After-school activities are often an integrated part of school. It is also becoming increasingly common for day care activities and school to be housed in the same building. In addition, different ways are being tried of facilitating the transition between pre-school institutions and school, *inter alia*, through special programmes for 6-year-olds.

Child care activities are usually operated by the municipalities. As a complement to the activities conducted on municipal premises, the municipality employs **family child care** minders to care for children aged 1 to 12 years in the minder's own home. Private day care and after-school centres are also becoming increasingly common. In many municipalities, these centres receive a compensatory transfer payment from the municipal funds.

The aims and responsibilities of the pre-school institutions and after-school centres have been set out in pedagogical programmes issued by the National Board of Health and Welfare. Together with the parents, one of the tasks of the pre-school institution is to integrate the child into society. Its activities, which should be planned in close cooperation with the parents, should be based largely on the childrens' background, their interests, previous experiences and special needs.

Pre-school institutions cover the following main areas: cultural activities, such as language, drama, music and art, painting and pottery; nature studies and community life. These topics manifest themselves through play, creative activities, daily tasks, etc. There are also daily outdoor activities throughout the year. Pre-school education does not convey school education *per se*, but it should provide preparatory training for school.

Teachers

All staff in public child care institutions are civil servants and are employed by the municipalities. Pre-school institutions are staffed by teachers and child care attendants, while recreation instructors and child care attendants work in after-school centres. Pre-school teachers also cooperate in various ways with teachers at the lower level of compulsory school.

The director or supervisor of the pre-school institution is responsible for the regular planning of the centre's work. The staff works in teams where the particular knowledge and interests of each member of staff can be utilized. Parents are encouraged to participate in the activities whenever possible.

The training course for pre-school teachers and recreation instructors takes place at universities, university colleges or institutes of education. The study programmes have been extended from 2 1/2 to 3 years with effect from the academic year 1993/94. They lead to a University Diploma in Child and Youth Training. Child care attendants are trained in special 2-3 year programmes in the upper secondary school; in 1995 all these programmes will be 3 years in duration (see 4.3). There are also special courses, such as those for bilingual persons wanting to work primarily with immigrant children. Most family child minders in family day care have followed an introductory course of 90-100 hours, or longer training, such as the child attendant's course.

Responsibility for in-service training rests with the municipalities, but it is not compulsory; the availability and content of such training can vary enormously from one area to another.

Statistics 1992

Institutions	13,949*	Children	503,589
– day care centres	7,359	– day care centres	315,550
– after-school centres	3,103	– after-school centres	127,146
– part-time groups	2,488	– part-time groups	60,893

* family day care not included.

Staff	98,642	Staffing ratio*	
– pre-school teachers	44,435	– day care centres	4.9
– recreation instructors	8,791	– after-school centres	11.5
– child care attendants	39,683	– part-time groups	16.9

* number of children per full-time employee.

3. Compulsory education – primary and lower secondary education

Compulsory education in Sweden takes the form of a 9-year comprehensive school (*grundskola*) for children aged 7 to 16. However, since 1991 children have had the right to start compulsory school at the age of six years, if their parents so desire and if the municipality has the capacity to provide this opportunity. The option should be available in all municipalities by the school year 1997/98. In the school year 1992/93, 70 % of the municipalities were able to offer children the option of starting school at the age of six. In October 1993, 5.3 % of the pupils starting school that year were 6 years old or younger. The Government has had a special commissioner investigating the consequences of extending compulsory schooling to ten years. The commissioner's final report has been sent for review to the government agencies and municipalities concerned.

Compulsory elementary schooling was formally introduced in Sweden in 1842. A process of reform, destined to take many years, began in the 1940s with the aim of extending compulsory schooling. The 9-year compulsory comprehensive school was decided by Parliament in 1962, and fully implemented in the school year 1972/73. Today, it is regulated by the Education Act of 1985 and amendments of 1991, 1992, 1993 and 1994.

The compulsory school system comprises compulsory school (*grundskolan*), Sámi school (*sameskolan*) for Sámi-speaking children in the north of the country, special schools (*specialskolan*) for children with certain handicaps (for example, children with impaired hearing, vision or speech disabilities) and compulsory school for the mentally disabled (*särskolan*).

Almost all pupils (over 98%) attend schools run by the municipalities, usually in their local area. The Education Act states, however, that parents and pupils should be able to make a choice concerning compulsory education. To the extent that it is possible, parents' wishes for their children to attend a particular public school within the municipality should be considered. Parents and pupils should also be free to choose between public and private schools. As from the school year 1993/94, a pupil can attend a public school outside his/her home municipality. The municipalities are obliged to provide pupils with all the materials necessary for school work. Particular emphasis is put on textbooks, etc. covering essential parts of a specific subject or a group of subjects. All compulsory schooling is coeducational and provided free of charge.

The school year is divided into two terms and comprises 40 weeks with not less than 178 school days (Monday-Friday) and 12 days of holiday. The autumn term lasts from the end of August to the end of December, the spring term from the beginning of January to the beginning of June. The exact dates vary from year to year and from one municipality to another.

Attendance is compulsory for a maximum of 190 days per year and eight hours per day (six hours in the first two years of school). Under certain circumstances, however, pupils could be exempt from otherwise compulsory teaching. This applies, for example, to pupils belonging to a religious community which is authorized by the Government to arrange instruction in religious studies corresponding to the instruction given in school.

3.1 Pre-reform system

The general objectives of the compulsory school are laid down in chapter 4 of the Education Act: 'Education in the compulsory school shall aim at providing pupils with the knowledge and skills and the additional training needed to participate in society. All this shall provide the basis for further education in the upper secondary school.'

Compulsory school is currently divided into three levels:

- **lower level**   1st-3rd year
  (*lågstadiet*)
- **intermediate level**   4th-6th year
  (*mellanstadiet*)
- **upper level**   7th-9th year
  (*högstadiet*)

Education at lower and intermediate level could be classified as primary education and upper level education as lower secondary education. In the Swedish education system, however, no such distinction is made.

Lower and intermediate level schools exist in most residential areas and have one or two classes per year, which gives a total of 150-300 pupils per school. There are, however, both larger and smaller schools, the latter mainly in sparsely populated rural areas, where classes can be made up of pupils from two or three different years. Upper level schools are normally larger, with 150-600 pupils and two, three or more classes per year. In recent years, there has been an increase in the number of schools covering all levels.

Pupils frequently attend the same school all the way through lower and intermediate levels, although at intermediate level they usually change teachers. Teachers at both these levels take the children for practically all subjects; there are specially-trained teachers for music and very often for craft subjects, pictorial studies and physical education from intermediate level onwards. At upper level, pupils are taught by several different subject teachers specializing in two or three subjects. Upper level often brings a change of school as well.

Work in school is organized in such a way that two or more classes, usually from the same year, make up a single working unit. In addition to class or subject teachers, remedial teachers and pupil welfare staff, e.g. a social welfare officer, psychologist and school nurse, can be attached to every such unit. The staff making up every unit of this kind constitute a working team with the task of planning, developing and evaluating the work to be done – a process in which the pupils are also entitled to participate.

There are no regulations concerning class sizes but classes are normally larger at intermediate and upper levels than at the lower level. In the school year 1992/93, the average number of pupils per class was 22.1 for the whole of compulsory school.

Curriculum

At present, all schools in the compulsory school system have their own centrally compiled curricula. Centrally compiled curricula for the compulsory comprehensive school have succeeded one another since 1962. The curriculum now in force was introduced in 1980 and fully implemented in the school year 1982/83. As compared to the earlier curricula, which contained detailed instructions on school work, subject by subject, the current curriculum lays down goals and guidelines of a more general nature. It also includes timetables specifying the number of periods per week (lessons) at each 3-year level for each subject.

The curriculum puts a great deal of emphasis on training the pupils in basic skills – reading, writing and arithmetic – all the way through school. Similarly, a great deal of attention has to be paid to providing the pupils with a basic knowledge of civics, natural science and technology. Increasing emphasis is being put on cultural affairs and artistic activity in school work.

Individual teaching subjects are covered by syllabi in which the subject matter is divided between the levels. Natural science subjects and social science subjects, respectively, have a common syllabus and are often taught on an interdisciplinary basis. The distribution of the periods specified in the timetable and of the stipulated subject matter of various subjects is left to the individual school to decide. On an experimental basis, the local education authority may also make adjustments to the timetables for the intermediate and upper levels in order to provide scope for local specialization, i.e. in-depth studies in some classes of a particular subject or a group of subjects.

At lower and intermediate levels all pupils take the same subjects. English is compulsory from the 3rd or 4th year.

In each year of the upper level, pupils have a choice of optional courses of varying length for between 3 and 4 periods per week. The options offered must include 3-year courses in French, German and home languages (i.e. when this is not Swedish); more than 50% of pupils in year 7 opt for German and around 17 % for French. Other elective subjects – for example, artistic-practical or scientific-technical subjects – are offered at the discretion of the local education authority. Locally determined electives are subject to the stipulation that they must be suitable for both boys and girls and must not be associated with any traditional sexual bias or constitute further studies of a particular school subject. In some cases, double options are offered on an experimental basis. Girls generally choose 3-year language courses, while boys are more evenly divided between languages and local options.

Swedish as a second language is a compulsory subject for all pupils who need it. Furthermore, it is the duty of municipal authorities to organize voluntary home language instruction for all pupils using a language other than Swedish for their everyday communication with at least one of their parents. The most common home languages taught in compulsory school are Finnish, Spanish and Arabic.

At all levels, time is to be reserved for project studies, i.e. detailed studies which teachers and pupils choose to undertake within the framework of compulsory subjects. At both intermediate and upper levels the curriculum provides for free activities (i.e. activities chosen by pupils out of personal preference) for a certain compulsory number of periods. Free activities are designed to put children in touch with associations and activities outside school and to encourage them to develop their initiative and creativity.

Vocational **guidance** is provided above all at the upper level, when work experience is arranged at workplaces of various kinds. During their compulsory schooling pupils must complete between six and ten weeks of vocational guidance.

Assessment and qualifications

Pupils' progress is monitored on the basis of continuous assessment. There are no examinations in compulsory school.

At present, no marks are awarded for the first seven years of school. Marks only have to be awarded in all subjects in years 8 and 9 of compulsory school, in both the autumn and spring terms, as a basis for upper secondary school entrance.

Marks are awarded on a five-point scale, the highest award being five and the average three. These marks are relative, i.e. they refer to the average national level of achievement in each subject. There are no specified percentages for the numbers of pupils receiving the various awards, but the number of twos and fours in a class should not normally exceed the number of ones and fives. A three indicates the average achievement of all pupils in the country, but the average award in an individual class may be higher or lower than the national average.

There are, however, various standardized achievement tests, primarily aimed at measuring achievement corresponding to the award 3. The tests should be 'normative' for that mark, thus guaranteeing a certain measure of nationwide comparability. Comparisons between different classes refer solely to test results in each individual subject. Compulsory schools also inform parents of their children's progress and difficulties through interviews.

All pupils receive a compulsory school leaving certificate (*grundskolabetyg*) which qualifies them to apply for upper secondary school, irrespective of the optional subjects taken at the upper level of compulsory school and the marks they have been awarded.

3.2 Post-reform system

The recent modifications to the legislative framework for the school system have involved fundamental changes in the control and organization of the schools, as well as in the conditions under which individual schools are able to operate. In December 1993, Parliament adopted legislation laying down new curricular guidelines for the whole school system, geared to the new objective and result-related administration of the school system. As further described below, this will mean extensive changes in the curriculum, syllabi and timetables, and in the marking system for compulsory school in the next few years. The new system will take effect in the 1995/96 school year for years 1-7 of compulsory school, compulsory school for the mentally disabled and special school, and for the whole of Sámi school. Pupils already in the 7th to 9th years will be able to finish school under the present system, but the reform will be fully implemented as from the 1997/98 school year.

Curriculum

In the new curriculum, emphasis will be placed on the conveyance of knowledge, norms and values as the primary objectives of the school. The objectives of education, to be pursued through teaching, are expressed as the aims of education; and the objectives which all pupils must be given a chance of achieving, as the educational requirements. The objectives should be formulated in such a way that their achievement can be evaluated.

The compulsory school will no longer be divided into levels. Instead, the new national syllabi for each subject are to state the objectives which are to be achieved by the end of the fifth and ninth year of school. This will provide an opportunity for nationwide evaluation of school achievements after the fifth year.

The syllabi will also indicate the aims of education and the purpose, structure and character of each subject, including each individual subject within the areas of natural science and social science. Teachers will, however, be given great freedom when planning their teaching and choosing their working methods and subject matter.

In order to ensure equivalent standards throughout the country, a timetable has been laid down by Parliament; this will be attached to the Education Act as from 1 July 1995. It will indicate a minimum guaranteed teacher or supervisor-led instruction time to be covered in units of 60 minutes over the 9 years, divided between different subjects and groups of subjects. The local education authorities are free to decide on a more extensive timetable. The timetable also provides increased scope for individual electives involving more intensive study of one or more subjects. Teachers themselves, within the framework of the timetable, will decide upon the allocation of teaching time between different years. The only restriction will be that imposed by the syllabus assessment at the end of the fifth and ninth year. In the new timetable, more time is allotted to courses in second foreign languages. *Inter alia*, Spanish is introduced as an alternative to German and French among the optional subjects that each municipality is obliged to offer. Local or individual electives may also include a third foreign language.

The curriculum will make clear the responsibilities of all members of the school community. It is also aimed at strengthening the opportunities and duties for pupils and their families to be involved in decisions in school matters.

Compulsory school principals have been given overall responsibility for educational **guidance**. They have to ensure that the pupils receive guidance on the educational choices offered at the school as well as guidance on further studies and vocational training.

The new curriculum will be common to the whole of the compulsory school system. However, some adjustments will be made to educational objectives in order to accommodate the special needs of pupils in special schools and in schools for the mentally retarded.

Subject	Hours today Max. Hours	Hours from 1 July 1995 Min. Hours
Art education	246	230
Domestic science	112	118
Physical and health education	537	460
Music	246	230
Crafts	358	282
Swedish	1498	1490
English	470	480
Mathematics	895	900
Geography		
History		
Religion		885
Social sciences		
	1588	
Biology		
Physics		800
Chemistry		
Technology		
Foreign language	246	320
Pupils' choice	112	470
Child studies	22	
Extracurricular activities	151	
Experience weeks at various workplaces	161	
Miscellaneous	75	
Total	6717	6665
of which choice of school (decided locally)	440	410

Assessment and qualifications

The new marking system is to be objective and achievement-related instead of relative. It will be geared to special achievement criteria which are to be devised in conjunction with the syllabi so as to make it clear to teachers and pupils which achievements are necessary for the award of a certain mark. Final awards of nationwide validity are to be given in the eighth year. Final awards will be on a three-point scale: passed, passed with distinction, and passed with exceptional distinction.

Comparability will be achieved by means of national tests. Diagnostic tests in reading, writing and arithmetic should be administered in all municipal schools at the end of the second year. All municipal schools are also to administer subject tests in Swedish, English and mathematics at the end of the fifth and ninth years. Swedish tests are also to be administered at independent schools.

All pupils will receive a leaving certificate (*grundskolabetyg*).

3.3 Teachers

In order to qualify, teachers must have completed a Swedish teacher training programme or its equivalent in another EFTA country or a Member State of the EU. Unqualified teachers may be employed for a certain length of time if qualified staff are not available.

Teachers are civil servants. They normally hold posts with conditional tenure, full-time or part-time.

Teachers in compulsory school are trained at universities, university colleges or institutes of education. The majority of teachers of general subjects now in service have been trained as follows: Class teachers for years 1-3 and 4-6 have completed separate integrated training programmes lasting 2 ½ years and 3 years respectively; whilst subject teachers for years 7-9 have a university or college degree in their subject(s), plus a diploma awarded on completion of a one-year course in the theory and practice of teaching.

A new integrated study programme was introduced in the academic year 1988/89. There are two branches in the programme: for teachers of years 1-7 and 4-9 respectively. A one-year course in the theory and practice of teaching is common to all students. Training for years 1-7 takes 3 ½-4 years. Students can choose between three different variations of the basic curriculum and may also specialize in one of two different subject areas.

Trainees for years 4-9 may specialize in one of five areas, and study between 3 ½ and 4 ½ years, depending on their specialization. They could also extend their subject studies to qualify for service in the upper secondary school. As from the academic year 1992/93, there is an alternative training route for teachers of years 4-9, where subject studies in different combinations are followed by one year of practical pedagogical training.

Remedial teachers follow an extended study programme, lasting for one year or more, after their basic training as compulsory school teachers. Teachers of practical and artistic subjects are trained at special university colleges. They can specialize in one area but are also able, within a training programme for compulsory school teachers, to opt for a combination of their main subject with one or two others.

Supervised teaching practice, equivalent to one term's full-time study, is a requirement in all teacher training.

Responsibility for in-service training is divided between the State and the municipalities. The National Agency for Education must ensure that in-service training courses are available in all parts of the country, whilst the local education authorities are obliged by law to ensure that all school staff are adequately trained. For teachers in post, universities and colleges arrange in-service training courses of varying length, from one week to 20 weeks. The local education committee decides which teachers to send. In addition, all teachers are obliged to take part in school-based in-service training for five days a year, and in training activities after school hours.

3.4 Statistics 1993

Pupils	893,932	Schools	4,826
of which		of which	
Sámi school	111	Independent schools	166
Independent schools	13,689		
Teachers (public schools)	84,011	Teacher/ pupil ratio (full-time posts)	8.3/100 pupils

4. Post-compulsory education – upper secondary education

Upper secondary education has passed through a period of reforms and developments in the last 25 years. In 1970, the different types of schools for academic and vocational education that existed at upper secondary level were amalgamated into one school, the *gymnasieskola*, designed to accommodate all young adults. The final leaving examination of the former *gymnasium*, which prepared for university studies, had been abolished two years earlier. During the 1970s and the 1980s, a number of measures were taken to improve upper secondary schooling, so as to match the needs of the labour market and higher education to the wishes and requirements of young people. At the end of the 1980s, a reform of the structure of the upper secondary school was initiated, which in 1991 led to major alterations to the 1985 Education Act. A new system of upper secondary education was introduced in the 1992/93 school year; this will be fully implemented by the school year 1995/96.

Since 1 July 1992, municipalities have been obliged, under the Education Act, to provide upper secondary schooling for all pupils leaving compulsory school. This applies to all residents up to and including the first six months of the year of their 20th birthday. Over 95% of compulsory school leavers apply for upper secondary school and nearly all of them are accepted. As mentioned above, a compulsory school leaving certificate qualifies pupils to apply for upper secondary school, irrespective of the optional subjects taken at the upper level of compulsory school. However, in accordance with a decision by Parliament in the autumn of 1993, in order to be eligible for upper secondary school, as of the 1998/99 school year, pupils will be required to have pass grades in Swedish, English and mathematics from the compulsory school.

Most upper secondary studies take place in schools under municipal responsibility. However, studies in agriculture, forestry, horticulture and certain caring occupations take place in schools run by the County Councils. All upper secondary schooling is coeducational and provided free of charge. There are also a number of independent (private) upper secondary schools.

Upper secondary schools are generally located in larger municipalities with pupils usually coming from several different municipalities. Most of the large upper secondary schools include a variety of study programmes and courses. Certain programmes, e.g. for physical education, are organized for pupils from all over the country.

The number of pupils in an upper secondary school varies between 300 and 1,500. Various types of education within one school can be located in different buildings, and in many places upper secondary pupils and students in municipal adult education share the same building. In sparsely populated areas, there are upper secondary schools which collaborate with the upper level of compulsory school and with an upper secondary school in a larger municipality. The number of pupils per class does not usually exceed 30 in theoretical/academic study programmes and courses and 16 in practical/vocational ones.

Most of the independent upper secondary schools are found in the major urban areas and there are great variations between them in terms of programmes on offer. The average number of pupils in independent upper secondary schools is approximately 100, as compared with about 700 in municipal schools.

The school year is arranged in the same way as in compulsory education (see 3.).

4.1 Pre-reform system

Upper secondary school is divided into about 25 different lines (*linjer*) of two, three or four years' duration and some 500 specialized courses, grouped in the following sectors:

– Languages, social sciences and artistic activities – 2- and 3-year lines;

– Caring professions, social services and consumer education – 2-year lines;

– Economics, commerce and office work – 2- and 3-year lines;

– Industrial trades and crafts – 2-year lines and, experimentally, 3-year lines;

– Technology and natural sciences – 2-, 3- and 4-year lines;

– Agriculture, forestry and horticulture – 2-year lines.

Most lines are practical/vocational lines of two years' duration. In principle, the 3-year lines prepare pupils for university-level studies. The 4-year lines provide access, after three years, to higher technical studies. The lines are subdivided in subsequent grades into several 'branches' and 'variants'. The specialized courses range in duration from a week to two years, and they provide vocational education in a wide variety of fields. There are also study programmes of various lengths which build on the programmes of upper secondary school already studied.

Municipal upper secondary schools are also – through their supervisory activities and by providing a certain amount of tuition – responsible for apprenticeship training, the greater part of which is provided at workplaces outside the school system.

In 1991/92, nearly 50 % of those who completed their studies in one of the lines of the upper secondary school had followed a 3-year theoretical programme, roughly 40 % had followed a 2-year vocational one. The majority of those entering the upper secondary school today choose a 3-year programme. The distribution of pupils by sex is fairly even in the upper secondary school as a whole, but there are considerable variations between different lines and courses.

Curriculum

The general curriculum for the upper secondary school dates from 1970. In 1992, the objectives and guidelines in the curriculum were revised to suit the new school administration system for schools. These apply to all upper secondary education until the new curriculum comes into effect. All lines and specialized courses under the old regulations have their own timetables and syllabi. Swedish, English, physical education and civics and work experience are compulsory in all study programmes. Foreign languages are compulsory subjects in all academic lines and many vocational ones. The 2-year vocational lines have only a few general subjects, but pupils who take these lines can opt for one or more general subjects and reduce their vocational education instead. English and mathematics are the most popular optional subjects. Pupils in 3- and 4-year lines have to carry out special projects for a certain number of lessons. In some programmes, time is reserved for extracurricular purposes.

Assessment and qualifications

In upper secondary school, as in compulsory school, there are no examinations, and marks are awarded according to the same basic principles. At present, this means that there are no definite requirements for the various marks; a pupil's knowledge is compared nationally with that of other pupils doing the same course. Upper secondary pupils are awarded marks for all subjects every term.

Teachers use centrally compiled achievement tests in order to ensure the highest possible degree of uniformity in the marking system. Other forms of assessment are written tests, classroom observations of pupils' behaviour and class conferences (which involve all the teachers taking the class in question discussing individual pupils' achievements).

An upper secondary school leaving certificate (*gymnasiebetyg*) is awarded to all pupils after at least a two-year study programme including a specified amount of Swedish and English. The certificate meets the general eligibility requirements for higher education.

4.2 Post-reform system

In the new upper secondary school all education is organized in study programmes (*program*) of three years' duration. The new vocational programmes are designed to confer wider and deeper knowledge than the pre-reform vocational studies. The pupils are also given increased choice with respect to the content of their own education, as well as greater possibilities to influence the teaching methods and the forms of assessment. Specialized courses as they exist at present will be abolished.

There are 16 nationally determined programmes, 14 of which are primarily vocationally oriented and two preparing primarily for university studies. Most national programmes are divided into branches for the second and third year. In addition to the national branches that are drawn up centrally, municipalities may choose to set up local branches adapted to local needs and conditions.

The national programmes are:

- **Arts programme** – broad basic education leading to employment within arts-related occupations;

- **Business and administration programme** – leading to employment in commerce and administration in private business and public administration;

- **Construction programme** – leading to employment in the construction industry, building or civil engineering;

- **Child recreation programme** – leading to employment in child care, after-school and recreational activities, health care, sports and libraries;

- **Electrical engineering programme** – leading to employment in the installation, repair and maintenance of electrical, telecommunications and electronic equipment;

- **Energy programme** – leading to employment in, for example, electricity and power stations, heating, ventilation and sanitation installations and related work aboard ships;

- **Food programme** – leading to employment within food processing, sales and distribution;

- **Handicraft programme** – leading to employment within different handicraft and trade occupations, with a large part of the education being located at workplaces;

- **Health care programme** – leading to employment within the health, dental care and support service sectors;

- **Hotel, restaurant and catering programme** – leading to employment as, for example, a receptionist, a conference organizer, a waiter or a chef;

- **Industry programme** – leading to employment within industrial production, including programming and operating computer-controlled machines and processes;

- **Media programme** – leading to employment within advertising, various forms of design and production of graphic media;

- **Natural resource use programme** – leading to employment in agriculture, forestry, horticulture and animal husbandry;

- **Natural science programme** – leading to further studies in mathematics, science subjects and technology;

- **Social science programme** – leading to further studies in social sciences, economics and languages;

- **Vehicle engineering programme** – leading to employment in the repair and maintenance of cars, lorries and machines.

The educational aims of the national programmes are set out in programme goals. The programmes must give a broad basic education within the vocational field, as well as providing the foundation for further studies on completion of the upper secondary school.

Pupils who have requirements which are not provided for within the national programmes can opt to follow a **specially designed programme**, for which the pupil, in cooperation with the school, designs an individual syllabus for the whole period of study. Pupils who are unsure of what to study can also follow **individual programmes** of varying length and content, after which they may transfer to one of the national programmes, a specially designed programme or apprenticeship training. The third year can be replaced by a supplementary course to obtain, for example, skills other than those provided in the programme initially chosen.

The **apprenticeship training programme** comprises vocational training organized by the employers involved and education in the upper secondary school, mainly in core subjects.

All pupils who are entitled to education in a national programme can apply to any school in the country. Municipalities must offer a comprehensive selection of national programmes, and capacity for the various programmes must be adapted to pupils' preferences. If a municipality is unable to provide all programmes, the local authority can enter into an agreement to cooperate with other municipalities. Two or several municipalities, which together provide education in a national programme, constitute a cooperation region for that programme.

The national programmes and the national and local branches are to be built up from courses within different areas. A subject syllabus can consist of a number of short courses, both within the programme selected and from other programmes. Course goals are set out in syllabi which are common to upper secondary schools and municipal adult education.

Curriculum

The following core subjects are common to all programmes:

Core subject	Min. guaranteed instruction-time per three-year programme in hours
Swedish	200
English	110
Civics	90
Religious studies	30
Mathematics	110
Nature studies	30
Sports & health studies	80
Aesthetic activities	30

In addition to the core subjects, pupils take subjects which are specific to their programme. All pupils must also carry out a project during their course of studies. In all programmes, time is set aside for local supplements or practical work connected with subjects, as well as for individual choice to allow pupils to choose additional subjects and courses within the national programmes.

The timetables, which are now attached to the Education Act, express in units of 60 minutes the minimum guaranteed teacher or supervisor-led instruction time. This is 2,400 hours for the vocationally-oriented programmes and 2,180 hours for academically-oriented programmes, over the three years. The local education authority or school decides when different subjects are to be studied and how long the lessons should be.

In the vocationally-oriented programmes, at least 15% of the pupils' total time is to be spent on training at a place of work. The school will be responsible for procuring such training opportunities and for supervising pupils during this training.

The new common curriculum, with specific objectives set for each type of school, came into effect on 1 July 1994. As in the new curriculum for compulsory school, the objectives stated in the curriculum for the non-compulsory schools are of two kinds: objectives that education should strive towards; and those that everybody must be given the opportunity of achieving. The set of basic values which are to influence the activities of the school and the demands imposed on pupils and school staff will be set out in six different sections: Knowledge; Norms and values; Pupil responsibility and influence; Choice of education – work and civic life; Assessment and grades; Responsibilities of the head teacher.

In order to provide criteria, apart from the number of teaching hours, to determine whether an educational programme is completed, a points system has been introduced, whereby a pupil obtains a certain number of points on completion of a course with the minimum pass result, i.e. when the knowledge and skills that the course aims at providing have been acquired. These points are based on the number of hours allocated in the timetable to each course, irrespective of the number of hours taken to attain the objectives. An educational programme consisting primarily of courses preparing for higher education shall thus represent in total at least 2,180 upper secondary points, and a programme where a large part is vocational in content shall thus represent at least 2,400 points. No courses may consist of less than 30 hours or the equivalent number of points. The hours and points for courses that are normally studied over several years should be divided up between each year. This should be done on the basis of the structure of the individual subject or block of subjects in relation to the syllabus. The syllabus, which is drawn up in such a way as to ensure continuity with compulsory school, states the aims of the course and also the knowledge and skills that all pupils should have achieved on completion of the course. The teaching of Swedish and English is further strengthened and bilingual education (where a foreign language is used as the language of instruction for certain subjects), which today is offered by a limited number of schools at both upper secondary and compulsory school level, is promoted.

The principals of upper secondary schools have been given the overall responsibility for educational **guidance**. They have to ensure that pupils obtain guidance on the educational choices offered at the school and on further studies and vocational training. Vocational guidance is concerned both with the labour market as a whole and with individual sectors. Practical guidance on working life is also organized in theoretical lines. In vocational lines, contact with working life is an integral part of teaching. Schools and the world of work cooperate partly through the joint vocational committees for the vocational lines of local upper secondary schools. Some municipalities also have joint planning committees.

Assessment and qualifications

Within the new marking system for the upper secondary schools, which is gradually being implemented, the award of marks will be a continuous process. Marks will be awarded on completion of every course and not for individual subjects or for each term. Marks will also be given for special project work.

Marks will be awarded on a four-category scale: Failed, Passed, Passed with distinction and Passed with exceptional distinction. The criteria for awarding marks will be specified in the different syllabi; to support this, centrally compiled tests will be developed in certain subjects.

The leaving certificate will contain a record of the marks for all courses in upper secondary education. All three-year programmes will meet the general requirements for access to studies at institutions of higher education. The two programmes preparing for higher education will also meet most of the specific entrance requirements.

4.3 Teachers

Teachers of general subjects have a university degree in two or three subjects. They have also received one year's training in the theory and practice of teaching, subsequent to their subject studies. The minimum requirements for a University Diploma in Education for Upper Secondary School, valid from the academic year 1993/94, are four years' study – 2 years for the main subject, 1 1/2 years for other subjects (2 years for modern languages, Swedish, civics or artistic-practical subjects) and one year's pedagogical training. Upper secondary schools also have subject teachers with a PhD. degree or similar qualification.

All teachers are civil servants and may work full-time or part-time.

Vocational teaching in upper secondary schools is provided by subject teachers with advanced economic or technical qualifications or by vocational teachers who have completed vocational training and studies in vocational theory. They also have long experience of their trades and have undergone teacher training at university institutes of education.

The major task for the in-service training of teachers in upper secondary school and municipal adult education is to supplement subject qualifications so as to bring them more in line with the qualifications needed in the new programmes within upper secondary education.

4.4 Statistics 1993

Pupils	313,662
of which	
municipal schools	218,216
country council schools	28,876
independent schools	5,570
Teachers (municipal and county council schools)	29,398
Schools	638
of which	
independent schools	59
Average teacher/pupil ratio	7.2/100
(full-time posts)	pupils

5. Higher education

Higher education is divided into undergraduate studies and postgraduate studies and research.

In 1977, practically all post-secondary education, i.e. all university-type education and non-academic colleges for different kinds of vocational education and training, was incorporated into one system, the *högskola*. The system included a strong element of national planning and regulation, and the aims and length as well as the location and financing of most study programmes were laid down by Parliament. Until 1989, the State also established the curricula for each programme.

After the change of Government in the autumn of 1991, a major reform was initiated with the aim of deregulating the unitary system of higher education and giving greater autonomy to the individual institutions of higher education. The reform was adopted by Parliament in 1992, and on 1 July 1993 a new Higher Education Act came into effect. Under the system now in force the capacity of different programmes and the allocation of grants between institutions will be influenced by the requirements of the individual students and the achievements of the individual institutions in terms of both quality and quantity. The organization of study and range of courses on offer are determined locally, and students have been given increased freedom of choice of study route within the framework of a new internationally valid Degree Ordinance, attached to the 1993 Higher Education Ordinance.

The purpose of the institutions of higher education, as stated in the Higher Education Act of 1993, is to provide education and carry out research and artistic development; there should be a close connection between these two main duties. Emphasis is placed on quality and the effective use of available resources. Equality between men and women should be observed in all aspects of higher education. Universities and university colleges should also promote an understanding of other countries and international relations.

State institutions are:

- The Universities of Uppsala, Lund, Gothenburg, Stockholm, Umeå and Linköping;

- 15 university colleges in different parts of the country;

- Single-faculty institutions, i.e. the Karolinska Institute (Medicine and Dentistry), the Royal Institute of Technology, the Stockholm Institute of Education and the University College of Physical Education and Sports;

- 7 smaller university colleges in Stockholm for various areas of Arts.

Under the auspices of the County Councils, there are twenty-six Colleges of Health Sciences, which provide preparatory programmes for work in the paramedical professions.

State run universities and university colleges are central government agencies and their employees are civil servants.

Admission

To be admitted to higher education in Sweden, a student must first fulfil the general eligibility requirements which are common to all programmes or courses, and then meet the specific eligibility requirements which are usually imposed on applicants by the individual university or university college. The latter vary according to the field of education.

The general eligibility requirements for undergraduate education are: the successful completion of a 3-year national programme of the upper secondary school or other equivalent Swedish or foreign education; or the acquisition of the equivalent level of knowledge, e.g. through work experience. Applicants with a mother tongue other than one of the Nordic languages must possess the requisite knowledge of Swedish, e.g. acquired through a one-year preparatory course. All applicants are required to have a very good command of English.

Responsibility for the admission and selection of students rests with the institutions themselves. Within a generally formulated framework, they are able to decide what selection criteria will be used for admission to their courses and whether the admission procedure will be carried out locally or by using the central service provided by the National Agency for Higher Education.

For the selection of students, one or more of the following criteria are applicable: school marks; results in the university aptitude test (a national, non-compulsory test which is common for all institutions of higher education) or a special test (e.g. interviews); or previous education and work experience.

During the 1970s and 1980s, the capacity of the Swedish higher education system was nearly constant, with a total number of entrants of between 40,000 and 45,000 per year, in spite of a considerable increase in demand. Since 1991, however, there has been a steady expansion in the total number of places for undergraduate studies and by the mid-1990s student numbers will have increased by about 30%.

Roughly 30 % of young persons go on to higher education after completion of their compulsory and upper secondary schooling. Apart from students coming straight from school, the post-secondary student population includes a relatively large proportion of mature students, i.e. students who have previously acquired various amounts of work experience.

Fees/Student finance

Higher education is free of charge. The post-secondary study assistance scheme applies to students in undergraduate education at universities, university colleges and certain other establishments, as well as to students aged 20 and over attending upper secondary school and other forms of upper secondary schooling. This study assistance consists of a non-repayable grant, plus a larger repayable loan, awarded for both full-time and part-time studies.

The Government has announced that there are to be changes in the study assistance scheme.

Academic year

The academic year comprises 40 weeks, divided into two semesters. The autumn term usually runs from the middle or end of August to mid-January, the spring term runs from mid-January to the beginning of June. There is usually a two-week teaching break at Christmas.

Courses/Qualifications

In the new system of undergraduate education, students are able to choose their study route freely and to combine different subject courses into a degree. For study intended to lead to a degree, courses may be combined to form an educational programme (*utbildningsprogram*), if the university or university college so wishes.

The requirements for various courses of study are set out in the Degree Ordinance. All courses and educational programmes also have to follow curricula established by the individual university or university college. Undergraduate studies are available in the form of study programmes or as single-subject courses. A first degree programme generally takes between 2 and 5 1/2 years to complete. The single-subject courses vary in length from 5 weeks to 1 1/2 years.

The average number of study hours is 40 hours per week for full-time studies, including individual studies and group work. Study time is measured in points; one week's full-time study is equivalent to one point and one term's full-time study to 20 points.

Instruction takes the form of lectures to large groups (up to around 300 students) and seminars of about 30 students. Students are also expected to participate actively in group work, laboratory work and seminars. The language of instruction is usually Swedish, but a great deal of the compulsory course literature is in English.

A number of programmes include practical training in the relevant industry or the public sector. Sometimes the practical training takes place during the summer vacation. In many programmes a large part of the final term is devoted to work on a degree project or thesis. Students carry out these projects individually or in small groups.

There are two kinds of first degrees – general and professional. The professional degrees (*yrkesexamen*) are awarded upon completion of programmes of varying length (2 to 5 ½ years), leading to specific professions, e.g. University Diploma in Medicine or Education (for upper secondary school).

The general degrees are:

- **Diploma** *(högskoleexamen)* after studies amounting to not less than 80 points (2 years of study).

- **Bachelor's degree** *(kandidatexamen)* after completion of at least 120 points (at least 3 years of study), including 60 points in the major subject and 10 points for a thesis.

- **Master's degree** *(magisterexamen)* after studies amounting to not less than 160 points (4 years of study), including 80 points in the major subject and 20 points for one thesis or for two (10 points each).

Assessment

All courses are subject to continuous examination, written and/or oral. There are, however, no final examinations which cover an entire three or five-year programme. This means that the students have to be prepared to give proof of the knowledge they have acquired every three or four weeks.

Marks are generally awarded on a three-level scale: Fail, Pass and Pass with distinction. Some courses are only graded Fail and Pass, and some faculties, *inter alia*, Engineering and Law, have other grading systems.

Teachers

As from the academic year 1993/94, each university and university college is entitled to decide on the establishment of chairs and the appointment of staff. The teaching staff are grouped into the following main categories: professors, senior lecturers, lecturers and research assistants. Since 1986, duties of different kinds – teaching, research, personal study, educational counselling and administration – have been included in the same appointment. Professors have some teaching commitments but are mainly engaged in research. Senior lecturers must have a doctorate and be active in both research and teaching. Lecturers are not required to have a doctorate. To be appointed, they must also have displayed proficiency in teaching undergraduates.

Statistics 1992

Students	257,000
of which	
postgraduate studies	15,800
undergraduate studies	230,500
distance education	10,700

United Kingdom

England and Wales

Northern Ireland

Scotland

ENGLAND AND WALES

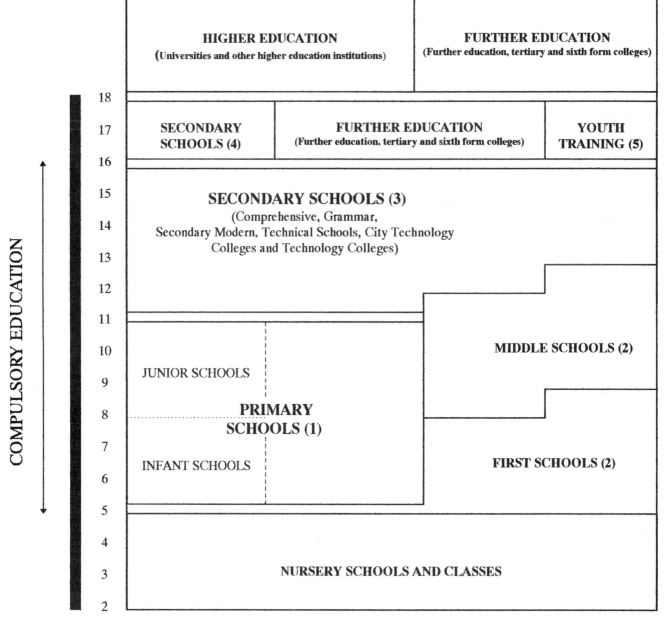

1. Some areas have separate schools, known as infant and junior schools, within primary education.
Infant schools and primary schools may include pupils in nursery classes.
2. Two tier (primary and secondary schools) and three tier (first, middle and secondary schools) systems exist side by side according to the provision within each individual LEA (local education authority).
3. All secondary pupils in Wales and over 90% of secondary pupils in England attend non-selective comprehensive schools covering the 11 to 16 or 11 to 18 age group. Most other children attend grammar schools for the 11 to 18/19 age group or secondary modern schools for the 11 to 16 age group. There are also a few technical schools and, more recently, City Technology Colleges and Technology Colleges.
4. Classes in secondary schools for pupils over 16 are known as sixth forms, and are subject to Schools Regulations. Sixth form, tertiary or further education colleges also provide education for pupils over 16. All three types of colleges are now subject to Further Education Regulations, and offer a range of academic and vocational courses.
5. Youth Training is delivered through contracts with independent training providers (often private employers). It lasts two years and is organized in "units of competence".

·········· = division in the level / type of education.

NORTHERN IRELAND

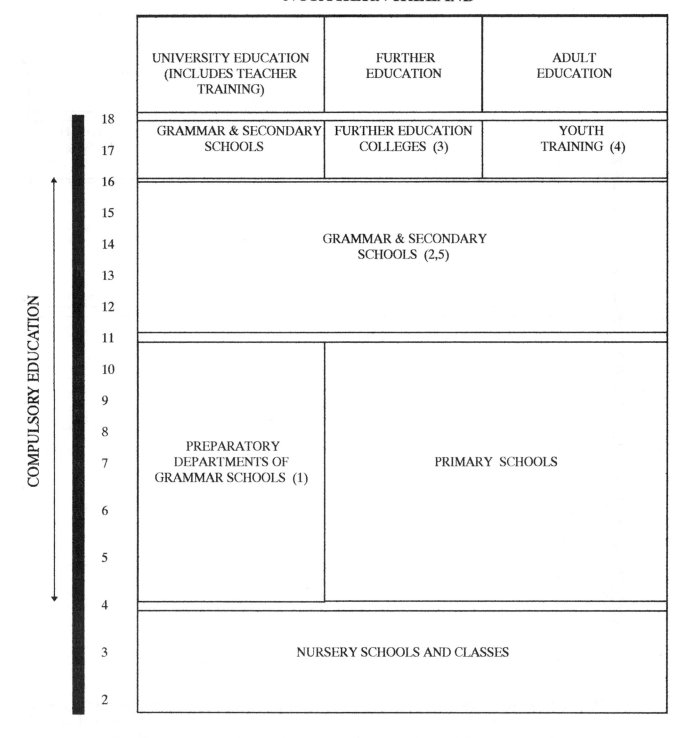

1. Preparatory Departments of Grammar Schools charge fees.
2. Secondary education is at present selective. On the basis of tests pupils go to either grammar schools or secondary schools. Both provide a similar range of courses, grammar schools for 11- to 18-year-olds and secondary schools for 11- to 16-year-olds (many secondary schools offer post-16 opportunities).
3. Further education colleges provide a range of academic and vocational courses for persons over compulsory school age.
4. Youth Training is provided by Training Centres, Community Workshops and FE colleges.
5. In some areas of NI , secondary education between the ages of 11 to 14 is provided in Junior High Schools.

SCOTLAND

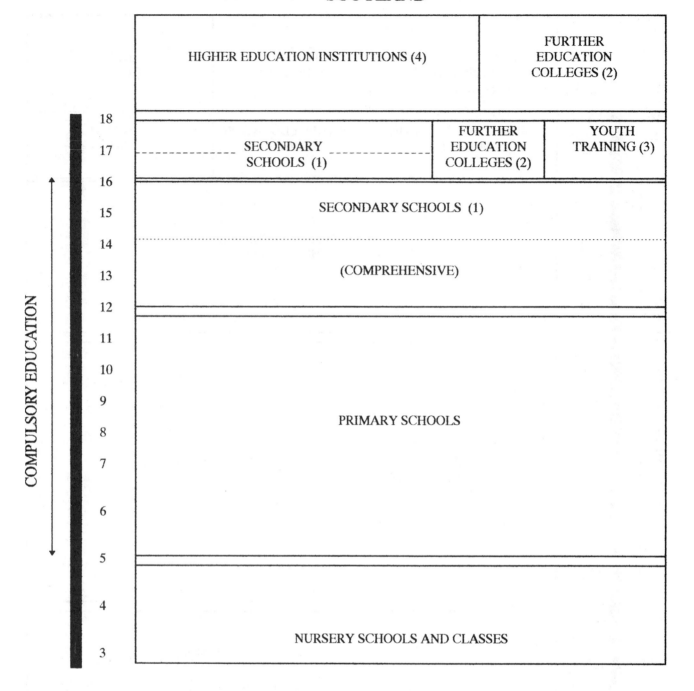

1. 99% of Scottish education authority secondary schools are comprehensive schools offering all types of courses to pupils of all abilities. 90% provide 6 years of education (4 years of compulsory and 2 years of optional secondary education). Pupils may leave at 16. Examinations usually taken at age 17 provide access to tertiary education.

2. Further education colleges offer courses in academic and vocational subjects from craft to degree level. They accept pupils currently attending secondary school for some courses. FE colleges also provide courses for the "off-the-job" component of the Youth Training scheme.

3. Youth Training is delivered through contracts with independent training providers (often private employers). It lasts 2 years, and is organized in "units of competence".

4. Higher Education Institutions comprise universities, former technological institutions, arts and health care colleges and teacher training institutions.

·········· = division in the level / type of education

– – – – · = alternative beginning or end of level / type of education

United Kingdom

1.1 Background

The United Kingdom consists of Great Britain (England, Wales and Scotland) and Northern Ireland. It has a constitutional monarchy and the Sovereign is Head of State and Head of Government. The Government comprises the Legislature (Parliament), the Executive (the Cabinet, which consists of about 20 Ministers, who are usually Heads of the Government Departments and are chosen by the Prime Minister) and the Judiciary. Parliament consists of the Queen, the House of Lords and the House of Commons. Most of the work of Parliament is conducted in the House of Commons which is composed of 650 elected Members, including 38 for Wales, 72 for Scotland and 17 for Northern Ireland. The Conservative Party won the last General Election in 1992 and currently has the majority in the House of Commons.

The United Kingdom is the union of four separate countries. Its Constitution is not contained in any single document but comprises statute, common law (precedent) and convention. The nature of the union means that there may be separate statutes, laws and conventions in the four constituent countries. In the case of education, separate legislation exists for England and Wales, for Scotland and for Northern Ireland respectively. The Secretaries of State for Wales, Northern Ireland and Scotland are Ministers in the UK Government and responsible to Parliament for the operation of their respective Offices and for legislation.

Local Government in England, Wales and Scotland is organized on a two-tier basis. In England and Wales, there are currently 53 Counties subdivided into 369 District Councils, a further 6 Metropolitan Counties subdivided into 36 District Councils, and London, which is divided into 32 Boroughs and the Corporation of the City of London. There are, however, plans for reorganization. In Scotland, there are 9 Regional Councils, subdivided into 53 District Councils, and 3 Island Councils which perform the functions of both Regional and District Councils in their areas. In Northern Ireland, there are 26 single-tier District Councils.

The established church in England is the Church of England, which is Protestant Episcopal, and in

Scotland, it is the Presbyterian Church of Scotland. There is no established church in Wales or in Northern Ireland.

The official language in England by custom and practice is English, but in Wales both English and Welsh are used in official documents. English is the official language in Scotland, with Gaelic as a national language, spoken by some 80,000 Scots. English is also the official language of Northern Ireland.

The UK covers an area of 94,247 square miles (50,663 for England, 8,018 for Wales, 30,414 for Scotland and 5,452 for Northern Ireland).

In 1992, the population of the UK was 57,801,000. Of this number, 48,208,000 lived in England, 1,594,000 in Northern Ireland, 5,107,000 in Scotland and 2,891,000 in Wales.

1.2 Basic principles: education

Education provision is based on the principle that all children between the ages of 5 and 16 must receive full-time education, either by attendance at school or by approved alternative provision. The curriculum should be balanced and broadly based and be suited to the child's age, ability, aptitude and to any special educational needs he or she may have. All children between the ages of 5 and 16 are entitled to free education. Any subsequent full-time education provided at schools or at further education institutions is also free for students up to the age of 19. Students attending higher education institutions must pay fees, often covered by their grants (see Higher Education).

1.3 Distribution of responsibilities

Education in the UK (England, Wales, Northern Ireland and Scotland) is characterized by its decentralized nature. Responsibility for different aspects of the service is shared between Central Government, local government, churches and other voluntary bodies, the governing bodies of educational institutions and the teaching profession.

Overall responsibility for all aspects of education lies with the Department for Education in England, the Welsh Office, the Scottish Office Education Department and the Department of Education for

Northern Ireland. The Departments of Health and of Social Security are responsible for some pre-school provision and the Employment Department for specific education initiatives. Overall responsibility for training lies with the Employment Department in England and the Welsh Office in Wales (in consultation with the Employment Department),with the Scottish Enterprise and the Highlands and Islands Enterprise in Scotland, and with the Training and Employment Agency in Northern Ireland. The provision of publicly financed education has traditionally been the responsibility of local government. In England and Wales, responsibility for financial and related administration has been transferred from Local Education Authorities to the governing bodies of individual schools and colleges. Training schemes are delivered locally in England and Wales by Training and Enterprise Councils (TECs) and in Scotland by Local Enterprise Companies (LECs). All higher education institutions in the UK are autonomous.

The fact that the education systems for England and Wales, for Northern Ireland and for Scotland are subject to independent legislation results in variations with respect to the organization, administration and control of the education systems and in the educational terminology and the designation of educational institutions. For clarity, the descriptions which follow are arranged in three sections, to outline the separate systems in England and Wales, in Scotland and in Northern Ireland respectively. These descriptions do not apply to Guernsey, Jersey, the Isle of Man and the Scilly Isles.

1. Responsibilities and administration

1.1 Administration

Central Government

The Department for Education (DFE) is responsible for all aspects of education in England, whilst the Employment Department (ED) is responsible for vocational training programmes and for some special education initiatives. The Welsh Office (WO) is responsible for both education and training in Wales. (See Vocational Training below.) In general terms, it may be said that the central authorities:

- determine national aims and formulate national policy, including the National Curriculum and assessment of pupils of statutory school age;

- commission research and support work on the development of the school curriculum and public examinations;

- set minimum standards of education provision and monitor both the quality and the cost effectiveness of provision.

Central authorities have the power to intervene if individual Local Education Authorities or the governing bodies of educational institutions do not discharge their duties satisfactorily. Central authorities also have at their disposal important means of influence and control, particularly the allocation of certain resources – for example, by granting permission to borrow money for school building programmes and by awarding Grants for Education Support and Training for specific purposes.

The Department for Education (DFE) is also responsible (under section 62 of the Education Act 1944) for the supply and training of school teachers.

The Secretary of State for Education lays down criteria with which courses of initial teacher training must comply if they are to lead to Qualified Teacher Status (QTS). The Secretary of State is responsible, under the Teachers' Pay and Conditions Act 1991, for determining teachers' pay and conditions of service. The DFE publishes guidance to assist LEAs and schools to implement legislation and other regulations.

The DFE is headed by the Secretary of State for Education. He is assisted by one or more Ministers of State.

The Secretary of State for Wales, assisted by a Minister of State, exercises those functions concerning education and training which are exercised in England by the Secretary of State for Education. However, although he is responsible for the supply of teachers, matters relating to teachers' qualifications and remuneration remain the responsibility of the Secretary of State for Education.

In accordance with the Education Act 1993, the School Curriculum and Assessment Authority (SCAA) in England and the Curriculum and Assessment Authority for Wales (known by its Welsh acronym ACAC) share responsibility for ensuring that the National Curriculum and its associated assessment at Key Stages develop within a clear framework of values and standards.

With regard to examinations in England, there is a national code of practice, but administrative responsibility lies with the four GCSE Examining Groups and the five GCE Examining Bodies, which are private companies set up on a geographical basis.

The Welsh Joint Education Committee (WJEC) acts as the examining body in Wales for GCSE, for GCE and for technical examinations in further education institutions. The WJEC also coordinates and makes provision for a wide range of curriculum materials in relation to the Welsh language.

Local Government

Under the Education Act 1944, the provision and organization of publicly funded school education and adult education are the responsibility of local councils (Counties, Metropolitan Boroughs and London Boroughs), which have designated responsibility as Local Education Authorities (LEAs). There are 116 LEAs in England and Wales. Following major changes as a result of recent legislation, their principal duties are as follows:

- to plan and provide school places (acting in conjunction with the Funding Agency for Schools where appropriate);

- to monitor school admissions policies and arrange for parental appeals;

- for LEA-maintained schools, to set budgets, to allocate funds, to publish information on funding for individual schools, to review the local management of schools scheme and to set term and holiday dates;

- to monitor the quality of education and to take initial action in LEA-maintained schools identified as being 'at risk';

- to assess and make provision for pupils' special educational needs;

- to provide educational psychology and education welfare services (and take action to secure school attendance);

- to arrange school transport for pupils, as appropriate;

- to make provision for the education of children who cannot attend school (for example, children in hospitals or children in Pupil Referral Units);

- to administer student awards (financial support for students attending courses of higher and further education); and

- to provide education for adults and services for young people outside school hours (the Youth Service).

LEAs also have powers to make additional provision as they consider appropriate. Each LEA has an Education Committee which determines and monitors the execution of these responsibilities, but the day-to-day administration of education is delegated to the Chief Education Officer (sometimes known as the Director of Education), who is assisted by professional and technical staff and advisers. However, the Education Act 1993 abolished the legal requirement that LEAs appoint an Education Committee.

Successive legislation has extended the individual financial and managerial responsibilities of LEA-maintained schools. Under the Education Reform Act 1988 and subsequent regulations, the governing bodies of all LEA-maintained secondary and primary schools have a delegated budget to cover most of the school's running costs. This is known as local management of schools. LEAs' delegation schemes must be approved by Central Government. LEAs were required to prepare schemes for the delegation of budgets to special schools by April 1994, to be implemented in 1996/97, or earlier at the request of the individual school. Local management of schools does not apply to nursery schools.

Institutions

Maintained, or publicly funded, **schools** fall into three categories: county schools, voluntary schools and self-governing grant-maintained schools. County schools are established and fully funded by Local Education Authorities (LEAs) and managed by the governing body of each school. They are non-denominational. Voluntary schools are established by religious or charitable bodies, but their recurrent expenditure and the majority of their capital expenditure is met by LEAs. The founding body retains some control over the management of these schools. A third category, known as self-governing grant-maintained schools, was created by the Education Reform Act 1988. These are county schools which have opted out of LEA control and receive their funding through the Funding Agency for Schools (FAS) or, in Wales, the Welsh Office. Any LEA-maintained school can, following a secret postal ballot indicating that the majority of parents wish to do so, apply for grant-maintained status. Self-governing grant-maintained schools are funded at the same level as LEA-maintained schools, but they receive an additional allowance to compensate for the loss of certain services normally provided by the LEA. By mid-August 1994, 1,000 schools in England and 16 in Wales had been granted self-governing grant-maintained status.

The Education Act 1993 makes provision for voluntary schools and special schools to apply for self-governing grant-maintained status.

Under local management of schools, the governing bodies of all LEA-maintained schools are responsible for the management, administration and maintenance of schools and the appointment, management, appraisal and dismissal of teachers.The LEAs, however, technically remain the employers of teachers. The LEA, the governing body and the head teacher share responsibility for delivering the National Curriculum. In practice, much of the day-to-day management of a school is delegated by the governing body to the head teacher.

The governing body of each self-governing grant-maintained school is responsible for all aspects of the management of its affairs, including decisions about the budget and employment of staff. It is the formal employer of its teachers.

The governing body of LEA-maintained schools comprises representatives of the LEA, the community, the parents and the teaching staff of the school. The head teacher is an ex-officio member but may choose whether to be a full voting member. The governing body of self-governing grant-maintained schools has no LEA representatives and the head teacher must be a full voting member.

The Further and Higher Education Act 1992 granted autonomous status as Further Education Corporations to existing colleges of **further education** (both general and specialist), tertiary colleges and sixth form colleges which had at least 15% of their students (in full-time equivalent terms) attending full-time courses or who attended courses on release from employment. These, and a few other 'designated institutions', comprise a new further education sector (see 4.). The Act transferred the control of and responsibility for provision from LEAs to the further education institutions.

The administration of institutions in the FE sector is the responsibility of the corporation or governing body, the head of the corporation (known as the principal), and its senior management. The principal is responsible for the organization, direction and management of the institution, including the determination of academic activities, after consulting the academic board, and for student discipline. Corporations consist of 10-20 members, including the principal and a member from the local Training and Enterprise Council (see

also Vocational Training below). Other members are drawn largely from local business and industry, but also include staff and student members (and, in former sixth form colleges, parents). Most institutions are organized into departments under the leadership of a head of department, who is responsible for all courses within the department. Heads may delegate responsibility for sections of the department to senior lecturers. At course level, there may be a course tutor who acts as coordinator for the course team and is responsible to the head of the department for the quality of the course. In larger institutions, several departments may be grouped into faculties or schools.

All **higher education institutions** (see 6.) are autonomous bodies, with full responsibility for educational provision and internal organization. Universities and some other higher education institutions award their own degrees and diplomas but the qualifications of smaller institutions must be validated by a university. Individual institutions determine teaching and assessment methods but their standards must satisfy the Higher Education Funding Councils. Institutions awarding their own degrees must have appropriate external academic and professional points of reference.

The overall head of a university is the Vice-Chancellor. The head of the administrative section is usually called the Registrar. The most senior governing body is the Court, which comprises senior staff and elected external members, and determines matters of general policy. The next most senior body is the university Senate, which normally consists of professorial staff, heads of departments and representatives of other interests, such as non-professorial staff and trade unions. It takes decisions on matters which are beyond the competence of faculties. Universities group related departments into faculties for administrative purposes. All members of the teaching staff are members of the appropriate faculty and the faculty is required to take certain actions and decisions, such as approving new courses and formally awarding degrees. Other higher education institutions have similar internal divisions.

1.2 Inspection

Under the Education (Schools) Act 1992, overall responsibility for school inspections lies with Her Majesty's Chief Inspector of Schools (HMCI) for

England and for Wales respectively. The office of HMCI in England is known as OFSTED (the Office for Standards in Education), that in Wales as the Office of HMCI (Wales).

All educational institutions which receive grants from public funds are subject to external evaluation. Schools in England are inspected on a four-yearly cycle in accordance with the Education (School Inspection) (No 2) Regulations 1993. Schools in Wales are inspected on a five-yearly cycle, in accordance with the Education (School Inspection) (Wales) (No 2) Regulations 1993. The new system was implemented for secondary schools in September 1993 and for primary and special schools in September 1994.

OFSTED comprises a professional arm and an administrative arm. The professional arm is Her Majesty's Inspectorate (HMI), comprising around 220 HM Inspectors, who are responsible for quality assurance for the new system, and for interpreting and reporting on inspection findings. The administrative arm is responsible for developing the range of regulatory and financial functions.

The Education (Schools) Act 1992 also created three categories of school inspectors: Registered Inspectors, Professional Team Members and Lay Inspectors. Registered Inspectors are trained team leaders who are contracted to conduct school inspections on behalf of Her Majesty's Chief Inspector (HMCI). Professional Team Members may have expertise in a particular aspect of a school's work, for example, finance or management or a curriculum area. Lay Inspectors are expected to contribute a common-sense view of a school, from the perspective of someone who has never been professionally involved in education; they may be drawn from the local community or from industry and commerce. Both Professional Team Members and Lay Inspectors are trained to use the Framework for Inspection.

Following the implementation of the Further and Higher Education Act 1992, the Inspectorate of the Further Education Funding Council (FEFC) for England is responsible for assessing the quality of education provision within its sector, and the Quality Assessment Division of the Higher Education Funding Council (HEFC) for England monitors the quality of higher education provision. The FEFC for Wales shares a Quality Assessment Division with the HEFC for Wales and may, under the Act, request the Office of HMCI Wales to inspect further education institutions.

1.3 Financing

The cost of education for pupils who attend **Local Education Authority (LEA)-maintained schools** is shared between Central and Local Government. Each LEA incurs both capital and recurrent expenditure on education. The majority of expenditure is recurrent and covers teachers' salaries, other institutional expenditure and the cost of LEAs' central services.

Recurrent expenditure incurred by LEAs and governing bodies is met partly by grant from Central Government and partly by income from the Council Tax and charges for local authority services. The Central Government grant is based on the Government's standard assessment of the authority's expenditure needs as compared with the income it raises locally. Arrangements are similar in Wales but all Central Government funding for Wales is provided through the Welsh Office.

Capital expenditure covers buildings and equipment. The total amount that a local authority may spend as capital expenditure is also determined annually by Central Government. In addition, LEAs may bid for additional funding from the Department for Education's and the Welsh Office's Grants for Education Support and Training. This funding, a large proportion of which must be devolved directly to schools, is for certain priority projects identified by the Secretary of State.

LEAs set a budget for the whole education service in their area. They determine the funding for individual schools in accordance with the local management of schools formula. The school governing body and head teacher are informed of the school's total annual budget for the year and are entirely responsible for its expenditure.

Maintained primary and secondary schools may not charge for tuition, books and stationery. However, the Education Reform Act 1988 allows LEAs and governing bodies to charge for some extracurricular activities provided outside school hours. Charges may not be made for any activity during the school day (except for individual music tuition which is provided other than to fulfil the requirements of a prescribed public examination or the National Curriculum). Likewise, charges may not be made for activities outside school hours which are provided as part of an examination syllabus or which fulfil statutory requirements of the National Curriculum or religious education. Schools may, however, invite parents to make voluntary contributions.

Under the provisions of the Education Act 1993, the Funding Agency for Schools (FAS) was established in April 1994 to assess and administer the grants payable to **self-governing grant-maintained (GM) schools** (see Institutions above) in England. When the percentage of pupils educated in GM schools in an LEA area exceeds 10% in either the primary or secondary phase, the FAS takes on joint responsibility with the relevant LEA for ensuring that there are sufficient schools for that phase. When the percentage of pupils educated in GM schools in an LEA area exceeds 75%, the FAS takes over full responsibility for ensuring that there are sufficient schools. By November 1994, the FAS was operating in 48 LEAs. Additional funding is available to schools from the FAS by means of the Special Purposes Grants.

The Act makes provision for the Secretary of State for Wales to establish the Schools Funding Council for Wales if necessary. Since few schools in Wales have chosen to become self-governing grant-maintained schools, there are no plans to do so at present and the schools are funded through the Welsh Office.

Following the implementation of the Further and Higher Education Act 1992, **further education institutions** are mainly funded by Central Government through the Further Education Funding Councils for England and Wales respectively. A block allocation of recurrent funding is paid to each FE institution every year. Colleges may receive additional income from student fees or by marketing their services.

Higher education institutions are mainly funded by Central Government through the Higher Education Funding Councils for England and Wales respectively and through student fees. Some research is funded through seven Research Councils. All institutions are encouraged to seek additional finance through sponsorship, by obtaining research commissions from commercial or industrial firms and by marketing their services.

The Funding Councils base their decisions as to funding levels on projected and desired student numbers.

1.4 Independent institutions

Schools outside the maintained sector (known as private or independent schools and colleges) receive no grants from the State, but are financed from fees and endowments. They must be registered with the Department for Education or the Welsh Office, which can require them to remedy deficiencies in their premises, accommodation or instruction. Independent schools and colleges for pupils and students of all ages charge fees.

The Education Act 1980 made provision for the Assisted Places Scheme. Under the Scheme, the Government enables academically able children to attend one of the participating independent schools, by paying all or part of the fees, according to the parents' income. The participating schools are chosen on the basis of proven academic merit and curriculum breadth.

Independent schools are not required to implement the National Curriculum, but they must satisfy inspectors that their curriculum is of the requisite depth and breadth for the age, aptitudes and abilities of their pupils and for any special educational needs which they may have.

The Education Reform Act 1988 also made provision for the establishment of a new category of independent school for pupils aged 11 to 18 years, the city technology college (CTC) or city college for technology of the arts (CCTA). CTCs are intended to extend parents' choice between schools and to pioneer new approaches to the delivery of the curriculum, with an emphasis on science and technology, or in the case of the CCTAs, an emphasis on the technology of the creative and performing arts. These colleges are managed by their sponsors or promoters, who are expected to meet, or make a substantial contribution towards, the cost of buildings and equipment. The Department for Education pays the staff salaries and the recurrent expenditure, subject to the college's fulfilling a mutually agreed contract. Unlike other independent schools, CTCs may not charge tuition fees and are required to offer education to pupils without reference to academic ability. Also, unlike other independent schools,

CTCs must provide the National Curriculum as a condition of their grant. The first CTC opened in September 1988 and by September 1993 there were 15 CTCs and one CCTA in operation in England. There are no CTCs in Wales.

Most private **further education** institutions are accredited by the British Accreditation Council for Independent Further and Higher Education, which was set up by bodies responsible for the maintenance of academic standards to define, monitor and improve standards in independent further and higher education institutions in Britain.

The only **higher education** institution in the UK which is independent of Government finance and whose degrees are nationally recognized is the University of Buckingham.

1.5 Advisory and consultative bodies

Education policy is influenced by the work of a wide range of consultative bodies providing advice for Central Government Departments as well as for Local Education Authorities. Parents, teachers, school governors and students may make representation to Government through national bodies, as may other bodies representing political, religious and social interest groups.

From time to time, the Government may set up a committee of enquiry which normally produces published reports examining specific aspects of the education service (e.g. Curriculum Organization and Classroom Practice in Primary Schools: a Discussion Report.(London: DFE, 1992)).

1.6 Vocational training

The Secretary of State for Employment takes the lead in setting targets and priorities for training in Great Britain as a whole and also has particular responsibilities for vocational training in England, exercised by the Employment Department through the Training and Enterprise Councils (TECs). In Wales, the responsibility for training rests with the Welsh Office and TECs contract directly with the Secretary of State for Wales.

TECs operate on a geographical basis. There are, however, a number of autonomous bodies which exercise responsibilities for training across industrial sectors (Industry Training Organizations) and for specific occupations or groups of occupations (Lead Bodies). Various examining bodies (see 4.) award qualifications, some of which are subject to accreditation by the National Council for Vocational Qualifications.

The provision of training courses is the responsibility of some 500 further education institutions, several hundred managing agents (some of which may be colleges), private enterprise training organizations and individual employers.

There are 82 **Training and Enterprise Councils (TECs)** in England and Wales. They are independent companies whose aim is to involve local industry in the identification of training needs and the organization of training so that local training needs may be met effectively. TECs are responsible for the delivery of Government-funded training schemes such as Youth Training (see 5.). In meeting the training needs of their local area, TECs cooperate with further education institutions in planning course provision and by funding specially designed courses through the Work-related Further Education scheme. All further education college governing bodies include representatives of the TEC. At national level, TECs are represented on the Further Education Funding Councils. TECs also have responsibilities for developing links between education and industry.

Industry Training Organizations (ITOs) foster the development of training within their particular industry. They provide advice and information to employers and specify standards of competence in their industry, including the development of National Vocational Qualifications.

Lead Bodies (LBs) comprise representatives of employers and employees in an occupational field and are responsible for determining the standards of competence associated with specific occupations or groups of occupations. Many of the Lead Bodies are also ITOs.

2. Pre-school education

In England and Wales, pre-school or nursery education is the education of children from two to five years old, preceding the statutory period of education. Sometimes children are admitted to full-time schooling (reception class) before the age of five; these children are known as 'rising fives'.

Provision is made either through the local authorities or by voluntary and independent bodies. The law does not oblige Local Education Authorities (LEAs) to make educational provision for children below the statutory school age of 5 years, but the Government's educational expenditure enables LEAs and school governing bodies to make provision for children aged between two and five years, if they wish to do so, for example by converting spare primary accommodation for nursery education. However, LEAs have a duty to ensure that appropriate provision is made for children between two and five who are identified as having special educational needs, although this may not be LEA provision.

Admission to LEA nursery schools and nursery classes is governed by criteria defined by the schools on the basis of admission policies established by each LEA. These may include the child's educational and psychological needs, where he or she lives and whether he or she has brothers and sisters attending the school. Local authority Social Services Departments may also provide day nurseries, which accept children below the age of five years. Education and Social Services Departments are required to collaborate in their care for the under-fives and may combine the services offered by a nursery school and a day nursery. Admission to day nurseries provided by local authority Social Services Departments and to combined nursery centres is based on the degree of the child's need for specialist help and the family's ability to provide for the child's health and educational needs. Both types of pre-school establishment are subsidized by Central and Local Government, but, whilst fees may be charged for day nursery care, nursery schools and classes maintained by LEAs do not charge fees.

In addition, there are private nursery schools and pre-school play groups organized by parents and voluntary or independent bodies, some of which charge fees.

In 1993 in England, 51% of children aged three and four attended maintained nursery or primary schools and a further 4% attended private or special schools. During 1991/92 in Wales, a total of 68.5% of children of this age attended maintained nursery or primary schools and a further 1.5% attended private or special schools. If all forms of day care provision are taken into account, it is estimated that over 90% of children receive some provision before reaching the age of five. In November 1994, the Government stated its intention to provide, over time, pre-school places for all children aged four whose parents wish to take them up.

The principal goal of pre-school education provided in nursery schools and classes is to develop children's social, intellectual, linguistic, physical and cognitive skills and their personality. Day nurseries generally emphasize their function as guardians and care providers, who ensure the children's physical well-being.

Nursery schools or classes provided by LEAs are normally open five days per week from about 9.00 a.m. to 3.00 p.m. during term time. They are closed during normal school holidays. Schools must provide at least one-and-a-half hours of suitable activities during every half-day session on which a school or class meets. Independent nursery schools have a similar timetable. The majority of children attend for one session on each school day, either morning or afternoon. Publicly maintained and independent day nurseries and combined nursery centres admit and care for children for the entire day. They usually open from 7.30 a.m. to 6.00 p.m. throughout the year.

Children in nursery schools may be grouped according to age, depending on the size of the classes. Children in day nurseries are in mixed age groups. The Children Act 1989 recommends a minimum of two members of staff for every 26 children in nursery classes and for every 20 children in nursery schools; one member of staff should be a qualified teacher and the other a qualified nursery assistant. In day nurseries, a ratio of one to eight is recommended.

Curriculum and assessment

There are no specific legal regulations for the curriculum, teaching methods or assessment in nursery schools and classes. The management and staff of each institution jointly determine the programme of activities. In 1989, a report by Her Majesty's Inspectorate recommended that teachers refer to nine areas of learning: artistic, social, linguistic, mathematical, moral (civics), physical, scientific, technological and spiritual (religion).

Teachers

See 7.

Statistics 1992/93

	Pupils	Teachers	Nursery schools
England	53,200 (FTE)	1,600	561
Wales	1,029 (full-time) 2,525 (part-time)	113	52

FTE – full-time equivalents.

3. Compulsory education

The compulsory school age is from 5 to 16. All children must receive appropriate full-time education, by regular attendance at school or otherwise, from the beginning of the school term which follows their fifth birthday. At present, pupils who reach the age of 16 before 31 January in an academic year may leave school at Easter, and those who reach 16 between 1 February and 31 August may leave on the Friday before the last Monday in May. It is intended to introduce a single School Leaving Date in 1995/96, after which a pupil who reaches the age of 16 after the beginning of the school year, but before the beginning of the next school year, ceases to be of compulsory school age on the School Leaving Date. The School Leaving Date will be determined by Order of the Secretaries of State and will probably fall in the later part of June. The academic year runs from 1 September to 31 August.

The Education Act 1944 requires that there should be three phases of education: primary, secondary and further. It defines a junior (primary) pupil as one who has not reached the age of 12, a senior (secondary) pupil as one aged between 12 and 18 years. Further education covered all provision for those aged over the compulsory school age who were not attending school; however, the Education Reform Act 1988 defines a fourth level, higher education, that is, advanced level education for students normally over the age of 18. Since 1964, legislation has permitted the establishment of middle schools, which normally provide a four-year course for pupils aged between eight and twelve years, or nine and thirteen years. Middle schools are classified either as 'middle schools deemed primary' (if the average age of pupils is under 11) or as 'middle schools deemed secondary' (if the average age of pupils is over 11) for statistics and funding purposes. In January 1992, there were 1,036 middle schools in England. There are no middle schools in Wales.

Two-tier (primary and secondary) and three-tier (first, middle and secondary) systems exist side by side, according to the provision within each individual Local Education Authority.

The **school year** consists of 380 (half-day) sessions. The actual dates of terms and holidays are determined annually by the individual governing bodies of self-governing grant-maintained schools and by the LEA Education Committee in consultation with the governing bodies of schools maintained by them. In general, the school year runs from about the first week of September to the third week of July. It is divided into three terms with a long summer break of about six weeks in July and August and shorter breaks of two to three weeks at Christmas and Easter, and one week in the middle of each term. The **school week** normally runs from Monday to Friday, although in independent boarding schools pupils may also have lessons on Saturday. The **school day** is divided into two sessions, one in the morning (usually between 9 a.m. and 12 noon) and one in the afternoon (usually between 1 p.m. and 3.30 p.m.). Children under eight years of age must receive at least three hours of secular instruction per day. For children aged eight and over, the minimum is four hours of secular instruction. Subject to these minimum requirements, and to the requirements of the National Curriculum, Local Education Authorities or school governing bodies have discretion concerning the arrangement of the timetable. There are no fixed number of lessons per week. DES Circular 7/90, Management of the School Day,

suggests the minimum weekly lesson times as 21 hours for pupils aged 5 to 7 years, 23½ hours for pupils aged 8 to 11 years and 24 hours for pupils aged 12 to 16 years.

Following the Education Reform Act 1988, the statutory period of education is divided into four Key Stages. Key Stage 1 (age 5 to 7 years), Key Stage 2 (age 7 to 11 years), Key Stage 3 (age 11 to 14 years) and Key Stage 4 (age 14 to 16 years).

3.1 Primary education

Primary education comprises Key Stage 1 (age 5 to 7) and Key Stage 2 (age 7 to 11) of compulsory education, although schools may admit children who are younger. In some areas, there are separate schools for each phase, known as infant and junior schools respectively. Publicly maintained primary schools are generally coeducational.

Most primary schools are supported from public funds and administered by Local Education Authorities (LEAs). There are some independent primary schools, which are usually known as pre-preparatory (age 5 to 8 years) or preparatory (age 8 +) schools.

LEAs and school governing bodies are responsible for establishing admissions policies. Priority may, for instance, be given to children who live closest to the school or who have brothers and sisters at the school.

Pupils are placed in a class according to their age and at the end of each school year they normally progress to the next class. In exceptional circumstances, generally serious illness, the parents and the school may decide that a child would benefit educationally from an extra year in a particular class. Some primary schools are organized in mixed-age groups, and at Key Stage 2 the core subjects may be taught in classes divided into groups according to learning ability. However, children aged five to eleven are generally taught by year group in mixed-ability classes with one teacher in charge of teaching all subjects to a class. Teachers remain with the same class for one year; in small schools they may have the same class for more years. In some schools, there are also specialist teachers for physical education and music and, more rarely, for foreign languages.

In accordance with the Education Reform Act 1988, all maintained schools in England and Wales must provide the National Curriculum (see Curriculum, assessment and qualifications below). There are no final examinations or certificates at the end of primary education.

3.2 Secondary education

Secondary education covers school-based provision for young people aged 11+ to 18+. Compulsory secondary education lasts until the pupil is 16 years of age. Secondary schools usually admit pupils at age 11 but, in areas where three-tier systems exist, pupils may transfer at age 12, 13 or 14. Secondary schools provide a general education for pupils in Key Stage 3 (age 11 to 14) and Key Stage 4 (age 14 to 16), although some schools also cater for pupils of post-compulsory age up to age 18. Alternatively, pupils aged 16 may continue their post-compulsory education in a further education institution (see 4.).

All secondary school pupils in Wales and over 90% of secondary school pupils in England attend comprehensive schools, which provide a wide range of secondary education for all or most of the children of a district, without reference to ability or aptitude. In some areas, pupils are admitted to secondary schools on the basis of their performance in selection tests, taken at the age of 11, or on the basis of special aptitude, for example in science, technology or art. Grammar schools provide a mainly academic education for pupils selected by examination from the age of 11 to 18 or 19. Modern schools provide a general education for pupils who have failed or have not taken the examination up to the minimum school leaving age of 16; their pupils may stay on beyond that age. Technical schools also provide a general education, but put considerable emphasis on technical subjects. The Education Act 1993 allows all schools to select up to 10% of their pupils on grounds of ability or special aptitude. Schools that are currently non-selective and which wish to select over 10% of their pupils on such grounds must apply to the Secretary of State for a change in status. Under the Education Act 1993, self-governing (grant-maintained) schools and voluntary schools which secure additional income by appointing up to four business sponsors to their governing bodies may then also apply for additional

support from the Government to become Technology Colleges, in which pupils study technology, science and mathematics in greater depth. Forty-two schools had been approved as Technology Colleges by July 1994. In 1993, approximately 3.8% of all pupils in England attended grammar schools, 3.5% attended secondary modern schools and 1% attended technical schools.

As at primary level, pupils are placed in a class according to their age and at the end of each school year they progress to the next class, unless, in exceptional circumstances, the parents and the school decide that a child would benefit educationally from an extra year in a particular class. Classes may be mixed-ability throughout the school, but pupils may be divided by ability into whole classes or 'streams' or they may be grouped according to ability for individual subjects. Such grouping may be introduced at the discretion of the school but is not normally introduced until after the first year. Pupils are taught by specialist teachers for most of their subjects. At secondary level, each lesson lasts around 35 to 40 minutes.

In accordance with the Education Reform Act 1988 and subsequent regulations, all maintained schools and city technology colleges (see Independent institutions) in England and Wales must provide the National Curriculum (see Curriculum, assessment and qualifications below).

3.3 Curriculum, assessment and qualifications

The law requires that all pupils receive a broad, balanced **curriculum**, appropriate to their age, abilities, aptitudes and to any special educational needs which they may have.

The National Curriculum (which requires certain subjects to be studied) and Programmes of Study (which define the content to be covered) have been phased in since autumn 1989. The law prevents prescription of the time to be spent on each subject, although guidelines are offered. LEAs, governing bodies and head teachers of individual schools are jointly responsible for ensuring that the basic curriculum, which comprises the National Curriculum and religious education, is delivered.

The basic curriculum must include:

1. the National Curriculum, comprising:

   - the **core** subjects: English, mathematics and science. In Welsh-medium schools in Wales, Welsh is a fourth core subject; and

   - the **other foundation** subjects: technology, history, geography, art, music and physical education and – for pupils aged 11 to 16 only – a modern foreign language. In schools in Wales which are not Welsh-medium, Welsh is a further foundation subject.

Greater flexibility is being introduced during Key Stage 4 so that, from 1996, the mandatory curriculum for this Key Stage will be: full General Certificate of Secondary Education courses in English, mathematics and science; short courses in technology and, in England only, a modern foreign language; physical education; religious education and sex education. In Wales, there will be no compulsory requirement for a modern foreign language and, until 1999, Welsh ceases to be compulsory at this Stage. This flexibility means that there should be room in the timetable for schools to offer pupils aged 14 to 16 a choice of subjects, including vocational options, in addition to those required by the National Curriculum.

2. Religious education and a daily act of collective worship for all school pupils, including those over compulsory school age, unless parents request otherwise. The nature of the religious education and collective worship must conform to a syllabus agreed with the local Standing Advisory Councils on Religious Education (SACREs). It should be broadly Christian, although, at the request of parents, religious education and worship may be provided according to a particular denomination, or according to a different faith.

The curriculum should, at appropriate stages, also include: careers education; health education; other aspects of personal and social education; cross-curricular coverage of gender and multi-cultural issues. These and other aspects, such as economic awareness, environmental education, political and international understanding, (including an awareness of European identity and European historical, cultural, economic and social aspects), may be taught in a cross-curricular way. For some pupils, further study within these areas may form part of their formal curriculum, as may other subjects such as a second foreign language, home economics or classical studies.

Teachers are responsible for determining **teaching methods and materials**. There are no prescribed texts at primary or secondary level, except those which are required to meet the needs of examination syllabuses set by examining groups, for example literature texts.

A continuous **assessment** of pupils' progress and attitudes is carried out by their teachers, who may set their own internal tests and examinations. In addition, towards the end of each of the first three Key Stages, teachers monitor pupils' progress against Level Descriptors for each of the National Curriculum subjects. Pupils are also assessed by means of National Curriculum Tests – restricted until 1996 to English and mathematics at the end of Key Stage 1 and English, mathematics and science at the end of Key Stages 2 and 3. Under the Reports on Individual Pupils' Achievements Regulations 1992, schools are required to send parents an annual report on their child's progress in each subject and, in addition, must provide all school-leavers with a National Record of Achievement (NRA), in which achievements in all subjects and any qualifications or credits gained must be noted.

Assessment of pupils at the end of Key Stage 4 is linked to the main external examination for secondary school pupils aged 16: the General Certificate of Secondary Education (GCSE). The GCSE may be taken in a range of single subjects. There are no regulations governing the minimum or maximum number of subjects to be taken by a pupil at any one time. Accordingly, a certificate is issued listing the grade a candidate has achieved in each subject. The grade awarded may be based partly on course work done throughout a period of up to two years, as well as on the final examination. Candidates are awarded one of seven grades (A-G); they must reach the minimum standards for Grade G for a subject to be included on a certificate. A starred A grade (A*) was introduced in 1994 to indicate outstanding achievement in a given subject.

In England and Wales, GCSE examinations are administered principally by five separate Examining Groups, which are subject to a national code of practice. The main features of GCSE examinations are:

- syllabuses based on national criteria;

- differentiated assessment (different papers or questions for different ranges of ability);

- grade-related criteria (grades to be awarded on absolute rather than relative performance).

All courses which are taught to pupils of statutory school age, and which lead to an external qualification, must have been approved by the Secretaries of State for Education and for Wales.

Teachers

See 7.

Statistics 1992/93

	Pupils	Teachers	Schools
Primary			
England	4,165,400	179,400	18,828
Wales	262,267	12,286	1,697
Secondary*			
England	2,964,700	184,000	3,773
Wales	189,729	12,111	225
Independent**			
England	560,200	53,000	2,263
Wales	11,164	1,162	65

* Most secondary schools also provide post-compulsory courses (see below)
** Nursery, primary and secondary schools.

In January 1993, maintained schools (including self-governing grant-maintained schools) catered for 92.5% of the total school population in England and Wales. Independent schools, including the city technology colleges, provided for the remainder.

4. Post-compulsory education

Post-compulsory education includes further education, adult and continuing education and higher education. (For higher education provision, see 6.). Further education may be provided in school sixth forms (subject to Schools Regulations) and also in further education institutions (subject to Further Education Regulations).

The Further and Higher Education Act 1992 defines further education as 'full-time and part-time education suitable to the requirements of persons over compulsory school age (16 years) including vocational, social, physical and recreational training'. Further education institutions include sixth form colleges, tertiary colleges and further education colleges. Sixth form colleges entered the new further education sector on 1 April 1993, having previously been in the schools sector. These autonomous institutions receive funding through the Further Education Funding Councils for specific types of courses known as *Schedule 2 Courses*. These are:

- courses which prepare students to obtain a vocational qualification;

- courses which prepare students for the General Certificate of Secondary Education (GCSE) or the General Certificate of Education Advanced Level (GCE A Level) or Advanced Supplementary (AS) examinations;

- basic English or mathematics;

- English as a second language;

- Welsh language or literacy courses in Wales;

- independent living and communication skills courses for people with learning difficulties, which prepare them to participate in any of the above courses.

Traditionally, young people stayed on at school or transferred to a sixth form college to follow academic courses (GCE A Levels) or transferred to a further education or tertiary college to study vocational courses. However, the distinction between the post-compulsory courses offered in schools and further education colleges is becoming blurred. Many further education institutions have for some time offered a wide range of academic as well as vocational courses for young people over the age of 16, and schools are now being encouraged to offer vocational as well as academic courses. Whereas schools offer post-compulsory education on a full-time basis, further education institutions offer courses full-time, part-time, or on day-release or block-release for students in employment.

Success in the GCSE examinations is not officially required for access to post-compulsory school education, but it allows pupils to evaluate their aptitude for higher education. The individual school decides admission policy. Pupils are usually admitted on the basis of their past educational and personal record. Likewise, there are no formal qualifications for admission to a further education institution, although individual courses may have specific requirements with regard to previous achievement.

Students enrolled on full-time courses are required to devote the whole of their time to their studies. Part-time courses are offered for students who can attend college during the day and/or evening, normally for a full academic year. Day-release courses are for employees released by their employer to attend courses on one or two days per week. Block-release courses are for employees released by their employers for one or more periods of full-time study per year. Block-release courses average up to 19 weeks per academic year.

The academic year runs from 1 September to 31 August, with breaks at Christmas, Easter and during the summer, although certain courses may be offered during these holiday periods. Classes are offered during the day and in the evenings.

The overall proportion of 16-year-olds in post-compulsory education rose in the five years up to 1992/93 from 65% to 80%, with an increase in the proportion of those receiving full-time education and a corresponding decrease in the proportion of those receiving part-time education. The pattern for 17- and 18-year-olds is similar, with 55% of 17-year-olds and 34% of 18-year-olds now in full-time education.

In 1992/93, half of 16-year-olds and about three-fifths of 17-year-olds were following GCE A level and/or GCE AS courses. The remainder were following courses leading to examinations, including GCSE and Business and Technology Education Council (BTEC) courses. Of the 17-year-olds, about 5% were on GCSE courses, with the remainder taking BTEC and other courses.

4.1 Academic courses

Curriculum, assessment and qualifications

Young people who wish to go on to university or other higher education institutions usually study subjects to General Certificate of Education Advanced Level (A Level). A Level is the main external examination offered in schools at upper secondary level. General Certificate of Education Advanced Supplementary (AS) examinations were introduced in 1989 to broaden the curriculum of A Level pupils by enabling them to take examinations in subjects that complement or contrast with their main subject areas. An AS examination is equivalent to one half of an A Level.

The syllabus and examinations of A Levels and AS courses are set by General Certificate of Education (GCE) Examining Groups, most of which are attached to universities. There are five GCE Examining Groups in England and one in Wales. A Level and AS are single-subject examinations and candidates may attempt any number, although most pupils take between two and four subjects at A Level, or the AS equivalent. Examinations are generally taken at the age of 18 following a two-year course, but they may be taken earlier if the candidate is ready. Candidates may receive one of five 'pass' grades (A-E), a 'narrow failure' (F) or be ungraded for each subject in which they are examined.

Depending on its size, an educational institution may offer between eight and thirty subjects at A Level, in different combinations. Each subject requires six to ten hours' work (including private study) per week over two years full-time, and often builds on the curriculum studied up to GCSE Level. The AS courses take half the time required by A Levels – normally spread over two years – but are equally demanding intellectually. In principle, there is no limit on the permutations of A Level and AS examinations which pupils may choose. However, in practice, pupils' choice may be restricted by what an individual school can offer in terms of subjects and by its timetable. Pupils in schools must, by law, receive religious education. The school may also require them to follow courses such as physical education, personal and social education, general studies and careers education. Courses may also be taken on a part-time basis at further education institutions, or syllabuses may be studied independently.

In addition to A Level and AS courses, pupils in post-compulsory education (either in a college or school sixth form) may take courses in preparation for GCSE examinations.

4.2 Vocational courses

Curriculum, assessment and qualifications

Although traditionally offered in further education institutions, vocational courses are increasingly being made available in schools. In both cases, the courses follow syllabuses set by one of the examining and awarding bodies, such as the Business and Technology Education Council (BTEC), the RSA Examining Board, the City and Guilds of London Institute (C&G) and the London Chamber of Commerce and Industry (LCCI). An AS examination in the built environment, which blends academic and vocational study, has also been available from one of the GCE Groups since September 1994.

BTEC approves vocational courses in a wide range of subjects such as business studies, management and engineering and design. Qualifications are awarded at three levels: First, National and Higher National.

The RSA offers examination and assessment schemes in all aspects of business studies, including clerical and secretarial skills, information technology and foreign languages. Qualifications are awarded at four levels from Vocational Certificates through to Higher Diplomas.

The C&G offers over 1,100 examinations at various levels in technical and vocational subjects, ranging from agriculture to retail distribution and from construction to hotel and catering studies. It works closely with industry to ensure that courses are relevant to the needs of employers. Assessments and examinations are competence-based, that is, they are designed to measure practical skills, knowledge, aptitude and experience.

The LCCI offers single-subject Certificates, Group Certificates and Group Diplomas at three levels in a wide variety of subjects.

In 1986, the Government set up the National Council for Vocational Qualifications (NCVQ) to oversee and validate qualifications awarded by the examining bodies. The Government has introduced two new qualifications: National Vocational Qualifications (NVQs) and General National Vocational Qualifications (GNVQs). These are intended to replace the vocational qualifications currently offered by the examining and awarding bodies as the main national provision for vocational education and training. The examining bodies will continue to set the broad parameters for syllabuses designed by individual institutions and to award qualifications.

National Vocational Qualifications (NVQs) are specific vocational qualifications aimed at young people who have left full-time education. They may be obtained by successfully completing courses offered by one of the above examining bodies and which comply with the competence-based criteria laid down by the NCVQ. Alternatively, they may be obtained by showing 'competence' in an occupation as defined in the 'statement of competence' from one of the Lead Bodies (see 1.) for industrial sectors or occupations. 'Competence' is defined as a combination of relevant skills, knowledge and understanding and the ability to apply them. Units of competence which may have been achieved in a range of different ways and over a period of time may be combined into an NVQ. An awarding body may accept a variety of evidence to show that someone has achieved the necessary level of competence.

The system of credit accumulation operates through the National Record of Achievement (NRA) (see 3) and was introduced to provide a common system of recording unit-credits awarded by different bodies, in different education and training programmes, in different locations and over varying periods of time. Currently, accreditation covers Levels 1-4 of the NVQ, that is, qualifications up to higher technician levels and their equivalents.

General National Vocational Qualifications (GNVQs) are aimed at young people over compulsory school age who remain in full-time education. They are intended to provide a comprehensive preparation for employment as well as an accepted route to higher-level qualifications. The first pilot schemes for GNVQs started in September 1992 and new subject areas will be phased in at the various levels until 1995, when the scheme will be fully operational. The 14 subject areas will be: health and social care; business; management; art and design; manufacturing; science; distribution; construction and the built environment; engineering; media, communication and the performing arts; agriculture and the environment; hospitality and catering; leisure and tourism; and information technology. GNVQs will be validated by the existing vocational examining boards and approved by the NCVQ. Most subject areas will be available at three levels: foundation, intermediate and advanced:

- GNVQ Foundation requires 3 mandatory units of study, plus 3 optional units from different vocational areas, plus Level 1 of the core skills in communication, application of number and information technology. It is equivalent to 4 GCSEs at grades D to G or 1 NVQ level 1. It takes approximately 1 year to complete;

- GNVQ Intermediate requires 4 mandatory units of study, plus 2 optional units, plus Level 2 of the core skills in communication, application of number and information technology. It is equivalent to 4-5 GCSEs at grades A to C or 1 NVQ level 2. It takes approximately 1 year to complete;

- GNVQ Advanced requires 8 mandatory units of study, plus 4 optional units, plus Level 3 of the

core skills in communication, application of number and information technology. Additional units may be studied if desired. It is equivalent to 2 GCE A Levels or 1 NVQ level 3. It takes approximately 2 years to complete.

The Government has set a target of 25% of young people aged 16 starting GNVQ courses by 1996, and, as the long term objective, 50% of all those aged 16 and 17 taking GNVQs.

GNVQs are primarily qualifications for students over compulsory school age, but pupils under the age of 16 may study some units (where the requirements of the National Curriculum allow) and acquire credits which can be carried forward towards a full qualification in post-compulsory education.

4.3 National targets for education and training

The Confederation of British Industry (CBI) has promoted the use of vocational qualifications as the means for setting 'world class targets' for developing skills in the UK work force. These have been endorsed by the Government as official national training targets.

Foundation Learning Targets

1. By 1997, at least 80% of all young people should attain NVQ Level 2, or its academic equivalent, in their foundation education and training.

2. All young people who can benefit should be given an entitlement to structured training, work experience or education, leading to NVQ Level 3 or its academic equivalent.

3. By the year 2000, at least half of the age group should attain NVQ Level 3 or its academic equivalent, as a basis for further progression.

4. Education and training provision should develop self-reliance, flexibility and breadth.

Lifetime Learning Targets

1. By 1996, all employees should take part in training or development activities.

2. By 1996, at least half of the employed work force should be aiming for qualifications or units within the NVQ framework, preferably in the

context of individual action plans and with support from employers.

3. By the year 2000, 50% of the employed work force should be qualified to at least NVQ Level 3 or its academic equivalent.

4. By 1996, 50% of organizations with 200 or more employees should be 'Investors in People' (the Government programme which aims to encourage employers to invest in training and to develop and evaluate training strategies which are driven by standards and related to business goals).

4.4 Education – industry links

Several initiatives are in operation which are intended to bring schools closer to the world of employment.

– *The Technical and Vocational Education Initiative* (TVEI) is a collaborative project funded by the Department for Education and the Employment Department, in which the Training and Enterprise Councils have a key advisory role. All Local Education Authorities (LEAs) are now operating TVEI. TVEI is complementary to the objectives of the National Curriculum and aims to make the curriculum of pupils aged 14 to 18 – whether at school or college – more relevant to adult and working life. It adopts a practical, problem-solving approach to learning and encourages the use of new technology throughout the curriculum. TVEI programmes are designed and managed by individual LEAs in line with their own strategies and circumstances, but their proposals must meet nationally agreed TVEI criteria. TVEI will run until 1997.

– *Compacts* are agreements between employers, young people, schools and colleges and training providers in some LEAs. Employers endeavour to provide a job with training, or training leading to a job, for every participating young person who has achieved a set of agreed personal and educational goals and objectives in terms of regular attendance and academic achievements. Every school and college involved undertakes to support and encourage young people in the achievement of standards and competencies. Compacts are funded by the Employment Department.

– *Education-business partnerships* aim to bring coherence and coordination to local education-industry collaboration. Funded through Training and Enterprise Councils, they coordinate activities which span all age ranges and sectors, from primary through to further and higher education. Each partnership consists of representatives from education, business and the local community.

4.5 Teachers

See 7.

4.6 Statistics

In September 1993, in addition to post-compulsory education in school sixth forms, there were 465 further education institutions funded by the Further Education Funding Council in England, with 920,500 full-time students and 184,100 part-time students. During 1992/93, there were, in Wales, 24 further education institutions, with 37,905 students (full-time equivalents).

Because of varying definitions, there are no precise figures for adult education institutes (AEIs) but returns made by Local Education Authorities in November 1992 suggest that there were approximately 1,500 AEIs in England and 300 in Wales. There were 89 private further education institutions in England and 2 in Wales.

5. Vocational training

5.1 Youth Training

The management of the main initial vocational training programme, Youth Training (YT), has been transferred from the Employment Department to the Training and Enterprise Councils (TECs). Youth Training offers a guarantee of vocational training to school-leavers under 18 years old who are neither in employment nor receiving full-time education. Young people between the ages of 18 and 25 may also be eligible for YT even if they are employed. YT provides broad-based vocational training, both on-the-job and off-the-job, and planned work experience. It enables trainees (with some exceptions for young people with special training needs) to work towards a qualification equivalent at least to Level 2 in the framework established by NCVQ. Completion of an individual's training plan may take more than two years, especially where the aim is to obtain qualifications at Level 3 or Level 4.

YT is delivered through contracts with a range of training providers (including private employers and further education institutions) and is based on the achievement of NVQs. TECs may develop and deliver different patterns of education and training to enable young people to gain qualifications. All arrangements must meet minimum requirements and lead to NVQs or their equivalent.

On completion of training, a YT trainee receives a National Record of Achievement, which is a personal record of experience, achievements and qualifications gained during YT, to demonstrate his/her suitability for further education, training or employment.

The level of funding for YT training is negotiated between the TEC and training provider, taking into account factors such as the needs of trainees, the qualifications offered and the local demand for skills. Payment to training providers depends on local arrangements but is usually based on the number of training weeks delivered and the qualifications gained.

5.2 Training Credits

A training credit is an entitlement to training to approved standards for young people who have left full-time education to join the labour market. Each credit has a specific value and can be presented by a young person to an employer, or to a specialist training provider, in exchange for training. Training credits aim to increase the motivation of young people by giving them purchasing power in the training market place. The scheme currently operates in some areas only and covers about 20% of 16- to 17-year-old school-leavers. The Government intends that by 1996 all 16- to 17-year-olds leaving full-time education will be offered a training credit.

6. Higher education

There is no single coherent body of legislation dealing with higher education but the Further and Higher Education Act 1992 introduced many reforms.

Higher education is defined in the Education Reform Act 1988 as 'education provided by means of a course of any description mentioned in Schedule 6 of that Act.' The courses listed are:

- a course for the further training of teachers or youth and community workers;

- a post-graduate course (including a higher degree course);

- a first degree course;

- a course for the Diploma of Higher Education;

- a course for the Higher National Diploma or Higher National Certificate of the Business and Technology Education Council, or the Diploma in Management Studies;

- a course in preparation for the Certificate in Education (which accords Qualified Teacher Status);

- a course in preparation for a professional examination at higher level; and

- a course providing education at a higher level (whether or not in preparation for an examination).

The main providers of higher education are the universities and other higher education institutions, including specialist institutions such as agricultural, art and theological colleges. Some higher education is provided by colleges of further education. The Open University provides higher education courses through distance learning. All higher education institutions are autonomous.

There remain some structural differences between institutions commonly referred to as the "old" universities and those referred to as the 'new' universities, although such differences are disappearing. The Further and Higher Education Act 1992 allows all higher education institutions to include the word 'university' in their title, subject to their fulfilling certain criteria. Most 'new' universities were previously polytechnics, but permission to use the word 'university' has also been granted to some other higher education institutions.

Each institution decides which degrees and other qualifications it offers and the conditions which apply. Some universities, for historical reasons, specialize in certain areas, for example, technological studies (institutions originally set up as technological colleges but which were later granted university status) or applied studies (the former polytechnics) but all offer a wide range of courses. With effect from 1992, all higher education institutions applying for permission to use the title university must offer courses that cover a specified range of broad curriculum areas.

Admission

Prospective full-time students for first degree or Higher National Diploma courses apply to individual institutions through a central clearing-house, the Universities and Colleges Admissions Service (UCAS). Each higher education institution has its own admissions policy. In general, applicants are required to have at least three passes in General Certificate of Secondary Education (GCSE) examinations at grade C or above and two passes, in different subjects, at General Certificate of Education Advanced Level (or the equivalent AS passes – see 3. and 4.). In practice, due to the competition for places, most institutions require levels of qualifications considerably above the minimum. Alternative qualifications (including vocational qualifications) are becoming more generally acceptable and many institutions welcome applications from older candidates who have work experience but who may lack the formal qualifications usually required. Access courses, which prepare adults without formal qualifications for higher education studies, are offered in many further education institutions, often in collaboration with higher education institutions.

The more popular the course, the higher the level of qualifications required from prospective students. By the same token, courses that fail to attract students may lower their requirements. Some courses require previous study in the subjects, others do not.

There is no official policy of numerus clausus, but the Secretary of State for Education sets quotas for teacher training courses, and the Department of Health, in consultation with the profession and the regional Health Authorities of the National Health Service, sets quotas for student places on medicine and dentistry courses.

Fees/Student finance

Fees are charged by all higher education institutions.

Fees for first degrees are usually paid by students' Local Education Authorities (LEAs) in England and Wales, although Central Government refunds expenditure where such awards are considered mandatory. The LEAs also award maintenance allowances, graded according to the students' and their families' income. Students wishing to continue studying for higher degrees and other postgraduate courses may apply for bursaries or awards (which include elements to cover fees and maintenance) to the appropriate body: the Department for Education, one of the seven Research Councils or a professional body. A limited number of awards are available from individual institutions. Loans are also available to all students.

Academic year

The full academic year for higher education runs from 1 September to 30 August. Organization of courses is at the discretion of the individual institution but follows similar patterns. For first degrees, student attendance is normally required from a date varying from the beginning of September to the beginning of October through to the end of June, with breaks lasting between three and five weeks at Christmas and Easter. The organization of teaching traditionally reflected this three-term system but institutions are increasingly organizing their teaching along the two-semester system, although this does not necessarily involve changing the dates of required attendance.

Courses/Qualifications

A first degree course normally lasts for three years, although certain courses are longer (for instance, students of foreign languages are normally required to study or work for an additional year in the country of the target language). A few institutions have introduced accelerated two-year first degrees on an experimental basis. Students on accelerated courses have shorter holidays than those on traditional courses. First degree courses lead to the title of Bachelor – the most common are Bachelor of Arts (BA) and Bachelor of Science (BSc). Requirements for attendance and length of courses for postgraduate study vary according to the nature of the course. Masters' degrees require a minimum of one year's full-time study or the part-time equivalent. However, many courses require two years' study or the part-time equivalent.

Many institutions operate Credit Accumulation and Transfer Schemes (CATs). The aim is to help students create a personal programme of studies to complete a degree. Within CATs, credit may be given for previous study or work experience. CATs also facilitate degree-completion by students who are unable to undertake one continuous period of study. Institutions may also form local consortia to operate a common CAT scheme, thus enabling students, where appropriate, to follow certain courses at institutions other than their own but for which they will be given credit towards their degree.

Assessment

Assessment procedures are determined by the individual institution, but for first degrees, all require students to take examinations. It is now rare for the final mark awarded to depend completely on student performance in final examinations; most institutions base a component of the degree class on examinations taken during the period of study, especially those taken at the end of the second year, and many also base a component on a form of continuous assessment.

Statistics

In **England**, in June 1993, there were 72 universities, including the Open University. One of these, the University of London, has 8 Schools which are separately funded. There were a further 48 higher education institutions. Some higher education is also provided at 75 further education institutions. Between all three categories of institution, there were a total of 828,806 full-time and sandwich students and 391,758 part-time students. In addition, there is 1 private university. In **Wales**, there were 2 universities, including one federal institution with 6 constituent colleges in different towns or cities. There were a further 9 higher education institutions. Some higher education was provided at 2 other institutions. In the three categories of institutions, there were a total of 59,515 students, giving a full-time equivalent of 52,587 students.

7. Teachers

School teachers employed in maintained schools at all phases (nursery, primary, including reception classes, and secondary) are required to have Qualified Teacher Status (QTS). There are currently seven models of training which lead to QTS. The two traditional routes are the concurrent model and the consecutive model.

The concurrent training model usually involves four years of full-time teacher training leading to an education degree, normally the Bachelor of Education (BEd). This training is offered by university-level higher education institutions and comprises a mixture of subject studies, theoretical classes and practical teaching activities. Prospective primary teachers specialize in either early years, including the nursery phase, or the later stage of primary education, and training must cover the subjects of the primary curriculum, although students may concentrate on certain areas. Prospective teachers of specialist subjects at secondary level study their specialist discipline as well as educational and professional studies. All four-year concurrent education degrees for primary teachers must include at least 25 weeks' experience in schools (from 1996, this will be extended to 32 weeks). Concurrent degrees for secondary teachers must include at least 32 weeks' school experience.

The consecutive training model involves three or four years of study in a specialist subject(s) leading to a first degree, followed by one year of professional training leading to the Postgraduate Certificate in Education (PGCE). The PGCE focuses on education theory and practical teaching skills. All PGCE students training to be primary teachers must spend at least 15 weeks gaining practical experience in schools (from 1996, this will be extended to 18 weeks). New regulations require students preparing to become secondary school teachers to spend at least 32 weeks in schools.

Alternative routes include the articled teachers scheme, the licensed teachers scheme, a special training scheme for teachers who have received their training outside the European Union and school-centred initial teacher training. The Open

University, the main UK distance learning provider, has developed part-time courses leading to the PGCE, for which the first students were admitted in February 1994.

Although students specialize in certain phases of education during training, QTS allows holders to teach at all levels.

Participation in in-service training is one of the professional duties of teachers. The statutory conditions of service provide for all full-time teachers to have at least five working days when they are not required to teach pupils. The Department for Education expects at least three of these days to be used for in-service training.

The teaching staff in maintained nursery schools are assisted by nursery nurses or assistants, many of whom hold the Diploma of the National Nursery Examination Board (NNEB) or similar qualification. Social Services Department day nurseries are staffed mainly by qualified nursery nurses (NNEB). Independent schools and nurseries may have qualified or unqualified staff.

Teachers in further education institutions are subject to separate regulations from those which apply to school teachers. They are not obliged to have Qualified Teacher Status but they are encouraged to undertake specialist training for further education teachers, such as the courses leading to the Certificate in Education (FE), the Graduate Certificate in Education (FE) or the City and Guilds' Further and Adult Education Teachers' Certificate. Most further education teachers of vocational subjects start teaching on a part-time basis while still employed in industry or commerce. They have an average of ten years' experience in their profession before starting to teach. Some lecturers of general education subjects may have taught in schools and have Qualified Teacher Status.

Teachers in higher education institutions are not required to have Qualified Teacher Status, except for teacher-trainers, who are also required to have substantial teaching experience in schools.

Teachers are not civil servants. Appointment to an established post may be made at one of two levels of tenure: an open-ended or a fixed-term contract. Teachers may be employed on a full-time or a part-time basis.

1. Responsibilities and administration

1.1 Administration, financing and advisory bodies

Central Government

The **Department of Education for Northern Ireland** (DENI) has central responsibility for the administration of the education service in Northern Ireland. The main concerns of the DENI are the formulation of national policies for education and the maintenance of consistency in national standards. It is responsible for the broad allocation of resources for education, for the rate and distribution of educational building and for the supply, training and superannuation of teachers. The DENI is headed by the Secretary of State for Northern Ireland, assisted by a Minister of State. It comprises two divisions, each led by an Under-Secretary, and the Education and Training Inspectorate, led by the Senior Chief Inspector (see Inspection below).

Since 1 April 1994, the **Northern Ireland Council for the Curriculum, Examinations and Assessment** (CCEA) has been responsible for keeping under review and advising the DENI on all aspects of the curriculum, assessment and examinations: publishing and distributing material relating to the curriculum, assessment and examinations for information and consultative purposes; the conduct and moderation of assessments of pupils at ages 8, 11 and 14; and the conduct, moderation and award of public examinations at all levels.

The **Council for Catholic Maintained Schools**, which was established by the Education Reform (Northern Ireland) Order 1989, has responsibility for all Catholic maintained schools.

Local Government

There are five Education and Library Boards (Boards) in Northern Ireland. They have statutory responsibility for the provision of services. They must ensure that there are sufficient schools and colleges to meet local needs for primary, secondary and further education. The Boards employ teachers and are wholly responsible for the schools under their management, which are known as controlled schools. However, they have no powers to inspect the quality of education in the schools which they control. They are responsible for enforcing school attendance and provide a curriculum advisory and support service to all the schools in their area. The Boards' expenditure on these services is 100% grant-aided by the Department of Education for Northern Ireland (DENI). The salaries of all school teachers and all lecturers in further education are paid by the DENI as a matter of administrative convenience.

Institutions

In Northern Ireland, there is a variety of management arrangements for **publicly funded (grant-aided) schools.** However, all of them are managed by individual Boards of Governors and have their recurrent costs met through budget shares under the Local Management of Schools (LMS) scheme. This is funded by the DENI either direct to schools or through the Education and Library Boards.

Controlled schools are owned by the Education and Library Boards, which are responsible for all capital works.

Catholic maintained schools are owned by Roman Catholic Church trustees and their teachers are employed by the Council for Catholic Maintained Schools. Capital works are eligible for 100% capital grants from the DENI.

Maintained schools are owned by voluntary bodies and their Boards of Governors employ all teaching staff. Capital works are eligible for capital grants from the DENI at the rate of 85% or 100%.

Voluntary grammar schools are owned by trustees and their Boards of Governors employ all staff. Capital works are eligible for capital grants from the DENI, largely at the rate of 85% or 100%.

Grant-maintained integrated (GMI) schools comprise a new category of primary and post-primary school established by the Education Reform (Northern Ireland) Order 1989. Existing schools may seek integrated status if a majority of pupils' parents at a non-integrated school vote by secret ballot to do so. The provision for GMI status is exclusive to Northern Ireland.

GMI schools are owned by charitable trusts and managed by Boards of Governors. Capital works are eligible for 100% capital grants from the DENI.

The GMI schools and some small elements of the controlled sector, such as special schools and controlled integrated schools, serve pupils of all religious denominations but, with only minor exceptions, most other schools are attended mainly by either Roman Catholics or Protestants. However, it is Government policy to encourage integration between Protestant and Roman Catholic schools where there is a local desire for it.

No fees are charged at controlled or maintained schools. Fees are charged at voluntary grammar schools, but education is free to all pupils who are awarded a non-fee-paying place, who make up about 96% of the pupil numbers.

The Education Reform (Northern Ireland) Order 1989 reflects many of the provisions of the Education Reform Act 1988 for England and Wales, but includes provisions which are particular to Northern Ireland. The introduction of formula funding and the delegation of financial and managerial responsibilities to Boards of Governors is one of the key reforms. The underlying principle of the Schemes is to delegate as many financial and managerial responsibilities as is consistent with the discharge of their statutory duties by the DENI and the Council for Catholic Maintained Schools. All nursery, primary and secondary schools and further education colleges have been funded on the basis of

an agreed formula since April 1991. Secondary schools and colleges received delegated budgets from that date and delegation is being extended to primary schools on a voluntary basis.

Unlike those in England and Wales, **further education colleges** are not autonomous institutions. The Education and Library Boards are responsible for the management of further education institutions in their respective areas. The Education Reform (Northern Ireland) Order 1989 requires the Boards to establish schemes for the local management of the colleges. Each college must have a governing body to which the Boards delegate the functions of staff management and control of the college budget.

All **higher education institutions** are autonomous bodies.

The DENI is advised on the planning and funding of higher education by the Higher Education Funding Council for England (HEFCE) and by the Northern Ireland Higher Education Council (NIHEC), which formally came into being on 1 April 1993.

1.2 Inspection

The Education and Training Inspectorate is the main source of professional advice for the DENI, and the sole group with responsibility for inspection in the education service in Northern Ireland. The Inspectorate assesses standards throughout the education system and advises the DENI about education in Northern Ireland as a whole, as well as in individual institutions. It seeks to maintain and, where necessary, contribute to improving standards by reporting weaknesses where they exist and by disseminating examples of good practice. The Inspectorate also assesses and reports to the DENI and to the Department of Economic Development on the vocational education and training of young people and adults in grant-aided courses.

1.3 Independent schools

There are very few independent schools in Northern Ireland and they do not cater for a significant part of the school population. These schools are not grant-aided and receive no direct funding for recurrent or capital costs. There is no Assisted

Places Scheme in Northern Ireland as the independent sector admits non-fee-paying pupils.

1.4 Vocational Training

The Training and Employment Agency, launched on 2 April 1990, is responsible for Government training programmes and the employment service activities in Northern Ireland. It operates as an executive agency within the Department of Economic Development.

The Agency's overall aim is to assist economic growth by ensuring the provision and operation of training and employment services. The Agency provides industrial skills training for young persons and adults in its network of twelve Training Centres. The Centres also provide sponsored training for industry, which may be provided in a Training Centre or on company premises.

The Training Agency is encouraging each of the key sectors of industry to form sector representative bodies (SRB), which will represent the opinions of employers and other parties on individual sector training needs. It is also expected that a number of sectors will establish training organizations, which will operate on a commercial basis providing training and assistance within sectors.

2. Pre-school education

Nursery education is provided in nursery schools and in nursery classes attached to primary schools. There is also an active network of voluntary playgroups. The Government's policy on early years provision is currently under review.

Statistics 1992/93

Pupils	4,005 (FTE)
Teachers	164 (FTE)
Schools	88

FTE: full-time equivalents.

3. Compulsory education

Children who have attained the age of 4 years on or before 1 July must start school at the beginning of the following September. In accordance with the Education Reform (Northern Ireland) Order 1989, the school leaving date for all pupils is 30 June and all those who reach the age of 16 on or before that day, or whose sixteenth birthday falls between that day and the start of the next school year, may leave school on that day.

The Education and Libraries (Northern Ireland) Order 1986 stipulates three stages of education: primary, secondary and further. There are no middle schools.

3.1 Primary education

The majority of children up to the age of 11/12 years are educated in primary schools. However, some children are educated in the preparatory departments of grammar schools. Fees are charged by these preparatory departments.

The dates of terms and holidays are set by the Education and Library Boards for controlled schools. For all other schools, the dates of terms and holidays are set by the relevant school authorities and approved by the appropriate Education and Library Board. The school year runs from the beginning of September to the end of June, with 8 weeks' summer holidays, and two weeks at both Christmas and Easter.

Pupils under the age of 8 years must receive not less than three hours of instruction per day (other than religious education) and all other pupils must receive not less than four-and-a-half hours of such instruction, in two daily sessions. The curriculum, syllabus and timetable are subject to the approval of the DENI.

The Education Reform (Northern Ireland) Order 1989 makes provision for a common Northern Ireland curriculum for pupils in compulsory education (see Curriculum, assessment and qualifications below).

3.2 Secondary education

Secondary education normally begins when pupils reach the age of 11. There are two main types of post-primary school: grammar and secondary schools. Grammar schools provide a range of courses for pupils between 11 and 18 years old whilst secondary schools provide a similar range of courses for the 11-16 age group; some secondary schools offer post-16 opportunities.

Following the Education Reform (Northern Ireland) Order 1989, parents may express their choice of school for their child; schools must accept pupils up to their capacity and must publish admissions criteria to be applied if over-subscribed. Only grammar schools may include the academic ability of a pupil in these criteria.

Grants equal to tuition fees are paid to the schools from public funds for the vast majority of pupils attending schools of secondary education.

3.3 Curriculum, assessment and qualifications

The education provided in a school is determined by the school authorities with due regard to the ages, abilities and aptitudes of the pupils. However, the Education Reform (Northern Ireland) Order 1989 makes provision for a common curriculum, known as the Northern Ireland Curriculum, for pupils in compulsory education in grant-aided schools. In addition to religious education, the curriculum of all children of compulsory school age (other than those in independent schools) is required to include five areas of study (six in secondary schools): English; mathematics; science and technology; the environment and society; creative and expressive studies; and language studies (secondary and Irish-speaking schools only). Within each area of study, at least one subject is compulsory during certain years of compulsory schooling.

Every pupil's performance in the compulsory subjects will be formally assessed against specified attainment targets, through centrally determined arrangements, at ages 8, 11, 14 and 16. Assessment arrangements are being piloted. At the end of the compulsory school phase, most pupils take the General Certificate of Secondary Education (GCSE) examinations (for details of these, see England and Wales).

Teachers

See 7.

Statistics 1992/93

	Pupils [1]	Teachers [1]	Schools
Primary [2]	189,909	8,534	957
Secondary [3]	145,512	9,583	234
Independent [4]	963	96	18

[1] Full-time equivalents.
[2] Includes 3,633 pupils and 140 teachers in preparatory departments which are attached to grammar schools.
[3] Most secondary schools also provide post-compulsory courses (see below).
[4] Nursery, primary and secondary schools.

4. Post-compulsory education

Post-compulsory education is provided in schools (sixth forms) and in further education colleges.

The same types of academic and vocational courses are offered at post-compulsory level in Northern Ireland as in England and Wales (see England and Wales).

Statistics 1992/93

	Students [1]	Teachers [1]	Institutions
Further Education Colleges	37,905	2,883	24

[1] Full-time equivalents.

5. Vocational training

5.1 Youth Training Programme

The Youth Training Programme (YTP) provides a 2-year programme for 16-year-old school-leavers combining training, further education and work experience in the first year, followed by either employment with training or more specialized full-time training in the second year.

In contrast to England and Wales, where youth training is mainly employer-led, the YTP is organized by Training Centres, Community Workshops and further education colleges in cooperation with employers who provide work experience places. Training providers must have Recognized Training Organization (RTO) status.

5.2 Jobskills

Jobskills is a two-year pilot scheme to develop a single training programme, which will, in time, replace the Youth Training Programme and the Job Training Programme and will offer training for all entrants to the labour market, and to the unemployed. The aim of the initiative is that trainees should obtain qualifications at National Vocational Qualification (NVQ) Level 3 or equivalent. The funding structure provides financial incentives to both the training organizations and trainees for such attainment. Jobskills also offers flexible funding levels and duration of training to meet individual needs.

6. Higher education

In June 1993, there were two universities and two other higher education institutions, both Colleges of Education which provide only teacher education. Higher education provision in Northern Ireland is comparable with that elsewhere in the UK, but at the same time takes the particular circumstances of Northern Ireland into account.

Fees/Student finance

Fees for first degrees are usually paid by students' Education and Library Boards. The Boards also award maintenance allowances, dependent on the students' or their families' income. Students wishing to continue studying for higher degrees and other postgraduate courses apply to the institution itself or, for certain discretionary awards for courses leading to Diplomas or Certificates, to the Boards; if they wish to continue their studies in England, Wales or Scotland, they apply to the appropriate Research Council or professional body; if they wish to continue their studies in the Republic of Ireland, they apply to the DENI.

Statistics 1992/93

	Students [1]	Teachers [1]	Institutions
Colleges of Education	1,380	135 [2]	2
Universities	23,841	1,403 [2]	2

[1] Full-time equivalents except where stated – see note (2).
[2] Full-time figures only.

7. Teachers

Training takes place at the two universities and at the two specialist Colleges of Education. The DENI sets annual quotas to ensure that the supply of newly trained teachers is consistent with demand.

There are two traditional routes which lead to recognition as a qualified teacher: the concurrent model which leads to a degree in education, normally the Bachelor of Education (BEd); and the consecutive model, which leads to the Postgraduate Certificate in Education (PGCE). The Open University, the main UK distance learning provider, is currently developing part-time courses leading to the PGCE. Although students specialize in certain phases of education during training, a teacher recognized as a qualified teacher by the DENI may teach at all levels.

Each of the five Education and Library Boards employs teachers in all controlled schools and further education colleges in its area. The Council for Catholic Maintained Schools is the employer of all teachers in Catholic maintained schools. The school's Board of Governors is the employing authority for teachers in maintained schools (other than Catholic maintained schools), in voluntary grammar schools and in grant-maintained integrated schools. Teachers are public employees, without guaranteed tenure. Appointment to an established post at a school may be made at one of two levels of tenure: a permanent appointment or a temporary appointment on a fixed-term contract.

Further education lecturers are not required to have teaching qualifications, but those who do not must hold an approved qualification, such as a university degree or a vocational qualification in the subject they wish to teach. Holders of approved vocational qualifications must also have achieved a pass at grade C or above in the General Certificate of Secondary Education in English and have three years of industrial or business experience.

Teachers in higher education institutions are not required to hold teaching qualifications, except for teacher-trainers, who are also required to have substantial teaching experience in schools.

1. Responsibilities and administration

1.1 Administration

Central Government

The Secretary of State for Scotland is responsible to the Parliament of the United Kingdom for the overall supervision and development of the education service in Scotland and for legislation affecting Scottish education, through the Education Department of the Scottish Office (SOED). The SOED broadly determines national aims and standards, formulates national policy, commissions policy-related research and issues guidelines in the area of curriculum and assessment and, together with the General Teaching Council, oversees teacher training and supply. In practice, the Secretary of State delegates day-to-day responsibility to a Minister of Education. The Secretary of State is advised by the Inspectorate (see Inspection below) and by the national bodies dealing with the development of the curriculum (Scottish Consultative Council on the Curriculum, Scottish Vocational Education Council) and with public examinations (Scottish Examination Board and Scottish Vocational Education Council).

Local Government

The provision of publicly funded education is the responsibility of the 9 Regional Councils and 3 Islands Councils, which are known as education authorities. They have a statutory duty to provide adequate and efficient school education, to make provision for special educational needs and to provide the teaching of Gaelic in schools in Gaelic-speaking areas. They are responsible for the construction of buildings, the employment of teachers and other staff and the provision of equipment and materials. They exercise responsibility for the curriculum taught in schools, taking account of national guidance.

Each Regional and Islands Council has an Education Committee composed of elected local councillors, and representatives of the main churches and teachers' groups. The committee is responsible for making policy decisions on educational provision, within the framework of national law and regulations. The executive functions, however, are fulfilled by an Education Department, headed in each case by a Director of Education who may have one or more deputes and a number of assistant directors.

Institutions

The School Boards (Scotland) Act of 1988 requires that education authorities establish a School Board for each **school** (except nursery schools) under their management. The Boards comprise elected parent and staff members and other coopted members of the local community. The Director of Education (or his nominee) and the local Regional or Islands Councillor also have the right to attend Board meetings and speak, and the head teacher of the school is the Board's chief professional adviser. Boards have powers which are broadly consultative.

In 1993, education authorities were invited to prepare draft schemes for the devolved management of schools in which 80% of the school's budget would rest with the head teacher. School Boards would have a specific consultative role. In 1994, these schemes began to be put in place, with devolved budgets covering staffing, furnishings, repairs, supplies, services and energy costs. All schemes are expected to be fully in place by 1996, with the exception of those for small schools and special schools.

The Self-Governing Schools Etc (Scotland) Act of 1989 enables parents to vote by ballot to remove their school from local authority control and make it self-governing. The school is run, and its staff employed, by a Board of Management consisting of parents, teacher representatives, the head teacher and members coopted from the local community. A self-governing school remains within the public sector, is not allowed to charge fees and is funded direct by Central Government.

Under the Further and Higher Education (Scotland) Act 1992, most of the **further education colleges** transferred from local authority control and became incorporated bodies, funded by the Secretary of State through the Scottish Office Education Department. Three colleges, in Orkney and Shetland, remain under education authority control. Each college of further education is managed by a Board of Management, at least half of whose members have experience of, and capacity in, industry, commerce or employment. The colleges have well established links with local industry and commerce, and the Board includes a nominee of the Local Enterprise Company. The Scottish Office has delegated substantial powers to these Boards, and colleges are now able to undertake commercial activities.

As in the rest of the UK, **higher education institutions** are autonomous. Universities and certain other higher education institutions have powers to award their own degrees; the remainder have validation arrangements with another higher education institution.

1.2 Inspection

All educational institutions (schools and further education colleges) receiving grants from public funds are subject to inspection. Her Majesty's Inspectors report directly to the Scottish Office Education Department (SOED) on the provision of education in schools and can advise the Secretary of State on any relevant educational topic. The Inspectorate is headed by a Senior Chief Inspector and there are Chief Inspectors responsible for major policy sectors and geographical areas. National responsibility for each subject is held by a Staff Inspector. In 1994, there were 105 HM Inspectors in Scotland. Universities and other higher education institutions are not subject to inspection by HM Inspectorate in the same way. The Scottish Higher Education Funding Council (SHEFC) has its own provision for quality assessment, based on institutions' self assessment and peer review, in which HM Inspectorate act as lead evaluators.

Education authorities also carry out quality assessment of the various aspects of the educational provision which they make and some employ teams of local inspectors to carry out this work.

1.3 Financing

Education is the most expensive service provided by local authorities. Public sector school education is provided free to the pupils, as are books and stationery. The cost of education in publicly funded schools is met from resources raised by the local council tax, non-domestic rates and from an annual grant (the Revenue Support Grant) payable from the National Exchequer. Once the education budget is agreed, the Education Committee in each local authority then decides on the level of support to be given to its schools and colleges. Thereafter, the Education Department in each authority is responsible for implementing the Education Committee's policies and ensuring that the money allocated under the approved budget headings is spent appropriately. These arrangements apply to current expenditure on salaries, running costs, teaching materials and a few other items.

Capital expenditure, however, on new buildings, equipment or major modernization projects is controlled by the Government through the SOED and the funds for this are allocated on the basis of an evaluation of plans prepared by local authorities on a 5-year basis updated or revised each year.

Further education is funded directly by the Secretary of State for Scotland. Forty-three of the further education colleges are incorporated and receive grant-in-aid directly from the Scottish Office Education Department. However, the 3 further education centres in Orkney and Shetland, which are integrated with school education, are managed by the Islands' Councils which receive 100% grant from the SOED for further education.

The funding of higher education is through the Scottish Higher Education Funding Council (SHEFC) which receives funds from the Secretary of State and distributes them to the individual institutions, according to formulae which are subject to review. Funding includes resources for capital projects and for teaching, the latter based on subject groups and the number of students.

1.4 Independent schools

In Scotland there are 2 categories of independent school: those run by the private sector; and those which are subsidized by the Government (known as 'grant-aided') for children with sensory or physical impairment. The latter get most of their finance from Central Government or from the education authorities which place children in them. Private sector schools must cover all their expenses, generally by charging school fees.

Independent schools provide education to some 5% of the school age population in Scotland. They must be registered with the SOED and are open to inspection. Central Government may require them to improve their premises, accommodation or teaching. Under the Education (Scotland) Act of 1981, the Assisted Places Scheme extended parents' right to choose schools. The scheme works on the basis of fee remission related to parental income and allows those pupils selected on this basis to attend independent schools. There are 55 schools in this scheme in Scotland, slightly under half the total number of independent schools, involving 3,040 pupils.

1.5 Consultative Bodies

The education system is supported by 9 agencies linked, in most cases through their funding, to the Scottish Office Education Department (SOED). These are:

- The Scottish Consultative Council on the Curriculum (SCCC), a body on which the teaching profession and various educational interests are represented and which advises on the schools curriculum.

- The Scottish Examination Board (SEB), a statutory body which has responsibility for the Scottish Certificate of Education and all Government-sponsored assessment in schools.

- The Scottish Vocational Education Council (SCOTVEC), the national body in Scotland with responsibility for developing, awarding and accrediting vocational qualifications.

- The Scottish Further Education Unit (SFEU), the centre established for curriculum development in the further education (VET) sector.

- The Scottish Community Education Council (SCEC), the national body whose role is to provide a support service for adult basic and continuing education, youth work and community development.

- The Scottish Council for Educational Technology (SCET) whose main duties are to offer information, publications, open learning resources, software, film, video and training associated with the use of technology in education.

- The Scottish Council for Research in Education (SCRE), which carries out research on all aspects of education and acts as a national forum for debate about educational research issues in Scotland.

- The Scottish Higher Education Funding Council (SHEFC), a statutory body established in 1993 to administer the funding of all Higher Education Institutions, including universities, and to oversee evaluative procedures for such institutions.

- The General Teaching Council for Scotland (GTC), established in 1965 and statutorily responsible for maintaining a register of teachers in Scotland and for the establishment and monitoring of professional teaching standards.

1.6 Vocational training

In 1989, the Government announced the creation of 22 Local Enterprise Companies (LECs) in Scotland, which would give local industry the responsibility for training, enabling local needs to be met more effectively.

Following the Enterprise and New Towns Act of 1990, the Secretary of State for Scotland set up in 1991 two overarching enterprise bodies: Scottish Enterprise; and Highlands and Islands Enterprise. Each has training, enterprise and environmental responsibilities, to be implemented through networks of LECs. Responsibility for the delivery of adult and youth training in Scotland has since then rested with these two bodies, which administer to LECs those funds granted for the purpose by the Scottish Office. The main programmes for young and adult unemployed are run by managing agents and training managers under contract to the LECs.

2. Pre-school education

Pre-school provision is made by a number of agencies and groups. Local authorities make non-mandatory provision through both their education departments (nursery schools or nursery classes in primary schools) and their social work departments (day nurseries). Voluntary organizations run pre-school playgroups, most of which are affiliated to the Scottish Pre-School Playgroup Association. A substantial number of other forms of provision for young children are organized by commercial interests or parents. There exists also a system of accredited child-minders, employed to look after children under the age of 3. Priority is given by nursery schools to 4-year-olds before 3-year-olds, and to children referred by social work departments, educational psychologists or health services. In many areas pre-school facilities may not be available, but of those 3- and 4-year-olds who in 1992 were able to gain a place, 36% went to nursery schools, 38% to playgroups, 15% went to child-minders and 5% were in day nurseries.

Once children are accepted for a pre-school establishment place, they attend weekly for a variable number of sessions (a session being half a day), which will depend on local arrangements and conditions. Day nurseries often look after some children all day every day.

The facilities offered by education authorities in nursery schools and nursery classes and by social work departments in day nurseries are provided free of charge. This does not preclude small charges being made for certain activities.

There is no fixed curriculum in pre-school education, which aims to promote children's thinking, help them express themselves, acquire understanding of the world around them, improve their motor skills and develop good behaviour and sound social relationships. Nursery school pupils' progress is continuously assessed, discussed with parents and made the basis of further activities and objectives.

There is no statutory requirement for primary schools to receive information about children's pre-school experience, but most pre-school establishments, especially local authority nursery schools and day nurseries, do provide some form of progress report on the 5-year-olds who have been with them.

Teachers/Staff

In nursery schools and classes and in day nurseries, the staff normally comprises teachers, nursery nurses and auxiliaries.

Teachers in nursery schools in Scotland have to be registered with the General Teaching Council of Scotland as being fully trained primary school teachers. Many also hold an additional qualification in early education. Nursery nurses qualify through a two-year course at a college of further education. No formal qualifications are demanded of auxiliaries.

Statistics 1993/94

Pupils	48,127
Teachers	964
Schools	758

Source: Scottish Office Education Department, 1994.

3. Compulsory education

As in England and Wales, compulsory education in Scotland begins around the age of 5 and lasts until 16. The leaving dates for pupils who have reached age 16 are the end of the Christmas term or the last day in May.

Compulsory education is divided into primary (ages 5 to 12) and secondary (ages 12 to 16). Post-compulsory secondary education is from 16 to 18, and pupils usually remain in the same institution for that purpose.

4. Primary education

Normally, children enter primary school at about the age of 5 and follow a 7-year course; they transfer to secondary schools at about the age of 12. Schools vary in size according to the community they serve; a one-teacher rural school may serve a much bigger area than a large city primary school.

Schools are coeducational and organized in classes by age. Usually, one teacher is responsible for teaching all subjects to a class, often assisted by specialist teachers for specific subjects. In the larger primary schools there will be more than one class at each stage, the normal maximum class size being 33 by regulation. In smaller schools, children of more than one age may be combined in one class with one teacher. As far as possible, the education authorities will try to keep such composite classes to a limit of 25 pupils. In the very smallest schools where there are fewer than 20 children, one teacher will teach all the children in one class. Three broad stages are normally distinguished in primary schools: P1 to P3 (the infant or early education stage); P4 and P5 (the middle stage) and P6 and P7 (the upper primary stage). There is no selection or streaming by ability between classes and no repeating of years.

The school year covers 3 terms and must last 190 days. The actual dates of terms are determined by each education authority. The school year lasts from the third week of August to the beginning of July, with breaks of one week in October and 2 weeks in December/January and March/April.

There is no legislation as to the pattern of the school day and week, but it is usual for there to be 2 sessions per day – one in the morning and one in the afternoon – for five days per week (Monday to Friday). The primary school week normally lasts 27.5 hours in five days of 5.5 hours each. The number and duration of lessons is determined by each head teacher in consultation with the class teachers.

In general terms, the purpose of primary schooling is to provide a broad basic education concentrating on enabling children to read, write and count but also introducing them to ways of examining and understanding their environment, past and present, helping them to express themselves through art, music and physical activity, and developing their awareness of religious, moral and social values.

Curriculum and assessment

The curriculum is not imposed by any central authority, but the SOED recommends, through Guidelines, that primary education be based on a number of broad curricular areas, set in an appropriate balance. These are: language, mathematics, environmental studies (including aspects of geography, history, science, basic understanding of society and local government, technology, information technology and health education), expressive arts, religious and moral education.

The entire primary curriculum, reaching into early secondary level, has been subject to development since 1988 in close consultation with practising teachers. This has been effected through the 5-14 Development Programme, implementation of which is well under way. It is expected to be fully in place by 1999. As part of this programme, National Guidelines have been published by the Government covering each of the above 5 areas of the curriculum (language, mathematics, environmental studies, expressive arts and religious and moral education), together with assessment and reporting.

For assessment purposes, 5 levels of attainment are specified in each area of the curriculum. These are used by teachers to plan the curriculum and monitor pupil progress and attainment. A continuing process of classroom assessment through observation and task-setting is supported by the use of national tests in reading, writing and mathematics. These tests will help to ensure that teachers' assessments are in line with nationally agreed standards. Pupils are promoted automatically to the next class, and repeating the year is not permitted.

The Government has also initiated (in 1993) the introduction of modern languages in the primary school. This involves a phased expansion, built on the experience of earlier piloting.

There is no certificate or final examination at the end of primary education.

Pupil guidance is the responsibility of teaching staff.

Teachers

See 7.

Statistics 1993/94

	Public	Independent
Pupils	438,863	12,387
Teachers	22,473	119
Schools	2,342	20

Source: Scottish Office Education Department, 1994.

5. Secondary education

More than 99% of pupils in education authority secondary schools in Scotland attend coeducational comprehensive schools offering all types of courses to pupils of all abilities and aptitudes. 90% of these schools provide education on an all-through basis covering four years of compulsory and two years of optional secondary education. Because of local circumstances there are some comprehensives at which courses may last only 2 or 4 years. Pupils may, however, transfer at the end of their second and fourth years to a six-year comprehensive. In the remote and sparsely populated areas, where secondary schools do not provide a full range of courses, parents have the option of sending their children to the comprehensive school serving the area, rather than to the local school. All secondary schools offer a general education, with some vocationally-oriented courses for those who wish them.

Secondary education is divided into three broad stages, each of which has a different emphasis. The first 2 years (S1 and S2) provide a general education, following the 5-14 Guidelines, while the third and fourth years (S3 and S4) have elements of specialization and of vocational education for all. Together they constitute lower secondary education. The final stage (S5 and S6) is one of greater specialization and forms upper secondary education.

Pupils have different specialist teachers for different subjects. They may be taught as a whole class or in groups within the same class in order to differentiate teaching. Classes have no more than 30 pupils in earlier years, no more than 25 in later years. In certain practical subjects, e.g. science, the number of pupils is restricted to 20.

The school year, week and day are organized as at primary level. Each lesson lasts around 40 minutes, but schools have considerable freedom to decide on the pattern of their own timetables.

Lower secondary education

Curriculum

At lower secondary level, in the four years of compulsory education, the curriculum is divided into two stages, as mentioned above, each lasting two years.

The Scottish curriculum is not prescribed by law, and education authorities and head teachers have considerable freedom to decide what courses should be available in any individual school. All schools, nevertheless, are expected to follow certain guidelines recommended by the Secretary of State for Scotland.

The first two years of secondary education are coincident with the last two years of the 5-14 curriculum. Curriculum and assessment at this stage are therefore covered by the National Guidelines for the 5 curriculum areas: language, mathematics, environmental studies, expressive arts and religious and moral education. Similarly the 5-14 Guidelines on assessment and reporting apply at this stage. The aim of the 5-14 programme is to aid planning and sustain pupil progress and transfer from primary to secondary school.

At the end of the second year of compulsory secondary education decisions are taken by pupils as to what subjects they will follow. Although some selection of subjects for more specialized study is possible, the general aim is to maintain a well-balanced curriculum for all pupils.

Schools are recommended to design their curriculum for S3 and S4 using the following 8 'modes': language and communication, mathematical studies and applications, scientific studies and applications, social and environmental studies, technological activities and applications, creative and aesthetic activities, physical education, religious and moral education.

All subjects taught fall within the scope of one or other of the 8 'modes' and every pupil should study at least one subject from each of them.

Whatever structure of curriculum is adopted, the Government regards it as essential that English, mathematics, science and a modern language are studied by all pupils in compulsory secondary education. A major reform of the curriculum completed between 1983 and 1993 brought in new ways of teaching and assessing traditional subjects and introduced a number of multidisciplinary courses, together with a range of short courses and modular vocational courses.

Assessment and qualifications

Pupils are subject to continuous assessment according to the internal procedures of each school and are promoted automatically to the next class.

In the first two years of lower secondary education (S1/S2), assessment is carried out in accordance with the 5-14 National Guidelines which are described in the previous section. Thereafter, courses in chosen subjects may lead, depending on pupils' performance, to Scottish Certificate of Education examinations at Standard Grade, normally taken at age 16. This certificate takes into account performance in examinations (gradings from 1 to 7) and the school's own assessment of pupils. Standard Grade is awarded at 3 levels: Credit, General and Foundation. It is not necessary to receive this certificate in order to proceed to upper secondary school.

Short modular courses, taken separately by pupils, may be components of General Scottish Vocational Qualifications (GSVQs). In addition, some school pupils take complete GSVQ programmes, which are designed to articulate with the new SVQs. (GSVQs and SVQs are described in 6.)

Upper secondary education

Upper secondary education is offered in six-year secondary schools and in further education colleges (see Vocational Education and Training).

There are no restrictions on pupils staying on at school beyond the age of 16, although schools usually assume minimum standards for certain courses and will advise pupils whether it is sensible for them to take on a longer or shorter time to achieve their intended awards.

The aim of this stage in secondary education is to build on achievements in the earlier years, to prepare pupils for future years, whether in work, leisure or further study, and to offer a broad and rewarding educational experience.

Curriculum

Up to 1994, courses leading to the Scottish Certificate of Education examination at Higher Grade, giving access to higher education, formed the core of the post-compulsory curriculum. These were sometimes followed by a Certificate of Sixth Year Studies. This position is now in the process of changing.

A national Development Programme related to the reform of upper secondary education began in 1994, following consultation on proposals from the Howie Committee. In S5 and S6, courses of the Scottish Examination Board (SEB) and the Scottish Council for Vocational Education (SCOTVEC) will be brought into a unified curriculum and assessment structure. Higher Grades will remain, but courses to Highers will be modular and drawn from both SEB and SCOTVEC provision, so that pupils can study vocational and academic courses at demanding levels. The recommended study time for each subject at Higher Grade will be extended from 120 to 160 hours, and there will be a mixture of internal and external assessment.

In addition, Advanced Higher courses will be developed, incorporating and replacing the existing Certificate of Sixth Year Studies, and building on the Highers to provide coherent, challenging 320-hour courses to be followed over 2 academic years.

Other courses, based mainly on existing National Certificate modules, will continue to be offered to meet the needs of pupils for whom Highers are too immediately demanding. National Certificate modules, introduced in 1985 by SCOTVEC, comprise 40-hour blocks of work and are mainly vocational in orientation. Each module successfully attained attracts an award on the National Certificate administered by SCOTVEC. Some students will take combinations of courses and modules which meet the requirements for General Scottish Vocational Qualifications (GSVQs), or which are based on coherent programmes of general education, and these awards will be known as National Certificates.

For the more able pupils, Higher modules may be accredited in S4. The stage restriction on taking Standard Grade will be waived to allow those capable of gaining Standard Grade at Credit level at S3 to do so. To provide progression for the most able students at the early stage of secondary education, a new level F will be introduced into the 5-14 curriculum structure.

The reforms will take effect from 1997/98.

Assessment and qualifications

Arrangements for administering the awards will be developed by the SOED, SEB and SCOTVEC. The objectives of the reforms include higher standards of attainment, recognized qualifications for all, an even gradient of progression and a range of courses offered, allowing pupils to progress at the fastest pace of which they are capable. Assessment at Higher Grade is currently by external examination following formal written examinations set internally in each school to determine the likely performance in the external examinations. Pupils also have folio or project work which is submitted to the teacher for assessment. The external examinations for Higher Grade are primarily in written form, and are set by the SEB. The award of a minimum of 3 Higher Grades with 2 additional Standard Grades gives access at present to higher education, including universities.

Assessment for SCOTVEC modules is institution based (school, college or workplace). Standards are sampled by teams of 'verifiers' nominated by the SCOTVEC. The nationally agreed criteria will be primarily concerned with a pupil's competence in carrying out an activity or process, and pupils who have successfully completed each 40-hour module are credited accordingly in their Record of Education and Training. These may be taken as free-standing modules or as recognized groupings called 'clusters' or in larger groupings called 'General Scottish Vocational Qualifications' (GSVQs). Groups of modules at graded levels allow progression to Higher National Certificates and Diplomas, which are an alternative route to higher education. Further details are found in the section on Vocational Education and Training.

Teachers

See 7.

Statistics 1993/94

	Public	Independent
Pupils	311,898	19,396
Teachers	24,326	2,716
Schools	410	66

Source: Scottish Office Education Department, 1994.

6. Vocational education and training

Non-advanced vocational education takes place primarily in post-compulsory further education colleges, although schools also offer vocational modules in the National Certificate. Vocational education may continue into higher education, provided by the higher education institutions including universities, teacher training institutions and other educational institutions offering a variety of advanced level courses, both academic and vocational in nature.

6.1 Further education

A typical further education college offers a wide range of courses at non-advanced and advanced levels. The courses are mainly vocational in kind and include both theoretical and practical work. It is standard practice for 16- to 18-year-olds in employment to be given day-release or block-release from work to attend colleges of further education. The needs of industry and students are met by the provision of a number of types of course:

- vocational and general education for post-16 students and trainees;

- link courses for school pupils;

- industrial pre-employment training serving specific employer needs;

- off-the-job training for the Youth Training programme;

- vocational and non-vocational evening classes;

- access to higher education.

Further education colleges continue to increase their provision of updating and retraining courses for local industries.

At the non-advanced level, students undertake National Certificate courses based on modules or short units of study normally to be completed in 40 hours. The description of each module specifies the level of knowledge and prior qualifications required. Students can study modules either part-time, e.g. 5 or 6 per year, or full-time, e.g. 25-27 per year. A course is made up of a number of modules taken during a year. Performance is continuously assessed internally by college lecturers by reference to nationally agreed criteria of success. Achievement in each module is recorded on a Record of Education and Training awarded by the Scottish Vocational Education Council (SCOTVEC). There are approximately 3,000 such modules available.

The National Certificate modular courses allow progression to advanced level courses, to courses in higher education and to advanced examinations of some professional and technical bodies and trade associations.

SCOTVEC completed a major reform of its advanced level qualifications in 1993, the central features of which are unitization of the Higher National Certificates and Diplomas (HNC and HND) qualifications and the introduction of two new qualifications, Scottish Vocational Qualifications (SVQs) and General Scottish Vocational Qualifications (GSVQs).

SVQs are nationally recognized awards for specific occupations, designed to standards set by industry. They are built up from units which bring together groups of related skills within a framework of five progressive levels. Because SVQs have been developed in partnership with employers they are accepted as a guarantee of a person's ability to do a particular job well.

GSVQs are broad-based qualifications made up from National Certificate modules and are being developed to complement the system of SVQs. They are specifically designed to meet the needs of 16- to

19-year-olds at school or in further education, and adult returners. They are especially suitable for people entering or returning to work as they provide training in a range of core skills; but they also allow progression to higher education. The GSVQ framework also comprises five progressive levels.

SVQs and GSVQs are analogous to the NVQs and GNVQs available in England, Wales and Northern Ireland, accredited by the National Council for Vocational Qualifications (NCVQ).

Statistics 1992/93

Students	
Full-time	15,192
Part-time	27,688
Teachers	5,594
Institutions	46
(FE Colleges)	

6.2 Youth Training

Responsibility for Youth Training (YT) rests with the Local Enterprise Companies (corresponding to the Training and Enterprise Councils in England and Wales). The scheme offers a guarantee of 2 years' vocational training for young people under 18, leading to nationally recognized vocational qualifications. In Scotland's case, qualifications are awarded by the Scottish Vocational Education Council (SCOTVEC). YT offers a broad-based vocational education and training, including planned work experience and enables trainees to work towards a qualification equivalent at least to level II in the SVQ framework. The training, to which there is no predetermined pattern, is offered through contracts with independent training providers. It is organized in so-called 'units of competence' (modules) which relate to occupations in all sectors of agriculture, industry and commerce and which also cover the development of 4 general areas of competences: occupational skills; transferable core skills (numeracy, literacy, communication, computer literacy and information technology); ability to transfer particular skills and knowledge to new situations; personal effectiveness such as planning, problem-solving and interpersonal skills.

6.3 Training Credits

The 1991 White Paper 'Education and Training for the 21st Century', announced the Government's intention to extend the training credits scheme each year with the aim of offering one by 1996 to every 16- and 17-year-old leaving full-time education. A training credit is defined as an entitlement to train to approved standards for young people who have left full-time education to join the labour market. Each credit carries a monetary value and can be presented by a young person to an employer or specialist training provider, in exchange for training. It is hoped by this to increase the motivation of young people to train by giving them purchasing power in the training market place.

7. Teachers

All teachers in Scottish local authority schools must hold an academic qualification to degree level, with an appropriate professional qualification. The Teaching Qualification (Primary Education) entitles the holder to teach general subjects in primary schools and may be obtained by taking a 4-year Bachelor of Education (BEd) Degree Course at a teacher training institution, or by taking another degree followed by a one-year course at a teacher training institution. The Teaching Qualification (Secondary Education) entitles the holder to teach a particular subject and is awarded to candidates who hold an appropriate degree and who have completed a one-year postgraduate training course at a teacher training institution. For physical education, entry to teaching is by means of a 4-year BEd course; for music and technological education, entry is either through the postgraduate route or by way of a BEd. The BEd combines general and professional education and 30 weeks' school placement. Postgraduate courses last 36 weeks, 22 of which are spent on school placements for training in secondary education, and 18 of which are similarly spent for training in primary education.

An alternative route is the concurrent pre-service teacher training programme of the University of Stirling. The programme leads to either an Honours Degree plus Diploma of Education or a General Degree plus Diploma of Education. Students at Heriot-Watt University may take the Stirling concurrent programme with a degree in order to train as teachers of mathematics or physics.

The annual intake to teacher training courses takes account of the demand for teachers and is set by the Secretary of State for Scotland after consultation with the General Teaching Council for Scotland, local authorities and teacher training institutions.

Entry to the teaching profession in Scotland, for teachers who wish to work in education authority schools, is through registration with the General Teaching Council for Scotland. Registration is not mandatory for teachers in further education, although many teachers in further education colleges have taken courses of training and are registered.

Teachers are employees of the education authorities.

Scottish teachers spend 5 days per year undergoing in-service training and are contracted to devote, in addition, up to 50 hours during the year to in-service training and personal professional development.

8. Higher education

The Further and Higher Education (Scotland) Act of 1992 created the Scottish Higher Education Funding Council, removing the dividing line which existed between the former central institutions and the universities. Four central institutions have since become universities, bringing the total number of Scottish universities to 12. The remaining 10 colleges offer courses up to degree level but are not universities. They are now known as Higher Education Institutions. Higher education institutions offer a wide range of vocationally oriented courses, ranging from law, medicine, science, engineering and computing to health care, art and design, music and drama and teacher training, as well as the more traditional 'academic courses' (e.g. the liberal arts and humanities).

Admission

The usual entry qualification for higher education courses is a group of passes in Standard Grade and Higher Grade examinations set by the Scottish Examination Board for the award of a Scottish Certificate of Education. Alternatively, for a Higher National Certificate Course, which may in turn lead on to a diploma or a degree, a cluster of appropriate passes at National Certificate level may be acceptable.

Student finance

The SOED Students' Allowances Scheme provides support for Scottish students on most full-time courses of higher education up to first degree or equivalent level. Assistance for students attending other full-time, and all part-time, courses is the responsibility of the education authorities.

Academic year

The academic year is divided into 3 terms of approximately 10 weeks each, with the exception of Stirling, which has established a 2-term year based on the American system. Many of the colleges which were not part of the traditional university structure have longer terms and different working patterns.

Courses/Qualifications

In Scotland, degrees are awarded for the successful completion of a 3-year full-time course at an appropriate level (an Ordinary Degree) or a 4-year course which is more specialized and normally more demanding (an Honours Degree). The traditional Scottish first degree in arts, humanities and languages is known as a Master of Arts (MA), equivalent to a Bachelor's degree in England. Increasingly, institutions in Scotland are offering first degrees with the title of Bachelor, as in engineering or education.

HNC courses normally last one year and most HND courses 2 years, if taken full-time.

Many courses, especially in science and engineering, are sandwich courses, with students spending periods of professional training or work experience in a professional environment or industry. Such courses normally take a year longer to complete than full-time courses.

At the level of individual modules and elements of courses, of increasing significance within Scotland is the Scottish Credit Accumulation and Transfer Scheme (SCOTCATS). This allows students to gain credit in one institution for courses which they have taken in another.

Assessment

Assessment of students is most likely to be by written examinations, traditionally at the end of each academic year, but now varies considerably according to the institution and course. In some courses, assessment is on the basis of work submitted during the course or on a large piece of work done in the student's own time. Where appropriate, there will also be practical examinations as in the sciences or in oral proficiency in languages. The actual assessment is normally carried out by the department in which the student is studying, but there will also be one or more external examiners from another institution or institutions who will sample some of the course work and examinations and in some cases give oral examinations to students.

Statistics 1992/93

Students	
Full-time	105,291
Part-time	19,012
Academic Staff	
Former SOED funded Central Institutions and Colleges of Education	2,995
8 Traditional Universities	7,471
Total	10,466
Higher Education Institutions	22

* Includes Lecturers, Senior Lecturers, Principals and Department Heads.

Iceland

ICELAND

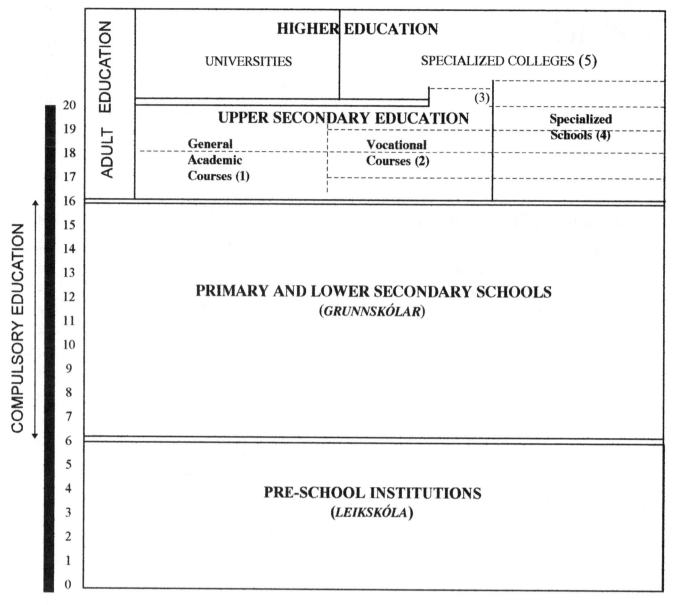

1. Courses conclude with the matriculation examination *(studentsprof)* in both grammar schools and comprehensive schools. Two-year courses are also offered in preparation for specialized study requiring general qualifications for admission. Completion of the *studentsprof* entitles students to commence study at higher level.

2. Vocational courses may last 1/2 to 4 years and are offered at comprehensive, vocational and specialized schools. Courses generally include practical training in a workplace.

3. Master craftsman course of 1 to 2 years after completion of the journeyman's certificate.

4. According to existing legislation these schools operate at upper secondary level, but the courses offered by some of them correspond to higher level.

5. Colleges of higher education which do not have research obligations.

----- = alternative beginning or end of level / type of education.

1. Responsibilities and administration

1.1 Background

Iceland has a population of 262,000, of which 151,000 live in the capital Reykjavík and its suburbs. The country covers 103,000 square kilometres.

Iceland is a republic with a parliamentary democracy. The President is elected by popular vote for a four-year term. Executive power lies with the Cabinet formed by the political parties. The Government must have the direct or indirect support of the majority of the Icelandic Parliament, the *Althing*, which has 63 members. Parliamentary elections are held at intervals of four years or less.

Local government is exercised by 195 local authorities.

Icelandic is the language spoken in Iceland. The Evangelical Lutheran Church, to which 95% of the population belong, is the official state church.

The employment sectors in 1991 were: agriculture 5.4% of the workforce; fishing and fishing industry 11.4%; industry except fishing industry 12.5%; construction 9.8%; wholesale, hotel and restaurant 14,6%; communication 6.9%; banking and insurance 8.4%; public service 18.5%; unspecified 12.4%.

In 1993, 4.4% of the workforce was unemployed.

1.2 Basic principles: education

A fundamental principle of Icelandic education is that everyone should have equal opportunities to acquire education, irrespective of sex, economic status, geographic location, and cultural or social background.

At the pre-school level, teaching and education are carried out with clear goals in mind under the guidance of specially trained personnel.

The main purpose of compulsory schooling (ages 6 to 16 years) is to prepare pupils for life and work in a continuously developing, democratic society. The organization of the school as well as its work should, therefore, be guided by tolerance, Christian values and democratic cooperation.

At the upper secondary level, which normally covers the 16 to 20 year age group, all pupils who have completed their compulsory education should be able to find a programme of study that suits them. The primary aims of upper secondary education are to prepare pupils for life and work in a democratic society by offering them suitable opportunities to learn and develop individually, and to prepare them for employment through specialized studies leading to vocational qualifications or further study.

Universities are charged with the task of carrying out research and offering higher education programmes in different subjects as stipulated by the legislation governing each institution. These institutions contribute to the expansion of knowledge by using scientific working methods and results. They decide what research they carry out.

The main purpose of adult education is to encourage equality of opportunity among adults without regard to location, age, gender, occupation or previous education.

1.3 Distribution of responsibilities

The Icelandic Parliament, the *Althing*, is legally and politically responsible for the education system. The *Althing* determines its basic objectives and administrative framework. All education comes under the jurisdiction of the Ministry of Culture and Education, with the exception of the schools of agriculture which come under the Ministry of Agriculture.

The Ministry of Culture and Education is responsible for implementing legislation at all levels from pre-school and primary education through secondary and higher levels, as well as adult education. The Ministry is in charge of planning educational improvements and issuing regulations, and bears the final responsibility for all official developments and experimental work in schools.

The system of education has to a large extent been decentralized, as part of a general trend in Icelandic society towards decentralization, both with regard to responsibilities and decision-making. The new Primary and Lower Secondary Education Act now before Parliament makes provision for the operation of these schools to be transferred completely to the local authorities.

At present, local authorities are responsible for the provision of pre-school and compulsory school facilities and contribute to the financing of compulsory education. Individual institutions at all levels enjoy limited autonomy.

1.4 Administration

Central administration

The Ministry of Culture and Education is directed by the Permanent Secretary, who acts on the instructions of the Minister. The Minister is aided by his assistant and special advisers on individual projects. The Ministry is divided into three offices: the Minister's Office, which includes three sections (administration, financial affairs and international relations), the Department of Education and Research and the Department of Culture. Each of these sections and offices is under the control of a Director. These main offices and sections handle the daily administration of the education system and the development of education policy.

The Ministry lays down the framework and policy for pre-school education, including its educational role, and sets the general policy regarding the methods used. The Ministry issues the National Curriculum Guide for compulsory education, which is intended both to provide the detailed objectives necessary to implement the law and to offer guidelines as to how they should be achieved in practice. In addition to the National Curriculum Guide, the Ministry issues guidelines on the proportion of total teaching time to be devoted to individual subjects for each year. The Ministry is responsible for the Curriculum Guide for upper secondary education, which describes the various programmes of study available, their objectives and course content.

The upper secondary curriculum guide provides for pupil assessment, for instance in the form of examinations and reports, requirements for continuing from one unit to the next and the minimum requirements for completing certain final examinations.

The National Centre for Educational Materials (under the auspices of the Ministry of Culture and Education) develops and publishes educational materials for compulsory school and distributes them to pupils free of charge.

The only standardized examinations are taken by pupils at the conclusion of compulsory education. They are set, graded and organized by the Institute for Educational Research. These examinations are held in Icelandic, mathematics, Danish and English.

The Institute for Educational Research is an independent institution funded by the State through the Ministry of Culture and Education. Its main function is to carry out research on education. It also offers assistance to teachers and other individuals on questions concerning educational research and development. It advises the Ministry of Culture and Education concerning the National Curriculum Guide.

The Upper Secondary Schools' Coordination Committee, which is composed of the principals of all the schools in question and is headed by the Minister of Education or his representative, is responsible for coordinating the activities of upper secondary schools.

Constitutionally, each higher education institution is directly responsible to the Minister of Culture and Education.

Regional administration

There is no regional administration at pre-school level. The local authorities are responsible for pre-school education in their respective administrative area.

Iceland is divided into 171 local authorities and eight educational regions which deal with matters concerning compulsory education. The Regional Office of Education, located in each educational region, is headed by a Regional Education Officer who represents the Ministry of Culture and Education in his region. The Regional Office is responsible for planning, monitors teaching and other educational services, and supervises counselling, psychiatric help, and school development and innovation work.

In each educational region, an Educational Council coordinates the efforts of local authorities in the region concerned. Members of the Educational Council are elected by the local authorities or the Association of Local Authorities in the region in question. The Educational Councils work together with the Regional Office to encourage cooperation between schools and improve efficiency.

There is no regional administration at the upper secondary and higher education levels.

Local administration

The establishment of pre-school facilities is the responsibility of local authorities, while their professional operation is supervised by the Ministry of Culture and Education.

Pre-school education is controlled by the pre-school board (*leikskólanefnd*) (or the school board – *skólanefnd* – in those local authorities where there is one body responsible for both of these areas) which supervises pre-school education affairs in the local authority concerned. The boards are composed of representatives appointed by the political parties or organizations which have been elected to the local administration. The number of members varies according to the size of the local authority, but most often there are five politically appointed representatives, in addition to the representatives of parents, the school principal and pre-school director, who have the right to attend meetings and state their opinions or make suggestions.

The local authorities are in charge of employing pre-school directors and other personnel.

In the larger local authorities supervisors of pre-school services work together with the pre-school board to advise on and supervise the activities of the pre-school institutions in the area concerned.

A school board is responsible for compulsory education affairs for each local authority. The school board is to ensure that all children of school age in the area receive the instruction prescribed by law. It is also to see to it that school premises and other facilities are satisfactory. The school board is composed of representatives appointed by the political parties or organizations which have been elected to the local administration. The number of members varies according to the size of the local authority, but most often there are five politically appointed representatives, in addition to the representatives of parents, the school principal and pre-school director, who have the right to attend meetings and state their opinions or make suggestions.

There is no local administration at the upper-secondary and higher education levels.

Institutional administration

The institutional administration of education varies according to the level.

Pre-school directors control the activities of each pre-school facility on behalf of those responsible for its operation. They are responsible for planning the educational activities of pre-school institutions and hold regular meetings with pre-school staff regarding these activities.

Primary and lower secondary schools are directed by the principals. They both direct and are responsible for the operation of the school according to the direction of the Ministry of Culture and Education. Each principal consults with his teachers at regular staff meetings, as well as with the school board and the regional educational officer. Principals are appointed by the Ministry of Culture and Education, acting on the advice of the school board, the teachers' council and the regional educational officer. The principal is responsible for employing teachers in consultation with the school board.

Primary and lower secondary pupils may establish a pupil council to look after, for instance, social affairs and other matters linked to pupil welfare. Student or pupil council representatives are entitled to attend and make proposals at meetings of the principal and teachers' council or staff meetings whenever questions regarding the organization of school activities are being discussed.

Most primary and lower secondary schools have parents' associations, which have no formal power but can influence decision-making at staff meetings and meetings of school boards, where they are allowed to attend and make proposals.

Every **upper secondary** school has a school board composed of representatives from the Ministry, the local authority, teachers and pupils. Its main function is to make suggestions about courses offered and to prepare budget proposals.

The daily operation of upper secondary schools is directed by the principals. They are responsible for ensuring that school activities are in accordance with the laws, regulations, academic curricula and other administrative provisions currently in effect, and are within the bounds of the school budget. Each principal consults with his teachers at regular staff meetings. Principals are given fixed-term or permanent appointments by the Ministry of Culture and Education. The principal is responsible for employing teachers, school counsellors and librarians, as well as part-time teachers and other school staff, in consultation with the school board.

The school council (*skólastjórn*) is composed of the principal, vice-principal and pupils' and teachers' representatives. The council assists and advises the principal in the daily operation and administration of the school.

Upper secondary schools have pupil councils (*nemendaráð*). The pupil council has the right to comment on and make proposals regarding, for instance, the aims of instruction, instructional materials and form of instruction. A pupil council representative sits on the school board.

Vice-chancellors (*rektor*) are responsible for the daily operation of educational institutions at the **higher education** level.

Internal administration at both the University of Iceland and the University of Akureyri is controlled by the University Council, which is composed of the Deans of the faculties, two members elected by the faculty and staff as a whole, two to four student representatives, and the *rektor*, who chairs the Council. Representatives of the administrative staff sit as non-voting members on the Council.

The University College of Education is governed by a school council which is composed of the *rektor*, seven representatives of permanent faculty members, one representative of temporary faculty members, one representative of the non-teaching staff, two representatives from the College's experimental school, and three student representatives.

The school boards of publicly operated institutions are appointed by the Minister of Culture and Education, acting on the advice of parties associated with the school. Private colleges are privately administered, but have one representative from the Ministry of Education on their board.

1.5 Inspection

There is no inspectorate as such in Iceland.

The Ministry of Culture and Education is responsible for the control and supervision of educational activities in Iceland. This responsibility includes the collection and processing of data concerning education. Most larger local authorities have supervisors of pre-school services who advise on and supervise pre-school activities carried out by the local authorities on behalf of the pre-school board and in cooperation with the directors of pre-school institutions. The Regional Offices of Education supervise studies and instruction in lower secondary schools in their area and ensure that they are in accordance with applicable laws and regulations.

1.6 Financing

Local authorities pay almost the entire cost of pre-school education. They are also responsible for the initial capital investment and the cost of operating and maintaining compulsory school installations and equipment, including the renewal of educational equipment. The local authorities finance their services from taxes.

The operating costs of upper secondary education are funded by the State. Construction costs and initial capital investment for equipment are divided between the State and the local authorities, with the former paying 60% and the latter 40%.

The State pays the salaries of teachers and school administrators at all levels of education except the pre-school level.

The University and University Colleges are under the jurisdiction of and are wholly financed by the State. University-level institutions receive annual budget allocations which they administer themselves.

Compulsory education, including textbooks and materials, is completely free but at upper secondary level and in higher education only tuition is free of charge.

1.7 Private schools

Education in Iceland has traditionally been organized within the public sector and there are very few private schools in the country.

Any primary and secondary schools established and owned by individuals or institutions must be accredited by the Ministry of Culture and Education. All of them receive public funding. Only 4% of children attend privately operated pre-school institutions and 1.8% of primary and lower secondary pupils are in private schools.

At upper secondary level there is one private school; there are three at higher education level.

1.8 Advisory body

The Industrial Training Board (*Idnfrædslurád*) serves as an advisory body at upper secondary level.

Its purpose is to advise the Ministry of Culture and Education on general policy and the organization of industrial instruction, trades certification and factory training. The Industrial Training Board comments on proposals regarding the syllabus in both practical and theoretical vocational training and proposals for standards concerning equipment and facilities, and submits its own proposals regarding the organization of supervision and control of industrial instruction. The Board submits to the Ministry of Culture and Education proposals on the implementation of apprenticeship agreements. Interested parties in industry appoint the eight members of the Board and the Ministry selects a chairman.

The Minister of Culture and Education appoints education committees in various vocational fields. The Industrial Training Board nominates three representatives to each education committee while the Minister appoints the chairman and secretary of each. The committees discuss the organization of instruction, each within its own area, and make proposals regarding the instructional syllabus.

The Fishing Industry Training Board (*Frædslurád sjávarútvegs*) is composed of eight members. In cooperation with the Minister of Culture and Education, the Board formulates overall policy and the organization of training in the fishing and aquaculture industries. It also comments on proposals for programmes of study and individual courses of instruction in both practical and theoretical subjects connected with the fishing industry. Interested parties in the fisheries sector nominate six representatives to the Board; the Ministries of Culture and Education and of Fisheries each appoint one additional member.

A Council for Adult Education advises the Government on matters of planning and priorities in adult education.

2. Pre-school education

Pre-school education is governed by Act No. 78/1994. Pre-school education is the first level in the school system and is intended for children who have not yet reached the age of compulsory schooling. This is considered to begin on 1 September of the year in which the child reaches the age of six years. Children are not required to attend pre-school education, but the aim is to provide all children with the opportunity to do so if their parents so wish.

Most pre-school facilities are established by the local authorities (with a permit from the Ministry of Culture and Education). Other parties may also operate a pre-school facility in consultation with the local authority and after receiving a permit from the Ministry. Almost all private pre-school institutions receive financial support from the municipality, so very few are run on a totally private basis.

All parents pay fees for their children to attend pre-school education; these vary according to the length of time per day the child attends. Single parents pay 30-50% less than couples. Parental contributions cover roughly 30% of the operating costs of publicly run pre-school institutions. The fees in privately run pre-school institutions are around 15-20% higher than in the public ones.

Approximately 75% of children aged three to six years attend pre-school education, and approximately 15% of children two years of age or younger. Children may attend for from four to nine hours daily. It is up to parents to decide on the length of time each child attends, and it varies according to the local authority concerned whether the requests of parents as to length and type of pre-school attendance can be met. Children from single-parent families and of students have priority for full-day (nine-hour) pre-school places in many local authorities.

Most of the pre-school institutions operate 11 months of the year, i.e. they close for one month during the summer.

Each pre-school institution operates as an independent institution, almost always in facilities which have been specifically designed for the purpose. As a general rule, children attend the pre-school institution which is closest to their home. Pre-school education is coeducational. Only one pre-school institution has separate groups for the two sexes.

Pre-school institutions vary in size, each including from one to four groups. Most have from 40 to 80 children, with 18 to 20 in each individual group. The children are generally divided into groups by age, but there are also instances where children of various ages are put into the same group, especially in smaller institutions. Teachers are normally assigned to a particular group, but may be asked to change groups if the organization of work requires it. They normally remain with the group for the whole day. The groups are usually reorganized when the pre-school institution re-opens each autumn and the teachers are assigned to a new group.

The Ministry of Culture and Education establishes the curriculum for pre-school education and sets out its educational and developmental role and the general policy regarding the methods used. The main educational objectives at pre-school level are:

- to provide children with safe conditions in which to play and a healthy environment in which to grow up;

- to give children the opportunity of participating in games and activities and to enjoy the more varied educational opportunities provided in groups under the direction of pre-school teachers;

- to place emphasis on encouraging, in cooperation with the parents, the all-round development of the children in accordance with the individual nature and needs of each child and to strive to offer them the emotional and physical support needed to enjoy their childhood;

- to encourage tolerance and open-mindedness in the children and to provide them with equal opportunities to develop;

- to support their Christian ethical development and lay the foundations for children to become independent, conscious, active and responsible participants in a democratic society which is constantly and rapidly changing;

- to foster the children's creative and expressive abilities in order to strengthen their self-image, feelings of security and ability to solve problems in a non-agressive manner.

Curriculum

The current pre-school educational programme is based on a child-centred ideology, where emphasis is placed on childhood as a separate stage of development with special qualities which must be borne in mind; the individual development and needs of each child must be the focal point. The educational programme at pre-school level corresponds to the National Curriculum Guide at compulsory school level. The educational programme deals with a number of areas:

- caring and daily routine;

- play and playing conditions;

- speech and speech stimulation;

- visual creativity and expression;

- music, sound and movement;

- nature;

- society.

All of these areas are integrated; there are no clear demarcation lines between them as in the case of traditional school subjects. Pre-school education is intended to bridge the gap between caring for children and educating them, supporting their all-round development and thus preparing them for primary school and life itself.

Children in pre-school education learn mainly through play and other activities, by encountering and participating, under normal and tangible circumstances. First-hand experience is considered very important. Considerable emphasis is placed on positive interaction between the teacher and child and on democratic cooperation.

Assessment

Teachers are not required to assess the position or progress of children at this level. Many pre-school teachers do, however, carry out informal assessment as a means of gaining better understanding of the children's development and progress.

According to legislation, the Ministry of Culture and Education is required to formally organize cooperation between pre-school and primary school levels. At present, individual schools cooperate informally.

Teachers/Staff

In pre-school institutions 36% of the staff are qualified pre-school teachers, while 7% of the staff have various other types of teacher training and 57% are untrained.

Pre-school teachers are required to complete a three-year course of studies at the Icelandic College for Pre-school Teachers. Most of the students who enter this college have completed upper secondary school, although the minimum requirement, according to regulations, is the completion of a two-year general preparatory course at an upper secondary school. The main emphasis is placed on education and general development at the pre-school level. The programme is divided into academic subjects (two-thirds) and practical training (one-third) in a pre-school institution under the supervision of a qualified pre-school teacher. It has become quite common for qualified pre-school personnel to supplement their education after having worked for a minimum of three years in a pre-school institution. In-service training for pre-school teachers is not required by law.

Qualified pre-school teachers are employed by the institutions on a full-time or part-time basis. Pre-school teachers, like all other teachers, are civil servants.

Statistics 1992

Approximately 75% of children aged 2 to 6 years attend pre-school institutions. Some 15% of children aged 0 to 2 years attend pre-school institutions.

Pre-school centres	220
Qualified pre-school teachers (36% of staff)	620
Teachers with other training (7%)	120
Untrained personnel (57%)	970
Children per pre-school teacher 0-2 years of age	3-4
Children per pre-school teacher 3-6 years of age	6-8

3. Compulsory education

The law governing primary and lower secondary education, Act. No. 49/1991, makes attendance at school compulsory for all children from 6 to 16 years of age (ten school years).

One aim of educational policy in recent years has been to raise the general level of education by extending the duration of compulsory education. Before 1984, eight years of education, from age 7 to 15, were compulsory. In 1984 this was extended to nine years, concluding with the pupil's 16th year. The Act concerning compulsory education No. 63/1974 gave all children in Iceland the right to attend school from the age of six years, if their parents so wished. In 1990, compulsory education was extended to ten years instead of nine, i.e. it became mandatory for all children to start school at the age of six years.

Primary and lower secondary education

There is no division between primary and lower secondary education: they form part of the same school level and take place in the same school, grunnskóli (pl. grunnskólar). In general, pupils attend the school which is nearest to their home in the school district within which they live. Most schools cover the entire age span from 6 to 16 years. There are no entrance requirements at this school level, and all children are accepted at the age of six years. The enrolment rate is 100%.

There is no charge to pupils for compulsory schooling. The Government supplies pupils in grunnskólar with teaching materials and textbooks free of charge.

The size of schools varies greatly depending upon their location. In urban areas the largest schools have up to 1,000 pupils, while in rural areas there are many small schools, some of which have fewer than ten pupils. One-half of all grunnskólar have fewer than 100 pupils. All grunnskólar are coeducational.

Pupils are grouped by year according to their age, and progress automatically from one year to the next.

There are no formal connections with other levels of education, but there are numerous examples of informal exchanges between the various levels with regard to individual pupils, subject matter and instruction.

The school year begins on 1 September and lasts for nine months, or until 31 May. The school year is divided into two terms, autumn and spring. The actual teaching time is somewhat shorter, however, due to school and public holidays and the cancelling of classes for various reasons, including in-service training for teachers and organizational and preparatory work. There are about 174 school days each year, but the number of days of actual teaching varies. The school principal is responsible for drawing up a teaching timetable at the beginning of each school year in consultation with his or her teaching staff.

Smaller rural schools generally have only a single teaching shift, i.e. all pupils attend school at the same time, but many of the larger schools in urban areas are unable to accommodate all their pupils at the same time due to a shortage of space. Classes are then staggered, with one portion of the pupils attending school during the earlier part of the day and the remaining portion during the latter part of the day.

Classes are held five days each week. School hours vary.

Act No. 49/1991 defines the main objectives of grunnskóli. The role of the schools is 'to prepare pupils for life and work in a continuously developing democratic society. The educational methods shall, therefore, be guided by tolerance, Christian ethics and democratic cooperation.' On the basis of this law, the Ministry of Culture and Education issues regulations and the National Curriculum Guide. These provide the details of how the law is to be implemented and define more clearly the educational role of the grunnskólar and, accordingly, the main objectives of instruction in individual subjects.

In addition to the National Curriculum Guide, the Ministry issues guidelines on the proportion of total teaching time to be devoted to individual subjects each year.

Curriculum

The number of hours of teaching varies according to the age of the pupils. The law provides for the following minimum number of teaching hours (i.e. each of 40 minutes' duration):

Year	1	2	3	4	5	6	7	8	9	10
Teaching hours per week	25	25	25	26	28	30	32	34	34	34

At the end of ten years of compulsory education, the pupils' scheduled school time will have been divided among the various subjects in approximately the following proportions:

Icelandic	18%
Mathematics	15%
Arts and crafts	20%
Foreign languages	9%
Natural sciences	6%
Social studies	7%
Religious study	3%
Physical education	10%
Optional subjects, misc. extra study	12%

Icelandic, mathematics, arts and crafts, home economics, music, social studies, natural sciences and physical education are subjects which all pupils study throughout their grunnskóli. Danish is studied from the 6th year onwards (11-year-old pupils) and English from the 7th year. In the 10th year (the final year of compulsory education) all pupils study Icelandic, mathematics, English, Danish and physical education, while other subjects are electives.

All pupils are generally expected to cover the same subject material at roughly the same speed. Pupils having difficulty are provided with remedial teaching, primarily in Icelandic and mathematics, but remain with their class for most of their lessons. Teachers choose teaching methods suited to their pupils, their instructional aims and the conditions under which they teach. In general, an attempt is made to provide as much variety as possible.

Teaching based on the school's immediate environment generally takes the form of special field trips which are most often linked to studies in traditional subjects.

A public institution, the National Centre for Educational Materials, is responsible for producing **teaching materials** and receives an annual budget appropriation for this purpose. Because of the extremely small market, it is not possible to have a wide range of textbooks for all subjects. Individual schools and teachers may choose which materials they use when alternatives are available.

Assessment

Examinations and other forms of assessment, usually written, are carried out by individual teachers and schools. Assessment is not standardized between different schools and teachers. Reports on the progress of pupils can take various forms, such as grades given in letters or numbers, and descriptions, either in written or oral form, and may be made at regular intervals throughout the school year and at the end of each year. The purpose of assessment by the school and teacher is first and foremost to back up study and teaching and to provide pupils and their parents with information on how their studies are progressing.

In the last week of April in the 10th and final year of their compulsory schooling, all pupils sit the same compulsory written examinations in Icelandic, mathematics, English and Danish. These examinations are set, graded and organized by the Institute for Educational Research. Grades of 1 to 10 are awarded on the basis of referenced criteria. The purpose of these nationally coordinated examinations is primarily to provide an indication of each pupil's standing at the end of compulsory education and assist him/her in choosing a course of upper secondary education. At the end of compulsory schooling, all pupils receive certificates (*grunnskólapróf*) stating their grades in both the nationally coordinated examinations and other studies completed at the schools they attended.

All pupils are legally entitled to upper secondary education regardless of their achievement in primary and lower secondary school. Schools may require pupils to enrol in preparatory courses in individual subjects if the grades they have received at the conclusion of *grunnskóli* do not meet the required entrance standards.

Home-room or advisory teachers (*umsjónarkennarar*) are intended in particular to offer pupils advice on their studies and their study choices. Special school counsellors are relatively few and are found primarily in the largest schools.

Teachers

At primary level (1st to 7th year), the same teacher instructs his/her class in most subjects. At lower secondary level (8th to 10th year), teachers generally teach one or more subjects to a number of different classes. These teachers are usually specialists in those subjects. They may or may not continue with the same group from one year to another.

To qualify as a teacher at the upper secondary level 30 credits in education are required in addition to a diploma or degree in vocational or university training (BA or BSc). Three institutions offer studies leading to such qualifications. Teachers who have completed these courses are also qualified to teach at the compulsory level. Teaching practice lasts from 10-14 weeks depending on the institution.

Teachers are civil servants employed by the State and work either full-time or part-time.

Participation in in-service training or continuing education is not compulsory, but collective bargaining agreements provide for teachers to attend training courses at least every third year. Each year teacher training institutions offer a variety of courses, both during the school year and in the summer. Collective bargaining agreements make provision for teachers to devote up to 153 hours during the period from June 1 to August 31 to preparing their teaching programme for the coming year, including attending in-service courses.

Statistics 1993

	Grunnskóli	Private schools
Pupils	41,400	788
Schools	210	6
Number of teachers (qualified teachers and instructors lacking full teaching qualification)	3,362	
Full-time positions they hold	2,743	

4. Upper secondary education

Upper secondary education is governed by Act No. 57/1988 and subsequent amendments. The law provides a framework for education at this level by defining the main objectives of upper secondary education and the various responsibilities of the State, local authorities, individual institutions and their staff.

The law defines the purpose of upper secondary education as follows:

– to prepare pupils for life and work in a democratic society by offering them suitable possibilities to learn and develop;

– to prepare pupils for employment through specialized studies which lead to vocational qualifications;

– to prepare pupils for further study in specialized schools and at university level by providing them with the necessary education and practical training.

In the 1970s extensive reforms were carried out within upper secondary education. One of the objectives was to coordinate general and vocational training into one comprehensive system and give equal status to practical and academic education. Both theoretical and practical studies offered at upper secondary institutions are conceived within a common framework, not the least so that credits obtained for study completed at one institution can be transferred to others offering comparable units of instruction.

The main types of upper secondary schools are:

– Grammar schools (*menntaskólar*) which offer a four-year academic programme of study leading to matriculation, i.e. the university entrance examination (*stúdentspróf*). Pupils who complete the course satisfactorily are entitled to apply for admission to university.

– Industrial-vocational schools (*idnmenntaskólar*) which provide almost exclusively vocational courses that prepare pupils for skilled trades. They also offer studies leading to a technical matriculation examination.

– Comprehensive schools (*fjölbrautaskólar*) which provide academic courses comparable to those of the grammar schools and vocational training comparable to that offered by industrial-vocational schools, as well as other specialized vocational training courses.

– Specialized vocational schools (*sérskólar*) which offer training for specific occupations.

In some rural communities where there are no upper secondary schools, lower secondary schools offer additional courses in basic subjects equivalent to the first year of upper secondary education. Pupils completing these studies can then continue at upper secondary schools in other communities.

Upper secondary education is not compulsory and all schools at this level are coeducational. The size of upper secondary schools varies; the largest schools have around 1,500 pupils, while the smallest have from 50 to 100. All schools operate independently, but there is cooperation between them concerning the courses offered and the requirements for their successful completion.

While there is no charge for tuition in public schools, pupils in upper secondary schools are required to pay an enrolment fee. In addition, in many vocational courses pupils have to pay for the cost of materials, and all pupils have to supply their own textbooks. No grants are made to cover these costs.

After completing primary and lower secondary education pupils are entitled to commence study at the upper secondary level regardless of their performance in final examinations at the lower secondary level. If a pupil's academic standing is lower than a prescribed minimum, he/she must begin by attending special preparatory courses in basic subjects and improve his/her standing before commencing regular studies at upper secondary level.

Approximately 85% of the pupils who complete primary and lower secondary education enter upper secondary school directly; the drop-out rate is, however, considerable. Pupils at this level of education are usually 16 to 20 years of age. The average age of pupils beginning a vocational course is higher, as many of them enter employment after completing their compulsory schooling or enrol in general academic programmes before commencing vocational study at upper secondary level.

The percentage of pupils in the various courses of study was as follows in the school year 1992/93:

	Male	Female	Total	
General studies	1,581	1,487	3,068	17.07%
Languages	364	1,147	1,511	8.41%
Fine Arts	227	491	718	4.00%
Education	360	931	1,291	7.18%
Social sciences	701	1,395	2,096	11.66%
Commerce	906	791	1,697	9.44%
Natural sciences	1,435	1,286	2,721	15.14%
Technical-vocational studies	3,057	347	3,404	18.94%
Agricultural study, restoration	485	465	950	5.29%
Health care	30	484	514	2.86%

The school year lasts for nine months, i.e. from 1 September to 31 May. In most schools, the year is divided into autumn and spring terms. The length of the school day is approximately eight hours. Pupils generally attend 30 to 40 lessons per week, with each lesson lasting 40 minutes.

Some upper secondary schools also offer evening classes. The courses offered at evening school are selected from those provided at day school on the basis of demand. Evening classes are intended in particular for adults who are not in a position to attend school in the daytime because of their jobs.

Curriculum

The curriculum guidelines issued by the Ministry of Culture and Education describe the various courses available, their objectives and subject content.

Most upper secondary schools operate according to a unit-credit system. This means that the course content of each subject is divided into units, each of which can be completed in a single term, or one-half of the school year, given a specific number of lessons per week. At the beginning of each term, the pupil selects course units according to prescribed rules and has the possibility of increasing or decreasing the speed with which he/she completes the course of study, depending on his/her personal situation. Pupils who select the same course unit thus form a group, but traditional class groups do not exist.

A pupil's progress is measured by the number of credits completed. As a general rule, one credit represents two lessons per week for one term, or one-half of a school year.

The individual schools decide on the organization of their curricula and, to a certain extent, on how many hours they devote to teaching individual subjects as long as they remain within the limits set by their financing.

The content of each course of study is divided between core subjects, which all pupils are required to take, specialized subjects, which depend on the emphasis of the study, and optional or elective subjects.

A number of courses of study lead to the matriculation or university entrance examination. All of them share a common core of subjects, including the following in the proportions indicated: Icelandic, 12% of the total; foreign languages, 19%; social sciences, 8%; sciences, 9%; mathematics, 9%; computer studies, 2%; physical education, 6%. The proportion of optional subjects varies between the different courses of study from 2% to 18%. A further 17% to 33% is devoted to the subjects that characterize the particular courses of study. In a language stream, for instance, the study of foreign languages constitutes 40% of the entire content.

Subjects included in vocational courses of study can be grouped as follows: general academic subjects, theoretical vocational subjects and practical vocational subjects.

All trainees for certified trades must take at least 25 credits in general academic subjects, including four credits in Icelandic, eight in modern foreign languages, two in social science, four in mathematics, two in bookkeeping and five in electives. Physical education is also compulsory. The number of specialized subjects varies between different courses and so does the extent of practical training.

Teaching may take the form of lectures, discussions between teacher and pupils and independent work by the pupil, both within and outside school. Teachers decide which textbooks they use.

Assessment and qualifications

Examinations are compulsory and pupils cannot normally continue without passing them. A few schools allow pupils to continue without sitting examinations in some courses if they have shown very good results during the term.

Pupils who are successful in the examinations held at the end of each term in each subject have completed those course units. Even though pupils are permitted to repeat individual course units up to three times, a four-year course of study should not take longer than 5 1/2 years. Individual schools may, however, choose to make exceptions to the above-mentioned rule. Examinations are normally written, although they may also be oral. Following the examinations, pupils receive a statement of their results and a list of all the credit units completed. There are no standardized examinations; examinations are set and graded in each school by the individual teachers. In all schools, grades are given in whole numbers from 1 to 10. The minimum grade required to complete each course unit and to be entitled to continue in the subject in question is 5. Pupils who do not achieve the required minimum must repeat the course unit. In schools operating according to the traditional class-group system, pupils who do not achieve the required minimum must repeat the year.

On completion of a course of study, pupils are awarded a certificate (*prófskírteini*) listing all the course units completed, the grades awarded and the number of credits taken in each subject area. This certificate entitles pupils to apply for admission to institutions of higher education such as university, or certifies that a pupil has completed a certain preparatory course of vocational studies, which means that he/she may enter certain specialized vocational schools.

Most schools offer educational **guidance**, which includes assistance in the choice of a course of study, in organizing studies and in setting up a study plan, in addition to special counselling if and when study-related problems arise.

General academic courses

At the upper secondary level, general academic education is primarily organized as a four-year course leading to matriculation, but two-year courses are also offered. Such courses are usually intended as preparatory studies for other courses within the school or at specialized vocational schools.

Traditional grammar schools and upper secondary comprehensive schools are virtually the only schools offering education leading to matriculation. There are basically six courses of academic study leading to matriculation. These are studies in languages, sociology, economics, physical education, natural sciences and physics. Additional fine arts studies, in music, for example, may lead to matriculation, as does a technical programme offered as a follow-up to vocational training.

It takes, on the average, eight semesters (four years) to complete a course leading to matriculation. In schools with a unit-credit system, 140 study units are required. About two-thirds of the course leading to matriculation are of a general nature and are common to all courses of study.

Only the comprehensive schools offer two-year courses of upper secondary study consisting of 70 study units. The main areas of study are education, physical education and commerce. They are organized as a part of the course leading to matriculation (70 units of the 140 required) and pupils in these shorter courses can therefore continue on to matriculation.

Vocational courses

Vocational training takes place in comprehensive schools, industrial-vocational schools and specialized vocational schools. The length of the courses offered varies from one to ten semesters. Many forms of vocational training award pupils certification for certain types of employment. This applies especially to study in certified trades, but also to some other studies, such as the training of nurses assistants and qualified skippers.

Study leading to full qualification in certified crafts and industrial trades can take 3 to 4 years. Pupils have the choice of one of the following avenues:

– an apprenticeship agreement with a master craftsman;

– one year of basic academic and practical study (*grunndeild*) at a vocational school or a comprehensive school, followed by an apprenticeship agreement with a master craftsman;

– one year of basic academic and practical study followed by another year of specialized academic and practical study (*framhaldsdeild*) at a vocational school or a comprehensive school, followed by an apprenticeship agreement with a master craftsman.

In each case, basic studies and the theoretical part of vocational courses are the responsibility of the schools, while practical training is carried out in the workplace, in accordance with a contract with a master craftsman. The apprentice receives payment from the employer during the training periods as provided for by wage agreements. If he/she receives practical training at school the apprenticeship is shortened accordingly.

The first option is the one most pupils avail themselves of. Under the agreement, the master craftsman accepts responsibility for the practical training of the apprentice. The master craftsman is to keep a record of the completion of the various sections of the contract. In all educational regions there is a trade supervisor, who is responsible for checking on the fulfilment of the contract.

Pupils can choose courses from ten different vocational fields in this sector of upper secondary education, including printing, construction and woodwork, tailoring, food industries, metalwork, electrical trades, and hair-and-beauty trades. Each field is divided into a number of specialized courses of study.

When an apprentice has completed his/her course of study at the school, normally after four or five years, he/she takes a journeyman's examination, which qualifies him/her to pursue the trade concerned. The journeyman's examination is the responsibility of a special examining committee, including representatives from both sides of industry. It defines the requirements and sets and grades the journeyman's examination, which consists of both practical and theoretical sections and may be held over a period of one to ten days, depending on the trade.

A pupil who has passed his/her journeyman's examination can become a master craftsman after a certain period of work experience and further studies at a vocational school offering the appropriate instruction. A master craftsman has the right to supervise work in his/her field.

In addition to studies in authorized crafts and trades, comprehensive schools also offer specialized vocational training courses lasting 1 to 4 years, for example, in the sectors of health care and commerce.

The Chief of Police in Reykjavik (or competent authority elsewhere in the country) formally issues certificates in accordance with an earlier tradition still in effect.

The following vocational schools specialize in a particular field. Admission to some is restricted to pupils who have completed one to two years of general studies at an upper secondary school. All of these schools are controlled by their own specific legislation.

Seamen's and navigational colleges (*sjómanna- og styrimannaskólar*) are intended to prepare pupils for positions as officers aboard fishing and merchant vessels. They offer 1 to 4-year courses of study, each leading to a variety of different certificates depending on the size and type of vessel.

The Fish Processing College (*Fiskvinnsluskólinn*) educates and trains skilled workers for the fish processing industry.

Marine engineering colleges (*vélstjórnarskólar*) are intended to prepare pupils for positions as engineers on fishing and merchant vessels, as well as other types of mechanical engineering work. They offer two-, four- or five-year courses of study, each leading to a different certificate depending on the size and type of engine.

The Technical College of Iceland (*Tækniskóli Islands*) offers education and training in many different fields. This school operates partly at the upper secondary level of the education system but mainly at the higher education level. A two-year course of follow-up studies after completion of the journeyman's certificate leads to a final examination similar to a physics matriculation examination. The school offers a 2½-year course of study for technicians after completion of the appropriate journeyman's certificate (as well as three- and four-year BSc programmes in various technological fields at university level).

Fine art colleges (*listaskólar*) train pupils both in the visual arts and music. In addition to artistic studies, pupils can choose certain courses of study offering vocational training. The Icelandic College of Fine Arts (*Myndlista- og handídaskóli Islands*) offers four-year courses of study in various branches of visual art.

Agricultural colleges (*bændaskólar*) prepare pupils for employment in agriculture and horticulture.

The Icelandic College for Pre-school Teachers (*Fósturskóli Islands*) prepares pupils to teach at the pre-school level. Most of the pupils who enter this college have passed the matriculation examination, although the minimum requirement, according to the legislation, is the completion of a two-year preparatory course of general study at an upper secondary school. The programme is thus considered to be at higher education level although the college has not been accredited with higher education status.

The Icelandic College of Social Pedagogy (*Throskathjálfaskóli Islands*) offers a three-year programme of study (after matriculation or a similar examination) for professionals in institutions for mentally disabled individuals.

Teachers

Legislation stipulates that upper secondary teachers of academic subjects should have completed at least four full years of university education. At least two of these should be in a major subject and one year should be devoted to the study of education and instructional methodology. This course of study is offered at the University of Iceland. A comparable course of study completed at a university abroad is also accepted as fulfilling this requirement.

Teachers are paid by the State although they are hired by individual schools to teach the subject(s) in which they have specialized. In-service training courses are held annually.

Teachers of vocational subjects or other technical subjects at a vocational school must be qualified in the field in which they teach or be a master craftsman in the trade in question and have, in addition, a minimum of two years of experience working in the trade. In addition, they are required to have completed a one-year course of study in education and instructional methodology.

Plans for the future

At present, the laws concerning both primary and lower secondary education and upper secondary education are under review. The review is being conducted on the basis of experience gained from the present educational arrangements at these levels. When it has been completed various changes to the school system may be expected, with the aim of ensuring better service for the pupils and more effective education. The structure of education leading to matriculation is to be revised. With regard to vocational training, the aim is to involve employers in the organization of practical training to a greater extent than is presently the case and to give the development of vocational training priority in educational affairs.

5. Higher education

The modern Icelandic system of higher education dates back to the foundation of the University of Iceland in 1911. The University of Iceland remains the principal institution of higher education in Iceland but, in addition, there are two more specialized universities and several small colleges that offer programmes at the higher education level.

There is no general legislation covering higher education as a whole in Iceland.

Constitutionally, each higher education institution is directly responsible to the Minister of Culture and Education. The law governing the operation of each institution defines its main role in education and research, the degrees granted and length of the various programmes offered, the competent administrative authorities and the form of their control, and the structure of their internal organization and administration. Within the framework of the available appropriations the individual institutions draw up and update their programmes, determining their aims, scope and duration, and the form and content of courses.

Institutions of higher education

Most of the higher education institutions are run by the State, while three are operated by private bodies in cooperation with the State. There are two types of higher education institutions in Iceland: universities and colleges. Universities have research responsibilities and offer more than one course of study. Colleges offer specialized training courses at higher education level, but do not generally carry out research. Their teaching is, however, based on the results of university research.

Universities

There are three universities in Iceland with research responsibilities, offering more than one course of study. The University of Iceland offers courses of study in all traditional university subjects, while the other two universities are more specialized and offer fewer courses of study.

The University of Iceland is composed of nine faculties with research and teaching responsibilities. The faculties are: arts, dentistry, economics and business administration, engineering, law, medicine, natural sciences, social sciences and theology. Most faculties are further divided into departments. The university offers postgraduate studies in most faculties.

The University of Akureyri consists of four departments: health sciences, management study, fishery studies and education.

The University College of Education is responsible for the education of teachers for the compulsory school level. It also offers a Master of Education (MEd) programme with specialization in curriculum studies, special education, educational administration, or educational theory.

Colleges

Colleges in Iceland offer technical and vocational courses as well as courses in the arts. Most colleges specialize in a single field of study. Some colleges belong formally to the secondary school level, but operate in practice at higher education level. Studies are offered in the following areas: physical education, social pedagogy, pre-school education, drama, music, fine arts and applied arts and design, computer studies, management, building technology and electrical technology, laboratory and radiology technology, and agricultural science.

Admission

Most institutions of higher education require matriculation from an Icelandic upper secondary school or equivalent education. For some vocational studies at colleges, additional work experience may be required. Colleges may limit the number of students admitted. The schools of fine arts hold entrance examinations and have admission restrictions.

Universities may set specific requirements as to specialization at the secondary level for some programmes of study. There is no ceiling on the number of students admitted. However, in the medicine, nursing and physiotherapy programmes of the faculty of medicine and in the faculty of dentistry, the number of students allowed to continue after the end of the first term is limited.

Students are selected on the basis of competitive examinations held at the conclusion of the first term. Both the University College of Education and the University of Akureyri admit only a limited number of students.

Registration of first year students at universities and colleges usually takes place from the end of May until the middle of June. Applications must be submitted before registration takes place. Applications are sent directly to the selected institutions on special application forms which may be obtained from each institution. The University of Iceland also admits new students to the spring semester, with applications accepted during the first two weeks of January.

Fees/Student finance

Apart from registration fees there are no tuition fees at Icelandic universities. State run colleges charge only small registration fees. Colleges run by private parties have tuition fees.

Icelandic students attending university or college are eligible for student loans from the Icelandic Government's Student Loan Fund. The total loan received per annum depends on the income of the student (and his/her spouse, as appropriate). Repayments commence two years after study has been completed.

Academic year

In most institutions of higher education the academic year lasts from September to May and is divided into two semesters, autumn and spring. The autumn semester starts at the beginning of September and lasts until 21 December. The spring semester lasts from the beginning of January until the end of May. The University College of Education has a summer session extending from 1 June until 31 August.

Courses/Qualifications

Non-university degrees

A diploma or certificate is awarded after 2-3 years of post-secondary college study in physical education, social pedagogy, pre-school education, drama, fine arts and applied arts and design, computer studies, management and building and electrical technology. The University of Akureyri awards a diploma in management after two years of study.

A certificate is awarded to students who have completed 3 years of study on a degree course in the Instrumental Teacher Training Departments, the Vocal Teacher Training Department, and the Department of Theory and Composition at the Reykjavík College of Music. Graduates from the Department of Music Education receive a professional music teacher's certificate for the compulsory primary and lower secondary school level.

First university degrees

The BA degree is awarded to students who have completed 3 to 4 years of study on a degree course at the University of Iceland in the fields of arts, theology or social sciences and who have satisfactorily completed the final thesis or research project.

The BSc degree is awarded to students who have completed 3 to 4 years of study on a degree course in the fields of economics, natural science and medical subjects at the University of Iceland; nursing, fishery studies, and total quality management at the University of Akureyri; agricultural science at the Agricultural College at Hvanneyri; and technical and engineering subjects at the Icelandic College of Engineering and Technology.

The BEd degree is awarded to students who have completed 3 years of study on a degree course in teacher education at the University College of Education and the University of Akureyri. The BEd degree represents professional teacher certification at primary and lower secondary school level.

The BPhilIsl degree (Baccalaureatus Philologiae Islandicae) is awarded after completion of the programme in Icelandic for foreign students offered at the University of Iceland. This degree is on the same level as the BA programme.

The final examination in Engineering. Four-year courses of study in the Faculty of Engineering at the University of Iceland conclude with this degree. Studies are in civil, mechanical and electrical engineering and are accredited by the Association of Chartered Engineers in Iceland. Students who pass the final examination are awarded the title 'chartered engineer' by the Ministry of Industry and Commerce.

The Candidatus degree is only offered at the University of Iceland and qualifies the holder for a special office or profession. It is an academic/professional degree in the fields of theology, medicine, pharmacy, law, business administration and dentistry. The degree title candidatus/candidata is followed by the Latin title for the relevant subject field. Thus *cand. theol.* in theology, *cand. juris* in law, *cand. med.* and *chir.* in medicine, *cand. odont.* in dentistry, *cand. pharm.* in pharmacy, and *cand. oecon.* in business administration.

Postgraduate degrees

The MS degree is awarded after two years of postgraduate study in the faculties of medicine, economics, engineering and natural sciences at the University of Iceland and the successful completion of a major thesis/research project.

The MA degree is awarded after two years of postgraduate study in the humanities and the social sciences at the University of Iceland and the successful completion of a major thesis/research project.

The MEd degree is awarded after two years of postgraduate study at the University College of Education and the successful completion of a major thesis/research project.

The University of Iceland also offers one-year courses of study leading to postgraduate certificates in education, social work, and journalism and mass communication.

Doctorate degrees are only awarded by the University of Iceland. According to its regulations, the University College of Education is also allowed to award a doctorate degree, but it has not yet exercised this right.

Assessment

Student assessment is usually based on written or oral examinations and individual assignments. University degrees are only awarded after students have written a final thesis or completed a research project.

Norway

NORWAY

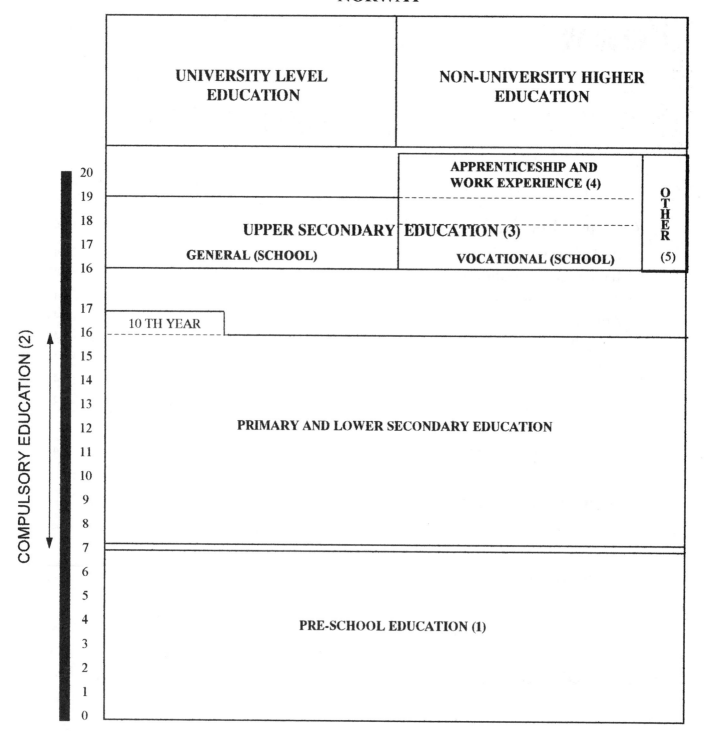

1. School entry age will be lowered to 6 years.
2. There are nine years of full-time compulsory education, to be extended to 10 years within a few years.
3. Upper secondary schools provide 3 years of general and vocational education after the 9th or 10th year of lower secondary education, with the final year examination qualifying for higher education.
4. The norm for apprenticeship training is 2 years of vocational training in upper secondary school followed by 1 or 2 years of practical training in industry.
5. Courses not included in the Act concerning upper secondary education.

‒ ‒ ‒ ‒ ‒ = alternative beginning or end of level / type of education

1. Responsibilities and administration

1.1 Background

Norway has approximately 4.2 million inhabitants in an area of 324,000 square kilometres. The country is divided into 19 counties and 439 municipalities, of which 47 are towns. Oslo, the capital, has roughly 460,000 inhabitants.

A relatively small Sámi population, estimated at approximately 20,000 people, has its own language and its distinctive culture and is centred mainly in the northernmost county of Finnmark.

At national level, political power is invested in the *Storting* (the Parliament). The 165 members of the *Storting* are elected for four-year terms. Since 1986 the Government has been led by a Prime Minister representing the Social-Democratic Party. Since 1981 almost half the ministerial posts have been held by women. This applies to Conservative as well as Social-Democratic Governments.

Culturally, the population has always been fairly homogeneous. The common language is, however, divided into two branches (*nynorsk* or 'new Norwegian' and *bokmal* or 'book Norwegian') which have co-existed as the country's two official languages for about a hundred years. The proper balance to be accorded to the two versions requires special efforts with regard to educational and cultural policies.

As a general rule, Sámi pupils in compulsory schools are entitled to education in their own language.

Nearly 90% of the population belongs to the Evangelical Lutheran Church of Norway.

In 1993, the working population was employed as follows: agriculture, hunting, forestry and fishing 5.5%; oil extraction, mining and quarrying, manufacturing, electricity, gas and water supply 16.9%; construction 5.8%; wholesale and retail trade, restaurants and hotels 17.4%; transport, storage and communication 7.9%; financing, insurance, real estate and business services 7.6%; community, social and personal services 38.7%.

The unemployment rate was 5.3% in 1994.

1.2 Basic principles: education

The overall objective of Norwegian education policy is to provide equal opportunities for all, irrespective of sex, geographic location, and economic, social or cultural background. The aim is to offer all children an education which is adapted to their individual abilities.

Increased knowledge and competence are guiding principles for educational planning and development at all levels of education for the early nineties. Attention is focused on the content and quality of education. Special emphasis is being placed on preparing the young for the information society, the new technologies and a scientific environment, and, at a time when conservation of the environment is very much in focus, environmental education is gaining importance and will be an area of primary concern.

Under the recent reforms emphasis has been placed on strengthening the provision for foreign language teaching and learning. Attention has also focused on school administration and educational leadership.

In order to provide possibilities for life-long learning it is considered important that a broad spectrum of further training and other study possibilities should be accessible to adults. High priority is also given to research and to the recruitment of research workers. Strengthening the sector of higher education is particularly relevant in this respect.

1.3 Distribution of responsibilities

The *Storting* defines the overall aims of public compulsory, secondary and higher education; it lays down their structure and organization, the responsibility for running them and their sources of funding.

The Government exercises its authority in matters of education through the Ministry of Education, Research and Church Affairs. This Ministry covers all levels of education from primary and secondary to higher education, including adult education. Agriculture and veterinary medicine remain under the Ministry of Agriculture. Pre-school education is the responsibility of the Ministry for Children and Family Affairs.

Municipalities are responsible for the provision of child care services and for primary and lower secondary schools. Counties provide upper secondary schools. There is a special Vocational Training Committee for apprenticeship training.

Regional colleges of higher education are organized under a system of Boards on which county authorities have major representation.

Universities are state institutions but enjoy a considerable degree of autonomy.

1.4 Administration

Central

The Ministry of Education is responsible for all tasks relating to the entire education system. As offices for the Government and the Minister, the Ministry's departments prepare questions/issues for the *Storting* and the Government. The Ministry is also responsible for following up decisions made in the *Storting*.

The Minister is the head of the Ministry and his advisers are two State Secretaries and a political adviser. The Ministry comprises 7 Departments:

- Department of Administration;

- Department of Church Affairs;

- Department of Primary and Lower Secondary Education;

- Department of Upper Secondary Education;

- Department of Adult Education;

- Department of Higher Education;

- Department of Research.

According to the law, the Ministry of Education draws up Curriculum Guidelines for compulsory school, the most recent of which were adopted by the *Storting* in 1987. The Curriculum Guidelines lay down a binding framework for work in the school and the subject matter which all pupils are required to study at their own ability level. The national authorities assist the schools to some extent by providing extra material to guide the teachers further in some areas of study.

The Ministry is also responsible for establishing the main curriculum and timetables for upper secondary school and organizing the school leaving examinations. The curricula are to a large extent developed on the basis of local initiatives or the initiatives of various bodies of experts.

A new General Section of the curriculum has been drawn up, including general curriculum principles for compulsory education, upper secondary education and adult education in school and industry. This document will provide an ideological basis for curriculum development within all these educational sectors.

Other responsibilities of the Ministry include school management training, in-service training and school development programmes.

National Education Offices for regional administration were established in each county (Oslo and Akershus have one in common) in 1992 to carry out tasks delegated by Central Government. The head of each Office is a Director of Education.

County

The counties are responsible for providing upper secondary education. Each county has a County Education Committee elected by the County Council, which is responsible for schools being run in accordance with current laws and regulations and being kept within given standards. The Committee is also responsible for the intake of students and for the appointment/employment of teachers, and assists in school development. The tasks of the Committee are carried out by the County Chief Education Officer. For apprenticeship training there is a special Vocational Training Committee in each county, which is responsible for the administration of the contracts, approves the firms and companies, organizes the examinations and issues the certificates.

Municipal

The municipalities are responsible for running the primary and lower secondary schools (compulsory education). The authority dealing with education is the Municipal Education Committee, which is appointed by the Municipal Council. The Municipal Council consists of representatives of the various political parties in proportion to their respective local strength. Representatives are elected for four-year terms. All responsibility for budgeting, school buildings and the appointment/employment of teachers lies with the municipality. The tasks of the Municipal Education Committee are carried out by the Chief Education Officer. Within the framework of the Curriculum Guidelines the Municipal Education Committee, the individual school and the individual teacher can influence the content of teaching through local curricula and work plans. Pupil participation is a basic principle of the Curriculum Guidelines.

Institutional

The principal of each **school** is its administrative and educational head. However, each individual teacher is free to adopt the methods that are most appropriate for his or her classes. There is widespread cooperation between teachers, fostered partly by the existence of regular planning days when teachers from a school or a district meet to discuss matters of common interest, often

pedagogical matters. As far as teaching materials are concerned, a distinction is made between textbooks and supplementary materials. Textbooks are subject to approval by the appropriate authority; books which have not been approved may not be used. Supplementary materials, on the other hand, can be used freely without official approval being needed.

In February 1992, the Government set up a commission to propose new legislation for the **universities, university colleges and state colleges**. Based on the proposals put forward by the commission, a Bill was presented to the *Storting* in the summer of 1994 concerning a common Act on higher education.

The universities are state institutions but have traditionally enjoyed a considerable degree of autonomy. Universities and university colleges are represented in the National Council of Universities, which has been established to coordinate the activities of the institutions and contribute to a national policy on higher education. Questions concerning degrees, examinations and normal periods of study at the institutions of higher education are decided by the Government.

As from August 1994, 98 public non-university institutions were organized as 26 state colleges. Each will have its own internal board. The details of the system of administration will be decided upon when the Government has dealt with the new Act on higher education.

1.5 Inspection

There are no inspectorates, or the equivalent to inspectorates in Norway. However, the National Education Offices established in each county in 1992 are invited to discuss educational matters with the Ministry.

1.6 Financing

All public and, to a certain extent, private education and training is subsidized by Central Government.

A major step in the direction of decentralization of decision-making was made by the introduction of a new sector grant system in 1986. The former earmarking of grants to primary and secondary education from central to municipal/county authorities was then abolished and replaced by a system, under the General Purpose Grant Scheme, where each of these authorities receive one lump sum covering all Central Government subsidies for school education and culture as well as health services.

Municipal and county services are financed by different sources of income. The most important sources are taxation (approximately 50%), Central Government transfers (approximately 40%) and fees and charges, etc. (approximately 10%). The General Purpose Grants Scheme takes into account and equalizes variations in expenditure requirements and tax revenues between counties and municipalities. With regard to education, the most important criteria are 'share of the population aged 0-15' (municipalities) and 'share of the population aged 16-18' (counties). Municipalities and counties now have greater autonomy and better possibilities for planning their economy.

Upper secondary schools are mainly financed by the county. The costs in this sector vary considerably from one county to another. State subsidies mainly cover expenses for the setting up of extra classes to guarantee education for 16- to 19-year-olds, a state initiative started in 1988 to avoid unemployment.

Extra state subsidies and provisions are also made to avoid regional disparities, e.g. for state schools or courses in some trades which cannot be organized in each region and for several schools for pupils with special needs. There are also special measures for the three northernmost counties.

Education in public institutions is provided free of charge. In compulsory primary and lower secondary education textbooks are also free of charge.

Students at public institutions of higher education are not required to pay tuition fees. However, a small fee has to be paid each term to the Student Welfare Organization by all students.

1.7 Private schools

Norway has few private schools compared with other countries (approximately 5% of primary and lower and upper secondary schools). They have primarily been considered as supplementary and not designed to compete with public education.

Fees may be charged at private schools. However, these schools usually also receive public funding. The Act relating to State Grants to Private Schools was implemented in 1985.

Private schools at primary and lower and upper secondary level receive a certain rate of public funding, which usually corresponds to 75 or 85% of the schools' total expenses. The rate is decided according to the type of school.

1.8 Advisory bodies

A characteristic feature of the Norwegian education system has been the large number of advisory bodies concerned with specific types of education. At national level, this contributed to a highly complex and unsystematic form of organization. Consequently, when a White Paper on this matter was approved by the *Storting* in June 1991, a number of advisory bodies, such as the National Council for Primary and Lower Secondary Education, the National Council for Upper Secondary Education and the National Council for Adult Education were dissolved as from 1 August 1992. A National Centre for Educational Resources was affiliated to the Ministry. The National Council for Vocational Training was retained. The Sámi Education Council and the National Parents' Committee for home – school relations in compulsory education were also retained. The training councils were also retained but they may be merged into larger units. Contact with the employers' and employees' associations and users will be maintained by establishing a system of meetings and ad hoc committees for areas not covered by agreements. There is a National Council for Teacher Education to assist the Ministry of Education in matters related to teacher training, which has a mainly advisory function.

2. Pre-school education

Pre-school institutions are generally referred to as child care institutions (*barnehager*) and are regulated by the Child Care Institution Act of 6 June 1975 and subsequent amendments. Child care institutions cover the age group 0 to 6 years.

Attendance is not compulsory and there are no formal entrance requirements. Any limitations are linked to capacity and costs. The development of new child care institutions varies from one municipality to another, and a shortage of places mainly affects children under 3 years.

Parents normally have to contribute financially to have their child in a child care institution. There are, however, a few exceptions. Parents on low income or whose child has physical handicaps may apply for a free place; their expenses are then paid by the municipality. The amount parents contribute varies from one child care institution and from one municipality to another. All approved institutions receive financing from the state authorities.

Provision of child care services is the responsibility of the municipalities. A large part of the overall service is provided by private organizations, under municipal supervision. The Central Government covers part of the annual costs of all approved private and public institutions, at present an average of about 35-40%. The remaining costs are shared between the municipality and the parents. The municipality decides whether it wishes to subsidize privately owned institutions.

53% of all children between the ages of one and six years attend child care institutions. The coverage is low for the youngest children, increases with age, and is over 80% for 6-year-olds. Parental leave of absence has recently undergone reforms which make it possible to benefit from the right to parental leave in a more flexible manner. The need for child care for the youngest children will be reduced in the future in view of these reforms.

Child care institutions serve a dual function. On the one hand they contribute to the education of children of pre-school age, and on the other hand they provide care during parents' working hours. At present there is no national plan regarding the general aim of pre-school education but such a plan should be presented in the spring of 1995.

In general, there are three types of child care institutions in Norway: ordinary child care institutions (*vanlige barnehager*), family child care institutions (*familiebarnehager*) and open child care institutions (*åpne barnehager*). They are all coeducational.

Ordinary child care institutions, which are the most common, are normally divided into departments which are again split into groups consisting of children either in the age-group 0 to 3 or 3 to 6. The youngest children are organized in groups of 8 or 9, while the older ones are in groups of 16 to 20 children. According to the Act relating to Child Care Institutions and subsequent amendments, the norm is one pre-school teacher for 14 to 18 children over the age of three, and one teacher per 7 to 9 children under the age of three, when the children spend more than six hours a day in child care institutions. Principals and departmental leaders should be qualified pre-school teachers or the equivalent. The rest of the staff are mainly assistants; there are generally 1 or 2 assistants for each group.

Family child care institutions are mainly aimed at younger children. This type of child care is organized in private homes, and involves small groups of children; no more than 3 to 5 children in each group. They are under the supervision of a pre-school teacher who normally supervises several homes.

The third type of child care is in open child care institutions. Parents with children in an open institution can bring their children whenever they want within the working hours of the institution. These institutions can be regarded as places where pre-school teachers, parents and children can meet.

Children may attend child care institutions full-time or part-time. Ordinary child care institutions are usually open at least 41 hours per week. 80% are open more than 30 hours per week (63% of children attending child care institutions or educational programmes do so for more than 30 hours per week). All types of child care institutions are usually open for five days per week and have a holiday period of four weeks in addition to the public holidays.

There are no formal links between child care institutions and primary schools. However, within the next few years school entry age will be lowered to 6 years, and experiments are underway to provide a gradual transition from child care to primary school. This includes all-day school programmes for 6-year-olds consisting of short periods of formal teaching, combined with recreational pre-school activities. Under an amendment to the Act relating to Child Care Institutions, as from the autumn of 1991 all municipalities have been entitled to establish voluntary education programmes for 6-year-olds. Education programmes for 6-year-olds are available at 813 locations, 569 of which are open more than 30 hours a week.

Curriculum

In 1992 a Government-appointed commission proposed a curriculum for child care institutions. The commission recommended five basic themes: society, religion and ethics; aesthetics; language and communication; nature and environment; physical activities. Together with this proposal, the Government has during 1994 put forward a Bill for child care institutions which will amend the Child Care Act of 1975.

Assessment

Up to now there has been no national plan regarding the general aim of pre-school education and no standard method for the assessment of children's progress. The monitoring of progress has tended to be concentrated around the child's ability to function socially as part of a group. If children show signs of social, emotional or other kinds of disturbance, special educational measures may be introduced.

Teachers/Staff

Pre-school teachers follow 3 years of training at a teacher training college. Students receive training in educational theory and practice, aesthetics, social science and the Norwegian language. There is no formal training for teaching assistants. Some of them have only completed compulsory school, but others have attended courses in upper secondary education relevant for work in a child care institution.

Staff in child care institutions may work full-time or part-time. Both categories are well represented amongst pre-school teachers and assistants.

Statistics 1993

	Children	Staff*	Institutions**
Ordinary	180,994	Not available	Not available
Family	9,066	Not available	2,085
Open	Not available	Not available	Not available
Total	190,060	46,394	5,630

* Over 90% of staff are women. Approximately 30,000 are employed in public institutions and 16,400 in private ones. 10,800 staff are qualified pre-school teachers.

** The number for family institutions refers to the number of homes. This is not the same as the number of institutions because a family child care institution may be made up of one or more homes.

3. Compulsory education

Seven years of compulsory education has been law since 1889. The Education Act of 1969 introduced 9 years of compulsory schooling for all children between 7 and 16 years of age. In a White Paper submitted in 1993 the Government proposed that compulsory education should be extended by providing schooling from the age of six.

Within the next few years, children will start school at the age of six and compulsory education will be extended to 10 years.

Primary and lower secondary education
(Grunnskole)

According to the Education Act of 1969, the purpose of primary and lower secondary education should be: '.....in agreement and in cooperation with the home, to help to give pupils a Christian and moral upbringing, to develop their mental and physical abilities, and to give them good general knowledge so that they may become useful and independent human beings at home and in society. The school shall promote intellectual freedom and tolerance, and strive to create good forms of cooperation between teachers and pupils and between school and home.'

The compulsory school is divided into two main stages with the first one divided into two blocks:

- the primary stage (*barnetrinnet*): years 1 to 6 (age 7 to 13)
  first block: years 1 to 3
  second block: years 4 to 6

- the lower secondary stage (*ungdomstrinnet*): years 7 to 9 (age 13 to 16).

Some schools also offer an optional tenth year. Primary schools (*barneskoler*) are for pupils in years 1 to 6, lower secondary schools (*ungdomsskoler*) are for pupils in years 7 to 9. Some schools have pupils at both stages (*1-9-skoler* or *kombinerte skoler*). No division is made between these two levels of education, regarded as a continuous period. Pupils who attend a primary school usually pay a one-day visit in year six to the school they will be attending the following year.

Compulsory education in public institutions is provided free of charge. School materials are also free. Fees are charged at private schools. There are no entrance requirements.

Compulsory education is completely comprehensive. The aim is to provide all children with an education which is adapted to their individual abilities. Compulsory schools are coeducational. The classes are organized by age. Neither subject nor level of competence is a determining factor. Each class is kept together as a heterogeneous unit at least from the first to the sixth year and even to the ninth year. During the eighth and ninth years pupils are allowed to choose elective subjects in addition to the compulsory subjects, but class units remain unchanged for all except the elective courses which are organized by subject. There is no repeating of years. Pupils at both primary and lower secondary level automatically progress to the next class.

Teachers in compulsory school are in general allocated by class, but in lower secondary schools there are some subject specialists (such as for the second foreign language, home economics and physical education).

As a rule, the teacher should have the same group of pupils for as many classes as possible. Consequently, classes tend to have the same teacher from the 1st year to the 6th year and change when entering lower secondary school and when starting the 7th year. There are, however, many exeptions to this rule, and the most common is to change teacher after the 3rd year.

As it is considered important that children should attend school without having to leave their families, there are a large number of small schools in remote and sparsely populated areas. In 1993/94, of a total number of 3,326 primary schools, 1,475 had more than one age group in each class (fådelte skoler). Some of them have as few as 6 pupils or less and are ungraded, i.e. all pupils are together in the same classroom. 1,851 schools, either at primary or lower secondary stage or with children at both levels, have pupils in every class (fulldelte skoler). In 1993/94, there were around 18.3 pupils per class at the primary stage and around 22.6 at the lower secondary stage.

Since 1994, the school year has been 38 weeks for pupils and teachers. Up to 1994 it had consisted of 37 weeks for pupils and 38 weeks for teachers (teachers had to spend one week of the school year in in-service training or organized planning) The total number of hours per year did not change. There is a five-day school week and the time spent at school per week varies from 16 to 20 hours in the first year to 30 hours in the final years.

A major concern in primary education at present is to provide after-school care and extracurricular activities for the pupils. The central education authorities have developed models and contributed information, guidance and evaluation in this connection.

Curriculum

The Curriculum Guidelines indicate the allocation of time to the various subjects in terms of weekly lessons per subject for each of the three-year (years 1 to 3, 4 to 6 and 7 to 9) blocks of compulsory education. Each school then decides within this framework how many weekly lessons there will be per subject each year. During the first six years, Norwegian, mathematics, English, civics, religious instruction, music, arts and crafts, physical education and free class discussion constitute a common compulsory curriculum. Practical work and social and cultural work has to be integrated into all subjects. Home economics is compulsory

from the fourth year. Since 1992, English, the most important foreign language taught in Norwegian schools, has been compulsory from the third year. Schools may also choose to introduce English as a compulsory subject from the first year.

In addition to the introduction of social studies and natural sciences, a number of optional subjects are taught at the lower secondary stage. The number and type of optional subjects may vary from one school to another. Particularly in social sciences and natural science subjects the Curriculum Guidelines attach great importance to integrating teaching across traditional subject boundaries.

Vocational **guidance** and information about the world of work are integrated as important parts of education, and a temporary work placement (1 week) is a compulsory component of lower secondary education.

A special section on Sámi education is included in the Guidelines. Teaching hours and subjects are distributed in a way which takes into consideration the right of the Sámi population to non-discriminatory education.

The Guidelines also contain syllabuses for mother tongue teaching and for Norwegian as a second language for linguistic minority groups.

Throughout primary school education, work in class councils and pupil's councils is considered to be of great importance. Knowledge of democratic systems and decision-making processes, supplemented by practical experiences, is intended to help pupils to express their own views and opinions so that they will be able to play an active part in the community. The class councils and pupil's councils are mostly linked to the general running of the school.

The Norwegian education authorities give high priority to environmental education. The strategy of the Ministry is to integrate environmental education into all parts of education and to involve different authorities and bodies at regional and local level in this.

There are no prescribed **textbooks**, but all textbooks must be submitted for approval to the central authorities. This requirement does not apply to supplementary materials.

Assessment and qualifications

The Curriculum Guidelines propose various forms of assessment at all levels. Emphasis is placed on forms of assessment which are suitable for providing guidance to pupils and stimulating the learning process. It is laid down that parents and guardians must be informed of their child's progress at least twice a year, either through personal meetings or by means of written reports. There is no formal assessment at all during the six years of primary school. Children's progress is based solely on teachers' observations.

At the lower secondary stage pupils are awarded marks for compulsory subjects at least twice a year. The teachers are responsible for giving these marks, and they are usually based on both written tests and pupils' work in class. The marks are on a scale including the letters S, M, G, NG and LG, where S represents the best mark and LG the worst. Pupils are also given marks from this scale for their final examination.

A final written examination is organized by the public authorities in the ninth year. All pupils sit a written examination in at least one subject from Norwegian, mathematics and English. There is no formal written assessment in optional subjects. Most pupils also take an oral examination in one or more subjects, including religion, social sciences and natural sciences, in addition to those already mentioned. The central authorities decide which pupils take this examination, but the examination is set by each school. The pupils' teacher sets the questions but the marks are awarded by a teacher from another school.

On leaving school, all pupils receive a leaving certificate (*Vitnemål*) indicating the subjects taken, the latest marks for the years' work and the examination results. The marks are used as one of the more important criteria for selecting the area of study in upper secondary school.

Close to 100% of all pupils complete compulsory schooling. At the end of compulsory education, approximately 0.5% of pupils follow an optional tenth year of lower secondary education, approximately 94 to 95% enter general or vocational upper secondary education, and 4% to 5% enter employment or unemployment. Most pupils continue in upper secondary schools in the same area.

Teachers

Teacher training in Norway takes place either at teacher training colleges or at universities. Often there will be a combination of the two. Until 1994, teachers in primary and lower secondary schools had to follow three years of study in a teacher training college. From 1994 onwards this has been extended to four years. Teachers in lower secondary schools may also have been trained through four to six years of university study and, in addition, compulsory teacher training at a university or teacher training college, including teaching practice; up to 1994 this had consisted of a half-year course, but from now on the course is being extended to one year.

Teachers educated at teacher training college may teach all subjects at all levels. Teachers who are university educated may only teach those subjects in which they have passed a university examination.

Teachers in compulsory schools are employed by the municipal authorities. Most of them work full-time, but a large number of teachers work part-time, especially in primary schools. The school year allows for five planning days each year, which are often used for in-service training. Educational Acts state that teachers have a duty to attend in-service training to ensure that their education is in accordance with the national guidelines.

Statistics 1993/94

	Primary Grades 1-6	Lower secondary Grades 7-9	Combined grades Grades 1-9	Total
Pupils	309,981	156,41	466,400*	
Teachers (1992/93)			53,124**	
Schools	2,076	481	769	3,326

* If special classes and pupils in the optional grade 10 are included, the number is 467,865.
** 36,213 working full-time and 16,911 part-time.

4. Post-compulsory education

Upper secondary education

Upper secondary education normally covers the 16 to 19 age group, or the period from the tenth to the twelfth year of education and training, including general and vocational education at upper secondary schools, vocational training at technical schools and apprenticeship training (see 5.).

In the 1970s and 1980s extensive reforms were carried out within upper secondary education (the Act concerning Upper Secondary Education of 21 June 1974 regulates upper secondary education in schools, whereas the Act concerning Vocational Training of 23 May 1980 regulates vocational/apprenticeship training in industry). One of the objectives was to coordinate general and vocational training in one comprehensive system and to give equal status to practical and theoretical education. A White Paper endorsed by the *Storting* in 1992 laid the foundation for a future reform of upper secondary education, by which it will be transformed quite radically in the years to come. Implementation of the reforms started in the autumn of 1994. The necessary reforms of curricula and organization will be accompanied by a reform of school evaluation and teacher and management training.

In principle, upper secondary education is available to all pupils who have successfully completed their nine-year compulsory education. Although normally attended by pupils from 16 to 19 years of age, there has been a recent increase in the enrolment of older pupils who wish either to complete or to continue their education. Approximately 25% of pupils in upper secondary education are over 20 years of age.

There is, basically, only one type of school at this level of education: the upper secondary school (*videregående skole*), administered by the regional authority, the county. Upper secondary schools are generally of modest size and are invariably coeducational; their pupils are recruited from the lower secondary schools in their areas. School buildings are used by one set of pupils per day, but are generally available for adult education courses in the evenings.

As from 1994 everyone has a formal right to three years of upper secondary education. Entrance to the individual courses will be decided by factors such as the applicants' grades from lower secondary school and age and work experience in the case of older pupils.

General and vocational education in schools

The Act concerning upper secondary education in schools stipulates that upper secondary education should prepare pupils for an occupation and for participation in civic affairs, provide the basis for further education and serve as an aid to personal development. It should contribute to increasing pupils' knowledge and understanding of basic Christian values, the Norwegian national cultural heritage, democratic ideas and scientific method and thought.

The Act implies, *inter alia*, a coordination of general and vocational education. Equal status is given to practical and theoretical studies and it should be possible to combine them within one course. The large majority of upper secondary schools are combined schools, i.e. schools offering both general studies and vocational training, and all schools established since the Act came into force in 1974 have been of this type.

Within the framework of the upper secondary school there are at present 10 areas of study:

General Area of Study; Technical and Industrial Subjects; Aesthetic Subjects; Fishing Trade Subjects; Maritime Subjects; Physical Education; Commercial and Clerical Subjects; Home Economics; Social Services and Health Subjects; and Agriculture and Rural Subjects.

Approximately 45% of 16-year-olds enrol in the General Area of Study at present; this percentage seems likely to rise in the near future, with the forthcoming amalgamation of the General Area of Study with the area of study for Commercial and Clerical Subjects. Pupils taking courses in the General Area of Study are preparing for further study; other courses lead to apprenticeships and to work, but pupils in vocational areas of study are also given the opportunity to gain the additional qualifications they need for higher studies.

At present all areas of study have the same basic structure:

- Foundation course: one or two years;

- Advanced courses: one or two years;

- Shorter courses.

The two-year foundation course combines the general subjects normally taken in the one-year foundation course in the general area of study with the vocational subjects from the one-year foundation course in a vocational area of study. This permits the pupil to keep his/her options open, being free to choose either the academic or the vocational direction after the two-year course. However, only a small minority of pupils take the two-year foundation course. The table on p. 452 shows the distribution of compulsory subjects during each of the normal three years of the general area of study.

An area of study may be divided into different branches. Within the General Area of Study the division into branches was abolished as from the school year 1990/91, and a new model was introduced opening the way for greater flexibility of choice across the former branches. Within most of the areas of study there are a number of different foundation courses (109 until 1994, but the number has been reduced to 13 because of Reform-94). Further specialization is provided in Advanced Course I and in Advanced Course II.

Pupils choose the area of study they wish to follow; some of these are more difficult to enter than others, and in this case it is primarily the level of marks gained at lower secondary school which is decisive. However, disabled pupils are given priority, and places are reserved for those who need special attention. Classes are organized by subject. Pupils automatically progress to the next class, no matter what grades they obtain in the end-of-year examinations. Level of ability is not a determining factor, except in so far as limited capacity in certain areas makes the selection of pupils necessary. When there are not enough places at Advanced Course I and Advanced Course II level, marks determine which pupils are given the opportunity of proceeding to the next year, and pupils with poorer marks are sometimes forced to move horizontally instead of vertically in the system.

All pupils have between 30 and 35 lessons per week over the approximately 38-week school year; small variations are found between courses.

Curriculum

The table on the next page shows the distribution of subjects and teaching periods within the General Area of Study, according to the current model. These are the compulsory subjects within this, the largest, area of study. The table shows that compulsory subjects total 28 periods per week in the first year in this area of study; the first year is, in effect, a continuation of general education, without any opportunity to specialize. In the second year, the number of compulsory subjects drops to 17, leaving at least 13 periods a week for specialization; here the pupil chooses the subjects in which he or she wishes to specialize. In the third year, the difference between 14 and 18 compulsory subject periods per week is explained by the requirement that pupils should study a second foreign language (in addition to English) for at least three years. If the pupil has studied a second foreign language at lower secondary school, the language can be dropped after two years at upper secondary; if, however, the second foreign language was started at upper secondary school, the pupil must study it for four periods weekly in each of the three years. The award of a certificate is dependent upon the pupil having at least 90 periods in total, i.e. an average of at least 30 periods in each of the three years.

General area of study

Comon core subjects	Level/periods			Total
	Foundation	Advanced		
	Year 1	2	3	
Norwegian	4	5	5	14
Religion	0	0	3	3
A-language*)	5	0	0	5
B-language	4	4	0	8
C-language	4	4	4	12
Social studies	2	0	0	2
Geography	0	3	0	3
History I	0	3	0	3
Modern history	0	0	3	3
Science (biology, chemistry, physics)	5	0	0	5
Mathematics	5	0	0	5
Physical education	3	2	3	8
Total common core subjects for pupils with B-language	28	17	14	59
Common core subjects for pupils with C-language	28	17	18	63
Optional subjects and study area subjects for pupils with B-language				31
Optional subjects and study area subjects for pupils with C-language				27

* A-language = first foreign language (English).
  B-language = second foreign language based on introductory course at lower secondary school.
  C-language = foreign language for beginners.

For all pupils there is an additional compulsory foreign language course (minimum 3 hours) which can be taken in any of the three years; they can choose which of the languages on offer at the school they wish to take.

Whenever possible, the concept of equality and international responsibility should play an important role in education. Questions related to aesthetics, ethics, philosophy and religion should also be part of education at upper secondary level.

In order to integrate environmental education into education at upper secondary level, the Ministry of Education has established a system of cooperation with the directors of education and the Education Committees in the counties. Contacts between schools and local communities are encouraged, and these have grown recently. Many schools have close and constructive links with local commerce and industry.

All schools have an adviser whose task is to provide **guidance** to pupils on the choice of course and career. Many schools organize guidance sessions at the start of the school year.

There are no prescribed **textbooks**, but all textbooks must be submitted for approval. This requirement does not apply to supplementary material.

Assessment and qualifications

Most of the grades awarded in the upper secondary school are Grades for Overall Achievement (*standpunktkarakterer*). These are based on the pupils' work during the school year, including practical work, work in class, homework, tests and, in some cases, project work and group work. Grades are awarded by the subject teacher each term. The grades are awarded on a scale from 0 (lowest) to 6 (highest); decimal points are not used.

The same grading system is used for end-of-year examinations (compulsory for both general and vocational training). Most examinations in written subjects are organized by public examination boards. Papers are assessed centrally by groups of experienced teachers. As a safeguard against possible errors, a separate commission of examiners has been established to deal with appeals. Their decision is final.

Examinations are either written, oral, a combination of the two or practical. In the General Area of Study written examinations in Norwegian composition are compulsory. In addition, pupils normally take at least two written examinations. In the area of study for Clerical and Commercial Subjects the pupils normally take four written examinations, two in the third year and one in each of the first two years. In both these areas of study a certain percentage of the pupils, drawn by lot, also take an oral examination during which the class teacher acts as examiner and an external assessor, appointed for the occasion, awards the marks. In vocational areas of study, local assessment based on overall achievement (see above) and testing is the norm. Exceptions include electrical trades where national standards must be met and national examinations are set.

At the end of their studies, pupils are awarded a certificate (*Vitnemål*) listing the subjects they have taken – general subjects, subjects related to their chosen area of study and electives. Marks recorded on certificates are those awarded by the subject teacher indicating the pupil's level of achievement in the subject, with the addition, in some cases, of examination marks.

Every year, examinations are held for external candidates. This category of examinees includes adults who are in employment and wish to qualify for further studies.

Teachers

Teachers in upper secondary schools are subject specialists; this applies both in the General Area of Study and in vocational areas of study. The subjects that they are qualified to teach therefore determine both their appointment to a specific school and their allocation to classes. Teachers of academic subjects have completed four to six years of university studies and are normally qualified to teach two or three different subjects; teachers of vocational subjects have full trade qualifications. Both groups of teachers have, in addition, completed compulsory teacher training; until 1994 this had consisted of a full-time, half-year course, but from now on the course is being extended to one year. In some areas, e.g. commercial and clerical subjects, teacher training is an integral part of the students' higher education.

Teachers in upper secondary education are employed by the regional authorities. Their workload allows for five planning days each school year; these planning days are often used for in-service training. More emphasis is currently being placed on in-service training in connection with the introduction of sweeping changes (Reform-94).

Statistics 1991/92

Pupils	195,050 (full-time)
Teachers	23,680 (FTE)
Schools	582

FTE: full-time equivalents.

Reform

The expansion and developments in upper secondary education during the last twenty years or so have made it necessary to reform the system. Reforms are therefore being introduced from August 1994 (Reform-94).

– There is at present too much specialization at the foundation course level; the number of foundation courses is being drastically reduced from well over 100 to 13.

– Many vocational courses have acted as bottlenecks, where pupils could not proceed to the next level, and have instead moved horizontally in the system to take a new foundation course, or else have dropped out of the system; a 3-year progressive system is now guaranteed.

– Contact between schools and commerce and industry is not as good as it should be; schemes are being developed to improve coordination between schools and working life.

– The present rules for admission to higher education are complicated and confusing; better opportunities are being provided for progress from vocational training to higher education.

The statutory right to upper secondary education which young people have had since 1 August 1994 is to be matched by the provision of an adequate number of school places in the regions. All young people who wish to do so will be able to gain the qualifications they need for a craft certificate or other vocational certificate, or for study at an institution of higher education. (Young people with special needs will be provided for, and a follow-up service for young people outside the educational system will be strengthened.)

New syllabuses are being drawn up in which clear goals are set and where a modular structure will, it is hoped, ensure flexibility while maintaining national standards.

Technical College

Technical Colleges (teknisk fagskole), whose history is different from that of upper secondary schools, are now part of upper secondary education. They have traditionally offered further vocational qualifications within a broad range of trades, and have acted as a stepping stone to higher education. They now offer two-year courses to students who already have trade skills, practical experience in employment, and/or upper secondary education. As a consequence, students tend to be somewhat older than the average upper secondary pupil. In 1992/93, 5,879 pupils attended technical colleges: 5,346 boys and 533 girls.

Technical Colleges currently offer courses in engineering, motor mechanics, drilling technology, production technology, electric power, electronics, house building, chemistry, machinery, food technology, process technology, welding technology and heating, ventilation and sanitary technology.

Pupils who pass the technical college examination are awarded a vocational certificate, which also qualifies them for further technical studies.

A number of colleges offer a one-year course of additional studies in certain subjects.

5. Apprenticeship

Apprenticeship and vocational training in Norway must be seen in the light of what is said above about the structure of upper secondary education. The trend towards combined schools and the parallel effort to avoid higher status being awarded to specific areas of study have resulted in a greater integration of practical and theoretical subjects. This in turn makes it difficult to provide statistics based on an assumption of the separation of study and training at this level.

Apprenticeship training, including the craft examination, is regulated by the Act concerning Vocational Training of June 1980. According to the Act apprenticeship training aims to promote the development of skill in, understanding of and responsibility in craftmanship in relation to craft, occupation and society. The central body under this Act is the National Council for Vocational Training. Each craft or industry has a training council which produces training plans, curricula and examination regulations. The training plans and curricula are approved by the Ministry of Education. Each county has a Vocational Training Committee which administers apprenticeship contracts, approves training companies, organizes tests, etc. The main associations of employers and of employees are given a key role in the administration of the Act and the development of the training programmes covering the various trades under the Act.

The apprenticeship training system at upper secondary level in Norway is based on close cooperation between school and working life and on a combination of schooling and apprenticeship. Most trades and crafts have an apprenticeship period of 3 or 4 years (full-time). The norm for training is two years of vocational training in an upper secondary school (classroom teaching and practical experience in the school workshop), followed by a period of practical training (one or two years) in industry. It is, however, also possible to attend apprenticeship school one day a week, with in-firm training four days a week. The firms responsible for on-the-job training have to be approved by the local Vocational Training Committee. Each firm must have a trained specialist, called a training manager, in charge of the training. The training manager, together with the employee's representatives, is responsible for seeing that the establishment provides adequate training opportunities and that the training curriculum laid down for the craft or trade is followed.

From 1994, in accordance with the proposals of Reform-94, more weight has been placed on general subjects in vocational training; the foundation course in all vocational areas of study will include at least 11 periods of general subjects per week (Norwegian, English, mathematics, science and physical education) while 22 periods per week will be available for subjects directly related to the area of training.

Apprentices have to be paid a regular wage, which is determined by the appropriate wage agreement, and an apprentice can only be laid off if the training establishment is not able to provide work suitable for on-the-job training for a transitional period, or if both parties agree. Training establishments which enter into contracts with apprentices receive a state subsidy, the size of which is currently uncertain, although it is expected to rise. Firms are also recompensed for the supervisory work involved during training and testing. In some trades, the labour market training authorities subsidize equal status measures, and some counties give additional grants.

The relationship between schools and industry/firms is expected to develop further and improve in the 1990s. The development of schools into regional/local resource centres is also seen as a step towards closer cooperation between schools and firms, industry, etc.

Assessment and qualifications

There is continous assessment and regular, formal testing during the first two school-based years (see 4. Assessment and qualifications). During the in-company training period, the company is responsible for determining when and how assessment should be conducted. A centrally monitored final examination for the craft certificate is set. The examination consists of a practical and a theoretical part. The theoretical part is considered to have been taken when the apprentice has passed the final examination for the appropriate course at upper secondary school. The practical part varies a great deal depending on the trade involved. In some trades the practical work has to be done in the course of a day, in others the candidate may spend weeks on it. The work must be assessed by the examination board.

On completion of the apprenticeship, a trade skills test (*Fagprøve*) or journeyman's test (*Svenneprøve*) is taken, leading to the award of a trade skills or journeyman's certificate. In a few subjects the trade skills examination can be taken on completion of advanced course II, but in most cases a period of practical experience is needed in order to satisfy requirements. On certain conditions it is possible to take the trade skills or journeyman's test without having been an apprentice.

During the school-based training, **guidance** is provided by advisers. During on-the-job training it is provided by the training manager. Later, the Government employment advisory service is available.

Teachers

Vocational teachers in schools are required to have a full trade qualification, a minimum period of work experience, one year of additional education in their field, and to have completed a half-year teaching course (see 4. Teachers).

They are appointed full-time or part-time. Like other teachers in upper secondary education, they are employed by the county authorities, and are expected to keep up-to-date with developments in their subject areas and follow relevant in-service training courses.

Statistics

In 1992, 6,945 apprentices received the certificate awarded on passing the trade skills or journeyman's test. In the same year 9,276 new apprenticeship contracts were signed, while the total number of apprenticeship contracts in operation was 19,955. Approximately 10% of these contracts were with public companies.

6. Higher education

The Ministry of Education, Research and Church Affairs is responsible for all public higher education with the exception of the agricultural, veterinary and military sectors. Agriculture and veterinary medicine remain under the Ministry of Agriculture.

Institutions offering higher education can be divided into two main sectors: the university sector and the college sector.

There are four universities (Oslo, Bergen, Trondheim and Tromsø); and 6 specialized colleges at university level (the Norwegian College of Agriculture in Ås near Oslo, the Norwegian School of Economics and Business Administration in Bergen, the Norwegian College of Physical Education and Sport, the Oslo School of Architecture, the Norwegian State Academy of Music and the Norwegian College of Veterinary Medicine, all in Oslo).

Although the four universities cover most of the traditional fields of study (with some exceptions for the University of Tromsø), there is some specialization. The University of Trondheim is the central institution for technology, whereas the University of Tromsø has special educational and scientific commitments to studies related to northern Norway.

The Free Faculty of Theology and the Missionary College in Stavanger provide studies in Theology.

A large number of non-university institutions of higher education offer programmes lasting for one to four years. Longer courses and graduate programmes of up to six years have also been introduced at some of the institutions. Most programmes are oriented towards specific professions, their graduates becoming professional or para-professional personnel in areas such as teaching at pre-school and at compulsory school level, engineering, social work, administration, economics, electronics-based data, health professions, libraries, journalism, etc.

Most of the undergraduate programmes offered by the state colleges and other non-university institutions can easily be transferred to undergraduate degree programmes at the universities.

New guidelines for the organization of higher education have been drawn up by the Government in a White Paper adopted by the *Storting* in 1991. The basic idea is to link institutions of higher education together in an integrated 'Norway Network' in order to create a structural framework for increased cooperation and communication between the institutions.

As from 1 August 1994, 98 public non-university institutions were organized into 26 state colleges.

About 15% of the student population is enrolled in private institutions of higher education.

Admission

The normal requirement for access to higher education is the completion of three years of study in general subjects at the upper secondary level, or in some areas of study in technical and vocational subjects. Admission may also be granted to students with a different background if the institution considers it to be equally relevant for a particular field of study. The White Paper of June 1992 proposed that a general matriculation standard be introduced, providing entry to all types of higher education. Minimum requirements will include two components:

- Successful completion of three years of upper secondary education including Foundation Course, Advanced Course I and Advanced Course II (regardless of area of study) or possession of a recognized vocational qualification/trade certificate.

- Studies corresponding to a specific level of attainment, determined in periods per week, within the following general subject areas: Norwegian (14); English (5); social studies (6); mathematics (5); science/environmental studies (5).

Admission to many areas of study, at both universities and non-university institutions, is very competitive. At present, they have different rules for the selection of students, but it is planned to make them more standardized.

Fees/Student finance

Studies in public institutions of higher education are free of tuition fees, but a small fee has to be paid each semester to the student welfare organization.

The State Educational Loan Fund provides financial support for the students in the form of scholarships and loans granted twice a year. These are mainly to cover expenses for accommodation, food and study materials.

Academic year

The academic year is normally divided into two terms:

- Autumn term from mid-August to mid-December

- Spring term from mid-January to mid-June.

Faculty studies generally begin in August. However, certain programmes admit students only in the spring term.

At some institutions a summer term was introduced in 1992. This lasts for about two months with dates varying from one institution to another.

Courses/Qualifications

The degrees awarded by universities and other institutions of higher education vary from one institution to another. The titles of degrees, the examinations concerned, and the normal duration of studies are decided by the Government. Decisions on subject areas to be included in an examination are taken by the Ministry of Education.

A lower degree (*cand.mag.*) may be taken in the faculties of arts, social sciences, and mathematics and natural sciences at universities and at state colleges. The duration of studies is approximately 4 years for arts and social sciences, and 3½ years for mathematics and natural sciences. As a minimum requirement one subject must be studied for at least 1½ years, and another subject must involve study over at least one year. The degree may be composed of subjects from one faculty or several. Equivalent education from other institutions of higher education in Norway or abroad can also be taken into account.

Non-university institutions offer one-year programmes of 'foundation studies' and specialized two- and three-year programmes of 'intermediate studies'. They all lead to the title '*Høgskolekandidat*' (College Graduate). The *cand.mag.* degree may be awarded to students who, according to certain regulations, have successfully completed at least four years of study. Within this system it is possible to become a Graduate in Economics and Business Administration or Engineering in specially designed programmes (2 years of economic-administrative studies plus 2 years of advanced studies in Economics and Business Administration, or 3 plus 2 years of Engineering).

Graduates with a *cand.mag.* degree may study for a higher degree in the same main subject. An important part of this degree is independent research work in the form of a thesis. Study of a main subject takes approximately 3-4 terms (1½-2 years) and leads to the title *cand.philol.* in the arts, *cand.polit.* in the social sciences, and *cand.scient.* in mathematics and natural science, or graduate engineer.

Another higher degree (*mag.art.*) taken at universities, has stricter requirements concerning previous marks obtained and a thesis. It usually represents a total period of study of approximately 7 years. A further higher degree, the licentiate, may be taken in specific subjects.

Professional degrees awarded at the universities normally require 6-7 years' consecutive study:

theology (*cand.theol.*), law (*cand.jur.*), medicine (*cand.med.*), pharmacy (*cand.pharm.*), dentistry (*cand.odont.*), psychology (*cand.psychol.*), education (*cand. paed.*), sociology (*cand.sociol.*), economics (*cand.oecon.*), economics and business administration (*siv.økon.*) and engineering (*siv.ing.*).

The specialized colleges with university status offer professional degrees in the following: agriculture (*cand.agric.*), architecture (*siv.ark.*), economics and business administration (*siv.økon.*), veterinary medicine (*cand.med.vet.*), engineering (*siv.ing.*), theology (*cand.theol.*), music (*cand.musicae*) and physical education and sports. These studies usually take 4½-5 years.

Doctorates are awarded on the basis of high level research conducted over a number of years leading to the successful defence of a substantial thesis.

A number of universities and university colleges have also introduced degree programmes modelled on the English education system, designed to further internationalization. In these programmes the language of teaching and examination is English.

Assessment

Student assessment is decided by the institutions. It usually takes the form of both written and oral examinations at the end of courses. Marks range from 6.0 to 1.0, where 1.0 is the best mark and 4.0 is the pass mark.

Reforms

Since 1987 various aspects of higher education have been thoroughly reviewed, and three different Royal Commissions have concentrated on the following areas: the main system of higher education and research; teacher training; and conditions for foreign students in Norway. In 1991 the Government presented a White Paper on Higher Education aimed at a thorough revision of several of the most important issues discussed in the reports of the three commissions mentioned above. As a follow-up to this White Paper the system of higher education is now going through a period of substantial reform. A new Bill concerning a common Act on higher education was presented to the *Storting* in the summer of 1994.

EURYDICE NETWORK
Editing of the document

Eurydice European Unit
Rue d'Arlon 15
B-1040 Brussels
Editor: J. Martin-Bletsas

National Contributions

BELGIQUE/BELGIE
Unité Belge d'Eurydice (Communauté française)
Ministère de l'Education, de la Recherche et de la Formation
Secrétariat Général
Cité Administrative de l'Etat
Boulevard Pachéco 19, Bte 0, 7e étage
B-1010 Bruxelles
National contribution: D. Barthélémy

Belgische Eurydice-Eenheid
(Vlaamse Gemeenschap)
Ministerie van de Vlaamse Gemeenschap
Departement Onderwijs
Centrum voor Informatie en Documentatie
Koningsstraat 71
B-1000 Brussel
National contribution: joint responsibility

DANMARK
Eurydice's Informationskontor i Danmark
Undervisningsministeriet
Frederiksholms Kanal 25 D
DK-1220 København K
National contribution: joint responsibility

BUNDESREPUBLIK DEUTSCHLAND
Eurydice – Informationsstelle im
Sekretariat der Ständigen Konferenz der Kultusminister der Länder
Nassestrasse 8
D-53113 Bonn
National contribution: Dr G. Jonen

Eurydice – Informationsstelle beim
Bundesministerium für Bildung und Wissenschaft
Heinemannstrasse 2
D-53170 Bonn

ELLAS
Eurydice
Ministry for Education and Religious Affairs
Mitropoleos 15
GR-10185 Athens
National contribution: joint responsibility

ESPAÑA
Unidad Nacional de Eurydice
Centro de Investigación y Documentación Educativa
c/ San Agustín 5
E-28014 Madrid
National contribution: joint responsibility

FRANCE
Unité Nationale d'Eurydice
Ministère de l'Education Nationale
Direction des Affaires Générales,
Internationales et de la Coopération
Sous-Direction des Affaires Multilatérales
Bureau de l'Information sur les Systèmes Educatifs et la Reconnaissance des Diplômes
Rue de Grenelle 110
F-75357 Paris
National contribution: joint responsibility

IRELAND
Eurydice Unit / E.C. Section
Department of Education
6th floor – Apollo House
Tara Street
Dublin 2
National contribution: joint responsibility

ITALIA
L'Unità Nazionale di Eurydice
Ministero della Pubblica Istruzione
Biblioteca di Documentazione Pedagogica
Palazzo Gerini, Via Buonarroti 10
I-50122 Firenze
National contribution: joint responsibility

LUXEMBOURG
Unité Nationale d'Eurydice
Centre de Psychologie et d'Orientation Scolaires
Route de Longwy 280
L-1940 Luxembourg
National contribution: joint responsibility

NEDERLAND
Dienst van Eurydice
Bibliotheek en Documentatie
Ministerie van Onderwijs, Cultuur en Wetenschappen
Postbus 25000
2700 LZ Zoetermeer
National contribution: Drs N. van der Noordt

ÖSTERREICH
Bundesministerium für Unterricht
und kulturelle Angelegenheiten
Abt. I/6b
Minoritenplatz 5
A-1014 Wien
National contribution: joint responsibility

PORTUGAL
Unidade de Eurydice
Ministério da Educação
Departamento de Programação e
Gestão Financeira (DEPGEF)
Av. 24 de Julho 134
P-1300 Lisboa
National contribution: joint responsibility

SUOMI / FINLAND
Eurydice Finland
National Board of Education
P.O. Box 380
SF-00531 Helsinki
National contribution: joint responsibility

SVERIGE
Eurydice Unit
Ministry of Education and Science
Drottninggatan 16
S-10333 Stockholm
National contribution: K. Henriksson, E. Wiberg

UNITED KINGDOM
Eurydice Unit London
National Foundation for Educational Research
The Mere, Upton Park
Slough, Berkshire SL1 2DQ
National contribution: Dr J. Le Métais, Dr H. Hayes

Eurydice Unit Scotland
Scottish Office Education Department
International Relations Branch SOED
Room 801
Jeffrey Street, 43
Edinburgh EH1 1DN
National contribution: joint responsibility

ISLAND
Ministry of Culture and Education
EURYDICE Unit
Sölvholsgata 4
IS-150 Reykjavik
National contribution: joint responsibility

NORGE
Royal Norwegian Ministry of Education, Research
and Church Affairs
Eurydice Unit
Akersgaten 42
P.O. Box 8119 Dep.
N-0032 Oslo
National contribution: A. Andersen, J.P. Strømsheim, D. MacCulloch, A.M. Fetveit

MEMBERS OF CEDEFOP'S DOCUMENTARY INFORMATION NETWORK

BELGIQUE/BELGIË
FOREM /CIDOC *(Office communautaire et régional de la formation professionnelle et de l'emploi/ Centre intercommunautaire de documentation pour la formation professionnelle)*
Bd. de l'Empereur 11
B-1000 Bruxelles
Fax. 322 + 502 54 74

VDAB/ICODOC *(Vlaamse Dienst voor Arbeidsbemiddeling en Beroepsopleiding/ Intercommunautair documentatie-centrum voor beroepsleiding)*
Keizerlaan 11
B-1000 Brussel
Fax. 322 + 502 54 74

DANMARK
SEL *(The Royal Danish School of Educational Studies for Teachers at Technical and Commercial Colleges)*
Rigensgade 13
DK-1316 Køenhavn K
Fax. 4533 + 14 42 14

BUNDESREPUBLIK DEUTSCHLAND
BIBB *(Bundesinstitut für Berufsbildung)*
Referat K4
Fehrbelliner Platz 3
D-10702 Berlin
Fax. 4930 + 8643-2607

ELLAS
OEEK *(Organization for Vocational Education and Training)*
1, Ilioupoleos Street
17236 Ymittos
GR-Athens
Fax. 301 + 92 54 484

ESPAÑA
INEM *(Instituto Nacional de Empleo)*
Condesa de Venadito, 9
E-28027 Madrid
Fax. 341 + 377 58 81/377 58 87

FRANCE
Centre INFFO
Tour Europe Cedex 07
F-92049 Paris la Déense
Fax. 331 + 477 374 20

IRELAND
FAS *(The Training and Employment authority)*
P.O. Box 456
27-33, Upper Baggot Street
IRL-Dublin
Fax. 3531 + 668 26 91

ITALIA
ISFOL *(Istituto per lo sviluppo della formazione professionale dei lavoratori)*
Via Morgagni 33
I-00161 Roma
Fax. 396 + 884 58 83

LUXEMBOURG
Chambre des métiers du G.-D. dc Luxembourg
2, Circuit de la Foire internationale
B.P. 1604 (Kirchberg)
L-1016 Luxembourg
Fax. 352 + 42 67 87

NEDERLAND
CIBB *(Centrum Innovatie Beroepsonderwijs Bedrijfsleven)*
Pettelaarpark 1
Postbus 1585
NL-5200 BP's-Hertogenbosch
Fax. 3173 + 12 34 25

ÖTERREICH*
Bundesministerium für Unterricht und Kunst
Abt./Dept.: II/7
Minoritenplatz 5
AT-1014 Wien
Fax. 431 + 531 20 41 30

PORTUGAL
SICT *(Servicio de Informação Cientifica e Tecnica)*
Praça de Londres, 2-1ºAndar
P-1091 Lisboa Codex
Tel. 3511 + 849 66 28
Fax. 3511 + 80 61 71

SUOMI/FINLAND
National Board of Education
Utbildningsstyrelsen/Opetushallitus
Hakaniemenkatu 2Ms.
FI-00530 Helsinki
Fax. 3580 + 77 47 78 69

SVERIGE*
Swedish Education and Science Ministry
SE-10333 Stockholm
Fax. 468 + 723 17 34

UNITED KINGDOM
IPD *(Institute of Personel and Development)*
IPD House
35 Camp Road
UK-London 4UX
Fax. 44181 + 263 33 33 (IPD)

---

* provisional contact point until a network member is formally nominated

European Commission

Structures of the education and initial training systems in the European Union

Luxembourg: Office for Official Publications of the European Communities

1995 — 464 pp. — 21 × 29.7 cm

ISBN 92-826-9319-8